JURISDICTION AND THE AMBIT OF THE CRIMINAL LAW

Jurisdiction and the Ambit of the Criminal Law

Michael Hirst

OXFORD
UNIVERSITY PRESS

*This book has been printed digitally and produced in a standard specification
in order to ensure its continuing availability*

OXFORD
UNIVERSITY PRESS

Great Clarendon Street, Oxford OX2 6DP

Oxford University Press is a department of the University of Oxford.
It furthers the University's objective of excellence in research, scholarship,
and education by publishing worldwide in

Oxford New York

Auckland Cape Town Dar es Salaam Hong Kong Karachi
Kuala Lumpur Madrid Melbourne Mexico City Nairobi
New Delhi Shanghai Taipei Toronto
With offices in
Argentina Austria Brazil Chile Czech Republic France Greece
Guatemala Hungary Italy Japan South Korea Poland Portugal
Singapore Switzerland Thailand Turkey Ukraine Vietnam

Oxford is a registered trade mark of Oxford University Press
in the UK and in certain other countries

Published in the United States
by Oxford University Press Inc., New York

ISBN 978-0-19-924539-0

General Editor's Introduction

This book constitutes the first major examination of the rules on the territorial and extraterritorial application of English criminal law, including cross-border offences and those committed at sea or on aircraft. In many criminal justice systems these topics are regarded as part of the foundations of criminal law, and they are therefore prominent in teaching and writing. This has never been true of this country, and the author argues that this may explain some of the confusions and misunderstandings in judgments, statutes, and official reports to which he draws attention. Michael Hirst has taken an interest in this subject for many years, and the depth of his research into and reflections on the state of the law is manifest in this volume. It is a significant and scholarly addition to the series.

Andrew Ashworth

Preface

When I took up my first academic post in 1976, at the University College of Wales, Aberystwyth, I was surprised to find that the topic set for my first tutorial class in criminal law was 'criminal jurisdiction'. This was not a topic that I had studied as a student, and the textbooks contained almost nothing on it. It seemed a strange and difficult topic with which to commence a first-year course on criminal law. I had expected to start off with something more basic: something on the elements of an *actus reus*, perhaps. It took me a while to realize that the tutorial was indeed focused on such things. There can be no *actus reus* in English criminal law unless the events in question take place within the ambit of that law, and there can be no more basic issue in criminal law than that concerning its area of application.

The more I looked into this topic, the more interested in it I became. It was clearly of fundamental importance, and was generating a rich vein of case law, and yet it featured only infrequently in published works on criminal law. Here then was an ideal research opportunity. In due course, it formed the subject of my master's thesis and of my first five publications. I was then advised to move on to other things; but I vowed that I would eventually return to my first area of interest, and in due course I was able to do so. This work is the result.

This is not a work on 'international criminal law'. Nor is it a work on comparative law, extradition, mutual legal assistance, or the investigation of international crime. I touch occasionally on each of those subjects, but claim no great expertise in relation to any of them. My subject is the territorial and extraterritorial ambit of English criminal law. This is closely linked with the jurisdiction of the courts which enforce that law, and the term 'jurisdiction' is widely used to refer to it, but jurisdiction is strictly a procedural matter, whereas questions of ambit are fundamental to our understanding of the criminal law itself. Where and to whom does this law apply?

The answers to that apparently simple question proved even more difficult and complex than I expected them to be, and the need for rationalization and reform proved even more acute. The law, to put it bluntly, is a mess, and it is becoming a more complex mess with each passing year. This much will doubtless become clear to any reader, but I hope that readers will also come away with some idea of how things might be changed for the better.

I must thank a number of people who have assisted or encouraged me in the preparation and completion of this work. My former colleague, Professor John Andrews, unwittingly started things off by setting that unusual tutorial question in 1976. He also supervised the master's thesis in which my interest in the subject was first developed. Professor Andrew

Ashworth helped to nurture that early interest when he was Editor of the *Criminal Law Review*. As General Editor of this monograph series, he encouraged me to develop and refine my original proposal, and he has read and commented most helpfully on draft chapters that were e-mailed to him very late in the day and at a very busy time of the year. My colleague, Professor Richard Card, and Mike Williams of Wolverhampton University, have also read and commented on draft chapters, as has my wife and colleague, Patricia Hirst. Chris Carleton and David Teasdale of the United Kingdom Hydrographic Office provided invaluable assistance and information in connection with the location of bay-closing lines and territorial limits generally. I must also thank my colleague, Professor Richard Ward, who encouraged me to take the study leave I foolishly imagined I could manage without, and helped to cover for me when I took that leave. Lastly, I must thank John Louth and his colleagues at Oxford University Press for their patience, tolerance, and enthusiasm as I repeatedly asked for (and was given) more time and more words to play with. This work has benefited from each of these contributions. Responsibility for any remaining errors or deficiencies is my own.

I have generally attempted to state the law as of 1 May 2003, but have also included references to legislation that has been enacted but not yet brought into force, and provisions in Bills currently before Parliament, where these appear likely to have a significant effect on the current law.

Michael Hirst

Leicester
May 2003

Contents

Table of Cases   xi
Tables of Legislation   xvii
Table of Statutory Instruments   xliii
Table of Conventions and Treaties   xlvii

1. Ambit and Jurisdiction in English Criminal Law   1
2. Historical, International, and Other Influences   28
3. The Limits of Territorial Jurisdiction   60
4. Cross-frontier Offences   110
5. The Extraterritorial Application of English Criminal Law 201
6. Maritime and Aviation Offences   282
7. Rethinking the Ambit of the Criminal Law   324

Select Bibliography   349
Index   355

Table of Cases

ACLU v. Reno (No.3) (2000) 217 F d 162 . . . . .186, 190
Adelino Enriquez v. Procurator Fiscal, Lerwick [2001] Scot HC 51 85
Air India v. Wiggins [1980] 1 WLR 815 . . . . .6, 14, 41, 226
Aitchison v. Bartlett 1963 SLT 17 65
Al-Fawwaz, Re [2002] 1 All ER 545 . . . . .22, 50, 111, 157, 263
Al-Mudaris v. Al-Mudaris [2001] All ER (D) 288 (Feb) 236
Anderson v. Alnwick District Council [1993] 3 All ER 613 . . . . . .72, 73
Andreas Lemos, The *see* Athens Maritime Enterprises Corp. v.
   Hellenic Mutual War Risks Association (Bermuda) (The Andreas
   Lemos) [1983] 1 All ER 590
Anglo-Norwegian Fisheries [1951] ICJ Rep 116 76
Antonelli v. Secretary of State for Trade and Industry [1998]
   1 All ER 997 22
Arrest warrant of 11 April 2000; Democratic Republic of
   Congo v. Belgium (The *Yerodia* Case) [2002] ICJ Rep 3 . . . . . . .20, 40
Athens Maritime Enterprises Corp. v. Hellenic Mutual War
   Risks Association (Bermuda) (The Andreas Lemos)
   [1983] 1 All ER 590 . . . . .53, 304
Attorney-General for Canada v. Attorney-General for Ontario
   [1937] AC 326 40
Attorney-General of Israel v. Eichmann (1961) 36 ILR 5 40
Attorney-General's Reference (No. 1 of 1982) [1983] QB 751. . .176, 177

Baindail v. Baindail [1946] P 122 234
Barwick v. South Eastern Railway Co. Ltd [1920] 2 KB 387;
   [1921] 1 KB 187 (CA) 71
Bennet v. Hundred of Hartford (1650) Style 233 32
Bingham's Case (1600) 2 Co Rep 91(a) .32, 199
Blackpool Pier Co. v. Fylde Union (1876) 41 JP 344 71
Board of Trade v. Owen [1957] AC 602 . . . . .138, 175, 176, 177
Buvot v. Barbuit (1737) Cases t. Talb 281 35

Chahal v. UK [1996] 23 EHRR 413 143
Chung Chi Cheung v. The King [1939] AC 160 . . . . .35, 36
Clark (Inspector of Taxes) v. Perks [2001] EWCA Civ 1228 288
Cox v. Army Council [1963] AC 48 . . . . .3, 4, 203, 212

Doe v. Roe (1998) 955 P 2d 951 186
DPP v. Doot [1973] AC 807 . . . . .110, 135, 154, 155, 156

DPP v. Stonehouse [1978] AC 55 . . . . .117, 118, 122, 153, 154,
                                                        155, 156, 173

Embleton v. Brown (1860) 3 El & El 234 . . . . .70, 71

Fagernes, The [1927] P 311 . . . . .75, 86
Forbes v. Cochrane (1824) 2 B & C 448 282
Fortuna, The, unreported, 31 March 1860; Public Record Office
    Reference: MT9/11, file 4126/60 94
Franconia case see R v. Keyn (1876) 2 Ex D 63

Gibson v. Ryan [1968] 1 QB 250 65

Harman v. Bolt (1931) 47 TLR 219 61
HM Advocate v. Abdelbaset Ali Mohmed Al Megrahi
    [1999] Scot HC 248 . . . . .111, 320, 338

Jan Mayen Case (Denmark v. Norway) [1993] ICJ Rep 38 107
Joyce v. DPP [1946] AC 347 . . . . .49, 219, 220, 560

Lacy's Case (1582) 1 Leon 270 . . . . .32, 199
Lawson v. Fox [1974] AC 803 120
Leda, The (1856) Swabey Adm 40 77
Liangsiriprasert v. US Government [1991]
    1 AC 225 . . . . .29, 136, 155, 157,
                          158, 175, 177, 218, 246, 264, 281, 332, 343
Libman v. R [1985] 2 SCR 178 . . . . .43, 160
LICRA and UEJF v. Yahoo! Inc and Yahoo! France,
    Tribunal de Grand Instance de Paris, 22 May 2000 . . . . .48, 192–3
Loose v. Castleton (1978) 41 P & CR 19 73
Lotus Case (France v. Turkey) (1927) PCIJ Rep,
    Series A, No.10 . . . . .44, 46, 51, 52, 284

MacKay v. The Queen (1980) 114 DLR (3rd) 393 212
MacLeod v. Attorney-General for New South Wales
    [1891] AC 455 . . . . .29, 233
Magellan Pirates, The (1853) Ecc and Ad 81 303
Minquiers and Ecrehos Case; France v. UK [1953] ICJ Rep 17 61
Mortensen v. Peters (1906) 8 F (J) 93 41

Oteri v. The Queen [1976] 1 WLR 1272 . . . . .282, 283, 285

Parlement Belge, The (1878–9) 4 PD 129 40
Pianka v. The Queen [1979] AC 107 53
Piracy Jure Gentium, Re [1934] AC 586 303
Post Office v. Estuary Radio Ltd [1968] 2 QB 740 . . . .81, 82, 88, 90, 91

Prosecutor v. Anto Furundzija Case No. IT-95917/1,
  10 December 1998 245
Public Prosecutor v. Ashby (1999) 93 AJIL 219 ....21, 212

R v. Abdul-Hussain [1999] Crim LR 570 317
R v. Allen (1872) LR 1 CCR 367 236
R v. Anderson (1868) XI Cox CC 198 286
R v. Andrews-Weatherfoil Ltd [1972] 1 WLR 118 208
R v. Atakpu [1994] QB 69 ....24, 25, 26, 170, 171, 182
R v. Athos (1722) 8 Mod 144 226
R v. Ayres [1984] AC 447 147
R v. Azzopardi (1843) 1 Car & Kir 203 231
R v. Banks (1873) 12 Cox 393 151
R v. Baxter [1972] 1 QB 1 ......121, 122, 135, 153, 154, 155, 156, 173
R v. Beck [1985] 1 WLR 22 166
R v. Bernard (1858) 1 F & F 240 139
R v. Berry [1985] AC 246 ....118, 119
R v. Black [1995] Crim LR 640 ....229, 230
R v. Bow Street Metropolitan Stipendiary Magistrate,
  ex p Pinochet Ugarte (No. 3) [2000] 1 AC 147; [1999] 2 All
  ER 97 .....17, 19, 20, 38, 49, 54, 136, 157, 227, 245, 260, 281, 336
R v. Bruce (1812) Russ & Ry 243 74
R v. Carr and Wilson (1882) 10 QBD 76 286
R v. Casement [1917] 1 KB 98 ....33, 219, 220
R v. Chambers (1709) (unreported) 226
R v. Cope (1922) 16 Cr App R 77 151
R v. Cox [1968] 1 WLR 88 ....176, 177
R v. Cumberworth (1989) 89 Cr App R 187 ....292, 294, 296
R v. Cunningham (1859) Bell 72 74
R v. Dawson (1696) 13 St Tr 451 303
R v. Delandro (1865), unreported 94
R v. Devon Justices, ex p DPP [1924] 1 KB 503 ....84, 286
R (on the application of Lewin) v. DPP [2002]
  EWHC 1049 (Admin); [2002] All ER (D) 379 (May) 231
R v. Dudley and Stephens (1884) 14 QBD 273 ....228, 297
R v. Dyfed County Council, ex p Manson (1994),
  unreported, 18 February 73
R v. Earl Russell [1901] AC 446 232
R v. El-Hakkaoui [1975] 1 WLR 396 ....119, 120
R v. Ellis [1899] 1 QB 230 ....118, 124, 125
R v. Evans (1977) 64 Cr App R 237 133
R v. Faulkner (1976) 63 Cr App R 295 133
R v. Fellows and Arnold [1997] 2 All ER 548 ....189, 191
R v. Forsyth [1997] 2 Cr App R 299 164

R v. Forty-Nine Casks of Brandy (1836) 3 Hagg Adm 257 70

R v. Généreux (1992) 88 DLR (4th) 110 212

R v. Goldman [2001] All ER (D) 157 (July) 135

R v. Gomez [1993] AC 442 171

R v. Gordon-Finlayson, ex p an Officer [1941] 1 KB 171 283

R v. Governor of Brixton Prison, ex p Levin [1997] QB 65 . . . . .128, 159

R v. Governor of Brixton Prison, ex p Rush [1969] 1 WLR 165 .114, 138

R v. Governor of Pentonville Prison, ex p Khubchandani
(1980) 71 Cr App R 241 114

R v. Governor of Pentonville Prison, ex p Naghdi
[1990] 1 All ER 257, 114 137

R v. Governor of Pentonville Prison, ex p Osman
[1990] 1 WLR 277 . . . . .111, 128, 129, 158, 169, 171, 341

R v. Guildhall Magistrates' Court, ex p Jarrett-Thorpe
(1977) *The Times*, 6 October 16

R v. Harden [1963] 1 QB 8 . . . . .114, 125, 137, 158, 165

R v. Helsham (1830) 4 C & P 394 231

R v. Hindawi (1988) 10 Cr App R (S) 104 . . . . .317, 321

R v. Hinks [2001] 2 AC 241 128

R v. Hooper (1734) W Kel 190 6

R v. Howe and Bannister [1987] 1 AC 417 118

R v. Howlett (1967) *The Times* , 4 February 73

R v. Ireland [1998] AC 147 184

R v. Jakeman (1983) 76 Cr App R 223 127

R v. Jameson [1896] 2 QB 425 . . . . .6, 129, 226, 277

R v. Johnson (1805) 6 East 583 129

R v. Johnson [1964] 2 QB 404 126

R v. Karte and Panayi (1988) Cr App R 266 133

R v. Kay (1887) 16 Cox 292 233

R v. Kelly [1982] AC 665 . . . . .7, 84, 199, 293, 296

R v. Kent Justices, ex p Lye [1967] 2 QB 153 . . . . .62, 69, 80, 81, 86

R v. Keyn (1876)
2 Ex D 63 . . . .36, 37, 38, 39, 40, 71, 77, 78–9, 94, 95, 105, 200, 288

R v. Kohn (1979) 69 Cr App R 395 . . . . .160, 176, 177

R v. Krause (1902) 66 JP 121 . . . . .135, 151, 153

R v. Kular Mohan Singh (2000), unreported, 18 April 201

R v. Lambert [2002] 2 AC 545 275

R v. Latif and Shazad [1996] 1 WLR 104 . . . . . .126, 136, 157, 173, 261

R v. Lewis (1857) Dears & Bell 182 . . . . .8, 110, 117, 199

R v. Liverpool Justices, ex p Molyneux [1972]
2 QB 384 . . . . .13, 84, 291, 292, 294, 328

R v. Lopez (1858) Dears & Bell 525 293

R v. Lynch [1903] 1 KB 444 219

R v. Lyons [2002] 4 All ER 1028 40

R v. Mackenzie and Higginson (1910) 6 Cr App R 64 . . . . .122, 126
R v. McLeod (1993) (unreported) 201
R v. Manning [1998] 4 All ER 876 . . . . . . .114, 117, 157, 164, 166, 177
R v. Martin [1956] 2 QB 72 . . . . .11, 314
R v. Miller [1983] 2 AC 161 118
R v. Mills (1995) Crown Court, Croydon 36
R v. Ministry of Defence, ex p Walker [2000] 2 All ER 917 . . . .265, 266
R v. Most (1881) 7 QBD 244 148
R v. Moussa Member [1983] Crim LR 618 .317
R v. Munton (1793) 1 Esp 62 6
R v. Musson (1858) 8 El & Bl 900 70
R v. Naini [1999] 2 Cr App R 398 . . . . .138, 157, 176
R v. Nanayakkara [1987] 1 WLR 265 166
R v. Natji [2002] All ER (D) 177 (Feb) 147
R v. Naylor [1962] 2 QB 527 . . . . .11, 12, 314
R v. Ofori (1994) 99 Cr App R 223 . . . . .24, 25
R v. Ofori (No.2) (1994) 99 Cr App R 223 . . . . .36, 181
R v. Okolie [2000] All ER (D) 661 . . . . .24, 181
R v. Page [1954] 1 QB 171 . . . . .33, 203, 231
R v. Perrin [2002] All ER (D) 359; [2002]
   EWCA Crim 747 . . . . .8, 48, 110, 188, 189, 191, 193, 342
R v. Preddy [1996] AC 815 . . . . .125, 159, 160, 170
R v. Ransford (1874) 13 Cox CC 9 .135, 151
R v. Robert Millar (Contractors) Ltd and Millar [1970]
   2 QB 54 . . . . .130, 131, 132, 154, 192, 208, 250, 329, 343
R v. Rooney [2001] All ER (D) 299 (Dec) 271
R v. Sagoo [1975] 2 All ER 926 235
R v. Sansom [1991] 2 All ER 145 . . . . .135, 156, 175, 177
R v. Sarwan Singh [1962] 3 All ER 612 235
R v. Sawoniuk [2000] 2 Cr App R 220 . . . . .201, 231, 241
R v. Sawyer (1815) Russ & Ry 294 231
R v. Scott (1979) 68 Cr App R 164 136
R v. Secretary of State for the Home Department, ex p Puttick [1981]
   1 All ER 776 203
R v. Serafinowicz (1997) unreported, 18 January 201, 241
R v. Serva (1845) 1 Cox CC 292 231
R v. Smith [1996] 2 BCLC 109, 43 164
R v. Spear [2002] 3 All ER 1074 . . . . .23, 212, 213, 215
R v. Stoddart (1909) 2 Cr App R 217 125
R v. Thompson [1984] 1 WLR 962 159
R v. Tirado (1974) 59 Cr App R 80 125
R v. Tomsett [1985] Crim LR 369 128
R v. Topping (1856) Dears 647 . . . . .233, 329
R v. Towner (2001) unreported, 18 June (Crown Court
   at Maidstone) 271

R v. Vickers (1975) 61 Cr App R 48 133
R v. Waddon [2000] All ER (D) 502 189
R v. Wall (1802) 28 St Tr 51 . . . . .34, 209
R v. Wall [1974] 1 WLR 930 131
R v. Whitaker [1914] 3 KB 1283 273
R v. Wille (1987) 86 Cr App R 296 128
Radwan v. Radwan [1972] 3 All ER 967 103
Rees v. Secretary of State for the Home Department [1986]
    AC 937 . . . . .51, 264
Republic of Bolivia v. Indemnity Mutual Marine Assurance Co. Ltd
    [1909] 1 KB 785 305
Rose Mary, The [1953] 1 WLR 246 36
Ryan v. Ross [1963] 2 QB 151 65

Secretary of State for the Home Department v. Rehman [2002]
    1 All ER 122 143
Secretary of State for Trade v. Markus [1976]
    AC 35 . . . . .7, 9, 118, 123, 124, 125, 158, 178, 200
Shufflebottom v. Chief Constable of Greater Manchester Police
    [2003] EWHC 246; (2003) *The Times*, 13 February 22
Sir Henry Constable's case (1601) 5 Co Rep 106a 70
Soering v. UK (1989) 11 EHRR 439 203
Sunday Times v. UK (No.1) [1979] 2 EHRR 245 190

Tarling v. Government of Singapore (1978) 70 Cr App R 77 176
Thai-Europe Tapioca Service v. Government of Pakistan [1975]
    1 WLR 1485 36
Thompson v. The Queen (1989) 169 CLR 1 230
Tracey, ex p Ryon, In re (1989) 166 CLR 518 212
Treacy v. DPP [1971] AC 537 . . . . .6, 8, 11, 34, 39, 42, 43, 46, 55, 110,
                                 114, 115, 118, 121, 124, 160, 168, 341
Trendex Trading Corporation v. Central Bank of Nigeria [1977]
    QB 529 . . . . .35, 36
Triquet v. Bath (1764) 2 Burr 1478 35
Twee Gebroeders, The (1800) 3 C Rob 162 77

US v. Aluminium Corp. of America (1945) 148 F 2d 416 47
US v. Cargo of the Brig Malek Adhel (1844) 43 US 210 303
US v. Yunis (No.2) (1988) 681 F Supp 896 .51

Wanderer II, The , unreported, Stranraer Sheriff Court
    (1998) April 87, 91

Tables of Legislation

United Kingdom

Access to Justice Act 1999 .... .69
Act for the Trial of Murders and Felonies in Several Counties
   1548 2 & 3 Edw. 6, c. 24 .... .31
Act of 9 Geo. 4, c. 31 .... .226
Act of 15 Ric 2, c. 3 (1391) .... .285, 286, 302
Act of 26 Hen. 8, c. 13 .... .219, 226
Act of 43 Geo. 3, c. 31 .... .226
Admiralty Offences Act 1844 .... .34, 68, 78
Admiralty Offences (Colonial) Act 1849
   s 1 .... .285
Air Force Act 1955 .... .211, 214, 225
   Pt II .... .216
   s 70 .... .212, 237
   s 191 .... .225
   s 192 .... .225
   s 193 .... .225
   s 194 .... .225
   s 195 .... .225
   s 196 .... .225
   s 197 .... .225
   s 209 .... .214
   s 218 .... .225
   Sch. 5 .... .214
An Act to punish Governors of Plantations in this Kingdom for Crimes
   by them committed in the Plantations (11 Will. 3, c. 12) .... .209
Antarctic Act 1994 .... .207, 217
   s 7 .... .278
     (1) .... .278
      (a) .... .278
      (b) .... .278
      (c) .... .278
      (d) .... .278
      (e) .... .278
      (f) .... .278
      (g) .... .278
   s 21 .... .202, 217, 278
   ss 21–4 .... .228

Antarctic Act 1994 (*cont.*):
  s 22 217
    (1)(a) 217
      (b) 217
    (2) 217
  s 23 . . . . .217, 278
  s 24 . . . . .217, 278
  s 31 5
Antarctic Minerals Act 1989 217
Antarctic Treaty Act 1967 217
Anti-terrorism, Crime and Security Act 2001 . . . . .247, 332
  s 44 251
  s 47 . . . . .25, 253
    (1) 252
      (a) 252
    (6) 252
    (7) 252
    (9) 252
  s 50 252
    (1) 252, 253
    (6) 253
  s 108 . . . . .274, 275
  ss 108–10 274
  s 109 . . . . .204, 207, 274, 275
    (1) 274
      (a) 274
      (b) 274
    (2) 274
      (a) 274
      (b) 274
    (3) 274
  s 110 275
  s 113 251
  s 113A 251
  s 114 251
Armed Forces Act 1976 216
  s 7 216
  s 57 216
Army Act 1955 . . . . .211, 224, 225
  Pt II 214, 216
  ss 24–69 214
  s 29 214
  s 35 214
  s 36 214

s 55 214
s 56 214
s 57 214
s 68 214
s 68A 214
s 70 . . . . .23, 212, 213, 231, 237
    (1) 212
    (2) 212, 214
    (3) 214
    (4) 213
    (5) 117, 200, 213
    (6) 213
s 191 225
s 192 225
s 193 225
s 194 225
s 195 225
s 196 225
s 197 225
s 209 214
    (1) 214
    (2) 214
        (a) 214
        (b) 214
s 220 225
Sch. 5 214
Aviation and Maritime Security Act 1990 . . . . . .207, 247, 301, 306, 316
Pt I 314, 323
Pt II 258, 306, 308
s 1 . . . . .314, 323
    (1) 323
        (a) 323
        (b) 323
    (2) 323
        (a) 323
        (b) 323
    (3) 323
    (4) 323
        (a) 323
        (b) 323
    (7) 323
    (9) 323
s 9 . . . . .306, 308, 310
    (1) 306, 307

Aviation and Maritime Security Act 1990 (*cont.*):
   (2) 306, 309, 310
     (a) 307
     (b) 307
     (c) 307
  s 10 . . . . .306, 308, 310
  s 11 . . . . .309, 310
   (1) 309
     (a) 309
     (b) 309
     (c) 309
   (2) 309
     (a) 309
     (b) 309
   (4) 309
   (5) 309, 310
   (7) 309
  s 12 . . . . .306, 309, 310
   (1) 309
   (6) 310
  s 13 . . . . .309, 310
   (4) 310
  s 14 310
   (1) 306, 310
   (3) 310
   (4) 310
  s 18 311
  s 19 . . . . .311, 312
   (1) 311
   (2) 311
     (a) 311
     (b) 311
   (3) 311
  s 20 311
  s 21 311
   (1) 312
   (3) 312
  Sch. 3 . . . . .311, 312
   para. 9 312
Aviation Security Act 1982 . . . . .54, 106, 138, 247, 314, 322
  s 1 . . . . .307, 316, 317, 320, 321, 323
   (1) 317
   (2) 317, 322

(a) 317
(b) 317, 318
s 2 . . . . .316, 319, 320, 321, 323
  (1) 316, 320
    (a) 316, 319
    (b) 316, 319, 320
  (2) 316, 319, 320
    (a) 319
    (b) 319
  (3) 319
  (4) 319, 322
    (a) 319
    (b) 319
  (5) 319
  (6) 319
    (a) 319
    (b) 319
  (7) 319
    (a) 319
    (b) 319
s 3
  (1) 316, 321, 323
  (3) 316, 321
  (5) 321, 322
    (a) 321
    (b) 321
    (c) 321
    (d) 321
  (6) 321, 322
s 4 . . . . .316, 322
  (1)(a) 322
s 6 323
  (1) 228, 317, 318, 321
  (2) 322
s 8 323
s 21A 316
s 21B 316
s 21C 316
s 21D 316
s 38 318
  (3) 318
  (b) 319
Backing of Warrants (Republic of Ireland) Act 1965 22

Behring Sea Award Act 1894 277
  Sch. 1 277
Biological Weapons Act 1974 247
  s 1 . . . . .213, 251, 252, 267
  s 1A 204
British Nationality Act 1948 . . . . .210, 222
  s 1(3) 205
  s 3 . . . . .210, 292
    (1) 204–7, 228, 232, 277, 330
      (a) 205
      (b) 205
British Nationality Act 1981 . . . . .207, 222, 292
  s 37 205
    (1)(a) 206
      (b) 206
  s 51 . . . . .205, 210, 228, 277
    (1) 79, 205, 206, 232
      (a) 206
      (b) 206
  Sch. 3 205
British Overseas Territories Act 2002 206
  s 3 206
Channel Tunnel Act 1987 . . . . .41, 99–100
  s 10 99
    (1) 99
  s 14 99
Chemical Weapons Act 1996
  s 2 . . . . .213, 251, 252, 267
  s 3(2) 251
  s 11 213
Child Abduction Act 1984
  s 2 257
Civil Aviation Act 1949
  s 6 . . . . .12, 314
    (1) 12
Civil Aviation Act 1982 . . . . .12, 54, 106
  Pt IV 105
  s 81 105
  s 92 . . . . .4, 105, 106, 314, 315, 318
    (1) 315
    (1A) 315
    (1B) 315
    (2)(a) 316
    (2A)–(2C) 315

(4) 257, 316
(5) 315
s 101 315
s 106 . . . . .105, 106
Sch. 13, Pt III 300
   para. 6(5) 300
Civil Aviation (Amendment) Act 1996
s 1 315
Commonwealth Secretariat Act 1966 19
Companies Act 1985 179
Computer Misuse Act 1990 . . . . .112, 151, 185, 193
s 1 . . . . .194, 195, 196, 197
s 2 . . . . .194, 195, 196
s 3 . . . . .187, 194, 195, 196, 198
s 4 . . . . .194, 195
   (1) 195, 196
      (a) 195
      (b) 195
   (2) 195, 196
      (a) 195
      (b) 195
   (3) 196
      (a) 195
      (b) 195
   (4) 196
      (a) 196
      (b) 196
   (6) 195
s 5 195
   (2) 195, 196
      (a) 196
      (b) 196
   (3) 195, 196
      (a) 196, 198
s 6 197
   (1)(a) 197
      (b) 197
   (2)(a) 197
      (b) 197
   (3) 197
s 7(1) 198
   (2) 198
   (3) 197
   (4) 197

Computer Misuse Act 1990 (*cont.*):
    (a) 197
    (b) 197
  s 8 ....194, 197
   (1) 196
  s 9(1) 195
Consular Relations Act 1968
  s 1 ....18, 103
  Sch. 1 103
Continental Shelf Act 1964
  s 1(7) 299
  s 3(1) 299
Courts Act 1971 33
  s 3 18
  s 6 11
  s 12 18
  Sch. 1 18
  Sch. 2 18
Crime and Disorder Act 1998
  s 36(3)(b) 218
  Sch. 10 218
Criminal Attempts Act 1981
  s 1 ....137, 198
   (1) 198
   (4) 114
    (a) 137
    (b) 137
    (c) 137
  s 1A 138, 172, 173, 174, 198
   (1) 173, 174
   (2)(a) 173
    (b) 173
Criminal Damage Act 1971 6
  s 1 ....253, 262, 265
Criminal Jurisdiction Act 1802 210
  s 1 209
Criminal Jurisdiction Act 1975 204
  s 3 249
   (1)(a) 249
    (b) 249
   (2) 249
  s 7 249
Criminal Justice Act 1925 33
Criminal Justice Act 1948 210

s 31 . . . . .5, 11, 210
s 80 3
Criminal Justice Act 1967 286
Criminal Justice (Scotland) Act 1980
    s 78 253
Criminal Justice Act 1987
    s 1(5) 339
    s 4 339
    s 9(3) 145
    s 12 147
Criminal Justice Act 1988 246
    s 32 339
        (1A) 335
    ss 93A–93C 180
    s 134 . . . . .39, 245, 246
        (1) 245
        (2) 246
Criminal Justice (International Cooperation) Act 1990
    Pt I 334
    s 18 310
    s 19 310
Criminal Justice Act 1993 . . .112, 115, 126, 133, 162, 163–78, 180, 181
    Pt 1 . . . . .1, 9, 48, 111, 114, 116, 126, 129, 137, 158,
                        161, 164, 166, 170, 178, 187, 198, 275, 341, 345
    Pt V 179
    s 1(2) 23
        (4) 23
    s 2 . . . . .165, 172
        (1) 174
        (3) 165, 174
    s 3(1)(a) 166
        (2) 147, 175
        (3) 172, 173
        (4) 166
        (6) 172
    s 4(a) 170, 171
        (b) 168, 169, 170, 172, 174
    s 5(1) 162, 175
        (2) 138, 173, 174, 197
        (3) 164, 177, 178
            (a) 177
            (b) 177
            (c) 177
        (4) 23, 164, 174

Criminal Justice Act 1993 (*cont.*):
    (a) 174
    (b) 174
  (5) 164
s 6(1) 177, 178
  (2) 174
  (4) 177
s 52 179
  (1) 179
  (2) 179
s 62 179
  (1) 179
    (a) 179
    (b) 179
    (c) 179
  (2)(a) 179
    (b) 179
s 71 . . . . .133, 345
  (5) 134
    (a) 134
    (b) 134
    (c) 134
    (d) 134
    (e) 134
    (f) 134
Criminal Justice (Terrorism and Conspiracy) Act 1998 . . . .23, 139, 142,
                          162, 165, 171, 175, 198
s 5 . . . . .142, 144, 148, 269
Criminal Justice and Police Act 2001
s 33 271
  (2)(c) 271
  (4) 271
Criminal Justice and Public Order Act 1994
s 51 272
s 160 . . . . .191, 192
Criminal Law Act 1967 . . . . .283, 285
s 4(1) 137
s 5(1) 137
s 10 227
Sch. 3 227
Criminal Law Act 1977
s 1 . . . . .25, 137, 147, 148, 175, 177, 218
  (1) 138, 143, 144, 145, 146
  (4) 23, 138, 139, 142, 143, 144, 148

s 1A 23, 25, 26, 139, 142, 143, 144, 146, 147,
148, 149, 150, 171, 175, 269, 343
(1) 144
(2)(a) 144
(b) 144
(3) 145, 147
(4) 145
(5) 147
(a) 145
(b) 145
(c) 145
(6) 145
(7) 145
(8)(a) 145
(b) 145
(c) 145
(9) 145
(10) 145
(11) 145
(12) 145
(13) 146
(14) (a) 146
(b) 146
s 2 144
s 3 144
s 4 . . . . .144, 147
(5) 146
(6) 146, 147
s 5 144
s 9 104
Sch. 13 148
Criminal Law Amendment Act 1885
s 2 122
Criminal Procedure (Scotland) Act 1995 .84
s 11(1) 229
Criminal Procedure and Investigations Act 1996
s 31(3) 145
Customs and Excise Management Act 1979 300
s 5(2) 157
s 170(2) 127, 130, 131
Dangerous Dogs Act 1991
s 3 16
Deep Sea Mining (Temporary Provisions) Act 1981 279

Deep Sea Mining (Temporary Provisions) Act 1981 (*cont.*):
  s 1(1) 279
    (2) 279
    (3) 279
Diplomatic and Other Privileges Act 1971 18
Diplomatic Privileges Act 1964 ....16, 19
  s 2(1) 103
  s 3 17
  Sch. 3 ....103, 104
Drug Trafficking Act 1994
  ss 49–52 180
Estate Agents Act 1979
  s 3(1) 22
European Communities Act 1972
  s 11(1)(a) 272
    (2) 224
Explosive Substances Act 1883 ....247, 249–50, 252, 260, 267
  s 2 ....202, 204, 208, 248, 249, 257, 258,
               262, 265, 267, 309, 310, 318, 319, 323
  s 3 ....202, 204, 208, 249, 257, 258, 267
    (1) 249
    (2) 249
  s 4(1) 119
  s 5 ....250, 267
  s 22 202
Extradition Act 1870 ....22, 50
  s 2 ....22, 50, 111
    (4) 148
  s 6(1)(c) 203
    (d) 203
  Sch. 1 ....22, 158, 263
Extradition Act 1989 22
Finance Act 2000
  s 144 130
Financial Services and Markets Act 2000
  s 397 ....123, 178
    (1) 178
    (2) 178
    (3) 178
    (6) 178
      (a) 178
      (b) 178
      (c) 179
    (7) 178, 179

(a) 179
(b) 179
Firearms Act 1937 97
  s 16 119
Firearms Act 1968
  s 16 257
  s 17(1) 257
Fisheries Act 1981 108
Fishery Limits Act 1976
  s 1(1) 107
    (3) 107
    (4) 107
  s 8 . . . . .85, 108
  s 40 85
Foreign Enlistment Act 1870 276
  s 4 . . . . .204, 276, 277
  s 16 276
Forgery and Counterfeiting Act 1981
  ss 1–5 165
  ss 14–17 165
  s 20 165
  s 21 165
Geneva Convention (Amendment) Act 1995 . . . . .237, 238
  s 1(1) 238
Geneva Conventions Act 1957 . . . . .238–40, 241, 243
  s 1 . . . . .7, 213
    (1) 238
    (1A) 239
Genocide Act 1969 . . . . .237, 242
Herring Fishery (Scotland) Act 1889 41
Hijacking Act 1971 . . . . .314, 317
Immigration Act 1971
  s 24 131
    (1)(a) 131
  s 25 133
  s 25A 131, 132
    (5) 132
  s 25B 131, 132
    (4) 132
Immigration and Asylum Act 1999
  s 80 207
Indecency with Children Act 1960
  s 1 141
Insolvency Act 1986 179

International Criminal Court Act 2001 . . . . .207, 238, 242–4
  s 51 . . . . .213, 237, 242
    (1) 242
    (2)(a) 242
      (b) 242
  ss 51–4 204
  s 52 . . . . .152, 213, 237
    (1) 242
    (2)(a) 242
      (b) 242
    (3) 242
  s 54(1) 272
    (3) 272
    (4) 272
  s 55 242
  ss 58–61 204
  Sch. 8 . . . . .243, 244
  Sch. 9 272
  Sch. 10 242
International Organizations Act 1968 104
International Organizations Act 1981 104
Internationally Protected Persons Act 1978 . . . . .104, 249, 258, 262, 264
  s 1 . . . . .218, 248, 263
    (1) 149, 262
      (a) 262
      (b) 262
    (2) 262
    (3) 262
    (5) 262, 263
      (a)–(c) 263
  s 2 262
Interpretation Act 1978 64
  s 17(2)(b) 299
  Sch. 1 . . . . .3, 4, 61, 204
Ireland Act 1949
  s 1(2) 205
Island of Rockall Act 1972
  s 1 61
Judicature (Northern Ireland) Act 1978
  s 46(3A) 294
Justices of the Peace Act 1979
  s 2(1)(a) 101
Justices of the Peace Act 1997
  s 1 69

Landmines Act 1998 207
  s 2
    (1) 279
    (2) 279
  s 3 279
    (1) 279
    (2) 279
    (3) 279
      (a) 279
      (b) 279
Larceny Act 1916
  s 29 115
  s 32(1) 114
Limited Liability Partnership Act 2000
  s 1(2) 208
Local Government Act 1972 72
  Pt IV 61
  s 20 61
  s 72 . . . . .71, 72
    (1) 71
  s 73 61
  Sch. 1, Pt III 63
Local Government Act (Miscellaneous Provisions) Act 1976
  s 17 69
    (3) 69
Magistrates' Courts Act 1980 93
  s 1(2)(b) 69
    (e) 69
  s 2(1) 69
    (2) 69
    (3) 15, 297, 327
    (4) 11, 14, 15, 69, 285, 297, 327
  s 3(1) 69, 75, 76
    (3) 69, 105
  s 3A 84, 94, 293
  s 3B 69
  s 24 15
  s 33 194
Malicious Damage Act 1861
  s 72 68
Marine, etc., Broadcasting (Offences) Act 1967 81
Matrimonial Causes Act 1973
  s 47(1) 234

Merchant Shipping Act 1854
  s 267 . . . . .297, 298
  s 521 . . . . .93, 94, 95
Merchant Shipping Act 1867 286
  s 11 . . . . .95, 295
Merchant Shipping Act 1894 . . . . .7, 12, 292
  s 684 13
  ss 684–7 12
  s 685 . . . . .93, 94, 95
  s 686 . . . . .95, 291, 292, 293, 294
    (1) 291, 293, 294
  s 687 . . . . .95, 294, 296, 297
Merchant Shipping (Registration, etc.) Act 1993 293
  para. 61 292
  Sch. 4 292
Merchant Shipping Act 1995 . . . . .12, 13, 15, 205, 218, 280,
                                                      282, 285, 287, 289, 327
  Pt II 289, 290, 327
  Pt V 289, 290
  s 1(1) 288
    (b) 288
   (2) 288
   (3) 289
  s 2 . . . . .68, 288
  s 14 14
    (5) 14
  s 17 290
  s 57(1) 13
  s 60 13
  s 85 289
  s 144(3) 289
  s 219 96
  s 279 . . . . .12–14, 289
    (1) 13
    (2) 13
    (3) 13, 14
  s 280 . . . . .74, 94, 95, 96, 289, 290, 293, 327
  s 281 . . . . .7, 14, 68, 84, 95, 181, 204, 228, 289,
                                        290, 291, 293, 294, 295, 296, 298, 310, 328
    (a) 291
      (ii) 295, 296
    (b) 291
  s 282 . . . . .5, 96, 228, 289, 290, 293, 294, 295, 296–8, 310

(1) 296
   (a) 296, 297
   (b) 296, 297
(2) 296
(3) 296
s 307 290
s 308 289
   (4) 288
s 313 . . . . .290, 295
Sch. 13 . . . . .84, 94, 293, 294
Merchant Shipping Amendment Act 1855
  s 21 95
Merchant Shipping and Maritime Security Act 1997
  s 26 304
  Sch. 5 304
Misuse of Drugs Act 1971
  s 3(1) 311
  s 5(1) 213, 214
  s 20 133
  s 36 133
Nationality, Immigration and Asylum Act 2002
  s 143 . . . . .131, 133, 207
  s 145 132
  s 146 . . . . .132, 207
Naval Discipline Act 1866 . . . . .84, 286, 292
  ss 117–18 286
Naval Discipline Act 1957 . . . . .211, 214, 216, 224, 292
  s 42 . . . . .23, 212, 237
  s 93 225
  s 96 225
  s 100 225
  s 118 214
  Sch. 3 214
Nuclear Explosions (Prohibition and Inspections) Act 1998
  s 1 . . . . .213, 251, 253
Nuclear Material (Offences) Act 1983 . . . . .252, 258
  s 1 253
   (1)(a) 253
    (b) 253
    (c) 253, 254
    (d) 253
   (2) 253
  s 2 254

Nuclear Material (Offences) Act 1983 (*cont.*):
  s 6(1) 253
    (2) 253
  Sch. 1 253
Obscene Publications Act 1959 188
  s 1(3) 188, 189
    (a) 188
    (b) 188, 189, 190
  s 2(1) 188
Offences Against the Person Act 1828
  s 8 199
  s 22 232
Offences Against the Person Act 1861 ....13, 226, 227, 228, 260
  s 4 ....135, 148, 149, 151
  s 9 ......3, 12, 120, 139, 204, 206, 226, 227–32, 260, 261, 280, 321
  s 10 ....113, 198, 199
  s 18 ....149, 253, 262, 309, 318, 319, 323
  s 20 ....253, 262, 309, 310, 318, 319, 323
  s 21 ....262, 309, 310, 318, 319, 323
  s 22 ....262, 309, 310, 318, 319, 323
  s 23 ....149, 262, 309, 310, 318, 319
  s 24 ....149, 262, 309, 310, 323
  s 28 ....149, 257, 262, 309, 310, 318
  s 29 ....149, 257, 262, 318, 319, 323
  s 30 ....257, 262
  s 55 256
  s 56 ....256, 262
  s 57 ....4, 206, 232, 233, 235, 236, 329
  s 68 68
  s 78 310
Offences at Sea Act 1536 67
Offences at Sea Act 1799 ....67, 78
  s 1 ....5, 67, 68
Official Secrets Act 1911 ....221, 224
  s 1 ....15, 223
    (1)(a) 222
    (b) 222
    (c) 222
  s 3 222
  s 10 ....204, 224
    (1) 221
    (2) 222
  s 12 222
Official Secrets Act 1920 221

s 1 223
s 2 223
  (1) 223
s 3 223
s 7 223
s 8(3) 222, 223
Official Secrets Act 1989 . . . . .221, 223
  s 8(1) 221, 224
  (4) 221, 224
  (5) 221, 224
  s 11(5) 224
  s 15(1)(a) 224
    (b) 224
Oil and Gas (Enterprise) Act 1982
  s 22 299
Outer Space Act 1986 . . . . .207, 278–9
  s 12 278
    (4) 278
    (6) 279
      (a) 279
      (b) 279
Perjury Act 1911 272
  s 1 . . . . .113, 272
    (4) 200, 272
      (a) 200
      (b) 200
      (c) 200
    (5) 200, 272
      (a) 200
      (b) 200
  s 8 272
Petroleum (Production) Act 1934 82
Petroleum Act 1987
  s 21 300
  s 23 300
Petroleum Act 1998 82
  s 10 . . . . .299, 300, 310
    (8) 299
    (9) 299
  s 12 300
    (1) 300
      (a) 300
      (b) 300
    (2) 300

Petroleum Act 1998 (*cont.*):
s 12 (2)(a), (b) 300
    (c)–(f) 301
  (3) 301
    (a) 301
    (b) 301
  (4) 301
  (5) 301
    (a) 301
    (b) 301
Pilotage Act 1987 301
Piracy Act 1698 303
Piracy Act 1721 303
Piracy Act 1744 303
Police Act 1996
 s 30 80
Prevention of Corruption Act 1906 274
 s 1 ....273, 274
  (4) 274
    (a) 274
    (b) 274
Prevention of Corruption Act 1916 275
Prevention of Fraud (Investments) Act 1958
 s 13 178
  (1)(b) 123
Private International Law (Miscellaneous Provisions) Act 1995 234
Proceeds of Crime Act 2002
 Pt 7 ....171, 180
 s 327 180
 ss 327–9 26
 s 328 180
 s 329 ....26, 180
 s 335(2) 180
  (3) 180
 s 340 ....26, 171, 180
  (2)(b) 181
  (11)(d) 181
Protected Persons Act 1978 247
Protection of Aircraft Act 1973 ....314, 317
Protection of Children Act 1978
 s 1 ....191, 270
Protection of Military Remains Act 1986 280
 s 2
  (1)(a) 280

(2) 280
(3)(a) 280
s 3 280
s 9(2) 280
Protection of Trading Interests Act 1980 48
Public Bodies Corrupt Practices Act 1889 274
s 1 . . . . .273, 274
Regulation of Investigatory Powers Act 2000
s 12(1) 98
Road Safety Act 1967
s 1 121
Road Traffic Act 1988 5
s 5 121
Sale of Offices Act 1809
s 14 210
Salmon and Freshwater Fisheries (Scotland) Act 1951 . . . . . . .10, 65, 66
s 22(2) 65
Salmon and Freshwater Fisheries Act 1975 . . . . .64, 65
s 37 64
s 39(2) 64
Sch. 4, Pt II, para. 3 64
Scotland Act 1998 108
s 115 84
s 126 84
Sea Fish (Conservation) Act 1967 108
s 2 108
(2) 108
s 14 108
s 22A 108
Sea Fisheries Act 1968
s 5(1) 108
s 10 108
s 14 109
Seal Fisheries (North Pacific) Act 1895 277
Sex Offenders Act 1997 .142, 201, 268, 332
s 7 . . . . .58, 141, 191, 270, 271, 333
(1) 270
(2) 204, 270
(3) 270
(4) 270
(5) 270
(6) 270
Sch. 2 270

Sex Offenders Act 1997 (*cont.*):
  para. 2(2) 270
Sexual Offences Act 1956
  s 20 257
  s 22(1)(b) 126
Sexual Offences (Conspiracy and Incitement) Act 1996 .....139–42, 269
  s 1 ....140, 142
  s 2 ....140, 141
    (1)
      (a) 140
      (b) 141
      (c) 141
    (2)
      (a) 141
      (b) 141
    (3) 141, 142
  Sch. 141
Slave Trade Act 1824 247
  s 1 246
  s 10 247
  s 11 247
Slave Trade Act 1873
  s 26 247
State Immunity Act 1978
  s 20 ....19, 20
Statute Law (Repeals) Act 1995
  s 1 209
  Sch. 1 209
Statute Law Repeals Act 1981
  Sch. 1 227
Statute Law Repeals Act 1993 303
Suicide Act 1961
  s 2 126
Suppression of Terrorism Act 1978 ....142, 228, 247, 249,
                                        254, 255, 256, 260
  s 4 ....143, 146, 149, 227, 232, 248, 254, 255, 256,
                                        257, 259–62, 321
    (1) 202, 256, 257, 258, 260, 261, 280, 298
      (a) 256
      (b) 256, 261, 262
    (2) 256, 257
    (3) 208, 256, 257, 258, 260, 261, 280
    (4) 261

(7) 148, 258, 283, 298, 321
   (a) 257
   (b) 257
   (c) 257
s 5(1) 259
s 8(1) 259
Sch. 1 256
Supreme Court Act 1981
s 46 297
   (2) 5, 11, 12, 14, 33, 68, 285, 302
s 46A 84, 94, 294
Taking of Hostages Act 1982 . . . . .247, 258, 264
s 1 264
Territorial Sea Act 1987 . . . . .41, 43, 80, 81, 82, 83, 97, 105
s 1(1) 86, 98
   (2) 83, 98
   (3) 86, 87, 91, 98
   (4) 82
   (5) 82
   (6) 82
s 2(1) 82
   (2) 82
Territorial Waters Jurisdiction Act 1878 . . . . .38, 79–80, 81,
                                  95, 100, 105, 289
Pt 1 22
s 2 . . . . .3, 4, 68, 79
s 3 . . . . .53, 79, 301, 312
s 4 79
s 6 306
s 7 . . . . .21, 79, 80, 82, 95
Terrorism Act 2000 247
Pt III 267
s 1 267
   (a) 150
   (b) 150
   (c) 150
s 2(a)–(e) 150
s 3 150
s 4(a)–(d) 150
s 5 150
s 15 267
s 16 267
s 17 267

Terrorism Act 2000 (*cont.*):

s 18 267

s 59 . . . . .144, 149, 150, 151

  (1)(a) 149

    (b) 149

  (2)(a)–(e) 149

  (3) 149

  (4) 149, 150

  (5) 149

s 60 150

s 61 150

s 62 .143, 247, 248, 251, 252, 254, 266, 267

  (1) 266

  (2) 267

s 63 . . . . .247, 268

  (1) 268

s 63A 258

s 63B 258

s 63C 52

s 63D 262

s 125(2) 142

Sch. 16 142

Theft Act 1968 . . . . .42, 285

s 1 . . . . .25, 165

s 3 . . . . .25, 26

  (1) 24, 25, 169

s 8 305

s 14 181

s 15 . . . . .116, 123, 165, 253

s 15A 165, 170, 173

s 16 165

s 17 165

  (1) 171, 172

    (a) 172

    (b) 172

  (2)(b) 172

s 19 165

s 20(2) 114, 165, 166

s 21 . . . . .115, 165, 253

s 22 . . . . .24, 180

s 24 . . . . .25, 26

  (1) 24, 181

  (4) 181

s 24A 165

Theft Act (Northern Ireland) 1969
  s 15 253
  s 20 253
Theft Act 1978
  s 1 165
  s 2 165
Theft (Amendment) Act 1996
  s 3 165
Tokyo Convention Act 1964 . . . . .54, 314
  s 1 106
  s 4 304
Town Police Clauses Act 1847
  s 28 118
Trade Descriptions Act 1968
  s 21 . . . . .132, 133
Transport Act 1968
  s 96 120
Treason Act 1351 . . . . .218, 219
Treason Act 1795 218
Treason Felony Act 1848
  s 3 221
United Nations Personnel Act 1997 .258, 264–6
  s 1 . . . . .265, 266
    (1) 265
    (2) 265
  s 2 . . . . .265, 266
  s 3 265
  s 4 265
Vagrancy Act 1824
  s 4 118
Value Added Tax Act 1994 301
Visiting Forces Act 1952 . . . . .21, 212
Wales and Berwick Act 1746 (20 Geo. 3, c. 42) 64
War Crimes Act 1991 . . . . .50, 201, 231, 237, 240–1, 242
  s 1
    (1)(a) 240
     (b) 241
    (2) 204, 241
  Sch. 8 244
    Art. 8(2) (c) 244
        (d) 244
Wireless Telegraphy Act 1949
  s 1 . . . . .81, 82
  s 6 . . . . .82, 98

AUSTRALIA

Broadcasting Services Amendment (Online Services) Act 1999 193
Crimes at Sea Act 1979 285

FRANCE

Code Penal
  Art. 113–6 ....43, 336, 337
Criminal Code
  Art. R. 645–1 192

GERMANY

Criminal Code
  s 5.2 49
  s 7.1 51

NEW ZEALAND

New Zealand Crimes Act 1961
  s 7 341

REPUBLIC OF IRELAND

Criminal Law (Jurisdiction) Act 1976 249
Explosive Substances Act 1883
  s 2 250

UNITED STATES

Omnibus Diplomatic Security and Anti-terrorism Act 1986 51
USC Title 18
  s 2332 51
    (d) 51
  s 3236 117

INTERNATIONAL

International Criminal Court Statute
  Art. 6 237
  Art. 7 244
  Art. 70(1) 272

Table of Statutory Instruments

Air Navigation Order 2000 (SI 2000 No. 1562) 105
British Antarctic Territory Order 1989 (SI 1989 No. 842)...................216
Channel Tunnel (International Arrangements) Order 1993
   (SI 1993 No. 1813)...41, 100
   Art. 3 101–2
   Art. 5 100
      (1) 100
      (2) 100, 101
      (3) 102
   Sch. 1 100
Channel Tunnel (Miscellaneous Provisions) Order 1994
   (SI 1994 No. 1405)..100
   Art. 5 101
      (3) 102
      (4) 102
   Sch. 2 102
Channel Tunnel (Security) Order 1994 (SI 1994 No. 570) 102
   Pt II..258
   Art. 3 102
Chicago Convention on Civil Aviation 1944
   Art. 1 105
   Art. 2 105
Civil Jurisdiction (Offshore Activities) Order 1987
   (SI 1987 No. 2197)...300
Civilians (Application of Part II of the Army Act) Regulations
   (A.O. No. 123 of 1956)..215
Continental Shelf (Designation of Areas) Order 2000
   (SI 2000 No. 3062)...299
Continental Shelf (Designation of Areas) Order 2001
   (SI 2001 No. 3670)
Criminal Damage (Northern Ireland) Order 1977
   (SI 1977 No. 426)
   Art. 3 ....253, 262
Criminal Jurisdiction (Offshore Activities) Order 1987
   (SI 1987 No. 2198)...5, 299, 300
   Art. 3 299
   Art. 4 300
Criminal Justice Act 1993 (Commencement No. 10) Order 1999
   (SI 1999 No. 1189)...164
Criminal Justice Act 1993 (Commencement No. 11) Order 1999
   (SI 1999 No. 1499)...164

European Union Extradition Regulations 2002 (SI 2002 No. 419) 22
Evidence (European Court) Order 1976 (SI 1976 No. 428) 272
Excise Goods (Sales on Board Ships and Aircraft)
  Regulations 1999 (SI 1999 No. 1565) 105
Fishery Limits Order 1999 (SI 1999 No. 1741)...................................108
Fishing Vessels (Safety of 15–24 Metre Vessels)
  Regulations 2002 (SI 2002 No. 2201) 290
Hong Kong (British Nationality) Order 1986
  (SI 1986 No. 948)..206, 228
  s 4 205
Inshore Fishing (Prohibition of Fishing and Fishing Methods)
  (Scotland) Order 1989 87
International Criminal Court Act 2001 (Commencement)
  Order 2001 (SI 2001 No. 2161) 237
International Maritime Organization (Immunities and Privileges)
  Order 2002 (SI 2002 No. 1826)..19, 104
Isles of Scilly Order 1978 (SI 1978 No. 1844)
  Art. 2(1)..61
Justices of the Peace (Commission Areas) Order 1999
  (SI 1999 No. 3010)...69
Magistrates' Courts Committee Areas Order 1999
  (SI 1999 No. 3008)...69
Magistrates' Courts Committee Areas (Amendment) Order 2001
  (SI 2001 No. 695)..69
Magistrates' Courts (Northern Ireland) Order 1981
  (SI 1981 No. 1675)..93
  s 17A 294
Merchant Shipping (Registration of Ships) Regulations 1993
  (SI 1993 No. 3138)
  reg. 89...288
Merchant Shipping (Dangerous or Noxious Liquid Substances in Bulk)
  Regulations 1996 (SI 1996 No. 3010) 313
  reg 5...313
  reg 39...313
Merchant Shipping (Prevention of Oil Pollution) Regulations 1996
  (SI 1996 No. 2154)...312
  reg 12...312
  reg 13...312
  reg 16...312
    (6) 312
  reg 38...312
Merchant Shipping (Prevention of Pollution) (Limits) Regulations
  1996 (SI 1996 No. 2128)..313
Merchant Shipping (Prevention of Pollution by Garbage)
  Regulations 1998 (SI 1998 No. 1377) 313

Offshore Installations (Safety Zones) Order 2002
(SI 2002 No. 1063)..300
Protection of Military Remains Act 1986 (Designation of Vessels and
Controlled Sites) Order 2002 (SI 2002 No. 1761)............................280
Scotland Act 1998 (Border Rivers) Order (SI 1999 No. 1746)
Art. 1(2)...65
Art. 6 ....65, 66
(2)..66
(4)..65
Art. 7 65
(4)..65
Scotland Act 1998 (Consequential Modifications) (No.2) Order
(SI 1999 No. 1820)..108
Scottish Adjacent Water Boundaries Order 1999
(SI 1999 No. 1126)..84, 92, 108
Suppression of Terrorism Act 1978 (Designation of Countries)
Order 1978 (SI 1978 No. 1245) 259
Suppression of Terrorism Act 1978 (Designation of Countries)
Order 1978 (SI 1978 No. 1529) 258
Suppression of Terrorism Act 1978 (Designation of Countries)
Order 1978 (SI 1978 No. 1530) 258
Suppression of Terrorism Act 1978 (Designation of Countries)
Order 1978 (SI 1978 No. 1531) 258
Suppression of Terrorism Act 1978 (Designation of Countries)
Order 1979 (SI 1979 No. 497) 259
Suppression of Terrorism Act 1978 (Designation of Countries)
Order 1980 (SI 1980 No. 357) 259
Suppression of Terrorism Act 1978 (Designation of Countries)
Order 1980 (SI 1980 No. 1392) 259
Suppression of Terrorism Act 1978 (Designation of Countries)
Order 1981 (SI 1981 No. 1389) 259
Suppression of Terrorism Act 1978 (Designation of Countries)
Order 1981 (SI 1981 No. 1507) 259
Suppression of Terrorism Act 1978 (Designation of Countries)
Order 1985 (SI 1985 No. 2019) 259
Suppression of Terrorism Act 1978 (Designation of Countries)
Order 1986 (SI 1986 No. 271) 259
Suppression of Terrorism Act 1978 (Designation of Countries)
Order 1986 (SI 1986 No. 1137) 259
Suppression of Terrorism Act 1978 (Designation of Countries)
Order 1986 (SI 1986 No. 2146) 259
Suppression of Terrorism Act 1978 (Designation of Countries)
Order 1987 (SI 1987 No. 2137) 259
Suppression of Terrorism Act 1978 (Designation of Countries)
Order 1989 (SI 1989 No. 2210) 259

Suppression of Terrorism Act 1978 (Designation of Countries)
Order 1990 (SI 1990 No. 1272) 259
Suppression of Terrorism Act 1978 (Application of Provisions)
(India) Order 1993 (SI 1993 No. 2533)...............................259
Suppression of Terrorism Act 1978 (Designation of Countries)
Order 1994 (SI 1994 No. 2978) 259
Suppression of Terrorism Act 1978 (Designation of Countries)
Order 2003 (SI 2003 No. 6) 259
Territorial Sea Act 1987 (Isle of Man) Order 1991
(SI 1991 No. 1722)...83
Territorial Sea (Limits) Order 1989 (SI 1989 No. 482) 83
Territorial Sea (Amendment) Order 1998 (SI 1998 No. 2564)..........83, 87
    Art. 2 83
Territorial Waters Order in Council 1964 ....43, 44, 76, 80–2, 93
    Art. 2(1)..87, 88
        (2)...88
    Art. 3 90
    Art. 4 ....87, 90, 91, 92
        (b)...87
        (c) 87, 91
    Art. 5 ....88, 90, 91
        (2)...87
Territory: Falkland Islands Courts (Overseas Jurisdiction)
Order 1989 (SI 1989 No. 2399)
    s 6...216
United Nations and International Court of Justice
(Immunities and Privileges) Order (SI 1974 No. 1261)........................18
United States of America (Extradition) Order
(SI 1976 No. 2144)..158, 263
United States of America (Extradition) (Amendment)
Order 1986 (SI 1986 No. 2020) 263

Table of Conventions and Treaties

Antarctic Treaty
  Art. III(1)(b) 217
  Art. IV 216
  Art. VIII 216
  Art. XXIV 217
Budapest Cybercrime Convention ETS No. 185 ....183, 184, 186
  Art. 2 183
  Art. 3 183
  Art. 4 183
  Art. 5 183
  Art. 6 183
  Art. 7 183
  Art. 8 183
  Art. 9 183
  Art. 10 183
Comprehensive Nuclear Test Ban Treaty 1996 252
Convention for the Amelioration of the Condition of the
  Wounded and Sick in Armed Forces in the Field 1949 .....237, 238, 245
  Art. 2 239
  Art. 49 238
Convention for the Amelioration of the Condition of Wounded, Sick and
  Shipwrecked Members of Armed Forces at Sea 1949 ....237, 238, 245
  Art. 2 239
  Art. 49 238
Convention on Combating Bribery of Foreign Public Officials in
  International Business Transactions 1997 273
Convention on the Conservation of Antarctic Marine
  Living Resources 1980 278
Convention on the Fight against Corruption involving Officials of the
  European Communities or Officials of Member States of the
  European Union 1997 273
Convention on the Prevention and Punishment of the Crime of
  Genocide 1948
  Art. 2 237
Convention Relative to the Protection of Civilian Persons in
  Time of War 1949 ....237, 238, 245
  Art. 2 239
  Art. 49 238

Convention Relative to the Treatment of Prisoners
of War 1949 ....237, 238, 239, 245
  Art. 2 239
  Art. 49 238
Council of Europe Criminal Law Corruption Convention 1999 273
European Convention on Mutual Assistance in
Criminal Matters 2000 334
European Convention on the Suppression of Terrorism
ETS No. 90 (1977) 254, 255, 330
  Art. 1 ....255, 256, 257, 258, 261
  Art. 2 256
    (1) 255
    (2) 255
  Art. 5 255
  Art. 6 ....255, 256, 257, 261, 262
  Art. 7 ....255, 256, 257, 258, 261, 262
First (Corruption) Protocol to the Convention on the
Protection of the European Communities' Financial Interests
(The Fraud Convention)..273
Geneva Convention on the High Seas 1958 ....36, 91, 303, 307
  Art. 7 89
Geneva Convention on the Territorial Sea and Contiguous Zone 1958
  Art. 7 ....44, 81
Hague Convention for the Suppression of Unlawful Seizure of
Aircraft 1970 ....54, 314, 317, 318
  Art. 3(3) 318
International Convention against the Taking of Hostages 1979 264
International Convention for the Prevention of Pollution
from Ships 1973...312
Montreal Convention for the Suppression of Unlawful Acts
against the Safety of Civil Aviation 1974.............54, 314, 317, 320, 322
OECD Convention on Combating Bribery of Foreign Public Officials
in International Business Transactions 273
Ottawa Convention on Anti-Personnel Mines 1997 279
Protocol Additional to the Geneva Conventions of 12 August
1949, and relating to the Protection of Victims of International
Armed Conflicts (Protocol 1)...238, 243, 245
  Art. 44 240
  Art. 45 240
  Art. 73 240
  Art. 85
    (3)...239
    (4)...239

Protocol for the Suppression of Unlawful Acts Against
the Safety of Fixed Platforms Located on the Continental
Shelf 1992..308, 309
Protocol for the Suppression of Unlawful Acts of Violence at
Airports Serving International Civil Aviation 1988.............................322
Rome Convention for the Suppression of Unlawful Acts against
the Safety of Maritime Navigation 1988 ....53, 307, 308, 309
Rome Treaty 1999...55
Sangatte Protocol Concerning Frontier Controls and Policing,
Cooperation in Criminal Justice, Public Safety and
Mutual Assistance...100
Art. 11 101
Art. 30 102
    (2) 101
Art. 38 ....101, 231
    (2)(a)...102
Schengen Convention
Art. 27 ....132, 133
Single Convention on Narcotic Drugs, New York 1961 133
Tokyo Convention on Offences and Certain Other Acts
Committed on Board Aircraft 1963..54, 314
Treaty in the Principles Governing the Activities of States in the
Exploration and Use of Outer Space 1967...104
Art. 6 278
Tripartite Agreement 100
Art. 11 102
United Nations Convention Against Torture and other Cruel,
Inhuman or Degrading Treatment or Punishment 1984.........20, 39, 245
Art. 1 245
Arts. 5–7 245
United Nations Convention on the Law of
the Sea 1982...28, 43, 86, 106, 312
Art. 2 76
Art. 3 76
Art. 5 88
Art. 7 ....83, 85
Art. 9 85
Art. 10 ....44, 85, 89
Art. 12 85
Art. 13 88
Art. 15 85
Art. 16 85
Art. 27 ....21, 52, 80
Arts. 55–7 106
Art. 56(a) 106

United Nations Convention on the Law of
the Sea 1982 (*cont.*):
  Art. 58(2)..305
  Art. 60 107
  Art. 73 107
  Art. 86 285
  Art. 91 ....283, 284
  Art. 92 283
  Art. 94 284
  Art. 101 ....53, 304
  Art. 102 304
  Art. 103 304
  Art. 111 36
  Art. 121 88
  Pt V..107
United Nations Convention on the Physical Protection of
  Nuclear Material 1980..253
United Nations Convention on the Prevention and Punishment
  of Crimes against Internationally Protected Persons 1973 262
United Nations Convention on the Safety of United Nations and
  Associated Personnel 1994...264, 266
United Nations Convention for the Suppression of the
  Financing of Terrorism 1999..268
  Art. 97 284
United Nations Convention for the Suppression of Terrorist
  Bombings 1998 267
Vienna Convention Against Illicit Traffic in Narcotic Drugs
  and Psychotropic Substances 1988......................................311
  Art. 17 311
Vienna Convention on Consular Relations 1963...................18
  Art. 17 18
  Art. 31 103
  Art. 41 18
  Art. 43 18
  Art. 71 18
Vienna Convention on Diplomatic Relations 1961 ....19, 104
  Art. 22 103
  Art. 29 16
  Art. 30 103
  Art. 31(1)..16
  Art. 32 104
  Art. 37 16
  Art. 39(2)..17
  Art. 41 15

1

Ambit and Jurisdiction in English Criminal Law

INTRODUCTION

The purpose of this work is to define, analyse, and explain the territorial and extraterritorial ambit of English criminal law or, in common legal parlance, the limits of English criminal jurisdiction. This topic has attracted considerable interest in recent years, largely because of concerns raised by international terrorism, fraud, and other forms of high-profile transnational crime; but it has suffered from many years of neglect, and remains largely misunderstood by the majority of criminal lawyers. This neglect and misunderstanding can be seen not only in the confused and unstructured development of the law itself, but also in the way in which the subject is covered (or not covered) within published works on English criminal law. Although a good deal has been written on the subject of criminal jurisdiction under international law,[1] there has been no comparable attempt to provide a comprehensive account of the very different issues that arise under English law.[2] In the standard practitioners' reference works on English criminal law and practice, consideration of the subject is subsumed within chapters dealing with matters of criminal procedure or police powers.[3] In textbooks on criminal

---

[1] This includes a number of recent publications which focus on 'international criminal law' and on the jurisdiction of the International Criminal Court and other international criminal tribunals. See, e.g., Kriangsak Kittichaisaree, *International Criminal Law* (2001); I. Bantekas, S. Nash, and M. Mackarel, *International Criminal Law* (2001); Antonio Cassese, *International Criminal Law* (2003).

[2] The periodical literature has fared somewhat better. Notable amongst the handful of major publications in this field is Glanville Williams's three-part article, 'Venue and the Ambit of Criminal Law' (1965) 81 *Law Quarterly Review* 276, which for many years provided the most scholarly and detailed published analysis of the subject from the viewpoint of English law; but much of the relevant law has changed since this was written, and its value is now largely historical. Two official publications are worthy of particular note. In 1978, the Law Commission published a report entitled, *The Territorial and Extraterritorial Extent of the Criminal Law* (Law Com. No. 91). The Commission's analysis of the law was incomplete and in places inaccurate, but the Report nevertheless contains some valuable guidance as to possible reforms. A later (1989) Law Commission Report, *Jurisdiction over Offences of Fraud and Dishonesty with a Foreign Element* (Law Com. No. 180), addressed some of the issues neglected in the 1978 Report, and led to the enactment of major reforms in Pt I of the Criminal Justice Act 1993.

[3] See *Archbold 2003*, Chapter 2; *Blackstone's Criminal Practice 2003*, section D1. See also the Law Commission's 1989 Report, *A Criminal Code for England and Wales* (Law Com. No. 177), para. 3.13. In the 2004 edition of *Blackstone's Criminal Practice*, the relevant material will, however, be moved to section A (General Principles).

law, it is often glossed over in a few paragraphs, or in many cases omitted in its entirety; and yet it involves issues that are utterly fundamental to any concept of 'English' criminal law. In what parts of the world and to what persons does that system of English law apply? Who, in other words, are its subjects, and what is its domain? When is an act such as theft, rape, or murder capable of being categorized as a crime under English law?

THE AMBIT OF THE LAW AND THE
ACTUS REUS OF AN OFFENCE

The fundamental importance of the above issues may be demonstrated by reference to the *actus reus* of almost any offence under English law. The *actus reus* generally consists not only of proscribed conduct and (sometimes) of the proscribed results of that conduct, but also of the circumstances in which that conduct, etc., is committed. The location or place of the conduct or its results, and/or the status of the person who is committing that conduct, may be relevant circumstances for the purposes of this *actus reus*. Most of the principal road traffic offences, for example, are capable of commission only 'on a road or other public place' and some can be committed only by persons who are disqualified or uninsured drivers. This much may be considered obvious; but it is less widely recognized that the country or other geographical location of the alleged crime, and in some cases the nationality of the alleged offender, may equally constitute relevant circumstances. To put it another way, issues that criminal lawyers generally classify as 'matters of jurisdiction' and look up in their reference works by turning to chapters on procedure, as if they were merely concerned with the powers or competence of the court, should properly be considered as elements relating to the *actus reus* itself.

Territorial or geographical limitations on the ambit or extent of specific criminal offences are usually implied rather than expressed. Such limitations may, for example, be presumed under well-established principles of statutory interpretation, but they may occasionally be expressed in the definition of the offence. This may be true even of a common law offence. Take, for example, Sir Edward Coke's classic definition of murder at common law:

Murder is when a man of sound memory and of the age of discretion unlawfully killeth within any county of the realm any reasonable creature *in rerum natura* under the King's peace, with malice aforethought either expressed by the party or implied by law, so as the party wounded or hurt, etc., die of the wound or hurt, etc., within a year and a day after the same cause.[4]

While most works on criminal law recite the greater part of this definition, including the perennially troublesome reference to the 'King's peace' and

---

[4] *Institutes*, vol. 3, 47.

the words dealing with the 'year and a day' rule that was abolished in 1996, most simply omit the clause in which Coke defines murder as an act committed 'within any county of the realm'. Fewer still attempt to explain that clause. If asked why it has been omitted, the authors would presumably reply that it is no longer applicable, because many cases of murder committed outside the realm are now offences punishable under English law. With respect, however, the creation of exceptions (even multiple exceptions) does not invalidate the general rule. Some murders committed outside the realm (for example, in adjacent territorial waters) may indeed be punishable as offences under English law, but only in strictly limited circumstances[5] for which specific provision has been made by legislation, and subject to any special restrictions imposed by that legislation. As far as the common law is concerned, Coke's original definition largely holds good.[6] Nor is this rule peculiar to murder. It governs all common law and statutory offences, save where (and to the extent that) some express provision to the contrary has been made. To put it another way, misconduct committed outside the realm cannot ordinarily amount to the *actus reus* of an offence under English law. It is not merely a question of jurisdiction but a question of criminal liability. This is an issue to which I will return later in this chapter.

DEFINING THE AMBIT OF THE CRIMINAL LAW

The answers to questions concerning the ambit of the criminal law are often surprisingly complex. Indeed, they are frequently a great deal more complex than they need to be. The general rule at common law is relatively simple, however. The criminal law of England extends over the realm of England and Wales and over all persons who are within the realm, but does not generally extend to things done outside it, even when done by British citizens. This applies both to common law and statutory offences, and is sometimes referred to as the principle of 'territoriality'. As Viscount Simonds said in *Cox v. Army Council*[7]: 'Apart from those exceptional cases in which specific provision is made in respect of acts committed abroad, the whole body of the criminal law of England deals only with acts committed in England.'[8] Like most rules of English law, however, this has become subject to numerous statutory qualifications and exceptions. To give just

---

[5] Notably under the Offences Against the Person Act 1861, s. 9, or the Territorial Waters Jurisdiction Act 1878, s. 2.

[6] The realm of England and Wales now includes Greater London and the Isles of Scilly, as well as the counties to which Coke refers (Interpretation Act 1978, Sch. 1).

[7] [1963] AC 48, 67.

[8] A judge would now refer to acts committed in 'England and Wales'. See the Interpretation Act 1978, Sch. 1. Only one criminal statute now in force still deems references to England to include Wales. This is the Criminal Justice Act 1948, s. 80.

a few examples: English criminal law governs behaviour aboard British ships,[9] whether these are at sea or in foreign ports or harbours; and it has also been made applicable (in so far as indictable offences are concerned) to acts committed within the territorial or internal waters adjacent to the coasts of England or Wales, even where such acts are committed aboard foreign ships.[10] Some offences, such as murder, bigamy, or torture, have been given specific extraterritorial ambits, so that cases may fall within English criminal jurisdiction even when the relevant acts were committed entirely within foreign countries;[11] and some individuals, such as those who are members of the British armed forces, remain subject to the general corpus of English criminal law when abroad, as well as to the laws of the state they are visiting or residing in at the time. These and many other special cases will be analysed and explained in the course of this work, but few are straightforward, and many are absurdly complicated. Before delving too deeply into them, it is necessary to examine the general rule in more detail.

Territoriality: the General Rule

Formulating an accurate statement of the general rule governing the ambit of English criminal law is not easy. The problem is one of distinguishing between the general rule itself and the principal exceptions or qualifications to it. Where does the general rule end, and where do the exceptions or qualifications begin?

Some might perhaps argue that Viscount Simonds's *dictum* in *Cox* v. *Army Council* (p. 3 above) was misleading, because the general corpus of English criminal law enjoys a much wider ambit than he suggests. Any formulation of a modern general rule should, on that view, include a reference to British ships, which fall within the jurisdiction of the Admiral, as now exercised by the ordinary criminal courts. By the same token, it should then also include references to things done in the territorial or internal waters adjacent to England and Wales,[12] or on British controlled aircraft in flight.[13] These are also governed generally by English criminal law, albeit by virtue only of specific legislation to that effect.

A new indictable offence, created tomorrow by Parliament, would indeed apply, without the need for any further jurisdictional provisions, to misconduct committed aboard British ships and aircraft, or within English

---

[9] This jurisdiction is derived from that of the Admiral, rather than from the common law. Not all British ships are 'United Kingdom ships', as defined by the Merchant Shipping Act 1995.

[10] Territorial Waters Jurisdiction Act 1878, s. 2.

[11] Offences Against the Person Act 1861, s. 57.

[12] Territorial waters are not an integral part of England and Wales, which are defined as the areas comprising their respective counties: Interpretation Act 1978, Sch. 1. Some internal waters lie within the realm, but most do not. See further Chapter 3 below.

[13] Civil Aviation Act 1982, s. 92.

territorial and internal waters; but it would also apply (*inter alia*) to many offshore oil and gas platforms;[14] to members of the British armed forces[15] and to Crown servants,[16] when they are stationed abroad; to British citizens who are passengers or stowaways on foreign ships;[17] and to 'United Kingdom nationals' in the unclaimed sector of Antarctica.[18] These cannot all be included within a statement of the general rule. Somewhere along the line, we have undoubtedly entered the realm of special cases and exceptions—but where? To find an answer, it is submitted that we must go back to the position at common law.

As previously explained, the common law of England did not originally apply beyond the shores of the realm. At common law, criminal courts had jurisdiction only over things done within their own counties, and the counties of the realm ended on the foreshore, where the dry land meets the open sea, in accordance with the current state of the tide.[19] The common law had no conception of territorial waters or of crimes committed abroad. These are all the creation of legislation. Viscount Simonds was therefore correct in saying that any extraterritorial application of English law depends on specific legislative authority. This is true even of jurisdiction over British ships at sea, because the ordinary criminal law of England (in contrast to the ancient jurisdiction of the Admiral and his deputies) applies to offences committed at sea only as a result of legislation.[20] Despite the existence of many significant qualifications and exceptions, the territoriality principle, as described by Viscount Simonds, should therefore be accepted as an accurate statement of the general rule in English law.

Territoriality and Criminal Legislation

A statute dealing with criminal liability under English law ordinarily ends with a provision indicating whether (and if so to what extent) that statute applies to Scotland or Northern Ireland. In many cases, a statute will not apply to either; and even where an offence-creating provision *does* apply to other parts of the United Kingdom, the general rule is that any offences committed within Scotland or Northern Ireland are offences under Scots or Northern Ireland law alone, and are not punishable under English law. Dangerous driving, for example, is punishable in England under the same provision of the Road Traffic Act 1988 as is dangerous driving in Scotland,[21] but English courts have no jurisdiction over an offence of dangerous

---

[14] Criminal Jurisdiction (Offshore Activities) Order 1987.
[15] See, e.g., the Army Act 1955, s. 70.   [16] Criminal Justice Act 1948, s. 31.
[17] Merchant Shipping Act 1995, s. 282.   [18] Antarctic Act 1994, s. 21.
[19] The low-water mark is often said to mark this boundary, but this is open to dispute. Harbours, creeks, and rivers may, however, lie within the body of a county. See generally Chapter 3 below.
[20] Namely the Offences at Sea Act 1799, s. 1, and the Supreme Court Act 1981, s. 46(2).
[21] There are some procedural differences. The Act does not extend to Northern Ireland.

driving committed in Scotland, nor do Scottish courts have any jurisdiction over such an offence committed in England. To put it another way, dangerous driving on one side of the border is not an offence on the other side. Similarly, where the rules of English law have been adopted within British overseas territories, such as the Falkland Islands, misconduct committed there cannot ordinarily amount to an offence within the jurisdiction of English courts.[22]

There is no need for a criminal statute to contain any express provision restricting its potential application over things done abroad, because there is a well-established presumption against the creation of extraterritorial liability. As Lord Reid explained in *Treacy* v. *DPP*[23]:

It has been recognised from time immemorial that there is a strong presumption that when Parliament, in an Act applying to England, creates an offence by making certain things punishable, it does not intend this to apply to any act done by anyone in any country other than England. Parliament, being sovereign, is fully entitled to make an enactment on a wider basis. But the presumption is well known to draftsmen, and where there is an intention to make an English Act or part of such an Act apply to acts done outside England, that intention is and must be made clear in the Act.

There is an even stricter presumption against any interpretation that would result in the imposition of liability on foreigners for things done entirely abroad. In *Air India* v. *Wiggins*,[24] the House of Lords approved a *dictum* of Lord Russell of Killowen CJ in *R* v. *Jameson*,[25] to the effect that such a construction will be avoided unless none other is possible.

Exceptions to the Principle of Territoriality

While the principle of territoriality is well established in English criminal law, it has hardly ever been free from statutory exceptions, and such exceptions are now far more numerous and extensive than ever before. There are usually good reasons for the creation of such exceptions. Many of them give effect to the United Kingdom's international obligations under multilateral Conventions, and are designed to combat some of the most dangerous or troublesome transnational crimes of today, including crimes against the safety of aviation and crimes involving the trafficking of illicit drugs. Nothing in *Air India* v. *Wiggins* or *R* v. *Jameson* prevents such exceptions extending to the acts of foreigners, provided that suitably clear and unambiguous words are used. Nor should it be assumed that the ambit of a given offence is governed only by the legislation that creates it. An offence may also acquire a limited extraterritorial ambit as a result of provisions contained within other enactments, whether passed before or since. The Criminal Damage Act 1971, for example, possesses no extraterritorial

---

[22] *R* v. *Hooper* (1734) W Kel 190; *R* v. *Munton* (1793) 1 Esp 62.
[23] [1971] AC 537, 551.   [24] [1980] 1 WLR 815.   [25] [1896] 2 QB 425.

ambit of its own, but there are several possible circumstances in which criminal damage committed abroad might nevertheless amount to an offence triable under English law. In *R* v. *Kelly*,[26] three British citizens were convicted at the Crown Court in Newcastle of committing criminal damage aboard the Danish-registered ferry, *Winston Churchill*, whilst they were passengers on that ship, outside British territorial waters. The House of Lords confirmed that their acts of vandalism aboard the ferry were offences against English criminal law by virtue of what is now section 281 of the Merchant Shipping Act 1995.[27] This deals with offences committed by British citizens aboard foreign ships 'to which they do not belong'. In those specific circumstances (and in several others), criminal damage becomes an 'extraterritorial offence'.

Although much of it is modern, the law governing extraterritorial offences has developed on an unsatisfactory piecemeal basis and suffers from a lack of coherent general principles, which successive legislative interventions have done nothing to rectify. Most such offences are also inherently difficult to prosecute, especially in light of the constraints imposed by English rules of evidence and procedure. Some extraterritorial offences appear to be 'paper tigers': Draconian and far-reaching on paper, but unused (and perhaps almost unusable) in practice. One of my aims in this work is to consider whether a more coherent, effective, and principled approach to extraterritorial crime could be adopted, and what form this might take.

The Extent of Territorial Jurisdiction

Even if we ignore, for the moment, the complications that may arise in respect of extraterritorial offences, we are still left with significant problems in defining the standard or territorial extent of the criminal law. There are two main reasons for this. The first is that the territorial boundaries of England and Wales are complex and are often surprisingly difficult to identify or define. The maritime boundaries, in particular, require very careful identification and analysis. There are no fewer than four distinct maritime zones within the waters adjacent to the coasts of England and Wales, each with its own distinct legal regime. The second (and in practice the more significant) reason is that it is increasingly common for offences to be committed across jurisdictional frontiers. A banking or investment fraud, for example, may be perpetrated against European investors by dishonest dealers operating from London.[28] A fraudulent inducement may deceive the victims into transferring funds to numbered bank accounts in Switzerland,

---

[26] [1982] AC 665.
[27] The provision then in force was s. 686(1) of the Merchant Shipping Act 1894. The 1995 Act is primarily a consolidation of pre-existing law.
[28] As in *Secretary of State for Trade* v. *Markus* [1976] AC 35.

which the fraudulent dealers hold or control. In a converse scenario, numerous victims in England and Wales have fallen victim in recent years to the notorious Nigerian '419' advance fee frauds,[29] credulously transferring substantial funds to accounts in Nigeria or neighbouring states, in the misguided belief that such payments will secure them a substantial share in a multi-million pound fund that is to be smuggled out of Nigeria with their assistance. In neither of these examples is it easy to identify a particular location at which the relevant offence can obviously be said to have been committed.

Such difficulties are by no means confined to fraud cases. A seaman stabbed in a knife attack aboard a foreign merchant ship on the high seas may be airlifted to a hospital in England, and subsequently die there of his wounds.[30] A blackmailer may post a letter in England, containing demands that are subsequently received and acted upon by his victim in Germany;[31] or a pornographer may set up a website based in the USA, containing obscene content that is accessed by surfers or subscribers in England.[32] These are just a few examples. Transnational or cross-frontier offences are by no means a new phenomenon, but they are becoming increasingly common and may take increasingly serious or complex forms, including, of course, terrorist offences that may involve the murders of hundreds or even thousands of victims.[33] In comparison with purely extraterritorial offences, which are rarely prosecuted, cross-frontier offences are more likely to give rise to legal difficulties and are far more likely to come before the courts.

There is often no simple answer to the question whether cross-frontier offences will be held to fall within the ambit of English criminal law. The relevant law is not always clear, nor is it generally based on any coherent policy or principle. All too often, the legal answer to such a question may turn on the precise wording of a particular offence-creating provision, even though that provision is most unlikely to have been drafted with cross-frontier jurisdiction issues in mind. Wider policy considerations are rarely identified in the case law and seldom have any significant effect on the outcome of a case. Judicial attempts to identify and apply such considerations, whilst laudable in principle, have generally proved unsatisfactory in practice, a notable example being Lord Diplock's argument, in *Treacy v. DPP*,[34]

---

[29] Named after the section of the Nigerian Criminal Code that applies to such frauds, which are perpetrated in enormous numbers and on a worldwide scale. For information on these and other common transnational frauds originating from West Africa (including the equally notorious 'magic money' scam), see www.met.police.uk/fraudalert/419.htm.

[30] An updated version of the facts of *R v. Lewis* (1857) Dears & Bell 182.

[31] As in *Treacy v. DPP* [1971] AC 537.

[32] As in *R v. Perrin* [2002] All ER (D) 359; [2002] EWCA Crim 747.

[33] The destruction of Pan-Am flight 103 over Lockerbie in December 1988, and the outrages committed in America on 11 September 2001 each illustrate the threat posed by the global terrorism phenomenon.   [34] [1971] AC 537, 561. See below, p. 34.

that the ambit of English criminal law should be limited only by the principles of 'international comity'. The idea that international comity (or the rules of international law) should determine the extent of English criminal law is an attractive one in some respects, and has gained a number of supporters, but it has never truly represented the position under English law, and Lord Diplock himself quietly abandoned the idea just a few years later.[35]

Legislation specifically formulated with cross-frontier issues in mind remains rare. Even where such legislation does exist (as, for example, in Part 1 of the Criminal Justice Act 1993) difficulties caused by questionable or defective drafting mean that it does not always achieve its aims. The development of a coherent and effective general principle for resolving problems of jurisdiction over cross-frontier crime presents a challenge that no law reform body has fully succeeded in meeting. The challenge, however, is one that must still be addressed.

AMBIT AND JURISDICTION CONTRASTED

Judges, law reporters, commentators, and Parliamentary draftsmen all tend to categorize questions concerning the ambit or applicability of the criminal law under the heading 'jurisdiction'. This practice has now become so widespread as to be almost universal, but 'jurisdiction' is a term with a number of possible meanings, and this ambiguity may sometimes lead to confusion.

References to 'jurisdiction' may indeed refer to the ambit or applicability of the law itself. Does English criminal law apply in a given locality or situation, or to the conduct of which this particular defendant stands accused? But they may instead refer to the jurisdictional competence of the court. Does this particular court have jurisdiction to deal with this defendant, and with the particular offence with which he is charged?[36]

A negative answer to the first of these questions must inevitably dictate a negative answer to the second, because proceedings in English criminal courts are invariably governed by English law. It may sometimes be necessary for an English criminal court to enquire into the law of a foreign country and take note of its effect,[37] but in no circumstances can an English court try

---

[35] See *Secretary of State for Trade* v. *Markus* [1976] AC 35.

[36] A third possible meaning (albeit one that is unlikely to be confused with the other two) concerns the right to take executive or police action in order to enforce the law or the decisions of the courts. See Geoff Gilbert, 'Crimes Sans Frontiers: Jurisdictional Problems in English Law' (1992) 63 *British Yearbook of International Law* 415, 416.

[37] As, for example, where the defendant is charged with handling (in England and Wales) goods allegedly stolen abroad. Evidence as to the relevant foreign law is essential in such cases.

a defendant for an alleged offence under a foreign system of law.[38] In this respect, the position of the criminal courts may be contrasted with that of the civil courts, who may indeed be required, in accordance with the rules of private international law, to apply foreign law in order to resolve a dispute over which they have properly assumed jurisdiction.

Once any question of ambit or applicability has been resolved, and it is clear that the act of which the defendant is accused would indeed amount to an offence under English law, any question as to the jurisdictional competence of a particular court will ordinarily be a procedural one. The Crown Court, for example, has only a limited original jurisdiction over summary offences; magistrates' courts have no jurisdiction to try offences that are triable only on indictment; and the jurisdiction of courts-martial is strictly governed by legislation.

Jurisdictional issues of the latter kind are not, for the most part, the issues with which this work is concerned, but there are some exceptions, because the distinction between the jurisdictional competence of the courts and the territorial ambit of the law is not always as clear as the above analysis might tend to suggest. The ambit of purely summary offences, for example, remains constrained in most cases by the territorially-limited jurisdictional competence of the magistrates' courts that deal with them. In exceptional cases, provision is made for the trial of summary offences committed abroad, or at sea, but one cannot assume, in the absence of any such provision, that the ambit of a summary offence extends even to things done within English territorial waters. Historically, the concepts of ambit and venue were once intertwined, and the procedural rules of venue exerted a powerful constraining influence on the ambit of the common law itself. The nature and extent of this influence will be considered in the following chapter.

Drawing Distinctions in Practice

One may sometimes come across a statement such as: 'English courts ordinarily have no jurisdiction over offences committed in France.' If the terms 'jurisdiction' and 'offence' are interpreted in a loose or general sense, this statement may be considered true. Persons who commit burglaries in France cannot ordinarily be tried or punished in English courts. An international lawyer might also observe that, save where the alleged burglar is a British citizen or a United Kingdom national,[39] the United Kingdom would

---

[38] There may seem at first to be an exception to this rule in respect of fishery offences committed on the River Tweed or its subsidiaries, because these are governed by the Salmon and Freshwater Fisheries (Scotland) Act 1951, even in reaches of the Tweed that lie entirely within England and within the jurisdiction of English courts. The better view, however, is that the 1951 Act is, to that limited extent, and despite its Scottish origin, an integral part of the law of England. See below, p. 65.

[39] This is not the same thing as a British citizen, although all British citizens are UK nationals. See below, p. 207.

have no right to assert any criminal jurisdiction over such a matter. Under international law, such a burglary would be none of the United Kingdom's business; and to assert jurisdiction in such a case might result in an official complaint by the French Government over what it would doubtless consider to be an unwarranted usurpation of French sovereignty.

As a matter of strict English law, however, the statement may be condemned as inaccurate. Burglary is an indictable offence, and under section 46(2) of the Supreme Court Act 1981 the Crown Court has 'exclusive jurisdiction in proceedings on indictment for offences wherever committed'.[40] The correct analysis is that a burglary committed in France is not ordinarily an offence under English law at all. In those exceptional cases in which a burglary committed in France *is* an offence under English law (as, for example, where the burglar is a British diplomat[41]), section 46(2) ensures that the Crown Court will indeed have jurisdiction to try that offence.[42] What section 46(2) does *not* do is to extend the ambit of ordinary criminal offences so as to make them applicable abroad. It is, in other words, a mere 'venue' provision.

In *Treacy* v. *DPP*,[43] Lord Diplock issued a rare judicial warning against the dangers of confusing questions of mere jurisdiction with questions concerning the ambit or applicability of the substantive law. The appellant in that case had posted a blackmail demand from England to a woman living in Frankfurt, and it was argued that the courts in England had 'no jurisdiction' to try him; but as Lord Diplock explained 'The question in this appeal is not whether the . . . court had jurisdiction to try the appellant . . . but whether the facts alleged and proved against him amounted to a criminal offence under the English Act of Parliament.'

Parliament's chronic inconsistency in its use of the term 'jurisdiction' is, however, a major problem in this context. Sometimes that term is used in order to extend the ambit of criminal offences, and sometimes it is used, as in section 46(2) of the Supreme Court Act 1981, in relation only to the power of a court to try an offence, assuming that the substantive law already applies to the conduct that is alleged to amount to that offence. In section 46(2), the particular context makes the proper meaning relatively easy to determine, but this is not always the case. Sometimes the courts have struggled to understand what Parliament actually meant.

This can be illustrated by contrasting the cases of *R* v. *Martin*[44] and *R* v. *Naylor*.[45] Martin was charged with the unlawful possession of opium aboard a British aircraft in flight between Bahrain and Singapore. The Dangerous Drugs Regulations then in force did not purport to have any

---

[40] This provision restates the rule originally laid down by the Courts Act 1971, s. 6.

[41] Diplomats are Crown servants, and are thus subject to the Criminal Justice Act 1948, s. 31.

[42] The diplomat's conduct would amount to an offence under English law by virtue of the Criminal Justice Act 1948, s. 31. As to the power of magistrates' courts to try an 'either way' offence committed abroad, see the Magistrates' Courts Act 1980, s. 2(4).

[43] [1971] AC 537, 559.   [44] [1956] 2 QB 272.   [45] [1962] 2 QB 527.

extraterritorial effect, but Martin was prosecuted on the basis of section 6(1) of the Civil Aviation Act 1949. This provided: 'Any offence whatever committed on a British aircraft shall, for the purpose of conferring jurisdiction, be deemed to have been committed in any place where the offender may for the time being be.' Devlin J held that Martin had committed no offence within the ambit of English criminal law. Section 6 of the 1949 Act was, he said, a mere venue provision. It ensured that if an offence was committed aboard a British aircraft there would be a court with jurisdiction to try and punish the offender, but it did not actually extend the ambit of any particular offences so as to make them applicable aboard such aircraft. He was thus interpreting that provision in the same way as we must now interpret section 46(2) of the Supreme Court Act 1981. The problem with Devlin J's ruling, however, was that it largely deprived the provision in question of any practical effect. There were at that time very few criminal offences with their own extraterritorial ambit, and even fewer that could be committed aboard an aircraft.[46] In *Naylor*, therefore, Lord Parker CJ (sitting as a trial judge) refused to follow Devlin J's interpretation, and construed section 6 as a provision that both extended the ambit of ordinary criminal offences and provided a venue for trial. Naylor could therefore be tried in England for an offence of larceny allegedly committed aboard a British aircraft in flight over the sea. In the context of this particular legislation, Lord Parker's interpretation made a great deal more sense.

Section 6 of the Civil Aviation Act 1949 was repealed by the Civil Aviation Act 1982, which clarified the position, but the problem of distinguishing between venue provisions and provisions that extend the ambit of the law remains alive in other contexts. A particularly troublesome example can be found in section 279 of the Merchant Shipping Act 1995.

Merchant Shipping Act 1995, Section 279

The Merchant Shipping Act 1995 is primarily a consolidation of earlier legislation, dating from 1894 to 1993, and the provisions headed 'Jurisdiction' (sections 279–282) are mostly derived from sections 684–687 of the Merchant Shipping Act 1894; provisions that Glanville Williams had previously condemned as 'illustrations of cloudy draftsmanship'.[47] The 1894 Act was itself a consolidation of earlier legislation, which means that some of the 1995 Act's jurisdiction provisions effectively date back to the Merchant Shipping Act 1854. Unfortunately, the passage of time has done little to clarify their meaning. The provisions consolidated in the 1894 Act were not

---

[46] Murder and manslaughter, for example, had extraterritorial effect by virtue of the Offences Against the Person Act 1861, s. 9, but this provision deals only with homicides committed 'on land outside the United Kingdom'.

[47] 'Venue and the Ambit of Criminal Law' (1965) 81 *Law Quarterly Review* 276, 409.

arranged into any coherent overall structure, and no attempt was made to use the term 'jurisdiction' consistently within the Act. While we have learned to expect this kind of thing from the consolidating legislation of the Victorian era,[48] it is most disappointing to find it repeated in a modern statute.

Whilst all four of the 'jurisdiction' provisions in the Act raise problems of interpretation, most are best considered at a later stage, in the specific context of maritime or coastal jurisdiction. Section 279, however, may usefully be considered at this juncture, because it provides such a good illustration of the confusion that may be caused by careless use of the word 'jurisdiction'. This section (which restates section 684 of the 1894 Act) provides:

(1) For the purpose of conferring jurisdiction, any offence under this Act shall be deemed to have been committed in any place in the United Kingdom where the offender may for the time being be.
(2) For the same purpose, any matter of complaint under this Act[49] shall be deemed to have arisen in any place in the United Kingdom where the person complained against may for the time being be.
(3) The jurisdiction under subsections (1) and (2) above shall be in addition to and not in derogation of any jurisdiction or power of a court under any other enactment.

The purpose of this provision is to ensure that courts within the United Kingdom are empowered to try offences created by (or consolidated within) the Act itself. As Ashworth J pointed out in *R* v. *Liverpool Justices, ex p Molyneux*,[50] it has 'no bearing whatsoever' on offences created by any other statutes, such as the Theft Acts. This much, at least, is clear; but is section 279 merely a venue provision, or does it give an extraterritorial ambit to every one of the numerous offences created under the Merchant Shipping Act 1995? Ashworth J had no need to address that question, and he did not do so, but Glanville Williams had previously argued,[51] in relation to the old section 684, that it could not have been intended to be anything more than a venue provision. There is no reported authority to guide us, but it is submitted that Professor Williams was correct. There are some provisions in the Merchant Shipping Act 1995 which surely cannot be intended to have an unqualified extraterritorial ambit. Section 57(1), for example, creates a summary offence relating to the wrongful wearing of merchant navy uniforms:

Subject to subsection (3) below,[52] if any person, not being entitled to wear the merchant navy uniform, wears that uniform or any part thereof, or any dress having

---

[48] The Offences Against the Person Act 1861 provides a further example.
[49] This appears to refer disciplinary matters, rather than criminal offences. See for example s. 60 of the Act.
[50] [1972] 2 All ER 471, 472.   [51] Op. cit., fn 47, 409.
[52] This exempts the use of uniforms in stage plays, etc., provided the uniform is not brought into contempt.

the appearance or bearing any of the distinctive marks of that uniform, he shall be guilty of an offence.

Parliament cannot have intended to make this an offence of universal application, akin to piracy. Since the nationality or status of potential offenders is not limited in any way, the offence must be limited by territory. An American citizen who attends a fancy dress ball in New York dressed as 'Captain Smith of the *Titanic*' cannot conceivably be guilty of an offence under English law, even if his uniform resembles a modern one. As the House of Lords accepted in *Air India* v. *Wiggins*,[53] the courts will avoid such an interpretation if any other be possible. Moreover, section 14 of the Act, which creates offences relating to the falsification, etc., of a ship's nationality, concludes by providing (in subsection (5)) that: 'this section applies to things done outside, as well as to things done within, the United Kingdom'. If section 279 provided an extraterritorial ambit to all offences under the Act, there would simply be no need for section 14(5).

Assuming that section 279 is indeed a mere venue provision, we may then ask whether it serves any useful or necessary purpose. As can be seen from subsection 279(3), it operates in addition to, and not in derogation of, any other enactments. Jurisdiction (meaning venue) in respect of indictable offences is already provided for, under section 46(2) of the Supreme Court Act 1981 and section 2(4) of the Magistrates' Courts Act 1980. In respect of such offences, there is no real need or use for a provision such as section 279. This leaves purely summary offences, of which the Act creates several. Ordinarily, any such offence must be tried within the commission area (which, outside Greater London, usually means the county) within which it was committed. Section 279 relaxes that rule by enabling a summary offence committed (say) in Liverpool to be tried by a court in Cardiff, if the accused is brought before that court. Similarly, a court in Southampton would be empowered to try a summary offence committed aboard a British ship at sea; but many of the summary offences created under the Act can be committed only aboard 'United Kingdom ships' (a category which excludes many small and unregistered British vessels), and jurisdiction over such offences is in any case provided by section 281 of the Act. Section 279 is thus a provision of very limited utility.

Jurisdiction over Summary Offences

In the context of purely summary offences, issues of jurisdictional competence sometimes assume a territorial basis, because a magistrates' court generally has jurisdiction over a summary offence only if it is committed within its own commission area, or within 500 yards of the boundary

---

[53] [1980] 1 WLR 815.

between that and another area.[54] Where no court appears to have jurisdictional competence over an alleged offence (whether expressly or by necessary implication) the obvious conclusion to be drawn is that the offence cannot be committed in those particular circumstances. No provision has ever been enacted to give magistrates' courts a general jurisdiction over summary offences committed outside their commission areas. This has a number of consequences. The first is that the ambit of most summary offences under English law does not ordinarily extend even to the territorial waters adjacent to England and Wales. The second is that, where summary offences are clearly intended to apply beyond county boundaries (as, for example, in the case of certain sea fishery offences, or of offences under the Merchant Shipping Act 1995) a specific venue provision is almost invariably inserted within the relevant legislation.

JURISDICTIONAL IMMUNITIES

The distinction between ambit and jurisdiction is also crucial to the laws governing diplomatic and other immunities. English criminal law applies to all individuals and other legal persons who come within the realm of England and Wales, or within the territorial or internal waters adjacent to the realm. In some limited circumstances, it may also apply to persons (even foreigners) who are outside the realm; but it does not necessarily follow that offences against English criminal law may be tried or punished in the courts. Within England and Wales (and within London in particular) several thousand individuals, most of whom are diplomatic agents or other persons connected with a diplomatic mission, enjoy immunity from criminal prosecution.

It must be emphasized that immunity from prosecution does not involve immunity from the duty to comply with the law. This is expressly recognized, for example, in Article 41 of the 1961 Vienna Convention on Diplomatic Relations, which warns that 'it is the duty of all persons enjoying such privileges and immunities to respect the laws and regulations of the receiving state'. A foreign diplomat in London has no right or licence to ignore the rules of English law. If he deliberately kills another person, he may therefore be guilty of murder at common law, and if he engages in espionage he may be guilty of an offence under section 1 of the Official Secrets Act 1911; but he may be prosecuted for that murder or espionage in England only if his government waives diplomatic immunity. If immunity is not waived, the diplomat may be declared *persona non grata* and expelled

---

[54] Offences that are triable either way present no such difficulty: see the Magistrates' Courts Act 1980, s. 2(3)–(4). Nor do youth courts encounter such difficulties in respect of their jurisdiction over indictable offences: see the Magistrates' Courts Act 1980, s. 24.

from the United Kingdom,[55] whilst any non-immune person who has aided
him or conspired with him may be left to face prosecution alone.

This work is concerned only peripherally with the law relating to
jurisdictional immunities, but a brief account of those who may be entitled
to claim immunity is appropriate. They include the following:

The Sovereign

At common law, the reigning King or Queen is wholly immune from
any form of criminal process.[56] Stephen described this rule as 'merely an
honorary distinction of no practical importance'.[57] In the political climate of
today, however, royal misconduct is no longer overlooked, and misconduct
by other members of the royal family has occasionally resulted in prosecution. The personal immunity of the sovereign has thus acquired real practical
significance. In November 2002, for example, the Princess Royal was
convicted of an offence under section 3 of the Dangerous Dogs Act 1991,
when one of her dogs attacked a passerby,[58] but the Queen could not have
been prosecuted had her dogs been involved in a similar incident.

Persons Entitled to Diplomatic Immunity

Diplomatic immunity under English law is governed by the Diplomatic
Privileges Act 1964, which directly incorporates scheduled provisions of the
1961 Vienna Convention on Diplomatic Relations. These include Article
29, by which 'The person of a diplomatic agent shall be inviolable. He shall
not be liable to any form of arrest or detention', and Article 31(1), by which
'A diplomatic agent shall enjoy immunity from the criminal jurisdiction of
the receiving State'. By Article 37, the same privileges and immunities extend
to 'the members of the family of a diplomatic agent forming part of
his household ... if they are not nationals of the receiving State'[59] and to
'members of the administrative and technical staff of the mission, together
with members of their families forming part of their respective households ...
if they are not nationals of or permanently resident in the receiving State';
but members of the service staff enjoy such immunity only in respect of acts

---

[55] Two alleged cases of murder in England provide contrasting examples of state practice
in this area. In April 1984, WPC Yvonne Fletcher was shot and killed by an unidentified
member of the Libyan People's Bureau in London, following which the Bureau was closed and
the staff expelled. Diplomatic immunity was not waived. In September 2002, the Colombian
Government waived the immunity of a member of their embassy staff, Sairo Soto-Mendoza,
following the fatal stabbing of a man outside a London supermarket in May that year.
Mendoza was then arrested and charged with the murder.

[56] Following the English Civil War, King Charles I was tried and executed for treason
and murder in 1648–9, but following the restoration of the monarchy his execution was
condemned as unlawful and many of those responsible were themselves executed for treason.

[57] *History of the Criminal Law of England*, vol. II, 3 (1883).

[58] See *The Guardian*, 22 November 2002. Previous royal prosecutions had been confined
to minor motoring offences.

[59] See *R v. Guildhall Magistrates' Court, ex p Jarrett-Thorpe* (1977) *The Times*, 6 October.

performed in the course of their duties, and the private servants of members of the mission have no immunities from the criminal law other than those (if any) admitted by the receiving state.[60]

By Article 39(2), the immunities of a diplomat 'shall normally cease when he leaves the country, or on expiry of a reasonable period in which to do so, but . . . with respect to acts performed . . . in the exercise of his functions as a member of the mission, immunity shall continue to subsist'. The reasoning behind section 39(2) was explained by Lord Browne-Wilkinson in *R v. Bow Street Metropolitan Stipendiary Magistrate, ex p Pinochet Ugarte (No. 3)*[61]:

The continuing partial immunity of the ambassador after leaving post is of a different kind from that enjoyed *ratione personae* while he was in post. Since he is no longer the representative of the foreign state he merits no particular privileges or immunities as a person. However in order to preserve the integrity of the activities of the foreign state during the period when he was ambassador, it is necessary to provide that immunity is afforded to his *official* acts during his tenure in post. If this were not done the sovereign immunity of the state could be evaded by calling in question acts done during the previous ambassador's time. Accordingly under Article 39(2) the ambassador, like any other official of the state, enjoys immunity in relation to his official acts done while he was an official. This limited immunity, *ratione materiae*, is to be contrasted with the former immunity *ratione personae* which gave complete immunity to all activities whether public or private.

The abuse of diplomatic privileges and immunities in England (and particularly in London)[62] has on occasion given rise to concern, notably following the murder of WPC Fletcher in 1984, although this was by no means a typical example of such abuse. In response to a report prepared by the Foreign Affairs Committee in 1985,[63] the Government published a White Paper, *Diplomatic Immunities and Privileges*,[64] which concluded that the United Kingdom's freedom of action in curbing such abuse was strictly limited, because the Vienna Convention effectively states what has now become customary international law.[65]

---

[60] The diplomatic immunities of a particular mission may be restricted or withdrawn by Order in Council if it appears that the corresponding immunities granted to British diplomats, etc., are similarly restricted or withheld (Diplomatic Privileges Act 1964, s. 3). As to jurisdiction over things done within diplomatic or consular missions and residences, see below, p. 102.

[61] [2000] 1 AC 147, 202.

[62] In 1993, there were 29 occasions on which diplomatic immunity was claimed by persons suspected of committing offences punishable by imprisonment for six months or more, and nearly 2,000 parking tickets were cancelled on that basis (although cars with diplomatic plates may still be towed away if they are causing an obstruction). See D.J. Harris, *Cases and Materials on International Law* (5th edn, 1998), 343 and 350.

[63] *The Abuse of Diplomatic Immunities and Privileges.*   [64] Cmnd. 9497 (1985).

[65] For a review of the Foreign Affairs Committee Report and the White Paper, see R. Higgins (1986) 80 *American Journal of International Law* 135. British practice in cases involving misconduct by accredited foreign or Commonwealth diplomats or members of their families remains as set out in an Interdepartmental Committee's 1952 *Report on Diplomatic Immunities* (Cmnd. 8460), 3–4.

Persons Entitled to Consular Immunity

Consular immunity is more limited than diplomatic immunity, and for most purposes excludes any immunity from criminal process or prosecution, save in respect of acts performed in the course of consular duties. By section 1 of the Consular Relations Act 1968, the immunities granted to consular officials, families, and associated staff are those laid down by the 1963 Vienna Convention on Consular Relations. The relevant provisions (which may, as with diplomatic immunities, be waived by the sending state) are set out in Schedule 1 to the 1968 Act. These include Article 41, which provides:

1. Consular officers shall not be liable to arrest or detention pending trial, except in the case of a grave crime and pursuant to a decision by the competent judicial authority.

2. Except in the case specified in paragraph 1 of this Article, consular officers shall not be committed to prison or liable to any other form of restriction on their personal freedom save in execution of a judicial decision of final effect.

Even this limited immunity is denied to consular officers who are United Kingdom nationals or who permanently reside here;[66] but consular premises enjoy more extensive immunity, which is examined in Chapter 3 below.

Two further points should be noted. The first is that, by section 3 and Schedule 2 to the Act, the limited privileges and immunities described above may be reduced or supplemented by Order in Council in accordance with any agreement between the United Kingdom and the foreign state concerned, so as, for example, to provide for the same inviolability and immunity from jurisdiction and arrest as is granted to diplomats. The second is that the immunities of Commonwealth or Irish consular missions are governed by Orders in Council made under section 12, as substituted by the Diplomatic and Other Privileges Act 1971.

Persons Connected with International Organizations

In respect of an international organization of which the United Kingdom is a member, section 1 of the International Organizations Act 1968 enables certain 'quasi-diplomatic' immunities to be granted to its officers or representatives by Order in Council. In practice, such immunities appear to be granted only sparingly, and the exact terms of such immunities vary from one case to another. The United Nations and International Court of Justice (Immunities and Privileges) Order 1974,[67] for example, grants full immunity only to judges of the International Court and to the UN Secretary-General

---

[66] See Art. 71. This does not affect immunity in respect of official acts, which are protected by Art. 43. By Art. 17, 'the performance of [diplomatic] acts by a consular officer shall not confer upon him any right to claim diplomatic privileges and immunities'.

[67] SI 1974 No. 1261.

or any Assistant Secretary-General. Other officers, counsel, assessors, and experts are accorded immunity only in respect of acts done or omitted in the course of their duties.[68] As with diplomatic immunities, these immunities may be waived by the organization in question.

The Commonwealth Secretariat Act 1966 makes broadly similar provision for officers of the Secretariat. By section 1 and Schedule 1, senior officers 'have the like privileges and immunities as are accorded by law to a diplomatic agent and the members of his family forming part of his household', whereas other officers or servants have immunity only in respect of acts or omissions done in the course of the performance of official duties.[69]

Foreign Heads of State and Government Ministers

Section 20 of the State Immunity Act 1978 provides that the Diplomatic Privileges Act 1964 shall apply (with appropriate modifications) to a foreign sovereign or head of state, his household and private servants, as it applies to 'the head of a diplomatic mission, to members of his family forming part of his household and to his private servants'. This provision was intended to clarify the extent of the immunity which formerly attached to heads of state at common law through the incorporation of customary international law,[70] but whether it was ever intended to reflect customary law with any precision is doubtful. The incorporation of specific rules derived from the Vienna Convention on Diplomatic Relations hardly suggests that any serious attempt was made to do so.[71]

The concept of personal sovereign immunity might once have been dismissed as of negligible practical importance in criminal cases. Stephen was indeed dismissive of it,[72] but he could never have foreseen the day that a former head of state would be brought before an English court accused of crimes against international law committed in his own country. The *Pinochet* case[73] demonstrated that questions concerning the scope of sovereign immunity may have real practical importance.

The *Pinochet* case has been the subject of extensive comment elsewhere.[74] Briefly, Senator Pinochet, the former general and President of Chile, was arrested on a Spanish extradition warrant during a visit to England.

---

[68] For a further example, see the International Maritime Organization (Immunities and Privileges) Order 2002 (SI 2002 No. 1826).

[69] This excludes immunity from civil, but not criminal, proceedings in respect of road traffic accidents. [70] See *Hansard* (HL) 16 March 1978, 1538, col. 1 (Lord McLusky).

[71] See Hazel Fox, 'The Pinochet Case No. 3' (1999) 48 *International and Comparative Law Quarterly* 687, 693. [72] *History of the Criminal Law of England*, vol. II, 3.

[73] *R v. Bow Street Metropolitan Stipendiary Magistrate, ex p Pinochet Ugarte (No. 3)* [2000] 1 AC 147.

[74] See, e.g., Ivor and Clive Stanbrook, *Extradition Law and Practice* (2nd edn, 2000), paras 6.44 *et seq.*; Hazel Fox, op. cit., fn 71 above; Kittichaisaree, *International Criminal Law*, 56. Certain other aspects of that case are considered in Chapter 5 below.

This accused him of numerous grave offences committed during his undoubtedly bloody years in office, including offences of conspiracy to commit torture, which was recognized to be a crime, wherever committed, under English, Spanish, and international law. But was he not entitled to claim immunity for any such crimes? As to this, the House of Lords recognized that Pinochet's immunity would have remained absolute before a British court, had he still been the Chilean head of state, because it would, in effect, have been the immunity of the Chilean state itself, which he would still have represented. Because he was now merely a former head of state, however, their Lordships concluded that, like a former diplomat, he was entitled to immunity from prosecution only in respect of acts done by him (or on his orders) in connection with his former office (immunity *ratione materiae*). This might still include immunity for grave and illegal acts such as murder; but a specific exception existed in respect of torture, because Chile, Spain, and the United Kingdom were all parties to the 1984 Convention against Torture and other Cruel, Inhuman or Degrading Treatment or Punishment, which outlawed any such conduct committed by or on the orders of state officials. By acceding to this Convention, Chile must be taken to have determined that no immunity *ratione materiae* should be capable of attaching to any such acts. Lord Browne-Wilkinson concluded:

If, as alleged, Senator Pinochet organised and authorised torture after 8 December 1988,[75] he was not acting in any capacity which gives rise to immunity *ratione materiae* because such actions were contrary to international law, Chile had agreed to outlaw such conduct and Chile had agreed with the other parties to the Torture Convention that all signatory states should have jurisdiction to try official torture (as defined in the Convention) even if such torture were committed in Chile. As to the charges of murder and conspiracy to murder, no one has advanced any reason why the ordinary rules of immunity should not apply and Senator Pinochet is entitled to such immunity.[76]

Section 20 of the 1978 Act deals only with heads of state, but the recent ruling of the International Court of Justice in the *Belgian Arrest Warrant* case[77] suggests that English common law may need to incorporate similar immunities in respect of the acts of heads of government and foreign ministers, etc., because if the Court's ruling is correct, such persons are similarly protected by customary law.[78]

---

[75] This is the date on which the UK ratified the Treaty. The double criminality principle was held to preclude extradition for crimes of torture allegedly committed before that date.

[76] [2000] 1 AC 147, 205.

[77] *Arrest Warrant of 11 April 2000: Democratic Republic of the Congo v. Belgium* (The *Yerodia* Case) [2002] ICJ Rep 3; see Xiaodong Yang, 'Immunity for International Crimes: a Reaffirmation of Traditional Doctrine' [2002] *Cambridge Law Journal* 242.

[78] As to the 'doctrine of incorporation' (i.e., the automatic incorporation of principles of customary international law within English common law), see below, pp. 35–40.

Visiting Forces

When foreign or Commonwealth armed forces are stationed on British soil, they do not enjoy the same absolute immunity from local jurisdiction that is accorded to diplomats; but criminal jurisdiction over such forces is ceded for some purposes to their own military authorities. The Visiting Forces Act 1952 defines the circumstances in which the United Kingdom will cede primary criminal jurisdiction to foreign military authorities, in accordance with the NATO Status of Forces Agreement 1951. Those countries that are members of NATO generally cede similar immunities to British forces based in or travelling through their own territories.

Crimes committed amongst the visiting forces or their families, etc., will be left to the jurisdiction of the visiting forces themselves if they do not affect the local populace, as are those committed in the course of official military, naval, or air force business, even if they do have such an effect. This extends, for example, to accidents resulting from the dangerous flying of military aircraft,[79] but the rape, robbery, or murder of a local citizen would be dealt with in the ordinary courts, under English law.

Crimes Committed Aboard Foreign Ships

English criminal law extends to conduct aboard any ship within United Kingdom territorial waters (excluding only those adjacent to Scotland), but in practice the potential for the exercise of such jurisdiction is limited. Foreign naval vessels or warships are wholly immune from any such interference, even in respect of offences committed within English ports or harbours. No arrest or investigation may therefore be carried out aboard such a ship, save in the unlikely event of a request or invitation from the flag state.

In respect of foreign merchant ships, section 5 of the Consular Relations Act 1968 imposes some restrictions on prosecutions. In certain cases prosecutions may not be instituted or entertained otherwise than at the request of, or with the consent of, a consular officer of the flag state. In respect of offences committed aboard foreign ships that are merely passing through territorial waters, Article 27 of the 1982 UNCLOS (law of the sea) Convention restricts the circumstances in which jurisdiction may be exercised by coastal states. English law reflects this not by granting immunities from jurisdiction, but by making any prosecution dependent on the consent of the Attorney-General, who may be expected to take account of any international sensitivities.[80]

---

[79] Cf. *Public Prosecutor* v. *Ashby* (1999) 93 AJIL 219 (American military aircraft crashing in Italy, causing civilian casualties: pilots tried under US military law).

[80] Territorial Waters Jurisdiction Act 1878, s. 7.

OFFENCES—BUT NOT UNDER ENGLISH LAW

Whilst an act done outside England and Wales cannot ordinarily be an offence under English law, that does not mean that it cannot be recognized as being an offence in some other sense, or that it cannot be described as 'stealing', 'murder', etc. There are indeed several ways in which English courts may recognize the criminal character of acts or events abroad that are not, in those circumstances, offences under English law.

In *Antonelli v. Secretary of State for Trade and Industry*,[81] for example, it was held that the Director General of Fair Trading was empowered under the Estate Agents Act 1979, section 3(1), to prohibit the applicant from practising as an estate agent on the basis of a conviction imposed on him in the USA for an act of arson committed there. This arson was not, strictly speaking, an offence under English law, but the Court of Appeal nevertheless held that it was 'an offence involving fraud or other dishonesty or violence' within the meaning of that section. This ruling was clearly correct, given the rationale behind the provision in question, which was to prevent dangerous, dishonest, or other unsuitable persons from practising as estate agents. A conviction for arson is no less relevant, for those purposes, when it is imposed for a crime committed in the USA.

The most obvious way in which the criminal character of a foreign offence may be recognized in England and Wales is through the law of extradition. Under the Extradition Act 1989, a fugitive may be extradited to face trial in a foreign state, a Commonwealth country, or the Hong Kong special administrative region,[82] on the basis of evidence that *prima facie* shows him to have committed recognized extradition crimes against the laws of the requesting state. In cases governed by Part I of the Extradition Act 1989,[83] these must ordinarily be offences committed within that state's own territory, or aboard one of its ships or aircraft, but by section 2 of the Act they may also take the form of conduct committed outside its territory if:

(1) in corresponding circumstances equivalent conduct would constitute an extraterritorial offence against the law of the United Kingdom punishable with imprisonment for a term of 12 months or more; or

---

[81] [1998] 1 All ER 997. See also *Shufflebottom* v. *Chief Constable of Greater Manchester Police* [2003] EWHC 246.

[82] As to extradition to the Republic of Ireland, see the Backing of Warrants (Republic of Ireland) Act 1965. As to extradition arrangements within the European Union, see also the European Union Extradition Regulations 2002 (SI 2002 No. 419). A new Extradition Bill was before Parliament as this work went to press. See below, p. 50.

[83] Different rules apply in cases where extradition arrangements with the other state are still governed by treaties which pre-date the 1989 Act. These remain based on principles derived from the Extradition Act 1870 and associated enactments. See Sch. 1 to the 1989 Act and *Re Al-Fawwaz* [2002] 1 All ER 545.

(2) the requesting state bases its jurisdiction on the nationality of the offender, the conduct constituting the offence occurred outside the United Kingdom and, if (hypothetically) it occurred in the United Kingdom, it would constitute an offence under the law of the United Kingdom punishable with imprisonment for a term of 12 months or more.

A further way in which English law may recognize the 'criminality' of conduct that is not itself punishable under that law is found in a number of provisions governing inchoate offences and/or secondary participation. Section 5(4) of the Criminal Justice Act 1993 provides an example:

A person may be guilty of incitement to commit a Group A offence[84] if the incitement—
(a) takes place in England and Wales; and
(b) would be triable in England and Wales[85] but for what the person charged had in view not being an offence triable in England and Wales.

A broadly similar rule in respect of conspiracy is found in section 1A of the Criminal Law Act 1977, but this is not confined to Group A offences. In each of these cases, the substantive offence must also be one that is triable under the law in force where that offence is to be committed. Neither provision envisages or allows for a substantive 'offence' that is not committed within the jurisdiction of any state; but section 1(4) of the Criminal Law Act 1977, as originally drafted, extended the law of conspiracy so as to include conspiracy to murder, 'notwithstanding that the murder in question would not be so triable if committed in accordance with the intentions of the parties to the agreement'. It is possible to imagine a murder that is not punishable under English law, or under the law of any other state whose jurisdiction over such an act would be recognized under English law. Assume, for example, that a British citizen diving on a wreck just outside British territorial limits deliberately kills his fellow diver. This cannot be murder at common law; nor (unless the murderer is, for example, a Crown servant or a seaman from a United Kingdom ship) would it be punishable as murder by reason of any exceptional statutory provision.[86] But the term 'murder' might still be applied to describe such conduct, and section 1(4) would thus have applied to a conspiracy formed in England and Wales, under which the commission of such a murder was agreed upon.[87]

---

[84] Namely, one of the offences of fraud or dishonesty listed in s. 1(2) of that Act.
[85] The wording here is unfortunate, because the incitement *is* (by definition) triable under English law. It ought presumably to have read, 'would be triable *at common law . . .* '.
[86] If the murderer is subject to military law or naval law, he commits a 'civil offence' under s. 70 of the Army Act 1955 or s. 42 of the Naval Discipline Act 1957, which is equivalent to, but legally distinct from, the common law offence of murder. See *R* v. *Spear and others* [2002] 3 All ER 1074.
[87] This part of s. 1(4) was repealed and supplanted by the Criminal Justice (Terrorism and Conspiracy) Act 1998, which does not have quite the same effect. See below, p. 142.

Acts committed abroad that are not themselves within the compass of English criminal law may also be recognized as 'criminal' for the purposes of the law of theft and of the law relating to the proceeds of crime. Section 24(1) of the Theft Act 1968 provides:

The provisions of this Act relating to goods which have been stolen shall apply whether the stealing occurred in England or Wales or elsewhere . . . provided that the stealing (if not an offence under this Act) amounted to an offence where and at the time when the goods were stolen; and references to stolen goods shall be construed accordingly.

Thus, if D steals property in Spain, in circumstances to which English criminal law does not apply, and E dishonestly handles that property or its proceeds in England, knowing of the circumstances, E may be guilty of handling stolen goods under English law; but it must be proved that the conduct of the thief was, at the time of the theft, punishable under Spanish law.[88]

What, then, if D himself brings the stolen goods from Spain to England? D cannot ordinarily be guilty of handling stolen goods, unless perhaps he 'dishonestly undertakes or assists in their retention, removal, disposal or realisation by or for the benefit of another person, or . . . arranges to do so',[89] but it has been cogently argued[90] that he should be guilty of theft not on the basis that theft is an ongoing act, but on the basis of section 3(1) of the Theft Act, which provides:

Any assumption by a person of the right of an owner amounts to an appropriation, and this includes, where he has come by the property (innocently or not) without stealing it, any later assumption of a right to it by keeping or dealing with it as owner.

D, so this argument goes, came by the property (albeit not innocently) in Spain without stealing it, because what he did in Spain was not theft under English law. Section 24(1) does not purport to be a universal definition of what is meant by stealing, but must instead be confined to its own context, namely the law relating to handling.[91]

Acceptance of this argument would require the rejection of the Court of Appeal's decision in *R* v. *Atakpu*.[92] The appellants in this case were originally convicted of conspiracy to steal. The conspiracy had been hatched in England, but the thefts had been committed in Frankfurt and Brussels when the appellants purported to hire luxury cars there. They clearly had no intention of returning these vehicles at the end of the hire period; instead they drove them to England, where evidently they planned

---

[88] It is not possible to rely on any presumption that foreign law will be similar to English law; nor can judicial notice be taken of foreign law for such a purpose: *R* v. *Ofori* (1994) 99 Cr App R 223; *R* v. *Okolie* [2000] All ER (D) 661.   [89] Theft Act 1968, s. 22.
[90] G.R. Sullivan and Colin Warbrick, 'Territoriality, Theft and *Atakpu*' [1994] *Criminal Law Review* 650.   [91] Ibid., 657–8.
[92] [1994] QB 69.

to dispose of them.[93] The appellants were stopped and arrested when they arrived with the cars at Dover.

As the law then stood, a charge of conspiracy to steal was indictable under English law only if the theft in question was (or would if committed have been) a crime under English law.[94] Clearly, the thefts committed in Frankfurt and Brussels were *not* crimes under English law. To succeed in the conspiracy charge, the prosecution in *Atakpu* therefore had to establish that the appellants committed theft in England when they brought the vehicles into Dover in accordance with the agreement. Bringing the cars to Dover was indeed part of the appellants' plan, but could it be classified as theft? Having once stolen the property in question, a thief does not repeat his original theft each time he uses or deals with it, but the argument might nevertheless have succeeded if the original stealing in Germany or Belgium could have been disregarded on the basis that it was not theft under English law. The conduct in Dover might then be regarded as involving an appropriation of property that had previously been acquired (dishonestly or not) *without* stealing,[95] and thus as 'original theft'. The Court of Appeal firmly rejected that view. Ward J said:

We reject the speculation that [the appellants] would not have come by the property by stealing it if an indictment for the theft would not lie because the theft occurred abroad. There is no reason to restrict the plain ordinary words of section 3 in such a narrow legalistic way. We note that one is guilty of handling stolen property under section 24 and the provisions of the Act apply whether the stealing occurred in England or Wales or elsewhere. 'Stealing' must have the same meaning in section 3 as it has in section 24. In our judgment, if goods have once been stolen, even if stolen abroad, they cannot be stolen again by the same thief exercising the same or other rights of ownership over the property.

As Sullivan and Warbrick point out, however, there are good reasons for *not* giving 'stealing' the same meaning in section 3 as in section 24:

The stealing referred to in section 3, in this context, refers to a theft within the terms of section 1. Section 24, of course, defines stolen goods for the purposes of offences relating to stolen goods. Such goods, within the terms of section 24, include goods not merely obtained by theft but goods obtained by blackmail and deception. It also, in this inclusionary vein, includes goods 'which have been stolen . . . whether the stealing occurred in England or Wales or elsewhere . . . provided that the stealing amounted to an offence . . . where the goods were stolen.' . . . 'Stealing' cannot bear this meaning when used in section 3. There would be no discernible purpose and ground for much confusion if, quite apart from thefts 'elsewhere', 'stealing' in section 3 is taken to be a reference to blackmail and deception as well as theft.

---

[93] The precise plans for disposal are not mentioned in the report, but in similar reported cases such as *R v. Ofori* (1994) 99 Cr App R 223, the stolen vehicles were found to be destined for export to Nigeria.

[94] This indeed remains true of any conspiracy charge brought under the Criminal Law Act 1977, s. 1; but see now s. 1A of that Act.   [95] Theft Act 1968, s. 3(1).

The fact is that if 'stealing' in section 3 takes in thefts elsewhere there would be no need in a later section concerned with extending the ambit of 'stealing' for limited purposes to make explicit reference to extraterritorial thefts. Section 24 testifies to the fact that conduct elsewhere is not within theft as defined in sections 1 to 6 and had to be explicitly brought in to extend the ambit, not of theft, but of stolen goods for the purposes of offences relating to stolen goods.[96]

Should the facts of *Atakpu* be repeated tomorrow, there are two possible ways (apart from extradition) under which justice might be done in England. The first is under section 1A of the Criminal Law Act 1977, although that would be possible only where some element of the conspiracy can be located within England and Wales. The second (which would be crucial in the absence of a conspiracy) is under sections 327–329 of the Proceeds of Crime Act 2002. Although these are categorized as 'money laundering' provisions, they are in fact capable of applying to a wide range of acts done in respect of the proceeds of criminal conduct, including the proceeds of the accused's own criminal conduct, and including the proceeds of conduct abroad that is not criminal but would have been criminal if committed in England and Wales.[97] A foreign thief who steals property abroad and brings it into England (even long after the event) commits a 'money laundering offence' under section 329 of the 2002 Act. It does not matter that he may have committed no other offence under English law.

ISSUES FOR FURTHER CONSIDERATION

I hope to have demonstrated in this chapter:

(1) that the territorial or extraterritorial ambit of a given criminal offence is not a matter of procedural law, but a matter concerning the *actus reus* of that offence;
(2) that English criminal law is primarily territorial, and that misconduct abroad cannot ordinarily be an offence under English law, although there are now many exceptions to that rule;
(3) that the distinction between issues of ambit and issues of jurisdictional competence is fundamental, even if those issues are related and easily confused;
(4) that diplomatic or other immunities from English criminal jurisdiction do not involve any exemption from the duty to comply with English law; and
(5) that English law may for certain purposes recognize the criminality of acts that do not fall within its own ambit and which are not therefore punishable as crimes under English law.

---

[96] [1994] *Criminal Law Review* 650, 658–9.   [97] See s. 340 of the Act.

Some of these points require further consideration. Chapters 3 and 4 below accordingly provide a more detailed examination of the territorial ambit of English criminal law. Chapter 3 considers the territorial limits within which the operation of English law is primarily confined, while Chapter 4 examines the problems that arise when the territorial principle is applied to transnational or cross-frontier offences.

Chapters 5 and 6 examine the extraterritorial application of English law. Chapter 5 principally addresses offences committed in other countries, but also discusses the rules of British nationality in so far as these determine who may or may not be subject to extraterritorial liability. Chapter 6 concentrates on maritime and aviation offences. These include offences committed on British ships and aircraft, but also universal offences such as piracy and hijacking, and offences that may be committed by British citizens on foreign ships, etc.

The law considered in those chapters is both complex and, in many cases, unsatisfactory. Chapter 7 accordingly considers how the existing rules might be reformed. Some of the suggestions advanced are original, but I also consider (and in some cases adopt or incorporate) suggestions that have been made by others. These range from mere matters of clarification and rationalization (for which there is ample scope) to substantial reforms that would involve a significant modification to the general ambit of English criminal law.

Before beginning a detailed examination of the relevant law, as it exists today, it may be useful to consider the historical influences that helped to shape it, and the rules of international law within which it has to operate. These are the subjects of the next chapter.

2

Historical, International, and Other Influences

INTRODUCTION

This chapter examines the origins of the rules that govern the ambit of English criminal law, and the factors that shaped them. How and why did English criminal law become so heavily dependent on the principle of territorial jurisdiction, to the virtual exclusion, until relatively recently, of jurisdiction based on nationality? Why, in contrast, are many other countries so much more willing to apply their criminal laws to acts committed by their nationals abroad? And why, in recent years, has Parliament created so many exceptions to the general rule that English criminal law does not apply abroad?

Historical factors will be addressed first of all. To some extent, at least, the restricted ambit of English criminal law may be considered a product of ancient and largely forgotten rules of common law procedure: rules that never troubled the civil law jurisdictions of continental Europe. This provides us with a starting point; but account must also be taken of the influence of public international law. The relationship between English law and international law is a complex one. English law does not always mirror international law, but it does generally seek to avoid any outright incompatibility, and where the United Kingdom has assumed jurisdictional responsibilities under the terms of international treaties or conventions, English law is almost invariably amended, where necessary, so as to ensure that those obligations can be discharged. Indeed, international treaty obligations now represent by far the most common reason for the creation of new exceptions to the territoriality principle, while the delimitation of the United Kingdom's maritime boundaries is squarely based on the provisions of the 1982 United Nations Convention on the Law of the Sea (the UNCLOS Convention). The importance of international law in the jurisdictional context is examined in the second part of this chapter. It must suffice for the moment to note that this influence is ongoing: it does not merely help to explain many of the rules we have now, but also limits (or in some cases dictates) the extent to which those laws may (or must) be changed in the future.

Pressure for change, and in particular for the enlargement or extension of the common law's narrowly territorial approach to jurisdiction, has not come exclusively from international law or from the United Kingdom's treaty obligations. It has also come from the changing face of crime and from the threat posed by new forms of crime. At one time, misconduct committed abroad was unlikely ever to come to the attention of the authorities in England, and was unlikely to concern them if it did. Any crimes (other than piracy or treason) committed abroad would have been seen as the sole concern of the relevant foreign authorities, or, in other words, as none of English law's business. This attitude was not unique to English law or to systems derived from it. In his *Commentaries on the Law of Scotland Respecting Crimes*,[1] David Hume wrote:

A person domiciliated here, whether a Scotsman or a foreigner, for any crime he may have committee abroad, is not liable to be tried by our courts. They are not instituted to administer justice over the whole world, but in our country, or a particular district of it only; and therefore, if the crime charged has been committed beyond those limits, they are neither called upon nor entitled to step forward for its correction.

In 1891, Lord Halsbury LC could similarly assert: 'All crime is local. The jurisdiction over the crime belongs to the country where the crime is committed ...'[2] Almost exactly 100 years later, however, Lord Griffiths, in what has proved to be a most influential ruling,[3] recognized that this narrowly parochial approach to criminal jurisdiction can no longer be considered satisfactory in the face of the challenge posed by modern forms of crime, such as international drug trafficking. He said: 'Unfortunately in this century crime has ceased to be largely local in origin and effect. Crime is now established on an international scale and the common law must face this new reality.'

The influence exerted by changing patterns of criminal conduct will be considered in the final part of this chapter. Historical considerations must, however, provide our starting point, and the early history of English criminal jurisdiction was dominated by the common law rules of venue.

The Influence of Venue

The common law generally required that any indictable offences—treason, felony, or misdemeanour—should be tried in the county in which the relevant acts were alleged to have occurred, by a jury drawn from the residents of that county. This doctrine of 'venue' made it difficult for English criminal law to have any extraterritorial application, and thus caused it to adopt the narrow principle of territoriality that (despite many modern developments) still lies at its core today.

---

[1] (1797) vol. II, 52.
[2] *MacLeod v. Attorney-General for New South Wales* [1891] AC 455, 458.
[3] In *Somchai Liangsiriprasert v. US Government* [1991] 1 AC 225, 241.

The old rules of venue are sometimes dismissed today as tiresome procedural requirements, full of haphazard exceptions and fictions, which formerly created unnecessary and perverse jurisdictional difficulties for the courts in cases where crimes were committed across county boundaries, or where it was not clear in which county the relevant events had taken place. This, indeed, is what the rules became during their later history. The original philosophy behind them made some kind of sense, however. To explain or understand it, one must consider the original role and operation of the early English juries.[4]

The earliest records relating to the jury in Norman and Angevin England suggest that it was used primarily for the adjudication of disputes relating to land. For many years following the Norman conquest, the traditional rituals of compurgation, ordeal, and battle remained the principal methods of determining guilt or innocence in criminal cases. Of these, trial by ordeal was the most widely used, until 1215, when it was condemned by the Lateran Council and lost the support of the Church. Trial by jury in criminal cases appears to have been developed in order to fill the gap left by the sudden abandonment of trial by ordeal, but its origins can be traced back at least as far as the Assize of Clarendon in 1166. This instituted the body we now know of as the grand jury or presentment jury, which gradually replaced private accusation as the principal method by which a suspect was committed for trial in the first place. The Assize of Clarendon required that:

For the preservation of the peace and the maintenance of justice, enquiries be made throughout each county and hundred by twelve legal men of the hundred and four legal men from each township, under oath to tell the truth; if in their hundred or their township there be any man who is accused or is generally suspected of being a robber or murderer or thief, or any man who is a receiver of robbers, murderers or thieves since our Lord the King was King.

The members of this body were local men who clearly were expected to act upon their own local knowledge. Similar considerations applied to the petty (or trial) jury which, after 1215, quickly established itself as the principal method of determining a suspect's guilt or innocence, once he had been indicted. Indeed, it appears that the petty jury was often composed of some, at least, of the members of the grand or presentment jury.[5] Formal witnesses were not employed to assist either body. Jurors might not always be fully informed when first sworn. They might have to make enquiries of their own, or even question witnesses in private; but the fundamental point was that a jury drawn from the *vicenage* was considered better qualified than

---

[4] There is an extensive literature on this subject. See, e.g., T.A. Green, *Verdict According to Conscience* (1985), Ch. 1; Mike MacNair, 'Vicenage and the Antecedents of the Jury' (1999) 17 *Law and History Review* 537; L.B. Thayer, *A Preliminary Treatise on Evidence at the Common Law* (1898), vol. I; S.F.C. Milsom, *Historical Foundations of the Common Law* (2nd edn, 1981).   [5] See Green, op.cit, fn 4, 15.

any other body to ascertain the facts at issue. Indeed, if a juror had not obtained for himself some knowledge of the matter involved by the date of the hearing, he could be excluded and someone else found instead. This being the case, strict rules were developed concerning the composition of juries and the extent of the areas over which jurors could be credited with having knowledge. These rules were central to the doctrine of venue.

The History of Venue Doctrine

It seems to have been accepted from the outset that jurors were unable try a matter arising from events that occurred in a different county from their own; but to begin with it was considered necessary, both in civil and in criminal cases, for a certain proportion of the jurors to come from a more strictly confined area. Some, at least, had to come from the relevant hundred within the county. This requirement proved troublesome in practice, and led to many disputes over the qualification of jurors, as a result of which it was abolished in civil cases in 1705, and was tacitly ignored by sheriffs when summoning juries for criminal cases from the mid-seventeenth century onwards.[6]

The broader venue doctrine, under which the jury had at least to be drawn from within the relevant county, lived on, but so awkward were some of its effects that legislative intervention was often necessary. In 1548, for example, there was passed 'An Act for the Trial of Murders and Felonies in Several Counties',[7] section II of which recited that the strictly-applied common law rules on venue produced the following problem:

It often happeneth . . . that a man is feloniously stricken in one county and after dieth in another county in which case it hath not been founden by the laws or customs of this Realm that any sufficient indictment thereof can be taken for that . . . the jurors of the county where such party died of such stroke being in a foreign county . . . *ne* the jurors of the county where the stroke was given cannot take knowledge of the death in another county although such death must apparently come of the same stroke and the said murdered and manquellers escape thereof without punishment.

To redress this situation, the Statute then provided:

That where any person or persons hereafter shall be feloniously stricken or poisoned in one county and die of the same . . . in another county that then an indictment thereof founden by jurors of the county where the death shall happen . . . shall be as good and effective in the law as if the stroke or poisoning had been committed . . . in the same county where the party shall die.

As quickly as statutes provided solutions to such problems, new and unforeseen variations of those problems would be discovered. The 1548 Act,

---

[6] See Matthew Hale, *Historia Placitorum Coronae* (1736) vol. II, 272.
[7] 2 & 3 Edw. 6, c. 24.

for example, only regulated jurisdictional conflicts between counties. As *Lacy's Case*[8] revealed, it did not affect the position between the jurisdiction of a county and that of the Admiral. According to Coke's account of this case:

Lacy struck Peacock and gave him a mortal wound upon the sea, of which Peacock died at Scarborough in the County of York, and Lacy was discharged of it, for those of the County of York could not enquire of the stroke . . . because it was not given in any county; and those of the Admiral's jurisdiction could not enquire of the stroke without enquiring of the death, and they could not enquire of the death, because it was *infra corpus comitatus*.

It took a further statute (that of 2 Geo. 2, c. 21) to remedy this defect. There were many such statutes and many 'judicial fictions'. One fiction, noted by Hale,[9] was that a thief carrying stolen goods into a new county was deemed to steal them again, so as to give the courts of that county jurisdiction over him.

The creation of these exceptions naturally tended to undermine the principle that jurors should base their verdict largely on their own knowledge of the relevant events. How could they have personal knowledge of events which, in reality, may have taken place far away, in a distant county? The truth, however, was that during the seventeenth century the function of the trial jury changed considerably. Witnesses became more widely used, both in civil and in criminal cases, and the privately-obtained knowledge of the jurors became less and less important. A significant landmark was the case of *Bennet* v. *Hundred of Hartford*,[10] in which the court ruled that any juror with independent knowledge of relevant events should give sworn evidence in court, and 'ought not to be examined in private by his companions'.

Once witnesses replaced this function of the jury, the real justification for the venue rules had ceased to exist; but instead of being abolished, the rules were allowed to linger on, subjected to more and more statutory and judicial exceptions and fictions. These so obscured and discredited the underlying doctrine that its origins and rationale were largely forgotten. Writing in 1893, Sir James Stephen noted that there were 18 statutory exceptions to the original doctrine (to say nothing of the numerous judicial fictions) and roundly concluded that, 'The only general interest attaching to these exceptions is that they prove that the general principle which requires so many exceptions must be wrong.'[11]

The Restricting Influence of Venue

The connection between the rules of venue and the territorial limitations on the ambit of English criminal law was entirely logical. Neither Parliament

---

[8] (1582) 1 Leon 270; also noted by Coke in his report of *Bingham's Case* (1600) 2 Co Rep 91(a).
[9] Op. cit., fn 6, 273.   [10] (1650) Style 233.
[11] *History of the Criminal Law of England* (1883) vol. I, 277.

nor the judges would create offences that could never be tried; and as Lord Goddard CJ observed in *R v. Page*[12]: 'One can see the procedural difficulty which would have occurred to the medieval lawyers who would be unable to understand how a jury consisting of persons drawn from the *vicenage* could have knowledge of crimes committed abroad, sufficient to present them to the Sovereign's court.' A medieval jury, which was deemed to have no knowledge of events outside its own county, could hardly be expected to know anything of events that might have occurred in Scotland or across the sea. Unless some special provision for trial was made, there could therefore be no such thing as an extraterritorial offence at common law.[13] In this way, the venue doctrine almost accidentally contributed to the principle of territoriality, under which events abroad were regarded as beyond the criminal law's concern.

During the medieval period, offences committed upon the sea (and in particular offences involving piracy) became triable in the courts of the Admiral and his deputies. The Admiral was a royal officer, and his courts followed civil or Roman law procedure, involving reliance on the testimony of witnesses. They were accordingly unaffected by the venue rules that limited the jurisdiction of the common law courts. The criminal jurisdiction of the Admiral was subsequently transferred to commissions exercising a specially modified form of common law procedure (omitting the usual venue requirements),[14] but this civil law influence helps to explain why piracy became the doyenne of extraterritorial offences under English law.

The Demise of the Venue Rules

The Criminal Justice Act 1925 sounded the virtual death knell of the jurisdictional limitations imposed by rules of venue. The Act allowed for prosecutions to be brought in any county where the accused was apprehended or in custody; and yet it was even then thought necessary to keep the underlying philosophy alive by 'deeming' the offence to have been committed in that county. The venue doctrine has now been abrogated in its entirety. The Courts Act 1971 created a unified Crown Court with jurisdiction over indictable offences committed anywhere in the world, and this jurisdiction is now restated in section 46(2) of the Supreme Court Act 1981. Some restrictions remain on the jurisdictional competence of magistrates over purely summary offences committed outside the counties or commission areas for which they are appointed, but except where offences are committed upon the sea, outside commission area boundaries, these seldom give rise to major difficulties in practice.[15] The restrictions, whilst obviously

---

[12] [1954] 1 QB 171, 175.
[13] This point was considered at length in *R v. Casement* [1917] 1 KB 98.
[14] See Edward East, *Pleas of the Crown* (1803), 794.   [15] See below, pp. 69–76.

analogous to the original venue rules, concern the competence of local officials rather than juries, and are thus distinguishable on that ground.

Surviving Influences

The old venue doctrine may thus help to explain how English law (and common law systems derived from English law) originally came to rely so exclusively on a territorial basis for its jurisdiction, and the absence of similar constraints in European civil law systems may help to explain why extraterritorial jurisdiction was more freely asserted under those systems; but one must not overlook other considerations. It is clear, for example, that the restrictions imposed by the venue doctrine soon ceased to be considered insurmountable. Jurisdictional problems could be solved if the will existed. From the time of Henry VIII, if not before, legislation was occasionally enacted in respect of offences committed abroad, and provision was made for the trial of such offences, either by special commissions or by ordinary courts and juries. Offences of treason and murder were amongst the first to be provided with extraterritorial ambits under special trial procedures that avoided the usual problems of venue.[16] Admiralty jurisdiction over piracy and crimes committed on British ships became exercisable by commissions that used common law procedures, once legislation had taken this jurisdiction away from the Admiral's own courts in 1536. From 1844 onwards, this jurisdiction was exercised by ordinary common law courts.[17] Crown servants, such as the governors of colonies or plantations, were made subject to English criminal law by the statute of 11 Will. 3, c. 12, in 1698.[18]

Parliament's failure to create a more generalized or widespread extraterritorial jurisdiction cannot therefore be explained wholly in terms of ancient procedural problems or historical accident. Why was nothing more done to enlarge the ambit of English law? In *Treacy* v. *DPP*,[19] Lord Diplock argued that the reason was to be found in rules of 'international comity'. Having noted that venue rules no longer imposed any restriction on the ambit of the law, he said: 'It would be an unjustifiable interference with the sovereignty of other nations over the conduct of persons in their own territory if we were to punish persons for conduct which did not take place in the United Kingdom and had no harmful consequences there.' This *dictum* formed no part of the *ratio* of *Treacy*, but it has been cited many times since, both in English cases and abroad. Unfortunately, it is incorrect,

---

[16] Under the statute of 33 Hen. 8, c. 23 (1541), now repealed.

[17] Admiralty Offences Act 1844.

[18] This jurisdiction was invoked in the notorious case of *R* v. *Wall* (1802) 28 St Tr 51, in which a former governor of Goree was hanged for the murder of a soldier who had died from the effects of an unlawfully imposed flogging.   [19] [1971] AC 537, 561.

because considerations of international law or comity impose no such general constraints on the ambit of a state's criminal law. In recent years, considerations of international law have tended to push English criminal law in the opposite direction—extending its ambit so as to enable the United Kingdom to discharge international responsibilities.

ENGLISH LAW AND INTERNATIONAL LAW

This work makes no pretence to be a treatise on public international law, but the rules of international law (and in particular, the United Kingdom's treaty obligations under that law) have had a major influence on the development of many of the current rules governing the ambit of English criminal law. The position under international law may also need to be considered, in some cases, as an aid to construing difficult or ambiguous rules of English law, and the United Kingdom's rights and obligations under international law have a significant bearing on the potential for future developments of its municipal jurisdiction. The importance of the international law dimension in this area cannot therefore be overlooked.

The Doctrine of Incorporation

The rules of customary international law (by which is meant those rules that are accepted by general state practice as binding upon the international community[20]) have long been considered an integral part of English common law, but only to the extent that they are not in conflict with Acts of Parliament or rules laid down by binding precedent. This 'doctrine of incorporation', as it is commonly known, can be traced back at least as far as the old case of *Buvot* v. *Barbuit*,[21] in which Lord Talbot declared that 'the law of nations, in its full extent is part of the law of England'. This *dictum* was later approved by Lord Mansfield in *Triquet* v. *Bath*,[22] in which it was held that a servant to the Bavarian ambassador to Great Britain was entitled to claim a measure of diplomatic immunity. More modern judicial statements and rulings supporting this doctrine can be found in the opinion delivered by Lord Atkin in *Chung Chi Cheung* v. *The King*,[23] in Lord Denning MR's judgment in *Trendtex Trading Corporation* v. *Central Bank of Nigeria*,[24]

---

[20] Customary law must be distinguished from 'mere usage' (common practice that is considered convenient rather than obligatory) and from rules established by treaties, which are binding only upon those states that are parties to the treaty. A multilateral treaty or convention may, however, codify, or subsequently come to represent, the rules of customary law.
[21] (1737) Cases t. Talb 281.   [22] (1764) 2 Burr 1478.   [23] [1939] AC 160, 168.
[24] [1977] QB 529.

and in a ruling made by Devonshire J in the unreported case of *R v. Mills*.[25]
In *Chung Chi Cheung*, Lord Atkin said:

The courts acknowledge the existence of a body of rules which nations accept amongst themselves. On any judicial issue they seek to ascertain what the relevant rule is and, having found it, they will treat it as incorporated into the domestic law, so far as it is not inconsistent with rules enacted by statutes or finally declared by their tribunals.[26]

In *Mills*, Devonshire J held that the provisions of the 1958 Geneva Convention on the High Seas dealing with the right of 'hot pursuit'[27] were declaratory of customary international law, and that the relevant rules were thus incorporated within English common law.

This does not mean that rules of customary international law can easily be relied upon at criminal trials or appeals governed by English law. In practice, any party seeking to rely on such rules is likely to face at least two major difficulties. To begin with, there will usually be existing English precedents to consider, and where these appear to provide an answer to the issue in dispute under ordinary principles of *stare decisis*, evidence of the development of a contrary rule of international law would not ordinarily be relevant. It is possible that international law may prevail where the earlier precedents can be shown to be based on a clear misunderstanding of customary international law, or where they are based on an obsolete rule of customary international law that has since been abandoned or modified, but this is by no means clear, because there are conflicting decisions of the Court of Appeal on this question.[28]

The second likely difficulty is one of establishing the existence and scope of the particular customary rule. In theory, courts may take judicial notice of the rules of customary international law,[29] and do not therefore require formal proof of that law in the shape of sworn expert testimony, etc.,[30] but in practice a court or judge will still need to be persuaded (by legal submissions and citations) of the content of the customary rule in question. The views of jurists have traditionally received greater acceptance and recognition in the field of international law than in English law, but the only primary evidence of customary law is state practice, and this must provide evidence of

---

[25] (1995) Crown Court, Croydon; noted by Gilmore, (1995) 44 *International and Comparative Law Quarterly* 949.　　　[26] See also *The Rose Mary* [1953] 1 WLR 246.

[27] I.e., the pursuit of an offending foreign vessel from a state's own territorial waters onto the high seas, in order to make an arrest. See now UNCLOS 1982, Art. 111.

[28] *Thai-Europe Tapioca Service v. Government of Pakistan* [1975] 1 WLR 1485; *Trendtex Trading Corporation v. Central Bank of Nigeria* [1977] QB 529.

[29] *R v. Keyn* (1876) 2 Ex D 63; *Chung Chi Cheung v. The King* [1939] AC 160.

[30] This contrasts with the position concerning matters of foreign law, which must be proved by admissible evidence (notably expert evidence) in the usual way. See *R v. Ofori (No. 2)* (1994) 99 Cr App R 223.

uniformity, consistency, and generality of state practice in the relevant area. Furthermore, there must be clear evidence of *opinio juris et necessitatis*: a belief within the international community that the practice in question is legally obligatory, or (where the existence of permissive rules are in question) a belief that the practice cannot legally be objected to.

The evidence of such practice (and of the requisite *opinio juris*) may be obtained from various sources. Ian Brownlie[31] identifies the following:

Diplomatic correspondence, policy statements, press releases, the opinions of legal advisers, official manuals on legal questions e.g. manuals of military law, executive decisions and practises, orders to Naval forces, etc., comments by governments on drafts produced by the International Law Commission, state legislation, international and national judicial decisions, recitals in treaties and other international instruments, a pattern of treaties in the same form, the practice of international organs, and resolutions relating to legal questions in the United Nations General Assembly.

The potential difficulties involved in satisfying English judges as to the incorporation of a rule of international law within English criminal law (and in particular a rule imposing or extending criminal liability) were demonstrated in the historic case of *R v. Keyn*.[32] A fatal collision occurred in the English Channel, some two miles from the Kent coast. The British steamer *Strathclyde* was rammed and sunk by the German steamer *Franconia*. Keyn, the master of the *Franconia*, was charged with manslaughter, and was convicted at first instance, on the basis that the collision had taken place within what were alleged to be British territorial waters. On appeal, the Crown sought to convince the Court for Crown Cases Reserved that despite the absence, in modern times,[33] of any formal British claim to sovereignty over coastal waters, customary international law automatically gave all littoral states the right to exercise criminal jurisdiction within three nautical miles of their shores, and that this principle was effectively incorporated within the common law. The nature of the argument was summarized by Brett JA[34]:

The question on both sides has been made to depend on whether such is or is not proved to be the law of nations. On the one side it is said there is evidence and authority on which the court ought to hold that such is the law of nations; on the other side it said there is no such evidence or authority. The evidence relied on for the Crown is an alleged common acquiescence by recognised jurists of so many countries, as to be substantially of all countries, and declarations of statesmen, and

---

[31] *Principles of Public International Law* (5th edn, 1998), 5.

[32] Otherwise known as The *Franconia* Case (1876) 2 Ex D 63. The background to this case is examined by Geoffrey Marston, 'The Centenary of the *Franconia* Case: The Prosecution of Ferdinand Keyn' (1976) 92 *Law Quarterly Review* 93.

[33] In past times, English kings had made grandiose claims to sovereignty over huge areas of water in the 'narrow seas' around Britain, but the court did not consider such claims to be valid or effective.   [34] (1876) 2 Ex D 63, 126–7.

similar declarations of English judges in court in the course of administering law. On the other side it is said that the declarations cited of the judges were opinions only, and not decisions; that there is no common acquiescence of jurists to the alleged effect, or declarations of statesmen; and that if there were, such acquiescence or declarations are not sufficient; that there should be acquiescence by governments declared in treaties or evidenced by acts of government.

By a majority of 7 : 6, the court eventually rejected the claim that English criminal law could be applied to conduct that had occurred aboard a foreign ship on the open sea. The failure of the Crown's case can in part be explained by the fact that it was unable to produce any substantial evidence of the requisite state practice. While some of the dissenting judges were impressed by the arguments of the jurists, those in the majority were not. Kelly CB looked for evidence of the supposed rule in practice, and declared that he had found none[35]:

Not one single instance of the exercise of such a jurisdiction is to be found in the history of the world from the beginning of time; and . . . no authorities of any number of writers . . . even if they were (which they were not) express and uniform to the same effect, can take away or impose conditions upon the right to free navigation of the high seas. . . .

The judgment of Cockburn CJ, which was by far the longest and most detailed of those given, appears to go furthest of all in its rejection of the Crown's case. He said:

Even if entire unanimity had existed . . . the question would still remain, how far the law as stated by the publicists had received the assent of the civilised nations of the World. . . Nor, in my opinion, would the clearest proof of unanimous assent on the part of other nations be sufficient to authorise the tribunals of this country to apply, without an Act of Parliament, what would practically amount to a new law.

Cockburn CJ's judgment appears to reject the incorporation principle itself, at least in so far as it might be used to impose or extend criminal liability under English law, although jurists are divided as to whether he rejects it generally.[36] In any event, other judges in the majority did not go so far. The Admiralty judge, Sir Robert Phillimore, expressly left the point open,[37] and it remained open to argument whether criminal liability could be imposed or extended (and not merely limited) under English law through the incorporation of rules of customary international law.[38]

Some of the issues that divided the court in *Keyn* appear more recently to have divided the House of Lords in the *Pinochet* case.[39] One of the issues

---

[35] (1876) 2 Ex D 63, 151.

[36] H. Lauterpacht, *Private Law Sources and Analogies of International Law* (1927), 76. See also Brownlie, op. cit., fn 31, 44.　　　　　　　　　　[37] (1876) 2 Ex D 63, 68.

[38] This is despite the fact that Parliament quickly expressed its dissatisfaction with the majority judgments in *Keyn* by enacting the Territorial Waters Jurisdiction Act 1878.

[39] *R v. Bow Street Metropolitan Stipendiary Magistrate and others, ex p Pinochet Ugarte (No. 3)* [2000] 1 AC 147.

that arose in that case was whether torture committed abroad prior to 29 September 1988 (when section 134 of the Criminal Justice Act 1988 came into force, creating a statutory offence of torture that could be committed anywhere in the world) could nevertheless be extraditable as a common law offence. Lord Millett argued that it could be, because in his view torture had for several years been recognized as a crime under international law. The 1984 Torture Convention,[40] to which section 134 gave effect, did not (on that view) create any new international crime but merely restated or codified an old one, which had been recognized as early as 1973,[41] and must therefore have been incorporated within the common law. He considered that section 134 had done little more than restate an existing common law offence:

Every state has jurisdiction under customary international law to exercise extra-territorial jurisdiction in respect of international crimes which satisfy the relevant criteria. Whether its courts have extraterritorial jurisdiction under its internal domestic law depends, of course, on its constitutional arrangements and the relationship between customary international law and the jurisdiction of its criminal courts. The jurisdiction of the English criminal courts is usually statutory, but it is supplemented by the common law. Customary international law is part of the common law, and accordingly I consider that the English courts have and always have had extraterritorial criminal jurisdiction in respect of crimes of universal jurisdiction under customary international law.[42]

This was revolutionary doctrine. Not since the defeat of the minority view in *R* v. *Keyn* had any English judge argued that international law might endow English common law with an inherent extraterritorial jurisdiction over crime. The orthodox view is that any extraterritorial extension of the ambit of English law must necessarily be statutory, and Lord Millett was forced to acknowledge that his view was a minority one: 'I understand . . . that your Lordships take a different view, and consider that statutory authority is required before our courts can exercise extraterritorial criminal jurisdiction even in respect of crimes of universal jurisdiction.'[43]

In contrast, Lord Phillips doubted whether customary international law had ever required states to assume such jurisdiction, save in respect of express treaty obligations:

I believe that it is still an open question whether international law recognises universal jurisdiction in respect of international crimes—that is the right, under international law, of the courts of any state to prosecute for such crimes wherever

---

[40] The Convention against Torture and Other Cruel, Inhuman or Degrading Treatment or Punishment 1984 (UN General Assembly Resolution 39/46, Doc A/39/51; Cmnd. 9593).

[41] 'The Republic of Chile accepts that, by 1973, the use of torture by state authorities was prohibited by international law and that the prohibition had the character of *jus cogens* or obligation *erga omnes*.': [2000] 1 AC 147, 275.   [42] Ibid., 276.

[43] Ibid. The majority view appears to be correct in principle. To some extent, Lord Millett appears to have relied on the same kind of reasoning as that upon which Lord Diplock relied in *Treacy* (see p. 34 above).

they occur. In relation to war crimes, such a jurisdiction has been asserted by the State of Israel, notably in the prosecution of Adolf Eichmann,[44] but this assertion of jurisdiction does not reflect any general state practice in relation to international crimes. Rather, states have tended to agree, or to attempt to agree, on the creation of international tribunals to try international crimes. They have however, on occasion, agreed by conventions, that their national courts should enjoy jurisdiction to prosecute for a particular category of international crime wherever occurring.[45]

This division of opinion, so reminiscent of *Keyn*, shows that the doctrine of incorporation remains a potentially troublesome one, and may be difficult to rely upon, even in modern times. Wherever possible, judges will look for treaties and for legislation that gives legal effect to such treaties, because this places them on much safer ground.

In some cases, however, there may be no such treaties or legislation. It is possible, for example, that an attempt will one day be made to prosecute (or extradite) a foreign prime minister or foreign minister, etc., in respect of an offence allegedly committed by that person when in office. No United Kingdom legislation grants such persons any immunity comparable to that granted to diplomats, heads of state, or even consular officials, but there is now clear evidence (in the form of a recent judgment of the International Court of Justice[46]) that such persons are entitled to immunity under customary international law, and it would be surprising if English courts failed to recognize and give effect to that immunity.

Treaties and English Law

International treaties or conventions, whether bilateral or multilateral, have in practice become the major source of modern public international law, or at least of binding obligations under international law. There can be no question, however, of treaty obligations being incorporated automatically into English municipal law. Such automatic incorporation would enable the executive to alter English law without the assent of Parliament.[47] Legislation is therefore required to implement any such treaty under municipal law. As Lord Atkin said in *Attorney-General for Canada* v. *Attorney-General for Ontario*[48]: 'There is a well-established rule that the making of a treaty is an executive act, whilst the performance of its obligations, if they entail alteration of the existing domestic law, requires legislative action.'

---

[44] *A-G of Israel* v. *Eichmann* (1961) 36 ILR 5.   [45] [2000] 1 AC 147, 288–9.

[46] *Arrest Warrant of 11 April 2000: Democratic Republic of the Congo* v. *Belgium* [2002] ICJ Rep 3; see Xiaodong Yang, 'Immunity for International Crimes: a Reaffirmation of Traditional Doctrine' [2002] *Cambridge Law Journal* 242.

[47] *The Parlement Belge* (1878–79) 4 PD 129. The decision of Sir Robert Phillimore in that case was reversed on other grounds ((1880) 5 PD 197) but is still considered to be good authority on this particular issue.

[48] [1937] AC 326. See also *R* v. *Lyons and others* [2002] 4 All ER 1028.

Some treaty obligations may be implemented by delegated legislation, if there is an earlier statute providing authority for the making of the necessary Order. Thus, the Territorial Sea Act 1987 provides the authority for various Orders amending the extent of the United Kingdom's territorial sea in accordance with treaty obligations; and the Channel Tunnel Act 1987 provides the requisite authority for the Channel Tunnel (International Arrangements) Order 1993, which implements a 1991 Protocol between the United Kingdom and France on frontier controls, policing and cooperation in criminal justice, etc., within the tunnel system. In the context of criminal jurisdiction, the most common reason for the enactment of legislation giving extraterritorial application to offences under English criminal law is that this legislation is necessary in order to implement the United Kingdom's jurisdictional obligations under multilateral treaties. This has accordingly become a more significant and far more visible influence on English criminal law than has the incorporation of customary law into the common law.

International Law and the Interpretation of Statutes

Where there is any ambiguity in the meaning or effect of a statute, it must be construed, if possible, in such a way as to avoid any conflict with the rules of international law. There is a presumption, in other words, that Parliament would not legislate so as to create a conflict with international law, although if a statute were to be passed that did clearly create such a conflict, it would be the duty of the courts to apply it. In *Mortensen* v. *Peters*,[49] the Scottish High Court of Justiciary upheld the validity of a by-law issued under the Herring Fishery (Scotland) Act 1889, banning the use of beam or otter trawling techniques in any part of the Moray Firth, most of which then lay outside British territorial waters. The Court accordingly upheld the conviction of the Danish master of a Norwegian-registered fishing boat for acts done on the High Seas, long before the recognition of wide exclusive fishery zones under international law. The enforcement of this law against the Norwegian fishing fleet created a serious of international incidents, and led to the repeal of the legislation a few years later, but its validity under Scots law had not been in doubt.

The presumption that Parliament does not intend to violate international law may well be related to a presumption noted earlier in this chapter: namely, that Parliament does not intend provisions creating criminal liability to be applicable to conduct in foreign countries. It is undoubtedly related to the presumption that where Parliament does create extraterritorial liability, it does not intend that liability to extend to foreign nationals.[50]

---

[49] (1906) 8 F (J) 93.   [50] See *Air India* v. *Wiggins* [1980] 1 WLR 815.

It would be a mistake, however, to conflate these presumptions as if they were all variants of the same rule.

This appears to have been the mistake made by Lord Diplock in *Treacy* v. *DPP*.[51] The question that arose in that case was whether the appellant had committed an offence of blackmail under English law by posting a blackmail demand from England to a victim in West Germany. The Theft Act 1968, within which the offence of blackmail is to be found, does not expressly confine its ambit to England and Wales, but this was to be presumed under the rule that Parliament would not ordinarily intend criminal legislation to apply abroad. What then of a cross-frontier offence such as in *Treacy*, where the perpetrator acted in England against a victim who was abroad? The majority view in *Treacy* was that it would still be an offence under English law if, but only if, on a strict construction of the legislation, the blackmail demand could be said to have been 'made' in England. This was not by any means a wholly satisfactory way of resolving such cases, but it was (and remains) the orthodox approach to such problems under English law. Lord Diplock, however, looked for a more principled solution, and argued that, following the demise of the venue doctrine, the only proper modern restrictions on the ambit of English criminal law were to be found in the rules of 'international comity' (by which presumably he meant the rules of international law). He said:

The Parliament of the United Kingdom has plenary power, if it chooses to exercise it, to empower any court in the United Kingdom to punish persons present in its territories for having done physical acts wherever the acts were done and wherever their consequences took effect. When Parliament, as in the Theft Act 1968, defines new crimes in words which as a matter of language do not contain any geographical limitation either as to where a person's punishable conduct took place or, when the definition requires that the conduct shall be followed by specified consequences, as to where those consequences took effect, what reason have we to suppose that Parliament intended any geographical limitation to be understood?

The only relevant reason, now that the technicalities of venue have long since been abolished, is to be found in the international rules of comity which, in the absence of express provision to the contrary, it is presumed that Parliament did not intend to break. It would be an unjustifiable interference with the sovereignty of other nations over the conduct of persons in their own territories if we were to punish persons for conduct which did not take place in the United Kingdom and had no harmful consequences there. But I see no reason in comity for requiring any wider limitation than that on the exercise by Parliament of its legislative power in the field of criminal law. There is no rule of comity to prevent Parliament from prohibiting under pain of punishment persons who are present in the United Kingdom, and so owe local obedience to our law, from doing physical acts in England, notwithstanding that the consequences of those acts take effect outside the United Kingdom.[52]

---

[51] [1971] AC 537.   [52] Ibid., 561.

As previously explained, this *dictum* was not part of the *ratio* of *Treacy*, but it has been cited many times since, not only in England but also in Canada.[53] Although superficially attractive, it overlooks the fact that English law has never asserted the full range of jurisdiction permitted to it under international law. A state may not ordinarily criminalize acts done by foreigners in foreign countries (although there are several exceptions to that rule), nor may it send its law enforcement agencies into foreign territory without the consent of the state concerned, but there is no rule in international law or 'comity' that forbids a state from holding one of its own citizens accountable, before its own courts, for things done in foreign territory. Most states (including the United Kingdom) do this to some extent, and some do it on a more general basis. The latter include most states with civil law systems incorporating a criminal code. By Article 113–6 of the French *Code Penal*:

French criminal law is applicable to any felony [*crime*] committed by a French citizen outside the territory of the Republic. It is also applicable to misdemeanours [*délits*] committed by French citizens outside the territory of the Republic, if these are punishable under the laws of the country in which they are committed. ...

The precise circumstances in which international law permits or restricts the assertion or exercise of extraterritorial criminal jurisdiction are considered below, but it must already be clear that the rules of international law cannot, by themselves, explain why the extraterritorial ambit of English criminal law has not become more extensive.

International Law and English Territorial Limits

In contrast to the position in respect of extraterritorial jurisdiction, there is a very close and obvious relationship between the rules governing territorial waters under international law and the maritime limits actually adopted by the United Kingdom. The Territorial Waters Order in Council 1964 and the Territorial Sea Act 1987 were drafted with a view to providing the United Kingdom with the widest territorial limits currently permissible under the international law of the sea. The United Kingdom has accordingly declared a territorial sea with a breadth of 12 international nautical miles, measured from the line of lowest astronomical tides (LAT) because this is the maximum breadth of territorial sea recognized under the 1982 UNCLOS Convention, which is now considered to reflect customary law. Similarly, bays and estuaries are claimed as internal waters wherever UNCLOS so permits, but the waters of Mounts Bay in Cornwall or of the Ribble estuary in Lancashire are not claimed as internal waters under English law, because neither qualifies as a 'juridical bay' under the Convention;[54] and so on.

---

[53] See, e.g., *R v. Smith* [1996] 2 BCLC 109, 125–6; *Libman v. R* [1985] 2 SCR 178.

[54] In order for an indentation on the coast to be a 'juridical bay' under international law, the area of waters enclosed by a line drawn between its natural entrance points must equal or

This does not mean that the United Kingdom has always claimed its full entitlement to territorial waters, etc. On the contrary, it has seldom, if ever, been amongst the first states to adopt or take advantage of emerging doctrines in this area;[55] and even when it has decided to do so, it has sometimes taken months or years for the necessary legislation to be enacted. What the United Kingdom tends *not* do is to claim territorial limits in excess of those that can clearly be justified under international law.

The precise jurisdictional regimes applicable within the United Kingdom's territorial limits nevertheless owe more to the peculiarities of English and Scots law and to British Constitutional law than to any rules of international law. The international lawyer, for example, distinguishes for jurisdictional purposes between a state's territorial waters and its internal waters, whereas the English lawyer must distinguish first between waters that are adjacent to England or Wales, or Northern Ireland, and waters that are adjacent to Scotland; and then between waters that are internal, in the sense of being a part of the realm at common law,[56] and waters that are internal merely because they lie to landward of the baselines from which the territorial sea is measured. To the English criminal lawyer, these distinctions have greater significance than any distinction between internal waters and territorial waters under international law.

CRIMINAL JURISDICTION IN INTERNATIONAL LAW

Several possible bases of criminal jurisdiction may be asserted by individual states, although some of these tend to be used only occasionally or exceptionally, and they do not all enjoy the same degree of recognition or acceptance under international law. In the *Lotus Case*,[57] the Permanent Court of International Justice examined the general principles governing criminal jurisdiction under international law and concluded that, whilst international law undoubtedly restricts the right of a state to *enforce* its laws by police action, etc., within the territory of another state, each state nevertheless enjoys considerable freedom to delimit the territorial and extraterritorial ambit of its own laws:

It does not . . . follow that international law prohibits a state from exercising jurisdiction in its own territory, in respect of any case which relates to acts which have

---

exceed the area of an imaginary semi-circle, the diameter of which is equal to that of the line (see UNCLOS, Art. 10, and see also the preceding 1958 Geneva Convention on the Territorial Sea and Contiguous Zone, Art. 7 of which was to identical effect). The 1964 Order in Council applies that rule, without modification.

[55] In the context of fishery limits, the UK initially opposed the adoption of 12-mile (and later 200-mile) fishery limits by states such as Iceland, before conceding their validity and in due course adopting similar limits itself.

[56] These are waters that lie *inter fauces terrae* (within the jaws of the land) at common law. See Chapter 3 below.   [57] *France v. Turkey* (1927) PCIJ Rep, Series A, No. 10.

taken place abroad, and in which it cannot rely on some permissive rule of international law. Such a view would only be tenable if international law contained a general prohibition to states to extend the application of their laws and the jurisdiction of their courts to persons, property and acts outside their territory, and if, as an exception to this general prohibition, it allowed states to do so in certain specific cases. But this is certainly not the case under international law as it stands at present. Far from laying down a general prohibition . . . it leaves them in this respect a wide measure of discretion which is only limited in certain cases by prohibitive rules . . . This discretion left to states by international law explains the great variety of rules which they have been able to adopt without objections or complaints on the part of other states.

This generally permissive approach to the subject of state jurisdiction has not been without its critics,[58] but it helps to explain the continuing diversity of state practice in this area. The ambit of English criminal law has enlarged considerably in recent years, taking advantage in some cases of the flexibility and discretion that international law permits. Certain limits have nevertheless been established, and in practice any claim to criminal jurisdiction will be based on one or more of the following principles.

The Territorial Principle

In international law, as in English law, the territorial principle of jurisdiction is considered to be of fundamental importance. The right to prescribe and enforce criminal prohibitions over conduct within a state's own territory is seen as an indispensable attribute of national sovereignty. The regular enforcement of criminal laws and the investigation, trial, and punishment of crime cannot easily be accomplished on anything other than a territorial basis, and the state within which criminal behaviour takes place is likely, in the vast majority of cases, to have by far the strongest interest in the suppression and punishment of that behaviour.

Although the predominance of the territorial principle is now firmly established throughout the world, issues may still arise concerning the proper limits or extent of territorial jurisdiction. In particular, there may be issues concerning the extent to which acts committed outside a state's borders may be prosecuted under the territorial principle, if they bring about prohibited consequences within those borders.

Cross-frontier Offences

The general rule is that claims to territorial jurisdiction may lawfully be made either on the basis that criminal conduct was committed within the territory of the state in question, or on the basis that criminal conduct

---

[58] See, e.g., J.L. Brierly, 'The *Lotus* Case' (1928) 44 *Law Quarterly Review* 154.

abroad took effect within that territory. As the Permanent Court of International Justice explained in the *Lotus Case*[59]:

No argument has come to the knowledge of the Court from which it could be deduced that states recognise themselves to be under an obligation towards each other only to have regard to the place where the author of the offence happens to be at the time of the offence. On the contrary, it is certain that the courts of many countries, even of countries that have given their criminal legislation a strictly territorial character, interpret criminal law in the sense that offences, the authors of which at the moment of commission are in the territory of another state, are nevertheless to be regarded as having been committed in the national territory, if one of the constituent elements of the offence, and more especially its effects, have taken place there.

In *Treacy v. DPP*,[60] Lord Diplock expressed a similar view:

Comity gives no right to a State to insist that any person may with impunity do physical acts in its own territory which have harmful consequences to persons within the territory of another State. It may be under no obligation in comity to punish those acts itself, but it has no ground for complaint in international law if the State in which the harmful consequences had their effect punishes, when they do enter its territories, persons who did such acts.

International lawyers often refer in this context to 'subjective' and 'objective' applications of the territorial principle. Subjective jurisdiction is that exercised by the state in which the conduct in question was instigated; objective jurisdiction is that exercised by the state within which the consequences of that conduct were felt. This terminology has seldom been adopted in English cases, however.[61]

While the subjective application of territorial jurisdiction presents few difficulties under international law, the objective variant can be more problematic. How does one define the constituent elements of an offence? How direct or immediate must the effects of foreign conduct be, before they can legitimately give jurisdiction to the state within which they have been felt? A conspiracy hatched in England to defraud the Irish subsidiary of a multinational company may bring about the ruin of the parent company in France, or of another subsidiary company in Germany. Financial losses may be suffered by shareholders in Belgium. Under international law, the English and Irish courts may undoubtedly claim jurisdiction on subjective or objective territorial principles, but the position of France, Germany, and Belgium is less clear.

Writers on international law generally assert that a legitimate exercise of the objective principle of territorial jurisdiction must be based on the occurrence of a 'significant' adverse effect within the state in question, or even

---

[59] *France v. Turkey* (1927) PCIJ Rep, Series A, No. 10.   [60] [1971] AC 537, 562.
[61] The approach of the English courts is fundamentally different. See below, pp. 113–129.

that it may be exercised 'only by the state where the primary effect is felt'.[62] In practice, many states seem unwilling to assert objective territorial jurisdiction unless the consequences that occur (or that are intended to occur) within their territory form a constituent element, and not merely a remote consequence, of the offence in question, as defined under their own laws. This indeed is the approach taken under English law, but it can lead to unsatisfactory results, because in English law the direct and intended consequences of a crime are not always defined as essential elements of that crime. As explained in Chapter 4 below, this may sometimes mean that English law is unable to assert itself over acts that would undoubtedly fall within the rightful jurisdiction of English courts as a matter of international law.

The Effects Doctrine and Anti-trust Law

The controversial 'doctrine of effects' which has long been associated most closely with US anti-trust law, is closely related to the principle of objective territorial jurisdiction, but is more flexible and more open to abuse. An early statement of the doctrine may be found in the judgment of the US Supreme Court in *US v Aluminium Corp. of America*[63]: 'Any state may impose liabilities, even upon persons not within its allegiance, for conduct outside its borders that has consequences within its borders which the state reprehends.'

There is nothing inherently objectionable in this, as long as the consequences in question are intended and/or directly result from the conduct; but problems may arise where those consequences are merely the remote or indirect effects of conduct that is legitimate in the jurisdiction where it takes place. This explains why US attempts to penalize foreign companies for restrictive trade practices that only indirectly affect US interests have been a frequent source of international dispute.[64] For the most part, these disputes have concerned civil matters, rather than criminal ones, but many of the underlying issues are the same in each case. The United Kingdom's objections to effects-based jurisdiction in anti-trust cases are set out in this *aide-memoire* to the European Commission[65]:

The United Kingdom government have . . . consistently objected to the assumption of extraterritorial jurisdiction in anti-trust matters by the courts or authorities of a foreign state when that jurisdiction is based upon what is termed the 'effects doctrine'— that is to say, the doctrine that territorial jurisdiction over conduct which has

---

[62] See Michael Akehurst, 'Jurisdiction in International Law' (1972–3) 46 *British Yearbook of International Law* 145, 154. The 1982 *Draft Restatement of US Foreign Relations Law*, Chapter 1, § 402, restricts the objective principle to conduct that 'has, or is intended to have substantial effect' within a state's territory.   [63] (1945) 148 F 2d 416, 443.

[64] See A.V. Lowe, *Extraterritorial Jurisdiction* (1983); Malcolm Shaw, *International Law* (4th edn, 1997), 483.

[65] 20 October 1969. See Lauterpacht, *British Practice* (1967), 58.

occurred wholly outside the territory of that state claiming jurisdiction may be justified because of the resulting economic effects of such conduct within the territory of that state. This doctrine becomes even more open to objection when . . . foreign corporations are made subject to penal sanctions.

The United Kingdom's objections were later backed by legislation, in the form of the Protection of Trading Interests Act 1980, and the issues involved have given rise to a great deal of case law and literature; but English criminal law makes no such use of the effects doctrine, and a detailed discussion of these issues will not be attempted in this work.

On the other hand, the objective territorial principle, if applied inappropriately, may itself produce some at least of the same problems, as for example where State A attempts to criminalize or impose other sanctions on a foreign national who, in State B, publishes internet-based material that is lawful in State B but which may be viewed or downloaded (and thus arguably 'published') in State A, where it is deemed to be obscene, subversive, or blasphemous. The 'frontierless' nature of the Internet has already triggered a series of such prosecutions, including prosecutions in English courts,[66] and it may be only a matter of time before a case of this kind triggers a significant international dispute.[67]

The Protective Principle

The principle of objective territorial jurisdiction must be distinguished from the 'protective principle', under which acts done wholly abroad may be criminalized if they involve attacks on or threats against a state's security or vital national interests. The counterfeiting of a state's currency provides an example. Many states criminalize this practice, even where the counterfeit currency is printed and circulated abroad. According to the Harvard Research Group's *Draft Convention on Jurisdiction with Respect to Crime*,[68] the protective principle is 'claimed by most states, regarded with misgivings in a few, and generally ranked as the basis of an auxiliary competence'. It is not, however, relied upon anywhere in English law, even in respect of activities, such as the counterfeiting of British currency, that are obviously capable of damaging vital British interests.[69]

---

[66] Notably in *R v. Perrin* [2002] All ER (D) 359 (Mar); [2002] EWCA Crim 747. See below, p. 187.

[67] See also the *Yahoo! Case*, in which US courts have refused to enforce orders made by a French court against *Yahoo! Inc.*, concerning the Internet sale of Nazi memorabilia, which is illegal under French law if accessible by Internet users in France (*LICRA and UEJF v. Yahoo! Inc and Yahoo! France*, Tribunal de Grand Instance de Paris, 22 May 2000: *Relié du Receiul Dalloz; Jurisprudence Dalloz*, 172).

[68] Reprinted in (1935) 29 *American Journal of International Law* Supp. 443.

[69] Counterfeiting is likely to be punishable as an offence under English law if any element of that offence occurs within England and Wales (see Pt I of the Criminal Justice Act 1993), but it is not and never has been an extraterritorial offence under that law.

A number of international lawyers[70] cite the notorious case of *Joyce* v. *DPP*[71] as a rare application of the protective principle under English law. This may in part be explained by the fact that some other countries categorize jurisdiction over extraterritorial treason on that basis,[72] but the only mention of the protective principle in *Joyce* is an isolated *obiter dictum* by Lord Jowitt LC, who said:

No principle of comity demands that a state should ignore the crime of treason committed against it outside its territory. On the contrary, a proper regard for its security requires that all those who commit that crime, whether they commit it within or without the realm, should be amenable to its laws.[73]

It is one thing for a judge to defend the exercise of jurisdiction in such terms, but it is quite another thing to say that the protective principle was relied upon in that case as the basis for the exercise of jurisdiction. Criminal liability was imposed because Joyce (the Nazi propaganda broadcaster popularly known as 'Lord Haw-Haw') was the holder of a British passport and was accordingly held to have owed allegiance to the British Crown, as if he were a British subject. Jurisdiction asserted under the protective principle does not depend on the status of the alleged offender but on the threat he poses to national interests. In normal circumstances, no alien would have owed any such allegiance; and could not therefore have been tried for treason, however much damage he might have caused to British interests. Had the protective principle indeed been the basis of Joyce's liability, his possession of a British passport would surely have been irrelevant.

The Offender's Nationality or Status

The right of a state to apply its criminal laws to the acts or omissions of its own subjects abroad is universally recognized under international law, and is asserted (albeit to greatly differing extents) by almost all states. As previously noted, states whose legal systems derive from English common law tend to rely much less on this principle than states whose legal systems are based on civilian traditions, and English law has tended, historically, to use it very sparingly indeed, but this does not mean that the United Kingdom questions or objects to its wider use by other states.

Under the doctrine of 'double criminality', the United Kingdom will not ordinarily extradite a fugitive to another state, in respect of a crime allegedly committed against that state's law, unless the alleged offence would also have been recognized as an offence under a comparable United Kingdom law.[74]

---

[70] Including Shaw, op. cit., fn 64, 469; but contrast Brownlie, op. cit., fn 31, 307.
[71] [1946] AC 347.   [72] See, e.g., the German Criminal Code, § 5.2.
[73] [1946] AC 347, 372.
[74] *R* v. *Bow Street Metropolitan Stipendiary Magistrate, ex p Pinochet Ugarte (No. 3)* [2000] 1 AC 147.

This tended for many years to cause difficulties in cases where the requesting state sought to base its claim to extradition on the nationality of the fugitive, rather than on the commission of an offence within its own territory. Given, for example, that English criminal law did not extend to acts of counterfeiting committed by British citizens abroad, English courts could not permit the extradition of a citizen of State X to that state on a charge alleging the commission of a similar offence in State Y, because in double criminality terms the extradition request would not have disclosed any equivalent offence under English law. For extradition purposes, the right of a requesting state to rely upon the nationality of the fugitive accordingly depended on whether this was one of those rare or exceptional cases (such as murder or manslaughter) to which English criminal law applied the same principle.

Since the United Kingdom does not question the right of other states to claim such jurisdiction over their nationals, the restrictions imposed by this rule were considered undesirable, and section 2 of the Extradition Act 1989 therefore relaxed the double-criminality rule to the extent that extradition may now be granted where:

(1) the requesting state bases its jurisdiction on the nationality of the offender;
(2) the conduct constituting the offence occurred outside the United Kingdom; and
(3) if that conduct had occurred in the United Kingdom, it would have constituted an offence under the law of the United Kingdom punishable with imprisonment for a term of 12 months, or any greater punishment.[75]

This does not, however, apply in cases where extradition arrangements between the United Kingdom and the requesting state are still governed by bilateral extradition treaties made under the Extradition Act 1870.[76]

Nationality is not the only status that may link a defendant to a particular state. States may in some cases invoke residence within the state or possession of that state's passport as sufficient links. Indeed, the United Kingdom has asserted such jurisdiction on at least one occasion,[77] and some recent legislation expressly makes residence within the United Kingdom a potential basis for the application of English criminal law.[78]

---

[75] This would have to be the case at the date of the commission of the alleged offence, and not merely at the date of the extradition request or hearing: see the *Pinochet* case, at pp. 38–40 above.

[76] See, e.g., *Re Al-Fawwaz* [2002] 1 All ER 545. The Extradition Bill introduced before Parliament in November 2002 will create further potential exceptions to the double criminality principle in respect of cases involving 'category 1 territories' and 'conduct that falls within the European framework list'. Crimes of racism or xenophobia, for example, may become extraditable under a European arrest warrant, even where the conduct alleged would not be considered criminal under English law.   [77] See *Joyce v. DPP* [1946] AC 347.

[78] As, e.g., under the War Crimes Act 1991.

'Passive Personality'—the Victim's Nationality or Status

A state that applies the 'passive personality' principle of jurisdiction may seek to punish foreigners for crimes committed against its own citizens abroad. Historically, this practice once aroused more opposition than any other basis of criminal jurisdiction. The United States was a particularly vehement objector,[79] and in the *Lotus* case the Permanent Court of International Justice expressly reserved its opinion as to the legality of a Turkish law which asserted the principle.[80] The number of states purporting to rely upon the principle has nevertheless increased during the last century, particularly in respect of terrorist crimes,[81] and now includes Germany,[82] Italy, and (most significantly) the United States itself.

Under USC Title 18, section 2332,[83] it is now a federal crime for a terrorist overseas to kill a United States national, attempt to murder a United States national, conspire to murder a United States national, or to engage in physical violence with the intent to cause serious bodily injury to a United States national or with the result that serious bodily injury is caused to a United States national.[84] In *US v. Yunis (No. 2)*,[85] for example, a Lebanese citizen was convicted in an American court of the hijacking of a Jordanian airliner in which US citizens had been travelling, the court relying on the passive personality principle as one of two possible bases of jurisdiction.[86]

This passive personality principle has not hitherto been adopted under English law, and cannot currently be relied upon by another state when seeking the extradition of a fugitive offender from the United Kingdom;[87]

---

[79] Notably in the *Cutting* case of 1887, in which the US objected to the exercise of such jurisdiction by Mexico. That case was never fully resolved, but proceedings against C were abandoned. See Judge Moore's dissenting judgment in the *Lotus* case, op. cit., fn 57.

[80] The dissenting judges in the court each expressly rejected the passive personality principle as a legitimate basis of jurisdiction under international law.

[81] See the *Third Restatement of US Foreign Relations Law*, vol. I, 240.

[82] The German Criminal Code, § 7.1, provides: 'German criminal law is applicable to crimes committed abroad against a German if such conduct is punishable by the law of the place where it occurred, or if no criminal law enforcement existed at the place where the crime was committed.'

[83] Inserted by the Omnibus Diplomatic Security and Anti-terrorism Act 1986.

[84] Prosecution for an offence under s. 2332 requires the written certification of the US Attorney-General, or his highest ranking subordinate with responsibility for criminal prosecutions, that, in his judgment, the offence was intended to coerce, intimidate, or retaliate against a government or a civilian population (see s. 2332(d)).   [85] (1988) 681 F Supp 896.

[86] A more controversial aspect of this case was the fact that Yunis had been seized by American forces on the high seas.

[87] This explains the rejection of the German Government's first extradition request in *Rees v. Secretary of State for the Home Department* [1986] AC 937, in which Rees had allegedly been involved in the kidnapping of a German citizen in Bolivia. A later warrant which relied on universal jurisdiction over offences involving hostage-taking was accepted, because the UK asserts a comparable jurisdiction.

but this may change if and when clause 53 of the Crime (International Cooperation) Bill becomes law. The Bill was introduced before Parliament in November 2002, and clause 53 would (*inter alia*) insert a new section 63C into the Terrorism Act 2000, by which a wide range of terrorist acts committed against United Kingdom nationals or residents outside the United Kingdom would become punishable as offences under English (or other United Kingdom) law.

Jurisdiction in Respect of Ships and Aircraft

International law has long recognized the right of a state to apply, and if necessary enforce, its criminal jurisdiction aboard ships that fly its flag, as if any acts committed aboard such ships had been committed within its own territory. As in the case of offences committed on land, jurisdiction to try offences may ordinarily be exercised on subjective or objective principles. Thus, should a ship registered in State A be fired on by persons aboard a ship registered in State B when on the high seas, jurisdiction over any offence caused aboard the former ship may be claimed by either of the states concerned. The general rule, however, is that the flag state would alone be entitled to board or detain a ship in order to make arrests, conduct a search, or seize evidence.[88] This is again consistent with the 'territorial' analogy.

Certain special rules must be noted. The first concerns 'incidents of navigation', such as collisions. The rule here is that jurisdiction to try an offence such as manslaughter may be asserted only by the accused's flag state, or by the state of which he is a national. If a ship registered in State A collides with a ship registered in State B, killing those aboard her, State B cannot therefore claim jurisdiction on an 'objective' application of the flag state rule.[89]

The second rule concerns offences committed aboard ships in the territorial or internal waters or ports of another state. Here the flag state and the littoral or port state may have concurrent jurisdiction, although the general practice of port states is not to interfere in respect of matters occurring aboard a foreign ship unless something happens to disturb the good order of the port itself. Where a ship is exercising a right of innocent passage through the territorial waters of another state, the general rule laid down by UNCLOS, Article 27, is that the littoral state should not board or exercise any jurisdiction over that ship unless asked to do so by the ship's master or the consul of the flag state, or unless the crime involved is one that disturbs the peace of the country or the good order of the territorial sea, or unless the action is necessary in order to suppress illicit traffic in narcotic

---

[88] See the *Lotus* case, op. cit., fn 57 above.
[89] See UNCLOS, Art. 97. This rejects the view of the PCIJ in the *Lotus* Case on that particular issue.

drugs, etc.[90] This rule concerns enforcement jurisdiction, rather than the ambit of the law or the subsequent prosecution of offences, but in practice it means that states will rarely apply their criminal law to foreign ships traversing their waters, even if they know of offences committed aboard them.[91]

The third rule concerns warships. These have complete immunity from any foreign enforcement jurisdiction and offences committed aboard them by members of the crew will in practice be the sole concern of the flag state. It is nevertheless possible that an officer from State A might be liable to punishment in that state for an offence committed while serving as a liaison officer, etc., aboard a foreign warship.

Lastly, from ancient times states have regarded piracy on the high seas (or piracy *jure gentium*) as an offence of 'universal jurisdiction' punishable by all states, and multilateral treaties now enable certain other maritime offences (such as the hijacking of ships) to be tried and punished on a similar basis. Indeed, some of these treaties (notably the 1988 Rome Convention for the Suppression of Unlawful Acts against the Safety of Maritime Navigation) are potentially of even wider application than the international laws dealing with piracy. This is because piracy *jure gentium*, as defined in UNCLOS, Article 101, can be committed only on the high seas, outside the territorial waters of any state, whereas the newer offences may equally be committed within territorial waters.

Piracy (or maritime robbery) is endemic in many parts of the world, but the offence piracy *jure gentium* is relatively rare, because the vast majority of piratical attacks (typically committed by armed gangs using small motor boats) occur within territorial waters, especially on ships that are stopped or riding at anchor, whilst awaiting a suitable tide to enter port. Such attacks are categorized as piracy by the International Maritime Organization and may be similarly categorized for marine insurance purposes,[92] but do not involve the crime of piracy under international law.

The influence of international law on English criminal law is very obvious in this context, because the definition of piracy in English law is based directly and expressly on the UNCLOS definition. This means that piratical attacks on shipping in territorial or internal waters can no longer be prosecuted as piracy under English law, even if the waters concerned are those adjacent to England and Wales itself, or if an attack is made by or against a British ship.[93]

---

[90] See *Pianka v. The Queen* [1979] AC 107.

[91] The Territorial Waters Jurisdiction Act 1878, s. 3, imposes restrictions on the prosecution of foreign nationals for offences allegedly committed in territorial waters, by requiring the consent of the Secretary of State to any such prosecution.

[92] *Athens Maritime Enterprises Corp. v. Hellenic Mutual War Risks Association (Bermuda) Ltd (The Andreas Lemos)* [1983] 1 All ER 590.

[93] Any such cases may instead be charged as robbery or assault with intent to rob. See below, p. 305.

Civil aircraft are also subject to the criminal jurisdiction of their state of registration when in flight,[94] although a concurrent jurisdiction over any offence may be asserted by any state over which the aircraft was flying at the relevant time. Acts that endanger the safety of civil aviation (including acts of hijacking or sabotage) are now punishable on a universal basis, by any state into whose hands the offenders may fall. Here again, the applicable provisions of English criminal law are closely derived from the relevant international conventions to which the United Kingdom is a party, and can only be fully understood by reference to the obligations that the United Kingdom has accepted under those Conventions.[95]

Universal Jurisdiction

Reference has already been made to piracy and to the hijacking, seizure, or sabotage of ships or aircraft. These are examples of offences that are subject to 'universal jurisdiction' under English criminal law, in accordance with international conventions that largely mirror customary international law. English law asserts such jurisdiction because this is permitted (and in some cases required) under international law. According to the US *Third Restatement of Foreign Relations Law*:

A state has jurisdiction to define and prescribe punishment for certain offences recognized by the community of nations as of universal concern, such as piracy, slave trade, attacks on or hijacking of aircraft, genocide, war crimes and perhaps certain acts of terrorism. ...

There are many such offences, including also torture, offences of violence committed against internationally protected persons, and crimes against humanity, some of which may be justiciable even when committed by persons who would otherwise be entitled to claim immunity from prosecution.[96]

Recent years have witnessed a major resurgence of interest in the concept of 'international criminal law'. This resurgence was triggered (*inter alia*) by the appalling events that occurred in Rwanda and in the former Republic of Yugoslavia. This resurgence of interest has manifested itself not only in criminal prosecutions brought by and within individual states,[97] but in the

---

[94] See the 1963 Tokyo Convention on Offences and Certain Other Acts Committed on Board Aircraft (UKTS 126 (1969), Cmnd. 4230), which was implemented into UK law by the Tokyo Convention Act 1964 and is now reflected in the Civil Aviation Act 1982.

[95] Notably the 1970 Hague and 1971 Montreal Conventions, which are considered in Chapter 6 below, along with the consolidated UK legislation (namely the Aviation Security Act 1982) that gives effect to those Conventions.

[96] See *R v. Bow Street Metropolitan Stipendiary Magistrate, ex p Pinochet Ugarte (No. 3)* [2000] 1 AC 147.

[97] In 1994, Refic Saric was convicted in Denmark of offences of torture; in 1997, Novislav Djajic was convicted in Germany of war crimes; and Nikola Jorgic was convicted later that year (also in Germany) of genocide and murder. All these offences were committed in the

establishment by the UN Security Council of *ad hoc* international criminal tribunals for Rwanda and the former Yugoslavia (the ICTR and ICTY) and, under the 1999 Rome Treaty, by the establishment of a permanent International Criminal Court at The Hague, which is empowered to try accusations of genocide, war crimes, and crimes against humanity in cases where trial in municipal courts is impossible or impractical.[98] The former Serbian leader, Slobodan Milošević, is currently on trial before the ICTY, charged with instigating crimes against humanity in Croatia and Kosovo, and genocide in Bosnia. This has been hailed as the most significant war crimes trial since the trial of the Nazi leaders at Nuremberg and of the Japanese war leaders in Tokyo following the end of the Second World War, but is otherwise just one of a substantial number of cases that have already been prosecuted before the ICTY and ICTR.[99]

The relationship between international law and English criminal law is one that will be noted and examined at numerous points throughout this Work. But if Lord Diplock in *Treacy* was wrong in suggesting that international law has replaced ancient venue doctrine as the principal limitation on the ambit of English law (and he was), some other explanation must be found.

OTHER CONSIDERATIONS

Given that international law would happily allow the United Kingdom significantly to expand the ambit of English criminal law, some other explanation must be found for the failure of English law to break free from ancient and obsolete historical constraints. One plausible explanation is that, until relatively recent times, there was little (if any) perceived need for widespread change. Until well into the twentieth century, things done abroad were most unlikely to come to the attention of the relevant authorities in England; and even if they did so, they would rarely have been considered the concern of any jurisdiction other than that of the state in which

---

former Yugoslavia. In 1999, a Swiss court convicted a Rwandan citizen of war crimes. See Fiona McKay, *Universal Jurisdiction in Europe* (1999). Recent prosecutions for war crimes dating back to the Second World War have often proved problematic. In 1988, John Demjanuk was sentenced to death in Israel on charges relating to murders committed by a guard known as 'Ivan the Terrible' in the Treblinka extermination camp in Poland. The sentence was not executed, however, and in 1993 the conviction was quashed, following the discovery of documents that tended to support Demjanuk's protests that he had been the victim of mistaken identity. Demjanuk was later allowed to return to the USA, although other charges against him were left unproven. There has been just one successful war crimes prosecution under English law. See below, p. 241.

[98] Not all states claim universal jurisdiction over such crimes, and some (such as the UK) do so only in specified circumstances. See below, p. 244.

[99] See Kriangsak Kittichaisaree, *International Criminal Law* (2001), 22.

they occurred. Crime, in other words, was generally considered to be entirely a local or territorial concern; and in those rare cases where it was not, the creation of an occasional statutory exception to the general rule sufficed.

Practical considerations must not be overlooked. Until relatively recently, evidential difficulties (affecting both the gathering and the presentation of evidence) would usually have been so formidable as to preclude prosecutions for extraterritorial offences. Even today, in an age of rapid and relatively affordable international air travel, it may prove very costly to arrange for police officers to conduct enquiries abroad,[100] but in the days before the advent of such travel, any officers sent to pursue such enquires might not expect to return for several weeks. As for witnesses, it is only in recent years that the rules of criminal evidence have been relaxed or modernized sufficiently to permit the use of written statements from those who are abroad, or of video links that enable live testimony to be received from abroad, and even today the use of such evidence is beset with restrictions. Witnesses may alternatively be flown to England and back in order to testify, but once again this option has only recently become a realistic one, and even today it is viable only in the most important and serious cases, where the costs involved are considered appropriate.

This is a subject to which I will return in the final chapter of this work, because when examining options for reform, the practical difficulties and expenses involved in prosecuting extraterritorial crime cannot be ignored.

The Rise of International Crime

Pressure for change has come in recent years from the rise of international or multinational crime. Such crime is not, of course, entirely a modern phenomenon. The illegal trafficking of opium and its derivatives, for example, has a long and shameful history. In China and the Far East, this trade was once supported and protected by Britain and other western countries, the Chinese Government being too weak to prevent it. Political and military considerations (and especially the need to secure alliances) have subsequently drawn many states, governments, and government agencies into varying degrees of complicity in the drugs trade,[101] but western countries also became the targets of much of this trade, and during the late nineteenth century, Britain, the United States, and many other countries began to suffer from substantial problems associated with opium addiction.[102] The scale of

---

[100] See below, p. 337.

[101] The American CIA, for example, became involved in drugs trading in Cambodia, Laos, and Vietnam during the 1960s; and certain Asian, Central American, and South American states are now notoriously dependent on their 'narcotics economies'.

[102] See John M. Martin and Anne T. Romano, *Multinational Crime* (1992), 52–5.

that problem, however, is utterly dwarfed by that of the illegal drugs trade today.

The enormous growth of international crime during the second half of the twentieth century may be attributed to several factors, many of which are closely related. First and foremost amongst these has been the development of increasingly rapid and affordable means of international transport and communication, including air travel, containerized shipping, and electronic communication systems. Criminals can thus travel rapidly, transport contraband efficiently, and communicate with each other (or with their victims) almost instantaneously across the world. The volume of legitimate traffic (in travellers, goods, and messages) is such that law enforcement agencies cannot hope to monitor it all, and the illegitimate traffic can be concealed within it. Closely related to this development is the internationalization or globalization of the business, banking, and financial industries. This provides prime targets for criminals to defraud, and also provides them with facilities that they may use in order to perpetrate, finance, and conceal their activities.

Two related social phenomena have also contributed to the trend away from purely domestic crime. One is the growth of organized criminal associations. The other is immigration. Some migrants, inevitably, are members of organized criminal groups. Thus it was that the Mafia or Cosa Nostra first came to America from Southern Italy and Sicily in the 1930s, and in similar fashion Triad gangsters have more recently spread from Hong Kong to England and America. In England, Caribbean immigration has brought with it the notoriously violent Jamaican gangsters known as 'Yardies', and so on. Such organizations may sometimes fight each other in 'turf wars', but they also do business with each other and with other criminal organizations, both in this country and elsewhere.[103]

Last but by no means least, political, military, and religious tensions within the modern world have spawned a new era of international terrorism. To give just a few examples, Palestinian and Irish Republican terrorism developed a significant international dimension during the latter part of the twentieth century, and small but violent international anarchist groups were active throughout much of Europe during parts of the 1970s and 1980s, but the scale of the threat posed by these groups has of course been far surpassed by that of militant Islamic terrorism, which reached previously unimaginable levels of violence, fanaticism, and sophistication in the suicide hijacking attacks on America of 11 September 2001. The Al-Qaeda organization, which is believed to have been responsible for those attacks, is truly multinational, with tentacles reaching into and out of Britain and many other countries in the West, to say nothing of its influence within Muslim states throughout the world. It is obvious that purely territorial

---

[103] See ibid., 64–5.

concepts of law and jurisdiction are inadequate in the face of such international operations. In response, United Kingdom anti-terrorist legislation has acquired an increasingly universal ambit during recent years, and further expansion is proposed in the Crime (International Cooperation) Bill, currently before Parliament.

Other Pressures for Change

The threat posed by organized international crime is not the only reason why the dominance of the territorial approach to jurisdiction has come under attack in recent years. Increased media coverage of events abroad has led to heightened awareness of cases involving misconduct by British citizens overseas. English soccer fans run riot in a foreign city as television cameras record the carnage; British tourists are exposed by undercover reporters as sexual abusers of children in Thailand; drunken British passengers are publicly accused of causing a serious disturbance on an American airliner flying outside British airspace; and so on. Incidents such as these have led, at various times, to intense criticism of English jurisdiction laws, and in some cases to the fear that such activities must inevitably tarnish the image of the United Kingdom abroad. Media exposure of the sex tourism scandal was a major influence leading to the enactment of reforming legislation,[104] which was designed to ensure that British sex offenders can now be prosecuted here for crimes committed against children abroad; but the other examples remain outside English jurisdiction, and extradition does not always provide a viable solution. Indeed, where football hooligans are concerned, foreign states often react by deporting the alleged offenders at the first opportunity, instead of prosecuting them. The last thing that such states are likely to do is to request the extradition of persons they have already deported.

An Overall Assessment

The above considerations together offer a plausible explanation for the way in which the rules governing the ambit of English criminal law have developed so far. To recapitulate: the very limited territorial ambit of the common law was originally shaped by procedural rules of venue that made any extraterritorial application almost impossible, and the principle of territoriality that developed was then maintained by a mixture of practical considerations and by a general feeling that things done abroad were not in any case the proper (and certainly not the urgent) concern of English criminal

---

[104] Notably in the Sex Offenders Act 1997, s. 7, as to which see below, p. 270.

law. In the last 40 years, however, revolutions have occurred in international travel, trade, finance, and telecommunications. These, together with the changing patterns of criminal conduct associated with them, have spawned numerous exceptions to the basic principle of territoriality, many of which have been required in order to comply with the United Kingdom's treaty obligations under international law. The basic principles themselves remain largely unchanged, but now look increasingly archaic and parochial.

3

The Limits of Territorial Jurisdiction

INTRODUCTION

It is increasingly common for legislation to be enacted in which new extraterritorial offences are created, or in which existing offences are given an extraterritorial ambit that they did not hitherto possess. This movement away from what was once an almost exclusively territorial approach to criminal jurisdiction may be welcomed, because exclusive reliance on territorial principles can sometimes be unduly restrictive, but its importance must not be overestimated. In England and Wales, as in all other countries (even those that claim extensive extraterritorial powers over their own citizens), the overwhelming majority of prosecutions brought before the criminal courts will inevitably continue to be based on territorial principles or, in other words, on the commission of offences wholly or partly within the normal territorial limits. A proper understanding of this territorial jurisdiction requires a working knowledge of the territorial boundaries by which it is constrained.

Issues of criminal jurisdiction are not, of course, the only reasons, or even the main reasons, why the precise location of the territorial boundaries is important. With one important exception (namely, the Scottish border) the boundaries that delimit the territorial ambit of English criminal law equally delimit the sovereign territory of the United Kingdom under international law. The right to assert and enforce criminal jurisdiction is just one incident of a state's sovereignty over territory. From economic, political, and military viewpoints, other incidents of sovereignty are more significant. Sovereignty over territory gives a state certain rights to regulate entry to it and to control access to the airspace above it; and like all littoral states, the United Kingdom seeks to conserve, control, or exploit any natural resources that are to be found in the seas or on or under the seabed adjacent to its coasts. These resources include oil, gas, and fisheries, and are matters of enormous economic and political significance.[1] The criminal law has an important part to play in securing and enforcing the national borders and

---

[1] See generally R.B. Clark, *The Waters Around the British Isles* (1987); Geoffrey Marston, *The Marginal Seabed* (1981). The power to regulate fisheries is, however, constrained by EU law.

in protecting such natural resources, but any jurisdictional issues that arise in this context are of secondary importance when set against other incidents of sovereignty.

The border between England and Scotland has no real significance under international law, but it is of fundamental importance under the constitution of the United Kingdom, because English law does not ordinarily apply in Scotland, and Scots law does not ordinarily apply in England and Wales.

There are also secondary or 'internal' jurisdictional borders within the main territorial limits. These include the boundaries between the commission areas within which magistrates' courts exercise summary jurisdiction, and also the coastal boundary between the realm itself and the territorial waters adjacent to it.

The United Kingdom has from time to time found itself involved in international disputes, and even wars, over territory, but in recent years these have not involved any disputes over the boundaries of the United Kingdom itself.[2] One might therefore suppose that all relevant boundaries would be the subject of precise and settled legal definition, and that they would be identified on published maps or charts. The reality, however, is rather different.

THE BASIC SCHEME

At a basic level, the territory over which the general body of English criminal law applies can be defined without any great difficulty. It embraces the mainland of England and Wales and all those islands that are constitutionally part of England or Wales.[3] It does not, however, include Scotland, Northern Ireland, the Channel Islands, or the Isle of Man.[4] Within England

---

[2] In 1953, the International Court of Justice held that the islands and rocks of the Minquiers and Ecrehos, which lie in the English Channel, near Guernsey, belonged to the UK rather than to France (*Minquiers and Ecrehos Case; France* v. *UK* [1953] ICJ Rep 17); but while the islands are British possessions, they are not a part of the UK itself. Fishery and continental shelf disputes have been more common: in recent years, the UK has been involved in disputes with Denmark and the Republic of Ireland in respect of competing claims over fishery zones and continental shelf in the North Atlantic.

[3] These include Anglesey, the Isle of Wight, the Scilly Isles, and Lundy Island. See *Harman* v. *Bolt* (1931) 47 TLR 219. By Sch. 1 to the Interpretation Act 1978, 'England' means, subject to any alteration of boundaries under Pt IV of the Local Government Act 1972, the area consisting of the counties established by s. 1 of that Act, Greater London, and the Isles of Scilly; and 'Wales' means the combined area of the counties which were created by s. 20 of the Act, subject to any alteration made under s. 73 (consequential alteration of boundary following alteration of watercourse). The Isles of Scilly are defined by reference to a map, copies of which are deposited at the offices of the Secretary of State, the Duchy of Cornwall, and the Council of the Isles of Scilly: Isles of Scilly Order 1978, SI 1978 No. 1844, Art. 2(1), as amended.

[4] Neither the Channel Islands nor the Isle of Man are strictly part of the UK. Rockall, which was annexed in 1955 and is the most recent addition to the land territory of the UK, forms part of the territory of Scotland: see the Island of Rockall Act 1972, s. 1.

and Wales, the criminal law applies to things done on, above, or below the land and also to things done on or within those tidal rivers, creeks, inlets, and harbours that lie within the realm. The realm ordinarily ends on the foreshore or sea beach, where the land meets the open sea; but legislation has created an adjacent belt of territorial and (within certain bays, etc.) internal waters, which are not strictly part of the realm but over which United Kingdom sovereignty and a substantial part of English criminal law now extends.

While this basic scheme is unremarkable, closer inspection reveals a multitude of complications and uncertainties. To the north, the location of the border with Scotland may be identified from large-scale maps produced by the Ordnance Survey,[5] but the position in respect of 'border crimes' may still prove complex. In particular, fishery offences committed on the border rivers (the Esk, Sark, and Tweed) are subject to special jurisdictional rules, under which Scottish fisheries legislation applies to English stretches of the Tweed and its tributaries, whilst English fisheries legislation applies to Scottish stretches of the Esk and Sark and their tributaries. Some specific fishery offences committed on or in respect of the lower Esk may be prosecuted in either country.[6]

The most troublesome complications arise in connection with maritime boundaries. English criminal law draws few distinctions between internal waters and territorial waters, *per se*, even though these two zones are regarded as quite distinct under international law; but it appears to distinguish, as far as summary offences are concerned, between waters that lie within (or between) the counties of the realm[7] and those that are classed as internal or territorial by virtue only of legislation establishing the United Kingdom's territorial limits. As a result, the ambit of summary offences is ordinarily[8] more limited than that of offences triable on indictment. Unfortunately, the precise lines of demarcation between those zones which are subject to local summary jurisdiction and those which are not remains unclear. Doubts even exist as to the legal status of the foreshore of the open sea when it is submerged by the tide. Does it then lie within or beyond the realm? Does it fall within the commission areas of local magistrates' courts? Are the seaward borders of the realm fixed, or do they ebb and flow with the tides?

To add to our difficulties, the location of the baseline from which the United Kingdom's territorial sea and fishery zone are measured is itself

---

[5] One of the principal functions of large-scale OS mapping is to identify administrative boundaries within the United Kingdom.   [6] See below, p. 63.

[7] Or, more specifically, within or between the commission areas for magistrates' courts, which outside Greater London are based on county boundaries.

[8] This is the rule that applies in the absence of some provision to the contrary. In some cases, however, provisions creating summary offences are expressly made applicable within territorial waters: see *R v. Kent Justices, ex p Lye* [1967] 2 QB 153.

a matter of some complexity. Whilst its location may sometimes be deduced from a study of the physical features shown on published charts, it is not itself marked on such charts, and such charts may in any case become inaccurate over a period of time. The low-water mark, along which this baseline ordinarily runs,[9] is a shifting contour that may change substantially from time to time, whether as a result of gradual processes or as a result of violent storms that may alter stretches of coastline overnight. Even quite recent charts may be out of date in some such respect, and in some localities the most recent charts may be several years old. The development of a new offshore sandbank (even one that appears only at low tide) may lead to a substantial enlargement of the territorial limits in that area. Nor, at present, do any officially published charts or enactments identify the numerous points at which the territorial baseline departs from the low-water mark in order to 'close off' the mouths of bays, harbours, and estuaries as internal waters. Lastly, consideration must be given to the maritime border between 'Scottish adjacent waters' and those adjacent to the rest of the United Kingdom, because English law cannot ordinarily apply in Scottish waters.[10]

While the maritime boundaries are the most problematic, issues may also arise as to the airspace above the realm or its adjoining waters, or as to the status of foreign embassies, High Commissions, and other diplomatic or consular premises within the realm. In each of these respects, the basic rule requires more detailed consideration.

THE BORDER WITH SCOTLAND

No legislation specifically defines the course of the Anglo-Scottish land border, nor does any such legislation give express statutory authority to those maps that purport to do so. This is a surprising omission, but is probably of no great practical importance. The Ordnance Survey was charged, under Schedule 1, Part III, to the Local Government Act 1972, with the task of 'mereing' the boundaries of the new local government areas in England and Wales, as established by that Act. The northern borders of the counties of Northumberland and Cumbria are local government boundaries within the meaning of that Act, but they are also the borders of the realm, and are marked as such on the relevant Ordnance maps. These maps may thus be regarded (albeit indirectly) as authoritative, should any issue arise as to the exact location of the Scottish border.[11]

---

[9] This is not the same low-water mark as that shown on Ordnance maps. See below, p. 72.

[10] As to the possible application of English criminal law within the territorial waters adjacent to Northern Ireland, see below, p. 83.

[11] On Ordnance maps, the western border is marked only up until the point at which the River Eden flows into the Solway Firth, and the eastern border is marked only as far as the

The Scottish border follows natural landmarks for much, but not all, of its length. These landmarks including the Scots Dike and substantial stretches of various rivers: notably the Eden (where it flows into the Solway Firth), the Esk, the Sark, and the Tweed, all of which are important salmon fishery rivers. For legal purposes, the Sark, which is a tributary of the Esk, is deemed to be a part of that river.

The riparian stretches of the border generally follow the *medium filum aquae* (the middle of the main channel) but do not always do so, because the line of the border along the Tweed is influenced by weirs, islands, or other special features. The *medium filum aquae* may not, in any event, mark the mid-point between the northern and southern banks of the river. West of Gretna, for example, the main channel of the Esk lies close to the northern shore, while several acres of shallow-water and tidal mudflats separate it from the English shore to the south. A final point to note is that the Tweed ceases to mark the border as it nears Berwick-on-Tweed. This ancient border town now lies wholly within England,[12] and the famous 'Royal Border Bridge', despite its name, does not carry the east coast main railway line into Scotland. The true border now lies some three miles to the north, and reaches the coast between Lamberton Beach and Marshall Meadows Bay.

For most purposes, the law governing criminal jurisdiction in border areas is simple. Scots law governs offences committed to the north of the border and English law governs those committed to the south of it.[13] Evidence as to the exact location of a crime may sometimes be problematic, but the law itself is clear. Fishery offences committed on the border rivers appear to constitute the only real complication.

The Salmon and Freshwater Fisheries Act 1975, which for most purposes applies only to England and Wales, applies also to the Esk and its tributaries (notably the Sark), including such parts of those rivers as lie within Scotland. It does not, however, apply to the Tweed, even though the lower reaches of that river lie wholly within England. Offences under this Act, if committed in Scotland, must nevertheless be proceeded against and punished in Scotland.[14] Another curious rule may be found in section 39(2) of the Act, which provides:

Where the minimum size of mesh of nets used for taking salmon prescribed by any provision of this Act or by any byelaw in force in any part of the Solway Firth within England is greater than that which may be lawfully used in the part of the

low-water mark on the coast. Beyond these points, the maritime boundaries between English and Scottish 'adjacent waters' are defined by other means. See below, p. 84.

[12] See the Wales and Berwick Act 1746 (20 Geo. 3, c. 42), which remained in force until supplanted by the Interpretation Act 1978.

[13] Such are the twists and turns of the border that in some places a person moving due north may briefly cross from Scotland into England, but that is of course exceptional.

[14] See s. 37 of the Act and Sch. 4, Pt II, para. 3.

Solway Firth within Scotland, the provision or byelaw shall have effect as if the minimum size of mesh so prescribed in relation to the part of the Solway Firth within England were such as may be so lawfully used as aforesaid in the part of the Solway Firth within Scotland.

This means, in effect, that Scots law prevails on the issue of net mesh size, even in respect of things done in England.

On the Tweed, the Salmon and Freshwater Fisheries (Scotland) Act 1951 applies, even to offences committed wholly within England. As with offences under the 1975 Act, jurisdiction over any offences nevertheless lies with the courts of the country in which they are committed. An English court may accordingly find itself applying a Scottish penal statute. As Diplock LJ explained in *Gibson* v. *Ryan*[15]:

It may seem a little odd that an English magistrates' court should be dealing with offences under a Scots Act, but in section 22(2) of the Act which deals with the river Tweed in which the alleged offence was committed, it is provided that: 'This Act . . . shall apply to so much of the river Tweed as is situated outwith Scotland as if it were situated in Scotland . . .' and there follows a proviso that offences committed in England against this Act shall be proceeded against and punished in England. That is how the magistrates got their jurisdiction.

In construing this legislation, an English court may need to consult Scottish precedents,[16] but this does not mean that the English court applies anything other than English criminal law. The Scottish statute is, for such purposes, an integral part of English law, albeit only in so far as it applies to the Tweed and its tributaries.

Lastly, the Scotland Act 1998 (Border Rivers) Order 1999, Articles 6 and 7, create offences of unauthorized fishing for salmon or sea trout in the Lower Esk (as defined in Article 1(2)) and of possession of unauthorized instruments for such a purpose.[17] The Order makes no distinction between England and Scotland, save in so far as Article 6(4) provides that a fishing licence issued by the (English) Environment Agency may authorize fishing only to the south of a line representing the *medium filum*, at low-water, of the main channel of the Esk. This is in fact the Scottish border, as shown on Ordnance Survey maps. By Article 7(4) of the Order:

Proceedings for an offence under this Article may be taken, and the offence may for all incidental purposes be treated as having been committed, in any place in the

---

[15] [1968] 1 QB 250.

[16] See, e.g., *Ryan* v. *Ross* [1963] 2 QB 151, another case involving poaching on the Tweed, in which Lord Parker CJ's interpretation of the Scottish Act was supported by citation from a recent decision of the Lord Justice-General (Lord Clyde) in *Aitchison* v. *Bartlett* 1963 SLT 17.

[17] By Art. 1(2), the 'Upper Esk' means that part of the River Esk lying upstream of a line drawn from a point at Ordnance Survey Grid Reference NY 3245 6632 on the western bank of the River Sark in a southerly direction to a point at Ordnance Survey Grid Reference NY 3245 6503 on the coast of Cumbria, and 'Lower Esk' means any part of that River downstream of that line. The seaward limits of the estuary of the Esk are defined in the Schedule to the Order.

Sheriffdom of Dumfries and Galloway or within the Commission of the Peace for Cumbria.

This is a unique provision, because it enables an Article 6 offence committed on the Lower Esk to be prosecuted either by English or by Scottish courts, without regard to the side of the border on which that offence was committed.[18] As a result, any possible evidential difficulties concerning that issue (which may be a problem when determining the jurisdiction of Scottish or English courts under the 1951 or 1975 Acts[19]) are simply avoided.

Fishery offences are by no means the only ones that can be committed in border areas. Difficulties may arise in other contexts where the precise location of a 'border crime' is unclear. Assume, for example, that the body of a murdered child is found floating in the border reaches of the Tweed or Esk. The evidence clearly points to D as the killer, but there is nothing to indicate where the crime was committed, and D is not minded to confess.[20] Jurisdictionally, such a crime may prove insoluble under either English or Scots law, because murder in England is not an offence under Scots law; nor is murder in Scotland an offence under English law.[21]

LITTORAL BOUNDARIES

The Historical Background

The rules that govern the ambit of English criminal law in coastal areas still bear the imprint of largely forgotten historical considerations. Some of these were peculiar to English law, and gave rise to distinctions that have no counterparts in civilian jurisdictions. Foremost amongst these was the distinction between common law jurisdiction and the criminal jurisdiction of the Admiral.

As explained in Chapter 2 of this work, the ancient common law rules of venue originally imposed severe limitations on the ability of common law

---

[18] It may even permit the prosecution in England of an Art. 6(2) offence of unauthorized possession committed deep within Scotland; but this is no more than a theoretical possibility.

[19] Where, e.g., the river forms the Scottish border and the alleged offence appears to have been committed somewhere close to mid-stream.

[20] The example is by no means fanciful, because broadly similar problems arose (but were overlooked) in the case of the serial child murderer, Robert Black. See below, p. 229. Other potentially problematic cases are not difficult to imagine. D, a pickpocket, steals P's wallet aboard an Anglo-Scottish train, somewhere between Newcastle and Edinburgh. P cannot be certain when the theft occurred. D admits the theft, but cannot, or will not, say when exactly he committed it. The difficulties here are basically the same as that in the murder example given above.

[21] In contrast, legislation ensures that an offence committed in the Channel Tunnel system will be triable in either England or France if its exact location is uncertain, as where it appears to have been committed on a train moving from one jurisdiction to the other. Similar rules should perhaps be enacted to deal with offences committed on or close to the Anglo-Scottish border, or on trains, etc., that cross the border.

courts to try offences committed outside the boundaries of their own counties. Offences committed upon the sea could, however, be dealt with by the Lord High Admiral or his deputies. The Admiral was a royal officer whose court applied civil rules of evidence and procedure, freeing it from the venue constraints that plagued the common law courts. The Admiral appears to have claimed an exclusive jurisdiction over offences committed on the high seas,[22] but there were bitter conflicts with the common law judges as a result of what was perceived by them to be a usurpation of their authority in respect of civil and criminal matters arising out of incidents occurring within the realm itself.[23] In 1391, the statute of 15 Ric. 2, c. 3, resolved this dispute by providing that the Admiral might exercise jurisdiction over such matters only in cases involving homicide or mayhem committed aboard 'great ships' within creeks, rivers, and havens, etc., and then only in respect of offences committed below the lowest bridges on such rivers.

Despite the considerable advantages provided by the Admiral's freedom from common law venue constraints, the rules of procedure and evidence in the Admiral's court apparently created problems of their own.[24] The preamble to the Offences at Sea Act 1536 alleged that the Admiral was frequently unable to deal effectively with serious maritime crimes, such as piracy, which were then a major threat to seaborne commerce:

Traitours pirotes theves robbers murtherers and confederatours uppon the see many tymes escape unpunished because the triall of their offences hath heretofore ben . . . after the course of the civile lawes the nature whereof is that they must playnley confesse . . . or els their offences be so . . . directly proved by witnes indifferente such as sawe their offence comyted which cannot be gotten but by chaunce at few tymes . . . by cause such offendours . . . murder and kill such psons being in the shipp . . . which shulde wytness ayenst them. . . .

The Act accordingly transferred the Admiral's criminal jurisdiction over such crimes to special commissions that proceeded (venue rules excepted) 'after the manner of the common law'.[25] The Offences at Sea Act 1799 then subjected all Admiralty criminal jurisdiction to common law procedures and penalties. Under section 1 of this Act (which remains in force):

All and every offence and offences which . . . shall be committed upon the high seas, out of the body of any county of this realm, shall be and they are hereby declared to be offences . . . liable to the same punishments respectively, as if they had been committed upon the shore. . . .

---

[22] See Stephen, *History of the Criminal Law* (1883), vol. 2, 25.

[23] These disputes were probably as much about the revenue produced by court fees and fines, etc, as about the exercise of authority *per se*.

[24] Because the common law judges were jealous of any perceived usurpation of their own powers, this may perhaps have led to unjustified criticism of Admiralty procedures, or to exaggeration of the problems involved.

[25] East, *Pleas of the Crown* (1803), vol. II, explains that these commissions consisted of two common law judges and one presiding Admiralty judge; but that it was by the common law judges that the prisoner was tried.

The Admiralty Offences Act 1844 completed the triumph of the common law in criminal cases by providing for trials of Admiralty offences to be held in the ordinary criminal courts, where indeed they are still tried today. The concept of a distinct Admiralty jurisdiction over crime nevertheless survives, and is still referred to in current legislation. Thus, section 2 of the Territorial Waters Jurisdiction Act 1878 provides that 'an offence committed . . . on the open sea within the territorial waters of Her Majesty's dominions is an offence within the jurisdiction of the Admiral', while section 46(2) of the Supreme Court Act 1981 provides that the Crown Court shall have exclusive jurisdiction in proceedings on indictment 'including in particular proceedings on indictment for offences within the jurisdiction of the Admiralty of England'.[26]

None of this would be of anything more than historical interest if Admiralty jurisdiction were wholly coextensive with that exercisable over offences committed ashore; but it is not, because Admiralty jurisdiction has never extended to offences other than those that are triable on indictment, while the legislation governing the summary jurisdiction of magistrates' courts does not ordinarily permit them to deal with summary offences committed outside the realm of England and Wales. At first sight, section 1 of the Offences at Sea Act 1799 might appear to permit this; but it is generally agreed[27] that this Act does not apply to summary offences. It was concerned only with the transfer of existing Admiralty jurisdiction, and the Admiral had no summary jurisdiction to be transferred. It is, in other words, a venue provision, rather than one that governs the territorial ambit of the substantive criminal law.

This is why, where summary offences are involved,[28] English criminal courts must continue to distinguish between waters that lie exclusively within Admiralty jurisdiction and those that lie within or between the boundaries of littoral counties, and thus within the limits of the commission areas that govern the ambit of local summary jurisdiction. This distinction is by no means coextensive with the internationally recognized distinction between internal waters and the territorial sea, because some internal waters clearly do not form part of any county or commission area within England and Wales.[29]

---

[26] This effectively restates the jurisdiction originally laid down in s. 6 of the Courts Act 1971. For other examples of surviving references to Admiralty jurisdiction over crime, see the Offences Against the Person Act 1861, s. 68, and the Malicious Damage Act 1861, s. 72.

[27] See, e.g., the Law Commission Report on the Territorial and Extraterritorial Extent of the Criminal Law (Law Com. No. 91, 1978), para. 70.

[28] Special rules govern offences committed aboard 'United Kingdom Ships' (i.e., ships and fishing vessels registered in the UK under the Merchant Shipping Act 1995, s. 2). Offences committed aboard such vessels when at sea are governed by s. 281 of the 1995 Act; but that section (which provides for jurisdiction over both summary and indictable offences) does not apply to small, unregistered British vessels, or to foreign-owned craft operating in British waters.

[29] See below, p. 76. See also Marston, *The Marginal Seabed* (1981), 258–9.

Counties and Commission Areas

Under section 2(1) of the Magistrates' Courts Act 1980, the general rule is that a magistrates' court has jurisdiction to try a summary offence only if this was committed within that court's own commission area. Outside the newly constituted Greater London Commission Area, these areas are defined by reference to magistrates' courts committee areas, which are in turn defined by reference to counties and local government areas within counties.[30]

There are some exceptions to the general rule, under which a magistrates' court may exercise jurisdiction over summary offences committed outside its commission area. By section 3(1) of the Act, for example, a court may try offences committed on or within 500 yards of the boundaries between two commission areas, or in any river, arm of the sea, etc., lying between two or more such areas. By section 3(3), any offence against any person or property committed in a vehicle or vessel on a journey or voyage between or across two or more commission areas may be dealt with as if it had been committed in any of those areas.[31] Legislation may also create summary offences (such as fishery offences) that expressly extend over the territorial sea or fishery zone, and courts must necessarily have jurisdiction to try such offences, even if no specific venue provision is included within the legislation in question.[32] Magistrates' courts nevertheless lack any general power to try summary offences committed outside their own commission areas.[33]

The Low-water Mark and the Foreshore

The low-water mark around the coast generally represents the lower boundary of the sea beach or foreshore.[34] It is marked on large-scale digital mapping produced by the Ordnance Survey, who refer to it as marking the

---

[30] Justices of the Peace Act 1997, s. 1; Justices of the Peace (Commission Areas) Order 1999 (SI 1999 No. 3010); Magistrates' Courts Committee Areas Order 1999 (SI 1999 No. 3008, as amended by SI 2001 No. 695). The counties of Devon and Cornwall and those of Avon and Somerset each constitute single unified commission areas. In Wales, several commission areas now incorporate more than one county. The Dyfed-Powys commission area, for example, now includes the counties of Ceredigion, Pembrokeshire, Carmarthenshire, and Powys.

[31] See also ss. 1(2)(b) and 2(2) of the Act. Under s. 3B (inserted by the Access to Justice Act 1999, but not yet in force), the trial of a summary offence may in some cases be transferred to a court which would not otherwise have jurisdiction to try it; but this assumes that the alleged offence originally fell within the jurisdiction of some other court from which it could be transferred. By-laws creating summary offences may be applied, for some purposes (such as for the regulation of boating or bathing), over waters lying up to 1,000 metres to seaward of the low-water mark. See the Local Government (Miscellaneous Provisions) Act 1976, s. 17. By s. 17(3), alleged offences 'may be inquired into and dealt with as if committed within the area of the authority'.

[32] *R* v. *Kent Justices, ex p Lye* [1967] 2 QB 153. In practice, a venue provision is always inserted. As to the issue of a summons or warrant in such a case, see the Magistrates' Courts Act 1980, s. 1(2)(e).

[33] Such a power does exist in respect of offences triable either way; see s. 2(4).

[34] For criminal law purposes, the high-water mark is of no great significance, although it may be in civil cases where questions arise as to the boundaries of coastal properties, etc.

'extent of the realm'.[35] As far as fixed structures are concerned, this may be a convenient rule to apply; but does it mark the limits of jurisdiction over summary offences? Of those few textbooks or publications which address the matter at all, most appear to assume that it does.[36] With respect, however, the authorities do not support that assumption.

The demarcation between Admiralty and common law jurisdictions originally depended not on lines marked on maps, but on the location of the water's edge at the relevant time, in accordance with the state of the tides. This seems to have been true both of civil and of criminal cases. As Sir Edward Coke explained in his report of *Sir Henry Constable's Case*[37]:

> When the sea flows and has *plenitudinem maris*, the Admiral shall have jurisdiction over everything done on the water between the high water mark and the low-water mark . . . and yet when the sea ebbs . . . everything done on the land when the sea is ebbed shall be tried at common law, for it is then parcel of the county and *infra corp' comitat.*

Constable's Case was a civil action concerning property rights in a wreck,[38] but similar assertions were made by William Hawkins in his *Treatise of the Pleas of the Crown*[39] and by Sir James Stephen in his *History of the Criminal Law of England*.[40] Some confusion was caused by *Embleton v. Brown*,[41] in which it was held that justices had jurisdiction to try the respondent for a summary fisheries offence committed over the submerged foreshore, but the court gave judgment in that case without considering all the relevant authorities and without hearing argument from the respondent, who was not represented. The judges tamely accepted the prosecution's contention that they were bound in this matter by *R v. Musson*, which Cockburn CJ described as, 'direct authority that such part of the sea is within the body of the adjoining county'.[42] *Musson*, however, does not decide any such thing. The *ratio* of *Musson* was that the part of a pier standing on the foreshore at Yarmouth could not be assumed to lie within a parish for rating purposes. Only one of the judges in *Musson* appears to

---

[35] The Ordnance Survey's 'Land-line' digital mapping system also shows boundaries between administrative areas and is widely relied upon by local authorities. Under the Ordnance Survey Act 1841, ss. 1 and 2, the identification of 'reputed' administrative boundaries is one of the principal functions of the survey, but s. 12 of the Act provides that actual boundaries are not to be defined, altered, or affected thereby.

[36] This view is stated in *Halsbury's Laws of England* (online version, Criminal Law, Evidence and Procedure, para. 623) and by the Law Commission (Law Com. No. 91, para. 29). See also Geoffrey Marston, 'Crimes on Board Foreign Merchant Ships at Sea: Some Aspects of English Practice' (1972) 88 *Law Quarterly Review* 357, 358; *Card, Cross and Jones, Criminal Law* (15th edn, 2001), para. 3.87.　　　　　　　　　　　　　　　[37] (1601) 5 Co Rep 106a.

[38] See also *R v. Forty-Nine Casks of Brandy* (1836) 3 Hagg Adm 257.

[39] 3rd edn, 1739, vol. 2, c. 9. Edward East, citing Coke, Hale, and Hawkins on this point, asserts that alternating common law and Admiralty jurisdiction between high and low water was a fact, 'past dispute': *Treatise of Pleas of the Crown* (1803), 803.　　　　　[40] Vol. 2, 26.

[41] (1860) 3 El & El 234.　　　[42] (1858) 8 El & Bl 900.

have expressed any view as to whether this part of the structure lay within the body of a county, a view which was both *obiter* and (given the fixed and permanent character of a pier) quite easily distinguishable from the facts of *Embleton v. Brown*.[43] Whatever may have been the authority of *Embleton v. Brown*, Cockburn CJ had evidently changed his mind by the time that he came to give his monumental judgment in the historic case of *R v. Keyn*,[44] in which he said:

> Whatever of the sea lies within the body of a county is within the jurisdiction of the common law. Whatever does not belonged formerly to that of the Admiralty and now belongs to the courts to which the jurisdiction of the Admiral has been transferred by statute. On the shore of the outer sea the body of the county extends so far as the land is uncovered by water. And so rigorous has been the line of demarcation between the two jurisdictions that as between high and low-water marks the jurisdiction has been divided . . . according to the state of the tide. Such was the law in the time of Lord Coke, and as regards offences such it is still.

Such was undoubtedly the position at common law. The question now is whether modern counties (and the corresponding commission areas) retain the same tidal boundaries for jurisdiction purposes. Given the Ordnance Survey's statutory duty to 'mere' administrative boundaries, and given the publication of Ordnance maps that show the low-water mark as the seaward 'extent of the realm', a plausible case might perhaps be made for concluding that such boundaries must now be considered fixed at the low-water mark, unless otherwise stated.[45] Section 72 of the Local Government Act 1972 has been cited in support of that view.[46] The material part of this section provides:

> (1) . . . every accretion from the sea, whether natural or artificial, and any part of the sea-shore to the low-water mark which does not immediately before the passing of this Act form part of a parish shall be annexed to and incorporated with—
>
> > (a) in England, the parish or parishes which the accretion or part of the sea-shore adjoins, and
> >
> > (b) in Wales, the community or communities which the accretion or part of the sea-shore adjoins,

---

[43] There may even be some doubt as to whether jurisdiction would exist to deal with a summary offence committed at the seaward end of such a pier. See G.S. Wilkinson, 'The Application of Enactments within English Territorial Waters' (1950) 13 *Modern Law Review* 40. Section 72(1) of the Local Government Act 1972 (which restates earlier legislation) may appear to deal with that problem, because it brings both natural and man-made 'accretions from the sea' within littoral county boundaries; but see *Blackpool Pier Co. v. Fylde Union* (1876) 41 JP 344, in which it was held that (in contrast to solid harbour walls, etc.) a pier was not an 'accretion from the sea'. See also *Barwick v. South Eastern Railway Co. Ltd* [1920] 2 KB 387; [1921] 1 KB 187 (CA).

[44] (1876) 2 Ex D 63, 168. See also the judgment of Sir Robert Phillimore, ibid., at 67.

[45] Areas of sea may in some cases be included within county boundaries. See, e.g., the Local Government Act 1972, s. 71.

[46] See, e.g., John Gibson, 'Territorial Principles and the Law Commission: a Comment' [1979] *Criminal Law Review* 778, 779.

in proportion to the extent of the common boundary.
(2) Every accretion from the sea or part of the sea-shore which is annexed to and
incorporated with a parish . . . under this section shall be annexed to and incorporated with the district and county in which that parish is situated.

Section 72, however, refers only to the status of the seashore. It makes no
reference to the status of the sea when it covers that shore. This is not merely
a quibble on words. There are sound practical reasons for distinguishing
between the status of the exposed foreshore, on the one hand, and that of
the submerged one, on the other, and there is nothing to suggest that the
1972 Act (or earlier legislation that it restates) was intended to alter the
status quo in that respect. There is certainly nothing to suggest that such
legislation was intended to have any effect on the limits of summary criminal
jurisdiction. There is a world of difference between questions concerning
the status of fixed structures, such as harbour walls or breakwaters, and
questions concerning jurisdiction over crime.

    The practical difficulties that may arise from the adoption of a fixed
low-water mark boundary become apparent as soon as one attempts to
define or apply the concept. The term, 'low-water mark' may in fact bear a
number of quite different meanings. Most maps show the line of median
low tides, or the low-water mean meridian tide line (LWMMT). This is the
contour currently depicted on the Ordnance Survey's digital mapping of
coastal areas in England and Wales. In contrast, Ordnance maps of
Scotland depict the low-water mark as that of a median spring tide. The
Scottish approach is to be preferred in at least one respect, because, to quote
Halsbury's Laws of England[47]: 'If the low-water mark of ordinary tides is
the boundary, then on many parts of the coast there are considerable tracts
of land left bare by the sea on three days in every lunar week which are not
part of the realm of England and not subject to the common law.'

    On modern Admiralty charts, produced by the United Kingdom
Hydrographic Office, the line depicted is that of the lowest astronomical
tides (LAT). This is an exceptionally low tide level that may be expected
approximately once every 18.6 years under average meteorological conditions.[48] The LAT line has been adopted as the standard baseline from which
the United Kingdom's territorial sea and fishery zone are each measured;
but because it differs quite significantly from the LWMMT line shown on
Ordnance maps, its adoption for that purpose offers no support for the

---

[47] Online version, 'Water', para. 1, fn 1. See also S.R. Hobday (ed.), *Coulson and Forbes on
the Law of Waters and of Land Drainage* (6th edn, 1952) and *Anderson v. Alnwick District
Council* [1993] 3 All ER 613.
[48] Highest and lowest astronomical tide lines are not absolute extremes, because severe
meteorological conditions can cause even higher or lower levels, respectively. The lowest
levels under these circumstances result from a 'negative surge', the converse of which is a 'storm
surge'. These lines are determined by inspecting predicted sea levels over a number of years.

argument that either should be taken to represent the extent of the realm for jurisdictional purposes.

Whichever type of low-water mark is depicted on a map or chart, the actual location of low water on any given day will depend on a combination of astronomical and meteorological factors. On most days, it will bear little resemblance to any line shown on any map or chart. The low-water mark during a spring tide may lie much further out than the low-water mark during a neap tide, when the gravitational effect of the sun and moon is at its smallest, the difference between the two depending (*inter alia*) on the slope of the foreshore itself. Where the foreshore is almost flat, the difference between one tide and another may be enormous. Furthermore, recent storms may cause even a fairly modern map to be inaccurate in its depiction of the tide lines.

This means that it may sometimes be difficult to know whether a particular offence was committed to landward or to seaward of the low-water mark, either because of doubts as to the location of the offence relative to that line, or because of doubts as to how the line should be defined. Such difficulties may not be everyday occurrences, but they can and do arise from time to time. In *Anderson v. Alnwick District Council*,[49] the local authority had passed a by-law prohibiting any person from digging for bait at Boulmer Haven, 'on such parts of the beach as lie above the low-water line'. The defendant was prosecuted for an alleged breach of this by-law, but denied the offence on the basis that he had been digging on a part of the beach that was exposed only during spring tides, well below the LWMMT line. On the particular facts of that case, the defence succeeded, because an Ordnance map showing the extent of the beach covered by the prohibition had been annexed to the by-law when it was approved by the Secretary of State, and the LWMMT line had been used on that map to delimit the boundaries of the protected area. Had there been no such map, it is clear that different considerations would have applied. The court would instead have followed the approach suggested in *Loose v. Castleton*,[50] in which Bridge LJ defined the foreshore as including, 'the whole of the shore that is from time to time exposed by the receding tide'.[51] Evans LJ, who gave the judgment of the court in *Anderson*, also seems to have accepted the concept of alternating jurisdictions, according to the state of the tide. He said: 'There is an overlap between the territorial jurisdiction which includes the foreshore and the Admiralty jurisdiction which may extend as far as the high-water mark.'[52]

Much of the above argument and analysis would be rendered unnecessary if magistrates' courts were given full powers of summary jurisdiction

---

[49] [1993] 3 All ER 613.   [50] (1978) 41 P & CR 19, 34.
[51] See also *R v. Dyfed County Council, ex p Manson* (1994) unreported, 18 February; cf. *R v. Howlett* (1967) *The Times*, 4 February.   [52] [1993] 3 All ER 613, 618.

over offences committed within the territorial sea or within internal waters. The failure of Parliament to provide magistrates with such jurisdiction is difficult to explain or justify. It means, for example, that no jurisdiction ordinarily exists to punish commonplace summary offences such as assault or battery, if these are committed by someone standing ankle deep in the surf on a public beach.[53] The law would not, however, be improved by making jurisdiction depend on the offender's position relative to a notional low-water mark as shown on a map or chart. On the contrary, that would merely give rise to evidential complications. A witness to a 'beach' crime can at least state whether the offence was committed on the exposed beach or in the sea, but he is unlikely to have much idea of its position relative to the LWMMT line.

Waters Lying *Inter Fauces Terrae*

At common law, criminal jurisdiction could be exercised over offences committed within tidal waters lying *inter fauces terrae*, regardless of the state of the tide, the theory being that such waters were (or were deemed to be) an integral part of the relevant counties.

The *fauces terrae* concept was a common law one, and was inevitably imprecise. According to Coke,[54] it was necessary that a man standing on one side of the shore should be able to see what another was doing on the opposite shore, but in *R v. Bruce*[55] the Court of King's Bench expressed a preference for an even vaguer test advanced by Hale,[56] according to which: 'The arm or branch of the sea which lies within the *fauces terrae*, where a man may reasonably discern between shore and shore is, or at least may be, within the body of a county, and therefore within the jurisdiction of the sheriff or coroner.' Hale's test unfortunately neglected to specify what it is that a man must be able to discern on the other side. It left no doubt as to the status of small harbours or narrow tidal creeks, but did nothing to resolve the status of major bays or estuaries, and this uncertainty was twice manifested in cases concerning the legal status of the Bristol Channel. The first of these was *R v. Cunningham*,[57] in which three seamen from an American merchant ship were charged with the unlawful wounding of a fourth, while their ship lay in the Penarth Roads, less than a mile from the Glamorganshire coast, and two miles to landward of a small island known as Flat Holms. The coast of Somerset lay 10 miles to the South and was visible from the Glamorgan coast on a clear day. The venue was laid in

---

[53] The Merchant Shipping Act 1985, s. 280, might be construed as giving such courts jurisdiction over offences committed aboard ships lying off the adjoining coast, but it has never been so interpreted by the courts. See below, p. 93.   [54] *Institutes*. vol, 3, 113.
[55] (1812) Russ & Ry 243.   [56] *De Jure Maris* (1787) i.iv.,10.
[57] (1859) Bell 72.

Glamorganshire, but the question of jurisdiction was reserved for the opinion of the judges of Queen's Bench. Counsel on each side directed their principal arguments on the status of the waters lying between Flat Holms and the Glamorgan mainland, but the court, in a short unreserved judgment, roundly declared that, 'The whole of this inland sea between the counties of Somerset and Glamorgan is to be considered as within the counties by the shores of which its several parts are bounded'.[58]

The Bristol Channel was over 11 miles wide at that point, but the judgment seemed to suggest that its waters might lie *inter fauces terrae* even in places where its breadth exceeded 20 miles. In a later civil case, *The Fagernes*,[59] Hill J, at first instance, came to that very conclusion, holding that the whole area enclosed by a line drawn between Bull Point, in Devonshire, and Port Eynon Head on the Gower peninsular could be so categorized.[60] He accordingly concluded that he had jurisdiction to hear a civil action *in personam* against the owners of an Italian freighter that had been involved in a collision with a British vessel in the Channel, over seven miles from the nearest land. If this were so, a criminal court would similarly have had jurisdiction over any offence (even one triable only summarily) arising out of the same incident, or committed in the same locality.

On appeal, however, this finding was reversed. The Attorney-General appeared at the invitation of the Court of Appeal, and informed the court that he had been instructed by the Home Secretary that, 'The spot where this collision is alleged to have occurred is not within the limits to which the territorial sovereignty of His Majesty extends'. This was deemed to be conclusive on the matter. As Atkin LJ explained: 'What is the territory of the Crown is a matter of which the court takes judicial notice. Any definite statement from the proper representative of the Crown . . . must be treated as conclusive. A conflict is not to be contemplated between the courts and the executive on such a matter. . . .'[61] No precise indication was offered as to where the limits of the *fauces terrae* in the Bristol Channel actually lay. The Court suggested that these extended at least to the point where the width of the Channel reaches six miles, but declined to speculate on how much further (if at all) they might extend.

Modern legislation dealing with jurisdiction over summary offences makes no express reference to any concept of the *fauces terrae*, nor is it one with which Ordnance Survey cartographers appear to be familiar. Section 3(1) of

---

[58] Nothing seems to have turned on the fact that the crime was committed within the limits of the Port of Cardiff. See Marston, *The Marginal Seabed* (1981), 253.

[59] [1927] P 311.

[60] These points fall close to those which are now considered to mark the 'natural entrance points' of the bay formed by the Bristol Channel, namely Worms Head (west of Port Eynon) and the Morte Stone, west of Bull Point in Devonshire.

[61] See further W.R. Edeson, 'The Prerogative of the Crown to Delimit Britain's Maritime Boundary' (1973) 89 *Law Quarterly Review* 364, 370–7.

the Magistrates' Courts Act 1980 (which restates earlier legislation) does, however, provide for jurisdiction to be taken over offences committed, 'in any harbour, river, arm of the sea or other water lying between two or more [commission] areas'. Such offences may be tried in either area. What, then, of waters that lie between different arms of the *same* commission area? There are waters in Plymouth Sound, for example, which would have been categorized as lying *inter fauces terrae* at common law but which no longer fall within section 3(1), because Devon and Cornwall now constitute a sigle unified commission area. Summary offences committed in such waters must presumably be triable by the courts of the commission area in question. In other words, section 3(1) presupposes the existence of the *fauces terrae* concept, which underpins it.

Despite the absence of any recent case law, the survival of the *fauces terrae* concept must therefore be assumed. It provides a common law gloss on the statutory limits governing jurisdiction over summary offences. It has not, at any rate, been supplanted or abolished by the Territorial Waters Order in Council 1964. As Geoffrey Marston explains:

The [1958] Convention and Orders in Council have not altered the area of tidal waters and the solum thereof which is within the county. There is thus a basic difference between the tidal waters within the county (inland waters) and the tidal waters on the shoreward side of the baseline of the territorial sea (internal waters).[62]

JURISDICTION OVER TERRITORIAL WATERS

All littoral states throughout the world now claim sovereignty (and thus criminal jurisdiction) over a territorial sea, and most, but not all, claim a territorial sea with a breadth of 12 nautical miles,[63] in accordance with Article 3 of the 1982 United Nations Convention on the Law of the Sea (the UNCLOS Convention). The right to assert sovereignty over a territorial sea is now universally recognized under customary international law, and some jurists go further, asserting that such sovereignty arises as a matter of legal obligation. They argue, in other words, that it is not be open to a littoral state to decline such sovereignty.[64] It is clear, however, that international law cannot require any state to claim the full 12 miles.[65] The United States, for example, restricted its territorial sea for many years to just six miles.

---

[62] *The Marginal Seabed* (1981), 259.

[63] A nautical mile is equal to 1,852 metres or 1.1508 statute miles, and is very close to the mean value of one minute of latitude.

[64] See, e.g., the minority judgment of Sir Arnold McNair in *Anglo-Norwegian Fisheries* [1951] ICJ Rep 116, 160. UNCLOS 1982 appears to take the same view, declaring in Art. 2 that, 'The sovereignty of a coastal state extends, beyond its land territory and internal waters . . . to an adjacent belt of sea, described as its territorial sea.'

[65] See Art. 3 of UNCLOS, which (in contrast to Art. 2) merely declares this to be the maximum limit of permissible claims.

In contrast, some states in Africa and Central or South America have claimed territorial seas of up to 200 miles, but their claims are not generally recognized elsewhere, except in so far as they involve jurisdiction to regulate fisheries, and some states have recently abandoned similar claims.

While the breadth of the United Kingdom's territorial sea is not controversial, there are nevertheless some difficulties in identifying its precise extent, because it is not yet marked on any officially published charts, and the criteria by which its baselines are defined remain open, in some cases, to conflicting interpretations. These will be explored in due course, but it may help first to consider the history of the United Kingdom's territorial sea.

The Historical Background

The common law, for reasons already explained, had no conception of criminal jurisdiction over any area of sea lying beyond the harbours, rivers, or creeks that are located *inter fauces terrae*. Any such jurisdiction could only have originated with the Admiral. The Admiral, and later those courts to which the Admiral's jurisdiction was transferred, did indeed claim jurisdiction over acts of piracy on the high seas and over offences committed on English (and later British) ships. Extravagant and unsubstantiated claims were even made during the seventeenth century to the effect that English sovereignty extended over the whole of the 'narrow seas' between England and continental Europe;[66] but there was little evidence to suggest that any general (non-piracy) criminal jurisdiction was actually asserted over foreign vessels in open waters beyond the *fauces terrae*.[67]

During the eighteenth century, some jurists argued that states should have the right to exercise sovereignty over such waters as could be controlled by their coastal artillery, but this would mean that the extent of waters controlled would vary according to the range and siting of the guns in question, and in 1782 the Italian jurist Galiani proposed the adoption of a standardized belt of one marine league, equal to three nautical miles. This gradually gained widespread support, notably in respect of claims to neutrality, in which vessels lying within one marine league of a neutral shore came to be considered immune from attack or seizure by foreign belligerents.[68]

During the nineteenth century, English courts came to accept the concept of territorial waters, including British territorial waters three miles in breadth,[69] but this did not mean that they recognized or asserted any right

---

[66] See T.W. Fulton, *The Sovereignty of the Sea* (1911); Geoffrey Marston, 'Crimes on Board Foreign Merchant Ships at Sea: Some Aspects of English Practice' (1972) 88 *Law Quarterly Review* 357, 367.

[67] See the judgment of Cockburn CJ in *R v. Keyn* (1876) 2 Ex D 65, 163–75.

[68] Similarly, ships of war were precluded from engaging in hostile operations whilst themselves within one marine league of a neutral shore: *The Twee Gebroeders* (1800) 3 C Rob 162.

[69] See, e.g., *The Leda* (1856) Swabey Adm 40.

to exercise criminal jurisdiction over foreign vessels within them. Not until 1876 did that question fall squarely before an appellate court.

The *Franconia* Case

In February 1876, the British steamer *Strathclyde* sank following a collision with the German steamer *Franconia* on the open sea within two miles of Dover Pier Head. A number of passengers on the *Strathclyde* were drowned, including Jessie Young, with whose negligent manslaughter Captain Ferdinand Keyn, master of the *Franconia*, was charged. Since the existence or extent of criminal jurisdiction within territorial waters had not been established in any previous case, the opinions of the Law Officers and Crown Counsel were sought in advance of any trial. They advised that the Central Criminal Court[70] did indeed have jurisdiction to try Captain Keyn, but contrary opinions were expressed elsewhere, notably within the Foreign Office, wherein it was feared that such a prosecution might set a dangerous precedent, in so far as it might lead in comparable cases to the prosecution of the masters of British ships by foreign courts.[71]

The trial was duly held and resulted in Keyn's conviction for manslaughter. His appeal, which generated enormous interest, was heard by 14 judges of the Court for Crown Cases Reserved, including Lord Coleridge CJ, Cockburn CJ, and the distinguished Admiralty judge, Sir Robert Phillimore.[72] By the narrowest of majorities,[73] it was eventually held Keyn had committed no offence within English jurisdiction. The precise *ratio* of the case is not easy to extract from the several majority judgments,[74] but all of the judges in the majority denied that the United Kingdom had asserted any right to criminal jurisdiction over foreign ships off the coast of England, and most denied that the realm of England included any territorial sea. In his monumental judgment, Cockburn CJ examined an enormous range of precedents and writings, both English and foreign, and concluded:

Taken together, decisions and dicta no doubt shew that the views and opinions of the foreign jurists as to a territorial sea have been received with favour by eminent judicial authorities of this country, and that the doctrine respecting it has been admitted in the construction of statutory enactments; but none of them go to the length of establishing, or even suggesting, that, independently of statute, the criminal law of

[70] This would have been the Central Criminal Court's Admiralty jurisdiction, derived from the Offences at Sea Act 1799 and the Admiralty Offences Act 1844.

[71] See Geoffrey Marston, 'The Centenary of the Franconia Case—The Prosecution of Ferdinand Keyn' (1976) 92 *Law Quarterly Review* 93, 97.

[72] It appears that the Lord Chancellor, Lord Cairns, was also minded to sit, but was dissuaded by Cockburn CJ on the basis that this would be unusual and improper, especially in a case of such enormous constitutional importance: see Marston, ibid., 106.

[73] The majority was one of 7 : 6. The fourteenth judge, Archibald J, died before judgments could be given, but it seems that he would have concurred with Cockburn CJ.

[74] See Marston, *The Marginal Seabed* (1981), 137.

England is applicable to the foreigner navigating these waters . . . and no assent on the part of foreign nations to the exercise of dominion and jurisdiction over these waters can, without an Act of Parliament, confer on the Admiral or any judge of this country a larger jurisdiction than he possessed before.[75]

The decision was highly controversial. Parliament was goaded into action, and the precedent set in *R* v. *Keyn* was effectively reversed less than two years later by the Territorial Waters Jurisdiction Act 1878, which (with some amendments) remains in force today.

The Territorial Waters Jurisdiction Act 1878

The 1878 Act was drafted for the specific purpose of abrogating the rule laid down in *R* v. *Keyn*. According to the preamble:

The rightful jurisdiction of Her Majesty . . . extends and has always extended over the open seas adjacent to the coasts of the United Kingdom and of all other part of Her Majesty's dominions to such distance as is necessary for the defence and security of those dominions. . . .

Section 2 of the Act provides:

An offence committed by a person, whether he is or is not a subject of Her Majesty, on the open sea within the territorial waters of Her Majesty's dominions, is an offence within the jurisdiction of the Admiral, although it may have been committed on board or by means of a foreign ship, and the person who committed such offence may be arrested, tried and punished accordingly.

By section 7, the term 'offence' means 'an act neglect or default of such a description as would, if committed within the body of a county in England, be punishable on indictment according to the law of England for the time being in force'. Summary offences were not therefore affected by the enactment.

Prosecutions under this Act of persons who are not British subjects[76] require the consent of one of Her Majesty's principal secretaries of state, who must certify that such proceedings are 'expedient'.[77] This was inserted in recognition of the fact that an offence committed aboard a foreign vessel in territorial waters may be of no real concern to the United Kingdom, and that a misguided prosecution by overzealous officers might be damaging to international relations. Any interference with the passage of the ship itself (for example, to make an arrest or obtain evidence) may also be unlawful

---

[75] (1876) 2 Ex D 65, 229.

[76] The term 'British subject', when used in an old statute such as this, now has the meaning given to it by s. 51(1) of the British Nationality Act 1981, i.e., a British or Commonwealth citizen. See below, p. 205. In the context of the 1878 Act, it would be more appropriate to obtain the Attorney's consent to any prosecution of a person who is not a UK national.

[77] Territorial Waters Jurisdiction Act 1878, s. 3. As to procedural and evidential matters concerning such certificates, see s. 4 of the Act.

under international law, save in a limited range of circumstances provided for under Article 27 of UNCLOS.[78]

The phrase, 'territorial waters' was initially defined by section 7 of the 1878 Act as meaning 'such part of the open sea adjacent to the coast of the United Kingdom . . . as is deemed by international law to be within the territorial sovereignty of her Majesty', but the section then continued:

For the purpose of any offence declared by this Act to be within the jurisdiction of the Admiral, any part of the open sea within one marine league[79] of the coast measured from the low-water mark shall be deemed to be open sea within the territorial waters of Her Majesty's dominions.

This two-part definition was at best curious and at worst confusing. One way of interpreting it was to read the second part as a definition of the minimum extent of the territorial sea, and the first part as a statement of its maximum potential extent. In other words, the territorial sea was to be *at least* three nautical miles in breadth, but could potentially be made wider, should public international law so permit. Alternatively, section 7 could be read as distinguishing between the extent of the territorial sea for general purposes and its extent for purposes concerning 'offences declared by this Act to be within the jurisdiction of the Admiral'. The former interpretation was much to be preferred, if only because it avoided the complications of territorial limits that vary according to the purposes for which they are being applied, but the latter interpretation was favoured by the Divisional Court in *R* v. *Kent Justices, ex p Lye*.[80] Thankfully, the Territorial Sea Act 1987 now ensures that the location, breadth, and extent of the territorial sea is the same for all purposes.[81]

Because it was concerned with the 'open sea', nothing in the Act was intended to derogate from the jurisdiction already exercisable at common law over waters *inter fauces terrae*. Not surprisingly, given the date of enactment, no provision was made for jurisdiction to extend over offences committed in the airspace above the territorial sea, and this may give rise to problems under modern legislation that appears to assume the contrary.[82]

The Territorial Waters Order in Council 1964

The Territorial Waters Order in Council 1964 was made, under the Royal Prerogative, for the purpose of extending British territorial limits in accordance

---

[78] These include cases in which help is requested by the ship's master or by a consular officer of the flag state, and cases involving drug trafficking.

[79] A distance equal to three nautical miles.

[80] [1967] 2 QB 153. See also the Law Commission, *Report on the Territorial and Extraterritorial Extent of the Criminal Law* (1978) Law Com. No. 91, paras 16–17.

[81] Police powers are now fully exercisable within territorial waters: see the Police Act 1996, s. 30.   [82] See below, p. 104.

with principles laid down by the 1958 Geneva Convention on the Territorial Sea and Contiguous Zone.[83] The breadth of the territorial sea itself remained unaltered until the enactment of the Territorial Sea Act 1987, but the Order in Council made various modifications to the location of the baseline from which the territorial sea was measured, pushing it, in many cases, well away from the low-water mark around the coast, notably by drawing 'closing lines' across the mouths of bays and estuaries.

Serious doubts were raised as to the Crown's power to exercise its prerogative in this way.[84] If such a power ever existed, had it not been abrogated by the enactment of the Territorial Waters Jurisdiction Act? Was it acceptable for the executive to side-step the need for Parliamentary assent before giving effect to international treaties under English law? Answers to these questions were provided by the courts within a few years of the Order being made, but the answers were not wholly clear or satisfactory.

The issue came before the courts because the enlargement of the territorial limits brought within them an unlicensed (or 'pirate') radio station which had hitherto been able to broadcast with impunity from Red Sands Tower, a disused anti-aircraft platform sited in the Thames estuary, beyond the *fauces terrae*.[85] Being sited on a fixed platform, the unfortunate broadcasters were unable to move the location of their transmitter, as a ship-borne radio station might have done. The courts nevertheless upheld the validity of the Order in Council in two cases brought against the broadcasters. The first was a criminal case, *R v. Kent Justices, ex p Lye*,[86] in which the Divisional Court upheld the jurisdiction of the Kent justices to convict the broadcasters of an offence under section 1 of the Wireless Telegraphy Act 1949. The second was a civil case, *Post Office v. Estuary Radio Ltd*,[87] involving an application by the Post Office for an injunction against the broadcasters, who had continued to operate despite their earlier criminal convictions.

The cases raised a number of complex issues concerning the proper interpretation both of the 1964 Order and of the 1878 and 1949 Acts. As far as the validity of the Order was concerned, the Divisional Court in *ex p Lye* had to decide this question only in so far as it concerned the jurisdiction of the local justices over that particular case, but the process by which they held the Order to be valid was by distinguishing between summary and

---

[83] Cmnd. 584 (1958).   [84] See Edeson, op cit., fn 61, 377.

[85] During the Second World War several pre-fabricated anti-aircraft forts or platforms were towed into shallow waters off the south-east coast of England and Thames estuary, and sunk into positions there, where they were used to engage enemy aircraft, e-boats, and V-1 flying bombs. Another of these forts, also situated outside the original three-mile territorial limit, has also given rise to troublesome jurisdictional issues. The history of Roughs Tower, otherwise known as the 'Principality of Sealand', is considered later in this chapter (see p. 97). As to offences in respect of pirate broadcasting (whether from ships, aircraft, or platforms) see now the Marine, etc., Broadcasting (Offences) Act 1967.   [86] [1967] 2 QB 153.

[87] [1968] 2 QB 740.

indictable offences. For the purposes of Admiralty jurisdiction over indictable offences, the extent of the territorial sea was fixed, said the court, by the second limb of section 7 of the 1878 Act. The 1878 limits could not be extended otherwise than by Parliament itself. In contrast, the first limb of section 7 was flexible enough to permit enlargement of the limits in line with international law, which is what the Order in Council had done.

The offence created by section 1 of the 1949 Act was a summary one, but section 6 of that Act expressly made it applicable to offences committed in territorial waters, and although (most unusually) no specific venue provision had been included, the court inferred that jurisdiction must necessarily lie with magistrates' courts within the adjoining county.

In *Post Office* v. *Estuary Radio Ltd*, the Court of Appeal appears to have recognized a general prerogative power, unqualified by any reference to the 1878 Act. Giving the judgment of the Court, Diplock LJ said:

> It still lies within the prerogative power of the Crown to extend its sovereignty and jurisdiction to areas of land or sea over which it has not previously claimed or exercised sovereignty or jurisdiction. For such extension, the authority of Parliament is not required. The Queen's courts, upon being informed by Order in Council or by the appropriate minister or Law Officer of the Crown's claim to sovereignty or jurisdiction over any place must give effect to it and are bound by it.[88]

This did not altogether silence doubts or criticism as to the validity or effect of the Order,[89] but any such doubts were finally put to rest by the Territorial Sea Act 1987, section 1(4) of which now provides that the Order shall have effect as if it had been made under the authority of that Act.

The Territorial Sea Act 1987

The Territorial Sea Act 1987 amended, but did not wholly supplant, the 1878 Act and the 1964 Order in Council. As previously explained, it removed much of the uncertainty that had previously dogged the law concerning criminal jurisdiction within territorial waters, by giving statutory authority to the Order in Council and by making it clear that the baselines established under that Order are now applicable for all purposes. The principal purpose of the Act was to extend the breadth of the United Kingdom's territorial sea to 12 nautical miles. This extension applies for almost all purposes. All other enactments, before or since, that contain references (however worded) to the United Kingdom's territorial sea must ordinarily be construed in accordance with that Act.[90]

---

88 [1968] 2 QB 753.   89 See Edeson, op. cit., fn 61, 378–80.
90 Territorial Sea Act 1987, s. 1(5). This does not, however, require references to specific distances (e.g., three miles) to be construed as references to 12 miles (s. 1(6)), nor does it affect the operation of earlier local Acts or of earlier enactments determining the limits within which harbour authorities or port health authorities have jurisdiction (s. 2(1)–(2)). Further exclusions apply in respect of regulations made or licences granted under the Petroleum (Production) Act 1934 or the Petroleum Act 1998 (Territorial Sea Act 1987, s. 2(4)).

Orders under the Territorial Sea Act 1987

Section 1(2) of the 1987 Act enables Orders to be made, varying the location and extent of any part of the territorial sea. The Territorial Sea (Limits) Order 1989,[91] made by authority of this provision, restricts the seaward boundaries of the United Kingdom adjacent to those of France at the Straits of Dover and adjacent to those of the Isle of Man. In each case, the restriction was necessitated by the narrowness of the sea lying between the jurisdictions, but Article 2 of the Order further departs from standard practice by marking the outer limits of territorial waters in the Straits of Dover with a series of six straight baselines,[92] rather than with a line tracing the exact median points between the English and French coasts.

Two further Orders have been made under the authority conferred by the Act, although neither directly concerns waters adjacent to England or Wales. The Territorial Sea Act 1987 (Isle of Man) Order 1991[93] extends the operation of the Act to the waters adjacent to the Isle of Man.[94] The Territorial Sea (Amendment) Order 1998[95] amends the Schedule to the 1964 Order in Council, so as to revise a series of straight territorial sea baselines that run off the west coast of Scotland between Cape Wrath and Laggan, on the Rinns of Galloway, in accordance with the most recent data and with Article 7 of the UNCLOS Convention.[96]

ENGLISH, SCOTTISH, AND NORTHERN IRISH WATERS

The Territorial Waters Jurisdiction Act 1878 drew no distinction between waters adjacent to England and Wales and waters adjacent to other parts of the United Kingdom, but the phrase 'jurisdiction of the Admiral' was deemed to include that of the Admiral of Ireland. Under the Criminal Law Act (Northern Ireland) 1967, offences 'triable in Northern Ireland by virtue of any jurisdiction in Admiralty' are now triable in accordance with the normal procedures governing trials on indictment in Northern Ireland.

In Scotland, the High Court of Justiciary has inherent jurisdiction over indictable offences committed anywhere within Scotland, including offences committed within Scottish territorial or internal waters. The jurisdiction of sheriffs' and district courts is generally confined, like that of English justices,

---

[91] SI 1989 No. 482.   [92] These are specified in the Schedule to the Order.
[93] SI 1991 No. 1722.
[94] The Isle of Man is not strictly a part of the UK; but it is a British possession and matters concerning foreign relations, etc., are handled by the UK.   [95] SI 1998 No. 2564.
[96] For the full background to this amendment (which was triggered by a failed prosecution under Scottish fishery laws), see Geoffrey Marston, 'Redrawing the Territorial Sea Baseline in the Firth of Forth' (2002) 51 *International and Comparative Law Quarterly* 279. No such baselines are used off the coasts of England or Wales, which are not so heavily indented and are not fringed by any significant chain of islands.

to their own commission areas, but under section 4 of the Criminal Procedure (Scotland) Act 1995,

... the jurisdiction of the sheriffs, within their respective sheriffdoms shall extend to and include all navigable rivers, ports, harbours, creeks, shores and anchoring grounds in or adjoining such sheriffdoms and includes all criminal maritime causes and proceedings (including those applying to persons furth of Scotland) provided that the accused is, by virtue of any enactment or rule of law, subject to the jurisdiction of the sheriff before whom the case or proceeding is raised.

A further question that may arise is whether any overlapping jurisdiction exists. Would it be a good defence in an English court, on an indictment alleging the commission of an offence within territorial waters, to show that the offence in question was in fact committed in waters adjacent to Scotland? The answer to this question appears to depend on whether the sole basis for jurisdiction is territorial. If the alleged offence was committed aboard a 'United Kingdom ship' on the high seas, even within Scottish internal waters,[97] any British court before whom the alleged offender appeared would have jurisdiction by virtue of section 281 of the Merchant Shipping Act 1995.[98] The same provision would apply if the alleged offence was committed at sea by a British citizen on a foreign ship to which he did not belong,[99] and an offence would also be triable in England if committed aboard a ship of the Royal Navy.[100] Where, however, the sole basis for claiming jurisdiction is that the offence was committed within territorial or internal waters, it appears that English jurisdiction now ends, as on land, at the Scottish border. This would be the case if, for example, both the defendant and the ship involved were foreign, or if the alleged offence was not committed on any ship. Under section 126 of the Scotland Act 1998, internal and territorial waters adjacent to Scotland are now deemed to be part of Scotland and thus (if only by implication) subject to Scottish criminal jurisdiction. The Scottish Adjacent Waters Boundaries Order 1999,[101] made under the authority of section 115 of the Scotland Act, uses a complex series of map coordinates to identify the boundaries between Scottish waters and those adjacent to England or Northern Ireland, including the adjacent 200-mile fishery zones.[102] The Order does not expressly state that Scottish waters

---

[97] There is no contradiction here: the 'high seas', under English law, include territorial and internal waters, and even harbours and rivers, 'where great ships go'.

[98] See *R* v. *Liverpool Justices, ex p Molyneux* [1972] 2 QB 384. Section 281 must be read in conjunction with Sch. 13 to the Act, which amends the Supreme Court Act 1981, s. 46A and the Magistrates' Courts Act 1980, s. 3A.   [99] See *R* v. *Kelly* [1982] AC 665.

[100] In *R* v. *Devon Justices, ex p DPP* [1924] 1 KB 503, an offence committed aboard the minelayer *HMS Princess Margaret* in the Scottish Naval base at Rosyth in the Forth Estuary was nevertheless held to be triable in Devon by virtue of the Naval Discipline Act 1866.

[101] SI 1999 No. 1126.

[102] On the east coast, seven coordinates are used. No fewer than 74 are required on the more complex west coast boundaries.

lie to the north of the boundary with England, or to the east of the boundary with Northern Ireland. The draftsman no doubt assumed that this went without saying; but in *Adelino Enriquez* v. *Procurator Fiscal, Lerwick*,[103] the appellant, a Spanish fisherman, relied on this omission to challenge the jurisdictional competence of the Scottish courts to try him for a fisheries offence allegedly committed within the Scottish fishery zone. The Boundaries Order, he argued, was fatally flawed in that respect. The High Court of Justiciary rightly gave short shrift to this argument, taking judicial notice of the very obvious fact that Scotland lies to the north of England.

No such rigid distinction has been made between English and Northern Irish or Manx waters. In section 8 of the Fishery Limits Act 1976, for example, 'relevant British fishery limits' are now defined as 'British fishery limits so far as they do not relate to the Scottish zone'. This suggests that English and Northern Irish jurisdictions are not mutually exclusive in respect of offences committed at sea.[104]

IDENTIFYING THE BASELINE OF THE TERRITORIAL SEA

The Position under International Law

One might reasonably suppose that the precise location of the United Kingdom's territorial sea baselines would be identified either on standard charts of coastal waters, or in some other published form. With some exceptions, however, this has not been done. The low-water line, which forms the greater part of the baseline, is a standard contour marked on Admiralty charts, as are the shores of islands and low tide elevations, whilst a system of straight baselines that delimits Scotland's territorial sea between Cape Wrath and Laggan is identified by a series of published geographical coordinates; but the location of 'bay closing' baselines is not currently published in any such way. This omission is surprising. The seaward limits of port authorities, for example, are clearly marked on Admiralty charts, but bay-closing lines are not, even though Article 16 of the UNCLOS Convention specifically obliges states to identify their baselines. It provides:

The baselines for measuring the breadth of the territorial sea determined in accordance with Articles 7, 9 and 10,[105] or the limits derived therefrom, and the lines of delimitation drawn in accordance with Articles 12 and 15 shall be shown on charts of a scale or scales adequate for ascertaining their position. Alternatively, a list of geographical co-ordinates of points, specifying the geodetic datum, may be substituted.

---

[103] [2001] Scot HC 51.
[104] There is a reference in s. 40 of the Act to waters adjacent to Northern Ireland, but only in the context of the financing of fishery protection measures.
[105] These deal with straight baselines, river mouths, and bays.

The United Kingdom has been a party to the Convention since 1994, but has yet to comply with this particular obligation. This omission is puzzling. The United Kingdom Hydrographic Office has in fact determined where, in its view, each and every bay closing line should be drawn, but does not officially publish this information.[106] One of the reasons sometimes given for this failure to publish is that shifting sandbanks, etc., may lead to changes in the relevant coordinates and make any published information inaccurate, but this is unconvincing because the same could equally be said of sandbanks as navigational hazards, with far more serious and immediate implications for mariners.

This failure to identify or publish national territorial baselines has given rise to protracted litigation in the past.[107] Section 1(3) of the Territorial Sea Act 1987 now provides a method of resolving such litigation, in the form of a certificate issued by the Secretary of State, but clearly this does not satisfy the publicity requirements of the treaty.

The Hydrographic Office is aware of the problem of non-compliance with the UNCLOS Convention, and has undertaken to produce a single chart of the United Kingdom depicting the principal bay closing lines. This will not be on a sufficiently large scale to enable smaller bay closing lines to be shown, and in that respect it will still fall short of full compliance with the treaty.

The Secretary of State's Certificate

By section 1(3) of the Territorial Sea Act 1987:

In any legal proceedings, a certificate issued by or under the authority of the Secretary of State stating the location of any baseline established under subsection (1) above shall be conclusive of what is stated in the certificate.

The idea of resolving a legal dispute by means of such a certificate is by no means revolutionary. On matters concerning the recognition of foreign states, territory, or governments, for example, such certificates have long been considered conclusive. In the context of civil proceedings, a statement made before the Court of Appeal by the Attorney-General, acting on the instruction of the Home Secretary, in *The Fagernes*[108] was considered to be conclusive as to the question whether a particular part of the Bristol Channel where a collision had occurred lay within the realm of England. In criminal proceedings, however, the Crown has traditionally refrained from acting as a judge in its own cause. As the Law Commission noted in

---

[106] The Foreign Office has, however, used diplomatic channels to notify the location of principal bay closing lines to states that are signatories to the European Fishery Convention: see Marston, op. cit., fn 96, 290.

[107] *R v. Kent Justices, ex p Lye* [1967] 2 QB 153; *Post Office v. Estuary Radio Ltd* [1968] 2 QB 740.　　　　　　　　　　　　　　　　　　　　　　[108] [1927] P 311.

their 1978 Report, 'There is an understandable reluctance on the part of [government] departments to be involved in the provision of certificates of this character'.[109] The Law Commission nevertheless argued that it would be proper for a certificate to be issued identifying the baselines from which the relevant limits should be measured. This 'neutral' information would not necessarily resolve the final outcome of the case, because evidence would still be admissible as to where the alleged incident took place relative to that baseline, but in practice such a certificate would usually be decisive. Section 1(3) of the 1987 Act is based on clause 2(2) of the Draft Jurisdiction Bill appended to the Law Commission's Report, and is clearly meant to apply both in criminal and in civil cases.[110]

Production of a certificate may indeed help to resolve any particular case to which it is relevant, but this does not satisfy the requirements laid down by the Convention, because it provides no general guidance as to where the baselines are to be found. Nor should it be assumed that such a certificate will necessarily be issued. On the contrary, in at least one recent case the Crown conspicuously omitted to adduce any such certificate, perhaps for the reasons identified above. In *The Wanderer II*,[111] the master and owners of a Scottish fishing boat were prosecuted for an alleged violation of the Inshore Fishing (Prohibition of Fishing and Fishing Methods) (Scotland) Order 1989, which purported to apply Article 4 of the 1964 Order in Council for the purpose of identifying the bay closing line of the Firth of Clyde. The defendants were successful in their submission that the 1964 Order did not in fact permit the adoption of the particular bay closing line used by the 1989 Order, and the defendants were acquitted.[112]

The Low-water Mark Baseline

Article 2(1) of the Territorial Waters Order in Council 1964 states that, except where otherwise provided, 'the baseline from which the breadth of the territorial sea adjacent to the United Kingdom, Channel Islands and Isle of Man is measured shall be the low-water line around the coast, including the coast of all islands comprised in those territories'.

Article 5(2) provides that permanent harbour works which form an integral part of the harbour system shall be treated as part of the coast. One may therefore measure the baseline from a structure such as a breakwater.

---

[109] Law Com. No. 91, para. 24.

[110] The only significant modification to the original draft clause is that s. 1(2) is not confined (as was the draft clause) to criminal cases.

[111] Stranraer Sheriff Court (1998) unreported; see Marston, op. cit., fn 96.

[112] The problem was that Art. 4(c) (where this is the provision relied upon) does not sanction the use of anything other than a single straight baseline to mark the limits of the bay, whereas the 1989 Order purported to rely on a pair of baselines linked by an island. This was held to be permissible only where Art. 4(b) applies. See now the Territorial Sea (Amendment) Order 1998 (SI 1998 No. 2564).

The term 'low-water mark' is not expressly defined by statute or by the Order in Council, but UNCLOS, Article 5, defines the baseline as the low-water line 'as marked on large scale charts officially recognized by the coastal state'. The contour currently depicted on modern Admiralty charts is the line of lowest astronomical tides, or LAT. Although such tides may be expected to occur only once every 18.6 years under normal meteorological conditions, this line must accordingly constitute the standard territorial sea baseline. Accurate determination of the line of LAT is often difficult, particularly in areas with large tidal ranges and gradually sloping fore-shores, but its adoption benefits the littoral state by maximizing the area and resources brought within its jurisdiction and control, and that is the principal reason behind its adoption by most states today.

Islands and Low-tide Elevations

Islands, however small, generate their own territorial seas, which may or may not merge with that of the mainland.[113] They need not be inhabited in order to have this effect. Even Rockall, 170 miles from the nearest inhab-ited territory, has a territorial sea, although in deference to Article 121 of UNCLOS, no fishery zone or area of continental shelf is claimed by the United Kingdom in respect of it.[114] In contrast, low-tide elevations generate no independent territorial sea of their own, but may, if they lie wholly or partly within waters that would in any event be part of the territorial sea, be treated as if they were islands, and may thus be used to delimit the baseline of the territorial sea.[115] Article 5 of the Order in Council provides definitions of the relevant terms.

The expression 'island' means a naturally formed area of land surrounded by water which is above water at mean high-water spring tides; and
the expression 'low-tide elevation' means a naturally formed area of drying land sur-rounded by water which is below-water at mean high-water spring tides.

These definitions focus on the position at mean high-water spring tides, but do not state whether a low-tide elevation must appear *above* water at any particular state of tide. The question of what is meant by a low-tide eleva-tion in the Order became a contentious issue in *Post Office* v. *Estuary Radio Ltd.*[116] Red Sands Tower, on which the offending transmitter was based, lies within three nautical miles of a sandbank known as the 'Middle Sand', that itself lay within three miles of the Kent shore. In the criminal proceedings, Middle Sand was assumed to be a low-tide elevation. In the civil case, however,

---

[113] Territorial Waters Order in Council 1964, Art. 2(1).

[114] Article 121 provides that 'rocks which cannot sustain human habitation or economic life of their own shall have no exclusive economic zone or continental shelf'.

[115] Territorial Waters Order in Council 1964, Art. 2(2); UNCLOS, Art. 13. Low-tide eleva-tions do not have this effect if they only lie within territorial waters as a result of the presence of other low-tide elevations.　　　　　　　　[116] [1968] 2 QB 740.

the defendants claimed that it rarely dried out, and submitted that a low-tide elevation must be one that dries out at mean low-water spring tides. O'Connor J, at first instance, found that Middle Sand did indeed contain drying sandbanks, as shown on Admiralty charts, but he did not find it necessary to establish how often they dried, or under what conditions. What mattered, he said, was that their exposure was something more than a once-in-a-generation occurrence, and there was ample evidence of that.[117]

Since the United Kingdom has subsequently adopted the concept of lowest astronomical tide as the definition of low water, this must now be the test to apply when identifying low-tide elevations.

Bay-closing Baselines

The use of bay-closing baselines is regulated under international law by UNCLOS, Article 10, which largely restates Article 7 of the 1958 Geneva Convention and is generally considered to reflect customary international law[118]:

1. This Article relates only to bays the coasts of which belong to a single State.
2. For the purposes of this Convention, a bay is a well-marked indentation whose penetration is in such proportion to the width of its mouth as to contain land-locked waters and constitute more than a mere curvature of the coast. An indentation shall not, however, be regarded as a bay unless its area is as large as, or larger than, that of the semi-circle whose diameter is a line drawn across the mouth of that indentation.
3. For the purpose of measurement, the area of an indentation is that lying between the low-water mark around the shore of the indentation and a line joining the low-water mark of its natural entrance points.
Where, because of the presence of islands, an indentation has more than one mouth, the semi-circle shall be drawn on a line as long as the sum total of the lengths of the lines across the different mouths.
Islands within an indentation shall be included as if they were part of the water area of the indentation.
4. If the distance between the low-water marks of the natural entrance points of a bay does not exceed 24 nautical miles, a closing line may be drawn between these two low-water marks, and the waters enclosed thereby shall be considered as internal waters.
5. Where the distance between the low-water marks of the natural entrance points of a bay exceeds 24 nautical miles, a straight baseline of 24 nautical miles shall be drawn within the bay in such a manner as to enclose the maximum area of water that is possible with a line of that length.
6. The foregoing provisions do not apply to so-called 'historic' bays, or in any case where the system of straight baselines provided for in Article 7 is applied.

---

[117] O'Connor J also concluded that Red Sands Tower lay within a bay formed by the Thames estuary, and thus within internal waters. The status and proximity of the Middle Sand was only significant, therefore, if he was mistaken as to the latter point. The Court of Appeal agreed that the estuary formed a bay, but declined to rule on the meaning of a low-tide elevation.

[118] See the statement made by the US Secretary of State concerning Bristol Bay in Alaska: (1963) 2 ILM 528.

Indentations or estuaries which satisfy this test are sometimes referred to as 'juridical bays'. The position in English law is governed by Articles 4 and 5 of the 1964 Order in Council, which provide:

4. In the case of the sea adjacent to a bay, the baseline from which the breadth of the territorial sea is measured shall, subject to the provisions of Article 3 of this Order—

(a) if the bay has only one mouth and the distance between the low-water lines of the natural entrance points of the bay does not exceed 24 miles, be a straight line joining the said low-water lines;

(b) if, because of the presence of islands, the bay has more than one mouth and the distances between the low-water lines of the natural entrance points of each mouth added together do not exceed 24 miles, be a series of straight lines across each of the mouths drawn so as to join the said low-water lines;

(c) if neither paragraph (a) nor (b) of this Article applies, be a straight line 24 miles in length drawn from low-water line to low-water line within the bay in such a manner as to enclose the maximum area of water that is possible with a line of that length.

5. In this Order:

(1) the expression 'bay' means an indentation of the coast such that its area is not less than that of the semi-circle whose diameter is a line drawn across the mouth of the indentation, and for the purposes of this definition the area of an indentation shall be taken to be the area bounded by low-water line around the shore of the indentation and the straight line joining the low-water lines of its natural entrance points, and where, because of the presence of islands, an indentation has more than one mouth the length of the diameter of the semi-circle referred to shall be the sum of the lengths of the straight lines drawn across each of the mouths, and in calculating the area of an indentation the area of any islands lying within it shall be treated as part of the area of the indentation.

The interpretation of these Articles was soon found to be problematic. As previously explained, the principal argument relied upon by the Post Office in *Post Office* v. *Estuary Radio Ltd* was that Red Sands Tower lay within a bay formed by the Thames estuary, and thus within internal waters, but in order to determine whether this was indeed the case, it proved necessary to examine the geography and dimensions of the estuary itself. What were its 'natural entrance points' and what kind of test should be used in order to identify them? If a line were to be drawn between these points at low water, would the area of water enclosed to landward of this line be greater than that of an imaginary semi-circle the diameter of which was equal to that of the line? In making that calculation, could fresh water in tidal zones of the river be included?

As to the problem of identifying the natural entrance points, various possible candidates were suggested. The Post Office argued that the relevant points were the Naze to the north and North Foreland to the south. On a simple cartographic test (merely looking a map) these do indeed appear to be the points at which the indentation of the coastline begins. With these as its entrance points, the estuary would clearly satisfy the 'semi-circle test' laid down by Article 5 of the Order in Council, although the actual location of the baseline would have to be set further to the west in accordance with Article 4(c).

In contrast, the defendants submitted that the natural entrance points should be ascertained by more sophisticated means, taking account of the geology of the coastal area, of the tide streams, and of navigational considerations, such as the position of lights and shoals. On that basis, they argued that the natural entrance points were Orfordness and North Foreland, in which case the estuary could not qualify as a 'juridical bay' under Article 4.

O'Connor J and the Court of Appeal each held that the cartographic test was the correct one to apply, and indeed the only one that foreign seamen or fishermen could be expected to rely upon. They accordingly concluded that the Thames estuary was a bay for the purposes of the 1964 Order in Council. During the course of the hearing, however, consideration was given to a third possibility, namely that the entrance points were Orfordness and Foreness. The estuary would then qualify as a bay if, but only if, areas of fresh water in the tidal reaches of the Thames and its tributaries at low tide were included in the 'semi-circle' calculation. Whether such waters could in fact be included was never decided, because different entrance points were eventually chosen, but Diplock LJ suggested that had it been necessary to decide the point, the Court would have considered the 1958 Convention and its *travaux préparatoires*, together with evidence of international practice.[119]

Because section 1(3) of the Territorial Sea Act 1987 now permits the Secretary of State to certify the location of any bay-closing baselines for the purpose of any legal proceedings, one might suppose that cases such as *Post Office* v. *Estuary Radio Ltd* would no longer prove difficult to resolve. As previously explained, however, the Secretary of State is not obliged to issue any such certificate, and in at least one recent Scottish case he omitted (or perhaps declined) to do so.[120]

Another important change has occurred since the days of *Post Office* v. *Estuary Radio Ltd*. Until 1987, the 24-mile maximum limit imposed on bay-closing baselines under the 1964 Order in Council meant that such baselines could be up to eight times longer than the standard three-mile belt measured from the coast around the bay. They could thus enclose large areas of water within a bay that would otherwise lie beyond English sovereignty or jurisdiction. On the other side of the baseline, substantial additional areas of high seas would be brought within the territorial belt. The 24-mile maximum remains in force as far as bay closing lines are concerned; but the standard breadth of the territorial sea is now 12 miles. This almost

---

[119] It is doubtful whether much guidance could have been gleaned from either the old or the new Convention, although they each provide that where a river flows directly into the sea, the baseline should be drawn directly across its mouth. This might perhaps be taken to suggest that fresh water should not be taken into account.

[120] See *The Wanderer II* (above, p. 87).

inevitably means that the waters enclosed by bay closing lines are waters that would in any case have fallen within British territorial limits. Waters lying to landward of territorial sea baselines thereby become internal waters, where previously they may only have been territorial. This may be significant under international law, in respect of rights to innocent passage, etc., and it may be significant in cases where restricted inshore fishery zones are defined by reference to such baselines, but is not generally a matter of great significance as far as English criminal law is concerned. To seaward, the 12-mile belt measured from a bay-closing baseline will still extend marginally further out to sea than one measured from the low-water mark around the bay, but the difference is much less pronounced than it was.[121]

The Principal 'Juridical Bays' of England and Wales

As previously explained, the United Kingdom has never published any official document or chart identifying the many bays over which sovereignty is claimed by virtue of Article 4 of the Territorial Waters Order in Council.

Table 3.1. Location of largest or strategically important bays

Name of bay	First point	Last point
Thames Estuary	Minnies Bay Rock	Clacton Martello Tower[122]
The Solent (east)	Dunnose	Selsey Bill
The Solent (west)	Durlston Head	Sun Corner
Plymouth Sound	Rame Head East	Wembury Ledge[123]
Falmouth Harbour	Manacle Point	Zone Point
Bristol Channel	Worms Head	The Morte Stone
Carmarthen Bay	Old Castle Head	Worms Head[124]
Milford Haven	St Anne's Head	Linney Head
St Brides Bay	St David's Head	The Cable[125]
Tremadoc Bay	Trwyn Cilan	Borth Sands
Holyhead Harbour	Trwyn Cliperau	Holyhead Breakwater[126]
Conwy or Beaumaris Bay	Great Ormes Head	Trwyn du[127]
Liverpool Bay	Taylors Spit Point	Point of Ayr
Morecambe Bay	Hipsford Spit	King Scar
Solway Firth	Ree of Ross	North Head[128]
Humber Estuary	Donna Nook	Spurn Head Spit
The Wash	Gore Point	Wainfleet Sand
Harwich Harbour	The Naze	Languard Point

[121] It will ordinarily be greatest at the centre of the bay closing line, but even this depends on the geography of the area, and on whether there are any nearby islands or headlands, etc.
[122] The natural entrance points of Orfordness and North Foreland lie more than 24 nautical miles apart.   [123] Linked via four points on the Mewstone rocks.
[124] Linked via West Beacon Point and Chapel Point.
[125] Linked via nine intermediate points, including Gwahan Island, Trwyn Sion Owen, The Table, and Middle Isle.   [126] Linked via two low-tide elevations.
[127] Linked via Puffin Island.
[128] The northern half of the Solway Firth falls within Scottish Adjacent Waters, as delimited by SI 1999 No. 1126.

The relevant data are held on file within the United Kingdom Hydrographic Office, however, and may be provided, if necessary, at short notice.

Table 3.1, above, uses data kindly provided by the Hydrographic Office in order to identify the largest bays claimed by the United Kingdom in respect of waters adjacent to England and Wales, together with a selection of smaller but strategically important examples.

The second and third columns of the table show the approximate points between which the relevant bay closing lines are drawn. These are ordinarily the natural entrance points of the relevant bay, but in the case of the Thames estuary the distance between these points exceeds 24 nautical miles, and the bay closing line is accordingly drawn further inshore. There are many more small bays, but it is not practicable to identify them all here.

A number of well-known English bays are not 'juridical bays' under international law or within the meaning of the 1964 Order, because they would fail to satisfy the 'semi-circle test' described above. Examples include Mounts Bay in Cornwall, Bideford Bay in Devon, and Lyme Bay in Dorset.

SHIPS LYING OFF THE COAST

It has been argued above that magistrates' courts in England and Wales would ordinarily have no jurisdiction to deal with summary offences committed within territorial waters off their coasts. United Kingdom ships provide exceptions to this rule,[129] but what of smaller, unregistered vessels, or foreign ships? Section 280 of the Merchant Shipping Act 1995 might appear to cover such vessels, but this is very doubtful, as we shall see.

Section 280 is arguably the most obscure jurisdiction provision currently in force in English criminal law. It is derived, with little modification, from section 685 of the 1894 Act, which was in turn derived from section 521 of the Merchant Shipping Act 1854. The rule it encompasses (whatever that may be) has therefore been in force for nearly 150 years, but in all that time there has been no significant reported judicial analysis of its purpose or effect. Few commentators have dared to examine it, and none has discovered a satisfactory role for it to serve today. Section 280 provides:

(1) Where the area within which a court in any part of the United Kingdom has jurisdiction is situated on the coast of any sea or abuts on or projects into any bay, channel, lake, river or other navigable water the court shall have jurisdiction as respects offences under this Act over any vessel being on, or lying or passing off, that coast or being in or near that bay, channel, lake, river or navigable water and over all persons on board that vessel or for the time being belonging to it.

(2) The jurisdiction under subsection (1) above shall be in addition to and not in derogation of any jurisdiction or power of a court under the Magistrates' Courts Act 1980 or the Magistrates' Courts (Northern Ireland) Order 1981.

---

[129] See below, p. 289.

To begin with, the reference to 'offences under this Act' is almost wilfully misleading, because provisions inserted into the Magistrates' Courts Act 1980[130] and the Supreme Court Act 1981[131] ensure that section 280 is not in fact so restricted. These provide that section 280 'applies to other offences under the law of England and Wales as it applies to offences under that Act'. But what does that provision actually mean?

Geoffrey Marston has shown that section 521 of the 1854 Act was almost immediately found to be a cause of confusion.[132] In an unreported case dating from 1860, Hartlepool magistrates held that they had no jurisdiction to deal with an assault committed on the Prussian ship, *Fortuna*, within three miles of the coast, but the Law Officers of the Crown advised the Board of Trade that the magistrates had been mistaken[133]:

We are of the opinion that in the case put, of a common assault having been committed on board a foreign ship lying off the English coast, but within British territorial jurisdiction, the magistrates possessing ordinary jurisdiction of the adjacent coasts are empowered by the 521st section of the Merchant Shipping Act, 1854, to adjudicate upon the matter, if regularly brought before them for adjudication. There is nothing in the terms of the section, or in other parts of the statute, to confine the operation of the section to offences occurring on board British ships; and the general rule is that, within the limits of the territorial jurisdiction, the municipal laws of a country bind foreigners, and persons on board foreign ships, as well as native-born subjects within the same limits . . .

The Law Officers added that an indictable offence committed in similar circumstances would equally be triable in England by virtue of that section. This advice was given on the assumption that the *Fortuna* was 'within the limits of the territorial jurisdiction' at the time. Foreigners and foreign ships within those limits were assumed to be subject to the rules of English law. That being the case, section 521 provided a venue for criminal trials where the lack of a suitable venue might otherwise have been a problem.

In the landmark case of *R* v. *Keyn*,[134] however, it was held that English criminal law did not apply to things done aboard foreign ships, other than those lying within creeks, harbours, or rivers *inter fauces terrae* and within the realm.[135] The very existence of a general criminal jurisdiction

---

[130] Section 3A, inserted by Sch. 13 to the 1995 Act. Similar provisions are made in respect of Northern Ireland law.

[131] Section 46A, inserted by Sch. 13 to the 1995 Act. Similar provisions are made in respect of Northern Ireland.

[132] 'Crimes Aboard Foreign Merchant Ships at Sea: s. 685 of the Merchant Shipping Act 1894' [1971] *Criminal Law Review* 520; see also Marston, 'Crimes on Board Foreign Merchant Ships at Sea: Some Aspects of English Practice' (1972) 88 *Law Quarterly Review* 357.

[133] 31 March 1860; Public Record Office Reference: MT 9/11, file 4126/60.

[134] (1876) LR 2 Ex D 63. See also the unreported case of *R* v. *Delandro* (1865), discussed by Marston at (1972) 88 *Law Quarterly Review*, 374.

[135] Namely, waters that lie within the borders of littoral counties, and thus form a part of the realm.

within territorial waters was accordingly denied. Of the seven judges who formed the majority in *Keyn*, only Cockburn CJ referred to section 521,[136] and he appears to have attached no significance to it, clearly assuming that it could not be intended to apply to things done aboard foreign ships. None of the six minority judges in *Keyn* mentioned that section at all, which is surprising, because it would seem to have offered at least some support for their view that a foreigner *could* be liable for an offence committed on a foreign ship off the English coast.

The ruling in *Keyn* seems to have deprived section 521 of any significance it might otherwise have enjoyed. Clearly, none of the judges in that case considered that section 521 extended the ambit of the law itself. Had they done so, they would necessarily have decided the case in favour of the Crown. As for jurisdiction in respect of offences committed aboard British ships, this was already covered by section 21 of the Merchant Shipping Amendment Act 1855 and by section 11 of the Merchant Shipping Act 1867 (the ancestors of section 281 of the 1995 Act) so this would not have been important.

The Territorial Waters Jurisdiction Act 1878 largely abrogated the ruling in *Keyn*; but in respect of the criminal law its application was expressly limited to indictable offences, defined in section 7 of the Act as acts, neglects, or defaults which would be indictable offences if committed within the body of a county in England. Such offences were deemed to be punishable 'within the jurisdiction of the Admiral' if committed within the territorial limits, and were therefore triable by any court exercising that jurisdiction, without the need for any further venue provision, such as section 521.

Irrelevant or not, section 521 was re-enacted as section 685 of the 1894 Act, where its career continued in total obscurity. Not once in the 100 years of that Act's existence was it the basis of a reported judicial decision. Its existence was ignored in the Law Commission's 1978 Report on the *Territorial and Extraterritorial Extent of the Criminal Law* in which sections 686 and 687 were discussed at length; and it was merely paraphrased, without explanation, in successive editions of *Archbold* and *Halsbury's Laws*. Glanville Williams[137] argued that section 685 could only be a venue section dealing with things done aboard British ships, because it was too vague as to its geographical extent to have any wider meaning, or to have any application to foreign ships. None of this prevented it from being re-enacted with minimal changes as section 280 of the 1995 Act, where it has remained, unused by the courts and unexplained by the few reference works which mention it at all. The probability is that it was re-enacted without any thought being given as to its meaning or relevance.

Could a use for section 280 now be found? There is one possible interpretation that might enable it to fulfil a useful purpose. This would involve

---

[136] (1876) LR 2 Ex D 63, 212.
[137] 'Venue and the Ambit of Criminal Law' (1965) 81 *Law Quarterly Review* 276, 410.

a return to the interpretation favoured by the Law Officers in 1860. Given that any summary offences committed in territorial waters will ordinarily be committed aboard vessels of some kind, and given that such offences are not triable under any other general provision, unless committed aboard a 'United Kingdom ship', such an interpretation would make some sense, and might save section 280 from its current obscurity.

STRUCTURES IN COASTAL WATERS

Prior to the development of the offshore oil and gas industry, with its drilling rigs, pipelines, and associated installations, the only offshore structures that raised potential issues as to the ambit of English criminal law were a small number of manned lighthouses, such as the Eddystone light, which stands on a low-tide elevation 14 miles from Plymouth; a handful of submarine mineral workings (mostly coal mines), some of which once extended beyond the old three-mile limit; and a few former military fortifications, notably a chain of prefabricated anti-aircraft platforms sunk onto the seabed off the Kent and Essex coasts during the Second World War. Moored lightships also raised possible jurisdiction issues, because their status as 'British ships' was not entirely clear.

Little was done to address any of the potential difficulties that might have arisen in respect of things done on or within such structures. Section 219 of the Merchant Shipping Act 1995 penalizes acts of damage to or interference with lighthouses, lightships, buoys, or beacons, but does not specifically address the status of any such navigational aids as might be sited beyond territorial limits. Applying normal principles of statutory interpretation, this means that acts committed against such navigational aids cannot ordinarily amount to offences under English law, unless committed by seamen from United Kingdom ships.[138]

The Law Commission's 1978 Report gave detailed consideration to the status of lighthouses and submarine tunnels, and proposed legislation to bring these within the ambit of English criminal jurisdiction, even in respect of purely summary offences,[139] but these proposals were never implemented,

---

[138] Merchant Shipping Act 1995, s. 282.

[139] Law Com. No. 91, paras 48–53. The Commission proposed the enactment of legislation to ensure that criminal jurisdiction could be exercised 'for offences committed outside the seaward limits of territorial waters. . . . in a submarine tunnel accessible only from land in England or Wales' (Draft Criminal Jurisdiction Bill, cl. 1(2)). Jurisdiction within mine workings lying beneath the territorial sea would not have been problematic under the Law Commission's proposals, because draft cl. 1(1) would have applied to offences committed 'on, under or above any land or water' within those limits. The extension of the territorial limit to 12 nautical miles in 1987 ensured that all surviving submarine mine workings lay entirely within the seaward limits; and none of these now remain in use.

and since the gradual automation of offshore lighthouses[140] (and the replacement of lightships with unmanned beacons) coincided with the decline of the coal industry and the closure of most of the pits involved, the issues involved were never likely to attract much Government interest.

While tunnels and lighthouses caused no problems in practice, the former offshore fortifications gave rise to some colourful and well-publicized legal problems. The story of Red Sands Tower, and of Estuary Radio Ltd, which operated from it, was examined earlier in this chapter (see pp. 81–2); but the story of Roughs Tower is in many ways the most colourful of all.

Roughs Tower, or the 'Principality of Sealand'

The 'Principality of Sealand', otherwise known as Roughs Tower, stands in shallow waters six miles east of Harwich, and was originally part of a chain of prefabricated anti-aircraft forts sited off the Kent and Essex coastlines during the Second World War. Red Sands Tower, of *Estuary Radio* fame, was a similar structure.[141] In 1967 the abandoned platform was taken over by a former British army officer, Roy Bates, who purported to establish an independent mini-state there. International recognition was never likely, but since the platform lay well outside the three-mile territorial limit then in force, there was no obvious basis on which English courts could regulate what was done upon it. In 1967 a half-hearted attempt was allegedly made to evict Bates and his family. This apparently led to shots being fired from the platform, and Bates was subsequently indicted on firearms charges at Essex Assizes.[142] Chapman J, however, ruled that the relevant firearms legislation[143] was 'clearly an Act intended to operate only within the ordinary territorial limits and on British ships'. Roughs Tower was not a British ship. Accordingly, no offence had been committed under English law.

Sealand almost inevitably become a lawless place. In 1978, for example, Bates and his supporters successfully launched an armed helicopter-borne assault on a group of German entrepreneurs who had seized it from them. The United Kingdom Government refused to become involved, even when a German citizen was held prisoner on the platform.[144]

Everything changed, from a legal standpoint, when the Territorial Sea Act 1987 came into force and enlarged the United Kingdom's territorial sea to a breadth of 12 miles. Although Bates attempted to parry this development

---

[140] The Eddystone light was automated in 1982. The last manned lighthouse was automated in 1987.

[141] Another of these platforms, 'Knock John', was also used as the base for a pirate radio transmitter.

[142] See *The Times*, 22 October 1968 and 8 August 2000. The Crown's case at the time, however, was that Bates had fired at Trinity House personnel working on navigation buoys nearby. [143] The Firearms Act 1937 (since repealed).

[144] See *The Guardian*, 5 September 1978. See also *Code*, issue 1 (2001), 44.

by proclaiming Sealand's own territorial waters the day before, this claim has gone unrecognized. The Home Office and the Hydrographic Office each insist that Sealand now falls squarely within English jurisdiction. According to the Home Office:

The United Kingdom does not recognise Sealand as an independent state and is not aware that anyone else does. It is sited within UK territorial waters and we would expect anyone resident on it to comply with all UK legislation, just like anyone else.[145]

Until recently, it appears that the authorities have been content to leave Bates and his principality alone. This may change, however, as a result of plans to lease the structure to an Anguilla-based (but American-managed) company, HavenCo Ltd, which would operate an extraterritorial 'data haven' there. The problem, from the United Kingdom's viewpoint, is that the proposal threatens to evade controls over e-commerce that would otherwise be imposed under the Regulation of Investigatory Powers Act 2000. Under section 12(1) of the Act, the Secretary of State may by Order impose on communications service providers 'such obligations as it appears to him reasonable to impose for the purpose of securing that it is and remains practicable for requirements to provide assistance in relation to interception warrants to be imposed and complied with'.

Should any real attempt be made to enforce English jurisdiction over Sealand, a certificate issued by the Secretary of State under section 1(3) of the Territorial Sea Act 1987 would be conclusive as to the location of the territorial sea baseline around the Essex coast. The Act does not authorize the Secretary of State to certify that a given location falls within the outer limits of territorial waters, but it is clear from section 1(1) and (2) that the outer limits of territorial waters may only vary from their standard 12-mile extent where an Order in Council so provides (as is the case in respect of the Straits of Dover). It is therefore difficult to see how the owners or tenants of Sealand could ever succeed in disputing British sovereignty over that platform.

Oil and Gas Installations

Oil or gas platforms situated within territorial waters give rise to no special jurisdictional issues, save in respect of summary offences, but since most such platforms are sited outside those limits, on the United Kingdom's continental shelf, the creation of a special statutory regime was found to be

---

[145] Quoted in *Code* (fn 144 above), 46. With respect, since Sealand lies within territorial waters, and not within the realm, it would appear that magistrates' courts would not ordinarily be able to try summary offences committed there, unless such offences were specifically made applicable in territorial waters, as was the case, e.g., under s. 6 of the Wireless Telegraphy Act 1949.

necessary. This regime is examined, along with other forms of extra-territorial maritime jurisdiction, at p. 299 below.

THE CHANNEL TUNNEL SYSTEM

The construction of the Channel Tunnel raised jurisdiction issues that were too obvious and serious to be ignored. Not only did the construction of the tunnel link create the first ever 'dry' border between England and France, but the operation of rapid and frequent international train services (including some non-stop services from Belgium) created frontier control and jurisdiction issues that were new to the United Kingdom. Extensive and detailed primary and secondary legislation has been enacted, in accordance with the relevant treaties and protocols, under which extraterritorial frontier control zones have been set up, enabling British immigration officers stationed in Calais, Lille, Paris, and Brussels (and aboard the Eurostar services in France and Belgium) to operate English frontier control laws, backed by English criminal law, on foreign territory. Other provisions address the issue of jurisdiction over crimes committed aboard or against the trains themselves.[146]

The Channel Tunnel Act 1987

The extent of UK territory and the ambit of English criminal law within the Channel Tunnel system are governed by the Channel Tunnel Act 1987 and various Orders made thereunder. Section 10 of the Act makes basic provision as to the legal status of the tunnel system. Under section 10(1):

The land comprising the tunnel system as far as the [French] frontier, so far as not forming part of the United Kingdom before the passing of this Act, shall ... be incorporated into England and form part of the district of Dover in the county of Kent, and the law of England shall apply accordingly.

The policing of the tunnel system within England is primarily the responsibility of the Kent force, aided if necessary by constables provided by the Strategic Rail Authority.[147] Section 10 of the Act still contains elaborate provisions which dealt with the status of the tunnel system during the course of its construction. Although still nominally in force, these are now of merely historic interest. They ensured that prior to the joining of the English and French halves of the tunnel, English law would apply to workings extending

---

[146] Events have shown that the biggest security risks to the UK, and to the Tunnel system itself, are posed by the international freight services. Large numbers of illegal migrants have been able to breach security controls on the continental side of the Tunnel. Freight services have repeatedly been boarded by illegal migrants, either in distant freight yards as far afield as Italy, or in the yards adjacent to the French entrance to the Tunnel itself. New security measures were introduced at the end of 2002, and these appear to have greatly reduced (but not eliminated) the problem.   [147] Channel Tunnel Act 1987, s. 14.

from the English side, even if these were to reach more than halfway across, but not, in the converse situation, to any workings extending more than halfway across from the French side.[148]

Orders under the Act

While the Channel Tunnel Act lays down the basic territorial boundaries within the tunnel itself, the jurisdictional regime within the tunnel system (or 'Fixed Link' as it is referred to in the relevant treaties and protocols) is augmented by the Channel Tunnel (International Arrangements) Order 1993, and the Channel Tunnel (Miscellaneous Provisions) Order 1994.[149] The first of these Orders (as amended)[150] gives effect to the Sangatte Protocol Concerning Frontier Controls and Policing, Cooperation in Criminal Justice, Public Safety and Mutual Assistance, which was entered into by the Governments of the United Kingdom and France in November 1991 and supplemented by an Additional Protocol on the Establishment of Bureaux Responsible for Controls on Persons Travelling by Train between France and the United Kingdom, which was signed at Brussels in May 2000.

The second Order, which deals with issues raised by through workings to Brussels, gives effect to a 'Tripartite Agreement' between the United Kingdom, France, and Belgium, which came into force on 1 December 1997.

Frontier Control Zones

The 1993 and 1994 Orders authorize British, French, and (in respect of through workings to Belgium) Belgian frontier control officers to operate in specified 'control zones' and 'supplementary control zones' (including the trains themselves) within each other's territory. Within these zones, they may exercise what are in effect extraterritorial powers of enforcement and even arrest under their respective frontier control laws.[151] Article 5 of the 1993 Order (as amended) gives offences under British frontier and immigration control enactments the necessary extraterritorial effect. Paragraphs (1) (2) provide:

(1) Any act or omission which—
  (a) takes place outside the United Kingdom in a control zone, and

---

[148] That part of the Channel Tunnel lying beneath the ordinary borders of the county of Kent would have fallen within English jurisdiction without the need for any special legislation, but the status of the undersea part would otherwise have been open to doubt. Nothing in the Territorial Waters Jurisdiction Act 1878 could be construed as extending to tunnels beneath the sea, nor, in any case, does that Act extend to purely summary offences.

[149] SI 1994 No. 1405.

[150] SI 1993 No. 1813. There have been numerous amendments to this original Order.

[151] 'Frontier controls' are defined in Sch. 1 to the 1993 Order as 'controls in relation to persons or goods, police, immigration, customs, health, veterinary and phytosanitary, and transport and road traffic controls'.

(b) would, if taking place in England, constitute an offence under a frontier control enactment,[152]
or any act or omission which—
(c) takes place outside the United Kingdom in a supplementary control zone, and
(d) would, if taking place in England, constitute an offence under an immigration control enactment,
shall be treated for the purposes of that enactment as taking place in England.
(1A) Summary proceedings for anything that is by virtue of paragraph (1) an offence triable summarily or triable either way may be taken, and the offence may for all incidental purposes be treated as having been committed, in the county of Kent or in the inner London area as defined in section 2(1)(a) of the Justices of the Peace Act 1979.
(2) Any jurisdiction conferred by virtue of paragraphs (1) and (1A) on any court is without prejudice to any jurisdiction exercisable apart from this Article by that or any other court.

By Article 5 of the 1994 Order, made in accordance with the Tripartite Agreement, broadly similar provisions govern through traffic to and from Belgium.

Offences Committed within the Channel Tunnel System

While the basic rule is that jurisdiction over offences committed within the tunnel system belongs to the state within whose territory they are committed, it is also recognized that difficulties may arise in proving the territorial locus of a crime, particularly where it is committed aboard a fast-moving train. The Sangatte and Tripartite Agreements each therefore make special provision for such cases. Article 38 of the Sangatte Protocol, which is incorporated into English law by Article 3 of the 1993 Order, makes the following provision as regards jurisdiction over offences committed within the tunnel system:

(1) Without prejudice to the provisions of Articles 11 and 30(2),[153] when an offence is committed in the territory of one of the two States, including that lying within the Fixed Link up to its frontier, that State shall have jurisdiction.
(2)(a) Within the Fixed Link, each State shall have jurisdiction and shall apply its own law:
(i) when it cannot be ascertained with certainty where an offence has been committed; or
(ii) when an offence committed in the territory of one State is related to an offence committed on the territory of the other State; or
(iii) when an offence has begun in or has been continued into its own territory;
(b) however, the State which first receives the person suspected of having committed such an offence (in this Article referred to as 'the receiving State') shall have priority in exercising jurisdiction.

---

[152] Defined as, 'an Act or an instrument made under an Act, for the time being in force, which contains provision relating to frontier controls'.
[153] These deal with control zones and with the status of officers working in adjoining states.

(3) When the receiving State decides not to exercise its priority jurisdiction under paragraph (2) of this Article it shall inform the other State without delay. If the latter decides not to exercise its jurisdiction, the receiving State shall be obliged to exercise its jurisdiction in accordance with its own national law.[154]

This is supplemented by Article 5(3) of the 1993 Order, which provides:

Where it is proposed to institute proceedings in respect of an alleged offence in any court and a question as to the court's jurisdiction arises under Article 38(2)(a) of the International Articles, it shall be presumed, unless the contrary is proved, that the court has jurisdiction by virtue of that Article.

In respect of Anglo-Belgian services, Article 11 of the Tripartite Articles, which form Schedule 2 to the 1994 Order, provides:

(1) Without prejudice to the provisions of Articles 4 and 14(2) of the Protocol attached as an annex to this Agreement, when an offence is committed on the territory of one of the three States that State shall have jurisdiction.
(2) When it cannot be ascertained where such an offence has been committed, the State of arrival shall have jurisdiction.

Article 5(4) of the 1994 Order makes similar provision to Article 5(3) of the 1993 Order as to the jurisdiction of an English court in such cases.

The above provisions now govern the jurisdictional ambit of a number of specific 'Channel Tunnel' offences (notably hijacking and sabotage offences under the Channel Tunnel (Security) Order 1994), as well as the ambit within the tunnel system of offences under the general body of English criminal law. Where, for example, it is clear that the alleged offence was not committed within the English sector of the tunnel, no jurisdiction may be asserted in England under the 1994 Security Order, save where the alleged offender was a British Officer who was at the time subject to Article 30 of the International Articles.[155]

DIPLOMATIC AND CONSULAR PREMISES

Foreign embassies, High Commissions, and other diplomatic premises (including the private residences of diplomatic agents) are inviolable, and may not be entered by the police or by any other agents of the United Kingdom Government except with the consent of the ambassador or head of

---

[154] Article 30 provides that officers of the adjoining State may not be prosecuted by authorities of the host State for any acts performed in the control zone or within the Fixed Link whilst in the exercise of their functions. In such a case, they shall come under the jurisdiction of the adjoining State, as if the act had been committed in that State.

[155] Channel Tunnel (Security) Order 1994, Art. 3. As previously noted, cases involving similar uncertainties may occur aboard Anglo-Scottish trains or in Anglo-Scottish border areas, but no such provision has been enacted to deal with such cases.

the mission.[156] Consular premises (or such parts of those premises as are used exclusively for the purpose of the work of the consular post) enjoy similar status.[157]

None of this alters the fact that diplomatic or consular premises sited on land in England and Wales are part of the territory of England and Wales. The concept of 'exterritoriality', under which diplomatic premises are deemed to be part of the sovereign territory of the sending state, is not one that has ever been adopted under English law, and it was expressly rejected by Cumming-Bruce J in *Radwan* v. *Radwan*.[158] The issue that arose in this case was whether the Consulate-General of the United Arab Republic in London was a part of the territory of that state, so that a *talaq* divorce obtained within those premises fell to be recognized under English law as a divorce obtained in a country outside the British Isles. The Egyptian Deputy Consul General asserted in evidence that the Consulate in London was indeed regarded as Egyptian territory on Egyptian soil; but after hearing argument from the Queen's proctor and having consulted extensively from works on public international law, Cumming-Bruce J concluded that this assertion had no basis in state practice and was almost universally rejected by jurists. He preferred the theory of 'functional necessity', under which the privilege of immunity is granted by the receiving state merely because this is necessary to enable the mission to carry out its functions. He also noted that no theory of exterritoriality is mentioned in either of the Vienna Conventions on diplomatic and consular relations. After quoting the relevant Articles, he concluded:

What is significant about those Articles is not so much what they say as what they do not say. If it was the view of the high contracting parties that the premises of missions were part of the territory of the sending state, that would undoubtedly be formulated and it would have been quite unnecessary to set out the immunities in the way in which it has been done.[159]

As far as the criminal law is concerned, the rejection of the exterritoriality theory is important for several reasons. It means that burglaries, assaults, etc. committed on or within such premises by intruders, or by other persons who have no diplomatic immunity, are triable in England and Wales as offences under the ordinary territorial principles of English law;[160] while summary offences committed therein fall within the local jurisdiction of magistrates' courts for the commission area within which the premises

---

[156] See the Diplomatic Privileges Act 1964, s. 2(1) and Sch. 3. This schedule incorporates the 1961 Vienna Convention on Diplomatic Relations, as to which see especially Arts 22 and 30.

[157] See the Consular Relations Act 1968, s. 1 and Sch. 1. The Schedule incorporates the 1963 Vienna Convention on Consular Relations, as to which see especially Art. 31.

[158] [1972] 3 All ER 967.   [159] Ibid., 975.

[160] See, e.g., *R* v. *Nejad* (1981) unreported, Central Criminal Court, in which it was not disputed that acts committed by terrorists who seized the Iranian embassy in London were justiciable as offences under English law.

are situated.[161] It also means that diplomats who commit such acts within the premises are guilty of offences under English law, for which they may be tried and punished if (but only if) their immunity is waived by their own governments.[162] Lastly, it means that acts done within British diplomatic or consular premises abroad cannot be regarded as 'quasi territorial' offences under English law.[163]

Premises of International Organizations

By the International Organizations Acts 1968 and 1981, and Orders made thereunder, designated international organizations, of which the United Kingdom and at least one other state are members, may 'to such extent as may be specified in the Order' be accorded privileges and immunities derived from those accorded under the 1961 Vienna Convention. Inviolability of premises may be awarded on that basis. The International Maritime Organization, for example, is entitled to 'the like inviolability of official archives and premises as, in accordance with the 1961 Convention Articles, is accorded in respect of the official archives and premises of a diplomatic mission'.[164] Other international organizations that benefit from such immunity include the United Nations and the International Court of Justice.[165]

JURISDICTION OVER AIRSPACE

There may still be some room for doubt as to the precise circumstances or basis under which persons aboard aircraft, airships, gliders, or balloons overflying the United Kingdom and/or its adjoining waters fall within the ambit of English criminal jurisdiction. At common law, the concept of territory has always included the airspace above it,[166] and acts done aboard

---

[161] This is particularly relevant to cases involving alleged summary offences under s. 9 of the Criminal Law Act 1977 (trespassing on premises of foreign missions, etc.).

[162] Diplomatic Privileges Act 1964, Sch. 3; Vienna Convention on Diplomatic Relations, Art. 32.

[163] Diplomats or other Crown servants working in such premises are generally subject to a personal form of extraterritorial liability under English law and offences committed against their premises or residences may be punishable as terrorist offences or as offences under the Internationally Protected Persons Act 1978 (see below, p. 262).

[164] International Maritime Organization (Immunities and Privileges) Order 2002.

[165] See above, p. 18.

[166] Territorial rights were historically said to extend *usque ad coelum et ad inferos* (up to the heavens and down to the depths) but cannot include outer space (see the 1967 Treaty on the Principles Governing the Activities of States in the Exploration and Use of Outer Space (Cmnd. 3519)). The exact point at which airspace ends and outer space begins has never been defined. One plausible suggestion is that outer space begins at the lowest possible perigee of an orbiting satellite. See McMahon, J., 'Legal Aspects of Outer Space' (1962) 38 *British Yearbook of International Law* 339.

aircraft in the skies above England and Wales must therefore be equated with acts done on the land. Even a summary offence would on that basis be triable within the commission area above which it was committed, assuming that this area could be identified.[167]

Acts committed in aircraft overflying territorial or internal waters are more problematic. The United Kingdom undoubtedly has sovereign rights over such airspace. This is recognized in Articles 1–2 of the 1944 Chicago Convention on Civil Aviation,[168] which almost certainly represent customary international law in that respect. Parliament has indeed applied customs and air navigation regulations to aircraft overflying the territorial sea,[169] but it does not follow that this must automatically be accompanied by an extension of the ambit of the ordinary criminal offences. As the *Franconia* case[170] demonstrates, the courts must look for evidence that Parliament has taken advantage of what international law permits. Lush J said in that case 'International law . . . . cannot enlarge the area of our municipal law, nor could treaties with all the nations of the world have that effect. That could only be done by Act of Parliament.'[171]

The problem is that Parliament has never expressly proclaimed the general application of English criminal law over any part of its maritime airspace. No such provision was made by the Territorial Waters Jurisdiction Act 1878 or by the Territorial Sea Act 1987, nor can those statutes be construed as applying to airspace by mere implication. Section 106 of the Civil Aviation Act 1982 appears at first sight to fill this gap. It provides:

(1) Except where the context otherwise requires, in any provision of this Act to which this section applies a reference to a country or territory or to the territorial limits of any country shall be construed as including a reference to the territorial waters of the country or territory, as the case may be; and a reference to a part of the United Kingdom shall be construed as including a reference to so much of the territorial waters of the United Kingdom as are adjacent to that part.

(2) This section applies to Parts III and IV of this Act, except sections 64 to 71 and 84.

Section 92 of the Act is the provision dealing with criminal offences aboard aircraft. This lies within Part IV of the Act, and is thus subject to section 106(1); but nowhere in section 92 (nor anywhere else in the Act) is it provided that English criminal law applies to offences committed above England and Wales. What section 92 provides is that United Kingdom (including

---

[167] The Magistrates' Courts Act 1980, s. 3(3), might assist in securing jurisdiction within a particular commission area, but only if an aircraft can be equated with a 'vehicle or vessel'.

[168] UKTS 8 (1953); Cmnd. 8742.

[169] See, e.g., the Air Navigation Order 2000 (SI 2000 No.1562) and the Excise Goods (Sales on Board Ships and Aircraft) Regulations 1999 (SI 1999 No.1565). See also the Civil Aviation Act 1982, s. 81 (dangerous flying over land or water).

[170] *R v. Keyn* (1976) 2 Ex D 63. See above, pp. 94–5.

[171] See also Bin Cheng, 'Crimes Aboard Aircraft' (1959) 12 *Current Legal Problems* 187; Glanville Williams, op. cit., fn 137, 284.

English) criminal law applies to British-controlled aircraft when in flight *elsewhere* than in or over the United Kingdom, and that English criminal law also applies to acts committed aboard a foreign aircraft elsewhere than in or over the United Kingdom, if the next landing of that aircraft is in England and Wales.[172] Nothing in the 1982 Act applies to acts done in aircraft over the United Kingdom itself.[173]

The draftsman evidently assumed that no statutory provision was needed in respect of crimes committed within the airspace above the United Kingdom's territorial limits. This was a correct assumption to make in respect of the skies above the realm itself, but since nothing has been done to apply the criminal law to the United Kingdom's maritime airspace, a 200-mile 'jurisdiction-free zone' may exist around the United Kingdom within which an airline passenger may with impunity commit almost any offence, other than one that endangers the safety of the aircraft.[174] This would be so bizarre and unsatisfactory that the courts will doubtless strive their utmost to avoid such a conclusion. They would probably conclude that English criminal law *must* apply, if only by necessary inference, to conduct anywhere within or above English territorial limits. Sections 92 and 106 may not so provide, but they do appear to assume it, and that may be good enough for the courts.

The Fishery Limits

Fishery Zones and Exclusive Economic Zones

The UNCLOS Convention entitles coastal states to claim an exclusive economic zone (EEZ), which is defined in Articles 55–57 as an area beyond and adjacent to the territorial sea:

... within which the coastal state has sovereign rights for the purpose of exploring and exploiting, conserving and managing the natural resources, whether living or non-living, of the waters superjacent to the sea bed and of the sea bed and subsoil, and with regard to other activities for the economic exploitation and exploration of the zone ...[175]

The EEZ must not be confused with the continental shelf (which may be much larger) over which a coastal state has more limited sovereign rights that do not extend to fisheries.[176] Within the EEZ, the rights and jurisdiction

---

[172] Subject, in this case, to certain double-criminality requirements. See below, p. 315. If the foreign aircraft lands in Scotland, the applicable law would be Scots law, but Scots law cannot apply to an act committed in the skies over England, or vice versa.

[173] The same was true of s. 1 of the Tokyo Convention Act 1967, which s. 92 replaced.

[174] Such offences may be punishable under the Aviation Security Act 1982. See below, p. 316.   [175] Article 56(a).

[176] Other than to the harvesting of sedentary species, such as sponges or (arguably) crabs.

of the coastal state, which must be exercised in accordance with the provisions of Part V of the Convention, include the exclusive right to construct or authorize the construction of artificial islands, structures, and installations, and to exercise jurisdiction over them.[177] Under Article 73, the coastal state may,

... in the exercise of its sovereign rights to explore, exploit, conserve and manage the living resources in the exclusive economic zone, take such measures, including boarding, inspection, arrest and judicial proceedings as may be necessary to ensure compliance with the laws and regulations adopted by it in conformity with this Convention.

The United Kingdom does not, however, lay claim to an EEZ as such. It claims, instead, an exclusive fishery zone. The reason for this was summarized by the British Government in a statement to the House of Lords in 1982:

We see no point at present in creating [an EEZ] in order to secure resources. The United Kingdom already has a fishery zone ... and since rights over our continental shelf ... are inherent and do no have to be proclaimed, there would be no advantage to the United Kingdom in declaring such a zone.[178]

British Fishery Limits

By section 1(1) of the Fishery Limits Act 1976, British fishery limits generally extend to a distance of 200 nautical miles, measured from the baselines from which the breadth of the territorial sea adjacent to the United Kingdom, the Channel Islands, and the Isle of Man is measured. Where the proximity of foreign coasts and foreign fishery limits leaves no room for a 200-mile limit to apply, the general rule is that the median line between the British baseline and the corresponding baseline of the other country forms the boundary between the two fishery zones, or between the British fishery zone and any exclusive economic zone (EEZ) claimed by that other country.[179]

In almost all cases, British fishery limits are governed by one or other of these rules. By section 1(3), however, an Order in Council may, 'for the purpose of implementing any international agreement or the arbitral award of an international body, or otherwise, declare that British fishery limits

---

[177] Article 60.

[178] See *Hansard* (HL) vol. 473, col. 46 (7 April 1986). Several other states similarly claim a fishery zone, rather than an EEZ. These claims are invariably recognized by other states, on the basis that they involve nothing that would not be included within an EEZ. In the *Jan Mayen Case (Denmark v. Norway)* [1993] ICJ Rep 38, Vice-President Ota expressed strong reservations as to the practice of maintaining fishery zones instead of EEZs, on the basis that such zones have no standing under UNCLOS, but this was a dissenting judgment.

[179] The median line is defined in s. 1(4) as 'a line every point of which is equidistant from the nearest points of, on the one hand, the baselines referred to in subsection (1) and, on the other hand, the corresponding baselines of other countries'.

extend to such other line as may be specified in the Order'. One such Order is currently in effect, namely the Fishery Limits Order 1999,[180] which delimits the waters between Scotland and the Faeroe Islands, and gives effect to an agreement between the Governments of Denmark and the Home Government of the Faeroe Islands, on the one hand, and the Government of the United Kingdom, on the other, resolving a long-standing dispute over fishery rights in that area. Being adjacent to Scotland, however, the waters affected by this Order do not fall within 'relevant' British fishery limits.

'Relevant' British Fishery Limits

The Scottish Adjacent Waters Boundaries Order 1999,[181] made under section 115 of the Scotland Act 1998, separates the Scottish fishery zone from those waters adjacent to England and Wales or Northern Ireland.[182] The Scottish fishery zone falls almost exclusively within Scottish jurisdiction. The ambit of most English (and Northern Irish) fishery laws is therefore limited to things done within 'relevant' British fishery limits, which are defined as 'British fishery limits so far as they do not relate to the Scottish zone'.[183] As far as English law is concerned, regulations made under the Sea Fish (Conservation) Act 1967, governing the design and construction of fishing nets or other fishing gear, may be applied to Scottish fishing boats, or to boats registered abroad, but only when this gear is carried 'in any waters adjacent to the United Kingdom and within relevant British fishery limits'.[184] Similarly, regulations made under section 5 of the Sea Fisheries Act 1968[185] apply to Scottish or foreign fishing boats (and things done by such boats and their crews) only when they are in waters within 'relevant British fishery limits'.

There are some exceptional provisions under which things done in Scottish waters may still be triable as offences under English law (or vice versa). For example, offences under section 10 of the Sea Fisheries Act 1968

---

[180] SI 1999 No. 1741.   [181] SI 1999 No. 1126.
[182] On the east coast, seven coordinates are used, and 74 on the west coast.
[183] Fishery Limits Act 1976, s. 8, as amended by the Scotland Act 1998.
[184] Sea Fish (Conservation) Act 1967, s. 2(2), as amended by SI 1999 No. 1820. Section 14 of the Act (inserted by the Fisheries Act 1981) provides that proceedings for offences under certain sections of the Act (including s. 2) 'may be taken, and the offence may for all incidental purposes be treated as having been committed, in any place in the United Kingdom'. This cannot, however, apply to acts that are not (by some other provision) declared to be offences in the first place. By s. 22A, an appropriately modified (but effectively quite distinct) version of the Act now applies to Scotland.
[185] These are Orders 'making provision for regulating the conduct of, and safeguarding, fishing operations and operations ancillary thereto, including provision with respect to the identification and marking of fishing boats and fishing gear' (see s. 5(1)).

(involving the obstruction of sea fishery officers, assaults committed on such officers, or failure to comply with requirements made by such officers) are capable of commission anywhere within British fishery limits, and not merely within 'relevant' limits; and such an offence may for all incidental purposes be treated as having been committed in any place in the United Kingdom.[186]

[186] Sea Fisheries Act 1968, s. 14.

4

Cross-frontier Offences

INTRODUCTION

For as long as the territorial principle remains a basis for criminal jurisdiction, the problems raised by cross-frontier (or transnational) offences
must be accommodated within that principle. Can an alleged offence be
said to have been committed within England and Wales if some elements of
that offence take place there, but others take place abroad? Unfortunately,
the complexities of the laws governing the territorial boundaries of England
and Wales are comfortably exceeded by those that may arise where such
offences are involved.

There can be no wholly straightforward solution to the problem of cross-
frontier offences, but the ways in which they are dealt with under English
law leave much to be desired. Cases are routinely decided on technicalities,
rather than on the basis of coherently developed policy considerations, and
the results are often bizarre and unjust. Special statutory rules apply in
some cases, but although most of these rules are of modern origin, and usually designed to give effect to policy considerations, they are often poorly
drafted and highly problematic in their operation. To make matters worse,
they share few common principles or patterns, and their proliferation over
recent years has arguably made the overall picture far more confused than
it was before.

There are two principal ways in which cross-frontier issues may arise in
proceedings under English law. The first is where the Crown seeks to prosecute a defendant for an alleged offence that has both English and foreign territorial elements. Most such cases involve problems of international fraud or
deception; but cases may also arise involving drug trafficking,[1] money laundering,[2] murder,[3] blackmail,[4] Internet pornography,[5] computer hacking,[6]

---

[1] As in *DPP v. Doot* [1973] AC 807.
[2] It is estimated that over US$1 billion stolen by the former Nigerian leader Sani Abacha
was laundered through London banks, but to date no prosecution has ever been brought in
England.   [3] As in *R v. Lewis* (1844) Dears & B 182.
[4] As in *Treacy v. DPP* [1971] AC 537.
[5] As in *R v. Perrin* [2002] All ER (D) 359 (Mar); [2002] EWCA Crim 747.
[6] As in the unreported, but well publicized, cases of Matthew Bevan and Richard Pryce, in
which teenage hackers from Cardiff and London gained access to Pentagon and Lockheed
computers in the USA. See below, p. 185.

and terrorist outrages.[7] Numerous cases involving cross-frontier jurisdiction issues can be found in the law reports, in contrast to the relative paucity of modern case law on purely extraterritorial offences. The extent of the difficulties that may arise in cross-frontier cases is reflected in the fact that a disproportionate number of those cases end up before the House of Lords.

The second way in which such crimes may come before the English courts is in the context of extradition proceedings. The United States may, for example, seek the extradition of a foreign fugitive, now in British custody, on a warrant relating to an alleged offence of international fraud or terrorism. It may be alleged that some part of that offence was (or was intended to be) committed within American territory,[8] even though it may have been instigated or planned abroad. An English court, in determining whether to recognize the American claim to jurisdiction, must ordinarily be satisfied that the alleged offence would have fallen within the ambit of English criminal jurisdiction, had an equivalent element of the offence been committed within England or Wales.[9] Here again, the volume of reported case law provides some indication of the practical importance and complexity of the issues.[10]

The volume of reported cases dealing with cross-frontier offences may also reflect the inadequacy and excessive technicality of the relevant law. Simpler laws might be expected to result in fewer appellate cases, and certainly in fewer cases before the House of Lords. This indeed was one of the objectives behind Part 1 of the Criminal Justice Act 1993, which attempts to simplify the problems caused by cross-frontier fraud, blackmail, and dishonesty offences, by providing a more rational and comprehensive basis for asserting jurisdiction over them. Its recent implementation, after many years of delay,[11] does indeed appear to have resulted in a sudden and dramatic fall in the number of transnational fraud cases coming before the appellate courts, but it remains too early to tell whether this is a mere flash in the pan. As explained later in this chapter, this legislation suffers from certain limitations, and by no means guarantees that English courts will have jurisdiction over all types of cross-frontier fraud offence. Once these

---

[7] *HM Advocate* v. *Abdelbaset Ali Mohmed Al Megrahi* [1999] Scot HC 248, provides an example from Scots law, in which a conspiracy, formed in Libya and put into operation in Malta, brought about the destruction of an American airliner in British airspace, over the Scottish town of Lockerbie. Had the fatal explosion occurred just a few minutes earlier, it would have occurred within English jurisdiction.

[8] This assumes that extradition is being sought on the basis of territoriality. If jurisdiction is claimed on an extraterritorial basis (which is possible) different considerations may apply. See *Re Al-Fawwaz* [2002] 1 All ER 545.

[9] An exception may sometimes apply where the requesting state claims extraterritorial jurisdiction on the basis of the fugitive's nationality (Extradition Act 1989, s. 2).

[10] See e.g., *R* v. *Governor of Pentonville Prison, ex p Osman* [1990] 1 WLR 277 and *Re Al-Fawwaz* [2002] 1 All ER 545.

[11] Part 1 of the Act was brought into force on 1 June 1999.

limitations are better understood by defence lawyers, one may find that the Act will generate a new line of case law.

The Structure of this Chapter

The range and complexity of special regimes and exceptions that apply to different types of cross-frontier crime necessitate the division of this chapter into a series of distinct sections. I will begin by examining the general rule, under which an offence is regarded as being committed in England and Wales if (and only if) it is completed there. This 'terminatory' approach to jurisdiction requires an analysis of the distinction between 'conduct crimes' and 'result crimes', because the moment at which a crime is completed depends on whether any (and if so what) proscribed results must be caused by the accused's conduct.

Having established and explained the general rule governing substantive offences, I will then examine the issues raised by cross-frontier participation in such offences (as where D, in Scotland, procures the commission of an offence by E, in England), and by inchoate offences with cross-frontier elements (as where D and E, in England, conspire to commit a robbery in France). A separate section is devoted to each, because it is necessary to deal in each case both with general rules and with exceptions, many of which are highly complex. Inchoate offences (and conspiracies in particular) are subject to so many special provisions and exceptions that it is sometimes difficult to ascertain where the general rule ends and the exceptions begin.

Some types of cross-frontier offence have proved more common and more troublesome than any other. A fairly brief perusal of the reported case law will show that cases of fraud or dishonesty have reached the appellate courts, in criminal or extradition proceedings, more frequently than all other types of cross-frontier crime combined. Most, but by no means all, offences of fraud, blackmail, or dishonesty are now subject to a relatively new and untried jurisdictional regime, established under the Criminal Justice Act 1993 but brought into operation only in June 1999. This new regime governs both substantive and inchoate offences, but has by no means broken free from the technicalities of the terminatory approach to jurisdiction, and perhaps may prove less effective than most lawyers suppose. A separate section is accordingly devoted to this regime, and to those cases of fraud and dishonesty that fall outside it.

The next section is devoted to 'cybercrime' and other offences involving computer misuse. The rise of such offences is a relatively modern phenomenon, and one that has enormous 'cross-frontier' potential. Crimes involving unauthorized access to computer systems and related forms of computer misuse are subject to a special jurisdictional regime established under the Computer Misuse Act 1990, whilst other offences, such as the distribution of obscene material over the Internet, may be governed (often unsatisfactorily) by the application of general principles.

Lastly, the shortest of these sections addresses two of the longest-established 'special cases', namely homicide and perjury. Section 10 of the Offences Against the Person Act 1861 (which largely re-enacts an earlier provision dating from 1828) lays down rules to govern cross-frontier homicide, in which the victim is struck or wounded in one country, or at sea, but dies in another country, or on land. This has proved to be a much less effective provision than initial reading might reasonably suggest. In contrast, section 1 of the Perjury Act 1911 contains comprehensive provisions to deal with cases of cross-frontier perjury.

Anyone who struggles through this chapter from beginning to end must inevitably be struck by the sheer complexity and inconsistency of much of the law it addresses. One of the principal objects of this work is to suggest a better way of dealing with cross-frontier crimes, but this chapter is quite long enough as it is, and my principal suggestion for reform will therefore be found in Chapter 7.

The General Rule

As explained in Chapter 2 above, the United Kingdom is fully entitled, under the accepted rules of international law, to extend its criminal jurisdiction over any misconduct committed within its own territory, even where such misconduct is directed against victims abroad; and it is equally entitled to extend its criminal jurisdiction to cases involving misconduct abroad (even on the part of foreign nationals) where this misconduct is directed towards, or against victims within, its territory. International lawyers classify such cases as 'subjective' and 'objective' variants of the territorial principle of jurisdiction, and each is universally recognized as a legitimate application of the territorial principle. Indeed, a state may legitimately adopt an 'inclusionary' (or all-inclusive) approach to territorial jurisdiction, incorporating both subjective and objective principles, either of which may be relied upon in any given case.

English criminal law has never embraced a straightforward approach of this kind. The occurrence of subjective or objective elements of a cross-frontier offence within the territory of England and Wales accordingly provides no guarantee that the offence will be regarded as having been 'committed' within English jurisdiction. To put it another way, English law cannot be said to have settled upon either a subjective or an objective (still less an inclusive) approach to territorial jurisdiction. As a result, the ability of the courts to exercise jurisdiction over cross-frontier offences has always been patchy and may in some respects appear quite arbitrary.

This can be demonstrated by considering the cases of *R* v. *Harden*,[12] *R* v. *Manning*,[13] and *Treacy* v. *DPP*.[14] In each of the first two cases, rogues who instigated serious transnational frauds involving conduct committed within England were nevertheless found to have committed no offences under English law. In *Harden*, the appellant, in England, practised a successful deception on a company in Jersey, as a result of which that company drew cheques in his favour and posted them to him. On an indictment alleging the obtaining of valuable securities by false pretences,[15] it was held that the only relevant 'obtaining' had been committed in Jersey, where the cheques were posted. No offence had been committed in England, even though the appellant had received the cheques there.

A similar problem arose in *Manning*, in which the appellant, a marine insurance broker, was held to have committed no offences under section 20(2) of the Theft Act 1968 when, from his office in Essex, he fraudulently induced Greek shipping companies to draw cheques in his favour. Section 20(2) creates an offence of dishonestly procuring the execution of a valuable security by deception. The deception was practised from England, but the cheques were drawn (or executed) in Athens. Under English law, that was where the act of procuring had been committed, outside the reach of English jurisdiction.[16]

Further examples of this sort could be provided,[17] and together they may easily give the impression that English law has adopted an 'objective' approach to territorial jurisdiction. In other cases, however, something resembling a subjective (or even an inclusionary) approach appears to have been adopted. In *Treacy* v. *DPP*, the House of Lords upheld the appellant's conviction for blackmail, even though the blackmail demands, which he posted on the Isle of Wight, were addressed to and received by his victim in Frankfurt. Their Lordships did not have to decide whether the appellant could have been convicted had he posted his demand abroad, addressed to and received by a victim in England, but the prevailing (*obiter*) view was that he could indeed have been.[18]

---

[12] [1963] 1 QB 8.   [13] [1998] 4 All ER 876.   [14] [1971] AC 537.

[15] Contrary to the Larceny Act 1916, s. 32(1) (since repealed).

[16] It is tempting to suppose that the appellants in the above cases must have committed some act that was contrary to English law. Did they not at least begin to commit their crimes in England? If so, why should they not be guilty of committing a criminal attempt? This would again be a perfectly acceptable approach under international law, but ignores the niceties of English law. The general rule is that an attempt cannot be an offence under English law unless the crime attempted would equally have been an offence if completed. See the Criminal Attempts Act 1981, s. 1(4); *R* v. *Governor of Pentonville Prison, ex p Naghdi* [1990] 1 All ER 257.

[17] See *R* v. *Governor of Brixton Prison, ex p Rush* [1969] 1 WLR 165; *R* v. *Governor of Pentonville Prison, ex p Khubchandani* (1980) 71 Cr App R 241.

[18] In cases of fraud or blackmail, such as those discussed above, special rules now apply by virtue of Pt 1 of the Criminal Justice Act 1993; and some jurisdictional lacunae have been filled as a result, but those cases remain valid illustrations of the principles that still govern most cross-frontier jurisdiction issues under English criminal law, and the provisions of the 1993 Act cannot properly be construed or applied unless those principles are first understood.

To international lawyers who are not familiar with English criminal law, the approach taken by the English courts in the above cases may appear to follow no intelligible pattern, but this is the case only if one attempts to analyse those cases in 'subjective territorial' or 'objective territorial' terms. There may be much to be said for the adoption of a relatively simple approach of that kind, but it does not represent, and has never represented, the approach adopted under English law. To make sense of the English cases (or indeed of the jurisdiction provisions now found in the Criminal Justice Act 1993) one must think instead in terms of what Glanville Williams christened the 'terminatory' or 'metaphysical' theory of jurisdiction.[19]

The Terminatory Theory of Jurisdiction

The essence of the terminatory theory is that a crime will be regarded as 'committed' only where it is completed, or where, in other words, its last constituent element takes place. This may seem, at first sight, to be just another name for the objective territorial principle of jurisdiction, but it is not the same thing, as can be seem from a closer examination of *Treacy* v. *DPP*. The appellant's blackmail demand in that case was posted in England and received by his victim in Frankfurt. On the basis of a simple objective territorial approach, one would doubtless conclude that the offence was committed within Germany. The terminatory theory, however, concentrates on the purely legal (or as Williams put it, the metaphysical) question of when and where the offence of blackmail was 'completed'. Was the receipt and successful communication of the blackmail demand an essential element of the offence? If so, was any further consequence required?

The *actus reus* of blackmail, as defined by section 21 of the Theft Act 1968, is complete upon the 'making' of an unwarranted demand with menaces. It does not require that the victim should be coerced into acceding to the demand. The view of the Criminal Law Revision Committee, on whose recommendations section 21 was based, was that the evil lay in the making of the blackmail demand, and not merely in the obtaining of any actual profit or advantage from such behaviour.[20] Parliament thus intended that the maker of such a demand should be liable to conviction for the full offence, even if his intent to gain or cause loss should be utterly frustrated.

This does not, however, answer the question of when exactly such a demand is 'made'. Williams had argued that a demand could not be made until it had been communicated,[21] and this was also the view of Lords Reid and Morris, who dissented in *Treacy*; but the majority view of the House

---

[19] 'Venue and the Ambit of Criminal Law' (part 3) (1965) 81 *Law Quarterly Review* 276, 518.
[20] Eighth Report, *Theft and Related Offences* (Cmnd. 2977), para. 117. This had also been the position under the Larceny Act 1916, s. 29.   [21] See op. cit., fn 19, 521.

of Lords (and of the Court of Appeal before them) was that the blackmail demand was made at the moment when the appellant posted his letter on the Isle of Wight. The offence was thus complete even before the victim became aware of it. On that basis, the offence was completed entirely within England, and the fact that the victim received the demand outside the jurisdiction, in Frankfurt, was irrelevant. As John Stephenson J explained when delivering the Court of Appeal's judgment in the same case:

We are willing to assume that the last constituent element does determine the place where the offence is committed. Where then is the offence of making a demand completed? The demand is not made when the threatening letter is written, because it may never be sent . . . but once the letter is posted, the demand is completed and the offence of blackmail is committed.[22]

Assume, however, that the appellant had instead sent his victim a letter containing a false representation of some kind, in the hope of tricking her into paying him a similar sum of money. Had he then been prosecuted on a charge of obtaining property by deception, contrary to section 15 of the Theft Act 1968, there could have been no question of that offence being complete on the posting of the letter, nor even on its arrival in the post at the victim's house in Frankfurt. It would have been necessary for the victim to read the letter and be deceived by it; but even that would not be enough: the offence would have been complete only when, as a result of that successful deception, the appellant finally obtained some or all of the money requested.

Applying the terminatory theory of jurisdiction, the court would then have had to ask *where* that obtaining took place. If the money had been obtained in England, the appellant could then have been convicted of an offence under English law; but no such offence would have been convicted if the money had been handed to him or his agent (or otherwise obtained) in West Germany or in some third country.

Applying this same logic to a hypothetical extradition request from Germany, a German claim to jurisdiction would have been recognized had the money, etc., been obtained in Germany, but if payment had been made and received in England or in a third country, such as Belgium, German jurisdiction over the crime would not have been recognized in an English court, and the extradition request would accordingly have been rejected.[23]

Criticism of the Terminatory Theory

Professor Williams by no means approved of the terminatory theory as a method of resolving cross-frontier jurisdictional issues. He was strongly of

---

[22] [1971] AC 537, 543.

[23] Part 1 of the Criminal Justice Act 1993 was intended to eliminate such complications, but it does not entirely succeed in so doing, as we shall see.

the opinion that a subjective or 'initiatory' approach to questions of territorial jurisdiction offered a better (and also a simpler) solution to the problem of transnational crimes. He advanced the terminatory theory in order to explain the practice of the courts when deciding such cases, but at the same time condemned it as based on 'spurious pseudo-logic':

It would be logical to assert that a crime is fully consummated when and only when the last necessary element takes place, because a denial of this proposition would involve a self-contradiction. But the time of consummation is not necessarily the same as the time of commission. The word 'commission' naturally refers to the defendant's physical act, in contradistinction to the term 'consummation' which refers to all the elements of the crime including the consequences of acts.

Take a case in which D shoots P, who dies in an ambulance on the way to hospital. Clearly, D does not become guilty of murder until P dies, but this logic should not require us to conclude that P was actually murdered in the ambulance. Such a conclusion would indeed be absurd; but absurd or not, the terminatory theory undoubtedly points to that conclusion. In the context of cross-frontier jurisdiction, a problem might arise if P were to be shot or stabbed by D in Scotland and later transferred to a specialist medical facility in London, where he died. Common sense recoils from the conclusion that P was murdered in London, but it would be interesting to see how, if at all, the courts could escape from the logic of the terminatory theory.[24]

Although Williams's theory is frequently cited in cross-frontier jurisdiction cases, it is relatively unusual for the judges to rely expressly upon it when reaching their decisions, although John Stephenson J's judgment in *Treacy* and Buxton LJ's more recent judgment in *R v. Manning*[25] provide examples of such reliance. In *DPP v. Stonehouse*,[26] Lord Salmon gratuitously dismissed Williams's analysis, saying:

I would only add on this part of the case that although I am aware that distinguished academic writers have placed some importance on what they describe as the 'terminatory theory' and the 'initiatory theory' of jurisdiction, I doubt whether these esoteric classifications are of any practical utility in deciding the present or any other case.

In contrast, the Law Lords have more frequently made use of ostensibly different terminology that is ultimately based on exactly the same underlying theory. This terminology involves the twin concepts of 'conduct crimes' and 'result crimes'.

---

[24] The answer to this problem cannot be found in s. 10 of the Offences Against the Person Act 1861: see *R v. Lewis* (1844) Dears & B 182 and below, p. 199. The US Code, Title 18, s. 3236, provides: 'In all cases of murder or manslaughter, the offence shall be deemed to have been committed at the place where the injury was inflicted, or the poison administered or other means employed which caused the death, without regard to the place where the death occurs'. See also the Army Act 1955, s. 70(5).   [25] [1998] 4 All ER 876.
[26] [1978] AC 55, 78.

Conduct Crimes and Result Crimes

The idea of dividing criminal offences into conduct crimes and result crimes appears to have originated in the first edition of Sir Gerald Gordon's *Criminal Law of Scotland*,[27] and made its first English appearance in Lord Diplock's speech in *Treacy* v. *DPP*. Conduct crimes may be defined as those in which proscribed behaviour on the part of the accused may in itself amount to the full offence, regardless of any consequences that may (or may not) follow from this conduct. A simple example may be found in section 4 of Vagrancy Act 1824. This creates an offence of indecent exposure 'with intent to insult a female', but does not require that any female should either see the indecent conduct or feel insulted by it. It accordingly creates a pure conduct crime, in contrast to the superficially similar offence created by section 28 of the Town Police Clauses Act 1847, under which the prosecution must prove that the accused's conduct caused passers-by to be 'annoyed, obstructed or endangered'. The latter offence is, of course, a result crime. Blackmail, as construed by the majority in *Treacy*, must also be a conduct crime, completed (and thus committed) by the act of posting the blackmail demand, although the dissenting Law Lords in that case evidently saw it as a result crime, in so far as they considered it necessary for the demand to be read and understood by the victim before they would regard it as having been 'made'.

Gordon's dichotomy provides a useful method of explaining the diverse *actus reus* elements required by different offences. The House of Lords has adopted it on several occasions, not just in the context of jurisdiction cases, but also in cases where they have sought to emphasize the need for proof of causation, or the absence of any such need.[28] By definition, causation issues cannot arise in the context of conduct crimes.

It is in the context of cross-frontier offences, however, that the dichotomy has been most widely employed, notably (but not exclusively) by Lord Diplock. Lord Diplock was the only member of the Appellate Committee to use it in *Treacy*, and even he did not make it a central part of his reasoning in that case, but since then it has figured more prominently in a series of cross-frontier cases, including *DPP* v. *Stonehouse*,[29] *Secretary of State for Trade* v. *Markus*,[30] and *R* v. *Berry*.[31] The precise terminology used is of marginal significance, however. Whether it is expressed in terms of conduct and result, last essential element, or even 'gist or kernel of the offence',[32] the courts invariably look for the concluding act or event that turns a mere act of preparation or attempt into the full substantive offence. The conduct crime/result crime dichotomy is arguably the most revealing way of analysing

---

[27] First published in 1967.

[28] See, e.g., Lord Hailsham's speech in *R* v. *Howe and Bannister* [1987] 1 AC 417 and Lord Diplock's speech in *R* v. *Miller* [1983] 2 AC 161.   [29] [1978] AC 55.

[30] [1976] AC 35.   [31] [1985] AC 246.   [32] As in *R* v. *Ellis* [1899] 1 QB 230.

that approach, but there is no real conflict between this and the terminatory theory of Glanville Williams. In either case, the courts consider an offence to be committed where it is completed.

Conduct Crimes

Crimes of unlawful possession are typical conduct crimes. In order to amount to a given offence, the possession in question may have to be accompanied by some kind of knowledge or ulterior intent, but no consequence or result need be caused by that possession. Section 16 of the Firearms Act 1968, for example, provides:

It is an offence for a person to have in his possession any firearm or ammunition with intent by means thereof to endanger life or cause serious injury to property, or to enable another person by means thereof to endanger life or cause serious injury to property, whether any injury to person or property has been caused or not.

In *R v. El-Hakkaoui*,[33] H appealed against his conviction for conspiracy to commit such an offence, on the basis that the weapon in question, although seized from the conspirators in England, was intended for use in France rather than England. The Court of Appeal held that this was irrelevant. Browne LJ said:

On a literal reading of section 16, there is nothing to limit the intention to endanger life or cause serious injury to property to endangering or injuring life or property in the United Kingdom. There is no such express limitation, and we can see no reason to imply such a limitation. In our view, there are only two elements which have to be proved to establish an offence under section 16: (a) that the defendant had a firearm in his possession in the United Kingdom and (b) that at the time when he had it in his possession in the United Kingdom he intended by means thereof to endanger life or cause serious injury to property. If these elements are proved, the offence is complete. It is quite irrelevant whether or not the intention was carried out. . . . In our view, the place where the intention would have been carried out, if it had been carried out, is equally irrelevant.[34]

Generally speaking, conduct crimes present few jurisdictional difficulties, if only because the *locus* of the relevant conduct is usually a simple question of fact. Problems of interpretation may arise, however, even in cases involving crimes of possession. In *R v. Berry*,[35] the appellant was convicted of an offence under section 4(1) of the Explosive Substances Act 1883, which provides:

Any person who makes or knowingly has in his possession or under his control any explosive substance, under such circumstances as to give rise to a reasonable suspicion that he is not making it or does not have it in his possession or under his control for a lawful object, shall, unless he can show that he made it or had it in his possession or under his control for a lawful object, be guilty [of an offence] . . .

---

[33] [1975] 1 WLR 396.   [34] Ibid., 400.   [35] [1985] AC 246.

The appellant designed and exported electrical appliances to Middle East countries, including Syria and Lebanon. He designed and built electronic bomb timers for export to that region, for use in terrorist activities. There was no question but that this would have been an offence under section 4 had the bombs been intended for terrorist use in England and Wales, but the defence argued that the position was different in so far as the devices were intended for export, because causing explosions, etc., or even murder, within a foreign country is not ordinarily an offence under English law.[36] The Court of Appeal agreed and quashed his conviction, *El-Hakkaoui* being distinguished on the basis that section 16 of the Firearms Act merely required an intent to endanger life, whereas the present offence required a purpose that was 'unlawful'. The conviction was restored by the House of Lords. Lord Roskill, with whose speech the other members of the Appellate Committee agreed, said:

This offence is a 'conduct crime' not a 'result crime', . . . the guilty conduct was shown by proof of the making of what was beyond peradventure an explosive substance within the definition. A guilty state of mind was shown by proof that that making was under such circumstances as to give rise to a reasonable suspicion that that making did not have a lawful object . . .[37]

The difference of opinion between the Court of Appeal and the House of Lords did not turn on whether the offence was a conduct crime (which was not in dispute) but on whether there had to be a purpose, or at least a 'suspected' purpose, that was criminal under English (rather than foreign) law. It was not strictly a jurisdiction question, but a matter of statutory interpretation.

A different type of problem arose in *Lawson v. Fox*.[38] The respondents in this case were charged (*inter alia*) with an offence under section 96 of the Transport Act 1968, which provides: 'Subject to the provisions of this section, a driver shall not on any working day drive a vehicle or vehicles to which this Part of this Act applies for periods amounting in the aggregate to more than ten hours.' The first respondent, F, had driven a heavy goods vehicle on a round trip to France and back, thereby exceeding the permitted 10-hour maximum, but most of those hours had been amassed in France. The question was whether the French hours could be counted when calculating whether his driving on the return leg in England was unlawful. The Divisional Court held that it could not and quashed his (and his employers') convictions, but the convictions were restored by the House of Lords. Lord Diplock said:

The offences are committed by driving *after* having previously driven for ten hours or being on duty *after* having previously been on duty for eleven hours, since the last period of rest of the required duration. They thus fall within that class of offence in

---

[36] The well-known exception created by the Offences Against the Person Act 1861, s. 9, applies only to murders committed by British citizens, etc.   [37] [1985] AC 246, 254.
[38] [1974] AC 803.

which the act which constitutes the offence consists of doing something after having previously done something else which was not itself unlawful. Another example of this class is the offence under section 1 of the Road Safety Act 1967[39] committed by a person who drives a motor vehicle on a road or other public place having consumed alcohol in such a quantity that the proportion thereof in his blood exceeds the prescribed limit. He may consume alcohol to his heart's content; he commits no offence until he starts to drive. . . .

There is a presumption . . . that Parliament, when enacting a penal statute, unless it uses plain words to the contrary, did not intend to make it an offence in English law to do acts in places outside the territorial jurisdiction of the English courts—at any rate unless the act is one which necessarily has its harmful consequences in England. But . . . it has no application to the offences with which the driver was charged. He was not charged with anything that he did in France. It is conceded that nothing that he did by way of driving or being on duty in the course of his employment in excess of permitted hours while he was in France or on the ferry outside British territorial waters, was unlawful.[40]

Julian Lew[41] has condemned this decision as 'contrary to both legal principle and common sense', but his criticism is surely misguided, because Lord Diplock's logic seems, with respect, to be quite beyond reproach. If Lew's argument were to prevail, drink-driving on English roads would cease to be criminal, provided only that the drinking was done in Scotland or abroad. The absurdity of that position is surely self-evident.

It is easy to suppose that a conduct crime can be committed only where the offender is physically present. In most cases, this will indeed be the case, but there are important exceptions. One such exception involves the concept of a 'continuing act'. Another may involve the concept of 'constructive presence'. The two concepts may indeed be used together. *Treacy v. DPP* arguably provides an example. Lord Hodson in that case addressed (*obiter*) the question whether a blackmail demand initially made abroad might nevertheless continue to be made in England if sent to a victim there:

It has been argued that this view of the construction of the Act gives a blackmailer a charter if he takes the trouble to cross the Channel and post his letter to a recipient in this country. I do not agree, but it is unnecessary to consider such a case which might involve deciding whether a demand made outside the jurisdiction could be treated as a continuous demand subsisting until the addressee received it.[42]

Whilst the issue was merely *obiter* on the facts of *Treacy*, it became central to the prosecution case in *R v. Baxter*.[43] The appellant attempted to defraud two football pool companies in Liverpool by falsely claiming to have sent them winning coupons. He posted his fraudulent claims from Northern

---

[39] See now the Road Traffic Act 1988, s. 5.   [40] [1974] AC 803, 808.
[41] 'The Extraterritorial Criminal Jurisdiction of English Courts' (1978) 27 *International and Comparative Law Quarterly* 168, 177.
[42] [1971] AC 537, 558.   [43] [1972] 1 QB 1.

Ireland, and when convicted in England of attempting to obtain property by deception, he appealed on the basis that although he may have attempted to commit a crime in England, the attempt itself had been completed in Northern Ireland. His appeal was dismissed. Delivering the judgment of the Court of Appeal, Sachs LJ said:

An attempt to commit a crime is established by proving an intent to commit it and in addition proving that in pursuance of that intent something has been done that is more than a mere preparation and is sufficiently proximate to the intended offence. . . . Obviously the period between the moment the proximate act or acts commence and the time they finally fail may vary immensely. At any moment of that period, however, it is plainly true to say of the offender, 'He is attempting to commit that crime'. It matters not whether on any particular set of facts the attempt is best described as a continuing offence (as where a time bomb set to explode at a given hour in this country is being sent by rail) or as a series of offences (as where there are a series of blows on a cold chisel to force a door open). If the time bomb is discovered on the train it matters not whether it is known on which side of some border it was placed there. At the moment of discovery it can plainly be said of the person who put it there that he is attempting to cause an explosion. The position is no different if what is being transmitted is a letter and the moment when its contents come to light occurs on the premises where it is meant to produce the intended result, an obtaining by deception of money from someone within the jurisdiction. . . . An alternative but no less effective way of expressing the matter is to say that he who despatches a missile or a missive arranges for its transport and delivery (essential parts of the attempt) and is thus committing part of the crime within the jurisdiction by the means which he has arranged. The physical personal presence of an offender within this country is not, according to our law, an essential element of offences committed here.[44]

Baxter thus establishes that a conduct crime may continue to be committed over a period of time, and not only where the offender is physically present. On that issue, *Baxter* was subsequently approved by the House of Lords in *DPP* v. *Stonehouse*.[45] *Baxter* does not represent the last word on jurisdiction over attempts, because later decisions suggest that the appellant might still have been convicted, even if his fraudulent letters had never reached English soil; but the judgment given by Sachs LJ may still be relied upon on in so far as it deals with the concepts of ongoing and remotely committed conduct.

---

[44] [1912] 1 QB 1, 11–12. See also *R* v. *Mackenzie* (1910) 6 Cr App R 64, which involved a charge of 'procuring or attempting to procure' a woman under the age of 21 to have 'carnal connection', contrary to s. 2 of the Criminal Law Amendment Act 1885. Upholding M's conviction, Lord Alverstone CJ noted that the attempted procurement began in Scotland, but continued as the victim was lured into England, where sexual intercourse took place. He said: 'We think, though the attempt might be completed before, that the full offence is not brought about until the procurer has gained his or her object, and the carnal knowledge has been attained. In our opinion, the offence was a continuing offence, and if any part of the offence took place in this country, there was jurisdiction to try it here.'   [45] [1978] AC 55.

Result Crimes

In contrast to conduct crimes, result crimes can be completed only if, when, and where the accused's actions bring about one or more proscribed consequences. The offence of obtaining property by deception, for example, cannot be committed by any mere act of the accused. Any false representation he makes must produce a 'double result'. It must first deceive another person and then, as a result of this deception, the accused must obtain property belonging to another, or enable another person to obtain or retain any such property.[46] Crimes involving unlawful homicide are similar in this respect: the accused's conduct must cause the victim some harm or injury; and this harm or injury must then be a substantial cause of the victim's demise.

Identifying the Proscribed Result

Identifying the proscribed result of a result crime will often be difficult. It may require the most careful analysis both of the legal provision or rule creating the offence, and of the facts that have been, or need to be, proved in the case in question. *Secretary of State for Trade* v. *Markus*[47] illustrates the complexities that may be involved, particularly in cases where the alleged offenders have deliberately created a complicated multinational operation to confuse possible investigations into their activities.

The appellant and others operated what Lord Diplock described as a 'gigantic international swindle', the victims of which were primarily resident in West Germany. He and his associates purported to set up an investment scheme, the 'Agri-Fund', ostensibly for the purpose of facilitating worldwide investment in food-producing industries. The sales operation was run by one of the appellant's companies, whose offices were in London, although the fund itself was managed by a Panamanian corporation of which M was also a director. German citizens were approached by salesmen in West Germany and induced to invest in Agri-Fund by purchasing share units. Applications were addressed to the London company. A prospective investor, having completed and signed an application form for shares or units in the fund, ordinarily handed over a cheque or other security in payment. The documents were then sent by the salesmen to the London office for processing. The London company then sent any cheques to a bank in Switzerland to be credited to its account there. Once this had been done, the investor's application was 'accepted' and a certificate for the appropriate number of shares in the fund was sent to him. The fund, however, was a sham: a mere device to defraud the investors. As a director of the London company, the appellant was charged (*inter alia*) with 'conniving at' offences committed by that company, contrary to section 13(1)(b) of the Prevention of Fraud (Investments) Act 1958. That provision (since repealed)[48] created

---

[46] Theft Act 1968, s. 15.   [47] [1976] AC 35.
[48] See now the Financial Services and Markets Act 2000, s. 397.

two offences: one of fraudulently inducing other persons to take part in certain types of investment arrangement; and another of inducing them to offer to do so.

The appellant was convicted, but argued on appeal that the defrauding of the investors (the persons induced) had taken place in West Germany and accordingly that he had not connived at the commission of any offence within the jurisdiction of the English courts. His appeals failed, both in the Court of Appeal and in the House of Lords, each of which agreed that while the would-be investors may have *offered* to take part in the investment arrangements when they filled out their applications and drew up their cheques in Germany, they *took part* in those investment arrangements only when the appellant's London company processed and accepted their applications. Lord Diplock attempted to clarify the general rule concerning the applicability of English criminal law to cross-frontier result crimes. He said:

> To answer this question in the instant case does not, in my view, call for any wide-roving enquiry into the territorial ambit of English criminal law. The offences with which the appellant was charged were 'result-crimes' of the same general nature as the offence of obtaining goods on credit by false pretences which was the subject of the charge in *R v. Ellis*.[49] That case is well-established authority for the proposition that, in the case of what is a result crime in English law, the offence is committed in England and justiciable by an English court if any part of the proscribed result takes place in England.[50]

This ruling was doubtless correct as a matter of English law, but it seems, with respect, to lend further weight to Glanville Williams's criticism of the terminatory approach to jurisdiction. A ruling that the appellant was guilty 'because he had masterminded the fraud from London' would have made perfect sense to anyone. The actual ruling, namely that the German victims had 'taken part' in investment arrangements in England, relied on legal metaphysics of the most obscure kind. It also made English jurisdiction a matter of serendipity rather than one of principle. Moreover, Lord Diplock's understanding of *R v. Ellis* appears to have altered significantly since he delivered his speech in *Treacy* just a few years before. In *Treacy*, his Lordship had said:

> In *R v. Ellis* it was held as a matter of decision that the English court had jurisdiction to try the offence if the obtaining took place in England although the false pretences were made only in Scotland. This is not inconsistent with the view that an English court would likewise have jurisdiction in the converse case where the false pretences were made in England and the obtaining took place only in Scotland, and I do not find the *dicta* in the several judgments to be sufficiently clear or consistent to be persuasive to the contrary.[51]

---

[49] [1899] 1 QB 230.
[50] [1976] AC 35, 61. Lord Diplock glosses over the fact that the 'result crime' of which the appellant was convicted required a final act performed by the offenders (acceptance of the victims' applications) in order to complete the offence.   [51] [1971] AC 537, 562.

Ellis is, on the whole, consistent with the terminatory theory of jurisdiction as applied in *Markus*, although it is only in Bruce J's judgment that one finds express articulation of that theory. Other judgments in *Ellis* refer to the 'gist or gravamen of the offence' as occurring in England, rather than in Scotland. The terminatory theory is, however, more clearly discernible in *R v. Stoddart*,[52] a few years later. The appellant had organized a competition which required competitors in England to predict the results of football matches and post their entries and stake money so as to reach him in Holland on the evening of the day on which the matches were played. No prizes were ever allotted because non-existent competitors were named as winners. The Court of Criminal Appeal held that when the letters containing postal orders were posted in England for transmission to Holland, the offence was at once complete, because the Post Office had been identified as the requisite method of communication, and it was therefore deemed to receive them on the appellant's behalf—an application of the well-known 'postal rule' from contract law.

The rule that enabled a conviction to be upheld in *Stoddart* led to the opposite result in *R v. Harden*,[53] where a company in Jersey posted cheques to London as a result of the appellant's false pretences. The court found evidence of an implied contractual agreement, under which the postal service was the specified method of communication. Delivery of the letters containing the cheques to the postal authorities in Jersey was therefore delivery to the appellant's agent, and the cheques were obtained in Jersey, beyond the jurisdiction of English law. *Harden* must, however, be contrasted with *R v. Tirado*,[54] in which the appellant, in England, obtained money from victims in Morocco by deceiving them into supposing that he would then find them employment in England. He was charged with attempting to obtain property by deception, but argued, by analogy with *Stoddart* and *Harden*, that he had obtained the payments as soon as they were made to his agent in Morocco. On the facts, though, the Court of Appeal ruled that this is not what had happened. The appellant had suggested to his victims that they might, if they wished, make use of a Moroccan bank, which on receipt of their payment would transmit that payment to him in England by bankers' draft,[55] but he had not specified the bank as the requisite method of communication, nor had he intimated to his victims that payment to the bank would be sufficient in itself. On the contrary, he had told them that they had to pay him, and had merely suggested using the bank as one possible method of so doing. The appellant's conviction was therefore upheld. *Tirado* illustrates once again the fickle effect of the terminatory approach

---

[52] (1909) 2 Cr App R 217.   [53] [1963] 1 QB 1.   [54] (1974) 59 Cr App R 80.
[55] We now know from *R v. Preddy* [1996] AC 815 that a charge of obtaining cheques or bankers' drafts by deception may be inherently problematic, even without regard to any possible jurisdiction issues, but such problems had not been recognized when *Tirado* was decided.

to jurisdiction. On the basis of precedent, it seems to have been quite rightly decided; but there is an alarming element of chance in the outcome.

The reader may perhaps be wondering by this stage whether such detailed analysis of fraud or blackmail cases can still be justified, given that Part 1 of the Criminal Justice Act 1993 has substantially altered the rules governing jurisdiction over such cases; but in my submission it is indeed justified, for at least two reasons. The first is that the general principles applied in the pre-Act cases remain applicable to most other cross-frontier offences, including some offences of fraud or dishonesty that are not covered by the 1993 Act. The second is that these general principles may sometimes prove crucial to the interpretation of the Criminal Justice Act provisions themselves, and may in some cases undermine their effectiveness, as I explain later in this chapter.

Offences of Procuring

Offences of unlawful procuring, such as procuring another person's suicide or attempted suicide,[56] or procuring a woman to have unlawful sexual intercourse with a third party,[57] are result crimes, which are committed only if, when, and where that proscribed result has been procured. If D, in England, procures E's suicide or attempted suicide in Scotland, no offence is committed under English law, because the procuring is complete only when the suicide attempt is made. Conversely, if D, in Scotland, procures V to go to England in order to have sexual intercourse there with a third party, he commits, in England, an offence of procuring unlawful sexual intercourse, when that intercourse takes place in England.[58] The Court for Crown Cases Reserved so held in *R v. Mackenzie and Higginson*.[59]

Causation Issues in Result Crimes

Causation is a highly complex topic in its own right, which cannot be addressed in any great detail here. It must suffice to note that causation issues or arguments (such as *novus actus interveniens*) that may arise in respect of purely English result crimes may equally arise in transnational ones, and may give rise to much the same problems. In *R v. Latif and Shazad*,[60] for example, the appellants were involved in a plot to smuggle heroin into Britain. The heroin was delivered by S to a supposed accomplice in Pakistan, who was in fact an undercover operative of the US Drug Enforcement Agency. It was then flown into Britain by a British customs officer, technically without lawful authority, and the appellants were lured to a meeting in London, where they were arrested. It was held that the

---

[56] Suicide Act 1961, s. 2.   [57] Sexual Offences Act 1956, s. 22(1)(b).
[58] *R v. Johnson* [1964] 2 QB 404.   [59] (1910) 6 Cr App R 64.
[60] [1996] 1 WLR 104.

importation by the customs officer, whilst unlawful, was a deliberate third-party act for which the appellants were not responsible. No substantive offence under section 170(2) of the Customs and Excise Management Act 1979 had therefore been committed by them, even though the proscribed result had (in one sense at least) occurred within the jurisdiction.[61]

In contrast, there was held to be no such *novus actus* on the facts of *R v. Jakeman*.[62] The appellant in that case travelled with two suitcases containing cannabis on an international flight scheduled to terminate in London. The flight was diverted via Paris, and she abandoned the cases at Charles de Gaulle airport, apparently because she had lost her nerve. The cases were (predictably) found by airport staff, who assumed them to have been misrouted and very helpfully sent them on to Heathrow. The cases were never collected but were eventually opened at Heathrow, and the cannabis was discovered, as was the ownership of the cases. The Court of Appeal upheld the appellant's conviction under section 170(2) of the Customs and Excise Management Act 1979. Wood J nevertheless said:

For guilt to be established the importation must, of course, result as a consequence, if only in part, of the activity of the accused. If, for example, in the present case the appellant had taken her two suitcases off the carousel at Charles de Gaulle airport in Paris, removed all the luggage tags, placed the suitcases in a left luggage compartment and thrown the key of that compartment into the Seine, and then subsequently, in a general emergency, all left luggage compartments had been opened, a well-known English travel label had been found on her suitcase and those suitcases had been sent to the Travel Agents' agency, care of Customs and Excise at Heathrow, then that undoubted importation would not be the relevant one for the purposes of a charge against her.

Problems of Classification

The orthodox view is that a given offence must either be a conduct crime in all cases, or a result crime in all cases. The categorization cannot vary from one case to another, according to the particular facts or the *modus operandi* involved. The orthodox view also claims that conduct crimes are rare and that result crimes are the norm. According to *Smith & Hogan*[63]:

True conduct crimes such as perjury are rare. The term has been widely interpreted by Glanville Williams to include rape and abduction—in these crimes you do not have to wait and see if anything happens as a result of what the defendant does. If the test is whether you have to 'wait and see', wounding is a conduct crime if committed with a knife, but a result crime if committed with a gun, crossbow or catapult. . . . These offences are best regarded as result crimes. A result has to flow from D's physical movements, whether you have to wait for it or not.

---

[61] S was nevertheless convicted of being concerned in an *attempt* to import heroin, contrary to the Customs and Excise Management Act 1979, s. 170(2).

[62] (1983) 76 Cr App R 223.   [63] J.C. Smith (10th edn, 2002), 30–31.

The authors of *Smith & Hogan* are doubtless right to argue that wounding must always be a result crime, because the offence is concerned not merely with D's physical actions (stabbing, shooting, etc.) but with the consequences of those actions, whether these are simultaneous with D's conduct or whether they follow several hours later. In either event, the prosecution must prove a causal link between the shooting, etc., and the wound. In some offences, however, the *actus reus* can take such a variety of forms that the orthodox view may become unworkable. Take, for example, the offence of theft. Although theft is generally assumed to be a result crime, many thefts will in practice be conduct crimes, because any act involving the assumption of one or more of the owner's rights to property must now be regarded as an appropriation. An example is provided by *R v. Governor of Pentonville Prison, ex p Osman.*[64] This was an extradition case in which the Hong Kong authorities sought the return of the applicant to face numerous charges relating to multi-million dollar banking frauds involving unauthorized loans on the international money market. It was held that the applicant and his fellow conspirators had *prima facie* committed full offences of theft in Hong Kong when they issued fraudulent telex instructions there, addressed to banks in New York, instructing these banks to make enormous loan payments to other US banks, for the account of companies in which the applicant and his associates were involved. It was held that the mere issuing of these instructions was in itself an act of appropriation committed in Hong Kong, and not a mere attempt to appropriate property in the USA. It would not have mattered, on that analysis, if officials in the banks concerned had instantly recognized the irregularity and refused to make the required payment.[65]

In contrast, cases in which D commits theft by dishonestly inducing or deceiving P into making a gift to him cannot be regarded as conduct crimes,[66] because D cannot be said to appropriate property merely by pleading for it. A theft of this kind is analogous to an offence of obtaining property by deception.

Nor, indeed, can it be assumed that theft, in a case such as *Osman*, must necessarily be committed at, or only at, the place from which D issues the fraudulent instructions. In *R v. Governor of Brixton Prison and another, ex p Levin,*[67] it was held that the applicant committed theft in the USA by

---

[64] [1990] 1 WLR 277. For further analysis of this case see below, pp. 169–71.

[65] See also *R v. Wille* (1987) 86 Cr App R 296 (dishonest drawing and issuing of a cheque without authority may in itself be theft). *R v. Tomsett* [1985] Crim LR 369 appears to be authority to the contrary. The appellant in that case issued fraudulent instructions from London, diverting $7 million held in a New York bank account to an account that an accomplice had previously opened in Geneva. It was held that any theft had been committed either in New York or in Geneva, rather than in London; but as the court explained in *Osman*, the possibility that the theft had been completed in London was not addressed in *Tomsett*, because counsel for the Crown had declined the court's suggestion that he should argue the point.

[66] As, e.g., in *R v. Hinks* [2001] 2 AC 241.   [67] [1997] QB 65.

fraudulently accessing the computer of a bank in Parsipanny, New Jersey. Beldam LJ distinguished *Osman* on the facts:

The court in ... *Osman* was concerned with the assumption of the right of the account-holder to give instructions and to have them met. Those instructions could be given by telex without more ado. Osman was simply sending an instruction to the correspondent bank in the United States. But in the present case no instructions could be given without first gaining entry into the Citibank computer in Parsipanny. No doubt there was an appropriation of the right of the client to gain access to the computer, but that is a different right of property, which ... had been appropriated by the applicant many times before he actually set about entering the computer for the purpose of giving any instructions. We see no reason why the appropriation of the client's right to give instructions should not be regarded as having taken place in the computer.

The problem of identifying relevant acts of appropriation remains highly troublesome, even in purely domestic cases with no transnational elements. Cross-frontier cases add to the difficulties. Part 1 of the Criminal Justice Act 1993 was intended to draw the sting from any jurisdictional difficulties that might otherwise arise in transnational theft, fraud, or blackmail cases, by giving English courts jurisdiction where any 'relevant event' that is 'required for conviction of the offence' occurs within England and Wales, but the effectiveness of this legislation is occasionally open to question. In particular, if *Osman* is correct, then the state within which the direct consequences of a transnational theft are felt may not necessarily be the *locus* of any 'relevant event' at all. The crime may already be complete. If so, the effectiveness of the 1993 legislation may be undermined.

CROSS-FRONTIER PARTICIPATION IN CRIME

Secondary participation in crime may take either of two cross-frontier forms. In the first, D may become involved in England as a secondary party to a crime committed by E abroad. In the second, D may become involved, whilst abroad, as a secondary party to an offence committed by E within the realm. The general rule, first established in *R v. Johnson*,[68] is that D may be liable as a secondary party to E's offence if, but only if, E has indeed committed an offence that is triable under English law. If, in other words, E has committed no such offence, nor then has D, even if E *has* committed an equivalent offence (e.g., murder) under a foreign system of law. If E has indeed committed an offence under English law, D must also be guilty of that offence, wherever he was when he provided the assistance or encouragement in question.

---

[68] (1805) 6 East 583. See also *R v. Jameson* [1896] 2 QB 425.

The operation of this general rule was well illustrated in the case of *R* v. *Robert Millar (Contractors) Ltd and Millar.*[69] A fatal accident occurred on a motorway in England. A worn and defective tyre on one of the appellant company's heavy goods vehicles blew out, and the vehicle crashed into an oncoming car, killing all six persons inside. It was established that Hart, the HGV driver, had known of the defective tyre, but agreed to use it when ordered to do so by Millar, the company's managing director. Hart admitted causing death by dangerous driving, and it was clear that Millar, and through him the company, had counselled and procured that offence. The only possible complications were that the company was registered in Scotland, and that Millar had been in Scotland when he persuaded Hart to drive the vehicle with the defective tyre, but the Court of Appeal held that none of this made any difference. Giving the judgment of the Court, Fenton Atkinson LJ identified two separate grounds on which the convictions of Millar and his company could be upheld[70]:

The offence of causing death by dangerous driving was committed in England by Mr Hart; but the appellants are guilty of participating in that crime and not of some self-subsisting crime on their own account and, therefore, they are in the same position as the principal offender and they are liable to be tried in this country. There is a second way of perhaps reaching the same result, and that is to be found set out very clearly in Fisher J's judgment in dealing with this matter at the Crown Court. He said:

> The offence of causing death by dangerous driving is plainly not committed until the death occurs, and in the present case the death occurred in England. Where an employer with actual or imputed knowledge of the defective mechanical state of the vehicle permits an employee to take that vehicle out on the road he is, so this indictment alleges, counselling and procuring the employee to drive that vehicle in that state, and it seems to me that the common sense of the matter is that that counselling and procuring is a continuous act which persists so long as the driver is driving the vehicle in that condition on the road.

Offences Analogous to Secondary Participation

In some cases, a person whom one might otherwise regard as a secondary party to an offence committed in England and Wales may instead be prosecuted for an analogous but legally distinct offence. A number of customs and excise or revenue offences take the form of 'being knowingly concerned' in proscribed conduct. Under section 144 of the Finance Act 2000, for example: 'A person commits an offence if he is knowingly concerned in the fraudulent evasion of income tax by him or any other person'. Similarly, under section 170(2) of the Customs and Excise Management Act 1979, an offence may be committed by any person who, in relation to any goods, is

---

[69] [1970] 2 QB 54.　　　[70] Ibid., 73.

'in any way knowingly concerned in any fraudulent evasion or attempt at evasion' of any duty chargeable, or of any prohibition or restriction, etc. on those goods.

Liability in such cases still depends on the commission of the other offence, namely a fraudulent evasion of income tax or of an act of smuggling. In *R v. Wall*,[71] it was accordingly held that the *Millar* principle applies to such cases, just as it applies to ordinary cases of secondary participation. The appellant in *Wall* was charged that, on 17 February 1973, he was knowingly concerned in the fraudulent evasion of restrictions imposed on the importation of cannabis, contrary to what is now section 170(2) of the 1979 Act. The cannabis had been seized on that date, when his co-defendants attempted to smuggle it through customs at Dover. He admitted meeting his co-defendants in Afghanistan, several weeks earlier, but was not proved to have done any act in connection with that offence in England and Wales on 17 February or on any other date. Cairns LJ, giving the judgment of the Court, said: 'So here there is one offence, that of being knowingly concerned in fraudulent evasion on 17 February 1973, and just as in *R v. Millar* the part played by the company was played earlier and in another country, so here if that was the only part played by the appellant he was indictable here for it.[72]

In some cases, however, the wording or structure of the relevant legislation may preclude the application of the *Millar* principle. Sections 25A and 25B of the Immigration Act 1971 (as inserted by section 143 of the Nationality, Immigration and Asylum Act 2002)[73] provide examples. These provisions address the growing problem of 'people smuggling'. Under section 24(1)(a) of the 1971 Act, it is an offence for any person who is not a British citizen to enter the United Kingdom without leave, or in breach of a deportation or exclusion order, etc. This offence (typically committed by asylum seekers) is triable only summarily. Under the new section 25A, however, a person who knowingly and for gain 'facilitates' the arrival in the United Kingdom of an asylum seeker commits an indictable offence for which he may be imprisoned for up to 14 years. A similar penalty may be imposed, under section 25B, on anyone who facilitates a breach of a deportation order, or who assists an excluded individual to arrive in, enter, or remain in the United Kingdom.

Offences under sections 25A or 25B appear to be distinct from complicity in a section 24 offence, and not just because they carry higher penalties. They are also distinct in that no unlawful entry need actually take place. 'Facilitate' does not mean 'procure'. If this is correct, it follows that the 'one

---

[71] [1974] 1 WLR 930.

[72] In an earlier work ((1981) 97 *Law Quarterly Review* 80, 94) I argued that *Wall* was wrongly decided on that issue, but on further reflection I am satisfied that the error was mine.

[73] In force, 10 February 2003 (SI 2003 No. 1).

offence' principle identified in *Robert Millar (Contractors) Ltd* cannot apply to those provisions. What then if D, in France, does an act which facilitates E's illegal entry to England? By sections 25A(5) and 25B(4), offences under sections 25A or 25B may be committed outside the United Kingdom, but only when committed by British citizens, British overseas citizens, British overseas territories citizens, British nationals (overseas), British subjects, or British protected persons.[74] Given the much publicized connections between 'people smuggling' and organized crime abroad, this limitation must be considered surprising. Many foreign criminal gangs are involved in smuggling operations of that type, but it seems that sections 25A(5) and 25B(4) cannot ordinarily apply to them, unless they operate within the jurisdiction. The law might in fact be more effective if illegal entry became an indictable offence with substantial penalties, because the foreign gangs involved might then be prosecuted as secondary parties under the *Millar* principle.[75]

Special Cases and Exceptions

The *Millar* principle is logical, but may be open to criticism in so far as it excludes persons in England and Wales who procure, encourage, or assist in the commission of offences against the laws of other countries. This might be considered unhelpful, or even give the impression that the United Kingdom condones such conduct. In some such cases, however, special provision has been made to permit prosecution under English law. Section 21 of the Trade Descriptions Act 1968 provides an example. This makes it an offence for a person in England and Wales[76] to 'assist in or induce' the application of a false trade description to goods abroad, but only where that false trade description suggests that the goods were made in the United Kingdom, or that they are used or endorsed by members of the British royal family. The dominant purpose behind this provision was not the protection of the overseas consumer, but the protection of the United Kingdom's reputation as a manufacturer of quality goods. No reference is made to foreign law: it does not therefore matter whether the other country in question even prohibits the application of false trade descriptions.

---

[74] These could collectively have been referred to as 'United Kingdom nationals' (see below, p. 207), but for some reason the new legislation does not use that terminology.

[75] Note also the obligations of other EU countries to investigate and prosecute such conduct within their territories, in accordance with their obligations under Art. 27 of the Schengen Convention. As to trafficking in persons for the purposes of prostitution, see the Nationality, Immigration and Asylum Act 2002, ss. 145 and 146.

[76] The Act applies to the whole of the UK, but assistance or inducement provided in Scotland would be an offence triable only in Scotland, and so on.

A different approach is adopted in section 20 of the Misuse of Drugs Act 1971, by which:

A person commits an offence if in the United Kingdom he assists in or induces the commission in any place outside the United Kingdom of an offence punishable under the provisions of a corresponding law in force in that place.[77]

Section 36 of the 1971 Act defines a 'corresponding law' as:

A law stated in a certificate purporting to be issued by or on behalf of the government of a country outside the United Kingdom to be a law providing for the control and regulation in that country of the production, supply, use, export and import of drugs and other substances in accordance with the provisions of the Single Convention on Narcotic Drugs signed at New York on 30th March 1961 or a law providing for the control and regulation in that country of the production, supply, use, export and import of dangerous or otherwise harmful drugs in pursuance of any treaty, convention or other agreement or arrangement to which the government of that country and Her Majesty's Government in the United Kingdom are for the time being parties.[78]

The corresponding offence under the relevant foreign law need not have any exact counterpart under English law. This underlines the fact that section 20 serves a wider purpose than section 21 of the Trade Descriptions Act. It was enacted for the purpose of giving effect to the New York Convention, and was intended to contribute to an international campaign against an international menace, rather than to protect narrow British interests. Courts must nevertheless look to the penalties imposed under the equivalent (or nearest equivalent) offence under English law when sentencing for an offence under section 20. It does not matter whether this is higher or lower than the corresponding offence under the relevant foreign law.[79]

Section 71 of the Criminal Justice Act 1993 addresses the problem of frauds against the European Community by making it an offence for a person in England and Wales[80] to assist in or induce conduct abroad that involves a serious offence (punishable with at least 12 months' imprisonment) under the law of another member state, provided that this offence is connected with community taxation, subsidies, restrictions, or prohibitions.[81]

---

[77] As to what may amount to 'assisting' for the purposes of s. 20, see *R* v. *Vickers* (1975) 61 Cr App R 48 and *R* v. *Evans* (1977) 64 Cr App R 237. As to the need for the principal offence to be committed (and not merely planned or prepared for) under the relevant foreign law, see *R* v. *Karte and Panayi* (1988) 86 Cr App R 266. It was held in that case that the appellants could not be guilty of assisting in the illegal importation of drugs into The Netherlands, because the consignment of drugs, *en route* from Spain, was intercepted and seized in English territorial waters. Was it not perhaps a case of assisting in an offence of attempted importation?

[78] The certificate is conclusive evidence of the law in question, but does not prove whether the conduct alleged by the prosecution amounts to that offence.

[79] See *R* v. *Faulkner* (1976) 63 Cr App R 295.

[80] The Act refers to persons within the UK, but conduct in Scotland or Northern Ireland would fall exclusively under Scots or Northern Irish law.

[81] See also s. 25 of the Immigration Act 1971, as substituted by s. 143 of the Nationality, Immigration and Asylum Act 2002. This provision (which gives effect to Art. 27 of the

Section 71(5) facilitates proof of the relevant law in the state concerned:

For the purposes of any proceedings for an offence under this section, a certificate purporting to be issued by or on behalf of the government of another Member State which contains a statement, in relation to such times as may be specified in the certificate—

(a) that a specified offence existed against the law of that Member State,

(b) that an offence against the law of that Member State was a serious offence within the meaning of this section,

(c) that such an offence consists in or includes the contravention of particular provisions of the law of that Member State,

(d) that specified provisions of the law of that Member State relate to, or are capable of having an effect in relation to, particular matters,

(e) that specified conduct involved the commission of a particular offence against the law of that Member State, or

(f) that a particular effect in that Member State in relation to any matter would result from specified conduct,

shall, in the case of a statement falling within paragraphs (a) to (d), be conclusive of the matters stated and, in the other cases, be evidence, and in Scotland sufficient evidence, of the matters stated.

This addresses only the content of the relevant foreign law. If there is any dispute as to what was done by the persons allegedly assisted or induced, the prosecution would have to prove this in the normal way. The use of the past tense in section 71(5)(e), as in section 71(5)(a) and (b), may be explained on the basis that it refers to the law of the member state at the times specified in the certificate. In other words, section 71(5)(e) deals with the question whether specified conduct, if proved, would amount to a specified offence; and even on this, it is not conclusive.

INCHOATE OFFENCES

Many cross-frontier offences involve inchoate offences of incitement, conspiracy, or attempt. These may take many forms and the territorial element in such an offence may be objective, subjective, or even intermediate. The inchoate offence may, in other words, be initiated within England and Wales but directed abroad; or it may be initiated abroad but directed towards a substantive offence within England and Wales; or it may be that certain things are done in England in furtherance of an ongoing conspiracy, etc., that has been initiated abroad and is ultimately intended to take effect there.[82]

Schengen Convention) makes it an offence for any person in England and Wales to facilitate the commission by some other person of a breach of immigration law within another member state of the EU. (It also creates similar offences under Scots and Northern Irish law, and a wholly extraterritorial offence in respect of acts done by British citizens, etc., outside the UK.)

[82] Conspiracy is, in practice, the most important and most widely charged of these offences. For obvious reasons, most major transnational crimes involve conspiracies, and conspiracy

Inchoate offences with cross-frontier elements may raise a number of jurisdictional issues, over and above those that arise in respect of substantive offences. Some of these complications may be unavoidable. Others arise as a result of statutory intervention, of which there has been a great deal in this area. The absence of any coherent overall strategy or guiding principle governing this area of law is reflected in a plethora of largely *ad hoc* statutory provisions, each of which appears to have its own unique features or quirks. Nor can any of these provisions be described as models of clear or precise drafting. Even the best of them are problematic in certain important respects. The worst examples are so badly flawed as to be incapable of serving any useful purpose.

Conduct Crimes or Result Crimes?

Inchoate offences may be divided, like substantive ones, into 'conduct crimes' and 'result crimes'. For jurisdictional purposes, however—for the purpose, in other words, of determining whether the incitement, conspiracy, or attempt amounts to an offence under English law—the implications of this dichotomy are by no means the same.

A criminal attempt is generally considered to be a classic example of a conduct crime. The attempt is committed once D's actions go beyond the stage of mere preparation, but this does not require any particular consequences to be caused. As *R v. Baxter*[83] shows, an attempt may take the form of ongoing conduct, but this does not prevent it from being a conduct crime.[84]

In contrast, incitement (whether in its basic common law form, or any of its statutory variants[85]) appears to be a result crime. This may seem surprising, because an offence of incitement may certainly be committed without producing its *desired* result. The person incited need not commit, or even agree or attempt to commit, the offence incited.[86] It appears, however, that the incitement must at least be communicated to the 'incitee'. A failure to communicate with the intended recipient (as where a letter is intercepted by the police, or sent to a man who cannot read it) could thus amount only to an attempt to incite.[87]

---

charges will often be laid in such cases, even where, as in *DPP v. Doot* [1973] AC 807, substantive offences may have also been committed. Where the proposed crime has been foiled, as in *R v. Sansom* [1991] 2 All ER 145, where a consignment of controlled drugs was intercepted and seized at sea before being imported into England, conspiracy may be the only appropriate charge.

[83] [1972] 1 QB 1.

[84] At one time, it was thought that D's conduct abroad must trigger some consequence or have some effect within the jurisdiction, before it could be said that D committed a criminal attempt within the jurisdiction. *Baxter* provides an example of such reasoning. If that were still the case, it would be very difficult to classify such attempts as conduct crimes, but such consequences are no longer considered necessary. See below, p. 155.

[85] Such as solicitation to murder, contrary to the Offences Against the Person Act 1861, s. 4.

[86] This seems to have been overlooked in *R v. Goldman* [2001] All ER (D) 157 (July).

[87] See *R v. Ransford* (1874) 13 Cox CC 9; *R v. Krause* (1902) 66 JP 121.

Conspiracy is more complicated. If A in Scotland suggests to B in England that they should together commit a crime in England, A becomes guilty of conspiracy only when the suggested course of conduct is agreed to by B. To put it another way, he must not only incite B, but also persuade him to agree. From A's viewpoint, therefore, conspiracy is clearly a result crime. In contrast, B, merely by agreeing to the proposal, may bring the conspiracy into existence. But at what point does B's agreement become effective? What if his agreement is not successfully communicated to A? There is no clear authority on this point.[88] In *R v. Scott*,[89] Geoffrey Lane LJ held that an intent to join a conspiracy cannot be indictable unless it has been communicated in some way, but this *dictum* was directed towards the issue of 'secret intent' and not to a communication that is lost in the post, or an e-mail that is sent to the wrong address. Nor does it address the question of an agreement that is only communicated when it reaches a fellow conspirator abroad. The exact moment and place at which a conspiracy is formed may thus be difficult to ascertain even as a matter of law, to say nothing of any factual uncertainties that may arise.

But does it necessarily matter whether the act of conspiracy (or of incitement or attempt) is committed in England and Wales or abroad? The answer for most purposes appears to be 'No'. A conspiracy or attempt to commit a substantive offence that is punishable under English law is now considered to be punishable on the same basis, even if that conspiracy or attempt is committed wholly or partly outside the jurisdiction.[90] There is no direct authority as to the position in respect of incitement, but logic suggests that all inchoate offences should be subject to the same rules. If so, what matters in such cases is the *locus* of the ulterior offence, rather than that of the inchoate conduct itself.[91]

The Ulterior Offence under English Law

In any case involving a possible inchoate cross-frontier offence, one must always begin by asking whether the ulterior offence (the substantive offence incited, attempted, or conspired at) is or would have been triable under English law if committed in accordance with the intention of the party or parties concerned. If not, there can ordinarily be no offence of incitement

---

[88] See generally G. Orchard, 'Agreement in Criminal Conspiracy' [1974] *Criminal Law Review* 297.   [89] (1979) 68 Cr App R 164.
[90] *Somchai Liangsiriprasert* v. *US Government* [1991] 1 AC 225; *R v. Latif* [1996] 1 WLR 104. See below, pp. 155–8.
[91] Even where the substantive offence is an extraterritorial one, such as torture, and is committed abroad, it appears that a conspiracy to commit this offence will generally fall within English jurisdiction, even if it too was committed abroad. This at least was the opinion of Lord Hope in *R v. Bow Street Metropolitan Stipendiary Magistrate, ex p Pinochet Ugarte (No. 3)* [1999] 2 All ER 97, 139. See below, p. 281.

or attempt under English law, nor can it be a case of statutory conspiracy under section 1 of the Criminal Law Act 1977. Since, for example, causing grievous bodily harm in France or Scotland is not ordinarily an offence under English law, incitement or attempt to commit such grievous bodily harm cannot ordinarily be an offence either, even if this incitement or attempt is committed within England and Wales. This was the position at common law, but in respect of attempts it is restated in section 1 of the Criminal Attempts Act 1981, which provides:

(1) If, with intent to commit an offence to which this section applies, a person does an act which is more than merely preparatory to the commission of the offence, he is guilty of attempting to commit the offence. . . .

(4) This section applies to any offence which, if it were completed, would be triable in England and Wales as an indictable offence, other than—

    (a) conspiracy (at common law or under section 1 of the Criminal Law Act 1977);

    (b) aiding, abetting, counselling, procuring or suborning the commission of an offence;

    (c) offences under section 4(1) (assisting offenders) or 5(1) (accepting or agreeing to accept consideration for not disclosing information about an arrestable offence) of the Criminal Law Act 1967.

The meaning of section 1(4) was examined by the Divisional Court in *R v. Governor of Pentonville Prison, ex p Naghdi*,[92] in which the US Government sought the applicant's extradition on a number of charges, including charges of attempting to obtain property (namely, irrevocable letters of credit) by deception. It was argued that the US authorities had failed to adduce a *prima facie* case to establish that the obtaining was intended to take place within US jurisdiction. Woolf LJ rejected this argument on the facts, but agreed with the legal assumptions behind it. He said:

Although the language of subsection (4) is not entirely clear, I am satisfied that subsection (4) in its reference to England and Wales is referring to the jurisdiction to try the completed offence. That means that, because of the decision in *R v. Harden*, where an attempted obtaining is alleged if the full offence would have been completed outside England and Wales, the attempt is not triable in England and Wales even though all the preparatory steps towards the commission of the full offence took place in England and the defendant had the necessary intent. Thus, taking an example which is relevant to this case, if false pretences are made in this country to obtain a letter of credit but the letter of credit is to be delivered abroad, then, even if the full offence is never completed and all the ingredients of the attempt occur in this country, there is no jurisdiction to try the attempt in this country.[93]

Naghdi involved attempts to commit acts that would now (if committed on or after 1 June 1999) be triable in England and Wales as 'Group A offences' under Part 1 of the Criminal Justice Act 1993, but the basic principle

---

    [92] [1990] 1 All ER 257.   [93] Ibid., 267.

remains valid, namely that an attempt in England to commit an 'offence' abroad is not punishable under English law unless the offence attempted would itself be so punishable.[94]

At common law, a similar rule applied to cases of conspiracy. As Lord Tucker said in *Board of Trade* v. *Owen*[95]: 'A conspiracy to commit a crime abroad is not indictable in this country unless the contemplated crime is one for which an indictment would lie here . . .' This observation was *obiter*, given that the case itself concerned conspiracy to defraud, but it was supported in a number of later cases. In *R* v. *Governor of Brixton Prison, ex p Rush*,[96] for example, the Canadian Government sought the extradition of the applicant for his role in a conspiracy, in Canada, to obtain valuable securities (cheques, etc.) by deception from victims in the USA. The victims of this conspiracy were deceived into despatching the cheques, etc., to Panama or Nassau, where they were paid into accounts operated by the conspirators. Thus, although the conspiracy was formed in Canada, the ulterior offences were committed either in the USA, or in Panama and Nassau. Applying the standard double-criminality test to the extradition request, it was held that no such conspiracy would have been indictable under English law had it been committed in England rather than Canada, and extradition was accordingly refused on that particular charge.

The position in *ex p Rush* would have been different had the offence conspired at been one that possessed an extraterritorial ambit under English law. Had the applicant (assuming him to be a Canadian citizen) conspired in Canada to commit bigamy or murder in the USA, the double-criminality test would not have been a problem, because a British citizen similarly conspiring in England would have been indictable under English law.[97]

Section 1(4) of the Criminal Law Act 1977 restates the common law principle in respect of a charge of statutory conspiracy under section 1(1). The offence conspired at need not itself be intended for commission within England and Wales, but it must be an offence that would, if committed, be triable under English law.[98]

Special Cases and Exceptions

One cannot fault the logic of the general rule described above, but in practice its effects may be far from satisfactory. Crimes against foreign law, if

---

[94] Section 5(2) of the Criminal Justice Act 1993 purports to create a limited exception to this rule, by inserting a new s. 1A into the Criminal Attempts Act 1981, but it is doubtful whether that provision is capable of applying to any case that could ever arise in practice. See below, p. 173.

[95] [1957] AC 602. See also *R* v. *Naini* [1999] 2 Cr App R 398, 416, *per* Lord Bingham CJ.

[96] [1969] 1 WLR 165.   [97] A similar rule applies to incitement or attempt.

[98] A number of offences are punishable under English law even if committed abroad (e.g., offences under the Aviation Security Act 1982 and murder or manslaughter committed by a

committed entirely abroad, are usually perceived to be the concern of the local courts and authorities; but when such offences are incited, conspired at, or attempted by persons acting (perhaps openly) within England and Wales, the idea that our criminal law may be powerless to intervene becomes a deeply disturbing one. Not only may it suggest contempt or indifference as to the harm such conduct may do abroad, and thereby tarnish the international reputation of the United Kingdom and its laws (especially in cases involving potential acts of terrorism against friendly states), but in addition there may be concerns as to whether such conspirators, etc., pose a threat to security at home. Extradition does not necessarily provide a satisfactory answer to such cases, especially where all relevant events occur within England and Wales.

Isolated exceptions to the general rule have existed for many years. There was originally a proviso to section 1(4) of the Criminal Law Act 1977, under which conspiracy to commit murder was made an offence, 'notwithstanding that the murder in question would not be so triable if committed in accordance with the intentions of the parties to the agreement'. There are no reported cases in which this proviso was invoked, and it has now been supplanted by more modern legislation,[99] but it potentially enabled English courts to try and punish a conspiracy in England to commit murder in Scotland or Northern Ireland, or a conspiracy formed by foreign nationals in England to commit murder in their own (or in some other) country.[100]

The number of exceptions to the general rule has grown substantially in recent years, not least because of public and media concern as to the apparent immunity previously enjoyed by certain groups of 'international criminals' operating within the United Kingdom. There are now many circumstances in which it may be an offence under English law to conspire or incite (but rarely, if ever, attempt) to commit a crime under some other system of law. The Sexual Offences (Conspiracy and Incitement) Act 1996 provides an example of this phenomenon, and was in some respects a model for later provisions of a similar kind.

The Sexual Offences (Conspiracy and Incitement) Act 1996

This Act, although largely supplanted by more recent legislation, was the first of a series of modern statutes creating new forms of inchoate offence.

British citizen on land outside the United Kingdom). Persons who conspire in England or Wales to commit such crimes abroad are therefore indictable under s. 1.

[99] See the Criminal Justice (Terrorism and Conspiracy) Act 1998, at p. 142 below, which added a new s. 1A to the 1977 Act.

[100] In neither of these cases would the substantive offence of murder be triable in England under the Offences Against the Person Act 1861, s. 9. The ancestry of the proviso to s. 1(4) can be traced back to Palmerston's Conspiracy to Murder Bill of 1858. This Bill, which never became law, was inspired by French protests over the impunity enjoyed by Italian emigrés in England, some of whom had recently been implicated in the Orsini bomb plot, an attempt to assassinate Napoleon III in Paris, in which a number of bystanders and guards had been killed when a bomb was thrown at the Emperor's carriage. (Cf. *R* v. *Bernard* (1858) 1 F & F 240).

It originated as a private member's Bill, but was passed with government support in response to widespread outrage as to the sexual exploitation of child prostitutes and other children by 'sex tourists' (including British citizens) in a number of third world countries, such as Thailand, Sri Lanka, Cambodia, and The Philippines. Although the sexual abuse of children was and remains illegal in such countries, it was clear that little in practice was being done there to prevent it, and western or Japanese 'sex tourists' were generally able to commit serious paedophile acts in such countries, with little fear of arrest or prosecution under local law. The sex tourism industry had been exposed by powerful media campaigns, and there was a strong feeling within Parliament that the United Kingdom should urgently take measures to outlaw it, at least as far as British participation in such conduct was concerned.

One possible response—indeed, the most obvious response—would have been the enactment of legislation making such acts extraterritorial offences under English (and Scots and Northern Ireland) law when committed by British citizens abroad. This was an approach that had been adopted by a number of countries, including Australia, that do not ordinarily assert extraterritorial jurisdiction based on nationality, but it was not at that time favoured by the British Government, who argued that the only proper and effective response would be to criminalize things done within the United Kingdom itself.[101] The 1996 Act therefore targeted not the actual abuse of children by British tourists in foreign countries (which acts remained, for the time being, outside the ambit of English criminal law), but the organization, advertisement, and facilitation of 'child sex tourism' within the United Kingdom. The law would clamp down upon British-based tour organizers, and on those who encouraged others to take part.[102]

Section 1 of the Act created a new offence of conspiracy in England to commit specified sexual acts abroad. These sexual acts had to involve offences under relevant local law, which, if committed in England and Wales, would similarly involve offences under English law. Section 1 was later supplanted and repealed by wider-ranging provisions contained in the Criminal Justice (Terrorism and Conspiracy) Act 1998, and no longer merits detailed analysis. Section 2 remains in force, although its practical importance has been degraded by later legislation. It provides:

(1) This section applies where—

(a) any act done by a person in England and Wales would amount to the offence of incitement to commit a listed sexual offence but for the fact that what he had in view would not be an offence triable in England and Wales,

---

[101] According to Home Office Minister, David MacLean, the enactment of extraterritorial provisions applicable to such cases would be nothing more than 'gesture politics'. The following year, however, such legislation was enacted after all.

[102] For a more detailed analysis of the background to this legislation, see Peter Alldridge, 'The Sexual Offences (Conspiracy and Incitement) Act 1996' [1997] *Criminal Law Review* 30.

(b) the whole or part of what he had in view was intended to take place in a country or territory outside the United Kingdom, and

(c) what he had in view would involve the commission of an offence under the law in force in that country or territory.[103]

(2) Where this section applies—

(a) what he had in view is to be treated as that listed sexual offence[104] for the purposes of any charge of incitement brought in respect of that act, and

(b) any such charge is accordingly triable in England and Wales.

(3) Any act of incitement by means of a message (however communicated) is to be treated as done in England and Wales if the message is sent or received in England and Wales.

This provision applies only where the conduct incited is *not* in fact a crime under English law; although such conduct may be 'treated as' a listed sexual offence in order to enable the incitement to be prosecuted in England. When, in the following year, the Government bowed to demands for the criminalization of child sex abuse by British citizens or United Kingdom residents abroad, and enacted the requisite legislation in section 7 of the Sex Offenders Act 1997, the earlier statute was rendered largely, but not entirely, otiose. The relevant provisions of the 1997 Act are examined in Chapter 5 below. It must suffice at this point to note that by providing an extraterritorial ambit to a wide range of sexual offences, including an even wider range of child sex offences than those listed in the 1996 Act, this left the 1996 provisions with almost nothing on which they could still attach. If, for example, D in England incites his friend, E, to join him on a 'sex holiday' to Bangkok, for the purpose of having sex with child prostitutes, he will now be guilty not of an offence under section 2 of the 1996 Act, but of incitement at common law. Section 2 becomes applicable only if D, in England, incites persons who are neither British citizens, nor resident in the United Kingdom—persons, in other words, to whom section 7 of the Sex Offenders Act 1997 cannot apply.

Assume, for example, that D, in England, writes to his paedophile friend, F, in Germany, suggesting that they meet up for a child-sex holiday in The Philippines. If F is not a British citizen, this may amount to incitement under section 2 of the 1996 Act.[105] D may argue that the act of incitement was committed only in Germany, when F read the letter. At common law

---

[103] This may be presumed, unless the defence serve notice on the prosecution under s. 3 of the Act, requiring the relevant foreign law to be proved.

[104] Defined in the Schedule to the Act as: rape of an under-16; unlawful intercourse with girls under 13, or with girls under 16; buggery of an under-16; indecent assault on a boy or girl under 16; and indecent conduct towards a child (as defined in s. 1 of the Indecency with Children Act 1960).

[105] Peter Alldridge appears to have overlooked this possibility in his otherwise useful analysis of the relationship between the 1996 and 1997 Acts: 'Sex Offenders Act 1997—Territoriality Provisions' [1997] *Criminal Law Review* 655, 657.

that argument might well have succeeded, because incitement requires successful communication to the incitee; but section 2(3) of the 1996 Act ensures that it cannot succeed in this case. D will accordingly be guilty of an offence under section 2.[106] Section 2(3) similarly applies in the converse type of case, where D, in Germany, incites E in England. It appears that a foreign Internet advertisement promoting child-sex tourism might equally constitute an offence by virtue of section 2(3), merely through its being read by an Internet surfer (or a police officer searching for such material) in England.[107]

Conspiracy to Commit an Offence under Foreign Law

The Sexual Offences (Conspiracy and Incitement) Act 1996 focused on just one type of ulterior offence (that is, the sexual abuse of children abroad) but on two types of inchoate offence. It was followed two years later by the Criminal Justice (Terrorism and Conspiracy) Act 1998, which extends to almost all types of ulterior offence but applies only in respect of conspiracies. Section 5 of this Act amends the Criminal Law Act 1977 by inserting a new section 1A. This creates a new and distinct variant of the offence of statutory conspiracy, by providing for the trial and conviction of persons of any nationality who conspire within England and Wales to commit acts outside the United Kingdom that would (if committed in accordance with the conspiracy) amount to offences under the relevant local law, and which would amount to offences under English law if committed within England and Wales. The original proviso to section 1(4) of the 1977 Act was evidently (if wrongly) considered otiose once the new section 1A was enacted, and it was accordingly repealed. Also repealed was section 1 of the Sexual Offences (Conspiracy and Incitement) Act 1996. As previously explained, this provision had already been stripped of any real importance by the enactment of the Sex Offenders Act 1997, and its remaining ambit was wholly subsumed within the new section 1A.

Background to the New Law

Whereas other provisions of the 1998 Act[108] were passed primarily in response to terrorist acts or threats connected with Northern Ireland, the genesis of section 5 must be found elsewhere. To some extent it was inspired by the Lloyd Committee's *Inquiry into Legislation Against Terrorism*.[109] The Lloyd Committee's Report advised that, despite the enactment of earlier legislation, such as the Suppression of Terrorism Act 1978, the

---

[106] If D's friend F were a British citizen, the offence of incitement would remain triable, even if 'committed' in Germany, by virtue of s. 7 of and Sch. 2, para. 3 to the 1997 Act.

[107] See Alldridge, op. cit., fn 102, 35. Cf. *R* v. *Perrin* [2002] All ER (D) 359 (Mar); [2002] EWCA Crim 747.

[108] Most of these were subsequently repealed by the Terrorism Act 2000, s. 125(2) and Sch. 16.   [109] Cmnd. 3420 (1996).

United Kingdom was becoming a haven for active international terrorists. The concerns raised by 'British connections' to acts of overseas terrorism were (and remain) amply justified. The presence of active foreign terrorists on British soil may pose only a limited threat to national security, if their only quarrel is with distant foreign states; but it may easily do great damage to the United Kingdom's relations with those states,[110] and to its image as a state which opposes terrorism in all its forms. Even though most of these suspected terrorists are not British nationals, there are often difficulties in securing their extradition or deportation,[111] and the Lloyd Report accordingly concluded: 'The most significant additional measure which the government can take is to amend the law of conspiracy so as to facilitate the prosecution of those who conspire here to commit terrorist acts abroad.'[112]

Nevertheless, the jurisdictional ambit of the new conspiracy provision goes well beyond anything recommended in the Lloyd Report.[113] It is confined neither to terrorist acts nor to offences that might be associated with terrorism. Indeed, most acts of international terrorism are now likely to involve one or more of the recognized extraterritorial offences under English law, which means that conspiracies to commit them will ordinarily fall within section 1(1) of the Criminal Law Act 1977, if entered into in England or Wales. If so, they cannot fall within the new section 1A at all. To put it another way, section 1A now appears to be applicable almost exclusively to *non-terrorist* offences. This was largely true when the 1998 Act was passed, and later legislation has further eroded what little application section 1A ever had to terrorist crime.[114] This paradox does not seem to have been appreciated by Parliament or the Government. As far as they were concerned, the threat posed by world terrorism was the principal justification for the enactment of the new measure.[115]

While the concerns highlighted by the Lloyd Report undoubtedly helped to secure the passing of the new conspiracy law, the detailed content of that

---

[110] Informal protests against the activities of alleged foreign terrorists in Britain had been made by a number of countries, including Algeria, Saudi Arabia, India, Egypt, and France. France made similar complaints as long ago as 1858, when the UK was accused of providing a haven for Italian conspirators who were implicated in the Orsini bomb plot against Napoleon III.

[111] See, e.g., *Chahal v. UK* [1996] 23 EHRR 413; *Secretary of State for the Home Department* v. *Rehman* [2002] 1 All ER 122.

[112] Op. cit., fn 109, para. 12.40. See also *Hansard*, vol. 317, col. 737. Note, however, that the proviso to s. 1(4) of the Criminal Law Act 1977 did in fact make it an offence for foreigners (such as exiled dissidents) to conspire in England to commit murder abroad, regardless of whether such a murder would have been justiciable under English law.

[113] See Colm Campbell, 'Two Steps Backwards: the Criminal Justice (Terrorism and Conspiracy) Act 1998' [1999] *Criminal Law Review* 941.

[114] See in particular the Terrorism Act 2000, s. 62, which created a new substantive offence of terrorist bombing outside the UK. Many (but not all) such bombings would already have been punishable under earlier legislation, such as the Suppression of Terrorism Act 1978, s. 4.

[115] See *Hansard* (HC) vol. 317, col. 737 (2 September 1998), in which the Home Secretary explicitly justified the measures as a response to the threat posed by international terrorism.

law appears to owe more to the proposals of an Interdepartmental Steering Committee, which had been established by the Home Secretary in 1996 in order to review the operation of criminal jurisdiction under United Kingdom law, and had reported later that year. While the Committee was primarily concerned with issues appertaining to extraterritorial jurisdiction, one of its proposals was that existing territorial offences of conspiracy and incitement should be extended so as to embrace acts of incitement or conspiracy directed to the commission of crimes under foreign law. The Committee considered the possible extension of those inchoate offences to specified offences only,[116] but eventually decided against that option:

The Committee acknowledged that, although there was some merit in directing efforts against substantive acts where there were identified mischiefs to address, the extent of existing and proposed extensions were so wide as to leave it difficult to justify not taking jurisdiction over conspiracy and incitement to commit any offence (possibly any indictable offence) abroad.[117]

The Committee made few detailed proposals as to the drafting of any legislation, other than to specify a double criminality test, under which, 'the behaviour . . . envisaged by the conspiracy or incitement would have to be an offence both in this country and in the country where it was planned to take place'. In the event, the proposals were acted upon only in so far as they related to conspiracy.[118] The way in which this was done is likely to prove problematic, for reasons that are explained below.

The Section 1A Offence

Section 1A of the Criminal Law Act 1977 (inserted by section 5 of the 1998 Act) provides:

(1) Where each of the following conditions is satisfied in the case of an agreement, this Part of this Act has effect in relation to the agreement as it has effect in relation to an agreement falling within section 1(1) above.[119]

(2) The first condition is that the pursuit of the agreed course of conduct would at some stage involve—
   (a) an act by one or more of the parties, or
   (b) the happening of some other event,
intended to take place in a country or territory outside the United Kingdom.

---

[116] Amongst those considered were sex tourism (which, as we have seen, was the subject of legislation enacted earlier that same year), together with football hooliganism and terrorism.

[117] *Review of Extraterritorial Jurisdiction: Report of the Interdepartmental Steering Committee* (1996), para. 2.37.

[118] An offence of incitement to commit terrorist crimes abroad was later enacted in the Terrorism Act 2000, s. 59. See below, p. 149.

[119] This means that s. 2 (exemptions from liability), s. 3 (penalties), s. 4 (restrictions on and consents to prosecution), and s. 5 (savings etc.) apply to s. 1A as they apply to s. 1(1); but some provisions in Pt 1 of the Act (notably s. 1(4)) cannot sensibly be made to apply to s. 1A.

(3) The second condition is that that act or other event constitutes an offence under the law in force in that country or territory.

(4) The third condition is that the agreement would fall within section 1(1) above as an agreement relating to the commission of an offence but for the fact that the offence would not be an offence triable in England and Wales if committed in accordance with the parties' intentions.

(5) The fourth condition is that—

(a) a party to the agreement, or a party's agent, did anything in England and Wales in relation to the agreement before its formation, or

(b) a party to the agreement became a party in England and Wales (by joining it either in person or through an agent), or

(c) a party to the agreement, or a party's agent, did or omitted anything in England and Wales in pursuance of the agreement.

(6) In the application of this Part of this Act to an agreement in the case of which each of the above conditions is satisfied, a reference to an offence is to be read as a reference to what would be the offence in question but for the fact that it is not an offence triable in England and Wales.

(7) Conduct punishable under the law in force in any country or territory is an offence under that law for the purposes of this section, however it is described in that law.

(8) Subject to subsection (9) below, the second condition is to be taken to be satisfied unless, not later than rules of court may provide, the defence serve on the prosecution a notice—

(a) stating that, on the facts as alleged with respect to the agreed course of conduct, the condition is not in their opinion satisfied,

(b) showing their grounds for that opinion, and

(c) requiring the prosecution to show that it is satisfied.

(9) The court may permit the defence to require the prosecution to show that the second condition is satisfied without the prior service of a notice under subsection (8) above.

(10) In the Crown Court the question whether the second condition is satisfied shall be decided by the judge alone, and shall be treated as a question of law for the purposes of—

(a) section 9(3) of the Criminal Justice Act 1987 (preparatory hearing in fraud cases), and

(b) section 31(3) of the Criminal Procedure and Investigations Act 1996 (preparatory hearing in other cases).

(11) Any act done by means of a message (however communicated) is to be treated for the purposes of the fourth condition as done in England and Wales if the message is sent or received in England and Wales.

(12) In any proceedings in respect of an offence triable by virtue of this section, it is immaterial to guilt whether or not the accused was a British citizen at the time of any act or other event proof of which is required for conviction of the offence.

(13) References in any enactment, instrument or document (except those in this Part of this Act) to an offence of conspiracy to commit an offence include an offence triable in England and Wales as such a conspiracy by virtue of this section (without prejudice to subsection (6) above).

(14) Nothing in this section—

(a) applies to an agreement entered into before the day on which the Criminal Justice (Terrorism and Conspiracy) Act 1998 was passed,[120] or

(b) imposes criminal liability on any person acting on behalf of, or holding office under, the Crown.[121]

Proceedings for an offence under section 1A may ordinarily be instituted only by or with the consent of the Attorney-General.[122] This is in recognition of the fact that dissidents in the United Kingdom who plot to oppose, overthrow, or protest against certain foreign regimes (such as Iraq's) may sometimes be perceived as champions of liberty both here and elsewhere in the world. A decision to prosecute under section 1A may therefore be politically sensitive.

The basic format of section 1A seems unnecessarily complicated. It would surely have been both easier and more effective to have amended or redefined section 1(1) of the 1977 Act so as to create a single offence of statutory conspiracy, but one that could be committed in either of two ways, namely:

(1) by conspiring anywhere in the world to commit an offence triable under English law; or

(2) by conspiring within English jurisdiction to commit an act abroad that would be an offence under English law if committed in England or Wales and would also be an offence under the law of the country where it was intended to be committed.

Regrettably, section 1A eschews that approach. Instead, it creates a new and distinct offence (statutory conspiracy triable by virtue of that section) which is mutually incompatible with the existing offence under section 1(1) but which may all too easily be confused with it. Assume, for example, that foreign conspirators agree, in London, to commit an act of murder in their own (or in a third) country. Is this a conspiracy under section 1(1), or a conspiracy under section 1A? The answer may be far from obvious, given the relative obscurity and complexity of many of the provisions that create extraterritorial offences.[123] Cases may even arise in which, owing to a lack

---

[120] Namely, 14 September 1998.

[121] This exempts both British agents and persons (such as foreign rebels or dissidents) who agree to act on their behalf in ways that may involve offences under local law.

[122] See s. 4(5). This rule is subject to any special arrangements made under s. 4(6).

[123] How many criminal lawyers are familiar with, e.g., s. 4 of the Suppression of Terrorism Act 1978? How many would know that a conspiracy in England to commit a murder in Brazil or Nigeria would be triable under s. 1A if the proposed murderer is a Pakistani, Nigerian, or US citizen, but triable only under s. 1 if the proposed killer is an Indian, Spanish, or Irish citizen?

of evidence as to the precise identity of the proposed crime or of its intended location or perpetrator, the answer simply cannot be established.

The real problem is that the legislation permits no overlap between the two provisions: if the proposed conduct would amount to an extraterritorial offence under English law, the conspiracy *must* be charged under section 1(1), and not under section 1A. To make matters worse, it may well be impossible to effect any last minute amendment or correction of an indictment, so as to substitute a charge under section 1A for one under section 1 (or vice versa), because of the need (under section 4 of the 1977 Act) to obtain consents to the instigation of prosecutions.[124]

Conspiracies to commit cross-frontier offences of fraud or dishonesty may give rise to particularly difficult problems. As explained at pp. 165–71 below, a substantive 'Group A' cross-frontier theft or fraud will fall within English jurisdiction if (but only if) a 'relevant event' takes place within England and Wales. Difficulties may arise, however, in distinguishing between 'relevant events' on the one hand and mere incidental results, on the other. If the defendants are charged with conspiracy to commit a Group A offence, the indictment must be laid under section 1 of the 1977 Act if the conspirators intended that a relevant event should take place within the jurisdiction, but under section 1A if they had no such intent.[125] Even if the intent of the conspirators is clear, there may be room for argument as to whether a given event would have been 'a relevant event' under section 2 of the 1993 Act. If the indictment is laid under section 1A, the defence might thus defeat it by requiring the prosecution to prove that *no* relevant event was intended to occur in England. It is all very unsatisfactory, and it suggests that nothing was learnt from the unfortunate period during which statutory conspiracy and conspiracy to defraud were considered to be mutually exclusive offences.[126]

Nor is this the only problem with the drafting of section 1A. Subsections (2) and (3) are also problematic, because they appear to assume that a conspiracy which does not relate to an offence triable under English law will be worth prosecuting only if it does at least involve an agreement to do something in 'a country or territory outside the United Kingdom' that would be an offence under the law of that country or territory. What, then, of a conspiracy to commit an offence (under foreign law) aboard a foreign ship? Assuming that no substantive offence under English law would be

---

[124] In particular, the Attorney-General's consent is required for any prosecution under s. 1A (see s. 4(6)) or (in some cases) for prosecutions under s. 1. As to the problem of amending indictments in cases requiring such consent, see *R v. Natji* [2002] All ER (D) 177 (Feb).

[125] A person may be guilty of conspiracy to commit such an offence whether or not any act or omission in relation to that offence occurred in England or Wales (Criminal Justice Act 1993, s. 3(2)).

[126] See *R v. Ayres* [1984] AC 447. The problem was resolved by the Criminal Justice Act 1987, s. 12. A similar solution might be apposite in relation to ss. 1 and 1A of the 1977 Act.

involved, such a conspiracy would appear to be unpunishable, because there is nothing in section 1A that applies to foreign ships.[127]

Further defects are not hard to find. What if there is a conspiracy in England to commit murder in Scotland or Northern Ireland? Or what if two divers conspire in England to murder a third during a planned dive on a wreck lying just outside territorial waters? In neither of these cases would the murder itself be triable under English law; but until the enactment of the Criminal Justice (Terrorism and Conspiracy) Act 1998, such conspiracies would have been indictable under section 1 of the 1977 Act, by virtue of the proviso to section 1(4). The repeal of this proviso has left a lacuna that the new section 1A does not fill. This lacuna was almost certainly unintentional, but there is no way in which section 1A can be interpreted so as to avoid it.[128]

Solicitation to Commit Murder Abroad

Although section 5 of the Criminal Justice (Terrorism and Conspiracy) Act 1998 conspicuously omits to address the issue of incitement to commit crimes under foreign law, section 4 of the Offences Against the Person Act 1861 remains in force. This may just possibly be construed as creating yet another exception to the general rule governing inchoate offences, but the better view is that it merely restates the common law of incitement in so far as that law relates to murder. It provides:

Whosoever shall solicit, encourage, persuade or endeavour to persuade, or shall propose to any person, to murder any other person, whether he be a subject of her Majesty or not, and whether he be within the Queen's dominions or not, shall be guilty of an offence. . . .

The phrase, 'whether he be a subject of her Majesty or not' may seem ambiguous, but it must in fact refer to the intended victim, rather than to the person incited.[129] This becomes clear if one examines the original text of section 4, which began with a reference to conspiracy in the following terms: 'All Persons who shall conspire, confederate, and agree to murder any person, whether he be a subject of her Majesty or not, and whether he be within the Queen's dominions or not. . . .'[130] The nationality or status of the victim would in any case have been irrelevant at common law, and on

---

[127] Ships and aircraft cannot automatically be equated with the territory of the flag state or the state of registration. Contrast the wording of the Extradition Act 1989, s. 2(4), or the Suppression of Terrorism Act 1978, s. 4(7).

[128] In the case of a conspiracy to commit murder in Scotland or Northern Ireland, it is at least likely that the courts of Scotland or Northern Ireland could deal with the matter; but the murder of a diver outside territorial waters might not be an offence under any law.

[129] See *R v. Most* (1881) 7 QBD 244. M's offence was to publish an article in England, advocating the assassination of European rulers.

[130] These words were repealed by the Criminal Law Act 1977, Sch. 13.

that basis it is doubtful whether section 4 adds anything of substance to the common law of incitement. Although it may apply to persons who, in England and Wales, incite the commission of murder abroad, the murder incited would have to be an offence triable under English law, because section 4 makes no provision to the contrary. Murder committed by a British citizen on land abroad would indeed be such an offence, but murder committed by a foreigner abroad would not be.[131]

Incitement to Acts of Terrorism Overseas

Section 59 of the Terrorism Act 2000 provides:

(1) A person commits an offence if—
    (a) he incites another person to commit an act of terrorism wholly or partly outside the United Kingdom, and
    (b) the act would, if committed in England and Wales, constitute one of the offences listed in subsection (2).

(2) Those offences are—
    (a) murder,
    (b) an offence under section 18 of the Offences Against the Person Act 1861 (wounding with intent),
    (c) an offence under section 23 or 24 of that Act (poison),
    (d) an offence under section 28 or 29 of that Act (explosions), and
    (e) an offence under section 1(2) of the Criminal Damage Act 1971 (endangering life by damaging property).

(3) A person guilty of an offence under this section shall be liable to any penalty to which he would be liable on conviction of the offence listed in subsection (2) which corresponds to the act which he incites.

(4) For the purposes of subsection (1) it is immaterial whether or not the person incited is in the United Kingdom at the time of the incitement.

(5) Nothing in this section imposes criminal liability on any person acting on behalf of, or holding office under, the Crown.

The explanatory note to this provision draws analogies with section 1A of the Criminal Law Act 1977, and asserts that it 'similarly makes it an offence for a person in England and Wales to incite terrorist acts abroad'. Some basic similarities do indeed exist, but section 59 is in fact a very different provision to section 1A of the 1977 Act. Although flawed in several respects, it is drafted in such as way as to avoid the worst of the pitfalls that now beset the law of conspiracy.

One important difference is that section 59 applies only to cases involving incitement to acts of terrorism. Incitement of another person to commit

---

[131] Unless, for example, the murder would be triable under the Suppression of Terrorism Act 1978, s. 4, or under the Internationally Protected Persons Act 1978, s. 1(1).

one of the specified offences abroad is not an offence under that provision unless it can be proved that the act incited was (or would have been) an act of terrorism as defined in section 1 of the Act. Section 1 provides:

(1) In this Act 'terrorism' means the use or threat of action where—
   (a) the action falls within subsection (2),
   (b) the use or threat is designed to influence the government or to intimidate the public or a section of the public, and
   (c) the use or threat is made for the purpose of advancing a political, religious or ideological cause.

(2) Action falls within this subsection if it—
   (a) involves serious violence against a person,
   (b) involves serious damage to property,
   (c) endangers a person's life, other than that of the person committing the action,
   (d) creates a serious risk to the health or safety of the public or a section of the public, or
   (e) is designed seriously to interfere with or seriously to disrupt an electronic system.

(3) The use or threat of action falling within subsection (2) which involves the use of firearms or explosives is terrorism whether or not subsection (1)(b) is satisfied.

(4) In this section—
   (a) 'action' includes action outside the United Kingdom,
   (b) a reference to any person or to property is a reference to any person, or to property, wherever situated,
   (c) a reference to the public includes a reference to the public of a country other than the United Kingdom, and
   (d) 'the government' means the government of the United Kingdom, of a Part of the United Kingdom or of a country other than the United Kingdom.

(5) In this Act a reference to action taken for the purposes of terrorism includes a reference to action taken for the benefit of a proscribed organisation.

It is in some respects surprising that this section deals only with incitement to acts of terrorism. The Interdepartmental Steering Committee that reported in 1996 favoured a much wider ambit for the offences of incitement and conspiracy, and in respect of conspiracy, section 1A of the 1977 Act reflects this view. There is no obvious reason why it should not be made an offence for a person in England to incite the commission of a serious crime of any sort within another state's jurisdiction.

Section 59 does not purport to create any extraterritorial offence, but section 59(4) provides that it is immaterial whether the person incited was within the United Kingdom at the time. This appears to suggest that the inciter must himself be within English jurisdiction, if he is to be triable under section 59.[132] If D, in England, incites E, in Ireland, to commit a

---

[132] Namely, within England and Wales, or aboard a British ship, etc. Separate provisions of the Act (ss. 60 and 61) apply to Scotland and Northern Ireland, whereas the purely extraterritorial

relevant act of terrorism in the USA, section 59 makes this an offence under English law, even though on normal territorial principles incitement is a result crime that is 'committed' only when and where the incitement is communicated. What then if D, in Ireland, incites E, in England, to commit a relevant act of terrorism in the USA? Assuming the act of terrorism is one that would involve an extraterritorial offence punishable under English law, D will be guilty of incitement at common law or (if it involves murder) of solicitation to murder under section 4 of the Offences Against the Person Act 1861. This is because, on normal territorial principles, the incitement is committed in England; but if the act incited is one that would be an offence only under US law, we have a problem. It cannot be a case of incitement at common law, because E has not been incited to commit an offence under English law; and it cannot be an offence under section 59 of the Terrorism Act, because E's presence in England is expressly deemed to be immaterial. The draftsman probably assumed that incitement is committed where it is uttered, rather than where it is communicated, but the case law is firmly against that proposition.[133] Fortunately, most substantive terrorist offences are punishable under English law, wherever and by whomsoever committed.

For most purposes, section 59 does not require any distinction to be drawn between cases in which the act incited would be punishable under English law and cases in which it would not. This is to be welcomed. Terrorist acts committed abroad will usually (but not inevitably) be punishable as extraterritorial offences under English law, and it may sometimes be difficult to establish whether the act incited would be so triable or not.[134] The incitement may even relate to some acts that would be triable in England and some that would not.[135]

A further possible criticism is that the Act fails to address the problem of incitement in one part of the United Kingdom to commit terrorist acts in another. If D in Birmingham incites E in London to commit an explosives offence in Belfast, no offence is committed under section 59, or indeed under any other provision in English law. It may well be the case that an

---

offences of terrorist bombing and terrorist finance, created by ss. 62 and 63, each apply throughout the UK.

[133] *R* v. *Banks* (1873) 12 Cox 393; *R* v. *Ransford* (1874) 13 Cox 9; *R* v. *Krause* (1902) 66 JP 121; *R* v. *Cope* (1922) 16 Cr App R 77. Had the draftsman followed the precedent established by the Computer Misuse Act 1990, and made the ambit of the s. 59 offence dependent on the establishment of a 'significant link with domestic jurisdiction', such problems would not have arisen.

[134] The notes to the Terrorism Act explain: 'The offence of incitement to specific acts commonly associated with terrorism (such as hostage taking or hijacking aircraft) is already available, by virtue of the extraterritorial jurisdiction established over such offences in the past—and elsewhere in this Act—in legislation implementing various international counter-terrorism Conventions. This provision will, therefore, fill in remaining gaps in the law.'

[135] This might be the case where some of the persons incited are British citizens and some are not.

offence of incitement has been committed under the law of Northern Ireland, despite the fact that nothing has yet occurred within Northern Ireland, but there is no direct authority on that question in the context of incitement, and the omission must therefore be considered a defect in the new legislation.

Conduct Ancillary to Genocide, etc., Committed Abroad

Section 52 of the International Criminal Court Act 2001, read in conjunction with section 55 of that Act, makes it an offence for any person within England and Wales to incite, attempt, or conspire to commit an act of genocide, a war crime, or a crime against humanity, or to aid, abet, counsel, or procure such an act, or to assist an offender or conceal the commission of an offence, even where the crime assisted or incited, etc., is (or is to be) committed abroad by persons who are not subject to English criminal law.[136] These provisions also create some fully extraterritorial offences, and are more closely examined in Chapter 5 below.

Inchoate Offences Initiated Abroad

Thus far, we have considered inchoate acts that are committed within England and Wales but directed towards the commission of offences abroad. In the obverse scenario, acts of conspiracy, incitement, or attempt may be committed wholly or partly abroad but with the object of committing or procuring the commission of substantive offences within England and Wales. Such acts might take a number of different forms. D, in Germany, may incite E (also in Germany) to commit an offence in England; or he may instead incite F, who is already in England. D may then enter into a conspiracy with E or F. He may eventually launch an attempt to commit the offence in England, without ever entering the jurisdiction. He may do this in one of several ways: by despatching a letter, fax, or e-mail; by making an international telephone call; by concealing an explosive device in a package; by hacking into a computer; and so on.

In most respects the law governing such acts is now reasonably clear. It has been established, for example, that D may become guilty of an inchoate offence under English law even if he has never physically entered English jurisdiction. It is also clear (despite the existence of some older authorities to the contrary) that a conspiracy or attempt may be triable in England and Wales, even if no 'overt acts' have been committed within the jurisdiction, no messages transmitted there, and no consequences caused there. There is little direct authority dealing with cross-frontier incitement, but it is

---

[136] The Act does not create offences of universal jurisdiction.

submitted that the same general principles must apply in such cases as apply in cases of conspiracy or attempt.

Acts or Consequences within the Jurisdiction

Applying normal 'terminatory' principles, one may sometimes find that D has in fact committed an inchoate offence within the jurisdiction, even if he has not entered it himself. If, for example, D in Germany mails or telephones F in England and incites him to commit an offence there, the offence of incitement (a result crime under English law) is committed in England, where the incitement is communicated.[137] Inchoate offences will often be 'ongoing'. Even if begun outside the jurisdiction, they may continue to operate within it (and vice versa).

A number of the older reported cases dealing with inchoate offences appear to have relied on this type of reasoning in order to justify the assumption of jurisdiction. In *R v. Baxter*,[138] for example, B's conviction for attempting to obtain property by deception from football pools companies in Liverpool was upheld on the basis that, although he had initially committed the attempt by posting his letters in Northern Ireland, the attempt was an ongoing act that spread into England when his fraudulent letters arrived in Liverpool.

Baxter was approved by a majority of the House of Lords in *DPP v. Stonehouse*,[139] in which the appellant, a well-known English politician, had faked his death by drowning in Miami, before flying out to Australia using a false passport and identity. He had previously arranged substantial life assurance cover in England, for the benefit of his wife.[140] Had he not been found a few weeks later, living in Australia, his wife might eventually have obtained the benefit of the relevant life policies. For obvious reasons, he had taken no positive action to further the attempt in England and Wales following his supposed demise, but as Viscount Dilhorne pointed out:

The false representations were made in Miami with the object of leading the insurance companies to believe that the appellant had died and of enabling his wife to obtain the sums for which his life was insured. If false representations had been made by him by post while in Miami with a view to obtaining goods or money in England, there is no doubt that the English courts would have had jurisdiction to try him for attempting to obtain property by deception (see *R v. Baxter*). Does it make any difference that they were not so communicated and that the communications of the false representations as to his death were not made by the appellant? I think not. The object of staging his death was that insurance companies should be led to believe him dead. He must have known that news of his death would receive the widest publicity. They were representations to the world, but intended to be acted on and believed in England. Knowing that they were bound to be

---

[137] See *R v. Krause* (1902) 66 JP 121.   [138] [1972] 1 QB 1.   [139] [1978] AC 55.
[140] His wife was not alleged to be a party to the deception.

communicated to England and that being his object, I do not think that the fact that he made no communication himself is of any significance in relation to the question of jurisdiction.[141]

Neither in *Baxter* nor in *Stonehouse* was it strictly necessary for the courts to decide whether an inchoate offence can be committed under English law where no relevant act or event has occurred within the jurisdiction, but the basis of the Court of Appeal's decision in *Baxter* was that the appellant committed no attempt within the ambit of English law until the first of his fraudulent letters arrived in England. This, in other words, was defined as the crucial event on which jurisdiction was founded. Lord Keith adopted a similar stance in *Stonehouse*:

In my opinion it is not the present law of England that an offence is committed if no effect of an act done abroad is felt here, even though it was the intention that it should be. Thus if a person on the Scottish bank of the Tweed, where it forms the border between Scotland and England, were to fire a rifle at someone on the English bank, with intent to kill him, and actually did so, he would be guilty of murder under English law. If he fired with similar intent but missed his intended victim, he would be guilty of attempted murder under English law, because the presence of the bullet in England would be an intended effect of his act. But if he pressed the trigger and his weapon misfired, he would be guilty of no offence under the law of England, provided at least that the intended victim was unaware of the attempt, since no effect would have been felt there.[142]

Nor was this line of authority confined to cases involving criminal attempts. In *DPP* v. *Doot*,[143] much the same view was taken in respect of jurisdiction over conspiracy. The House of Lords held in that case that a conspiracy by US citizens to smuggle cannabis from Morocco to England was indictable under English law, even though the conspiracy had originally been hatched abroad, but the decision was reached on the basis that the conspirators had entered the jurisdiction while the conspiracy was still in existence and some of them had actually imported the vehicles in which the drugs were concealed.[144] The leading speech was given by Lord Pearson, who said:

On principle . . . a conspiracy to commit in England an offence against English law ought to be triable in England if it has been wholly or partly performed in England. In such a case the conspiracy has been carried on in England with the consent and authority of all the conspirators. It is not necessary that they should all be present in England. One of them, acting on his own behalf and as agent for the others, has

---

[141] [1978] AC 55, 75.   [142] Ibid., 93.   [143] [1973] AC 807.

[144] In other words, the substantive offence had quite clearly been committed in England. This being the case, all parties to the conspiracy would have been triable in England, either as principal offenders or as secondary parties to the substantive offence. This would have been true even of any parties who remained outside the jurisdiction (See *R* v. *Robert Millar (Contractors) Ltd* [1970] 2 QB 54). It seems, therefore, that the prosecution's reliance on the conspiracy charge greatly complicated the proceedings. The cannabis was ultimately destined for export to the American market, but nothing turned on this fact.

been performing their agreement, with their consent and authority, in England. In such a case the conspiracy has been committed by all of them in England.[145]

In his concurring speech, Lord Salmon added:

If a conspiracy is entered into abroad to commit a crime in England, exactly the same public mischief is produced by it as if it had been entered into here. It is unnecessary for me to consider what the position might be if the conspirators came to England for an entirely innocent purpose unconnected with the conspiracy. If, however, the conspirators come here and do acts in furtherance of the conspiracy, e.g. by preparing to commit the planned crime, it cannot, in my view, be considered contrary to the rules of international comity for the forces of law and order in England to protect the Queen's peace by arresting them and putting them on trial for conspiracy, whether they are British subjects or foreigners and whether or not conspiracy is a crime under the law of the country in which the conspiracy was born.[146]

Where Nothing Happens within the Jurisdiction

The reasoning relied upon by the courts in *Baxter*, *Stonehouse*, and *Doot* was broadly consistent with the terminatory theory of jurisdiction as it applies to substantive offences. The courts looked for acts or events that could be seen as manifestations of the attempt or conspiracy committed within England and Wales. What, then, of cases in which the inchoate offence is stopped or abandoned (or simply fails) before any relevant acts or events can occur within England and Wales? If one focuses on the interests that the criminal law exists to protect, and asks why inchoate offences are punishable in the first place, one may well conclude that the absence of relevant events in England should make no difference to the position. As Lord Salmon said in *Doot*, 'a conspiracy to carry out a bank robbery in London is equally a threat to the Queen's peace whether it is hatched . . . in Birmingham or in Brussels'. In *Stonehouse*, Lord Diplock warmed to that theme, and while he had no difficulty in agreeing that the appellant's attempt to deceive the insurance companies had been furthered in England by media reporting, his preferred view was that such happenings were not essential. As for *Baxter*, Lord Diplock's view was that the Crown Court would have had jurisdiction in that case even if the fraudulent claims had been intercepted in the post in Northern Ireland.[147]

While the views expressed by Lord Diplock and others (including the authors of *Smith and Hogan*[148]) kept the argument alive, the real breakthrough occurred when Lord Griffiths delivered the advice of the Privy Council in *Somchai Liangsiriprasert v. US Government*.[149] The issue that

---

[145] [1973] AC 807, 827.   [146] Ibid., 833.   [147] [1978] AC 55, 67.

[148] In the 6th edn of *Criminal Law* (1988), the authors argued, 'Where D has gone beyond mere preparation, the better view is that it is immaterial that no effect occurs in England. Why should the result have been different if [Stonehouse] had been "rescued" from the sea and confessed before any report of his death appeared in England?'   [149] [1991] 1 AC 225.

fell to be decided in that case was whether Hong Kong could lawfully extradite to the USA a fugitive who had conspired in Thailand to export heroin to the USA, given that no overt acts in furtherance of the conspiracy had occurred in the USA. Since Hong Kong's extradition law was similar to English law in its application of the double-criminality rule, the answer to this question turned on whether the conspiracy would have been triable in Hong Kong had Hong Kong been the intended destination of the heroin. The answer provided by Lord Griffiths was affirmative: 'A conspiracy entered into in Thailand with the intention of committing the criminal offence of trafficking in drugs in Hong Kong is justiciable in Hong Kong even if no overt act pursuant to the conspiracy has yet occurred in Hong Kong.'

Although the case itself had no connection with England and Wales, Lord Griffiths expressly considered the position under English law. He could see no compelling reason why the courts should refrain from punishing foreign conspiracies or attempts to do harm in England and Wales, even if no overt act (or other consequence) has occurred here:

Why should an overt act be necessary to found jurisdiction? In the case of conspiracy in England the crime is complete once the agreement is made and no further overt act need be proved as an ingredient of the crime. The only purpose of looking for an overt act in England in the case of a conspiracy entered into abroad can be to establish the link between the conspiracy and England or possibly to show the conspiracy is continuing. But if this can be established by other evidence, for example the taping of conversations between the conspirators showing a firm agreement to commit the crime at some future date, it defeats the preventative purpose of the crime of conspiracy to have to wait until some overt act is performed in pursuance of the conspiracy.

Unfortunately in this century crime has ceased to be largely local in origin and effect. Crime is now established on an international scale and the common law must face this new reality. Their Lordships can find nothing in precedent, comity or good sense that should inhibit the common law from regarding as justiciable in England inchoate crimes committed abroad which are intended to result in the commission of criminal offences in England.

While this ruling was widely approved, its initial appearance by no means resolved the position under English law, because a decision of the Privy Council could not in itself supplant the authority of cases such as *Baxter*, *Stonehouse*, or *Doot*. In *R* v. *Sansom*,[150] however, the Court of Appeal adopted the same approach. The four appellants were charged with conspiring to import cannabis. The cannabis had been transported from Morocco in a vessel named the *Lady Rose* and transferred to a British fishing boat, the *Danny Boy*, on the high seas. The meeting of the vessels was observed on radar, and the *Danny Boy*, together with its crew and cargo, was arrested by customs officers in British territorial waters, before any

---

[150] [1991] 2 All ER 145.

offence of unlawful importation had been committed.[151] The *Lady Rose* and its crew were arrested in Plymouth.

At the trial, the defence submitted that the conspiracy was not an offence under English law, because it had been formed outside the jurisdiction. The trial judge rejected that submission and his ruling was upheld on appeal. Taylor LJ quoted at length from the opinion of Lord Griffiths in *Liangsiriprasert*, and concluded that this approach 'should now be regarded as the law of England on this point'.[152]

The validity of this approach under English law has now been placed beyond doubt following its repeated endorsement by the House of Lords in *R v. Latif and Shahzad*,[153] *R v. Bow Street Metropolitan Stipendiary Magistrate, ex p Pinochet Ugarte (No. 3)*,[154] and *Re Al-Fawwaz*.[155] The facts of *Latif* were examined earlier in this chapter (at pp. 126–7). While the appellants in that case may not have been guilty of any substantive offence of importation, it was nevertheless held that S became guilty of an attempt in Pakistan when he first arranged for the heroin to be exported to London. Lord Steyn, who delivered the unanimous opinion of the Appellate Committee, said:

The attempted evasion in Pakistan, as well as the attempted evasion in England, were respectively directed at importation into the United Kingdom and associated with an importation into the United Kingdom. . . . The English courts have jurisdiction over such criminal attempts even though the overt acts take place abroad. The rationale is that the effect of the criminal attempt is directed at this country. Moreover, as Lord Griffiths explained in *Liangsiriprasert* v. *US Government* . . . as a matter of policy, jurisdiction over criminal attempts ought to rest with the country where it was intended that the full offence should take place. . . .[156]

The issue that arose in *Re Al-Fawwaz* was whether three suspected Al-Qaeda terrorists could be extradited from the United Kingdom to the USA, on charges alleging conspiracy to murder US citizens, 'within the jurisdiction of the United States'. The alleged conspiracies were formed outside the territory of the USA and primarily related to murders that were to be committed by attacks on US diplomats, peacekeeping forces, or other citizens in the Middle East and Africa, although they did include possible offences on

---

[151] Under the Customs and Excise Management Act 1979, s. 5(2), goods brought in by sea are not 'imported' until the ship comes within the limits of the relevant port.

[152] There was also clear evidence that one of the alleged conspirators had furthered the conspiracy within England by commissioning the *Danny Boy* and sailing in her to collect the cannabis from the *Lady Rose*, but this does not detract from the support given to the ruling in *Liangsiriprasert*.

[153] [1996] 1 WLR 104.   [154] [2000] 1 AC 147.

[155] [2002] 1 All ER 545. Endorsement of Lord Griffiths' views on inchoate offences can also be found in *R v. Manning* [1998] 2 Cr App R 461 and *R v. Naini* [1999] 2 Cr App R 398.

[156] [1996] 1 WLR 104, 116. See also A.T.H. Smith, *Property Offences, The Protection of Property through the Criminal Law* (2nd edn, 1994), para. 1–37.

American soil. Could these largely extraterritorial conspiracies be said to involve offences 'within the jurisdiction of the United States' as required under the extradition treaty of 1972?[157]

The House of Lords held that it would suffice if such conspiracies:

(1) were triable as extraterritorial offences under US law; and
(2) would equally have been triable as extraterritorial offences under English law, had the United Kingdom been the requesting state and British nationals the target of the alleged conspiracies.

Liangsiriprasert was considered to be relevant to this issue, in so far as it concerned an extraterritorial conspiracy, and their Lordships each approved the approach taken by Lord Griffiths in that case. Lord Millett said:

> When Lord Griffiths referred to a conspiracy 'aimed at England' he was clearly thinking of a conspiracy to commit a crime in England. If a conspiracy to plant bombs in England would be triable in England, even though it was entirely inchoate and no bombs had yet been planted anywhere, a conspiracy to plant bombs in England and abroad where some bombs had already been planted abroad would be *a fortiori*. This is sufficient to uphold the jurisdiction in the present case, since a conspiracy to murder British subjects because they were British and for no other reason must be a conspiracy to murder them wherever they might be found, whether in England or elsewhere; and such a conspiracy is (*inter alia*) a conspiracy to commit a crime in England.[158]

CROSS-FRONTIER FRAUD OR DISHONESTY

Although international terrorism and drug trafficking cases understandably attract greater media attention, the majority of cross-frontier offences that come before the courts involve acts of theft, fraud, blackmail, or other forms of dishonesty.[159] Some involve massive and complex business, investment, or banking operations, as in *Secretary of State for Trade* v. *Markus*[160] or *R* v. *Governor of Pentonville Prison, ex p Osman*,[161] whilst others, such as *R* v. *Harden*,[162] involve relatively simple schemes, typically perpetrated or attempted by means of international telephone or postal services.

While the basic problem is by no means a new one, the technological revolution that occurred in the latter part of the twentieth century, together

---

[157] See SI 1976 No. 2144 and the Extradition Act 1989, Sch. 1.
[158] [2002] 1 All ER 545, 577–8.
[159] 'Dishonesty' is used here (as in Pt 1 of the Criminal Justice Act 1993) in a general sense, so as to include offences of forgery and counterfeiting, which do not in fact require dishonesty in the specific sense required by most offences under the Theft Acts.
[160] [1976] AC 35.   [161] [1990] 1 WLR 277.   [162] [1963] QB 8.

with the associated globalization of the banking industry and financial markets, inevitably led to a major increase in the number, size, and complexity of international frauds. It also made it easier for major international frauds to be perpetrated by individual employees or computer hackers. A notable example can be found in *R v. Governor of Brixton Prison, ex p Levin*,[163] in which the US Government produced evidence that L, in St Petersburg, Russia, had used his skill as a computer programmer to gain unauthorized access to the electronic fund transfer service of an American bank, Citibank NA in Parsipanny, New Jersey, from which he fraudulently made 40 transfers of funds totalling $US10·7 million from the accounts of clients of Citibank to accounts maintained by his associate (or by companies controlled by him) at a bank in San Francisco. L did all this without leaving his computer terminal in St Petersburg, but the Divisional Court nevertheless upheld an order to proceed with his extradition to America. As Beldam LJ explained:

The applicant's keyboard was connected electronically with the Citibank computer in Parsipanny; as he pressed the keys his actions, as he intended, recorded or stored information for all practical purposes, simultaneously on the magnetic disc in the computer. . . . The fact that the applicant was physically in St Petersburg is of far less significance than the fact that he was looking at and operating on magnetic discs located in Parsipanny. The essence of what he was doing was done there.[164]

A more mundane but troublesome example is provided by *R v. Thompson*,[165] in which a computer operator employed by a bank in Kuwait programmed the bank's computer there so as to skim funds from clients' accounts and credit them to his own. On his return to England, it was a relatively simple matter for him to arrange for the transfer of 'his' funds in Kuwait to new accounts he had opened in England. Whilst in some way this was a much simpler fraud than that practised in *Levin*, it was arguably more problematic in terms of English jurisdiction, because the original fraud appeared to have been perpetrated (and the funds initially obtained) entirely within Kuwait. The Court of Appeal eventually concluded that T had not obtained any property in Kuwait, because the fact that he had transferred the funds fraudulently meant that the sums supposedly credited to his account there were not really his, and therefore no *chose in action* had been created there in his favour.[166] He had obtained the funds only when they were transferred to his English accounts, and his conviction for

---

[163] [1997] QB 65.
[164] Ibid., 80–81. L's appeal (on other grounds) to the House of Lords was also dismissed: see [1997] AC 741.   [165] [1984] 1 WLR 962.
[166] The possible difficulties arising from the House of Lords' controversial ruling in *R v. Preddy* [1996] AC 815 had not then been appreciated.

obtaining property by deception was upheld. May LJ said:

We agree with the judge in the court below that the only realistic view of the undisputed facts in this case is that the six instances of obtaining charged in the indictment each occurred when the relevant sums of money were received by the appellant's bank in England.[167]

International fraud does occasionally become headline news, as, for example, in the case of Nick Leeson, the 'rogue trader' whose activities in Singapore caused the collapse of Barings, London's oldest merchant bank. Leeson was arguably a reckless fool, rather than a cynical fraudster, but his attempts to conceal his original losses in the Japanese derivatives market by further, even more disastrous, trading nevertheless involved international fraud on an almost unprecedented scale, the principal victim of which was Barings Bank, whose London office was deceived into advancing him the £ millions he needed to keep operating in Singapore. Few fraudsters have ever achieved the dubious distinction of bringing down a major English bank, but despite this, it is by no means clear that Leeson committed any offence under the rules of English law that were applicable at that time.[168]

Faced with modern forms of international fraud, the traditional 'terminatory' approach to identifying the *locus* of a crime, which had always been open to criticism, was increasingly made to look inadequate and (as one leading commentator put it) 'parochial to an embarrassing degree'.[169] This view was widely shared by the judges themselves, which is why the 'international comity' theory, first expounded by Lord Diplock in *Treacy* v. *DPP*,[170] appealed to so many of them, both in England and in other common law jurisdictions, such as Canada.[171] In the absence of legislation to implement it, Lord Diplock's comity theory may have lacked any real basis under English law, but it would, if implemented, have represented a major advance on the rules which did apply. Radical reforms evidently were needed, but it was to be nearly 30 years before any such reforms were brought into force, and even these were to fall short of Lord Diplock's all-inclusive vision.

---

[167] [1984] 1 WLR 962, 968. The Court appears to have ignored any possible objection that the same considerations must have applied to the later transfer of the funds to England. Leaving aside the *Preddy* issue, it is also doubtful whether a defendant who had practised a similar computer fraud within England would have escaped conviction on the basis that the funds credited to his account 'were not really his'. Cf. *R* v. *Kohn* (1979) 69 Cr App R 395.

[168] Leeson's case never reached the English courts. He was arrested in Germany, whence he was extradited to Singapore. He had apparently hoped that he would instead be extradited to stand trial in the United Kingdom. See Geoff Gilbert, 'Who has Jurisdiction for Cross-Frontier Financial Crimes?' [1995] 2 Web JCLI; http://webjcli.ncl.ac.uk.

[169] Smith, op. cit., fn 156, para. 1–34. [170] As to this theory, see above, p. 42.

[171] See e.g., *Libman* v. *R* [1985] 2 SCR 178.

The Road to Reform

In 1986, the Roskill Committee recommended that the Law Commission should look into the problem of cross-frontier fraud.[172] This was something the Commission had conspicuously failed to do in its earlier report on *The Territorial and Extraterritorial Extent of the Criminal Law*,[173] but the recommendation was quickly acted upon. The following year, discussions were held between the Law Commission's criminal law team and representatives from the Home Office Criminal Policy Department, leading to the publication of a Consultation Paper[174] and in 1989 to a major report, entitled *Jurisdiction over Offences of Fraud and Dishonesty with a Foreign Element*.[175] The draft Jurisdiction Bill appended to this report eventually formed the model (with minor modifications) for Part 1 of the Criminal Justice Act 1993.

The Law Commission Report

In sharp contrast to its previous, half-hearted examination of the problems caused by cross-frontier offences, the Law Commission's 1989 Report adopted, as its guiding principle, the view that the problem was a serious one that required drastic remedies:

First, international fraud is a serious problem that is practised in many different and ingenious forms. It is essential that persons who commit frauds related to this country should not be able to avoid the jurisdiction of this country's courts simply on outdated or technical grounds, or because of the form in which they clothe the substance of their fraud. *Second*, it is particularly important that this country, as a leading international financial centre, should have and should be seen to have effective means of taking action against fraudulent conduct connected with this country. That consideration applies whether the fraudulent conduct is criminal dishonesty within this country, or the planning or preparation, either in this country or abroad, of criminal dishonesty affecting this country; or the use of this country for the planning or preparation of criminally dishonest acts abroad. *Third*, the present rules of this country about jurisdiction in offences of dishonesty have become increasingly difficult, complicated and controversial to apply, partly because they have not adapted adequately to fraud itself becoming increasingly complicated. The new rules should be simple and straightforward, in order substantially to reduce the amount of valuable court time taken up by technical arguments.[176]

It is difficult to argue with any of these sentiments, expect perhaps by pointing out that even the simplest of cross-frontier frauds had proved capable

---

[172] *Report of the Fraud Trials Committee*, para. 3.17.
[173] Law Com. No. 91 (1978). See Michael Hirst, 'Territorial Principles and the Law Commission' [1979] *Criminal Law Review* 355.
[174] For a comment on the 1987 Consultation Paper, see L.H. Leigh, 'Territorial Jurisdiction and Fraud' [1988] *Criminal Law Review* 280.
[175] Law Com. No. 180.   [176] Ibid., para. 1.4.

of causing jurisdictional difficulties under the traditional terminatory approach. At first sight, the Commission's first principal recommendation appears to demand similar support and approval:

We consider that in the case of substantive offences of dishonesty the present highly technical rules of jurisdiction should be abandoned in favour of a simple provision that such offences should be triable in this country if any part of the conduct or any of the results forbidden by such crimes takes place here.

There is arguably a weakness in the thinking here. The weakness lies in the fact that the specific offences of fraud or dishonesty to which the original proposals applied (and the additional offences to which the Criminal Justice Act 1993 now applies) do not necessarily involve 'forbidden results' at all. The relevant offences may involve conduct that tends to cause *harmful* results, but such results are not necessarily 'forbidden'. They may not necessarily involve definitional elements of the relevant offences; and while the general statement quoted above might have allowed for some element of flexibility as to what was meant by 'forbidden results', the more detailed proposals and draft clauses that followed clearly do not, as we shall see when we examine the provisions of the 1993 Act.

The Commission rightly gave detailed consideration to inchoate fraud offences. The general thrust of the Commission's proposals in respect of inchoate offences was similar to that in respect of substantive fraud offences, namely, that jurisdiction should be extended to cover both inward and outward acts. It was proposed that an attempt in England to commit a fraud in another country should be made an offence under English law, as should an attempt abroad to commit a relevant offence of fraud in England, even if no effect or act in furtherance of that attempt occurred here; and similarly with incitement and conspiracy.[177]

The Commission's proposals relating to attempt and incitement were given effect in the 1993 Act, as initially were its proposals in respect of conspiracy, but section 5(1) of the 1993 Act, which contained the provisions in respect of statutory conspiracy, was superseded and repealed by the Criminal Justice (Terrorism and Conspiracy) Act 1998, without ever being brought into force.

Not all offences of fraud or dishonesty were included in the Law Commission's recommendations, although the very limited range of offences suggested in the initial consultation document was enlarged as a result of the consultation exercise. A few more offences (such as defrauding the public revenue) were included in the original legislation, and several more have been added by amendments to the Act, but the list remains far from all-inclusive. Some of those who responded to the consultation exercise argued in favour of including a much wider range of offences: perhaps

---

[177] Law Com. No. 180, paras 4.7, 4.11, and 4.14.

even extending it so as to include all indictable offences under English law. Declining to act on this suggestion, the Commission pointed out (quite reasonably) that their remit had been to consider only offences of fraud and dishonesty; and then added, less convincingly: 'Except in relation to offences of dishonesty, no commentator suggested that the present jurisdictional rules had been found to be defective in practice or to give rise to difficulty.'[178] With respect, it has been clear for many years that while cases of fraud and dishonesty make up by far the majority of reported cross-frontier offences, other types of offence (including homicide offences, trafficking in narcotic drugs or immigrants, and terrorist offences) have much the same potential for difficulty, and it is hard to think of any convincing argument as to why the same rules concerning territorial jurisdiction should not be made applicable to them. In respect of drug trafficking offences, the Commission offered a further explanation for not including these within the proposed new jurisdictional regime:

The United Kingdom's international obligations relating to the control of narcotic drugs have always been based on various multilateral treaties. . . . In our view it would be inappropriate to intervene in an area of the law the rules of which . . . have been formulated . . . in the context of the United Kingdom's international obligations.[179]

This is also open to argument. Because the Commission were engaged in proposing new rules as to the ambit of territorial jurisdiction, the fact that some offences were already subject to provisions creating extraterritorial liability ought not to have been a problem. Extraterritorial liability is almost always constrained by the nationality or status of the alleged offender, and in many cases derives its legitimacy from international treaty obligations; but in the territorial cases to which the Criminal Justice Act 1993 now applies, such considerations are not applicable.

The Criminal Justice Act 1993

Whatever criticisms might be made of omissions from the Law Commission's 1989 Report, there is no question but that it succeeded in highlighting the urgent need for reform of the rules governing jurisdiction over cross-frontier offences of fraud and dishonesty; and while there is ample scope for criticism of the specific reforms that were proposed, those proposals were widely welcomed as offering significant advantages over the rules they were designed to replace. It is therefore regrettable that it took no fewer than four years for the necessary legislation to be enacted, in Part 1 of the Criminal Justice Act 1993, and it is even more regrettable that this legislation was not brought promptly into force. Instead, it gathered dust for

---

[178] Ibid., para. 3.4.   [179] Ibid., paras 3.17–3.18.

another six years, while judges and commentators called for its implementation, and a number of scoundrels, who clearly would have been convicted
had the relevant provisions been in force, escaped their just deserts. The
financial implications of implementation may have been a factor here. It
was estimated in 1996 that the cost of implementation would be in the
order of £15 million per annum, of which an estimated £13 million would
fall to the courts and to the legal aid budget.[180] But non-implementation
brought substantial costs of its own, including financial costs. In *R v.
Manning*,[181] in which the appellant's conviction was reluctantly quashed
because his fraud had been completed abroad, Buxton LJ concluded his
judgment with a swingeing attack on the Government's failure to implement the legislation that would have enabled the conviction to be upheld:

We cannot leave this case without expressing our great concern at the present state
of the law. . . . [It] is deplorable that in this case we find ourselves forced to conclude
that plainly dishonest conduct with a strong connection with this country cannot be
tried here.

In our view, however, these defects in the present law regrettably cannot be put
right by action in this court, and probably cannot be put right at all save by legislation. That is indeed the view of Parliament, which took steps to reform the law in
Part 1 of the Criminal Justice Act 1993. That was passed by Parliament to introduce
a rational and comprehensive scheme that would give the courts of England and
Wales jurisdiction over cases of international fraud that had a connection with this
country but which were not necessarily completed here. . . . The legislative rules
would have operated to give the courts of England and Wales jurisdiction, plainly
and without argument, both in *R v. Smith* [182] and in the case before us. The legislation could not however be applied in either of those cases, or in *R v. Forsyth*,[183]
because it has never been brought into operation. Failure to implement those
provisions seriously undermines the role that the courts of England and
Wales should be playing in the battle against international fraud. It causes a quite
unjustifiable expenditure of public funds in litigation, as the present case amply
demonstrates. . . .

We add our voice to those of other courts to hope that the most unhappy outcome
of this case may finally demonstrate that Part 1 of the Criminal Justice Act 1993
should now be brought into operation without further delay.

That legislation was finally brought into force nearly a year later, on 1 June
1999. The Criminal Justice Act 1993 (Commencement No. 10) Order
1999[184] was intended to achieve this, but by oversight it failed to include
section 5(3), (4) or (5), and a further Order[185] was therefore required in
order to rectify this omission. As previously noted, section 5(1) of the 1993

---

[180] *Review of Extra-territorial Jurisdiction* (Home Office, 1998), para. 4.3. The remaining
costs would be incurred primarily in police investigations. As to the cost implications of conducting enquiries abroad, see below, pp. 337–40.   [181] [1998] 4 All ER 876.
[182] [1996] 2 BCLC 109.   [183] [1997] 2 Cr App R 299, 317.
[184] SI 1999 No. 1189.   [185] SI 1999 No. 1499.

Act had already been superseded and repealed by the Criminal Justice (Terrorism and Conspiracy) Act 1998, without ever coming into force.

Group A and Group B Offences

Part 1 of the Criminal Justice Act 1993 applies only to a specific range of offences, albeit a wider range than that first suggested by the Law Commission. These are divided into 'Group A' offences (substantive offences of fraud and dishonesty) and 'Group B' offences (incitement, conspiracy, or attempt to commit a Group A offence; and conspiracy to defraud). The full list of Group A offences is found in section 1(2) (as amended) and is now as follows:

(1) Offences under the Theft Act 1968, sections 1, 15, 15A, 16, 17, 19, 20(2), 21, 22, and 24A.[186]
(2) Offences under the Theft Act 1978, sections 1 and 2.
(3) Offences under the Forgery and Counterfeiting Act 1981, sections 1–5, 14–17, and 20–21.[187]
(4) The common law offence of cheating the public revenue.

Relevant Events

In respect of substantive offences, section 2 of the 1993 Act (and in particular section 2(3)) contains the key operative provisions. It provides:

(1) For the purposes of this Part, 'relevant event', in relation to any Group A offence, means any act or omission or other event (including any result of one or more acts or omissions) proof of which is required for conviction of the offence.

(2) For the purpose of determining whether or not a particular event is a relevant event in relation to a Group A offence, any question as to where it occurred is to be disregarded.

(3) A person may be guilty of a Group A offence if any of the events which are relevant events in relation to the offence occurred in England and Wales.

In other words, the occurrence of any essential element of a Group A offence within England and Wales will suffice to bring it within English jurisdiction, even if other essential elements occur abroad. This means, for example, that a dishonest deception practised in England or Wales, resulting in the obtaining of property from the victim in Switzerland or Scotland, will for the first time amount to an indictable offence under English law. It will no longer matter that the offence was 'completed' only by the obtaining of property outside the jurisdiction. *R v. Harden*, for example, would

---

[186] Sections 15A and 24A inserted by the Theft (Amendment) Act 1996, s. 3.
[187] Sections 14–17 and 20–21 inserted by SI 2000 No. 1878, Art. 1.

have resulted in the upholding of H's conviction had the 1993 Act been in force at the time.

One common cross-frontier offence that often resulted in unmeritorious acquittals under the old law was that of procuring the execution of a valuable security by deception, contrary to section 20(2) of the Theft Act 1968. This was because a cheque, bill, or other security may well be 'executed' in some country other than that wherein the fraudulent conduct is committed. In *R v. Nanayakkara*,[188] for example, the appellant and others had acquired several US Treasury social security orders that had previously been stolen in California. They attempted to have them credited to accounts in London banks, but not surprisingly this aroused suspicion. They were arrested and initially convicted of conspiring to procure the acceptance (that is the execution) of the orders in London. The Court of Appeal, however, held that the orders could only have been 'accepted' (had the fraud succeeded) in the USA,[189] and that there was accordingly no conspiracy to commit any offence under English law. Similarly, in *R v. Manning*,[190] the appellant's convictions for procuring the execution of cheques from his victims in Greece were quashed because, although the deception was practised from England, the signing or execution of the cheques was done in Greece.

The new regime introduced by the 1993 Act has made a substantial difference to this kind of case. Such an offence will now be considered to have been committed both where the deception is practised *and* where any execution takes place. As Buxton LJ observed in *Manning*, the problems faced by the Court of Appeal in that case would have greatly diminished, had Part 1 of the 1993 Act been in force at the time.

Section 3(1)(a) of the Act confirms that the nationality of the accused is irrelevant for these purposes. It is accordingly possible for an offence against English law to be committed by a foreign national who has never set foot in England or Wales and has never lived under that law.[191]

Identifying Relevant Events

The point at which the supposedly simple and all-embracing structure of the 1993 Act ceases to be either of those things is when one attempts to

---

[188] [1987] 1 WLR 265.
[189] 'Acceptance' in this context is a technical term derived from the Bills of Exchange Act 1882. It does not mean 'receiving of taking into possession'. See also *R v. Beck* [1985] 1 WLR 22.
[190] [1998] 4 All ER 876.
[191] Section 3(4) mysteriously qualifies this by providing that 'Subsection (1)(a) does not apply where jurisdiction is given to try the offence in question by an enactment which makes provision by reference to the nationality of the person charged.' No such qualification was found in the Law Commission's Draft Bill, and it is impossible to find any Group A or Group B offence to which it might relate. Because these are all deemed to be territorial offences, the universal rule is that such offences (even those concerned with the falsification of British passports, etc.) can be committed by persons of any nationality.

distinguish between 'relevant events' on which jurisdiction may be founded, and mere preparatory or incidental acts or events, on which jurisdiction may *not* be founded. At this point, the highly technical problems that arose under the old terminatory principle of jurisdiction seem destined to reappear, in some at least of their old complexity.

Should a court find itself struggling to decide what is meant by an act or event, 'proof of which is required for conviction of the offence', guidance might perhaps be found in the Law Commission Report in which the concept was first formulated. The Commission argued that:

Our courts should have jurisdiction to try a charge of one of the listed [i.e., Group A] offences if any event that is required to be proved in order to obtain a conviction of that offence takes place in England and Wales. That would, in particular, mean that where the definition of the offence forbids conduct producing a certain result our courts would have jurisdiction if any part of that conduct, or any part of the defined specified result, took place here. Similarly, our courts would have jurisdiction over crimes whose definition relates only to the accused's conduct . . . if any part of the conduct forbidden by the definition of the offence took place here.

We regard it as important, however, that jurisdiction should be taken by the courts of this country only if an element *required to be proved for conviction* takes place here. It would in our view be excessive, and would also lead to substantial arguments of jurisdiction of the type that we seek to avoid, if the courts of this country sought jurisdiction merely because a preparatory or incidental act or event that happened to form part of the narrative took place here.[192]

The Commission then provided an example of the kind of preparatory act that should *not* become a basis for English jurisdiction:

Armed with documents that contain false statements that he has previously prepared in London, D calls on V in Paris. He there produces the documents to V, in reliance on which V gives him a sum of money. The court would not have jurisdiction[193] since neither the deception nor the obtaining took place in England and Wales. . . .[194]

Does the drafting of the Act succeed in giving effect to that policy? The authors of *Arlidge and Parry on Fraud*[195] point out that should a court construe the Act without regard to the Commission's explanation, it might conclude that, *in the particular case before it*, proof that D originally prepared the fraudulent documents might be considered an essential part of the prosecution case, if his guilt is to be established, and in that sense it might be considered to be a 'relevant event'.[196] The authors concede, however, this

---

[192] Law Com. No. 180, paras 2.27–2.28.
[193] More accurately, it would not be an offence under English criminal law.
[194] Law Com. No. 180, para. 2.29, example (d).   [195] (2nd edn, 1996), para. 12-023.
[196] Further difficult cases might be envisaged. On a charge involving an alleged offence of handling stolen goods, is the original act of stealing a 'relevant event'? The point may be arguable because, unless the prosecution can prove a previous act of stealing, there can be no

would achieve precisely what the Law Commission wanted to avoid, and they also note that this way of interpreting the Act would (in a different context) give rise to a further difficulty:

> Sometimes the prosecution will frame its case in such a way that it has two or more alternative routes to conviction. If two false representations are alleged, for example, only one of them need be proved. It would seem to follow that neither of them is a relevant event . . . because neither is essential to the prosecution's case.[197]

This would, with respect, be so perverse an interpretation of the Act that one can be fairly confident that the courts will never adopt it. On the other hand, the courts might sometimes find it harder to deal with another potential problem, which is considered below.

Results that are not 'Relevant Events'

The harmful consequences of criminal activity are not necessarily defined as essential elements of the offence in question, and may not therefore be relevant events for the purposes of the 1993 Act. Of the Group A offences, around half appear to be conduct crimes of one kind or another. The offence of blackmail, for example, is complete as soon as the unwarranted demand is 'made' (say, by the posting of a letter) and it is not necessary for the demand to be communicated to the intended victim, or indeed to anyone at all. That was the *ratio* of *Treacy* v. *DPP*.[198] The Law Commission intended that the act of blackmail should be brought within English jurisdiction, both where the blackmailer makes his demand here (as was already the law) *and* where a victim in England or Wales is subjected to blackmail demands that are made from abroad, and it is generally assumed that section 4(b) of the 1993 Act ensures this. It provides:

> There is a communication in England and Wales of any information, instruction, request, demand or other matter if it is sent by any means:
> (i) from a place in England and Wales to a place elsewhere; or
> (ii) from a place elsewhere to a place in England and Wales.

The wording is unfortunate. Since the 'communication' of a blackmail demand is not itself a relevant event, section 4(b) arguably flails at thin air. As far as blackmail is concerned, what the Act *ought* to have said is that there is a 'making' of a demand in England and Wales in either of those two

---

conviction for handling. On the other hand, the original act of stealing is not ordinarily considered to form any direct part of the *actus reus* of handling. What matters is that the goods in question are stolen goods at the time of the handling. If the original stealing were to be regarded as a 'relevant event' on a charge of handling, this would bring foreign acts of handling within English jurisdiction whenever the property in question represents the proceeds of an offence of theft or blackmail, etc., committed wholly or partly within England and Wales. Some might regard that as a desirable interpretation, but it seems unlikely that it could have been intended.

[197] Op. cit., fn 195, para. 12-024.   [198] [1971] AC 571.

circumstances. That is not what it actually says, but it seems more than likely that a court would construe section 4(b) flexibly, so as to give effect to its intended meaning, in which case no great difficulty should arise in this particular context.

More complex issues may arise in theft cases. In some such cases, section 4(b) may prove effective; but in others it may not. *R* v. *Governor of Brixton Prison, ex p Osman*[199] illustrates some of the difficulties that may arise. The Divisional Court in that case had to decide for extradition purposes whether a series of banking thefts had been committed in Hong Kong or in the USA. Osman was the chairman of BMFL, the Hong Kong subsidiary of a Malaysian bank. It was alleged by the Hong Kong Government that he and his fellow directors had abused their positions by causing BMFL to make improper and undisclosed loans amounting to over $US800 million to the Carrian group of companies, which had subsequently become insolvent, so that the sums involved were effectively lost to BMFL. The exact methods by which the loans were made varied, but most were 'money market transactions' in which a dealing ticket was issued in Hong Kong for the amount of the loan, followed by a confirmation slip. Thereafter, BMFL would send a telex instruction to its correspondent bank in the USA, authorizing the transfer of funds to the Carrian group's correspondent bank there. That bank would in turn transfer the funds to the Carrian group's account in Hong Kong. The transactions were concealed from BMFL's parent bank. The property allegedly stolen as a result of each such transaction was a chose in action represented either by a debt due to BMFL from its correspondent bank in the United States, or by BMFL's contractual right to overdraw on its account there.

The jurisdictional issue that arose in respect of these transactions concerned the exact place and moment at which each of the offending appropriations was made. When and where was the relevant act of theft 'completed'? Could the Hong Kong Government show that the thefts were committed within its jurisdiction? The Divisional Court concluded that the mere transmission of the telex instruction from Hong Kong was a relevant act of appropriation. Lloyd LJ said:

The act of sending the telex is ... the act of theft itself, and not a mere attempt. It is the last act which the defendant has to perform and not a preparatory act. It would matter not if the account were never in fact debited. We can find no way of excluding the sending of the telex in such circumstances from the definition of appropriation contained in section 3(1) of the 1968 Act. ...

If we are right that the act of sending the telex was the act of appropriation, then the place where that act was performed, namely the place where the telex was dispatched, is the place where the chose in action was appropriated. ...

[199] [1990] 1 WLR 277.

It is unnecessary to consider whether there may have been a prior act of appropriation in Hong Kong when the dealing ticket was made out, or the confirmation slip issued.[200]

What, then, if it had been the USA, and not Hong Kong, that had sought Osman's extradition from England? Back in 1989, when these extradition proceedings took place, the position would have been unclear. If, however, Part 1 of the 1993 Act had been in force, the US Government would almost certainly have been able to rely on section 4(b), which would have resolved the problem by deeming the telex instruction to have been 'communicated' both in Hong Kong and in New York.[201]

On slightly different facts, however, section 4(b) may prove ineffective. Assume that D, in Germany, improperly and dishonestly issues instructions to V's bank in Switzerland, as a result of which that bank transfers funds from V's account to an account held by D's company or his associate at a bank in England. The fraudulent instructions that constitute the appropriation of V's property are neither issued nor received in England, and the theft of V's property appears to have been completed before any transfer is made to England.

Section 4(a) of the 1993 Act might at first appear to help. It provides that 'There is an obtaining of property in England and Wales if the property is either despatched from or received at a place in England and Wales'. There are nevertheless at least two reasons why it does not help, at least in respect of a charge of theft from V. The first is that section 4(a) does not deem the obtaining of property to be a relevant event, and in this case it seems unlikely that it could be considered one, because an effective appropriation of the property in question has already been committed in Germany or Switzerland. As the Court of Appeal made clear in *R* v. *Atakpu*,[202] once property has effectively been stolen abroad, a conviction for theft cannot be based on subsequent acts of appropriation committed within England and Wales. The second and decisive consideration is that, following the ruling of the House of Lords in *R* v. *Preddy*,[203] the transfer of funds between accounts cannot in any event be regarded as involving a transfer of property. The funds credited to D's account represent a new chose in action, created for his benefit, rather than one that previously belonged to V. A charge of obtaining a money transfer by deception, contrary to section 15A of the Theft Act 1968, should succeed on those facts, but this would have been the

---

[200] [1990] 1 WLR 277. As the Court of Appeal later noted in *R* v. *Atakpu* [1994] QB 69, theft can occur in an instant by means of a single appropriation, but it can also involve a course of dealing with property lasting longer and involving several appropriations before the transaction is complete. Once the transaction (that is, the theft) is complete, however, there can be no more thefts of that property by the same thief.

[201] A pedantic interpretation of s. 4(b) might hold that 'communication' of the instruction is not a relevant event, because mere sending is sufficient; but as explained above, this would be to ignore the obvious intent behind the drafting of that provision.

[202] [1994] QB 69.   [203] [1996] AC 815.

case even without the assistance of the 1993 Act, and has nothing to do with section 4(a). In other words, it does not seem that the 1993 Act makes any difference to such a case, one way or the other.

The facts of *Atakpu* may also be used to illustrate the limitations of the 1993 Act. The appellants in that case dishonestly purported to hire luxury cars in Germany and Belgium, but with no intention of returning them. Instead, they drove the cars to England, where they intended to sell them. It was held that the cars were stolen as soon as they were hired,[204] and that no further stealing was committed in England. Because the stealing was committed outside England and Wales, it could not amount to an offence under English law. There was thus no cross-frontier theft, but only thefts committed entirely within either Germany or Belgium; and since no relevant event took place in England, the 1993 Act would have made no difference at all as far as any charge of theft is concerned.[205]

Relevant Acts and False Accounting

The 1993 Act may have little impact on some other Group A offences. In *ex p Osman*, for example, some of the charges on which extradition was sought by the Hong Kong authorities were charges of false accounting, contrary to what would, in English law, have been section 17(1) of the Theft Act 1968. It was alleged that the applicant had falsified, or concurred in the falsification of, monthly returns made by BMFL to its holding company (BBMB) in Malaysia. In order to obtain extradition on those charges, the Hong Kong Government had to show that this false accounting was committed in Hong Kong, rather than Malaysia. Lloyd LJ said:

We do not think it is possible to lay down any general rule as to the place where the offence of false accounting is committed. In some cases it may be that it is at the place where the account is to be used. But in the present case it would be artificial to regard Malaysia as the place of making or concurrence, when the documents in question were prepared and created in Hong Kong, and relate to a business carried on by BMFL exclusively in Hong Kong. In our view the magistrate was right to hold that the offence of false accounting was complete when the documents were falsified, or when the material particulars were omitted.[206]

---

[204] Following *R* v. *Gomez* [1993] AC 442.

[205] See G.R. Sullivan and Colin Warbrick, 'Territoriality, Theft and *Atakpu*' [1994] *Criminal Law Review* 650. On a charge of conspiracy to steal, however, the Criminal Law Act 1977, s. 1A (inserted by the Criminal Justice (Terrorism and Conspiracy) Act 1998) has now transformed the position, assuming there is proof of a conspiracy formed or furthered, etc., in England and Wales. An alternative way of dealing with cases such as *Atakpu* would be to charge the defendants with offences under Pt 7 of the Proceeds of Crime Act 2002. Under these provisions, the possession, use, concealment, or transfer of the proceeds of criminal conduct is punishable on a similar basis to handling stolen goods; and 'criminal conduct' for these purposes includes conduct abroad that would have been criminal had it been committed within England and Wales (Proceeds of Crime Act 2002, s. 340). There would be no need, in such cases, to prove the content of any foreign law.   [206] [1990] 1 WLR 277, 297.

Lloyd LJ might usefully have distinguished here between two different offences created by section 17(1). Section 17(1)(a) creates an offence of falsifying or concealing, etc, an account or document required for accounting purposes; whereas section 17(1)(b) creates a quite separate offence of furnishing, or producing, or making use of any such account or document, knowing that it is or may be false or misleading. Lloyd LJ's ruling that an offence of false accounting was committed in Hong Kong seems unimpeachable; but would Hong Kong have been able to secure the applicant's extradition had he been charged with the equivalent of a section 17(1)(b) offence? Would Malaysia have been able to do so on a section 17(1)(a) charge? And would the 1993 Act have made any difference to either scenario, had it been applicable?

The answer to each of these questions would appear to be 'No'. Falsification was committed only in Hong Kong, whereas the false returns were produced to furnish information to BBMB only in Malaysia. Applying the 1993 Act, little if anything would seem to change. Any section 17(1)(a) offences were completed in Hong Kong by the preparation there of the false documents. These documents may have been intended for use in Malaysia, but neither the sending nor the communication of those documents to Malaysia could have been considered 'relevant events' for the purposes of section 2 of the 1993 Act. Conversely, the earlier preparation of the false documents in Hong Kong could not ordinarily have amounted to anything more than preparatory acts as far as any section 17(2)(b) offence was concerned. Only if the false information were furnished to BBMB by direct transmission from Hong Kong would any 'relevant event' have been deemed to occur in Hong Kong, and that by virtue only of section 4(b).

Attempts to Commit Group A Offences

The Criminal Justice Act 1993 deals with jurisdiction over attempts to commit Group A offences in two ways. Section 3(3) provides that a person may be convicted of an attempt to commit such an offence whether or not: (i) the attempt was made in England and Wales; or (ii) it had an effect there.[207] This does not of course mean that an attempt in Spain to commit a fraud in Portugal would automatically be punishable in England. Group A offences are not extraterritorial offences, and a fraud perpetrated in Portugal can only be a Group A offence if some relevant event (as defined in section 2 of the Act) is proved to have been committed in England and Wales.

There are two kinds of case to which section 3(3) might apply. The first is where an attempt to commit an offence in England is instigated from abroad. Where such an attempt actually causes or involves the receipt of a

---

[207] This rule does not apply to any offence of attempt charged under the Criminal Attempts Act 1981, s. 1A: Criminal Justice Act 1993, s. 3(6).

communication or some other event in England and Wales, jurisdiction would not in any case have been in doubt,[208] but it was not clear, at the time when the 1993 Act was drafted, whether it was necessary for some such effect of the attempt to occur within England. It now seems that the occurrence of such effects is in fact unnecessary.[209] In that respect, section 3(3) probably did no more than restate existing law.

The second kind of case to which section 3(3) might apply is where an attempt is made abroad to commit a Group A offence abroad, but in which it is intended that some relevant event will occur in England and Wales. Assume, for example, that D, in Nigeria, sends an e-mail or fax message to V, in Cardiff, inviting her to participate in a supposedly lucrative business venture there, but requiring an 'advance fee' payable to him in Nigeria. D is in fact attempting to pull off a classic Nigerian '419' scam, the object of which is to defraud anyone foolish enough to take part. On the face of it, therefore, he is attempting in Nigeria to commit an offence in Nigeria, because if V had succumbed to the fraud, she would have arranged for funds to be credited to a bank account there, and an offence under section 15A of the Theft Act 1968 would be completed only when that account was credited; but since the section 15A offence is a Group A offence, and since a relevant event (the deception of V) was intended to occur in England and Wales, a charge of criminal attempt (contrary to section 1 of the 1981 Act) would be triable in England and Wales, by virtue of section 3(3).

What, then, of a case in which a person in England attempts to commit a Group A offence abroad? It is submitted that any such attempt will necessarily be triable under section 1(1) of the Criminal Attempts Act 1981, because any Group A offence instigated from within England and Wales must by definition be indictable under English law; but section 5(2) of the 1993 Act unfortunately appears to assume the contrary, and it has amended the Criminal Attempts Act 1981 by inserting a new section 1A, which now provides:

(1) If this section applies to an act, what the person doing the act had in view shall be treated as an offence to which section 1(1) applies.

(2) This section applies to an act if
   (a) it is done in England and Wales, and
   (b) it would fall within section 1(1) above as more than merely preparatory to the commission of a Group A offence, but for the fact that the offence, if completed, would not be an offence triable in England and Wales. . . .

With respect, this provision ought never to have been enacted. It is fundamentally at odds with itself, because it is impossible for any case to arise to which it might apply. It cannot apply where the substantive offence in question would have been triable under English law; but acts done in England

---

[208] *R v. Baxter* [1971] 1 QB 1; *DPP v. Stonehouse* [1978] AC 55.
[209] *R v. Latif and Shahzad* [1996] 1 WLR 104.

by way of attempt to commit a Group A offence must inevitably be relevant events under section 2(1) of the 1993 Act, and any completed Group A offence must be triable under section 2(3), precisely because of its status as a Group A offence. This does not merely make section 1A a useless provision; it makes it a dangerous trap for unwary prosecutors or courts, who may be tempted to rely upon it instead of section 1, in cases where it is, in fact, inapplicable and in which any conviction obtained at trial would fall to be quashed on appeal.[210]

Incitement to Commit Group A Offences

The common law rules relating to incitement are modified by sections 4(b) and 5(4) of the 1993 Act. Section 4(b) provides that, in relation to Group A offences, there is a 'communication' in England and Wales of any information, instruction, request, demand, or other matter if it is sent by any means either to or from England and Wales. Since incitement appears to require communication of the relevant request or instruction, this provision enables incitement to be dealt with as an offence under English law, both where D in England incites E, who is abroad, and where D, from abroad, incites E in England.

Section 5(4) bears some resemblance to section 5(2) (see p. 173 above), but in contrast to that provision it does make sense in its own context. Section 5(4) provides:

A person may be guilty of incitement to commit a Group A offence if the incitement—
(a) takes place in England and Wales; and
(b) would be triable in England and Wales but for what the person charged had in view not being an offence triable in England and Wales.

D, in England, may, for example, incite E to steal from his employer in France. If E were to commit this theft, he could not ordinarily be guilty of any offence under English law, despite having been incited by someone in England, because the incitement would not be a 'relevant event' as far as E's liability was concerned. All relevant events would take place in France. At common law, therefore, D could not have been be guilty of incitement at all. Section 5(4) reverses this rule in respect of Group A offences. D must presumably be charged, in such a case, not with incitement at common law, but with incitement contrary to section 5(4) of the Criminal Justice Act 1993.[211]

---

[210] See *Blackstone's Criminal Practice 2003*, A6.38; J.C. Smith, *The Law of Theft* (8th edn, 1997) 1–22.

[211] Under s. 6(2), the defence may require the prosecution to prove that the act incited would have been criminal under the relevant local law.

Conspiracy to Commit Group A Offences

As previously noted, section 5(1) of the Criminal Justice Act 1993, which was to have implemented the Law Commission's proposals in respect of conspiracy to commit Group A offences, was repealed before it ever came into force. Jurisdiction over conspiracy to commit Group A offences is therefore governed primarily by the same provisions as apply to other statutory conspiracies, namely sections 1 and 1A of the Criminal Law Act 1977, as amended or inserted by the Criminal Justice (Terrorism and Conspiracy) Act 1998. A conspiracy in England to commit a Group A offence entirely within France would be triable under section 1A rather than section 1, because the substantive offence would not itself have been triable under English law. In contrast, a conspiracy to commit a cross-frontier offence in which relevant events are to occur in England and Wales would be indictable only under section 1 of the 1977 Act, and not under section 1A. There is no overlap or common ground: on a charge brought under section 1A, it must accordingly be a defence to show that the act conspired at would in fact have involved the commission of an offence under English law.

Section 3(2) of the Criminal Justice Act 1993 was not repealed with section 5(1). It provides:

On a charge of conspiracy to commit a Group A offence, or on a charge of conspiracy to defraud in England and Wales, the defendant may be guilty of the offence whether or not—
(a) he became a party to the conspiracy in England and Wales;
(b) any act or omission or other event in relation to the conspiracy occurred in England and Wales.

As previously explained, the decision of the Court of Appeal in *R* v. *Sansom*,[212] which followed that of the Privy Council in *Somchai Liangsiriprasert* v. *US Government*,[213] appears to have established much the same rule for conspiracy cases generally, but these cases were decided only after the Law Commission had drafted the provision that eventually became section 3(2). The enactment of that provision may perhaps have been unnecessary, but it does at least avoid any doubt as far as Group A offences are concerned.

Conspiracy to Defraud

The general rule at common law was that a conspiracy to defraud was not indictable under English law if the defrauding was intended to take place outside England and Wales. This rule was established in *Board of Trade* v. *Owen*,[214] in which O had allegedly conspired in England to defraud a department of the West German Government, in Germany. Delivering the

---

[212] [1991] 2 QB 130.   [213] [1991] 1 AC 225.   [214] [1957] AC 602.

opinion of the Appellate Committee, Lord Tucker said:

A conspiracy to commit a crime abroad is not indictable in this country unless the contemplated crime is one for which an indictment would lie here . . . It necessarily follows that a conspiracy of the nature of that charged in count 3 [i.e. conspiracy to defraud the West German Government]—which in my view was a conspiracy to attain a lawful object by unlawful means, rather than to commit a crime—is not triable in this country, since the unlawful means and the ultimate object were both outside the jurisdiction.[215]

On the other hand, jurisdiction could (and may still) be asserted at common law over conspiracies that have as their object an act of defrauding that *may* potentially take place within England and Wales, or within adjacent territorial waters. The House of Lords in *Board of Trade* v. *Owen* implicitly approved a ruling of Willes J in *R* v. *Kohn*[216] to the effect that a conspiracy to defraud marine insurance underwriters by causing the loss of a ship was indictable in England if it was contemplated that the ship 'might be destroyed off the bar at Ramsgate', even though the ship was eventually scuttled on the high seas.[217] *Board of Trade* v. *Owen* was subsequently applied in *R* v. *Cox*[218] and in *Attorney-General's Reference (No. 1 of 1982)*.[219] In the latter case, the Court of Appeal further held that a conspiracy to defraud does not become indictable under English law merely because the plan, if successful, would inevitably harm or imperil the financial interests of individuals or companies within England and Wales. It would be necessary for the actual *object* of the conspiracy to be sited within the jurisdiction, and not merely its incidental consequences or side effects. The defendants in *Attorney-General's Reference* had conspired in England to market whisky in the Lebanon, falsely labelled as Johnny Walker Scotch whisky. The company that owned the Johnny Walker brand was based in England, but as Lord Lane CJ explained: 'Had it not been for the jurisdictional problem, we have no doubt the charge against these conspirators would have been conspiracy to defraud potential purchasers of the whisky, for that was the true object of the agreement.'[220]

In the converse situation, where defendants abroad conspire to commit an act of fraud within England and Wales, it was eventually established that this may amount to an offence at common law, even if no consequence or effect of the conspiracy is ever felt within the jurisdiction. In *R* v. *Naini*,[221] Lord Bingham CJ summarized the common law position as follows:

First, in determining issues of jurisdiction, a distinction is to be drawn between charges of substantive offences and charges of conspiracy. That we regard as

---

[215] [1957] AC 602, 634.   [216] (1864) 4 F & F 68.
[217] See also *R* v. *Naini* [1999] 2 Cr App R 398.   [218] [1968] 1 WLR 88.
[219] [1983] QB 751. See also *Tarling* v. *Government of Singapore* (1978) 70 Cr App R 77 (discussed by J.C. Smith at [1979] Crim LR 220) and *R* v. *Naini* [1999] 2 Cr App R 398.
[220] [1983] QB 751, 757.   [221] [1999] 2 Cr App R 398, 416–7.

supported by the decisions in *Liangsiriprasert* v. *US Government* and *R* v. *Manning*. Secondly, it is clear that the courts of England and Wales have no jurisdiction to try a defendant on a count of conspiracy if the conspiracy, although made here, was to do something in a foreign country, or which could only be done in a foreign country. That proposition is supported by *Board of Trade* v. *Owen*, *R* v. *Cox* and *Attorney-General's Reference (No. 1 of 1982)*. Thirdly, in our view the authorities establish that the courts of England and Wales do have such jurisdiction if the conspiracy wherever made is to do something here or to do something which may be done here, whether wholly or in part, even if no overt act pursuant to the conspiracy is done in England and Wales. The residence of the party who suffers the loss does not determine where the crime of defrauding takes place. That conclusion is in our judgment supported by *R* v. *Kohn*, *Board of Trade* v. *Owen*, *R* v. *Cox*, *Liangsiriprasert* v. *US Government*, *R* v. *Sansom* and *R* v. *Manning*.

Section 5(3) of the Criminal Justice Act 1993 implicitly recognizes that a conspiracy abroad to defraud victims within England and Wales is already triable under English law, and addresses the more troublesome issue of conspiracies in England to commit frauds abroad. It provides:

A person may be guilty of conspiracy to defraud if—

(a) a party to the agreement constituting the conspiracy, or a party's agent, did anything in England and Wales in relation to the agreement before its formation, or

(b) a party to it became a party in England and Wales (by joining it either in person or through an agent), or

(c) a party to it, or a party's agent, did or omitted anything in England and Wales in pursuance of it,

and the conspiracy would be triable in England and Wales but for the fraud which the parties to it had in view not being intended to take place in England and Wales.

This means that if, for example, A and B agree in France to defraud C in Switzerland, and B (or B's agent) does anything in England in pursuance of that agreement, A and B may each become liable for conspiracy to defraud under English law.

Under section 6(4), however, the defence may serve notice on the prosecution, requiring them to satisfy the requirements of section 6(1), which provides:

A person is guilty of an offence triable . . . by virtue of section 5(3), only if the pursuit of the agreed course of conduct would at some stage involve—

(a) an act or omission by one or more of the parties, or

(b) the happening of some other event,

constituting an offence under the law in force where the act, omission or other event was intended to take place.

This is a remarkable provision, because at common law a conspiracy to defraud in England does *not* require the commission (or intended commission) of any substantive offence under English law. If it did so require, it would have been absorbed within the offence of statutory conspiracy under section 1 of the 1977 Act.

Given these significant differences between the requirements of the common law offence of conspiracy to defraud and those imposed by sections 5(3) and 6(1) of the 1993 Act, it is arguable that these provisions have created a new variant of the common law offence, rather than an enlargement of the common law one. Despite sharing many features of the basic common law offence, offences triable by virtue of section 5(3) are clearly distinguishable, to the extent that a conspiracy to commit the one cannot also be a conspiracy to commit the other, unless it involves two or more distinct objects (for example, to defraud X in England *and* Y in Scotland). If this analysis is correct, the new offence should be charged not as a simple common law conspiracy, but as a 'conspiracy contrary to section 5(3) of the Criminal Justice Act 1993 and common law.'

Offences that Fall Outside the Part I Regime

The regime introduced by Part I of the Criminal Justice Act 1993 now extends over a much broader range of offences than that which was originally proposed by the Law Commission, but some offences of fraud and dishonesty remain outside its ambit, and these include some which appear capable of cross-frontier commission. In some cases, the excluded offences are covered by jurisdictional provisions of their own. This is true, for example, of section 397 of the Financial Services and Markets Act 2000. Subsections (1) and (2) of that section create offences involving the making of false or misleading statements, or the concealment of relevant facts, with a view to inducing or dissuading other persons to buy, retain, dispose of, or exercise rights relating to investments. This is the kind of investment fraud that was originally punishable under section 13 of the Prevention of Fraud (Investments) Act 1958 and which featured in *Secretary of State for Trade* v. *Markus*.[222] Section 397(3) makes it an offence to 'rig the market' in any relevant investments by doing any act or engaging in any course of conduct which creates a false or misleading impression as to the market in or the price or value of any relevant investments. Potential jurisdictional issues are addressed in section 397(6) and (7), which provide:

(6) Subsections (1) and (2) do not apply unless—

(a) the statement, promise or forecast is made in or from, or the facts are concealed in or from, the United Kingdom or arrangements are made in or from the United Kingdom[223] for the statement, promise or forecast to be made or the facts to be concealed;

(b) the person on whom the inducement is intended to or may have effect is in the United Kingdom; or

---

[222] [1976] AC 35. See above, p. 123.

[223] Where the only United Kingdom connection is with Scotland or Northern Ireland, this would not suffice to bring such conduct within the ambit of English law (or vice versa).

(c) the agreement is or would be entered into or the rights are or would be exercised in the United Kingdom.

(7) Subsection (3) does not apply unless—

(a) the act is done, or the course of conduct is engaged in, in the United Kingdom; or

(b) the false or misleading impression is created there.

Subsection (7), in particular, may sometimes prove difficult to interpret (where is an act 'done' when it is 'done' over an international telephone or telex line?), but the basic cross-frontier issue has at least been addressed. The same may be said of insider dealing under Part V of the Criminal Justice Act 1993. Section 52 of that Act creates the basic offences of insider dealing (section 52(1)) and of encouraging such dealing or improperly disclosing inside information (section 52(2)). Section 62 then provides:

(1) An individual is not guilty of an offence falling within subsection (1) of section 52 unless—

(a) he was within the United Kingdom at the time when he is alleged to have done any act constituting or forming part of the alleged dealing;

(b) the regulated market on which the dealing is alleged to have occurred is one which, by an order made by the Treasury, is identified (whether by name or by reference to criteria prescribed by the order) as being, for the purposes of this part, regulated in the United Kingdom; or

(c) the professional intermediary was within the United Kingdom at the time when he is alleged to have done anything by means of which the offence is alleged to have been committed.

(2) An individual is not guilty of an offence falling within subsection (2) of section 52 unless—

(a) he was within the United Kingdom at the time when he is alleged to have disclosed the information or encouraged the dealing; or

(b) the alleged recipient of the information or encouragement was within the United Kingdom at the time when he is alleged to have received the information or encouragement.

In contrast, none of the numerous crimes created by the Companies Act 1985 or the Insolvency Act 1986 is subject to any special rules governing ambit or jurisdiction. This clearly excludes any possibility of full extraterritorial application, but, as Arlidge points out,[224] it leaves ample room for argument concerning the interpretation of provisions where the prohibited conduct or events have cross-frontier elements:

Taken to its logical conclusion, this . . . would suggest that there would be no offence under English law if an English company entered into a transaction abroad which would be prohibited if effected within the jurisdiction, such as a loan to one of its directors or the provision of financial assistance towards the acquisition of its

---

[224] *Arlidge and Parry on Fraud* (2nd edn, 1996), para. 12-005.

shares; but it may well be arguable that, in view of the mischief addressed by a particular offence (e.g., the looting of English companies' assets) Parliament cannot have intended that it should be possible for a company to evade the prohibition merely by arranging for the transaction to be effected through a foreign bank account.

Money Laundering, Stolen Goods, and Criminal Property

An offence of handling stolen goods, contrary to section 22 of the Theft Act 1968, is a Group A offence for the purposes of the Criminal Justice Act 1993, but the so-called 'money laundering' offences[225] created by Part 7 of the Proceeds of Crime Act 2002[226] are not. This is surprising, because money laundering is believed to be one of the most prevalent and (in financial terms) one of the most significant forms of cross-frontier crime, and is thus an obvious candidate for inclusion within the Group A list.[227] The money laundering offences nevertheless possess a cross-frontier ambit of a kind, because, while the offences must themselves be committed in England and Wales,[228] the money or other property to which they relate need not necessarily represent the proceeds of any crime committed within England and Wales, or indeed the United Kingdom. By section 335(2) and (3):

(2) Criminal conduct is conduct which—

    (a) constitutes an offence in any part of the United Kingdom, or

    (b) would constitute an offence in any part of the United Kingdom if it occurred there.

(3) Property is criminal property if—

    (a) it constitutes a person's benefit from criminal conduct or it represents such a benefit (in whole or part and whether directly or indirectly), and

    (b) the alleged offender knows or suspects that it constitutes or represents such a benefit.

---

[225] 'Money laundering' is defined in s. 340 of the Act as any conduct involving an offence (or attempted offence, etc.) under ss. 327, 328, or 329; but those sections in fact extend to many forms of conduct besides the laundering of cash sums, including the concealment, disguise, conversion, transfer, removal from the jurisdiction, acquisition, use or possession of 'criminal property' (which need not be money), or being concerned in arrangements, knowing or suspecting that these facilitate the acquisition, retention, use, or control of such property by another person.

[226] This combines and consolidates (with some amendments) offences previously found within ss. 93A–93C of the Criminal Justice Act 1988 and ss. 49–52 of the Drug Trafficking Act 1994. The troublesome dichotomy between offences involving the proceeds of drug trafficking and those involving the proceeds of other criminal conduct has been eliminated.

[227] During the 1990s, London allegedly became of one of the money laundering capitals of the world. British banks were certainly used by the Nigerian dictator General Abacha and his family to launder many of the £ millions looted from Nigeria during his reign in power. See 'Revealed: the questionable transactions routed via UK', *The Guardian*, 4 October 2001.

[228] Part 7 also applies to offences committed in Scotland or Northern Ireland, but such offences do not appear to be offences under English law or fall within the jurisdiction of English courts.

Money laundering committed abroad is in turn 'criminal conduct' within the meaning of section 340(2)(b),[229] and it follows that the mere possession or use, in England, of profits derived from such activity may be an offence under English law.

Apart from having Group A status under the Criminal Justice Act 1993, offences of handling stolen goods possess a broadly similar, but not identical, cross-frontier ambit to the money laundering offences. Theft Act offences (other than theft of mails under section 14 of the 1968 Act) do not ordinarily apply to conduct taking place wholly outside England and Wales, but section 24(1) of that Act, read in conjunction with section 24(4), ensures that property obtained outside the jurisdiction, by what would in England have been regarded as theft, blackmail, or deception, will be regarded as stolen goods within the jurisdiction if either:

(1) the stealing was (exceptionally) punishable as an extraterritorial offence under English law (as, for example, where the thief was aboard a British controlled aircraft, or was a British citizen aboard a foreign ship to which he did not belong);[230] or

(2) the stealing was punishable under the law then in force where it took place.

Thus, if C steals property in Spain, and D dishonestly receives it (or its proceeds) in England, knowing of the circumstances, D may be guilty in England of handling under section 22. It must be proved, however, that C's conduct was punishable as an offence under Spanish law. It is not possible to rely on any presumption that foreign law will be similar to English law, nor can judicial notice be taken of foreign law for such a purpose.[231]

The problems that may arise when the prosecution overlook this requirement are well illustrated by the case of *R v. Okolie*.[232] Two Mercedes cars were discovered in a container of 'bathroom fittings' at Tilbury Docks. The cars had been reported stolen in Germany, and were clearly on their way to Africa. The appellant was arrested when he attempted to pay for the shipment. On the face of it, it was a straightforward case; but the prosecution came to the trial without the requisite expert evidence of German law. When this was pointed out, they sought an adjournment, but were refused one. They did, however, adduce evidence that the owners of the cars had reported them as 'stolen' and the trial judge (whose task it was to determine issues of foreign law) accepted this evidence as sufficient. The trial proceeded and the appellant was convicted on both counts of handling. On appeal, however, the Court of Appeal noted that the

---

[229] See also s. 340(11)(d).   [230] Merchant Shipping Act 1995, s. 281.
[231] *R v. Ofori and Tackie (No. 2)* (1994) 99 Cr App R 223.
[232] [2000] All ER (D) 661.

persons who reported the alleged thefts were not experts in German criminal law. They were merely employees of the car hire company in Germany from which the cars had been stolen. Their crime reports were not admissible as evidence of German law. A retrial was ordered.[233]

This unfortunate waste of time and money might not have occurred had the charge been one of money laundering (for example, concealing, disguising, or transferring criminal property) under what is now Part 7 of the Proceeds of Crime Act 2002. This is because the content of foreign law is irrelevant for the purposes of a prosecution under the 2002 Act. It would be enough to prove that the stealing of the two cars in Germany would have been an offence if committed anywhere in the United Kingdom.

The 2002 Act might also provide a solution to the kind of problem that arose in R v. *Atakpu*.[234] Assuming that case to have been correctly decided, a person who steals property abroad and carries it to England cannot be guilty of stealing it again in England, nor can he be guilty of receiving stolen goods there; but he can be prosecuted for a 'money laundering offence' on the basis that he then possesses, uses, or conceals, etc., criminal property in England. It matters not that the original 'crime' was not committed within English jurisdiction or that it was committed by the defendant himself. While money laundering may lack 'Group A' status under the Criminal Justice Act 1993, its potential application to cases involving transnational crime may therefore be considerable.[235]

CYBERCRIME AND COMPUTER MISUSE

Crime on the Internet

Computer crime may take a wide variety of forms, but it is likely to give rise to jurisdictional problems only when it involves the international transmission of instructions, data, images, or other material, or where computer systems are unlawfully accessed or interfered with via international links.[236] It is, admittedly, possible for computer viruses to be disseminated internationally by circulating infectious programmes through the post, on compact or floppy disks, and disks containing images of child pornography may be circulated by similar means, but in practice the vast majority of jurisdictional problems that arise in this area involve misuse of the Internet.

The Internet (which includes Usenet newsgroups, e-mail and Internet Relay Chat (IRC) communications, and the World Wide Web) is frequently

---

[233] See Michael Hirst, 'Stolen Goods and Foreign Law' [2000] *Crime Online*, Commentary Archive, B4.132.　　　　　　　　　[234] [1994] QB 69. See above, p. 171.

[235] See *Blackstone's Criminal Practice* 2003, B22.15–16.

[236] This includes transmissions or access between different jurisdictions within the UK.

used as a vehicle for the commission of crimes, and its legitimate users are amongst the principal victims of such crimes. The term 'cybercrime' has been coined to describe this phenomenon, and this term has received a measure of official recognition through its adoption in a recent Council of Europe Convention. This, the Budapest Cybercrime Convention,[237] seeks to promote international agreement and cooperation over many of the problems to which such crimes give rise, including problems of jurisdiction, extradition, and enforcement.

Before attempting to examine the jurisdictional issues, it may help to consider the nature and variety of criminal conduct that may be committed via the Internet. The Cybercrime Convention identifies nine basic varieties of offence (or of conduct that it seeks to ensure will be treated as criminal by all contracting states).[238] These are:

(1) illegal access to computers and data (Article 2);
(2) the illegal interception of Internet communications (Article 3);
(3) the unlawful alteration, suppression, or deletion of data (Article 4);
(4) unlawful interference with the functioning of computer systems by the unlawful input, alteration, or deletion, etc, of data (Article 5);
(5) the improper use of devices or programmes (such as virus programmes or password sniffers) that are designed to facilitate the commission of any of the above offences (Article 6);
(6) computer-related forgery (Article 7);
(7) computer-related fraud (Article 8);
(8) the distribution, downloading, and possession of Internet child pornography (Article 9); and
(9) the infringement of copyright and related rights by means of a computer system (Article 10).

The Convention also addresses certain acts that may not themselves be cybercrimes, but which are intended to procure or facilitate the commission of such crimes. These include (in Article 6) the production, possession, and distribution of virus programmes or password sniffer devices, and (in Article 9) the filming or production of child pornography that is intended for subsequent Internet distribution.

While the Convention provides some indication of the wide range of offences that may be committed over the Internet, it can by no means be regarded as exhaustive. Its ambit is limited by the need to focus on matters on which most states can broadly agree. Individual contracting states may

---

[237] ETS No. 185. The Convention was opened for signature in November 2001, but has not yet been ratified by the UK.
[238] Note that, despite its title, the Convention applies not merely to Internet or 'cyber' offences, but to the misuse of computer systems generally.

have laws penalizing conduct that is not featured anywhere in the Convention. English law, for example, generally prohibits the publication of *any* obscene material (that is, any material that has a tendency to deprave and corrupt those who may view or read it) and this is by no means confined to child pornography. Threatening or abusive Internet communications, or other forms of online harassment, may similarly involve the commission of offences under English law, on much the same basis as threats, etc, which are communicated by letter or telephone;[239] but once again such conduct is not addressed by the Convention. Nor is the United Kingdom alone in creating offences that are not recognized in the Convention. French law proscribes the online marketing or display of Nazi memorabilia; German law prohibits online holocaust denial, and so on.

Other attempts have been made to identify and categorize the various forms of Internet criminality. David Wall,[240] for example, identifies four basic types of criminal behaviour that have caused concern over recent years. He calls them, 'cyberobscenity', 'cybertrespass', 'cybertheft', and 'cyberviolence'.

Cyberobscenity is primarily concerned with Internet pornography, and in particular with the dissemination of child pornography, much of which originates from abroad. Mainstream and fetishist pornography is widely distributed internationally via Usenet newsgroups, e-mail attachments, and private or commercial websites. Child pornography is less likely to be found on websites, because it is almost universally criminalized, and the use of newsgroups and e-mails offers those involved greater anonymity.

Much of the pornographic material available over the Internet is either lawful (judged by current British standards), or is at least unlikely to be considered worth prosecuting; but the Internet is also used as a means of publishing violent, perverted, and/or paedophile material that could not lawfully be produced, sold, or distributed in this country, even in licensed sex shops, and this is where the real problem lies.[241]

Cybertrespass involves unauthorized access to computer systems and to the data stored on them. Such offences may be sub-divided into 'cyber-vandalism', 'cyberespionage', and 'cyberterrorism'. Nightmare scenarios of this kind might involve the acquisition of acutely sensitive defence data by terrorists, spies, or other hostile agencies; but the vulnerability of such systems to online attack (and in particular to international or cross-frontier attack) has most graphically been demonstrated not by major terrorists or by

---

[239] See *R v. Ireland* [1998] AC 147.

[240] 'Policing and the Regulation of the Internet', in Walker (ed.), *Crime, Criminal Justice and the Internet* (*Criminal Law Review* Special Edition, 1998), 79.

[241] A particularly unpleasant form of Internet obscenity is the so-called 'squish' site, within which still and video images can be viewed showing the torture and deliberate crushing of small animals; but prosecutions have also been brought in respect of 'filthy' websites, that show images of coprophilia.

agents of hostile powers, but by amateur (often teenage) hackers using inexpensive computer equipment in their bedrooms. Thus, on numerous occasions during 1994, British teenagers Matthew Bevan, aged 19, and Richard Pryce, aged 16, reportedly gained access from their bedrooms to computers at NASA, at the USAF Command and Control Centre at the Griffiths Airforce Base in New York, and at the Lockheed Martin Aeronautics Company, triggering a massive security alert.[242] A few years later, Ehud Tenenbaum, an 18-year-old Israeli hacker, was responsible for what the US authorities conceded to be 'the most systematic and organised attempt ever to penetrate the Pentagon's computer systems'. Tenenbaum had planted a list of his own passwords in the Pentagon system and had allegedly passed them to other hackers.[243]

Cybertheft (or *cyberfraud*) is represented in the law reports by multi-million pound banking frauds such as *R v. Governor of Brixton Prison, ex p Levin*,[244] but may also take the form of modest frauds or scams directed at small companies or private individuals. The proliferation of personal Internet banking has opened up a new and potentially lucrative group of targets for online frauds.[245] Other examples of cyberfraud include fraudulent online auctions and fraudulent re-dialling scams, such as those in which web users surfing pornographic sites were tricked into subscribing to a service that, unknown to them, caused their modems to reconnect to the web via premium rate international telephone services originating in Russia. Numerous offences or attempted offences are committed involving the deliberate and dishonest infringement of copyright or other forms of intellectual property, while Nigerian '419' advance fee frauds and similar schemes may now be initiated by e-mail, as well as by fax or ordinary post.

Cyberfraud poses a threat not only to its direct victims, but to the maintenance of public confidence in the security of online financial or commercial transactions. This threat is particularly acute in cases where the fraudsters set up sites that purport to be owned by or linked to reputable financial institutions. In April 2001, the ICC's Commercial Crime Services' Commercial Crime Bureau, supported by its Cybercrime Unit, claimed to have foiled a multi-billion dollar advance fee cyberfraud conspiracy, by shutting down[246] a group of 29 fraudulent websites that were masquerading as sites operated by Euroclear, the clearing system for the settlement of Eurobond transactions, and Bloomberg, the leading supplier of international financial information.

---

[242] It was initially feared that sensitive data had been accessed by, or might be passed onto, a hostile power. Pryce pleaded guilty to an offence under the Computer Misuse Act 1990 and was fined. Charges against Bevan were dropped because of evidential difficulties arising from the highly complex and sensitive nature of the material available to the prosecution.

[243] See *The Guardian*, 21 August 2000.   [244] [1997] QB 65. See above, p. 159.

[245] See Wall, op. cit., fn 240, 81.

[246] The ISP concerned removed the offending websites following an approach from the Cybercrime Unit.

Cyberviolence is arguably a misnomer, but is used to refer to acts such as the sending of threatening e-mail messages or hate-mail and various other forms of online harassment, which are sometimes referred to as 'cyber-stalking'. It is probably the least significant of the five main categories of cybercrime, and the least likely to involve cross-frontier jurisdictional issues, but may of course be a very serious matter for those victims who are subjected to it.

Wall's categories are in some respects wider and more comprehensive than those used in the Cybercrime Convention; but malicious virus writers or virus mailers do not appear to fit easily into any of those four categories. Such persons may sometimes be cybertrespassers, but most are not. A fifth category, *'cybervandalism'*, should perhaps be added to Wall's original list. Cybervandalism used to be associated primarily with hackers, who delete files or modify data, etc, after gaining unauthorized access to a computer or computer system, or with acts of revenge committed by disgruntled or recently dismissed employees, but great damage and inconvenience may now be caused by the dissemination of a computer virus or worm, or by the circulation of hoax messages, advising computer users to find and delete 'dangerous' or 'infected' files on their machines: these files may in reality be essential system components, without which the victim's machine will be disabled.

Territorial Jurisdiction and Cyberspace

The unique geography of the Internet creates serious jurisdictional difficulties for both the civil and the criminal courts. Territorial frontiers do not exist in cyberspace, and territorially based laws may therefore seem out of place in such an environment. As the US Court of Appeals (Third Circuit) observed in *ACLU v. Reno (No. 3)*[247]:

The Internet has an international geographically-borderless nature. With the proper software, every website is accessible to all other Internet users world-wide.... Indeed, the Internet negates geometry... it is fundamentally and profoundly antispatial. You cannot say where it is or describe its memorable shape and proportions or tell a stranger how to get there. But you can find things in it without knowing where they are. The Internet is ambient—nowhere in particular and everywhere at once.

This admittedly shows only half of the picture. The physical hardware and operating systems on which the Internet depends—individual computers, web servers, mail servers, etc.—must ordinarily be based within the territory of some state or other, and information published on the Internet must ordinarily be uploaded, downloaded, and stored by persons who are within the jurisdiction of some state at that time. The problem is that material prepared in one jurisdiction may easily be uploaded to a web server in another,

---

[247] (2000) 217 F 3d 162, citing *Doe v. Roe* (1998) 955 P 2d 951.

and material uploaded to a web server may be accessed by computers running the requisite software almost anywhere in the world. A surfer may therefore have no idea that the site he is viewing is maintained in another country, while a person who maintains a website may have no idea that his site is being accessed, and its material downloaded, by a user in another country.

In some cases, these factors may not be a problem. A fraudulent e-mail sent from Canada to England raises precisely the same jurisdictional issues as a fax message, or indeed a conventional letter sent by air-mail, and such issues may be addressed by applying Part I of the Criminal Justice Act 1993 in the usual way. Similarly, damage caused to a computer system (or computer data) in England by a virus deliberately transmitted in an e-mail sent from abroad undoubtedly involves an offence committed within English jurisdiction,[248] because the damage is caused there; and so on.

Use of the Internet in such cases may sometimes add considerably to the difficulties of law enforcement agencies, especially in cases where the e-mail has been diverted via one or more 're-mailers' in order to disguise its true origins;[249] but if the facts can ultimately be established, the jurisdictional issues facing the courts are largely the same as those encountered in cases involving telephone calls, faxes, or letter-bombs. The same cannot, however, be said of cases in which objection is taken to the content of websites or web pages that are hosted by foreign Internet service providers (ISPs). These may, for example, be considered obscene, seditious, or blasphemous if judged under English law, but it is by no means obvious that English law has any right to judge them.

Jurisdiction over Internet Content

States may, if they wish, pass laws prohibiting individuals within their jurisdiction from producing, circulating, or acquiring specified forms of indecent, blasphemous, or other proscribed material. They may also prohibit the import or export of such material, and extend their criminal laws to acts committed by their own nationals abroad. In the context of the Internet, this means that a state may lawfully regulate or censor the content of websites, etc., hosted by ISPs located within its own territorial jurisdiction, and may prohibit persons within its territory (or in theory, its own nationals when abroad) from producing, accessing, or downloading proscribed material hosted on servers sited beyond its jurisdiction. Problems inevitably arise, however, if a state attempts to regulate or proscribe the content of

---

[248] Specifically, an offence under the Computer Misuse Act 1990, s. 3; see pp. 194–5, below.
[249] See David Davis, 'Criminal Law and the Internet: The Investigator's Perspective' in *Crime, Criminal Justice and the Internet* (*Criminal Law Review* Special Edition, 1998) 48, 53.

foreign websites, or material hosted by foreign ISPs, merely on the basis that such sites or materials have been or could be accessed by persons within its own territory.

One might reasonably suppose that the conduct of foreign companies or individuals on foreign territory should be the concern only of the relevant foreign courts, but this did not dissuade the Court of Appeal in *R* v. *Perrin*[250] from upholding the conviction of a French citizen in respect of the publication of obscene material hosted on a foreign web server. The appellant, a French citizen resident in London, was convicted of publishing an obscene article, contrary to section 2(1) of the Obscene Publications Act 1959. He formally admitted that he and his company were responsible for the publication of a website entitled 'sewersex.com', which was devoted to bizarre and disturbing sexual fetishes, including coprophilia or coprophagia, involving the use or consumption of human excrement. The site was primarily a credit card subscription site, and appears to have been based on an American server, but the preview page to this site (the one page in respect of which the appellant was convicted) was freely accessible by anyone who knew how to find it, anywhere in the world. The preview page was accessed by PC Ysart, an officer attached to the Obscene Publications Unit of the Metropolitan Police at Charing Cross police station. It was as a result of what this officer saw and recorded that the appellant was prosecuted.

The defence alleged that the website had been prepared, and the relevant material uploaded, abroad (presumably in the USA) and beyond the reach of English criminal jurisdiction. The Crown did not dispute this, nor indeed did it produce any evidence to identify the location of the website or to challenge the appellant's assertion that the material in question was lawful where it was hosted. The Crown relied instead on the argument that the obscene images had been published in England when displayed on the officer's computer in London, and that the offence had, on that basis, been committed in England. But had it?

'Publication' under the 1959 Act

The Obscene Publications Act 1959 defines the concept of publication, but it does so primarily for the purpose of defining those who may be described as publishers, rather than for the purpose of identifying the place at which publication occurs. Section 1(3) of the Act provides:

For the purposes of this Act a person publishes an article who—

(a) distributes, circulates, sells, lets on hire, gives, or lends it, or who offers it for sale or for letting on hire; or

(b) in the case of an article containing or embodying matter to be looked at or a record, shows, plays or projects it, or, where the matter is data stored electronically, transmits that data.

---

[250] [2002] All ER (D) 359 (Mar); [2002] EWCA Crim 747.

In *R v. Fellows and Arnold*,[251] it was held that images stored on a computer disk may be 'published' within the meaning of section 1(3), merely by permitting other persons to access and download those images. The Court of Appeal rejected the argument that publication must involve some form of active conduct and that providing access to the archive was passive conduct only; but neither in *Fellows* nor in section 1(3) itself is any consideration given to the question whether the downloading of a digitally stored image by a third party in another jurisdiction can amount to a publication of that image in that other jurisdiction by the person who provided access to it. Nor does the Court of Appeal appear to have given any active consideration to that issue in *Perrin*. Harrison J, who gave the judgment of the Court, merely referred to the Court's earlier decision in *R v. Waddon*,[252] saying: '. . . it is clear from the decision of this court in *R v. Waddon . . .*, that there is publication for the purposes of section 1(3) both when images are uploaded and when they are downloaded.' With respect, *Waddon* does not decide any such thing. At most, it contains some qualified *obiter dicta* in favour of that view. The obscene material in *Waddon* had been prepared by W in England and uploaded from England to a website in the USA, whence it was accessed and downloaded by the indefatigable PC Ysart in London. On those facts, the occurrence of a relevant transmission within the jurisdiction could not realistically be disputed. Giving the judgment of the Court of Appeal in *Waddon*, Rose LJ said:

[Counsel for W] conceding, as he did, that [W] . . . was involved both in the transmission of material to the website and its transmission back again to this country, when Constable Ysart gained access to the website, could not contend that publication did not take place in this country. . . .

[Counsel] invited the Court, which invitation . . . we did not accept, to rule upon what the position might be in relation to jurisdiction if a person storing material on a website outside England intended that no transmission of that material should take place back to this country. For the purpose of this appeal, it is unnecessary to embark on a consideration of the issues which may arise in relation to that matter, which will, no doubt, . . . depend upon questions of intention and causation in relation to where publication should take place. . . .

Rose LJ then added, in a passage he appears to have 'flagged' as an *obiter dictum*:

As it seems to us, there can be publication on a website abroad, when images are there uploaded; and there can be further publication when those images are downloaded elsewhere. That approach is, as it seems to us, underlined by the provisions of section 1(3)(b) as to what is capable of giving rise to publication where matter has been electronically transmitted.

---

[251] [1997] 2 All ER 548.   [252] [2000] All ER (D) 502.

This *dictum* was adopted without further analysis as part of the *ratio* of *Perrin*. With respect, however, the issues involved demand much closer attention. To begin with, section 1(3)(b) does not obviously support the concept of 'remote' publication. It provides that data may be published by transmitting it, but that does not mean (nor even does it suggest) that the act of publication occurs where the transmission is received. If it did, it would impose rules of English criminal law on foreigners (as well as on British citizens) in respect of conduct which may be committed entirely abroad, and which may not necessarily be considered unlawful there. It seems unlikely that Parliament could ever have intended the provision to be interpreted in that way, especially in a world where shared standards of sexual tolerance or permissiveness do not really exist.

The Human Rights Argument

Counsel for the appellant in *Perrin* reminded the Court of Appeal of the views expressed by the European Court of Human Rights in *Sunday Times* v. *UK (No. 1)*,[253] in which it was held that:

Firstly, the law must be adequately accessible: the citizen must be able to have an indication that is adequate in the circumstances of the legal rules applicable to a given case. Secondly, a norm cannot be regarded as a 'law' unless it is formulated with sufficient precision to enable the citizen to regulate his conduct: he must be able—if need be with appropriate advice—to foresee, to a degree that is reasonable in the circumstances, the consequences which a given action may entail.

How, counsel asked, could this test be satisfied in Internet cases where the publisher cannot know by whose laws his conduct may eventually be judged? The US courts (notably in *ACLU* v. *Reno*, at p. 186 above) have repeatedly rejected as unconstitutional attempts to enact laws that threaten to make the legality of unrestricted Internet publications in America dependent on whether their content would be considered offensive or harmful to minors on the basis of contemporary community standards. Even within the USA, community standards are thought to vary too widely to make such a test viable—unless of course the publishers submit to the standards of the most intolerant and restrictive state of all.

When one moves to a world stage, these problems are greatly magnified. Things that may be considered lawful in one country may be considered both offensive and criminal in another. The old maxim, 'When in Rome, do as the Romans do', becomes largely unworkable in cyberspace, if courts in other countries adopt the view that it is also done in their territory.[254]

---

[253] [1979] 2 EHRR 245.

[254] The 'frontierless' nature of the Internet means that the problem cannot be resolved by reference to that principle of European human rights law under which individual states may legitimately restrict freedom of expression within their own jurisdictions in accordance with their own conceptions of decency or morality.

Implications for Child Pornography

The ruling in *Perrin* might perhaps be welcomed by some on the basis that it would facilitate the prosecution of child pornography cases involving foreign-sourced material that is accessed within the jurisdiction. Child pornography, however, is unlikely to be prosecuted under the Obscene Publications Act. The production and distribution (or 'showing') of images of child pornography is usually prosecuted under section 1 of the Protection of Children Act 1978, which also criminalizes the publication of advertisements suggesting that the defendant distributes, or shows, or is prepared to show such images. Offences under that provision fall within the scope of section 7 of the Sex Offenders Act 1997, and are therefore capable of commission outside the United Kingdom;[255] but only where:

(1) the conduct in question also amounts to an offence under the law in force where it is committed; and
(2) the defendant is a British citizen or a United Kingdom resident.

A foreign child pornographer (not resident in the United Kingdom) who posts images of child abuse on a foreign Internet server does not therefore fall within the ambit of section 7. He may be guilty of an offence under English law, though, if (on the basis of the ruling in *Perrin*) he is deemed to have 'committed' that offence within England and Wales itself. As previously explained, the *Perrin* approach to this issue enables courts to ignore the question of whether the accused has any British connections or whether his conduct was unlawful in the country where it took place, thus bypassing the limitations that were deliberately built into the Sex Offenders Act.

On the other hand, it by no means follows that rejection of the *Perrin* approach would leave such persons in the clear. Most states now have strict laws against child pornography, and there is a substantial degree of international cooperation between the law enforcement agencies of different countries, an early example of which was Operation Starburst, which involved forces from Britain, Europe, North America, South Africa, and the Far East. In *Fellows and Arnold*, arrests were made in England, on the basis of information provided by the US authorities, who helped to trace the international distribution of paedophile material to F's computer at Birmingham University; and there have been many such cases since.

Furthermore, anyone in England and Wales who stores indecent photographic or pseudo-photographic images of child pornography commits a serious arrestable offence under section 160 of the Criminal Justice and Public Order Act 1994, whether the images have been downloaded from the Internet or not. It follows that anyone, anywhere, who knowingly

---

[255] Note that the Act gives English courts no jurisdiction over things done elsewhere in the UK.

assists in or procures that offence will be liable to conviction as a second-ary party to that offence. According to the Court of Appeal in *R* v. *Robert Millar (Contractors) Ltd*,[256] secondary parties to an offence, even if outside the jurisdiction themselves, '. . . are guilty of participating in that crime, and not of some self-subsisting crime on their own account, and therefore they are in the same position as the principal offender and they are liable to be tried in this country'.

Images of child pornography are unlikely to be freely accessible over the Internet, if only because of the very real danger of arrest and prosecution. Access tends to be protected by passwords that are given out only with care. Any website operator or newsgroup user who knowingly makes such images available to persons within England and Wales is therefore likely to possess the requisite *mens rea* for secondary liability under section 160.

The Yahoo! Case

The issue that arose in *Perrin* was similar in many respects to that behind the notorious 'Yahoo Case': *LICRA and UEJF* v. *Yahoo! Inc. and Yahoo France*,[257] in which a French court ruled that Yahoo! Inc., an American cor-poration, was in breach of a French law[258] prohibiting the sale or display of Nazi memorabilia, on the basis that such items were marketed via online auc-tions hosted on Yahoo's US portals.[259] Yahoo! Inc. was accordingly ordered: '. . . to take such measures as will dissuade and render impossible any and all consultation on Yahoo.com of the auction service for Nazi objects as well as any other site or service which makes apologies of Nazism or questions the existence of Nazi crimes'.[260] Yahoo was further ordered to pay a fine of 100,000 francs per day unless this injunction was complied with within three months, despite protests that full implementation was technically impossible.

In practice, the ruling was not enforceable without the support of the US courts; but the sale or display of such material is not illegal in the USA, and the US courts have so far upheld Yahoo's right to host anything on its US sites that is not contrary to US law, even if those US sites can in fact be accessed from France.[261]

---

[256] [1970] 2 QB 54. See above p. 130.

[257] Tribunal de Grande Instance de Paris, 22 May and 20 November 2000: *Relié du Receiul Dalloz; Jurisprudence Dalloz*, 172. See Carolyn Penfold, 'Nazis, Porn and Politics: Asserting Control over Internet Content' 2001 (2) *Journal of Information, Law and Technology* (http://elj.warwick.ac.uk/jilt).

[258] French Criminal Code, Art. R. 645-1. The proceedings nevertheless appear to have been civil in character.

[259] Yahoo France did not carry any such offending material, but was ordered to instruct its French Internet customers to terminate any searches leading to sites displaying content in breach of French law. It has complied with this injunction.

[260] English translation by Daniel Lapres of Lapres & Associés, Paris.

[261] Yahoo! Inc. subsequently banned some Nazi items from its auction site, but has not fully complied with the French ruling.

The *Yahoo Case* and *R* v. *Perrin* each involved clumsy attempts to apply domestic territorial laws to conduct that has no real link with the territory in question. The same criticism may be made of a sinister attempt, by state prosecutors in Zimbabwe, to prosecute *Guardian* correspondent Andrew Meldrum for an alleged breach of Zimbabwean media laws, on the basis that his newspaper's website, which carried the allegedly offending material, could be accessed online in Zimbabwe and was accordingly 'published' there.[262] Such prosecutions undermine the rights of citizens of State X to publish anything in State X that is lawful under the laws of that state, without having to worry as to whether such publications may be viewed in other countries and judged unlawful under other laws.

Australian law, which regulates Internet content more strictly than most, recognizes the impossibility of applying such controls to foreign websites or service providers. Instead, the Broadcasting Services Amendment (Online Services) Act 1999 (Commonwealth) requires Australian ISPs to take 'all reasonable steps' to prevent their subscribers from accessing 'prohibited content' from overseas.[263] In practice, this may often fail to prevent such access, but it must surely be preferable to approaches which attempt to impose one country's domestic media or obscenity laws on the rest of the world.

The Computer Misuse Act 1990

Persons who unlawfully hack into computers or computer networks may do so with any of a number of possible motives, and in some cases may do so merely out of curiosity or devilment. A person who goes on to commit acts of international fraud or espionage may be prosecuted for such offences in accordance with the jurisdictional principles applicable to them; but in most cases the first possible charges to be considered would be offences under the Computer Misuse Act 1990. Pranksters and virus-mailers are unlikely to be prosecuted under any other Act.

The Act was passed at a time when the Internet, as we know it, was still in the process of gestation; but its ancestors—military, financial, commercial, government, and university computer networks, in which individual computers and databases can be accessed internationally, via other computers or terminals—predate the Internet by several years. Some, at least, of the dangers posed by remote but unlawful computer access were therefore understood when the Act was drafted. As a result, it contains provisions that specifically address the problem of transnational computer misuse, of which Internet offences are now the most important variants.

---

[262] See *The Guardian*, 15 July 2002. A magistrate in Zimbabwe dismissed the charge, on the basis that Meldrum's article had merely reported certain allegations that were being made, and he was not guilty of irresponsible journalism.

[263] See Penfold, op. cit., fn 257, paras 2–3.

Offences of Unauthorized Access

Section 1 of the 1990 Act creates a basic summary offence of causing a computer to perform any function with intent to secure unauthorized access to any program or data held on that or any other computer. Section 2 creates a more serious offence, which is triable either way. This consists of the basic section 1 offence, coupled with an intent to commit (or to facilitate the later commission, whether by himself or by any other person) of an ulterior offence, such as theft, or an offence under section 3 (below), that is triable under English law and punishable by at least five years' imprisonment.[264]

In neither case is it necessary that any actual access to the target computer is achieved; nor need it even be possible. If, with the requisite _mens rea_, the hacker makes his own computer perform a function (as where he merely attempts to hack into another computer), he may commit a substantive offence under either of those sections. On normal territorial principles, therefore, the hacker sitting at his own computer in Scotland, whilst unsuccessfully attempting to gain illicit access to a computer in England, commits his offence entirely in Scotland, unless the target computer responds in some way, for example, by generating a password request, or indeed by sending him a curt 'access denied' reply. These general principles are supplemented, however, by extensive jurisdiction provisions contained in sections 4, 5, and 8 of the Act, which are examined at pp. 195–7 below.

Unauthorized Modification of Computer Material

Section 3 of the 1990 Act creates a further 'either way' offence that differs from the previous ones by requiring the actual modification of computer programs or data. To commit this offence, the accused must intentionally do any act which causes an unauthorized modification of the contents of any computer (whether permanent or temporary) with intent to impair the operation of any computer, to prevent or hinder access to any program or data held in any computer, or to impair the operation of any such program or the reliability of any such data.

This embraces most possible forms of cybervandalism or cyberterrorism, including the erasure or corruption of data and the infection of data, programs, or operating systems by computer worms or viruses.[265] On normal territorial principles, jurisdiction would lie where the relevant unauthorized modification takes place. On general principles of causation, a person who

---

[264] More specifically, it must be an offence for which the penalty is fixed by law, or for which a person aged 21 years or more (not previously convicted) may be sentenced to imprisonment for a term of five years (or might be so sentenced but for restrictions imposed by the Magistrates' Courts Act 1980, s. 33).

[265] See Yaman Akdeniz, 'Section 3 of the Computer Misuse Act 1990: an Antidote for Computer Viruses' [1996] 3 Web JCLI, http://webjcli.ncl.ac.uk.

releases a computer worm or virus, especially one that spreads via e-mail, etc., might well be held responsible for secondary or indirect infections, as well as primary or direct ones, but would not commit any section 3 offence within the jurisdiction merely because his own PC (from which the virus was dissipated) was sited there. Once again, however, the basic rules of territorial jurisdiction are supplemented by specific provisions, which substantially enlarge the ambit of the offence.

The Jurisdiction Provisions

The offences created by section 1–3 of the 1990 Act do not ordinarily possess any purely extraterritorial ambit, and (in contrast to the rules governing most extraterritorial offences) British citizenship is expressly made immaterial to any question of guilt;[266] but sections 4 and 5 make extensive provision for cases involving cross-frontier offences, and in some circumstances this may arguably (if perhaps unintentionally) give rise to something akin to full extraterritoriality. Section 4(1) and (2) provide:

(1) Except as provided below in this section, it is immaterial for the purposes of any offence under section 1 or 3 above—
(a) whether any act or other event proof of which is required for conviction of the offence occurred in the home country concerned; or
(b) whether the accused was in the home country concerned at the time of any such act or event.

(2) Subject to subsection (3) below, in the case of such an offence at least one significant link with domestic jurisdiction must exist in the circumstances of the case for the offence to be committed.

The Act applies to all parts of the United Kingdom, but as far as English law is concerned, the 'home country' means England and Wales.[267] The concept of a 'significant link with domestic jurisdiction' is elaborated in section 5(2) and (3):

(2) In relation to an offence under section 1, either of the following is a significant link with domestic jurisdiction—
(a) that the accused was in the home country concerned at the time when he did the act which caused the computer to perform the function; or
(b) that any computer containing any program or data to which the accused secured or intended to secure unauthorised access by doing that act was in the home country concerned at that time.

(3) In relation to an offence under section 3, either of the following is a significant link with domestic jurisdiction—
(a) that the accused was in the home country concerned at the time when he did the act which caused the unauthorised modification; or
(b) that the unauthorised modification took place in the home country concerned.

---

[266] Computer Misuse Act 1990, s. 9(1).   [267] See s. 4(6).

The position is relatively straightforward as far as offences under sections 1 and 3 are concerned. Such offences will be considered to fall within the ambit of English law in either of the scenarios identified in section 5(2) or (3) above. The would-be hacker in Poland who uses his own computer in an attempt to gain unauthorized access to a computer network in England may (at least in theory) be guilty of a section 1 offence in England by virtue of sections 4(1) and (2) and 5(2)(b), even if it turns out that his Internet connection has become inoperable and that access to any external computer (in England or elsewhere) is impossible. If he gains access and succeeds in modifying data on that computer network, he will commit an offence under section 3. Similarly, anyone in England and Wales who gains, or operates his own computer with intent to gain, unauthorized access to a foreign computer, may commit offences under English law by virtue of sections 5(2)(a) and 5(3)(a).

The position becomes complex and obscure only when one turns to section 2 of the Act. The jurisdiction provisions discussed above do not purport to apply to that section; but because the section 2 offence is merely an aggravated version of the basic offence under section 1, one might ordinarily have expected that the provisions governing section 1 (notably those set out in section 5(2)) would apply automatically to section 2. Section 4(3), however, makes special provision as to the ambit of section 2 offences, by dispensing with the 'significant link' requirement in any cases where the relevant ulterior offence would itself be triable under English law. It provides:

There is no need for any such link to exist for the commission of an offence under section 1 above to be established in proof of an allegation to that effect in proceedings for an offence under section 2 above.

A section 2 offence may thus be capable of commission *entirely* abroad, provided that the offender's ulterior intent relates to the commission of an offence that is punishable by at least five years' imprisonment under English law. The ulterior offence may even be an extraterritorial offence, in which case the section 2 offence requires no connection at all with England and Wales, and is itself fully extraterritorial.

Nor is this all. Section 4(4), read in conjunction with section 8(1), applies section 2 to cases in which the 'ulterior offence' is a territorial offence under a foreign system of law, and would have been an offence under English law if committed within England and Wales, provided that the underlying section 1 offence *does* have a significant link with English domestic jurisdiction. Section 4(4) provides:

Subject to section 8 below, where—

(a) any such link does in fact exist in the case of an offence under section 1 above; and

(b) commission of that offence is alleged in proceedings for an offence under section 2 above;

section 2 above shall apply as if anything the accused intended to do or facilitate in any place outside the home country concerned which would be an offence to which section 2 applies if it took place in the home country concerned were the offence in question.

This might cover a case in which D, in England, gains unauthorized access to a computer in the USA, with a view to doing something there that would have been punishable with imprisonment for five years or more if committed in England and Wales. Under section 8(1), however, criminality under local law is equally important in such cases:

A person is guilty of an offence triable by virtue of section 4(4) above only if what he intended to do or facilitate would involve the commission of an offence under the law in force where the whole or any part of it was intended to take place.

Jurisdiction over Inchoate Offences

Sections 6 and 7 of the 1990 Act address the problem of jurisdiction over inchoate offences. Section 6 provides:

(1) On a charge of conspiracy to commit an offence under this Act the following questions are immaterial to the accused's guilt—
    (a) the question where any person became a party to the conspiracy; and
    (b) the question whether any act, omission or other event occurred in the home country concerned.

(2) On a charge of attempting to commit an offence under section 3 above the following questions are immaterial to the accused's guilt—
    (a) the question where the attempt was made; and
    (b) the question whether it had an effect in the home country concerned.

(3) On a charge of incitement to commit an offence under this Act the question where the incitement took place is immaterial to the accused's guilt.

While this appears at first sight to be a highly significant set of provisions, it is doubtful whether it adds anything of substance to the general rules governing jurisdiction over inchoate offences. What matters in each case (although it is not spelt out in the provisions) is that the substantive offence in question must be one that would itself be triable under English law.[268]

Section 7 may be more significant, because it does at least extend the ambit of the law governing incitement. Section 7(4) provides:

Subject to section 8 below, if any act done by a person in England and Wales would amount to the offence of incitement to commit an offence under this Act but for the fact that what he had in view would not be an offence triable in England and Wales—
    (a) what he had in view shall be treated as an offence under this Act for the purposes of any charge of incitement brought in respect of that act; and
    (b) any such charge shall accordingly be triable in England and Wales.

In contrast, section 7(3) appears to have been drafted on the basis of the same inherent misconceptions that underlie section 5(2) of the Criminal

---

[268] In the case of attempt, the substantive offence must also be triable on indictment. Offences under s. 1 of the Act are not so triable.

Justice Act 1993 and section 1A of the Criminal Attempts Act 1981. Section 7(3) amends section 1 of the Criminal Attempts Act 1981, so as to insert the following additional provisions:

(1A) Subject to section 8 of the Computer Misuse Act 1990 (relevance of external law), if this subsection applies to an act, what the person doing it had in view shall be treated as an offence to which this section applies.

(1B) Subsection (1A) above applies to an act if—
  (a) it is done in England and Wales; and
  (b) it would fall within subsection (1) above as more than merely preparatory to the commission of an offence under section 3 of the Computer Misuse Act 1990 but for the fact that the offence, if completed, would not be an offence triable in England and Wales.

Like section 1A of the Criminal Attempts Act, section 1(1A) appears to be both useless and potentially misleading, because like section 1A it is hopelessly at odds with itself. If an act is done in England and Wales that is more than merely preparatory to the commission of an offence under section 3 of the 1990 Act, it must inevitably 'fall within subsection (1) above' (that is, it must be a regular criminal attempt within section 1(1) of the 1981 Act). There is in practice no way in which the intended section 3 offence could *fail* to be an offence triable in England and Wales, because the accused's conduct within England and Wales must necessarily provide a 'significant link with domestic jurisdiction' under section 5(3)(a) of the 1990 Act.

    Provisions dealing with conspiracy to commit offences under foreign law were originally included in section 7(1) and (2), but these have now been supplanted by provisions contained in the Criminal Justice (Terrorism and Conspiracy) Act 1998, which were examined earlier in this chapter.[269]

    While by no means models of clear drafting, the jurisdiction provisions in the 1990 Act do at least appear to have ensured that the relevant provisions of English criminal law extend to all hackers and 'virus mailers' who operate within England and Wales, as well as to all those who (directly or indirectly) attack, infect, or misuse computers situated within England and Wales without entering the realm themselves. This achievement is not matched by the comparable (and closely related) provisions contained in Part 1 of the Criminal Justice Act 1993.

HOMICIDE AND PERJURY

Murder and Manslaughter

Section 10 of the Offences Against the Person Act 1861 is one of the less well-known provisions of that Act, although it deals with offences of

---

[269] See above, pp. 142–8.

murder and manslaughter. It provides:

Where any person being criminally stricken, poisoned, or otherwise hurt upon the sea, or at any place out of England or Ireland, shall die of such stroke, poisoning, or hurt in England or Ireland, or, being criminally stricken, poisoned or otherwise hurt in any place in England or Ireland, shall die of such stroke, poisoning, or hurt upon the sea, or at any place out of England or Ireland, every offence committed in respect of any such case, whether the same shall amount to the offence of murder or of manslaughter, . . . may be dealt with, inquired of, tried, determined, and punished . . . in England or Ireland.

Section 10 was derived without amendment from section 8 of the Offences Against the Person Act 1828,[270] and addresses the type of problem that arose in *Lacy's Case*.[271] In Coke's account of this case:

Lacy struck Peacock and gave him a mortal wound upon the sea, of which Peacock died at Scarborough in the County of York, and Lacy was discharged of it, for those of the County of York could not enquire of the stroke . . . because it was not given in any county; and those of the Admiral's jurisdiction could not enquire of the stroke without enquiring of the death, and they could not enquire of the death, because it was *infra corpus comitatus*.

Nevertheless, the potential application of section 10 appears to be more limited than the unwary reader might suppose. In *R v. Lewis*,[272] the Court for Crown Cases Reserved held that section 8 of the 1828 Act could *not* apply where the fatal blow struck had been aboard an American ship on the high seas, even though the victim subsequently died ashore, after the ship had docked in Liverpool. It was held that the original blow could not be termed criminal (or 'felonious'[273]) under English law, because English criminal law had no application to things done on a foreign ship on the high seas. The position would have been different had the ship been British, or within an English port or harbour when the blow was struck. It would also have been different if the alleged offender had been a pirate, or a British subject who was not a member of the ship's crew;[274] but the provision could not be said to criminalize a blow that would not otherwise have been criminal.

Section 10 nevertheless remains applicable to cases in which the victim is injured in England and dies abroad. Such a scenario may seem rather improbable, but might arise where, for example, the victim is injured in Berwick-on-Tweed and then taken for specialist treatment to a hospital in Edinburgh, where he dies; or where a Canadian victim returns home following his discharge from hospital in England, only to die from unforeseen complications shortly afterwards. On facts such as those of *Lewis*, which

---

[270] 9 Geo. IV c. 34.

[271] (1582/3) 1 Leon 270; also noted by Coke in his report of *Bingham's Case* (1600) 2 Co Rep 91(a).   [272] (1857) Dears & B 182.

[273] 'Felonious' was the term used in the 1828 Act, and also in s. 10 of the 1861 Act, until the distinction between felonies and misdemeanours was abolished in 1967.

[274] See *R v. Kelly* [1982] AC 665.

seem more likely to arise in practice, it might now be argued that section 10 has become superfluous, because the terminatory principle of jurisdiction, as applied in cases such as *Secretary for State* v. *Markus*,[275] would apply English law to any case of murder or manslaughter in which the offence is completed (and thus committed) by the occurrence of the specified result (namely, the victim's death) within England and Wales. While such a conclusion may seem bizarre, it would be fully in accordance with the *Markus* type of approach.[276]

Perjury

Section 1(4) and (5) of the Perjury Act 1911 address the issue of cross-frontier perjury. Arrangements have long existed for sworn evidence or depositions to be taken in one country for the purposes of judicial proceedings in another. If wilfully false evidence is given by such means, questions then arise as to the *locus* of any crime of perjury. Subsections (4) and (5) provide an 'inclusionary' response:

(4) A statement made by a person lawfully sworn in England for the purposes of a judicial proceeding:

   (a) in another part of His Majesty's dominions; or

   (b) in a British tribunal lawfully constituted in any place by sea or land outside His Majesty's dominions; or

   (c) in a tribunal of any foreign state,

shall, for the purposes of this section, be treated as a statement made in a judicial proceeding in England.

(5) Where, for the purposes of a judicial proceeding in England, a person is lawfully sworn under the authority of an Act of Parliament:

   (a) in any other part of His Majesty's dominions; or

   (b) before a British tribunal or a British officer in a foreign country, or within the jurisdiction of the Admiralty of England;

a statement made by such person so sworn as aforesaid (unless the Act of Parliament under which it was made otherwise specifically provides) shall be treated for the purposes of this section as having been made in the judicial proceeding in England for the purposes whereof it was made.

---

[275] [1976] AC 35. See above, pp. 123–4.

[276] The terminatory theory appears to have been a twentieth century development, and was not recognized when *Lewis* was decided. In *R* v. *Keyn (The Franconia)* (1876) 2 Ex D 63, a majority in the Court for Crown Cases Reserved refused to uphold K's conviction for manslaughter, even though his negligent navigation of a German ship had caused the death of passengers aboard the British steamer, *Strathclyde*. The majority view was that since K was not himself within English jurisdiction at the time, and was not a British subject, it could not be right to subject him to the rules of English criminal law. Under the Army Act 1955, s. 70(5), an offence of murder or manslaughter shall be deemed, for the purposes of determining whether it was committed in the UK, to have been committed at the place of the commission of the act or occurrence of the neglect which caused the death, irrespective of the place of the death; but if this was thought to be the law in any event, it would not have been necessary to enact that provision.

5

The Extraterritorial Application of English Criminal Law

INTRODUCTION

There are numerous exceptions to the general rule that things done entirely abroad cannot amount to offences under English law. The greater part of this chapter, and of Chapter 6, is concerned with such exceptions. The extraterritorial ambit of English criminal law nevertheless remains more limited than that of many other countries, and in terms of actual prosecutions, the contrast with some European countries is very marked. In 1996, an Interdepartmental Steering Committee, established by the British Government to look into the subject of extraterritorial jurisdiction within the United Kingdom,[1] managed to identify only two recent examples of domestic prosecutions relating to offences committed abroad. One was a Scottish case involving a murder allegedly committed in Spain,[2] and the other was a forthcoming trial in England under the War Crimes Act 1991.[3] Several more prosecutions for extraterritorial offences have been brought since then under English law,[4] but the numbers involved remain extremely small. In contrast, data collected by the Council of Europe in 1990 reveal that courts in The Netherlands convicted 149 Dutch nationals for extraterritorial offences between 1981 and 1984: figures which do not include military personnel charged with offences while serving abroad. Comparable figures were recorded from Italy and Norway.[5]

The number of cases currently prosecuted does not, however, provide a meaningful indication of the importance or potential importance of the subject. Quite apart from the broader questions of principle involved (is it right, for example, that British citizens should be subject to rules of English

---

[1] *Review of Extraterritorial Jurisdiction* (Home Office, 1996).

[2] This was *HM Advocate* v. *McLeod* (1993) unreported, in which the accused was acquitted.

[3] This case was not identified, but it must presumably have been *R* v. *Serefinowicz* (1997) January. The trial in this case did not take place, because the defendant was found unfit to plead.

[4] Convictions upheld on appeal include *R* v. *Sawoniuk* [2000] 2 Cr App R 220 (war crimes) and *R* v. *Kular (Mohan Singh)* (2000) unreported, 18 April (murder). There have also been successful prosecutions under the Sex Offenders Act 1997 (see p. 271, below).

[5] In Italy, 30 prosecutions were recorded in 1981; in Norway, 47 were recorded in 1983. Most states, however, were unable to provide actual data: *Review of Extraterritorial Jurisdiction* (fn 1 above), Annex F.

criminal law when abroad?), the paucity of English prosecutions must in part be attributed to the limitations of the laws currently in force. The vast majority of offences under English law currently have no extraterritorial ambit. If more offences had such an ambit, and if English rules of criminal evidence and procedure facilitated prosecutions for extraterritorial offences by making greater use of live video-links or documentary evidence, one might expect to see many more such prosecutions.[6] Chapter 7 below considers whether this would be a desirable development. For the moment, however, our principal concern is with the law as it now stands.

The Forms of Extraterritorial Jurisdiction

Leaving aside the application of English criminal law to things done on British or United Kingdom ships, naval vessels, aircraft, or offshore mineral installations, over which the basis for exercising jurisdiction may best be described as 'quasi-territorial', English criminal law appears to recognize two distinct types of extraterritorial jurisdiction, or two distinct ways in which offences under English law may extend to conduct committed entirely abroad. The first is primarily 'offence-specific'. There are certain offences, such as murder, torture, or bigamy, to which legislation has given an express extraterritorial ambit. This extraterritorial ambit is usually specific not just to the offence, but to the category of person (such as United Kingdom nationals) who may be subject to it; and in a few cases it is limited to specific countries or localities with or in respect of which the United Kingdom has treaty obligations.[7]

'Universal jurisdiction', in which the nationality or status of the alleged offender is irrelevant, nevertheless characterizes a significant number of extraterritorial offences under English law. Most such offences are of modern origin, and give effect to international Conventions dealing with various forms of terrorism, or with crimes (such as the hijacking of aircraft) that are frequently associated with terrorism; but they also include torture, some war crimes, and an updated version of the ancient offence of piracy *jure gentium*, which has for centuries been punishable on a universal basis by any state into whose custody the alleged pirates are taken. Terrorism may now be likened to piracy, in that the terrorist, like the pirate, is widely perceived to be the common enemy of mankind.

---

[6] The much higher numbers of prosecutions recorded in Norway and The Netherlands may reflect the fact that those states either restrict or forbid the extradition of their own citizens, preferring to put them on trial at home. There is no suggestion that the United Kingdom would consider adopting such a policy, but Italy's extradition policy is closer to that of the United Kingdom.

[7] This is true, for example, of those offences given an extraterritorial application under the Suppression of Terrorism Act 1978, section 4(1). See also the Explosive Substances Act 1883, ss. 2 and 3, and the Antarctic Act 1994, ss. 21 and 22.

The second type of extraterritorial jurisdiction is not offence-specific, but instead subjects-particular (and in some cases quite narrow) categories of person to the general corpus of English criminal law when abroad, including many offences that are otherwise purely territorial in their ambit. Persons who are subject to this 'general' extraterritorial jurisdiction include Crown servants, seamen from United Kingdom ships, members of the British armed forces, and anyone else who is deemed subject to British service law. Such persons may be held liable for extraterritorially committed crimes such as theft, assault, or even dangerous driving,[8] which would otherwise have no extraterritorial ambit at all. A British serviceman, merchant seaman, or Crown servant who commits a specific extraterritorial offence, such as murder or torture abroad, may be tried in England on either basis.[9]

JURISDICTION AND EXTRADITION

Even where acts committed abroad potentially fall within the ambit of English criminal law, the policy of the United Kingdom is to recognize any stronger foreign claim to jurisdiction, by extraditing a fugitive offender to the country concerned. A British citizen who commits an extraterritorial offence, such as murder, in a foreign country will not ordinarily be tried for that offence under English law if the foreign country in question requests his extradition to face trial there, unless there are legal or political obstacles to such extradition.[10] Jurisdiction tends to be asserted only where such obstacles do exist, where no relevant extradition treaty applies, or where no request for extradition has been received. Where extradition is sought, no special rule is applied to British citizens or United Kingdom nationals, even in respect of extradition requests from countries that will not reciprocate by extraditing their own citizens to the United Kingdom.[11]

NATIONALITY AND STATUS

The imposition of liability for extraterritorial offences under English law, other than those committed aboard British ships or aircraft, depends in most cases on the nationality or status of the defendant. In most cases, he

---

[8] As in *Cox v. Army Council* [1963] AC 48.

[9] As in *R v. Page* [1953] 2 All ER 1355 (murder committed by a British soldier on land abroad).

[10] Human rights issues may raise such obstacles, notably where there are reasons to suppose that the fugitive will not receive a fair trial, or will face torture or death, should he be extradited. See the Extradition Act 1989, section 6(1)(c)–(d); *Soering v. UK* (1989) 11 EHRR 439; Stanbrook and Stanbrook, *Extradition Law and Practice* (2nd edn, 2000), §§ 1.50–56, 7.57, and 13.82.

[11] See Stanbrook and Stanbrook, op. cit., fn 10, §§ 6.83–6.93; *R v. Secretary of State for the Home Department, ex p Puttick* [1981] 1 All ER 776.

must hold a specified form of British or United Kingdom nationality, although in a few cases some alternative status, such as residence within the United Kingdom, may equally suffice, and in others (as noted above) the nationality or status of the defendant may be irrelevant.

The Varied Forms of British Nationality or Status

A wide range of expressions relating to the nationality or status of a defendant may be encountered in statutes imposing extraterritorial liability. The list of terms still in use includes:

(1) 'any subject of Her Majesty';[12]
(2) 'a British subject';[13]
(3) 'a British officer or subject';[14]
(4) 'a citizen of the United Kingdom and colonies';[15]
(5) 'a British citizen';[16]
(6) 'a United Kingdom national, a United Kingdom resident or a person subject to United Kingdom service jurisdiction';[17]
(7) 'resident in the United Kingdom';[18]
(8) 'resident in the United Kingdom, the Isle of Man or any of the Channel Islands';[19]
(9) 'a United Kingdom person'[20].

None of these terms is defined in the Interpretation Act 1978, although Schedule 1 to that Act formerly contained a definition of 'British subjects'. Furthermore, many of the most widely used terms are now obsolete and require reinterpretation in the light of more recent legislation. The process of deleting obsolete terms and inserting consequential statutory amendments does not appear to have been carried out with the usual degree of thoroughness in this particular context, and a certain amount of cross-reference between statutes may be needed in order to understand the current meaning or effect of the older ones. References in older (pre-1949) statutes to 'British subjects' or 'subjects of her Majesty' are a case in point. These must now be construed in the light of section 3(1) of the British

---

[12] Offences Against the Person Act 1861, s. 9.   [13] Foreign Enlistment Act 1870, s. 4.
[14] Official Secrets Act 1911, s. 10.
[15] Explosive Substances Act 1883, ss. 2 and 3 (as substituted by the Criminal Jurisdiction Act 1975).   [16] Merchant Shipping Act 1995, s. 281.
[17] International Criminal Court Act 2001, ss. 51–54, 58–61, etc. See also the Anti-terrorism, Crime and Security Act 2001, s. 109, which refers to 'a national of the United Kingdom'.
[18] Sex Offenders Act 1997, s. 7(2).   [19] War Crimes Act 1991, s. 1(2).
[20] Biological Weapons Act 1974, s. 1A (inserted by the Anti-terrorism, Crime and Security Act 2001).

Nationality Act 1948, section 51(1) of the British Nationality Act 1981, section 4 of the Hong Kong (British Nationality) Order 1986,[21] and section 1(1) of the British Overseas Territories Act 2002.

British Nationality Act 1948, Section 3(1)

References in older statutes to the extraterritorial liability of 'British subjects' or 'subjects of Her Majesty' would originally have extended to all subjects of the British Empire, colonies, and dominions, including those of Ireland; but section 3(1) of the British Nationality Act 1948 now provides:

A British subject or citizen of Eire who is not a citizen of the United Kingdom and Colonies shall not be guilty of an offence against the laws of any part of the United Kingdom and Colonies or of any protectorate or United Kingdom trust territory by reason of anything done or omitted in any country mentioned in subsection (3) of section 1 of this Act or in Eire or in any foreign country, unless—

    (a) the act or omission would be an offence if he were an alien; and

    (b) in the case of an act or omission in any country mentioned in subsection (3) of section 1 of this Act or in Eire, it would be an offence if the country in which the act is done or the omission made were a foreign country.

Provided that nothing in this subsection shall apply to the contravention of any provision of the Merchant Shipping Act 1995.

Section 3(1) must itself be construed in the light of later legislation, because the concept of citizenship of the United Kingdom and colonies ceased to exist when the British Nationality Act 1981 came into force, and that Act also repealed section 1(3) of the 1948 Act, so that the reference to it in section 3(1) is now a 'dead link'.[22] None of this has been reflected in amendments to section 3(1) itself. The one area in which that provision has been amended is through the substitution of a reference to the Merchant Shipping Act 1995 in place of the original reference to the Merchant Shipping Act 1894; but the revised reference makes no sense, because (in contrast to the 1894 Act) the 1995 Act does not create any criminal liability that even purports to be specific to British subjects. Indeed, the Act does not refer to British subjects at all.

When the British Nationality Act 1981 came into force, persons who previously were citizens of the United Kingdom and colonies acquired one of the new forms of British nationality created by that Act. By section 51, as amended, any reference in an earlier statute to a 'citizen of the United Kingdom and colonies' must now be construed as meaning a British citizen, a British overseas territories citizen,[23] a British overseas citizen, or one who

---

[21] SI 1986 No. 948.

[22] This must now be construed as a reference to Commonwealth countries, as defined in the British Nationality Act 1981, s. 37 and Sch. 3. References to Eire must (since 18 April 1949) be construed as references to the Republic of Ireland (Ireland Act 1949, s. 1(2)).

[23] Prior to 26 February 2002, these were known as British dependent territories citizens, although some legislation still refers to such territories as 'colonies'. There are currently

under the Hong Kong (British Nationality) Order 1986 is a British national (overseas). Of these categories, only British citizenship currently guarantees a right of abode within the United Kingdom itself, but all persons in these categories remain equally susceptible to English criminal jurisdiction under statutes that extend potential extraterritorial liability to 'British subjects', 'subjects of Her Majesty', or 'citizens of the United Kingdom and colonies'.

The limitations imposed by section 3(1) of the 1948 Act apply only to things done in foreign or Commonwealth countries, or in the Republic of Ireland. What, then, of a Commonwealth citizen who commits an act in Scotland, Northern Ireland, or the Channel Islands, or aboard a ship at sea, that is said to be an offence under English law when committed there by a British subject or by a subject of her Majesty? Assume, for example, that a Canadian citizen enters into a bigamous marriage in Scotland,[24] or that a Nigerian citizen commits an act of murder in Guernsey.[25] At first sight, it may seem that neither can be guilty of any offence under English law, because for most purposes the citizens of independent Commonwealth counties are no longer deemed to be 'British subjects' at all. Section 51(1) of the British Nationality Act 1981, however, provides:

(1) Without prejudice to subsection (3)(c), in any enactment or instrument whatever passed or made before commencement,[26] 'British subject' and 'Commonwealth citizen' have the same meaning, that is—
    (a) . . .
    (b) in relation to any time after commencement, a person who has the status of a Commonwealth citizen under this Act.

By section 37 of the 1981 Act:

(1) Every person who—
    (a) under the British Nationality Acts 1981 and 1983 or the British Overseas Territories Act 2002 is a British citizen, a British overseas territories citizen, a British national (overseas), a British overseas citizen or a British subject; or
    (b) under any enactment for the time being in force in any country mentioned in Schedule 3 is a citizen of that country,[27]
shall have the status of a Commonwealth citizen.

14 British overseas territories: Anguilla; Bermuda; British Antarctic Territory; British Indian Ocean Territory; the British Virgin Islands; the Cayman Islands; the Falkland Islands; Gibraltar; Montserrat; Pitcairn Islands; St Helena and Dependencies; South Georgia and the South Sandwich Islands; the Sovereign Base Areas of Akrotiri and Dhekelia in Cyprus; and the Turks and Caicos Islands. On 21 May 2002, British citizenship was conferred on all persons who were British overseas territories citizens immediately before that date, excluding those who were British overseas territories citizens by virtue only of a connection with the Sovereign Base Areas of Akrotiri and Dhekelia (British Overseas Territories Act 2002, s. 3).

[24] Offences Against the Person Act 1861, s. 57.

[25] Offences Against the Person Act 1861, s. 9. Guernsey is not a part of the UK (section 9 applies only to murder or manslaughter committed outside the UK), but neither is it a Commonwealth country or a British overseas territory. [26] Before 1 January 1983.

[27] The countries in question are currently: Antigua & Barbuda; Australia; The Bahamas; Bangladesh; Barbados; Belize; Botswana; Brunei; Cameroon; Canada; Republic of Cyprus;

The combined effect of these provisions is that a citizen of an independent Commonwealth country must still be considered a British subject for the purposes of construing pre-1983 legislation; and may become guilty of an extraterritorial offence under English law, on the same basis as a British citizen, in those limited circumstances to which section 3(1) of the 1948 Act does not apply. To put it another way, our Canadian bigamist may be convicted in England of an offence committed in Scotland; and our Nigerian murderer may be convicted in England of a crime committed in Guernsey. Is this really what Parliament intended?

United Kingdom Nationality

Most recently enacted legislation tends to limit any extraterritorial criminal liability to those who are 'United Kingdom nationals' or 'United Kingdom persons'.[28] United Kingdom nationality is a status originally identified for the purposes of European Community law, under which it means a person who falls to be treated as a national of the United Kingdom for the purposes of the Community Treaties.[29] The United Kingdom defines its nationals for those purposes as: British citizens; British overseas territories citizens connected with Gibraltar;[30] and British subjects under the British Nationality Act 1981 who have a right of abode within the United Kingdom. When used in the context of criminal jurisdiction, however, the term means:

(1) a British citizen, a British overseas territories citizen, a British national (overseas), or a British overseas citizen; or
(2) a person who under the British Nationality Act 1981 is a British subject; or
(3) a British protected person within the meaning of that Act.

Corporations and Legal Persons

The term 'United Kingdom person', which is widely used in modern statutes, applies to United Kingdom nationals, Scottish partnerships, and

---

Dominica; Fiji; Gambia; Ghana; Grenada; Guyana; India; Jamaica; Kenya; Kiribati; Lesotho; Malawi; Malaysia; Maldives; Malta; Mauritius; Mozambique; Namibia; Nauru; New Zealand; Nigeria; Pakistan; Papua New Guinea; Saint Christopher & Nevis; Saint Lucia; Saint Vincent & the Grenadines; Seychelles; Sierra Leone; Singapore; Solomon Islands; South Africa; Sri Lanka; Swaziland; Tanzania; Tonga; Trinidad & Tobago; Tuvalu; Uganda; Vanuatu; Western Samoa; Zambia; and Zimbabwe.

[28] These include the Outer Space Act 1986, the Antarctic Act 1994, the Landmines Act 1998, the Aviation and Maritime Security Act 2000, the Anti-terrorism, Crime and Security Act 2001, and the International Criminal Court Act 2001; but surprisingly the term is not used in ss. 143 or 146 of the Nationality, Immigration and Asylum Act 2002.

[29] See, e.g., the Immigration and Asylum Act 1999, s. 80.

[30] See the British Government's declaration of 28 January 1983 (Cmnd. 9062).

any other bodies incorporated under the law of any part of the United Kingdom, including 'limited liability partnerships'.[31] The term is used where it is considered that such entities should be subject to the same extraterritorial jurisdiction as individuals. In other cases, legislation refers to 'United Kingdom nationals and bodies incorporated under the laws of any part of the United Kingdom': a phrase which means much the same thing.[32]

Where extraterritorial jurisdiction is extended to corporations, as, for example, has been done in respect of offences involving corruption, a United Kingdom company may be punishable in England for the actions of its officers abroad, even where those officers are not United Kingdom nationals and are not themselves subject to English law. Whether the acts of such officers are capable of implicating the company in the first place is a question that must be answered in accordance with the ordinary rules governing corporate liability. In a corruption case, for example, it would be necessary for the prosecution to establish that the individual responsible had the status and authority which would make his acts the acts of the company itself,[33] or that he was acting on the instructions of one who had that authority.

Extraterritorial offences committed by the agents or officers of an overseas (foreign-registered) subsidiary of a United Kingdom company could not ordinarily be attributed to the parent company, although cases might conceivably occur in which the veil of incorporation could be lifted, so as to expose the subsidiary as the mere puppet of the parent company, or as a façade behind which the parent company attempts to hide.[34]

Jurisdiction Based on Foreign Nationality

In some cases, jurisdiction may be established over a crime committed abroad on the basis that the offender is a national of a specified foreign or Commonwealth country: notably under section 4(3) of the Suppression of Terrorism Act 1978, where the alleged crime is murder, manslaughter, or an offence under section 2 or 3 of the Explosive Substances Act 1883, and the alleged offender is a national of a 'convention country' within the meaning

---

[31] Limited Liability Partnership Act 2000, s. 1(2).

[32] In the normal course of events, one might expect that any extraterritorial prosecution brought against a Scottish or Northern Ireland corporation (or a Scottish partnership) would be brought only in Scotland or Northern Ireland, but there does not appear to be any rule to that effect; and circumstances might possibly arise in which it would be appropriate to prosecute a Scottish company in England in respect of an offence allegedly committed abroad—perhaps because other defendants in that case would naturally fall to be prosecuted in England. It is certainly possible for a Scottish company to be prosecuted in England as a party to an offence committed in England by one of its employees: see *R* v. *Robert Millar (Contractors) Ltd* [1970] 2 QB 54.   [33] *R* v. *Andrews-Weatherfoil Ltd* [1972] 1 WLR 118.

[34] As to lifting the veil, see generally S. Mayson, D. French, and C. Ryan, *Company Law* (19th edn, 2002), 147 *et seq.*

of the 1978 Act. The background to this extraordinary provision is explained later in this chapter (see pp. 254–61 below).

JURISDICTION OVER PARTICULAR CLASSES

Crown Servants

Crown servants, including diplomats and the governors, etc., of British overseas territories, may be tried and punished under English law for acts committed by them abroad, when acting or purporting to act in the course of their office, etc., if such acts would have been indictable offences had they been committed in England and Wales. There are sound reasons why this should be so. Historically, governors of colonies or plantations would once have appeared 'above the law' within their own domains, and the knowledge that they might one day have to answer for any crimes in an English court may sometimes have acted as a check on potential abuses of power. British diplomats are generally immune from the criminal jurisdiction of the states to which they are accredited, and clearly it would be wrong if they were also effectively immune from the jurisdiction of their own country. Furthermore, serious misconduct abroad by any servant or officer of the British Crown carries great potential for scandal and national embarrassment, but any such scandal, etc., may be reduced if the United Kingdom is seen to deal firmly with the misconduct following that person's expulsion or recall.[35]

The earliest legislation imposing extraterritorial jurisdiction over Crown servants dates back to 1698–9. The statute of 11 Will. 3, c. 12, entitled 'An Act to punish Governors of Plantations in this Kingdom for Crimes by them committed in the Plantations' (but which also applied to crimes committed by commanders-in-chief in colonial territories under their jurisdiction), was the basis of at least one notable prosecution, namely that of *R* v. *Wall*,[36] in which W, a former governor of Goree, was hanged for the murder, 20 years earlier, of a soldier who had died after an illegal flogging ordered by W. This statute was not repealed until 1995,[37] but was later supplemented by the Criminal Jurisdiction Act 1802, section 1 of which remains in force today. This provides:

From and after the passing of this Act, if any person who now is, or heretofore has been, or shall hereafter be employed by or in the service of his Majesty, his heirs or successors, in any civil or military station, office, or capacity out of Great Britain, or shall heretofore have had, held, or exercised, or now has, holds, or exercises, or

---

[35] It is also possible that any claim to diplomatic immunity would be waived by the UK, so as to permit trial and punishment in the host state where the crime was committed, but this would depend on the circumstances and nature of the crime, and also on those of the host state itself.
[36] (1802) 28 St Tr 51.   [37] Statute Law (Repeals) Act 1995, s. 1 and Sch. 1.

shall hereafter have, hold, or exercise any publick station, office, capacity, or employment, out of Great Britain, shall have committed, or shall commit, or shall have heretofore been, or is, or shall hereafter be guilty of any crime, misdemeanour, or offence, in the execution, or under colour, or in the exercise of any such station, office, capacity, or employment as aforesaid, every such crime, offence, or misdemeanour may be prosecuted or enquired of, and heard and determined . . . here in England.

Lastly,[38] section 31 of the Criminal Justice Act 1948 provides:

Any British subject[39] employed under His Majesty's Government in the United Kingdom in the service of the Crown who commits, in a foreign country, when acting or purporting to act in the course of his employment, any offence which, if committed in England, would be punishable on indictment, shall be guilty of an offence . . . and subject to the same punishment, as if the offence had been committed in England.

One may wonder why the 1802 provision was not simply repealed and supplanted by that of 1948, or subsequently repealed as obsolete and unnecessary. Had the drafting of the latter provision been amended just a little, this might indeed have happened; but as things now stand, the 1948 provision applies only to indictable offences committed by Crown servants in foreign countries and in the course of their employment, whereas the 1802 provision applies to offences committed by such persons anywhere in the world, as long as they were at the time employed in (or the holder of) an office or position somewhere outside Great Britain, and as long as the offence in question was committed in the exercise, etc. of that office, etc. Given that Commonwealth countries, Ireland, and British overseas territories cannot be considered 'foreign countries' under English law, it follows that the 1802 provision possesses a much wider ambit than the 1948 one, and thus remains of considerable importance.

The Law Commission examined the spread of offences in this area in the course of their 1978 Report,[40] and proposed a new provision that would have supplanted all of the existing legislation.[41] As in the 1948 Act, its ambit would have been confined to indictable offences committed by Crown servants acting or purporting to act in the course of their office or employment, but it would not be limited to things done in foreign countries, and would accordingly have permitted the repeal of the 1802 legislation as well as that of 1948.

---

[38] One may also note in this context the Sale of Offices Act 1809, s. 14; but although directed against crimes committed by colonial Governors, etc., this provision is specific to offences under the Sale of Offices Act itself.

[39] This must presumably be confined to British citizens, etc., by virtue of the British Nationality Act 1948, s. 3 and the British Nationality Act 1981, s. 51; but given that the British Nationality Act 1948 and Criminal Justice Act 1948 each received the Royal Assent on the same day, it is surprising that the term 'British subject' was used in the first place.

[40] Law Com. No. 91, paras 76–81.

[41] This may be found in cl. 8 of the Draft Criminal Jurisdiction Bill appended to the Report. It has never been enacted.

Where Crown servants enjoy the benefit of diplomatic immunity in the host state, a case might be made for extending this extraterritorial jurisdiction so as to embrace any indictable offences they might commit, regardless of whether they were acting or purporting to act as diplomats at the time. The Law Commission's suggestion was that such a case might adequately be dealt with by expulsion from the host state. With respect, this may not always be considered adequate at all. Cases may well arise in which the United Kingdom would be expected to take firm action over even the most private and personal crimes of its diplomats. If trial under English law is impossible, the only acceptable course remaining might be for the United Kingdom to waive diplomatic immunity and permit prosecution under local law. Even this might not be acceptable, however, if local law offers little chance of a fair trial or of humane punishment following conviction.

Persons Subject to Armed Service Law

The armed forces of the Crown have always been subject to special jurisdictional rules. Those serving in the British Army are subject to military law, under the Army Act 1955; those in the Royal Navy to naval disciplinary law, under the Naval Discipline Act 1957; and those in the Royal Air Force to air force law, under the Air Force Act 1955. These systems of law apply to all members of their respective services, whether at home, at sea, or abroad, and they also apply to certain civilians attached to or accompanying British armed forces abroad.[42]

For the most part, the laws of the armed services, which are distinct from the 'civilian' law of England, fall outside the scope of this work. In some cases, however, the distinction between service law and civilian criminal law is blurred. This blurring may occur in either of two ways. First, courts-martial and other service courts are often required to deal with 'civil offences' committed by persons subject to the laws of the service in question. Civil offences are defined in all three statutes as acts or omissions which are punishable by the law of England, or which would be so punishable if committed in England and Wales. Secondly, the legislation governing each of the armed forces creates certain specific offences (such as procuring desertion or unlawfully acquiring military stores) that may be committed by civilians who are not otherwise subject to service law at all. These offences, most of which have some extraterritorial effect, are triable by ordinary civilian courts in the United Kingdom, even where committed abroad, and are examined later in this chapter (see pp. 224–6 below). The class-based

---

[42] Service laws do not apply to the exclusion of English or other local law, and service personnel or attached civilians may sometimes find themselves before civilian courts, but in many cases service law is the primary form of jurisdiction applicable.

jurisdiction of service courts over ordinary 'civil offences' committed by persons subject to service law is considered here.

Visiting Forces Agreements and Concurrent Jurisdiction

Most, if not all, NATO countries have ceded extensive jurisdictional powers to the authorities of visiting forces stationed in or passing through their territories, in accordance with the NATO Visiting Forces Agreement 1951. Similar agreements may be made with other foreign and Commonwealth countries. The United Kingdom's own Visiting Forces Act 1952 gives effect to such agreements.[43] Crimes committed amongst the visiting forces or their families, etc., are generally left to the jurisdiction of the visiting forces themselves, if they do not affect the local populace, as are those committed in the course of official military, naval, or air force business, even if they do have such an effect. This extends to accidents resulting from the criminally negligent use of military aircraft,[44] or even to road traffic cases involving military vehicles,[45] but the rape, robbery, or murder of a local citizen would ordinarily be considered a suitable case for local civilian jurisdiction, as indeed would similar offences committed by servicemen in their own countries.[46]

The extraterritorial jurisdiction exercisable by British courts-martial and other British service courts in respect of civil offences committed by British servicemen or accompanying civilians must be viewed in that context, but the circumstances under which foreign civilian courts would claim jurisdiction in priority to such courts will be a question of the relevant foreign law.

Jurisdiction over Civil Offences

Section 70 of the Army Act 1955, which is in almost every respect identical to section 70 of the Air Force Act 1955,[47] provides:

(1) Any person subject to military law who commits a civil offence, whether in the United Kingdom or elsewhere, shall be guilty of an offence against this section.

(2) In this Act the expression 'civil offence' means any act or omission punishable by the law of England or which, if committed in England, would be punishable by that law; and in this Act the expression 'the corresponding civil offence' means the civil offence the commission of which constitutes the offence against this section. (2A)

---

[43] See above, p. 21.

[44] See, e.g., *Public Prosecutor* v. *Ashby* (1999) 93 AJIL 219 (American military aircraft crashing in Italy, causing civilian casualties: pilots tried under US military law).

[45] *Cox* v. *Army Council* [1963] AC 48; and see also *R* v. *Spear and others* [2002] 3 All ER 1074, 1080, *per* Lord Bingham of Cornhill.

[46] See *MacKay* v. *The Queen* (1980) 114 DLR (3rd) 393; *In re Tracey, ex p Ryon* (1989) 166 CLR 518; *R* v. *Généreux* (1992) 88 DLR (4th) 110.

[47] Section 42 of the Naval Discipline Act 1957 differs in several details, but the underlying principle is the same.

For the purpose of determining under this section whether an attempt to commit an offence is a civil offence, subsection (4) of section 1 of the Criminal Attempts Act 1981 (which relates to the offence of attempt) shall have effect as if for the words 'offence which, if it were completed, would be triable in England and Wales as an indictable offence' there were substituted the words 'civil offence consisting of an act punishable by the law of England and Wales as an indictable offence or an act which, if committed in England or Wales, would be so punishable by that law'.

(3)–(3H) [*deal with sentencing*]

(4) A person shall not be charged with an offence against this section committed in the United Kingdom if the corresponding civil offence is treason, murder, manslaughter, treason-felony or rape or an offence under section 1 of the Geneva Conventions Act 1957 or an offence under section 1 of the Biological Weapons Act 1974 or an offence under section 2 or 11 of the Chemical Weapons Act 1996 or an offence under section 1 of the Nuclear Explosions (Prohibition and Inspections) Act 1998 or an offence under section 51 or 52 of the International Criminal Court Act 2001.

In this and the following subsection the references to murder shall apply also to aiding, abetting, counselling or procuring suicide.

(5) Where the corresponding civil offence is murder or manslaughter, or an offence under section 1 of the Geneva Conventions Act 1957 or section 51 of the International Criminal Court Act 2001 consisting of the killing of a person, an offence against this section shall be deemed, for the purposes of the last foregoing subsection, to have been committed at the place of the commission of the act or occurrence of the neglect which caused the death, irrespective of the place of the death.

(6) A person subject to military law may be charged with an offence against this section notwithstanding that he could on the same facts be charged with an offence against any other provision of this Part of this Act.

The relationship between a section 70 offence and a corresponding offence under the civilian law of England was explained by Lord Rodger of Earlsferry in *R v. Spear and others*.[48] He said:

The effect of subsections (1) and (2) is, first, that where anyone who is subject to military law is guilty of an act or omission in England that would be punishable by the law of England, he is also guilty of an offence under section 70. Similarly, anyone who is guilty of an act or omission that would be punishable by the law of England if committed in England is guilty of an offence under section 70 wherever he commits it, whether in some other part of the United Kingdom or elsewhere in the world: *Cox v. Army Council*. So, for instance, a soldier or airman who possesses cocaine in England is guilty not only of an offence under section 5(1) of the Misuse of Drugs Act 1971 but also of an offence against section 70 of the Army Act or the Air Force Act, as the case may be, although he can, of course, be prosecuted for only one of them. If he possesses cocaine while on duty in Afghanistan, on the other hand, he does not commit an offence under section 5(1) of the 1971 Act since the legislation does not apply there, but he is guilty of an offence under section 70 of the relevant 1955 Act, because

---

[48] [2002] 3 All ER 1074, 1088. Lord Bingham of Cornhill, who gave the only other speech in that case, expressly agreed with Lord Rodger's analysis.

he would have been guilty of a contravention of section 5(1) if he had been in possession of the drug in England. Offences of this kind, which mirror offences under English criminal law, are referred to as 'civil' offences (section 70(2)). As section 70(3) makes clear, these civil offences are triable by court-martial.

The cases that fell to be decided in *Spear* all involved servicemen who were subject to military or air force law, so that the position of accompanying civilians did not arise for discussion, but section 209 of the Army Act, read in conjunction with Schedule 5 and regulations made thereunder, identifies those civilians who are subject to Part II (sections 24–143) as if they were subject to military law.[49] Section 209 distinguishes for this purpose between cases in which the forces are on active service and those in which they are not:

(1) Subject to the modifications hereinafter specified, where any body of the regular forces is on active service, Part II of this Act shall apply to any person who is employed in the service of that body of the forces or any part or member thereof, or accompanies the said body or any part thereof, and is not subject to military law, the Naval Discipline Act, or air-force law apart from this section or any corresponding provisions of that Act or the Air Force Act 1955 as the said Part II applies to persons subject to military law.

(2) Subject to the modifications hereinafter specified, Part II of this Act shall at all times apply to a person of any description specified in the Fifth Schedule to this Act who is within the limits of the command of any officer commanding a body of the regular forces outside the United Kingdom, and is not subject to military law, the Naval Discipline Act, or air-force law apart from this section or any corresponding provisions of that Act or the Air Force Act 1955 as the said Part II applies to persons subject to military law.

Provided that none of the provisions contained in sections 24 to 69 of this Act shall apply to a person by virtue only of this subsection, except—

(a) sections 29, 35, 36 and 55 to 57, and sections 68 and 68A so far as they relate to those sections, and

(b) in the case of persons falling within any description specified in paragraphs 1 to 4 of Schedule 5, section 34B and sections 68 and 68A so far as they relate to that section.

The specific military offences created under Part II of the Army Act ('Discipline and Trial and Punishment of Military Offences') fall outside the scope of this work. It must therefore suffice for present purposes to note that whereas all civilians employed by or accompanying forces on active duty anywhere are subject to the whole of Part II,[50] only designated classes of civilians come within Part II when such forces are not on active service, and then only to the limited extent specified in section 209(2). One of the limitations imposed by that subsection is that Part II (which includes section 70) does not then apply to civilians who are still within the United Kingdom.

---

[49] See also the Air Force Act 1955, s. 209 and Sch. 5; Naval Discipline Act 1957, s. 118 and Sch. 3.

[50] Some provisions in Pt II cannot in practice apply to civilians, because they refer to purely military activities (such as guard duty) that civilians would not be required to undertake, or to 'scandalous conduct by officers', etc.

The categories of civilians who are subject to service jurisdiction even when the relevant forces are not on active service are as follows[51]:

1 Persons serving Her Majesty, or otherwise employed, in such capacities connected with her Majesty's naval, military or air forces as may be specified for the purposes of this Schedule by regulations of the Defence Council, being persons serving or employed under Her Majesty's Government in the United Kingdom.

2 Persons who are employed by, or in the service of, any naval, military or air-force organisation so specified to which Her Majesty's Government in the United Kingdom is a party and are employed by or in the service of that organisation by reason of that Government being a party thereto.

3 Persons belonging to or employed by any other organisation so specified which operates in connection with Her Majesty's naval, military or air forces.

4 Persons who, for the purposes of their profession, business or employment, are attached to or accompany any of Her Majesty's naval, military or air forces in pursuance of an authorisation granted by or on behalf of the Defence Council or by an officer authorised by the Defence Council.

5 Persons forming part of the family of members of any of Her Majesty's naval, military or air forces and residing with them or about to reside or departing after residing with them.

6 Persons forming part of the family of persons falling within paragraphs 1 to 4 of this Schedule and residing with them or about to reside or departing after residing with them.

7 Persons employed by members of any of Her Majesty's naval, military or air forces.

8 Persons employed by persons falling within paragraphs 1 to 6 of this Schedule.

9 Persons forming part of the family of persons falling within either of the last two foregoing paragraphs and residing with them or about to reside or departing after residing with them.

The trial of civilians by British military courts abroad has long been a matter of controversy,[52] but may nevertheless be preferable, from a defendant's viewpoint, to the alternative of trial in a foreign court, under foreign law; and it may be more feasible in practice than a civil trial within England and Wales. Arguments that courts-martial are inherently lacking in independence and impartiality, and are thus incompatible with Article 6 of the European Convention on Human Rights, were recently rejected by the House of Lords in *R v. Spear and others*.[53]

---

[51] See the Civilians (Application of Part II of the Army Act) Regulations (A.O. No. 123 of 1956) as amended. Identical regulations apply to civilians working with or for the RAF or Royal Navy. The Regulations are not published as statutory instruments. It is not easy to identify any civilians who would *not* fall within the scope of these Regulations when working for or with the Army overseas, although in practice jurisdiction is not asserted over foreigners in respect of things done abroad. See Law Com. No. 91 (1978), para. 83.

[52] See, e.g., Gordon Borrie, 'Courts-Martial, Civilians and Civil Liberties' (1969) 32 *Modern Law Review* 35.   [53] [2002] 3 All ER 1074.

Standing Civilian Courts

Prosecutions of civilians for alleged extraterritorial offences under Part II of the Army or Air Force Acts of 1955[54] may in some cases be tried by a 'standing civilian court' in accordance with the provisions of the Armed Forces Act 1976. These are in effect magistrates' courts. By section 7 of that Act, the offences for which a civilian may be tried by a standing civilian court are offences committed outside the United Kingdom for which a court-martial may try a civilian, other than offences under section 57 (contempt of court, etc., in respect of a court-martial) or civil offences that would be triable only on indictment if committed within England and Wales.

English Criminal Law in Antarctica

In some cases, English (or United Kingdom) criminal law may be applicable to the acts or omissions of British scientists or observers, or of United Kingdom nationals generally, in Antarctica or in specified parts thereof. This extension of English criminal law can be understood only by reference to the legal status of Antarctica. Several states, including the United Kingdom, have made territorial claims to areas of that continent. These claims (which are not universally recognized[55]) have all been made on the 'sector' principle. States with sovereign rights to islands or other territory adjacent to Antarctica have drawn longitudinal lines linking the borders of those territories with the South Pole, and have claimed sovereignty over any Antarctic land territory enclosed within those lines. The sector claimed by the United Kingdom, which is primarily derived from its sovereignty over the Falkland Islands dependencies of South Georgia and the South Sandwich Islands,[56] is known as the British Antarctic Territory, and includes all the lands and islands of Antarctica extending from the South Pole to 60° S latitude between longitudes 20° W and 80° W. This Territory has its own law and courts,[57] including a Court of Appeal from which a further right of appeal lies to the Privy Council.[58] Only one sector of Antarctica remains unclaimed: this lies between 90° W and 150° W, and includes the area known as Marie Byrd Land.

By Article VIII of the 1959 Antarctic Treaty,[59] to which the United Kingdom is a party, claimant states have agreed that designated observers,

---

[54] Such courts do not have jurisdiction over civilians for offences under the Naval Discipline Act 1957.

[55] No such claims are recognized by the USA or by Russia, for example.

[56] This sovereignty (and most of the UK's claim to Antarctica) is disputed by Argentina.

[57] British Antarctic Territory Order 1989 (SI 1989 No. 842).

[58] Criminal and civil matters may also be dealt with by the courts of the Falkland Islands, which for those purposes apply the substantive law of the Territory: Falkland Islands Courts (Overseas Jurisdiction) Order 1989 (SI 1989 No. 2399), s. 6.

[59] UKTS 97 (1961); Cmnd. 1535. One purpose of the Treaty was to 'freeze' all existing claims to sovereignty or disputes over sovereignty: see Art. IV.

scientific personnel, and support staff working in Antarctica should be subject only to the jurisdiction of the states of which they are nationals, but this is without prejudice to any jurisdiction that may be exercisable over other persons entering Antarctica.

The Antarctic Act 1994

The general corpus of English criminal law was first made applicable to British scientists and observers in Antarctica by the Antarctic Treaty Act 1967.[60] The relevant provisions have since been supplanted by sections 22 and 23 of the Antarctic Act 1994. This also makes provision for English law to apply to United Kingdom nationals in the unclaimed sector, which is effectively *terra nullius* and therefore not subject to any local territorial law. Section 21 provides:

Where a United Kingdom national does or omits to do anything on any land lying south of 60 degrees South latitude and between 150 degrees West longitude and 90 degrees West longitude and that act or omission would have constituted an offence under the law of any part of the United Kingdom if it had occurred in that part, he shall be guilty of the like offence as if the act or omission had taken place in that part, and shall be liable to be proceeded against and punished accordingly.

In respect of British scientists and observers anywhere in Antarctica, section 22 provides:

(1) Where a United Kingdom national who—
    (a) is an Antarctic Treaty official,[61] and
    (b) is in any part of Antarctica, other than the area mentioned in section 21, for the purpose of exercising his functions as an Antarctic Treaty official,
does or omits to do anything, and that act or omission would have constituted an offence under the law of any part of the United Kingdom if it had taken place in that part, he shall be guilty of the like offence as if the act or omission had taken place in that part, and shall be liable to be proceeded against and punished accordingly.

By section 23, similar jurisdiction extends to United Kingdom nationals who are 'Convention officials'[62] aboard vessels in any part of the area south of the Antarctic Convergence for the purpose of exercising functions as Convention officials. The trial of summary offences is facilitated by section 24, which deems them to have been committed in any place in the United Kingdom.

---

[60] Note also the Antarctic Minerals Act 1989, most of which has also been repealed.

[61] Defined in s. 22(2) as a person designated as an observer by or on behalf of HM Government in the UK in accordance with Art. VII of the Treaty; a scientist who has been exchanged in accordance with Art. III(1)(b) of the Treaty, or is a member of the staff accompanying one of the above.

[62] Defined as any person designated as an inspector or observer by a Member of the Commission for the Conservation of Antarctic Marine Living Resources under Art. XXIV of the Treaty.

Merchant Shipping Act 1995

The Merchant Shipping Act 1995 contains jurisdictional provisions[63] that apply English criminal law generally to acts committed abroad by seamen from United Kingdom ships; or committed by British citizens in foreign ports or harbours, or aboard foreign ships 'to which they do not belong'. These provisions might logically be considered at this point, in that they apply the general corpus of English criminal law to specific classes, but those same provisions deal also with offences committed aboard United Kingdom ships, and they are best understood in the wider context of British maritime jurisdiction. I will accordingly defer consideration of these provisions until Chapter 6 below.

OFFENCES INVOLVING DEFENCE OR NATIONAL SECURITY

High Treason

With the exception of piracy, high treason appears to have been the first offence under English law to acquire an extraterritorial ambit. The explanation for this is obvious enough. The King's enemies at home might well seek support from, and give support to, his enemies abroad. This was not something to which the Crown could be indifferent merely because it might occur abroad. Treason committed abroad might constitute as great a threat to the Crown as treason committed within the realm.

Not all forms of treason share (or have ever shared) this extraterritorial ambit. Indeed, following the repeal of the Treason Act 1795 by the Crime and Disorder Act 1998,[64] only one extraterritorial form of treason survives, namely, that of adhering to the King's (or Queen's) enemies contrary to the Treason Act 1351. This provides: 'If a man be adherent to the King's enemies in his realm, giving to them aid and comfort in the realm, or elsewhere . . . that ought to be judged treason which extends to our lord the King . . .'

---

[63] In ss. 281 and 282.

[64] Section 36(3)(b) and Sch. 10. The 1795 Act formerly made it treason to plot or commit various offences against the life or person of the sovereign or his heir, 'within the realm or without'. 'Compassing or imagining' the death of the sovereign, or of his queen, or of their eldest son and heir, remains punishable under the Treason Act 1351, but this form of treason has no extraterritorial ambit. A conspiracy abroad to murder the sovereign, etc., within the realm would (on the basis of the general principle established in *Liangsiriprasert* v. *US Govt.* [1991] 1 AC 225) be punishable as a statutory conspiracy to murder, under s. 1 of the Criminal Law Act 1977, regardless of whether the conspirators commit any acts within the UK and regardless of whether they owe any duty of allegiance to the Crown, and any attacks or threats of attacks on the sovereign abroad (or on other official representatives of the UK abroad) would be punishable in England and Wales under s. 1 of the Internationally Protected Persons Act 1978, but no such conduct could now be prosecuted as treason.

The extraterritorial ambit of this form of treason is now firmly established by precedent, and in particular by the ruling of the House of Lords in *Joyce* v. *DPP*,[65] but it is by no means clear that their Lordships correctly interpreted the Act on that point. Did it really declare treason to be capable of extraterritorial commission, or did it merely provide that a man might commit treason by giving aid or comfort *within* the realm to the sovereign's enemies abroad? Either construction appears possible from the wording of the Act, but the historical context suggests that the latter is more likely to have been correct.

The 1351 Act was later augmented by the Act of 26 Hen. 8, c. 13 (now repealed). This undoubtedly had extraterritorial effect, and accordingly it made detailed provision for offences of treason committed abroad to be tried in England by special commissioners appointed for that purpose. Such provision would have been considered essential at that time, because under the common law venue rules then in force, no ordinary jury could have 'had cognisance' of offences committed abroad. How then (if at all) did the 1351 Act overcome the venue problem? If it did not, the obvious implication is that offences of high treason possessed no extraterritorial ambit until well into the reign of Henry VIII, but the statutes which provided that ambit are no longer in force.

Casement and Joyce

The correct historical interpretation of the 1351 Act was a crucial issue at the trial of Sir Roger Casement in 1916.[66] Casement went to Germany in 1916, in order to seek support for a rebellion against British rule in Ireland. He there incited Irish prisoners of war to fight the British, and was later arrested whilst attempting to smuggle arms into Ireland, prior to the Easter rising of 1916. He was charged with high treason, the indictment alleging that he had 'adhered to the King's enemies elsewhere than in the King's realm, to wit, in the Empire of Germany'; but at his trial, and at his appeal against conviction later that year,[67] it was argued that the indictment was invalid, and that the 1351 Act created no extraterritorial forms of treason.

The Court of Criminal Appeal accepted the contention that some special provision would be needed for the trial of any extraterritorial offence, but upheld Casement's conviction through reliance on the writings of Coke, Hale, and Hawkins, each of whom asserted that some form of trial would indeed have been possible.[68]

---

[65] [1946] AC 347.

[66] See G. Knott (ed.), *The Trial of Roger Casement* (2nd edn, 1927).

[67] *R* v. *Casement* [1917] 1 KB 98. See also *R* v. *Lynch* [1903] 1 KB 444.

[68] Despite the great reverence shown to Coke's writings by the judges in *Casement*, it is significant that none of the cases cited by Coke in support of his interpretation of the 1351 Act was found to have any obvious relevance to that issue. One was found to relate to a riot in Oxford. Hawkins' argument was merely that the offence *must* have been extraterritorial because it was so serious; and there was no real agreement between the ancient writers on how an extraterritorial offence would have been tried under the 1351 Act.

The ruling in *Casement* was followed and extended by the House of Lords in *Joyce* v. *DPP*. The principle that treason could be committed by adhering abroad to the King's enemies was scarcely questioned. The only contentious issue in *Joyce* was whether treason could be committed by a foreigner whilst abroad. Treason involves a breach of the subject's duty of allegiance to his sovereign. As a general rule, British citizens and other British nationals owe such a duty at all times, whereas foreigners owe such a duty only when living under the protection of the Crown. A foreigner (other than an enemy soldier, etc.) who enters the realm thereby comes within that protection, and a duty of allegiance arises in consequence. Joyce, however, had left the realm in possession of a British passport that had been issued to him on the mistaken assumption that he was a British subject at the time. He was in fact a US citizen by birth, and had never acquired British nationality, although he had lived within the United Kingdom almost continuously from the age of three. He used that passport to enter Nazi Germany shortly before the war broke out in 1939, and subsequently became a 'British' radio propagandist for the Nazis, as a result of which he acquired the contemptuous nickname 'Lord Haw-Haw'.

Following his arrest in 1945, Joyce was originally indicted as a British subject, but when this error was discovered a further count to the indictment was preferred, alleging that being 'a person owing allegiance to the King', he committed treason 'by adhering to the King's enemies . . . in the German realm . . . by broadcasting propaganda on behalf of the said enemies'. Upholding his conviction on that count, the House of Lords ruled (Lord Porter dissenting) that the protection afforded by possession of a British passport triggered a corresponding duty of allegiance, even though that passport had been wrongfully issued, and even though there was no evidence that Joyce ever invoked (or had any intention of invoking) its protection when in Nazi Germany.

Nor did their Lordships regard possession of a British passport as the only way in which a foreigner might incur such extraterritorial liability. They approved two passages in Foster's *Crown Cases*,[69] in which it was stated that:

Local allegiance is founded in the protection a foreigner enjoyeth for his person, his family or effects, during his residence here; and it ceaseth whenever he withdraweth with his family and effects . . . And if such alien, seeking the protection of the Crown, and having a family and effects here, should, during a war with his native country, go thither, and there adhere to the King's enemies for purposes of hostility, he might be dealt with as a traitor. For he came and settled here under the protection of the Crown; and, though his person was removed for a time, his effects and family continued still under the same protection. This rule was laid down by all the judges assembled at the Queen's Command Jan. 12, 1707.[70]

---

[69] (1762), 183–5.   [70] No other record of this 1707 resolution was found.

This appears to place a foreigner with a family resident in England in great difficulty, should war break out between the United Kingdom and his own country. In practice, it is now almost inconceivable that a treason charge would be preferred on such facts. Indeed, no charges of high treason have been brought in recent years, even in cases that might be thought to have warranted such charges.

Treason Felony

The lesser offence of treason felony also possesses some extraterritorial effect. By section 3 of the Treason Felony Act 1848:

If any person whatsoever shall, within the United Kingdom or without, compass, imagine, invent, devise, or intend to deprive or depose our Most Gracious Lady the Queen from the style, honour, or royal name of the imperial crown of the United Kingdom, or of any other of her Majesty's dominions and countries, or to levy war against her Majesty, within any part of the United Kingdom, in order by force or constraint to compel her to change her measures or counsels, or in order to put any force or constraint upon or in order to intimidate or overawe both Houses or either House of Parliament, or to move or stir any foreigner or stranger with force to invade the United Kingdom or any other of her Majesty's dominions or countries under the obeisance of her Majesty, and such compassings, imaginations, inventions, devices, or intentions, or any of them, shall express, utter, or declare, by publishing any printing or writing, or by any overt act or deed, every person so offending shall be guilty of an offence, and being convicted thereof shall be liable to imprisonment for life or any shorter term.

As with high treason, some forms of this offence possess no extraterritorial ambit: levying war, for example, clearly does not. The position in respect of offences of 'stirring a foreigner to invade the United Kingdom' is less clear, but given the archaic character of that offence, further consideration of that issue would not appear to be warranted.

Offences under the Official Secrets Acts

An extraterritorial ambit applies to all offences under the Official Secrets Acts 1911 and 1989, with the exception of the summary offences created by sections 8(1), (4), and (5) of the 1989 Act. The position in respect of offences created under the Official Secrets Act 1920 is more complicated, however.

Offences under the 1911 Act

Section 10 of the Official Secrets Act 1911 provides:

(1) This Act shall apply to all acts which are offences under this Act when committed in any part of His Majesty's dominions, or when committed by British officers or subjects elsewhere.

(2) An offence under this Act, if alleged to have been committed out of the United Kingdom, may be inquired of, heard, and determined, in any competent British court in the place where the offence was committed, or . . . in England . . .

The offences in question are those under sections 1(1)(a) of the Act (spying or sabotage in or around 'prohibited places'); section 1(1)(b) (making sketches, plans, models, or notes that may be useful to an enemy); section 1(1)(c) (obtaining, recording, or communicating secret codes or documents, models, etc., or information that may be useful to an enemy); and section 7 (harbouring spies or saboteurs, etc.). 'Prohibited places' are defined in sections 3 and 12 of the Act, and these clearly may include ships, aircraft, military establishments, and premises such as embassies, etc., situated outside the United Kingdom.

There are obvious and highly cogent reasons for the creation of an extraterritorial ambit in respect of some at least of these offences. It would indeed be bizarre if British officers or scientists engaged in secret defence work were able to avoid any criminal liability by travelling abroad before disclosing classified secrets to the agents of a potentially hostile power. There are equally obvious reasons for the restriction of this extraterritorial ambit to those who (reading section 10 of the Act in conjunction with the British Nationality Acts 1948 and 1981) are British citizens, British overseas territories citizens, British overseas citizens, British nationals (overseas), or British officers.[71] As the Franks Report stated in 1972, 'It seems right that . . . the servant of the Crown and the subject of the Crown should take with him everywhere in the world his duty under the Act to protect secrets of the State',[72] whereas a foreign national might be acting quite properly, within his own or a third country, in attempting to procure such information.

Offences under the 1920 Act

In respect of offences under the Official Secrets Act 1920, the principal source of confusion is section 8(3), which provides:

For the purposes of the trial of a person for an offence under the principal [i.e., the 1911] Act or this Act, the offence shall be deemed to have been committed either at the place in which the same actually was committed, or at any place in the United Kingdom in which the offender may be found.

As far as offences under the 1911 Act are concerned, this provision appears to make little sense. It makes no difference either to the ambit of the law (which is governed by provisions in the 1911 Act itself), or to the jurisdiction of any particular courts (because no summary offences are involved).

---

[71] The term 'British officer' is not expressly defined in the Act (an omission that troubled the Law Commission in Law Com. No. 91, paras 90–91) but must presumably include the holders of any office under the Crown, including any office or employment in any department of the Government of the United Kingdom, or of any British possession.

[72] Cmnd. 5104, paras 261–2.

It appears, in other words, to be an obsolete venue provision. Section 8(3) certainly cannot be construed as extending the ambit of espionage offences to the acts of foreign nationals abroad.

If section 8(3) is nothing more than a venue provision, it must be doubtful whether the offences created by the 1920 Act have any extraterritorial ambit at all. Section 2 of that Act admittedly contains references to offences committed abroad. Under section 2(1), for example, the fact that D has communicated or attempted to communicate with a foreign agent, 'whether within or without the United Kingdom', shall be evidence of the commission of an offence under section 1 of the 1911 Act. Section 2 does not create any offences of its own, however, and so its ambit merely corresponds to those of the offences to which it relates.

Section 1 of the 1920 Act does create additional offences, notably those concerning the unlawful possession or retention of official documents, and offences concerning the unauthorized use of uniforms, the falsification of reports, the impersonation of other persons, or the use of false documents, for the purpose of gaining admission to a prohibited place as defined in the 1911 Act. Section 3 meanwhile creates an offence of obstructing police or security forces in the vicinity of a prohibited place. Some commentators assume that these offences have an extraterritorial ambit by virtue of section 8(3), but it is submitted that this cannot be the case. Section 8(3) contains no provision for restricting the extraterritorial application of any such offence to British nationals or British officers. Any provision that was intended to extend the effective ambit of the law would inevitably have restricted its application in such a way. This leaves only section 7 of the 1920 Act, which provides:

Any person who attempts to commit any offence under the principal Act or this Act, or solicits or incites or endeavours to persuade another person to commit an offence, or aids or abets and does any act preparatory to the commission of an offence under the principal Act or this Act, shall be guilty of a felony or a misdemeanour or a summary offence according as the offence in question is a felony, a misdemeanour or a summary offence, and on conviction shall be liable to the same punishment, and to be proceeded against in the same manner, as if he had committed the offence.

Section 7 does not expressly apply to things done abroad, but it may arguably be construed as investing inchoate offences with the same ambit as substantive ones. If so, a British citizen in Syria who attempts (or merely prepares) to commit an offence under section 1 of the 1911 Act would be triable in England and Wales on the same basis as if he had committed the substantive offence. A French or Syrian citizen assisting him would not be so triable, because he could not have committed, in Syria, any offence under the 1911 Act.

Offences under the 1989 Act

The Official Secrets Act 1989 creates offences involving the unauthorized and 'damaging' disclosure of information, etc., by members or former members of the security and intelligence services, or in some case by Government contractors. This may include information concerning international relations or criminal investigations, as well as security, intelligence, defence, or military information. Once again, the nature and quality of the offences concerned demand some kind of extraterritorial ambit in order to be effective. Section 15 of the Act accordingly provides:

(1) Any act—
    (a) done by a British citizen or Crown servant; or
    (b) done by any person in any of the Channel Islands or the Isle of Man or any colony,[73]
shall, if it would be an offence by that person under any provision of this Act other than section 8(1), (4) or (5) when done by him in the United Kingdom, be an offence under that provision.

The excluded offences are each concerned with failure to safeguard information. They are triable only summarily and were not considered serious enough to warrant extraterritorial application, but they are nevertheless triable anywhere in the United Kingdom (and not merely within the local magistrates' commission area) by virtue of section 11(5) of the Act.

Unauthorized Disclosure of Euratom Secrets

The European Communities Act 1972, section 11(2), creates an offence in respect of European Atomic Energy Community (Euratom) secrets that is for most purposes to be regarded as an offence under the Official Secrets Act 1911, but this offence is not subject to section 10 of the 1911 Act. Instead, it prescribes its own extraterritorial ambit, as follows:

Where a person (whether a British subject or not) owing either—
    (a) to his duties as a member of any Euratom institution or committee, or as an officer or servant of Euratom; or
    (b) to his dealings in any capacity (official or unofficial) with any Euratom institution or installation or with any Euratom joint enterprise;
has occasion to acquire, or obtain cognisance of, any classified information, he shall be guilty of an offence if, knowing or having reason to believe that it is classified information, he communicates it to any unauthorised person or makes any public disclosure of it, whether in the United Kingdom or elsewhere and whether before or after the termination of those duties or dealings. . . .

Specific Offences under the Army, Air Force, and Naval Discipline Acts

The Army Act 1955, Air Force Act 1955, and Naval Discipline Act 1957 each create a number of specific offences, several of which possess an extraterritorial effect. Some of these offences are applicable only to persons subject to

---

[73] Colonies are now classified as British overseas territories. See above, p. 205, fn 23.

military, air force, or naval law, whilst others may be committed either by servicemen or by civilians who are deemed to be subject to the relevant parts of the Acts. Such persons are also subject, when abroad, to the general corpus of English criminal law, and may be tried by service courts or courts-martial for ordinary 'civil offences', such as theft or assault. This armed service jurisdiction was examined earlier in this chapter (see pp. 212–16 above). Other offences, however, are capable of commission by anyone, and are triable in the ordinary civilian courts of the United Kingdom, even when committed abroad.

The Extraterritorial Offences

Under the Army and Air Force Acts of 1955, offences that may be committed abroad include those of pretending to be a deserter (contrary to section 191); procuring and assisting desertion (section 192); obstructing or interfering with regular forces in the execution of their duty (section 193); aiding a malingerer with a view to enabling him to avoid military (or air force) service (section 194); unlawfully acquiring or procuring the disposal of army (or air force) stores (section 195); unlawfully dealing in service pay or pension documents, etc. (section 196); and unauthorized use of or dealing in military or air force decorations, etc. (section 197). Sections 191, 193, 196, and 197 apply to things done 'in the United Kingdom or in any colony', whereas sections 192, 194, and 195 apply to 'any person . . . whether within or without Her Majesty's dominions'.[74] Section 220 of the Army Act[75] then provides:

(1) In the United Kingdom or any colony, a civil court of any description having jurisdiction in the place where an offender is for the time being shall have jurisdiction to try him for any offence to which this section applies which is triable by a court of that description notwithstanding that the offence was committed outside the jurisdiction of the court:

Provided that such an offence committed in any part of the United Kingdom shall not be triable outside that part of the United Kingdom.

Section 93 of the Naval Discipline Act creates an offence of spying in Her Majesty's ships or vessels, or in Royal Naval establishments abroad. This offence is triable only by court-martial, even though it can be committed only by someone who is not otherwise subject to the Act, and it was until recently punishable by death.

None of the offence-creating provisions considered above expressly confines its extraterritorial ambit to British citizens or United Kingdom nationals, but such a limitation must nevertheless be implied, in accordance

---

[74] The Naval Discipline Act 1957 contains differently numbered provisions that are in most respects similar, but not identical. Section 96, for example, mirrors s. 191 of the Army and Air Force Acts in some respects, but applies 'within or without the UK', and thus has a wider ambit than either of the 1955 Acts.

[75] See also s. 218 of the Air Force Act and s. 100 of the Naval Discipline Act.

with the principle laid down by Lord Russell of Killowen CJ in *R* v. *Jameson*,[76] under which a statute will be construed as imposing extraterritorial liability on foreigners only if no other construction is possible.

MURDER, MANSLAUGHTER, AND BIGAMY

The Offences Against the Person Act 1861 contains provisions extending English criminal jurisdiction over acts of murder, manslaughter, or bigamy committed by 'subjects of Her Majesty' when abroad. These are amongst the best known and longest established of all extraterritorial offences, and yet neither fits easily into any general classification or grouping of such offences.

Murder and Manslaughter

Although Coke defined murder as a crime that could be committed only 'within any county of the realm',[77] it had in fact acquired an extraterritorial ambit some years before Coke penned his definition. Legislation extending jurisdiction over murders committed abroad can be traced back to the Act of 33 Hen. 8, c. 23 in 1541. This seems to have been enacted primarily in order that the Crown could, if it wished, select or manipulate the venue for trials for treason or misprision of treason committed 'within the King's dominions or without'. The Crown might, for example, have wished to ensure that alleged traitors were not tried within their own counties, lest they should have the benefit of support from sympathetic local jurors. The Act only applied to defendants who had been examined by the King's Council and who were 'vehemently suspected' of murder or treason; but since cases of murder would not ordinarily have attracted the interest of the Council in the first place, the inclusion of that offence within the Act has the appearance of a mere afterthought.[78]

Manslaughter first became an extraterritorial offence under the Act of 43 Geo. 3, c. 31. The legislation dealing with extraterritorial homicide was supplanted in 1828 by the Act of 9 Geo 4, c. 31, section 7 of which provided the common law courts with jurisdiction over cases of murder or manslaughter committed by any 'subject of his Majesty' on land outside the United Kingdom. This provision was in due course repealed and re-enacted in the 1861 consolidation, emerging as section 9 of the Offences Against the Person Act 1861, which remains in force today.

---

[76] [1896] 2 QB 425. Lord Russell's principle was approved by the House of Lords in *Air India* v. *Wiggins* [1980] 1 WLR 815.   [77] *Institutes*, vol. 3 (4th edn, 1670), 47.
[78] See M.J. Pritchard, 'The Army Act and Murder Abroad' (1954) 16 *Cambridge Law Journal* 232; *R* v. *Chambers* (1709 unreported), cited in *R* v. *Athos* (1722) 8 Mod 144.

The 1861 Act coexisted for many years with the Murders Abroad Act 1817, which remained in force until 1967.[79] This extended English jurisdiction to cases of murder or manslaughter committed in any place not within his Majesty's dominions, nor subject to any European state, nor within the United States of America, if the offender lived there or had sailed there in a British ship. The thinking behind this Act was that British expeditions to 'uncivilized' countries or unknown territories should enjoy some minimal protection from English law,[80] but it had become an anachronism long before its eventual repeal.

The Current Law

Section 9 of the 1861 Act remains the best known, but by no means the only, provision that may be applicable to cases of murder or manslaughter committed abroad. Another may be found in section 4 of the Suppression of Terrorism Act 1978, by which acts of murder or manslaughter (together with various other criminal acts) may be triable as offences under English[81] law:

(1) when committed by any person in a designated 'Convention country'; and
(2) when committed by a national of a Convention country (who is not also a British citizen, etc.) outside both the United Kingdom and that Convention country.

The background to this legislation, the range of offences to which it applies, and the identities of the relevant Convention countries are explored later in this chapter (see pp. 254–62 below). It must suffice for the moment to note just two things. The first is that the extraterritorial application of the 1978 Act does not depend on whether the offence is alleged to have been a terrorist one.[82] The Act makes no attempt to define terrorism, or to distinguish between terrorist and non-terrorist offences. The second is that section 4 of the 1978 Act may sometimes apply where section 9 of the 1861 Act does not.

Offences Against the Person Act 1861, Section 9

Section 9 of the Offences Against the Person Act 1861 provides:

Where any murder or manslaughter shall be committed on land out of the United Kingdom, whether within the Queen's dominions or without, and whether the person killed were a subject of Her Majesty or not, every offence committed by any

---

[79] The whole Act, 'so far as unrepealed', was repealed as 'obsolete and unnecessary' by the Criminal Law Act 1967, s. 10 and Sch. 3; but it appears to have been repealed for a second time by the Statute Law Repeals Act 1981, Sch. 1.

[80] See Glanville Williams, 'Venue and the Ambit of Criminal Law' (1965) 81 *Law Quarterly Review* 276, 400.

[81] The criminal laws of Scotland and Northern Ireland are similarly extended by the 1978 Act.

[82] This was acknowledged by the House of Lords in *R v. Bow Street Metropolitan Stipendiary Magistrate, ex p Pinochet Ugarte (No. 3)* [2000] 1 AC 147.

subject of Her Majesty in respect of any such case, whether the same shall amount to the offence of murder or of manslaughter, . . . may be dealt with, inquired of, tried, determined, and punished . . . in England or Ireland . . .

Although this provision is sometimes described as applying to murder or manslaughter committed 'by British citizens anywhere in the world', it is clear that its ambit is both wider and narrower than this. It is wider in that it now applies to British overseas citizens, citizens of British overseas territories, and British nationals (overseas) as well as to British citizens;[83] but it is narrower in that it does not apply things done at sea, in the air, or indeed in any other parts of the United Kingdom.[84] A British terrorist who destroys an airliner by means of a concealed bomb does not fall within the ambit of section 9, unless he also kills people on the ground somewhere outside the United Kingdom.[85] Nor may section 9 apply to things done on the Arctic ice-cap, or in any part of Antarctica that is comprised of ice-shelf rather than land.[86] There must even be serious doubt as to whether it could apply to things done on or in major lakes, harbours, or estuaries. Could the Great Lakes, for example, be described as 'land abroad' merely because they are land-locked?

Other provisions, not specifically concerned with homicide, may fill some at least of the section 9 lacunae identified above. Aside from section 4 of the Suppression of Terrorism Act, which has already been noted, a murder committed abroad may be punishable under English law if the killer is a Crown servant or a person subject to British military, naval, or air force law. Crimes committed in the air or at sea may be punishable under various statutory provisions, even (in some but not all cases) when committed aboard foreign ships or aircraft.[87] The shipwrecked mariners who resorted to cannibalism in *R v. Dudley and Stephens*,[88] for example, were prosecuted under what is now section 282 of the Merchant Shipping Act 1995, even though their vessel, the *Mignonette*, had foundered several days before they committed the act in question.

This leaves murder or manslaughter committed in other parts of the United Kingdom. Neither the 1861 Act nor the Suppression of Terrorism Act could apply in such cases.[89] This would not usually be a problem, because a suspected offender may simply be arrested in England on a Scottish or

---

[83] See British Nationality Act 1948, s. 3(1); British Nationality Act 1981, s. 51; Hong Kong (British Nationality) Order 1986.

[84] This does not include the Channel Islands or the Isle of Man.

[85] The destruction of Pan-Am flight 103 over Lockerbie involved the murders of 11 victims on the ground, but even if the killer had been British, the act was committed within the UK and s. 9 could not have applied. As to other possible offences, see Chapter 6 below.

[86] But see the Antarctic Act 1994, ss. 21–24.

[87] Notably under the Merchant Shipping Act 1995, ss. 281–282 and under the Aviation Security Act 1982, s. 6(1); but note the limitations identified below, at p. 321.

[88] (1884) 14 QBD 273.

[89] The United Kingdom is not itself a designated Convention country for the purposes of the 1978 Act.

Northern Irish warrant and sent for trial there. No extradition proceedings would be required. In some cases, however, major difficulties could arise. These difficulties may be illustrated by examining the case of the serial child killer, Robert Black.

In 1994, Black was convicted in Newcastle of the abduction and murder of three little girls. The offences were committed while Black was employed as a delivery driver, working routes between London and Scotland. His involvement in the murders was proved beyond any possible doubt, and his application for leave to appeal was refused by the Court of Appeal,[90] but a potentially grave jurisdictional problem seems to have escaped judicial consideration.

The details of the crimes are highly pertinent here. In the first, Caroline Hogg disappeared from outside her home in the Scottish town of Portobello in July 1983. Her body was found a month later beside a lay-by at Twycross in the English Midlands. It is clear that Black was responsible, but the cause of death could not be determined, and in particular there was no proof that she had been murdered in England rather than Scotland. Nor could any recognized evidential presumption have enabled that fact to be assumed without proof. This was potentially a major evidential problem, because murder in Scotland is not an offence under English law; nor is murder in England an offence under Scots law.[91] In the event, however, the defence assumed that section 9 of the 1861 Act prevented this from being an issue, and the point was not even addressed.

The problem also went unrecognized in relation to the murder of Susan Maxwell, who was abducted by Black at Coldstream on the Scottish border. Her body was found two weeks later, beside a lay-by a few miles from Twycross. Decomposition again made it difficult to deduce the time, place, or cause of death, but it was proved that Black had driven north to Dundee after abducting her, and that he had crossed back into England the next morning. Susan may or may not have been alive at that point.[92] Of Black's known victims, only Sarah Harper, who was abducted in Leeds and thrown (still alive) into the River Trent, could be proved to have been murdered in England.

Fortunately, Black's case was not one in which the jurisdictional problems (or indeed the defence's failure to identify them) carried any real risk of injustice, because his conviction for the murder of Sarah Harper was unimpeachable, and evidence of the other murders was admissible as similar fact

---

[90] *R v. Black* [1995] Crim LR 640. See Michael Hirst, 'Murder in England or Murder in Scotland? [1995] *Cambridge Law Journal* 488.

[91] Criminal Procedure (Scotland) Act 1995, s. 11(1).

[92] The prosecution may well have been aware of the possible difficulty, because they had taken the precaution in each case of adding charges of preventing lawful burial, contrary to common law—offences that clearly had been committed in England. See Michael Hirst, 'Preventing the Lawful Burial of a Body' [1996] *Criminal Law Review* 96.

evidence in support of it, wherever they may have been committed. The danger is that other cases might arise in which the conviction of a manifestly dangerous killer would indeed depend on there being clear proof that he killed in England rather than in Scotland, or vice versa. One need not resort to fanciful scenarios. Apart from the facts of *Black* itself, one might imagine a case in which the deceased's body is found in a car abandoned near to the Anglo-Scottish border, or in which her body is found floating in the Solway Firth.

A similar problem arose before the High Court of Australia in *Thompson* v. *The Queen*.[93] Thompson murdered two sisters by shooting them in the back of his car. Their bodies were found inside the burnt-out remains of the car in Capital Territory, following what had been made to resemble a crash, a few yards from the border with New South Wales; but had they been shot before or after the vehicle crossed the state border? The jury at the trial in Capital Territory were instructed to convict only if satisfied that the murders had been committed within that Territory, and this direction was upheld on appeal to the Federal court; but in the course of dismissing an application for leave to bring a further appeal, the judges of the High Court ruled that proof on balance of probabilities would suffice to establish the *locus* of the crime. Mason CJ and Dawson J reasoned that it would not be appropriate to require proof beyond reasonable doubt, because that high standard of proof was designed to reduce the risk of wrongful convictions and not to enable 'a wrongdoer clearly subject to the laws of one of two jurisdictions [to] escape the laws of both, even where such laws were identical . . .'.

As Deane J pointed out in his concurring judgment, this was a case in which each jurisdiction would have applied exactly the same law of murder, whereas:

> If the various states and territories constituting [Australia] were for the purpose of identifying the content of internal laws, to be treated as independent nations with their own discrete systems of common law, the conclusion that proof of locality was required beyond reasonable doubt would . . . be irresistible. . . .

Might *Thompson* be applied in an Anglo-Scottish case? This seems doubtful. Given that Scotland has always had its own discrete system of common law, *Thompson* would appear to be distinguishable on that basis.[94] Even if it were not, proof of any kind might have been difficult on the facts of *Black*.

Such problems might perhaps be resolved by a simple amendment to section 9 and its Scottish counterpart, so as to permit murders in one part

---

[93] (1989) 169 CLR 1.

[94] In some cases, it may be possible for a jury to infer, in the absence of evidence to the contrary, that the deceased was murdered in the country where his body was found; but there is no special presumption to that effect in English or Australian law. See *Thompson* v. *The Queen* (1989) 169 CLR 1, 14.

of the United Kingdom to be triable in any other part, on the same basis as when committed by a British citizen abroad. Limited reforms of this kind may nevertheless leave room for other problems to arise. A more radical solution would be to enact legislation that would enable any crime committed in England or Scotland to be dealt with in either jurisdiction, if the *locus* of the offence cannot be established.[95]

Prosecutions under Section 9

Actual reliance on section 9 or its predecessors appears to be infrequent. The handful of reported cases date mostly from the nineteenth century,[96] and although this legislation was considered at some length in *R v. Page*,[97] the assumption of jurisdiction in that case ultimately depended on what is now section 70 of the Army Act 1955, the appellant having been tried by court-martial in Egypt for the murder of a local man. Section 9 of the 1861 Act was significant only in so far as it supported the Crown's argument that the victim's nationality was irrelevant for the purpose of ascertaining jurisdiction under the Army Act. As Lord Goddard CJ explained, 'It is,...abundantly clear...that, had the appellant been brought to this country and tried here, the question as to the nationality of the victim could not have arisen.'

Section 9 has nevertheless been relied upon in at least one recent prosecution for murder abroad. In 1997, following a lengthy trial in the Crown Court at Bristol, Mohan Singh Kular was convicted of murdering his wife during a holiday in the Punjab. Eight police officers were flown to India to conduct a 16-week investigation there, and no fewer than 23 witnesses were flown to England from India in order to testify at the trial.[98]

The most recent case of extraterritorial murder to be featured in published law reports was one in which jurisdiction was provided by the War Crimes Act 1991 rather than by section 9,[99] but in May 2002 the Divisional Court refused a father's application for judicial review of a CPS decision not to bring a manslaughter prosecution in respect of the death of his son, who had died in Spain, whilst on holiday with friends.[100] It was clearly understood on

---

[95] Cf. Art. 38 of the Sangatte Protocol (above, p. 101). The problem is unlikely to arise as between England and Wales and Northern Ireland.

[96] These include *R v. Sawyer* (1815) Russ & Ry 294; *R v. Serva* (1845) 1 Cox CC 292; *R v. Helsham* (1830) 4 C & P 394 and *R v. Azzopardi* (1843) 1 Car & Kir 203.

[97] [1953] 2 All ER 1355.

[98] The jury failed to agree in respect of two other charges of murders allegedly committed in India.

[99] *R v. Sawoniuk* [2000] 2 Cr App R 220.

[100] *R (on the application of Lewin) v. DPP* [2002] EWHC 1049 (Admin); [2002] All ER (D) 379 (May). The applicant's son had been left by his friend, unconscious as a result of excessive drinking, in a car that was parked in the Spanish sun with its windows closed. When his body was discovered, outside temperatures had risen to nearly 30 degrees, but there was no evidence to prove that heat-stroke had been a cause of death, since he had probably died quite early that morning; and the court doubted in any event whether the friend had assumed any duty of care in respect of him.

all sides that jurisdiction would not have been a problem, had the evidence been sufficient to justify manslaughter proceedings in England.[101]

Bigamy

Bigamy first became an extraterritorial offence under section 22 of the Offences Against the Person Act 1828. This provision was supplanted by section 57 of the Offences Against the Person Act 1861, which provides:

Whosoever, being married, shall marry any other person during the life of the former husband or wife, whether the second marriage shall have taken place in England or Ireland or elsewhere, shall be guilty of an offence.... Provided, that nothing in this section contained shall extend to any second marriage contracted elsewhere than in England and Ireland by any other than a subject of Her Majesty, or to any person marrying a second time whose husband or wife shall have been continually absent from such person for the space of seven years then last past, and shall not have been known by such person to be living within that time, or shall extend to any person who, at the time of such second marriage, shall have been divorced from the bond of the first marriage, or to any person whose former marriage shall have been declared void by the sentence of any court of competent jurisdiction.

The offence is frequently associated with foreign marriages, if only because a would-be bigamist may believe that he can get away with such an offence if each marriage is celebrated in a different country. Prosecutions in England and Wales for extraterritorial offences of bigamy are nevertheless rare. There are several reported cases involving an original marriage abroad, followed by a second (bigamous) 'marriage'[102] in England and Wales. These latter cases do not, however, involve the commission of any extraterritorial offence. Although the existence of a valid first marriage is an essential component of the *actus reus*, the offence of bigamy is committed only when and where the supposed second marriage is celebrated. If that occurs within the realm, the offence is essentially a territorial one.

Bigamy can be described as an extraterritorial offence only where the second or bigamous marriage is entered into abroad. Reading section 57 in conjunction with section 3(1) of the British Nationality Act 1948 and section 51(1) of the British Nationality Act 1981, this may occur *either* where a British citizen, British overseas territories citizen, British overseas citizen, or British national (overseas) goes through a bigamous ceremony of marriage, anywhere in the world,[103] *or* where a Commonwealth citizen goes through

---

[101] Jurisdiction might have been asserted under s. 9, or under s. 4 of the Suppression of Terrorism Act 1978 (see p. 227 above).

[102] By definition, it cannot really be a marriage at all; but s. 57 makes sense only if construed as applying to married persons who *purport* to marry someone else.

[103] See *R v. Earl Russell* [1901] AC 446, in which the defendant was convicted by his peers on the basis of a bigamous marriage in Nevada. For an argument that s. 57 was wrongly

a bigamous ceremony of marriage anywhere other than in a foreign or independent Commonwealth country or the Republic of Ireland.

Section 57 of the 1861 Act applies within Northern Ireland as well as within England and Wales. This gives rise to a further complication. As a general rule, crimes committed in Northern Ireland or Scotland are the concern only of the courts of Northern Ireland or Scotland, even if the same legislation also applies in England and Wales. Where a foreign national commits bigamy in Northern Ireland, this general rule holds good. Where, however, the bigamist is a British or Commonwealth citizen, the extraterritorial ambit of the offence kicks in, giving English and Northern Ireland courts jurisdiction over offences both in their own territory and in each other's. The 1861 Act is not part of Scots law, in which bigamy remains a common law offence with no extraterritorial ambit, but this does not prevent an act of bigamy committed by a British or Commonwealth citizen in Scotland from being triable as an extraterritorial statutory offence under English or Northern Ireland law. In *R* v. *Topping*,[104] it was held that the defendant, a British subject, could properly be convicted of bigamy under English law, even though the bigamous marriage, and indeed the original marriage, had been solemnized in Scotland. The defendant lived in England, which explains how the matter came before the English courts in the first place, but residence or domicile is not strictly relevant to the ambit of the offence. A British citizen domiciled in Scotland, for example, would be guilty of an offence under section 57 if he were to marry bigamously in Australia, and would be triable for that offence in England and Wales, even though he would not be guilty of any offence under Scots law.

Polygamous Marriages under Foreign Law

In some countries, notably Islamic ones, polygamy may be considered lawful, and polygamous or potentially polygamous marriages are sometimes entered into by British (or British overseas, etc.) citizens in such countries. In English law, such marriages raise a number of difficult issues, both for the civil courts and for the criminal courts. These issues cannot be ignored when considering the extraterritorial reach of the offence of bigamy, because the validity of the original marriage must be established in any successful prosecution for bigamy.[105]

In English law, polygamous marriages are not regarded as marriages in the fullest sense of that term, but nor are they regarded as mere nullities.

---

applied in that case, see Williams, 'Venue and the Ambit of Criminal Law' (1965) 81 *Law Quarterly Review* 276, 402–6; and cf. *Macleod* v. *Attorney-General of New South Wales* [1891] AC 455.

[104] (1856) Dears 647.

[105] *R* v. *Kay* (1887) 16 Cox 292. See *Archbold 2003*, §31–18; *Blackstone's Criminal Practice 2003*, B2.93.

In accordance with the rules of private international law, a polygamous or potentially polygamous marriage lawfully celebrated in a country that permits such marriages will ordinarily be recognized by civil courts in the United Kingdom either for the purpose of granting matrimonial relief,[106] or for the purpose of invalidating any subsequent marriage by either of the parties in the United Kingdom. This does not mean, however, that such a marriage must necessarily be considered valid for the purpose of the criminal law of bigamy. In *Baindail* v. *Baindail*,[107] the Court of Appeal held that a potentially polygamous marriage entered into under Indian law sufficed to invalidate a subsequent marriage by the husband in England, but emphasized that the decision was not intended to affect the criminal law. Lord Greene MR said:

On principle it seems to me that the courts are for this purpose bound to recognise the Indian marriage as a valid marriage and an effective bar to any subsequent marriage in this country. . . . Counsel for the appellant . . . drew an alarming picture of the effect of our decision on the law of bigamy. . . [but] nothing that I have said must be taken as having the slightest bearing on the question of the law of bigamy which says under the statute 'Whosoever, being married, shall marry any other person during the life of the former husband or wife. . .' On the question of whether a person is 'married' within the meaning of that statute (which is a criminal statute) when he has entered into a [potentially polygamous marriage abroad] I am not going to express any opinion whatever. It seems to me a different question in which other considerations may well come into play. I hope sincerely that nobody will endeavour to spell out of what I have said anything to cover such a question.

A person domiciled in England and Wales (or in any other country that prohibits polygamy) cannot, as a matter of private international law, lawfully practice polygamy. This rule does not, however, invalidate a marriage that is only potentially polygamous. Section 5(1) of the Private International Law (Miscellaneous Provisions) Act 1995 provides:

A marriage entered into outside England and Wales between parties neither of whom is already married is not void under the law of England and Wales on the ground that it is entered into under a law which permits polygamy and that either party is domiciled in England and Wales.

Furthermore, a potentially polygamous marriage will become monogamous in certain circumstances, notably where the party who might otherwise have been entitled to take a second spouse[108] subsequently acquires a domicile of choice in a country that does not permit polygamy. This may happen,

---

[106] The Matrimonial Causes Act 1973, s. 47(1), provides: 'A Court in England and Wales shall not be precluded from granting matrimonial relief or making a declaration concerning the validity of a marriage by reason only that either party is, or has during the subsistence of the marriage, been married to more than one person.'   [107] [1946] P 122.

[108] That party is usually the husband. Islam, for example, permits polygyny but not polyandry.

for example, if the party in question settles permanently in England and Wales, thereby acquiring an English domicile of choice.[109]

As far as the criminal law is concerned, a British (or British overseas, etc.) citizen who practises polygamy abroad in accordance with local marriage laws generally commits no offence under section 57. This is not because his conduct is lawful where it takes place: Section 57 makes no reference to double criminality. It is because, as far as the criminal law is concerned, polygamous or potentially polygamous marriages are not deemed to be valid marriages at all. This is apparent from the decision of the Court of Appeal in *R* v. *Sagoo*.[110] The appellant was a Sikh, born and originally domiciled in Kenya, which was then a British colony. He entered into a potentially polygamous marriage there in 1959 at a time when such marriages were permitted under Kenyan law. In 1960, however, the Hindu Marriage and Divorce Ordinance of Kenya was passed. This applied to Sikhs and prohibited any future polygamous marriages, but it did not invalidate polygamous or potentially polygamous marriages solemnized before it came into force. In 1966 the appellant and his wife migrated to England, and became domiciled there. In 1973 he purported to marry another woman in England, while his original marriage was still subsisting, and for this he was duly charged with bigamy. There was no question of the appellant having any right to enter into a polygamous marriage in England (or indeed in Kenya), but his defence was that as far as English criminal law was concerned, the original (and potentially polygamous) marriage in Kenya was no marriage at all.

That argument may seem difficult to reconcile with the rules of private international law, as applied by the civil courts, but was fully in accordance with an earlier first instance ruling in the case of *R* v. *Sarwan Singh*.[111] Nor was it wholly rejected by the Court of Appeal in *Sagoo*. The Court upheld the appellant's conviction (and overruled *Sarwan Singh*) only on the much narrower basis that the Kenyan marriage had ceased to be potentially polygamous as a result of events that had occurred prior to celebration of the marriage in England. There were two such events, either of which would have sufficed to deprive the original marriage of its polygamous potential. One was that, by settling in England, the appellant had acquired an English domicile of choice. The other was that Kenyan law had ceased to permit polygamous marriages. The appellant had become monogamously married by the time of his second marriage, and he was accordingly guilty of bigamy. Had his first marriage remained potentially polygamous, however, it seems that he could not have been convicted of bigamy under English law either as a result of the invalid 'marriage' celebrated in England, or as a result of any second marriage he might have celebrated abroad.

---

[109] See *Ali* v. *Ali* [1968] P 564.   [110] [1975] 2 All ER 926.
[111] [1962] 3 All ER 612.

A better solution to the problem of polygamous foreign marriages made by British citizens might be to amend section 57, so as to exempt from its scope any foreign marriages that are lawful (i) under local law and (ii) under the personal laws of the parties, whilst *including* within its scope any person who purports to marry within the United Kingdom when either monogamously or polygamously married already. Some critics,[112] however, have questioned the need for the offence of bigamy to have any extraterritorial ambit at all. The traditional justification for the existence of this offence under English law is not that it involves any harm done to the other parties involved (although it may of course do so) but that it involves the 'prostitution of a solemn ceremony'.[113] If this is indeed the correct (and only) rationale behind the offence then there is no particular reason why English law should be concerned with bigamous marriages abroad.

CRIMES UNDER INTERNATIONAL LAW

Recent years have seen a resurgence of interest in international criminal law. Piracy and slave trading may no longer be of any great concern to the English courts, although neither has disappeared from the world scene, and piracy, in particular, is a very real problem in many parts of the world,[114] but recent years have seen significant legislation and litigation concerning war crimes, crimes against humanity, and crimes of state torture.

Genocide, War Crimes, and Crimes against Humanity

Genocide, war crimes, and crimes against humanity are potentially related or overlapping offences and may conveniently be considered together. Although they are all indictable as extraterritorial (and in some cases as universal) offences under English criminal law, they are better known as 'international crimes' (or crimes under international law) and have generally been prosecuted before international criminal tribunals[115] rather than before municipal courts. They are now the principal concern of the International Criminal Court at The Hague.[116] As international crimes, they have been

---

[112] Notably Williams, op.cit. fn 80 above, 407.

[113] See *R* v. *Allen* (1872) LR 1 CCR 367. Bigamy is not committed under s. 57 where a Muslim contracts an unregistered Islamic marriage in England without disclosing to his bride the existence of a previous and subsisting marriage. See *Al-Mudaris* v. *Al-Mudaris* [2001] All ER (D) 288 (Feb).

[114] Jurisdiction over piracy (and offences against aviation) is examined in Chapter 6 below.

[115] Namely, the International Military Tribunal at Nuremberg; the International Military Tribunal of the Far East (the Tokyo Tribunal); the International Criminal Tribunal for the Former Yugoslavia; and the International Criminal Tribunal for Rwanda. The Yugoslavia and Rwanda tribunals are subsidiary organs of the UN Security Council.

[116] Established by the International Criminal Court Statute, adopted in Rome in 1998.

examined in great detail elsewhere,[117] but such offences have been prose-cuted only very rarely under English law, and a relatively brief examination must therefore suffice in this work.

The position under English law is characterized by a confusing amount of overlapping legislation. Crimes of genocide, war crimes, and crimes against humanity committed on or after 1 September 2001 are now punish-able under sections 51 and 52 of the International Criminal Court Act 2001,[118] but the only extraterritorial jurisdiction provided under this legis-lation is confined to United Kingdom nationals, residents, or service personnel. The new offences apply alongside those created by section 1 of the Geneva Conventions Act 1957 (as amended by the Geneva Convention (Amendment) Act 1995) which apply on a universal basis (regardless of nationality) to all 'grave breaches' of the 1949 Geneva Conventions or of the First Additional Protocol to those Conventions. The jurisdiction pro-vided by the 1957 Act (as amended) is in some respects more extensive, but in other respects more limited, than that provided by the 2001 Act. Neither statute is retrospective, but a retrospective jurisdiction over war crimes committed in Nazi-occupied territory during the Second World War may be asserted under English law by virtue of the War Crimes Act 1991.

This impressive array of legislation has considerable symbolic importance in so far as it demonstrates the United Kingdom's abhorrence of such crimes, and much of it was necessary in order that it could discharge its obligations under public international law; but it has seen minimal use in practice. Indeed, few of these provisions have ever been considered or applied by English courts either in domestic prosecutions, or in extradition proceedings.

Genocide

Genocide may take several different forms, of which murder is just one. Common to each is 'an intent to destroy, in whole or in part, a national, ethnical, racial or religious group, as such'.[119] Because of their status as 'international crimes', acts of genocide are widely assumed to be offences of universal jurisdiction under English law, but they are not. The 1948 Genocide Convention did not require the assumption of any such jurisdic-tion, and the Genocide Act 1969, which first made acts of genocide punishable under English law, made no provision for extraterritorial jurisdiction, even over British nationals.[120]

---

[117] See, e.g., K. Kittichaisaree, *International Criminal Law* (2001); I. Bantekas, S. Nash, and M. Mackarel, *International Criminal Law* (2001).

[118] International Criminal Court Act 2001 (Commencement) Order 2001 (SI 2001 No. 2161).

[119] See the 1948 UN Convention on the Prevention and Punishment of the Crime of Genocide, Art. 2; ICC Statute, Art. 6.

[120] Such conduct would nevertheless have amounted to a 'civil offence' if committed abroad by a British serviceman or by any other person subject to armed service discipline: Army Act 1955, s. 70; Air Force Act 1955, s. 70; Naval Discipline Act 1957, s. 42.

As previously explained, acts of genocide (and ancillary acts of procurement, incitement, or assistance, etc.) may now be tried as specific extraterritorial offences under English law by virtue of the International Criminal Court Act 2001. This Act, which also applies to certain war crimes and crimes against humanity, is considered at p. 242 below. Before turning to it, however, it is necessary to consider some older legislation that remains in force alongside it.

The Geneva Conventions Act 1957

The four Geneva Conventions of 1949 (listed below) together reflected a determination by the international community to further outlaw and where necessary punish acts involving the murder, enslavement, maltreatment, or other abuse of prisoners of war or civilian populations: acts of the kind that had been so notorious a feature of the Second World War. Applying principles laid down in the Nuremberg and Tokyo war crimes trials, the Conventions apply the concept of individual (as well as of state) responsibility for grave breaches of their provisions. States party to the Conventions are obliged to provide effective penal sanctions for persons committing or ordering grave breaches of those Conventions, and to search for, arrest, and prosecute or extradite suspected offenders of any nationality who may be found within their territories.[121]

The Geneva Conventions Act 1957 gives effect to those obligations by creating offences of universal jurisdiction under English (and other United Kingdom) law. The Geneva Convention (Amendment) Act 1995 amended the 1957 Act so as to give similar effect to the first additional Protocol to the Conventions, which was added in 1977. Section 1(1) of the 1957 Act (as thus amended) now provides:

Any person, whatever his nationality, who, whether in or outside the United Kingdom, commits, or aids, abets or procures the commission by any other person of, a grave breach of any of the scheduled Conventions or the first Protocol shall be guilty of an offence.

The Conventions in question are the Convention for the Amelioration of the Condition of the Wounded and Sick in Armed Forces in the Field; the Convention for the Amelioration of the Condition of Wounded, Sick and Shipwrecked Members of Armed Forces at Sea; the Convention Relative to the Treatment of Prisoners of War; and the Convention Relative to the Protection of Civilian Persons in Time of War. These each apply:

. . . to all cases of declared war or of any other armed conflict which may arise between two or more of the High Contracting Parties, even if the state of war is not recognised by one of them. . . . [and] to all cases of partial or total occupation of the

---

[121] See Art. 49, common to each.

territory of a High Contracting Party, even if the said occupation meets with no armed resistance.[122]

Conventions cannot ordinarily be binding on states that are not parties thereto, but parties may nevertheless be bound by the Conventions in relation to a non-party, if the latter accepts and applies the provisions thereof.[123]

'Grave breaches' of the Conventions are defined by section 1(1A) of the 1957 Act and by provisions within each of the relevant Conventions. They vary as between each Convention, and depend in many cases on the circumstances or on the intent with which they are committed, but include the wilful killing of persons protected under the relevant Convention; torture or inhuman treatment, including biological experiments; wilfully causing great suffering or serious injury to body or health; and the wanton and extensive destruction or appropriation of protected property, if not justified by military necessity. The Prisoners of War Convention adds offences of forcibly conscripting prisoners into hostile forces, and of wilfully depriving prisoners of their right to a fair and regular trial. The Protection of Civilians Convention adds hostage taking and the unlawful deportation, transfer, or confinement of protected persons. Lastly, the first Protocol, which applies both to international conflicts and to armed conflicts 'in which peoples are fighting against colonial domination and alien occupation and against racist regimes in the exercise of their right of self-determination', adds a number of further potential breaches to the list. Article 85(3) of the Protocol identifies the following as grave breaches, 'when committed wilfully and in violation of the Conventions or the Protocol and causing death or serious injury to body or health':

- making the civilian population or individual civilians the object of attack;
- launching an indiscriminate attack affecting the civilian population or civilian objects in the knowledge that such attack will cause excessive loss of life, injury to civilians or damage to civilian objects;
- launching an attack against works or installations containing dangerous forces in the knowledge that such attack will cause excessive loss of life, injury to civilians or damage to civilian objects;
- making non-defended localities and demilitarised zones the object of attack;
- making a person the object of attack in the knowledge that he is *hors de combat*;
- the perfidious use . . . of the distinctive emblem of the red cross, red crescent or red lion and sun or of other protective signs recognised by the Conventions or this Protocol.

Article 85(4) adds the following acts, 'when committed wilfully and in violation of the Conventions or the Protocol':

- The transfer by the Occupying Power of parts of its own civilian population into the territory it occupies, or the deportation or transfer of all or parts of the population

---

[122] See Art. 2, common to each.   [123] Ibid.

of the occupied territory within or outside this territory, in violation of Article 49 of the Fourth Convention;

- unjustifiable delay in the repatriation of prisoners of war or civilians;
- practices of apartheid and other inhuman and degrading practices involving outrages upon personal dignity, based on racial discrimination;
- making the clearly recognised historic monuments, works of art or places of worship which constitute the cultural or spiritual heritage of peoples and to which special protection has been given by special arrangement . . . the object of attack, causing as a result extensive destruction thereof, where there is no evidence of the violation by the adverse Party of Article 53, sub-paragraph (b),[124] and when such historic monuments, works of art and places of worship are not located in the immediate proximity of military objectives;
- depriving a person protected by the Conventions or referred to in paragraph 2 of this Article of the rights of fair and regular trial.[125]

The Conventions (as opposed to the less widely accepted Protocol) are generally considered to reflect customary international law, and acts that would now amount to grave breaches of those Conventions were therefore criminal, under international law, even when committed during the Second World War. Nevertheless, the 1957 Act has no retrospective effect, and crimes dating from that period cannot be prosecuted under it. This partly explains the subsequent enactment of the War Crimes Act 1991.

The War Crimes Act 1991

The War Crimes Act 1991 is described in its long title as 'An Act to confer jurisdiction on United Kingdom courts in respect of certain grave violations of the laws and customs of war committed in German-held territory during the Second World War'. It was enacted in order that a small number of elderly war criminals might belatedly be brought to justice.[126] These were mostly former SS guards of Ukrainian, Latvian, or Lithuanian origin, who had subsequently become naturalized or domiciled in the United Kingdom. Section 1 of the Act provides:

(1) Subject to the provisions of this section proceedings for murder, manslaughter or culpable homicide may be brought against a person in the United Kingdom irrespective of his nationality at the time of the alleged offence if that offence—

  (a) was committed during the period beginning with 1 September 1939 and ending with 5 June 1945 in a place which at the time was part of Germany or under German occupation; and

---

[124] By using the monument, etc., for military purposes.

[125] By para. 2, acts described as 'grave breaches' in the Conventions are grave breaches of the Protocol 'if committed against persons in the power of an adverse Party protected by Articles 44, 45 and 73 of this Protocol [*refugees and captured combatants or persons who have taken part in hostilities, but excluding spies or mercenaries*] or against the wounded, sick and shipwrecked of the adverse Party who are protected by this Protocol, or against those medical or religious personnel, medical units or medical transports which are under the control of the adverse Party and are protected by this Protocol.'

[126] Similar laws have been enacted in Canada, Australia, and Israel.

(b) constituted a violation of the laws and customs of war.

(2) No proceedings shall by virtue of this section be brought against any person unless he was on 8 March 1990, or has subsequently become, a British citizen or resident in the United Kingdom, the Isle of Man or any of the Channel Islands.

This provision is unusual in that it has retrospective effect, creating offences under English law in respect of conduct that, when originally committed, was incapable of amounting to any such offence.[127] The equivalent offences created under the Geneva Conventions Act 1957 (above) have no such retrospective effect. If they had, the 1991 Act would not have been necessary. The ambit of the 1991 Act is not merely retrospective and extraterritorial: it is exclusively retrospective and extraterritorial. Given the narrow era and locality within which it applies, and given the ages of the offenders to whom it was intended to apply, its effective life-span was bound to be limited, and may already have run its course. Indeed, it was much criticized, even when first drafted, on the basis that it was already too late for justice to be done. Lord Shawcross, who had been the chief British prosecutor at the Nuremberg trials, argued[128]:

Revival of these sad and terrible matters by sensational trials of a small handful of aged men, which will take years to conduct and which will start with an assumption of guilt, will not help to promote understanding and friendship between the different peoples of the world, will not help eliminate the evils of anti-Semitism nor, still less, enhance respect for British justice.

Other critics argued that the Act would be unworkable for lack of reliable evidence, or because most of the identified suspects were too old or too frail to face trial. The highly unsatisfactory trial of John Demjanuk in Israel had previously heightened those fears,[129] and the first prosecution brought in England under the 1991 Act tended to confirm them. In *R v. Serafinowicz*,[130] the defendant, who was then aged 86, was found unfit to stand trial following a special hearing at the Central Criminal Court. He had been charged with a series of murders allegedly committed in Belarus in 1941 and 1942, but was found to be suffering from Alzheimer's disease.

Two years later, however, the first (and almost certainly the last) successful prosecution under the Act resulted in the conviction of Anthony Sawoniuk, a 78-year-old British resident who had formerly been a police officer from Belarus, on 18 charges of murdering Jewish civilians in collaboration with occupying Nazi forces. This conviction was upheld on appeal,[131] and it may thus be argued that the Act was not, after all, a total waste of time, money, and effort.

---

[127] See *R v. Sawoniuk* [2000] All ER (D) 154, *per* Lord Bingham of Cornhill CJ.

[128] Letter to *The Times*, 29 July 1989.

[129] Demjanuk's conviction was later quashed when new evidence came to light suggesting that he may have been a victim of mistaken identification. See above, p. 55.

[130] (1997) unreported, 18 January.

[131] *R v. Sawoniuk* [2000] All ER (D) 154. The prosecution case was relatively cogent because it rested primarily on the evidence of witnesses from Belarus who knew S as their local

The International Criminal Court Act 2001

By sections 51 of the International Criminal Court Act 2001:

(1) It is an offence against the law of England and Wales for a person to commit genocide, a crime against humanity or a war crime.

(2) This section applies to acts committed—
(a) in England or Wales, or
(b) outside the United Kingdom by a United Kingdom national, a United Kingdom resident or a person subject to UK service jurisdiction.

This is supplemented by section 52, by which:

(1) It is an offence against the law of England and Wales for a person to engage in conduct ancillary to an act to which this section applies.

(2) This section applies to an act that if committed in England or Wales would constitute—
(a) an offence under section 51 (genocide, crime against humanity or war crime), or
(b) an offence under this section,
but which, being committed (or intended to be committed) outside England and Wales, does not constitute such an offence.

(3) The reference in subsection (1) to conduct ancillary to such an act is to conduct that would constitute an ancillary offence in relation to that act if the act were committed in England or Wales.

Section 52 must be read in conjunction with section 55, under which ancillary offences are defined as inciting, attempting, or conspiring to commit an act of genocide, a war crime, or a crime against humanity; as aiding, abetting, counselling, or procuring such a crime; or as assisting an offender or concealing the commission of an offence. It is therefore an offence to incite, in England and Wales, the commission of genocide overseas, even if the perpetrators have no connection with the United Kingdom and are not subject to English criminal jurisdiction. Where the incitement or procuring, etc., is itself committed outside the United Kingdom, it may still be punishable under section 52 if committed by a United Kingdom national or resident, or by a person subject to British armed service jurisdiction.

The relationship between the 2001 Act and the Genocide Act 1969 is straightforward: the new Act repeals and supplants the 1969 Act,[132] and provides an extraterritorial ambit to the offence where none existed before. The relationship between the 2001 Act and the War Crimes Act 1991 is also straightforward: the 1991 Act is purely and narrowly retrospective, whereas the 2001 Act deals only with conduct committed on or after 1 September 2001. The only complication, therefore, is the relationship

police chief and watched as he murdered Jewish men and women by shooting them as they stood beside freshly dug graves. S did not dispute his identity, but claimed to be a 'friend' of the Jews, rather than a persecutor.

[132] The Genocide Act was repealed by Sch. 10 to the 2001 Act.

between the 2001 Act and the Geneva Conventions Act 1957, because neither of these Acts is retrospective, and both are now in force.

In the context of war crimes and crimes against humanity, the 1957 Act appears, at first sight, to be wider ranging than that of 2001. It has a universal ambit, regardless of nationality, whereas the extraterritorial ambit of the 2001 Act is governed by nationality or residence. During a Parliamentary debate on the International Criminal Court Bill, the Solicitor-General explained:

We ... have severe doubts about taking jurisdiction over people who have no substantial link with the United Kingdom. Historically, our practice has been to take universal jurisdiction only when it is obligatory as a result of an international agreement. The Torture Convention ..., the Hostage-taking Convention and the grave breaches of the Geneva Protocols [*sic*] are cases that involved obligations on our part to take universal jurisdiction, and we did so.[133] ... The Bill does not affect the universal jurisdiction that operates over grave breaches of the Geneva Protocols. That universal jurisdiction will remain. ... The Bill mirrors the provisions of the Geneva Protocols to a large extent.

This tells only half the story. In some other respects the 2001 Act has the wider ambit. This wider ambit arises, first, because the definition of a 'war crime' for the purposes of the 2001 Act extends not only to grave breaches of the Geneva Conventions, but also to many other 'serious violations of the laws and customs applicable in international armed conflict, within the established framework of international law'. These are listed in Schedule 8 to the 2001 Act, which incorporates the relevant provisions of the Statute of the International Criminal Court. The list includes many crimes that are also punishable as grave breaches of the First Protocol to the Geneva Conventions, but it extends to others besides, including the use of asphyxiating, poisonous, or other gases and the use of 'bullets which expand or flatten easily in the human body, such as bullets with a hard envelope which does not entirely cover the core or is pierced with incisions'.[134]

Secondly, the concept of war crimes is expanded under the 2001 Act so as to extend for some purposes to armed conflicts that are 'not of an international character'. Atrocities committed against persons taking no active part in the hostilities, including members of armed forces who have laid down their arms and those placed *hors de combat* by sickness, wounds,

---

[133] Contrary to the Solicitor-General's assertion, no such jurisdiction has yet been assumed under the second Protocol, which will apply to armed conflicts that take place in the territory of a Contracting Party 'between its armed forces and dissident armed forces or other organised armed groups which, under responsible command, exercise such control over a part of its territory as to enable them to carry out sustained and concerted military operations'. The 2001 Act applies to crimes committed during such conflicts.

[134] Popularly known as 'dumdum' bullets.

detention, or any other cause, may be dealt with under the Act on the same basis as if they were grave breaches of the Geneva Conventions.[135]

Thirdly, the 2001 Act applies to 'crimes against humanity', which need not be linked to armed conflicts. Such crimes are defined in Schedule 8 to the Act, which incorporates Article 7 of the ICC Statute, as:

... any of the following acts when committed as part of a widespread or systematic attack directed against any civilian population, with knowledge of the attack:

(a) Murder;

(b) Extermination;

(c) Enslavement;

(d) Deportation or forcible transfer of population;

(e) Imprisonment or other severe deprivation of physical liberty in violation of fundamental rules of international law;

(f) Torture;

(g) Rape, sexual slavery, enforced prostitution, forced pregnancy, enforced sterilisation, or any other form of sexual violence of comparable gravity;

(h) Persecution against any identifiable group or collectivity on political, racial, national, ethnic, cultural, religious, gender as defined in paragraph 3, or other grounds that are universally recognised as impermissible under international law, in connection with any act referred to in this paragraph or any crime within the jurisdiction of the Court;

(i) Enforced disappearance of persons;

(j) The crime of apartheid;

(k) Other inhumane acts of a similar character intentionally causing great suffering, or serious injury to body or to mental or physical health.

Trial in England or Extradition to the International Criminal Court?

The jurisdiction of the International Criminal Court (ICC) is not intended to supplant the jurisdiction of ordinary national courts, but rather to complement or supplement that jurisdiction. Individual states retain jurisdiction unless they are unable or unwilling to investigate and prosecute a crime themselves. In practice, however, a war criminal arrested in England and Wales is unlikely to fall within the ambit of the 2001 Act—unless he is a British national or resident, etc. This means that extradition, either to another country or to the ICC itself, may be required. Part 2 of the Act lays down an expedited procedure to govern the arrest and surrender of persons for trial before the ICC. This procedure is broadly similar to that which governs extradition to the International Criminal Tribunals for Yugoslavia

---

[135] See Sch. 8, Art. 8(2)(c). This does not apply to situations of internal disturbances and tensions, such as riots, isolated and sporadic acts of violence, or other acts of a similar nature: see Art. 8(2)(d).

and Rwanda but differs significantly from that used for extradition to other countries. The detailed content of extradition law and procedure lies outside the scope of this work.

Torture

The infliction of torture may, when connected with international wars, military occupations, or armed conflicts, involve 'grave breaches' of one or more of the 1949 Geneva Conventions, or of the First Protocol to those Conventions; but even where it is not connected with any such conflicts, it now amounts to an international crime by virtue of the 1984 United Nations Convention Against Torture and Other Cruel, Inhuman or Degrading Treatment or Punishment.[136] This applies to 'the intentional infliction of severe pain and of suffering . . . by or at the instigation of or with the consent or acquiescence of a public official or other person acting in an official capacity'.[137]

It is generally considered that torture offends against peremptory norms of customary international law (*jus cogens*), so that its criminality does not depend entirely on the application of the 1984 Convention. In *Prosecutor* v. *Anto Furundzija*,[138] the International Criminal Tribunal for the Former Yugoslavia held that this prohibition against torture has become 'one of the most fundamental standards of the international community' and 'signals to all members of the international community and the individuals over whom they wield authority that the prohibition of torture is an absolute value from which nobody must deviate'. This view was accepted by the House of Lords in *R* v. *Bow Street Metropolitan Stipendiary Magistrate, ex p Pinochet Ugarte (No 3)*,[139] in which Lord Browne-Wilkinson declared himself satisfied that, 'long before the Torture Convention, state torture was an international crime in the highest sense'.

Jurisdiction over torture, under English law, is nevertheless based firmly on the terms of the Convention, and upon the specific obligations it imposes. In particular, English criminal law and extradition law have each been amended so as to enable suspected torturers of any nationality either to be tried under English law, or extradited to another state with a greater interest in prosecuting, in accordance with the principle of *aut dedere aut punire* which underlies Articles 5–7 of the Convention. Universal criminal jurisdiction is established by section 134 of the Criminal Justice Act 1988, which provides:

(1) A public official or person acting in an official capacity, whatever his nationality, commits the offence of torture if in the United Kingdom or elsewhere he intentionally inflicts severe pain or suffering on another in the performance or purported performance of his official duties.

---

[136] UN General Assembly Resolution 39/46, Doc. A/39/51; Cmnd. 9593.
[137] Ibid., Art. 1.   [138] Case No. IT-95–17/1-T, 10 December 1998.
[139] [2000] 1 AC 147, 198.

(2) A person not falling within subsection (1) above commits the offence of torture, whatever his nationality, if—

(a) in the United Kingdom or elsewhere he intentionally inflicts severe pain or suffering on another at the instigation or with the consent or acquiescence—

(i) of a public official; or

(ii) of a person acting in an official capacity; and

(b) the official or other person is performing or purporting to perform his official duties when he instigates the commission of the offence or consents to or acquiesces in it.

This fell to be considered by the House of Lords in the *Pinochet* case. Although this case was primarily concerned with issues of extradition and with sovereign or state immunity, the need to apply principles of double criminality meant that Senator Pinochet could be extradited only on charges that disclosed conduct which would equally have involved offences under section 134. A majority of their Lordships concluded on that basis that extradition could be permitted only in respect of atrocities committed in Chile on or after 29 September 1988, the date on which section 134 came into effect. This seriously restricted the number of extraditable offences, because while thousands of victims were tortured by Pinochet's regime during the 1970s, only three cases were identified in the Spanish extradition request as having taken place on or after 29 September 1988.

Some of the alleged offences were charged as conspiracies to commit torture. In contrast to some other statutes that create extraterritorial offences, the Criminal Justice Act 1988 makes no express reference to conspiracies or to any other ancillary offences, but it was held that jurisdiction would arise in any event, on the basis of principles established by the Privy Council in *Somchai Liangsiriprasert* v. *US Government*.[140] If, in other words, a substantive offence has extraterritorial effect, a conspiracy (or presumably an attempt, etc.) to commit that offence will have a similar extraterritorial effect. This ruling has implications that go well beyond cases of conspiracy to torture, and these are examined later in this chapter.

The Slave Trade

Most of the nineteenth-century legislation dealing with slavery has now been repealed, but amongst the surviving provisions is section 1 of the Slave Trade Act 1843, by which:

All the provisions of the Slave Trade Act 1824 herein-before recited . . . shall be deemed to extend and apply to British subjects wheresoever residing or being, and whether within the dominions of the British crown or of any foreign country; and all the several matters and things prohibited by the Slave Trade Act 1824 . . . when committed by British subjects, whether within the dominions of the British crown

---

[140] [1991] 1 AC 225.

or in any foreign country, . . . shall be deemed and taken to be offences committed against the said several Acts respectively, and shall be dealt with and punished accordingly. . . .

Surviving provisions of the 1824 Act to which the above provision may apply include the offences of dealing in slaves (contrary to section 10) and embarking or serving aboard a slave ship (contrary to section 11).[141] While the practice of slavery remains alive in some parts of the world, the above legislation (which applies only to British citizens, etc.) has little if any practical application to that practice, and no longer merits detailed examination.

TERRORIST OFFENCES AND OFFENCES FREQUENTLY CONNECTED WITH TERRORISM

Many of the offences that possess an extraterritorial ambit under English law are of a type frequently associated with terrorism. These include murder and manslaughter (which have already been examined at pp. 226–31 above) together with offences under the Explosive Substances Act 1883, the Internationally Protected Persons Act 1978, the Biological Weapons Act 1974, and the Taking of Hostages Act 1982.[142] In addition, these and several other offences that might potentially be committed by terrorists have acquired an extraterritorial (or additional extraterritorial) ambit under specific anti-terrorist legislation, such as the Suppression of Terrorism Act 1978, the Terrorism Act 2000, or the Anti-terrorism, Crime and Security Act 2001. Each of these Acts has its own foibles, limitations, or peculiarities. Section 4 of the Suppression of Terrorism Act 1978, for example, substantially enlarges the ambits of several criminal offences, regardless of whether they are in fact committed for terrorist purposes, but it generally applies only to things done in designated 'Convention countries', or by the nationals of Convention countries elsewhere. In contrast, section 62 of the Terrorism Act 2000 provides a near-universal ambit for certain offences involving explosive, biological, or chemical devices, but only where these are committed outside the United Kingdom 'as an act of terrorism or for the purposes of terrorism'.

It is now recognized that the financing of terrorism, whether by money laundering, fund raising, or other means, is an evil that must be opposed with much the same vigour as terrorist atrocities themselves. Section 63 of

---

[141] By s. 26 of the Slave Trade Act 1873, offences under the Slave Trade Acts may '. . . be deemed to have been committed either in the place in which the offence was committed, or in any place in which the person guilty of the offence may for the time being be. . . . and the venue or local description in the margin may be that of the place in which the trial is held.'

[142] To that list, one might add offences under the Aviation Security Act 1982 or the Aviation and Maritime Security Act 1990, which are examined in Chapter 6 below.

the Terrorism Act 2000 extends the ambit of certain terrorist funding and money-laundering offences accordingly.

The overall picture is currently very confusing, because one may have to consider a whole range of potentially relevant provisions when deciding whether given conduct falls within the ambit of English criminal law. One course of conduct may be found to fall within that ambit several times over, whereas other, broadly similar conduct may fall outside each and every extraterritorial provision that one may attempt to apply to it. One may find, for example, that an Indonesian terrorist who guns down and kills Australian or US citizens in Bali ordinarily[143] commits no offence under English law, but that a German terrorist committing exactly the same act is indeed guilty of murder under that law.[144] If our Indonesian terrorist were to use a bomb he would be guilty of an offence under section 2 of the Explosives Substances Act 1883;[145] and if he were to commit an identical act in India, he would additionally become guilty of murder. Indeed, any Indian citizen who commits murder abroad, or any person who commits murder in India, may in theory be tried for that offence under English law, whatever weapon (if any) he uses and whatever motive he may have for the crime.[146]

The above examples merely give a flavour of the complexities, contradictions, and oddities involved. Faced with such a luxuriant growth of related or interwoven provisions,[147] it is difficult to know where to begin,

---

[143] Unless, e.g., the targets include internationally protected persons.

[144] This is because he is a national of a Convention country for the purpose of s. 4 of the Suppression of Terrorism Act 1978.

[145] By virtue of s. 62 of the Terrorism Act 2000.

[146] Once again, the explanation is to be found in s. 4 of the Suppression of Terrorism Act, which now applies to India and to Indian citizens as it applies to Convention countries and their nationals. See below, p. 259.

[147] This growth is clearly set to continue. Clause 53 of the Crime (International Cooperation) Bill, introduced into Parliament in November 2002, will insert new ss. 63A–63E into the Terrorism Act 2000, for the purpose of implementing the EU Framework Decision on Combating Terrorism 2002, which requires the UK to take extraterritorial jurisdiction over a wider range of terrorist offences than those covered by existing legislation. Article 9 of the Framework Decision requires member states to take responsibility for terrorist activities by their own nationals and residents, no matter where those acts occur. The proposed ss. 63A and 63B will accordingly provide an extraterritorial ambit to several existing extraterritorial terrorist offences, including weapons training or instruction and directing a terrorist organization; together with numerous offences of violence, criminal damage, forgery, and counterfeiting, where these are committed for terrorist purposes. These offences will be capable of extraterritorial commission only by UK nationals or residents (unless they are already subject to wider jurisdiction under existing legislation); but s. 63C will create an entirely new form of extraterritorial jurisdiction, based on the passive personality principle, over foreigners who commit certain acts of terrorist violence (or of forgery, etc.) against or in relation to UK nationals or residents, or against 'protected persons', such as diplomats or certain EU officials. Section 63D will supplement s. 1 of the Internationally Protected Persons Act 1978, by making further provision in respect of terrorist attacks or threatened attacks on UK diplomatic premises, residences, or vehicles abroad. Section 63E will specify any consents that may be required in respect of prosecutions for such offences.

but since the Explosive Substances Act 1883 is the oldest of the statutes involved, and the one that is most widely applied or extended by the newer anti-terrorist laws, it makes sense to begin with that.

Offences under the Explosive Substances Act 1883

Section 2 of the Explosives Substances Act 1883 (as substituted by section 7 of the Criminal Jurisdiction Act 1975) provides:

A person who in the United Kingdom or (being a citizen of the United Kingdom and Colonies) in the Republic of Ireland unlawfully and maliciously causes by any explosive substance an explosion of a nature likely to endanger life or to cause serious injury to property shall, whether any injury to person or property has been actually caused or not, be guilty of an offence and on conviction on indictment shall be liable to imprisonment for life.

Although this provision has only a very limited extraterritorial ambit of its own, it features prominently in the Suppression of Terrorism Act 1978, the Internationally Protected Persons Act 1978, and the Terrorism Act 2000, which between them extend its ambit significantly; and it is augmented by section 3 (another 1975 substitution) which provides:

(1) A person who in the United Kingdom or a dependency or (being a citizen of the United Kingdom and Colonies) elsewhere unlawfully and maliciously—

(a) does any act with intent to cause, or conspires to cause, by an explosive substance an explosion of a nature likely to endanger life, or cause serious injury to property, whether in the United Kingdom or the Republic of Ireland, or

(b) makes or has in his possession or under his control an explosive substance with intent by means thereof to endanger life, or cause serious injury to property, whether in the United Kingdom or the Republic of Ireland, or to enable any other person so to do,

shall, whether any explosion does or does not take place, and whether any injury to person or property is actually caused or not, be guilty of an offence and on conviction on indictment shall be liable to imprisonment for life, and the explosive substance shall be forfeited.

(2) In this section 'dependency' means the Channel Islands, the Isle of Man and any colony,[148] other than a colony for whose external relations a country other than the United Kingdom is responsible.

The Criminal Jurisdiction Act 1975 was primarily a Northern Ireland measure, and was mirrored by reciprocal legislation enacted in the Republic,[149] under a joint initiative to curb terrorist activity throughout the whole of Ireland. Most provisions of the 1975 Act (and its Irish equivalent) have no application to the rest of the United Kingdom; but because Irish terrorism had been responsible for many bomb outrages in England and elsewhere

---

[148] Colonies are now 'British overseas territories', but s. 3 has not been amended accordingly.
[149] Namely, the Criminal Law (Jurisdiction) Act 1976.

(for example, at British military bases in Europe), the Republic's version of the Explosive Substances Act 1883, section 2,[150] was amended so as to apply to offences committed by Irish citizens anywhere 'outside the state'. If not extradited, an Irish citizen accused of a serious explosives offence in England could thus be tried for that offence in the Republic. By way of reciprocity, a British (or British overseas, etc.) citizen who causes a dangerous explosion in the Republic may, if not extradited, be tried for that offence in the United Kingdom.

In contrast to the amended Irish legislation, the 1975 amendments to the United Kingdom version of the 1883 Act were not concerned with offences involving explosions outside the British Isles. Section 3 was, however, made applicable to British (or British overseas, etc.) citizens who conspire anywhere to cause 'section 2' explosions in the United Kingdom or the Republic, or who possess explosives for such a purpose. Furthermore, by section 5:

Any person who within or (being a subject of Her Majesty) without Her Majesty's dominions by the supply of or solicitation for money, the providing of premises, the supply of materials, or in any manner whatsoever, procures, counsels, aids, abets, or is accessory to, the commission of any crime under this Act, shall be guilty of felony, and shall be liable to be tried and punished for that crime, as if he had been guilty as a principal.

In so far as this section applies to secondary participation abroad in crimes committed within England and Wales, it appears to add nothing to the common law rule as stated in *R v. Robert Millar (Contractors) Ltd.*[151] Where, however, the principal offence is a section 2 offence committed by a British citizen in the Republic of Ireland, section 5 might meaningfully apply so as to extend English jurisdiction over any act of secondary participation abroad.

Offences Involving Chemical, Biological, or Nuclear Devices

Chemical and biological weapons have already been used to commit terrorist outrages in Japan[152] and in the USA.[153] There are fears that more virulent biological agents, such as smallpox, may one day be used, with the potential to trigger a catastrophic epidemic or pandemic, or even that nuclear (or 'dirty' radioactive) weapons may find their way into terrorist hands. Faced with these threats, the United Kingdom has significantly revised and extended the content and extraterritorial ambit of earlier legislation dealing with biological, chemical, and nuclear or radioactive weapons.

---

[150] The UK's 1883 Act (as amended) remains the basis for the Republic's own law on this area.
[151] [1970] 2 QB 54.
[152] Sarin gas was used in a terrorist attack on Tokyo underground system on 20 March 1995.
[153] A series of anthrax attacks occurred in the USA during late 2001, not long after the 11 September suicide terrorist attacks; but no firm link has been established between the anthrax attacks and international terrorism.

As a result of amendments made by section 44 of the Anti-terrorism, Crime and Security Act 2001, section 1 of the Biological Weapons Act 1974, which prohibits the development, production, stockpiling, transfer, acquisition, or retention of microbial or other biological agents, biological toxins, or biological weapons or delivery systems, now applies to acts done by British citizens and other 'United Kingdom persons' (including British corporations) outside the United Kingdom. Comparable offences under section 2 of the Chemical Weapons Act 1996 have acquired an identical extraterritorial ambit, by virtue of section 3(2) of that Act. If committed for terrorist purposes, however, biological or chemical weapons offences now possess a universal ambit, under section 62 of the Terrorism Act 2000.

By section 113 of the Anti-terrorism, Crime and Security Act 2001, a person who takes any action which involves the use of 'a noxious substance or other noxious thing' so as to cause serious violence or damage anywhere in the world, or who thereby endangers human life or creates a serious risk to the health or safety of the public or a section of the public in any country, or induces in members of the public the fear of such endangerment, etc., will be guilty of an offence if his conduct is designed to influence a government or intimidate the public or a section of the public anywhere in the world. Threats to take such action are also criminalized under this section. The substance in question may be a biological agent 'or any other natural or artificial substance, whatever its form, origin or method of production'.[154] This clearly includes chemical agents or weapons; but there is currently nothing in section 113 or in any supplementary provision that would give such offences a true extraterritorial ambit. Section 113 merely creates a territorial offence that is capable of either subjective or objective cross-frontier commission.[155] This will change, however, if and when clause 54 of the Crime (International Cooperation) Bill, currently before Parliament, is enacted and brought into force. This will add a new section 113A to the 2001 Act, which will provide:

(1) Section 113 applies to conduct done—
  (a) in the United Kingdom; or
  (b) outside the United Kingdom which satisfies the following two conditions.

(2) The first condition is that the conduct is done for the purpose of advancing a political, religious or ideological cause.

(3) The second condition is that the conduct is—
  (a) by a United Kingdom national or a United Kingdom resident;
  (b) by any person done to, or in relation to, a United Kingdom national, a United Kingdom resident or a protected person; or
  (c) by any person done in circumstances which fall within section 63D(1)(b) and (c) or (3)(b) and (c) of the Terrorism Act 2000.

As for nuclear weapons, section 1 of the Nuclear Explosions (Prohibitions and Inspections) Act 1998 creates an offence that will apply both to nuclear

---

[154] See s. 115.   [155] The same applies to s. 114, which deals with hoaxes, etc.

weapon test explosions and to terrorist explosions (but not to the use of nuclear weapons in the course of armed combat). It will apply extraterritorially to United Kingdom nationals and corporations, etc., but is not yet in force, and will not come into force until the implementation of the 1996 Comprehensive Nuclear Test Ban Treaty, which has yet to be ratified by the USA. In the meantime, section 47(1)(a) of the Anti-terrorism, Crime and Security Act 2001 (which, by section 47(9), will cease to have effect when the 1998 Act comes into force) makes it an offence for any person knowingly to cause a nuclear weapon explosion. As with the 1998 provision, section 47(9) applies to the acts of United Kingdom persons (including corporations) outside the United Kingdom.[156]

Section 47(1) creates further offences, with the same extraterritorial ambit, but these are intended to remain in force alongside the 1998 Act. They include offences of developing, producing, or possessing nuclear weapons, participating in the transfer of such weapons, or threatening to use them other than in the course of an armed conflict. Nuclear weapons are defined so as to include 'nuclear explosive devices that are not intended for use as weapons'.[157] This apparently is intended to include 'dirty' weapons in which conventional explosive devices are combined with industrial grade nuclear material that may cause widespread contamination.[158] Such devices might more accurately be defined as 'nuclear weapons that are not intended to cause nuclear explosions'. If (as is likely) such weapons use radioactive material taken from nuclear power stations, etc., rather than weapons grade material, they may also involve offences under the Nuclear Material (Offences) Act 1983, which is considered at p. 253 below.

The use of nuclear weapons by terrorists may also fall within the ambit of section 62 of the Terrorism Act 2000, under which jurisdiction is universal, but it falls only indirectly within that ambit, because section 62 does not apply to any specific nuclear weapons offences. Any charge alleging an offence committed by foreign nationals outside the United Kingdom would have to be laid under the Explosives Substances Act 1883, to which section 62 does apply.

Participation and Incitement

Section 50 of the Anti-terrorism, Crime and Security Act 2001 contains provisions dealing with secondary participation or incitement. By section 50(1), it is an offence to aid, abet, counsel, procure, or incite a person who is not a United Kingdom person to do a 'relevant act' abroad. Relevant acts are acts that would, if done by a United Kingdom person, be offences under section 1 of the Biological Weapons Act, section 2 of the Chemical

---

[156] See s. 47(7) of the 2001 Act.   [157] See s. 47(6).

[158] Semtex explosive might, for example, be combined with radioactive material such as spent fuel rods, stolen from a nuclear installation.

Weapons Act, or section 47 of the 2001 Act itself.[159] If committed by a United Kingdom person, an offence under section 50(1) is itself an extraterritorial offence, by virtue of section 50(6); but if committed by anyone else, the aiding, incitement, etc., must be committed within England and Wales, or abroad a British ship, etc., if it is to be punishable under English law.[160]

As far as acts of participation are concerned, section 50 evidently is intended to apply where a foreigner does anything in England and Wales that assists, etc., the commission of a relevant act abroad, but difficulties may arise where a foreigner in England is alleged to have incited persons who were abroad at the time of the incitement. As explained in Chapter 4 of this work, incitement is a result crime, and is committed only when and where the incitement is communicated.

Offences Involving Misuse of 'Peaceful' Nuclear Material

Conduct involving the theft, misuse, or threatened misuse of non-military nuclear material may be subject to universal jurisdiction under sections 1 and 2 of the Nuclear Material (Offences) Act 1983. This Act implements the 1980 UN Convention on the Physical Protection of Nuclear Material and, in accordance with that Convention, it applies only to nuclear material 'which within the meaning of the Convention is nuclear material used for peaceful purposes'.[161] Section 1 of the 1983 Act provides:

(1) If a person, whatever his nationality, does outside the United Kingdom, in relation to or by means of nuclear material, any act which, had he done it in any part of the United Kingdom, would have made him guilty of—

(a) the offence of murder, manslaughter, culpable homicide, assault to injury, malicious mischief or causing injury, or endangering the life of the lieges, by reckless conduct, or

(b) an offence under section 18 or 20 of the Offences against the Person Act 1861 or section 1 of the Criminal Damage Act 1971 or Article 3 of the Criminal Damage (Northern Ireland) Order 1977 or section 78 of the Criminal Justice (Scotland) Act 1980, or

(c) the offence of theft, embezzlement, robbery, assault with intent to rob, burglary or aggravated burglary, or

(d) the offence of fraud or extortion or an offence under section 15 or 21 of the Theft Act 1968 or section 15 of 20 of the Theft Act (Northern Ireland) 1969,

he shall in any part of the United Kingdom be guilty of such of the offences mentioned in paragraphs (a) to (d) above as are offences of which the act would have made him guilty had he done it in that part of the United Kingdom.

(2) In this section and in section 2 below, 'act' includes omission.

---

[159] No reference is made to participation or incitement in respect of an offence under s. 1 of the Nuclear Explosions (Prohibitions and Inspections) Act 1998. This appears to be an oversight.

[160] Or in Scotland, if it is to be punishable under Scots law (etc.).

[161] Section 6(1) and Sch. 1. A certificate signed by the Secretary of State shall be conclusive of any question raised as to that issue (s. 6(2)).

Section 2 of the Act similarly provides universal jurisdiction over related offences involving preparatory acts and threats, including threats to obtain nuclear material by theft, robbery, etc., contrary to section 1(1)(c).

Paradoxically, whereas conduct involving the misuse or unlawful detonation of military grade nuclear devices is generally subject only to a limited extraterritorial jurisdiction, based on United Kingdom nationality, under section 47 of the 2001 Act, offences involving less dangerous civilian grade material are subject to full-blown universal jurisdiction. It is never-theless difficult to imagine an offence involving weapons grade material being anything other than a terrorist offence, and as such it will in turn be subject to universal jurisdiction under section 62 of the Terrorism Act 2000.

The Suppression of Terrorism Act 1978, Section 4

Section 4 of the Suppression of Terrorism Act 1978 contains unique and far-reaching jurisdiction provisions, which in certain circumstances extend the ambit of English criminal law to acts committed by foreign nationals in foreign countries. Such acts need have no connection with the United Kingdom or with British citizens; nor (for reasons that are explained below) need they have the slightest connection with terrorism.

The provisions of the 1978 Act can be understood only by reference to the United Kingdom's treaty obligations under international law. This is not to say that those provisions precisely mirror or give effect to those treaty obligations. In some respects it is clear that they go well beyond any such obligations, and in other respects it appears that they may fall short. Without reference to those obligations, however, the provisions in the Act (and in particular the 'jurisdiction' provisions) make no sense at all.

The European Convention on the Suppression of Terrorism

The 1978 Act was passed for the purpose of enabling the United Kingdom to ratify the 1977 European Convention on the Suppression of Terrorism.[162] This Convention derived from a recommendation of the Council of Europe's Committee of Ministers in 1974. Alarmed by a spate of acts of international terrorism during the early 1970s, the Committee urged member states to take effective measures to ensure that such acts did not go unpunished, even if the perpetrators were found sheltering in a state other than the one in which the offence took place. In particular, it was urged that extradition arrangements between member states should no longer enable such criminals to rely on the political nature or motivation of their acts as a defence or bar to requests for their extradition.

---

[162] ETS No. 90 (1977); Cmnd. 7031.

The Convention and the 1978 Act are therefore each concerned primarily with rules relating to extradition. Article 1 of the Convention focuses for this purpose on acts that are usually committed for terrorist purposes (such as acts committed against the safety of civil aviation and attacks on internationally protected persons) and on acts involving kidnapping, hostage taking, or the use of bombs, parcel bombs, grenades, rockets, or automatic weapons—acts which often pose a 'collective danger' to human life, liberty, or safety and which are often associated with terrorism. It applies both to substantive offences and to attempts, and extends to secondary parties (those who 'participate as accomplices') as well as to principal offenders. It does not, however, attempt to define a terrorist offence, nor does it distinguish between a terrorist who takes a hostage or uses an automatic weapon and an ordinary bank robber who does so. It merely provides that, for the purposes of extradition between contracting states, such offences are not to be regarded as political offences, offences connected with political offences or offences inspired by political motives. Article 2(1) provides that a contracting state *may* choose not to regard as political or politically inspired any serious offence involving an act of violence against the life, physical integrity, or liberty of a person, even if that offence is not covered by Article 1; and Article 2(2) makes similar provision for crimes against property, if they involve 'a collective danger for persons'.[163]

This does not mean that an extradition request from another contracting state can never be refused, but only that it cannot be refused for any of the above reasons. Several states within the Council of Europe have constitutional rules that restrict their ability to extradite their own nationals, and other states (the United Kingdom included) may sometimes refuse an extradition request on the basis of concerns as to whether the fugitive will receive a fair trial in the state where the crime was committed. The right to refuse extradition in such cases is recognized in Article 5 of the Convention. Under Article 7, however, each contracting state is obliged to ensure that fugitives within their jurisdiction whose alleged offences fall within Article 1 are either extradited or referred 'without exception whatsoever and without undue delay to its competent authorities for the purposes of prosecution'. Such action would be futile if the requested state's 'competent authorities' lacked jurisdiction to prosecute the alleged offence; but Article 6 requires that:

Each contracting state shall take such measures as may be necessary to establish its jurisdiction over an offence mentioned in Article 1 in the case where the suspected offender is present within its territory and it does not extradite him after receiving a request for extradition from a contracting state whose jurisdiction is based on a rule of jurisdiction existing equally in the law of the requested state.

The highly unusual jurisdiction provisions in section 4 of the 1978 Act are designed to secure compliance with Article 6.

---

[163] These are not mandatory provisions, but they have been adopted in UK extradition law.

The Structure of the 1978 Act

Some statutes or statutory instruments implement treaty obligations within domestic law by including the text of the treaty within an appendix or schedule to the statute or instrument, and by declaring that this schedule is to have the force of law within the United Kingdom. The Suppression of Terrorism Act 1978 eschews that approach. Instead, it ploughs its own furrow, using different terminology and adopting a different structure to the Convention. This approach has inherent risks. While the Act attempts to ensure that the United Kingdom will always be able to discharge its minimum obligations under the Convention, and indeed goes further in some respects than the Convention demands, it seems likely that some lacunae exist, which may in certain (albeit unlikely) circumstances leave the United Kingdom in breach of its obligations.

In contrast to the Convention, the Act makes no attempt to limit its application by reference to the way in which offences are committed. Where Article 1 of the Convention refers to offences committed by means of automatic firearms, bombs, grenades, etc. (weapons typically associated with terrorism), the Act merely applies to specific offences, such as murder or manslaughter, without regard to the means by which such crimes are committed or to the motives of those involved. To that extent, its ambit is wider than the Convention requires. In respect of extradition to Convention countries, the Act takes full advantage of Article 2, and excludes from the scope of the 'political offence' exemption a wide range of offences involving harm, or the threat or risk of harm, to life, physical integrity, or liberty, not all of which are mandatory under Article 1. The relevant offences are listed in Schedule 1 to the Act, as amended. Our present concern, however, is with the ambit or jurisdiction provisions in section 4 of the Act.

Extraterritorial Jurisdiction under Section 4

Articles 6 and 7 of the Convention (the jurisdiction provisions) have no application to Article 2 offences, and this is reflected in section 4 of the 1978 Act, which applies only to a limited selection of the Schedule 1 offences. Indeed, section 4 does not even apply to all Article 1 offences, but the reason for this is that the omitted Article 1 offences already possess an adequate extraterritorial ambit by virtue of other legislation. Section 4(1)–(3) provide:

(1) If a person, whether a citizen of the United Kingdom and Colonies or not, does in a Convention country any act which, if he had done it in a part of the United Kingdom, would have made him guilty in that part of the United Kingdom of—

(a) an offence mentioned in paragraph 1, 2, 4, 5, 10, 11, 11B, 12, 13, 14 or 15 of Schedule 1 to this Act;[164] or

(b) an offence of attempting to commit any offence so mentioned,

---

[164] The relevant offences are: murder; manslaughter (or culpable homicide under Scots law); kidnapping (abduction or plagium under Scots law); false imprisonment; abduction offences under ss. 55 or 56 of the Offences Against the Person Act 1861, s. 20 of the Sexual Offences

he shall, in that part of the United Kingdom, be guilty of the offence or offences aforesaid of which the act would have made him guilty if he had done it there.

(2) [repealed]

(3) If a person who is a national of a Convention country but not a citizen of the United Kingdom and Colonies does outside the United Kingdom and that Convention country any act which makes him in that Convention country guilty of an offence and which, if he had been a citizen of the United Kingdom and Colonies, would have made him in any part of the United Kingdom guilty of an offence mentioned in paragraph 1, 2 or 13 of Schedule 1 to this Act,[165] he shall, in any part of the United Kingdom, be guilty of the offence or offences aforesaid of which the act would have made him guilty if he had been such a citizen.

In respect of ships and aircraft, these provisions are supplemented by section 4(7):

(7) For the purposes of this section any act done—

(a) on board a ship registered in a Convention country, being an act which, if the ship had been registered in the United Kingdom, would have constituted an offence within the jurisdiction of the Admiralty; or

(b) on board an aircraft registered in a Convention country while the aircraft is in flight elsewhere than in or over that country; or

(c) on board a hovercraft registered in a Convention country while the hovercraft is in journey elsewhere than in or over that country,

shall be treated as done in that Convention country; and subsection (4) of s. 92 of the Civil Aviation Act 1982 (definition of 'in flight' or, as applied to hovercraft, 'in journey') shall apply for the purposes of this subsection as it applies for the purposes of that section.

Section 4 seeks to ensure that should the United Kingdom for any reason refuse to extradite a fugitive to a Convention country in respect of any alleged offence falling within Article 1 of the Convention, it will at least be possible to try him for an equivalent offence under United Kingdom law, wherever this is required by Articles 6 and 7. The obligation of a requested state to refer such cases to its own prosecuting authorities arises, however, only where the original extradition request is based on a rule of jurisdiction that exists equally within its own law. In other words, the United Kingdom would be under no obligation to apply section 4 in a case where the requesting state relies on the nationality of the offender (rather than on territoriality) as the basis of its jurisdiction over him, unless the United Kingdom happens to assert a similar extraterritorial jurisdiction over its own nationals in respect of such an offence.

The offences to which Article 1 applies are all triable within some part of the United Kingdom if committed there, or if committed aboard a British

Act 1956, or s. 2 of the Child Abduction Act 1984; explosives offences under ss. 28–30 of the Offences Against the Person Act 1861, or ss. 2 or 3 of the Explosives Substances Act 1883; and firearms offences under ss. 16 or 17(1) of the Firearms Act 1968, or equivalent Northern Ireland legislation.

[165] These are murder, manslaughter, or culpable homicide and offences under ss. 2 or 3 of the Explosives Substances Act. In contrast to s. 4(1), criminal attempts are not included for the purposes of s. 4(3).

ship or aircraft, whether by a British citizen or by anyone else. If, therefore, a Convention country seeks the extradition of a fugitive in respect of an Article 1 offence allegedly committed within its own territory, or aboard one of its own ships or aircraft, it will be relying on a principle of jurisdiction that exists equally under English (or Scots, or Northern Irish) law. If it does not extradite him, the United Kingdom must therefore refer the case to its own prosecuting authorities without delay in accordance with Article 7, having first ensured that its courts have jurisdiction to try it. By giving Article 1 offences an extraterritorial ambit within all Convention countries (and aboard their ships or aircraft) section 4(1) and (7) thus seek to ensure that the United Kingdom is in a position to fulfil its obligations under that part of the Convention.

In contrast, only a minority of the offences to which Article 1 applies have any extraterritorial ambit under English law, other than by virtue of the 1978 Act itself. These currently include: murder; manslaughter;[166] offences under the Taking of Hostages Act 1982; offences under section 2 or 3 of the Explosive Substances Act 1883; offences under the Nuclear Material (Offences) Act 1983; offences under Part I of the Aviation Security Act 1982 (other than sections 4 and 7); offences under section 1 or Part II of the Aviation and Maritime Security Act 1990; attacks on diplomatic agents or other internationally protected persons (contrary to the Internationally Protected Persons Act 1978); attacks on UN personnel (contrary to the United Nations Personnel Act 1997); and (in very limited circumstances) offences under Part II of the Channel Tunnel (Security) Order 1994.

Most of these offences independently possess a 'universal' ambit under other United Kingdom legislation. No further jurisdiction provision in respect of them was therefore necessary in order to secure compliance with the Convention. The only Article 1 offences in respect of which further provision was considered necessary are those in which any separate extraterritorial ambit depends on the alleged offender possessing British or United Kingdom nationality, namely: murder; manslaughter/culpable homicide; and (in very limited circumstances) offences under sections 2 and 3 of the Explosive Substances Act 1883. These are accordingly the only offences to which section 4(3) of the 1978 Act applies.[167]

Convention Countries and other Designated Countries

The 1978 Act applies not only throughout the United Kingdom, but also to the Channel Islands,[168] the Isle of Man, and a number of British overseas

---

[166] Or, in Scots law, culpable homicide.

[167] The range of offences involved will greatly increase if and when the new ss. 63A and 63B are inserted into the Terrorism Act 2000 by the Crime (International Cooperation) Bill now before Parliament. This suggests that consequential amendments should be made to enlarge the scope of s. 4(3) of the 1978 Act, but no such amendments appear in the original version of the Bill. [168] SI 1978 Nos 1529–1531.

territories, such as Gibraltar, Bermuda, and the Falkland Islands;[169] but this does not affect the ambit of English criminal law or the jurisdiction of the English criminal courts under section 4, because cases arising following the arrest of a fugitive in Scotland or Bermuda will remain the sole concern of the Scottish or Bermudan courts. What matters as far as the ambit of English law is concerned is the number of states or jurisdictions that have been designated as 'Convention countries' by orders made under section 8(1) of the Act, together with any non-contracting states that have had the relevant provisions of the Act applied to them by orders made under section 5(1).

No fewer than 37 countries are currently designated under section 8(1).[170] Although a party to the Convention, the United Kingdom has not itself been designated as a Convention country, and is expressly distinguished from Convention countries within section 4 itself. As far as extradition issues are concerned, there would of course be no point in such designation; but jurisdiction issues may arise as between different parts of the United Kingdom, and it would be a mistake to suppose that the 1978 Act has any application to such cases.

Two additional countries have been designated by 'application of provisions' orders made under section 5(1). These are India[171] and the USA.[172] The order relating to India applies the whole Act to it, as if India were itself a Convention country, but the order relating to the USA deals only with extradition and does not extend to section 4 of the Act. This means that extradition proceedings between the United Kingdom and the USA cannot be resisted or frustrated in cases involving offences listed in Schedule 1 to the Act, merely because the fugitive claims to be a political or politically motivated offender, but no provision has been made to extend English criminal jurisdiction to offences committed in the USA or to offences committed by US citizens elsewhere in the world.

The Ambit of Section 4

Because the 1978 Act fails to distinguish between terrorist and non-terrorist offences, section 4 becomes applicable (in theory at least) to a potentially enormous range of non-terrorist scenarios. If, for example, a jealous husband in India stabs his wife in a quarrel and kills her, he thereby commits an

---

[169] SI 1985 No. 2019.
[170] See SI 1978 No. 1245 (designating Austria, Denmark, Germany, and Sweden); SI 1979 No. 497 (Cyprus); SI 1980 Nos 357 (Norway) and 1392 (Iceland); SI 1981 Nos 1389 (Spain and Turkey) and 1507 (Luxembourg); SI 1986 No. 271 (Belgium, The Netherlands, Portugal, and Switzerland); SI 1986 No. 1137 (Italy and Liechtenstein); SI 1987 No. 2137 (France); SI 1989 No. 2210 (Ireland); SI 1990 No. 1272 (Finland and Greece); SI 1994 No. 2978 (The Czech Republic and Slovakia); and SI 2003 No. 6 (Albania, Bulgaria, Estonia, Georgia, Hungary, Latvia, Lithuania, Malta, Moldova, Poland, Romania, The Russian Federation, San Marino, Slovenia, and Ukraine). [171] SI 1993 No. 2533.
[172] SI 1986 No. 2146.

offence of murder or manslaughter under English law,[173] by virtue of section 4(1), regardless of his nationality. This does not mean that he would be likely to face prosecution in England. Indeed, such a prosecution would be unlikely even if he were to flee from India and be arrested as a fugitive offender in England. Any prosecution in England and Wales under section 4 would require the consent of the Attorney-General,[174] and it seems unlikely that consent would be given in a case such as this, even if the fugitive's extradition to India were frustrated for some reason. This does not alter the remarkable fact that the homicide in question would indeed amount to an offence under English law.

Other examples of offences falling within section 4(1) might include the abduction of an unmarried girl in Portugal, a case of kidnapping or false imprisonment in Austria, firearms offences committed in Greece, or a case of attempted murder committed in Italy.[175] As previously explained, these may, but need not, have anything to do with terrorism.

Even in non-terrorist cases, the Attorney-General might sometimes be obliged to consent to the instigation of proceedings in England and Wales. This is because such cases may still fall within Article 1 of the Convention. Any case of kidnapping (for example) will do so, as will any offence involving the use of a bomb or an automatic firearm. If our jealous Indian husband were to kill his wife with such a weapon, it might therefore become necessary to prosecute him in England, should an extradition request from India be refused.

Even more remarkable jurisdictional oddities may (theoretically at least) arise under section 4(3) of the Act, in respect of homicides committed in countries that are not Convention countries. If, for example, a French citizen and an Israeli citizen take part in an illegal motor race on public roads in Serbia, and thereby cause a fatal accident, the former, but not the latter, may be guilty of manslaughter under English law, because France is a Convention country while Israel and Serbia are not. A British citizen committing such an act in Serbia could be tried for manslaughter under English law, by virtue of section 9 of the Offences Against the Person Act 1861. It follows that a French citizen would also be triable in England, by virtue of section 4(3) of the 1978 Act.

Explosives offences also fall within the scope of section 4(3); but this is of no practical significance, because the Explosive Substances Act 1883 has an extraterritorial ambit in respect of British citizens only in respect of crimes committed in the Republic of Ireland, and jurisdiction over citizens

---

[173] He also commits equivalent offences under the laws of Scotland and Northern Ireland.

[174] See s.(4).

[175] In *R v. Bow Street Metropolitan Stipendiary Magistrate, ex p Pinochet Ugarte (No. 3)* [2000] 1 AC 147, an allegation of attempted murder in Italy was held to fall outside the ambit of s. 4(1), but only because this allegation dated from a time prior to the passing of the 1978 Act. See *per* Lord Hope, at 234–5.

of Convention countries must similarly be limited under section 4(3). Ireland, however, is itself a Convention country, and any such offence committed on Irish territory must already fall within section 4(1) of the Act.

Consent to Prosecutions

In some cases, prosecutions brought under section 4 do not require the Attorney-General's consent. Section 4(4) requires such consent only in cases that would not amount to offences otherwise than under section 4 itself. If, therefore, a British citizen is accused of murder or manslaughter in Spain, an indictment might be laid by reference either to section 9 of the 1861 Act, or to section 4(1) of the 1978 Act, and in neither case would the Attorney General's consent be required.

Possible Lacunae under Section 4

There are dangers involved in any attempt to implement treaty obligations within national law by means of statutes that use wholly different language from the treaty itself. All too often, it will be discovered that the statute fails to comply in some respect; and so it is with section 4 of the 1978 Act. In most respects, section 4 deliberately exceeds the minimum demands of the Convention, but cases may nevertheless arise in which the United Kingdom would be unable to discharge its obligations under Articles 6 and 7 following the failure of an extradition request from a Convention country. The problem areas concern attempts to commit Article 1 offences. Assume, for example, that Cyprus (a Convention country) seeks to extradite a fugitive (D) from England. The basis of the extradition request is that whilst in Libya (which is not a Convention country), D attempted to commit a murder in Cyprus. His attempt failed at the outset, and no consequences of the failed attempt were ever felt within Cyprus itself. An attempt to commit an offence within England and Wales is now considered to be an offence under English law, even if the act of attempt is committed entirely abroad and produces no consequences here.[176] If the legal authorities in Cyprus regard the attempt committed in Libya as an offence within their own criminal jurisdiction, they would thus be relying upon a rule of jurisdiction that exists equally under English law. Such a case ought therefore to be triable as an offence under English law in accordance with Article 6 of the Convention.

Should extradition be denied for any reason, D's case would have to be referred to the Crown Prosecution Service in accordance with Article 7. But on what basis could the case be prosecuted? Section 4(1)(b) of the Act is the only provision that could conceivably be relevant, but this deals only with acts done 'in a Convention country'. It does not apply to acts done elsewhere, in an attempt to commit an offence within a Convention country.

---

[176] See *R v. Latif and Shahzad* [1996] 1 WLR 104.

If section 4(1)(b) cannot apply, the United Kingdom may find itself in breach of Articles 6 and 7.

The Internationally Protected Persons Act 1978

The Internationally Protected Persons Act 1978 gives effect to the 1973 UN Convention on the Prevention and Punishment of Crimes against Internationally Protected Persons,[177] to which the United Kingdom is a party. The Convention requires contracting states to deal effectively with persons who attack, abduct, imprison, or kill 'internationally protected persons', or who attack premises or vehicles ordinarily used by such persons. Such offenders must, if apprehended within a contracting state, be submitted to that state's prosecuting authorities or extradited to another state for trial there.

To comply with this obligation, it was first necessary for the requisite criminal jurisdiction to be established under United Kingdom law, and this was effected by sections 1 and 2 of the 1978 Act. Section 1(1) provides:

(1) If a person, whether a citizen of the United Kingdom and Colonies or not, does outside the United Kingdom—

(a) any act to or in relation to a protected person which, if he had done it in any part of the United Kingdom, would have made him guilty of the offence of murder, manslaughter, culpable homicide, rape, assault occasioning actual bodily harm or causing injury, kidnapping, abduction, false imprisonment or plagium or an offence under section 18, 20, 21, 22, 23, 24, 28, 29, 30 or 56 of the Offences against the Person Act 1861 or s. 2 of the Explosive Substances Act 1883; or

(b) in connection with an attack on any relevant premises or on any vehicle[178] ordinarily used by a protected person which is made when a protected person is on or in the premises or vehicle,[179] any act which, if he had done it in any part of the United Kingdom would have made him guilty of an offence under section 2 of the Explosive Substances Act 1883, section 1 of the Criminal Damage Act 1971 or Article 3 of the Criminal Damage (Northern Ireland) Order 1977 or the offence of wilful fire-raising, he shall in any part of the United Kingdom be guilty of the offences aforesaid of which the act would have made him guilty if he had done it there.

Section 1(2) and (3) impose a similar universal jurisdiction over acts of attempt, secondary participation, and threats to commit offences under subsection (1). Section 2 requires the consent of the Attorney-General before any prosecutions may be instituted in England and Wales.

---

[177] Cmnd. 6176.

[178] This includes any form of conveyance (s. 1(5)) and thus extends to aircraft and ships or boats.

[179] In respect of terrorist attacks (or threats of attacks) on UK diplomatic or consular vehicles or residences, the Crime (International Cooperation) Bill now before Parliament will insert a new s. 63D into the Terrorism Act 2000. This will enable jurisdiction to be taken over acts or threats of criminal damage, even where no diplomat or other protected person is in the vehicle or residence at the time.

'Protected persons' are defined by section 1(5) as:

(a) a person who at the time of the alleged offence is a Head of State, a member of a body which performs the functions of Head of State under the constitution of the State, a Head of Government or a Minister for Foreign Affairs and is outside the territory of the State in which he holds office;
(b) a person who at the time of the alleged offence is a representative or an official of a State or an official or agent of an international organisation of an intergovernmental character, is entitled under international law to special protection from attack on his person, freedom or dignity and does not fall within the preceding paragraph;
(c) a person who at the time of the alleged offence is a member of the family of another person mentioned in either of the preceding paragraphs and—
   (i) if the other person is mentioned in paragraph (a) above, is accompanying him,
   (ii) if the other person is mentioned in paragraph (b) above, is a member of his household.

While section 1 of the Act does not yet appear to have been invoked as the basis of jurisdiction in any reported case involving a prosecution under English law, it did fall to be considered by the House of Lords in *Re Al-Fawwaz and others*,[180] in which the US Government sought the extradition from the United Kingdom of three suspected Al-Qaeda terrorists on charges of conspiracy to murder American diplomats and other internationally protected persons, together with ordinary US citizens, in a series of attacks committed throughout the world.[181] The question that arose in that case was whether such conspiracies could be regarded as offences committed 'within the jurisdiction of the USA' for the purposes of Schedule 1 to the Extradition Act 1989 and of the 1976 Order in Council governing extradition arrangements with the USA.[182] It was held that the phrase 'within the jurisdiction of the USA' embraced both offences committed within the USA itself and offences committed within US extraterritorial jurisdiction, provided that the basis of this jurisdiction was matched by a corresponding jurisdiction under English law. Lord Millett said:

In political terms, what is alleged is a conspiracy entered into abroad to wage war on the United States by killing its citizens, including its diplomats and other internationally protected persons, at home and abroad. Translating this into legal terms and transposing it for the purpose of seeing whether such conduct would constitute a crime 'in England or within English jurisdiction', the charges must be considered as if they alleged a conspiracy entered into abroad to kill British subjects, including internationally protected persons, at home or abroad. Such a conspiracy would

---

[180] [2002] 1 All ER 545.
[181] The charges related in particular to attacks on US embassies in Nairobi and Dar es Salaam, in which many people had been killed.
[182] This is the United States of America (Extradition) Order 1976, SI 1976 No. 2144 (as amended by United States of America (Extradition) (Amendment) Order 1986 (SI 1986 No. 2020)), which incorporates the terms of the 1972 US/UK Extradition Treaty.

constitute a criminal offence within the extra-territorial jurisdiction of our courts.[183]

The Taking of Hostages Act 1982

The Taking of Hostages Act 1982 broadly follows the pattern set by earlier legislation in which universal criminal jurisdiction is asserted for the purpose of implementing the United Kingdom's treaty obligations: in this case the 1979 International Convention against the Taking of Hostages.[184] It differs from the earlier legislation, such as the Internationally Protected Persons Act 1978, by creating a specific new offence, namely, that of hostage taking, for which the maximum penalty is life imprisonment. Under section 1 of the 1982 Act:

(1) A person, whatever his nationality, who, in the United Kingdom or elsewhere,—
  (a) detains any other person ('the hostage'), and
  (b) in order to compel a State, international governmental organisation or person to do or abstain from doing any act, threatens to kill, injure or continue to detain the hostage,
commits an offence.

Although no prosecutions for this offence have been reported under English law, its existence enabled the West German Government to secure the extradition from England of Alan Rees in 1986, on a warrant alleging his involvement in the unlawful detention of a German citizen, Michael Wurche, the manager of Lufthansa operations in Bolivia, who was released only on payment of a ransom of US$1.5 million. Under German law, Rees might also have been tried for kidnapping, on the basis that his victim was a German citizen, but this was not acceptable as a basis for extradition under English law, because it was not one on which an English court could have asserted jurisdiction in comparable circumstances. The double-criminality test could be satisfied only by invoking the 1982 Act.[185]

The United Nations Personnel Act 1997

The United Nations Personnel Act 1997 implements the 1994 UN Convention on the Safety of United Nations and Associated Personnel,[186]

---

[183] [2002] 1 All ER 545, 577. Lord Millett concluded that there was, in any event, a conspiracy to commit murders on US territory, so that even if no internationally protected persons had been targeted, the conspiracy would have been triable on the basis of the principles laid down by Lord Griffiths in *Somchai Liangsiriprasert v. US Govt.* [1991] 1 AC 225, 250 (see above, pp. 155–6).	[184] UKTS 81 (1983); Cmnd. 9100.

[185] Subsequent proceedings before the House of Lords were reported as *Rees v. Secretary of State for the Home Office* [1986] AC 937, but the double-criminality issue was not discussed in those proceedings. See Stanbrook and Stanbrook, op. cit., fn 10, 123.

[186] See UN General Assembly Resolution 49/59 and Cm. 3363 (1994).

to which the United Kingdom is a party. The Convention prohibits attacks on UN personnel engaged in operations 'for the purpose of maintaining or restoring international peace and security' together with violent attacks upon the premises of any UN personnel, where such attacks are likely to endanger their safety, and requires contracting states to make any such attacks criminal offences under their national laws, although this protection does not extend to UN personnel engaged in enforcement operations under which such personnel are 'engaged as combatants against organised armed forces and to which the law of international armed conflict applies'. Section 1 of the Act 1997 provides:

(1) If a person does outside the United Kingdom any act to or in relation to a UN worker which, if he had done it in any part of the United Kingdom, would have made him guilty of any of the offences mentioned in subsection (2), he shall in that part of the United Kingdom be guilty of that offence

(2) The offences referred to in subsection (1) are—
   (a) murder, manslaughter, culpable homicide, rape, assault causing injury, kidnapping, abduction and false imprisonment;
   (b) an offence under section 18, 20, 21, 22, 23, 24, 28, 29, 30 or 47 of the Offences against the Person Act 1861; and
   (c) an offence under section 2 of the Explosive Substances Act 1883.

Section 2 of the 1997 Act gives extraterritorial effect to offences under section 2 of the Explosive Substances Act 1883 or section 1 of the Criminal Damage Act 1971 when committed in connection with attacks on premises or conveyances used or inhabited by UN workers and made when such workers are on or in such premises or vehicles. Section 3 creates a new universal offence of threatening to commit any of the above offences, if such threats are made in order to compel a person to do or abstain from doing any act.

By section 4, the term 'UN worker' is widely defined so as to include (*inter alia*) members of the military, police, or civilian component of UN operations, as well as UN employees, officials, experts, and persons deployed by humanitarian non-governmental organizations or agencies (such as Oxfam) by agreement with the UN Secretary-General, with a specialized agency, or with the International Atomic Energy Agency; but in accordance with the Convention, this definition excludes UN forces involved in armed enforcement operations against opposing military forces.

The scope of the 1997 Act, and its potential application to attacks on British peacekeeping forces abroad, was considered (*obiter*) by the House of Lords in *R v. Ministry of Defence, ex p Walker*.[187] The Act was not directly in issue in that case, because it involved an incident dating from 1995, when the applicant, an engineer in the British army, had been stationed in Bosnia as part of UNPROFOR, the UN peacekeeping force in that area. His regiment had been engaged in constructing a road and in helping to rebuild the

---

[187] [2000] 2 All ER 917.

economy of the area. The accommodation block in which they were based was shelled by a Serbian tank, and he suffered grave injuries, including the loss of his right leg.

The issue was whether the applicant was entitled to compensation under the Criminal Injuries Compensation (Overseas) Scheme. This Ministry of Defence scheme was designed to provide compensation similar to that payable to victims of violent crime in England and Wales, but was not applicable where the relevant act of violence was 'committed by an enemy where a state of war exists or a warlike situation is declared to exist'. There was no question but that soldiers attached to UNPROFOR qualified for protection under the 1994 UN Convention, but to succeed in his claim the applicant had to establish both that the attack was a 'criminal act' and that it was not 'committed by an enemy where a state of war exists or a warlike situation is declared to exist'. He succeeded on the first of these, but not on the second. It was held that the conduct of the unknown Serbian tank commander did indeed amount to a violation of the UN Convention, such as would now involve offences under sections 1 and 2 of the 1997 Act; but this did not prevent it from being 'warlike' conduct that fell outside the scope of the compensation scheme.

The ambit of the 1997 Act would not have been affected by the latter consideration. It is clear from *ex p Walker* that combatants who knowingly attack and kill UN peacekeeping forces that 'get in their way' will be guilty of murder under English law, on exactly the same basis as terrorists or as bandits who rob and kill UN aid workers for their money or provisions.

Terrorist Bombing and Explosives Offences

Section 62 of the Terrorism Act 2000 has been mentioned on a few occasions already, but it warrants independent consideration. Offences involving bombs or other explosive devices have long possessed an extra-territorial ambit under English law, but prior to the enactment and imple-mentation of section 62, this ambit was rarely universal. Universal jurisdiction was largely limited to crimes involving attacks on civil aviation, internationally protected persons, or UN personnel.

Section 62 of the 2000 Act possesses a universal ambit that appears, at first sight, to render the earlier extraterritorial provisions redundant in so far as explosives offences are concerned; but in contrast to those earlier pro-visions, section 62 is focused exclusively on acts committed 'for the pur-poses of terrorism'. It provides:

(1) If—
    (a) a person does anything outside the United Kingdom as an act of terrorism or for the purposes of terrorism, and
    (b) his action would have constituted the commission of one of the offences listed in subsection (2) if it had been done in the United Kingdom,
he shall be guilty of the offence.

(2) The offences referred to in subsection (1)(b) are—

(a) an offence under section 2, 3 or 5 of the Explosive Substances Act 1883 (causing explosions, etc.),

(b) an offence under section 1 of the Biological Weapons Act 1974 (biological weapons), and

(c) an offence under section 2 of the Chemical Weapons Act 1996 (chemical weapons).

Section 62 was enacted for the purpose of enabling the United Kingdom to ratify the 1998 UN Convention for the Suppression of Terrorist Bombings,[188] although in some respects it goes beyond what is strictly required under that Convention.[189] Section 62 is applicable to acts of terrorist bombing, wherever and by whomsoever committed, and whatever their targets.[190] It could thus extend (for example) to the bombing of a private residence, or to the attachment and detonation of a bomb under a car parked on a private driveway. In contrast, the Convention addresses only offences committed by means of explosives 'or other lethal devices' against 'a place of public use, a state or government facility, a public transportation system or an infrastructure facility'; and whereas section 62 gives universal effect to offences under the Explosive Substances Act 1883 that might involve nothing more than a risk of 'serious injury to property', the Convention addresses only acts or attempts[191] committed 'with intent to cause death or serious bodily injury, or with intent to cause extensive destruction... [which] results in or is likely to result in major economic loss'.

Terrorist Fundraising and Finance

Part III of the Terrorism Act 2000 creates offences of terrorist fundraising (section 15), using or possessing money for terrorist purposes (section 16), entering into or being concerned in terrorist funding arrangements (section 17), and 'money laundering' (section 18).[192] These offences are

---

[188] A/RES/52/164; Cm. 4662. This was ratified by the UK on 7 March 2001 but did not come into force until 23 May 2001.

[189] See Clive Walker, *Blackstone's Guide to the Anti-terrorism Legislation* (2002), 178.

[190] 'Terrorism' is defined in s. 1 of the Act. It must involve the use or threat of serious violence, endangerment of life, or serious damage to property; or actions that create a serious risk to the health or safety of the public or a section of the public in the UK or elsewhere, or actions that are designed seriously to interfere with or seriously to disrupt an electronic system. Such actions must be committed or threatened for the purpose of advancing a political, religious, or ideological cause, and must ordinarily be designed to influence any government or to intimidate the public or a section of the public of any country, although this last requirement is waived where the conduct in question involves the use or threatened use of firearms or explosives.

[191] Note that attempts and secondary participation in respect of offences under s. 2 of the 1883 Act are covered by ss. 3 and 5 of that Act, and thus fall within s. 62 of the 2000 Act.

[192] The term 'money laundering' is potentially misleading, because a s. 18 offence may in fact be committed by a person who enters into or becomes concerned in any arrangement which facilitates the retention or control, by or on behalf of another person, of terrorist property of any kind.

provided with a universal ambit by section 63 of the Act, which provides:

(1) If—
    (a) a person does anything outside the United Kingdom, and
    (b) his action would have constituted the commission of an offence under any of
sections 15 to 18 if it had been done in the United Kingdom,
he shall be guilty of the offence.

This has the remarkable effect of making it an offence under English law (and under the laws of Scotland and Northern Ireland) for US or Irish citizens to engage in IRA fund-raising activities within the USA, or for Egyptian nationals to launder Al-Qaeda property in Saudi Arabia. This sweeping universal jurisdiction is asserted by virtue of the 1999 UN Convention for the Suppression of the Financing of Terrorism,[193] although section 63 became law on 19 February 2001, before the Convention had come into force, and before it had even been ratified by the United Kingdom.

SEXUAL OFFENCES INVOLVING CHILDREN

The Sex Offenders Act 1997 extends the ambit of English (and other United Kingdom) criminal law in respect of a wide range sexual acts committed by British citizens or United Kingdom residents in countries outside the United Kingdom. Unusually, as far as recent extensions of criminal jurisdiction are concerned, this measure was not passed for the purpose of giving effect to obligations under any international Convention, but was instead a response to demands made by British MPs and by national and international pressure groups,[194] who were outraged by the sexual abuse of children by British citizens and others in third world countries, such as Thailand and The Philippines. One point repeatedly made by the pressure groups was that many other countries had already taken measures to extend their criminal jurisdiction over such conduct when committed by their own nationals abroad. New legislation had been enacted in some countries, such as Australia, and much attention had been focused on the trial and conviction in Sweden of Bengt Bolin, a Swedish citizen who had been exposed as the abuser of a 13-year-old boy in Thailand.[195] Sweden tried Bolin under its own law because of its refusal to extradite Swedish nationals to non-Nordic countries, and much of the evidence relied upon under Swedish law might well have been excluded in an English trial, but this did little to abate the demands for similar prosecutions to be made possible under English law.

As explained at p. 140 above, the Government initially declined to enact extraterritorial legislation in this area, insisting that such legislation would

---

[193] A/RES/54/109; Cm. 4663. See Walker, op. cit., fn 189, 180.
[194] Notably ECPAT (End Child Prostitution in Asian Tourism), the World Congress Against Commercial Sexual Exploitation of Children, and the UK Coalition on Child Prostitution and Tourism.
[195] See *Review of Extraterritorial Jurisdiction* (Home Office, 1996), Annex D.

in practice be unworkable and would amount to nothing more than an empty political gesture. Responsibility for sexual misconduct in foreign countries must remain, said the Government, in the hands of the foreign countries concerned. The Government did, however, support a private member's Bill, which eventually became the Sexual Offences (Conspiracy and Incitement) Act 1996. This made it an offence to conspire or incite,[196] by means of anything done in England and Wales, the commission of specified sexual acts abroad—acts that are not offences under English law but would be offences if committed within England and Wales. The idea was to strike at the British-based organizers of child-sex tourism, whose acts would be more easily prosecuted on the basis of evidence obtainable in the United Kingdom itself.[197] Shortly after the enactment of this legislation, however, the Government received the Report of an Interdepartmental Steering Committee, which had been established under the chairmanship of the Home Office to review the United Kingdom's policy on extraterritorial criminal jurisdiction. The wider findings and recommendations of the Steering Committee are examined in Chapter 7 below. For present purposes, it may be noted that while the Committee strongly agreed with the Government's opposition to the enactment of unenforceable legislation, and consequently saw little merit in any widespread or generalized extension of extraterritorial jurisdiction under English criminal law, it accepted that consideration should be given to extending the ambit of specific offences, where policy considerations appear to justify such a measure. The Committee did not identify any universal test for this purpose, but suggested that one at least of the following tests would have to be satisfied before consideration could be given to any new extensions of English law[198]:

(1) the offence is serious;
(2) by virtue of the nature of the offence, witnesses and evidence are likely to be available within the United Kingdom;
(3) there is international consensus as to the reprehensible nature of the crime and the need to take extraterritorial jurisdiction;
(4) the vulnerability of the victim makes it particularly important that offences are prosecuted;
(5) it is in the interests of the standing and reputation of the United Kingdom within the international community; and
(6) there is a danger that such offences would not otherwise be justiciable.

---

[196] The 1996 Act remains in force in respect of incitement, but its conspiracy provisions have now been supplanted by the wider-ranging jurisdiction contained in s. 1A of the Criminal Law Act 1977, as inserted by s. 5 of the Criminal Justice (Terrorism and Conspiracy) Act 1998.
[197] There do not, however, appear to have been any reported prosecutions under this legislation. [198] *Review of Extraterritorial Jurisdiction*, para. 2.21.

Offences committed against children by British sex tourists clearly satisfy many of these tests. Following publication of the Committee's Report, the Government accordingly relaxed its earlier objections, and major reforms were included in the Sex Offenders Act 1997, section 7 of which provides:

(1) Subject to subsection (2) below, any act done by a person in a country or territory outside the United Kingdom which—

    (a) constituted an offence under the law in force in that country or territory; and

    (b) would constitute a sexual offence to which this section applies if it had been done in England and Wales, or in Northern Ireland,

shall constitute that sexual offence under the law of that part of the United Kingdom.

(2) No proceedings shall by virtue of this section be brought against any person unless he was at the commencement of this section, or has subsequently become, a British citizen or resident in the United Kingdom.

(3) An act punishable under the law in force in any country or territory constitutes an offence under that law for the purposes of this section, however it is described in that law.

(4) Subject to subsection (5) below, the condition in subsection (1)(a) above shall be taken to be satisfied unless, not later than rules of court may provide, the defence serve on the prosecution a notice—

    (a) stating that, on the facts as alleged with respect to the act in question, the condition is not in their opinion satisfied;

    (b) showing their grounds for that opinion; and

    (c) requiring the prosecution to show that it is satisfied.

(5) The court, if it thinks fit, may permit the defence to require the prosecution to show that the condition is satisfied without the prior service of a notice under subsection (4) above.

(6) In the Crown Court the question whether the condition is satisfied is to be decided by the judge alone.

Schedule 2 to the Act lists the sexual offences to which section 7 applies. These are not by any means confined to sex-tourism offences but (with one exception) are restricted either by para. 2(2) of Schedule 2 or by their own terms, so as to exclude offences committed against victims who are aged 16 or above. The listed offences are: rape; unlawful intercourse with a girl under 13; or with a girl aged between 13 and 16; buggery and assault with intent to commit buggery; indecent assault on a boy or girl; indecent conduct (or gross indecency) towards a child; and offences under section 1 of the Protection of Children Act 1978 (that is, offences involving the taking, making, distribution, etc., of indecent photographs or pseudo-photographs of children). Offences under the 1978 Act need not in fact involve any child victim, because it may apply to cases involving pseudo-photographs,[199] in which

---

[199] A 'pseudo-photograph' is defined in that Act as an image, whether made by computer graphics or otherwise, which appears to be a photograph.

(for example) photographs showing adults engaged in sexual acts are digitally manipulated so as to suggest that one or more of the parties is a child.

Despite the Government's original scepticism as to the possible effectiveness of such legislation, there have already been at least two prosecutions under section 7 of the 1997 Act. Each resulted in conviction, but one conviction has since been quashed on the basis that the Act was not in force when the alleged offence was committed.[200] This was not in any event a typical sex-tourism case involving local child prostitutes, but a case involving the alleged rape of a 15-year-old girl by her mother's boyfriend, during a family holiday in Barbados. But for the date, however, it would indeed have fallen within the ambit of s. 7. In the second case,[201] the defendant pleaded guilty to four counts of unlawful intercourse with girls under the age of 13 and to 10 counts of making indecent photographs of children. He was sentenced to a total of eight years' imprisonment. The offences were committed in Cambodia and came to light when the defendant's wife found the photographs on his computer.

The effectiveness of this legislation cannot in any case be judged by the number of prosecutions. The real test is whether it has a significant impact on the British paedophile sex-tourism industry. Sex tourism, in the years before its criminalization, was a carefully planned activity, involving acts of abuse that were premeditated, rather than impulsive or opportunistic. British paedophiles contemplating trips abroad may now be aware that they will remain liable to prosecution under English law, and some may be discouraged or dissuaded by this. If only a few are dissuaded in this way, the legislation will have achieved something, to say nothing of the relevance of such legislation to the international image of the United Kingdom, which might otherwise have been seen as condoning such behaviour.

On the other hand, more might be achieved by the enactment of legislation that would enable (or even require) courts to impose travel restriction orders on convicted sex offenders. Such powers already exist in respect of convicted drug trafficking offenders, under section 33 of the Criminal Justice and Police Act 2001. Indeed, a court sentencing a drug trafficker to imprisonment for a term of four years or more is now under a duty to consider whether such an order might be appropriate, and is required to state its reasons should it decide *not* to impose one.[202] Pressure groups led by ECPAT have called for similar controls to be imposed on sex offenders,[203] but no such legislation has yet been enacted.

---

[200] See *R* v. *Rooney* [2001] All ER (D) 299 (Dec).

[201] *R* v. *Towner* (2001) unreported, 18 June (Crown Court at Maidstone).

[202] See s. 33(2)(c). Such an order may involve a direction under which the offender must surrender any UK passport held by him (s. 33(4)).

[203] See *The Guardian*, 28 July 1999.

Perjury and Related Offences

Offences under the Perjury Act 1911 do not, for most purposes, have any extraterritorial ambit. Section 8 of Act may at first appear to provide one. It states:

Where an offence against this Act or any offence punishable as perjury or as subornation of perjury under any other Act of Parliament is committed in any place either on sea or land outside the United Kingdom, the offender may be proceeded against, indicted, tried, and punished . . . in England.

As the marginal heading suggests, however, this is merely a venue provision, and is now obsolete.[204] The normal ambit of offences of perjury under section 1 of the Act is governed by sections 1(4) and (5), and those provisions would not have been necessary if section 8 gave an extraterritorial ambit to all offences under the Act.

A number of cross-frontier issues may arise in connection with perjury and related offences not only under section 1(4) or (5), but also where, for example, evidence is given in English proceedings via a video link, or by means of a written statement, by a witness who is abroad; but only two types of perjury appear to have a true extraterritorial ambit under English law, and neither arises under the 1911 Act itself. By section 11(1)(a) of the European Communities Act 1972, all relevant provisions of the Perjury Act 1911 are now applicable to statements made on oath before the European Court of Justice, or any court attached thereto, whether or not the person responsible is a British citizen;[205] and by section 54(1) of the International Criminal Court Act 2001:

A person intentionally committing any of the acts mentioned in Article 70.1 (offences against the administration of justice in relation to the ICC) may be dealt with as for the corresponding domestic offence committed in relation to a superior court in England and Wales.

Article 70(1) of the ICC Statute is set out in Schedule 9 to the Act. Section 54(3) identifies the corresponding English offences as perjury, witness interference or intimidation, contrary to section 51 of the Criminal Justice and Public Order Act 1994, and offences involving bribery or acts tending to pervert the course of justice, contrary to common law. If not committed in England and Wales, such offences are triable under English law only if committed outside the United Kingdom by a United Kingdom national, a United Kingdom resident, or a person subject to UK service jurisdiction.[206]

---

[204] Venue is no longer a problem for indictable offences (such as those under the 1911 Act).
[205] See also the Evidence (European Court) Order 1976 (SI 1976 No. 428).
[206] Section 54(4).

OFFENCES INVOLVING CORRUPTION

The International Background

Corruption, particularly the corruption of Government officials, has long been a scourge of international business transactions. Not only is it a problem for those who wish to do business in countries where corruption is widespread, and a particularly grave handicap for those who wish to compete honestly for contracts in which other parties may be prepared to offer bribes; but in addition it may seriously inhibit foreign investment and economic growth or development within third world countries in which corruption is perceived to be a major problem.[207]

Until recently, English law did not penalize acts of bribery or corruption committed by British nationals or corporations abroad, nor did it penalize the corruption of foreign Government officials; but the UK has become a party to a number of Conventions concerning corruption, which have prompted the enactment of legislation providing a wider ambit for existing corruption offences. These Conventions include the Convention on the Fight against Corruption involving Officials of the European Communities or Officials of Member States of the European Union; the Council of Europe Criminal Law Corruption Convention; the Corruption Protocol to the EU Fraud Convention; and the OECD[208] Convention on Combating Bribery of Foreign Public Officials in International Business Transactions.[209] The UK is also an active member of the Group of States against Corruption (GRECO) which monitors the implementation of the Council of Europe Convention.

The English Legislation

Bribery involving the holder of a public office still exists as a common law offence,[210] but has long been supplemented by statutory offences of corruption, which were created by section 1 of the Public Bodies Corrupt Practices Act 1889 and section 1 of the Prevention of Corruption Act 1906. In many respects, the law remains outdated, unclear, and unsatisfactory. Major reforms have been proposed by the Law Commission,[211] and in a later White Paper[212] the Government accepted the need for implementation of these proposals if and when the requisite Parliamentary time can be found.[213] Thus far, however, the only reforms actually implemented are

---

[207] V. Tanzi and H. Davaodi, 'Corruption, Public Investment and Growth' (1997) *IMF Working Paper* 97/139.

[208] The Organization for Economic Cooperation and Development.

[209] See Bantekas, Nash, and Mackerel, op. cit., fn 117, 269–73.

[210] *R v. Whitaker* [1914] 3 KB 1283.   [211] Law Com. No. 248 (1998).

[212] *Raising Standards and Upholding Integrity*, Cm. 4759, June 2000.

[213] Ibid. At the time of writing, a new Corruption Bill has been promised, and this will incorporate the extraterritorial elements introduced by the 2001 Act.

those concerning the jurisdictional ambit of the offences. These were effected by sections 108–110 of the Anti-terrorism, Crime and Security Act 2001, and came into force on 14 February 2002. The thinking behind them is set out in the White Paper[214]:

This could send a strong deterrent message that the UK is determined to act against corruption wherever it occurs. This is a message which would have real persuasive and dissuasive force and which would back up existing codes of conduct. It must not be forgotten that corruption is a major problem in developing and transitional countries, a problem which diverts scarce resources away from development and the eradication of poverty. Combating corruption should be an essential component of the efforts invested in the eradication of poverty and the relief of debt.

The Government has therefore considered the issue in considerable detail and, whilst recognising the practical problems associated with the prosecution of extra-territorial offences, believes that the balance of advantage rests with assuming juris-diction over its nationals for offences of corruption committed abroad. Such an assumption of jurisdiction would put beyond doubt the UK's commitment to join forces with the international community in the fight against corruption.

Section 108 of the 2001 Act amends existing offences so as to make these more widely applicable. It extends the common law offence so as to include the bribery of persons holding public office outside the UK. It amends the statutory offences so as to include the corruption of members, officers, or servants of foreign public bodies (under the 1889 Act) and the corruption of agents (under the 1906 Act). With regard to the latter, section 108 added a new subsection (4) to section 1 of the 1906 Act. This provides:

For the purposes of this Act it is immaterial if—

(a) the principal's affairs or business have no connection with the United Kingdom and are conducted in a country or territory outside the United Kingdom;

(b) the agent's functions have no connection with the United Kingdom and are carried out in a country or territory outside the United Kingdom.

Section 108 does not, in itself, create any extraterritorial liability; but it paves the way for section 109, which does. Section 109 provides:

(1) This section applies if—

(a) a national of the United Kingdom or a body incorporated under the law of any part of the United Kingdom does anything in a country or territory outside the United Kingdom, and

(b) the act would, if done in the United Kingdom, constitute a corruption offence (as defined below).[215]

(2) In such a case—

(a) the act constitutes the offence concerned, and

(b) proceedings for the offence may be taken in the United Kingdom.

---

[214] Cm. 4759, Ch. 2.

[215] Defined in subs. (3) as: (a) bribery at common law; (b) offences under the Public Bodies Corrupt Practices Act 1889, s. 1; and (c) bribes obtained by or given to agents contrary to the Prevention of Corruption Act 1906, s. 1.

There is no 'double criminality' requirement of the kind so often found in such provisions. It is therefore irrelevant whether an alleged act of bribery, etc., committed by a United Kingdom national in Ruritania would have amounted to a crime under Ruritanian law.

Section 109 applies to the acts of bodies incorporated in the United Kingdom, but not to the acts of subsidiary companies incorporated abroad. Given that many British companies do business abroad by means of their locally incorporated (and often locally staffed) subsidiaries, this imposes a major, if unavoidable, limitation on the ambit of the new law.

Lastly, neither section has any application to things done in Scotland. If D, a British citizen in London, bribes or attempts to corrupt E, in Glasgow, no offence is committed under English law unless it can be established that the offence was committed in England. But if D were to bribe F, in Ruritania, jurisdiction would not be a problem!

Restriction of the Presumption of Corruption

The notorious 'presumption of corruption' (which is imposed in some cases by the Prevention of Corruption Act 1916) is scheduled for abolition when the law of corruption eventually receives the fundamental overhaul promised by the Government. For the time being, however, it continues in force, albeit (most probably) in the form of a mere evidential burden on the defence.[216] Section 110 of the 2001 Act restricts the operation of the presumption to those cases where it applied before. It does not therefore apply to extraterritorial offences governed by sections 108 and 109.

Cross-frontier Issues

The problem of cross-frontier corruption is not addressed in the 2001 Act. What, then, of a bribe offered by D in England (by letter, e-mail, or telephone) to E in France or Scotland? Section 108 says nothing about this, which is surprising given that (according to the explanatory notes to the Act) it was intended to give effect to the proposals in the Law Commission's Report, which called for legislation drafted along the lines of Part I of the Criminal Justice Act 1993: legislation that would 'put beyond doubt the United Kingdom's ability to prosecute offences that do not occur wholly within the . . . jurisdiction'.

One might perhaps suppose that this would not be a problem in practice, because section 109 makes the relevant offences applicable to corruption committed abroad; but section 109 provides a solution to the cross-frontier problem only if and when the alleged offender is subject to that extraterritorial jurisdiction. If he is not a United Kingdom national or corporation, he will not be subject to it; nor, as previously noted, does the Act give English courts jurisdiction over acts of corruption in Scotland.

---

[216] See *R* v. *Lambert* [2002] 2 AC 545.

Foreign Enlistment

The Foreign Enlistment Act 1870 is described in its long title as 'an Act to regulate the conduct of Her Majesty's subjects during the existence of hostilities between foreign states with which Her Majesty is at peace'.[217] It attempts to prevent 'British subjects' from becoming involved in such wars, whether as mercenaries or as idealist volunteers, and creates a number of criminal offences to that end. Most of these offences are capable of commission only 'within Her Majesty's dominions', but by section 16:

Any offence against this Act shall, for all purposes of and incidental to the trial and punishment of any person guilty of any such offence, be deemed to have been committed either in the place in which the offence was wholly or partly committed, or in any place within Her Majesty's dominions in which the person who committed such offence may be.

This is primarily a procedural provision, concerning the trial of offences rather than the ambit of the legislation itself, but it does appear to extend the ambit of English law in one respect. Ordinarily, an offence committed (say) in Scotland or the Falkland Islands would be triable only in Scotland or the Falkland Islands, but section 16 enables it to be tried in another jurisdiction (such as England and Wales) if that is where the alleged offender is to be found. This might be useful where, for example, a series of offences have been committed in various parts of the United Kingdom or in various overseas territories.

Of the offences created under the Act (many of which now have a distinctly archaic character) only one appears to possess a 'full' extraterritorial ambit: namely, that created by section 4, which provides:

If any person, without the license of Her Majesty, being a British subject, within or without Her Majesty's dominions, accepts or agrees to accept any commission or engagement in the military or naval service of any foreign state at war with any foreign state at peace with Her Majesty, and in this Act referred to as a friendly state, or whether a British subject or not within Her Majesty's dominions, induces any other person to accept or agree to accept any commission or engagement in the military or naval service of any such foreign state as aforesaid, he shall be guilty of an offence against this Act . . . .

This is not the place to comment in detail on the limitations which restrict the practical utility of section 4; but it must be noted that it fails to prohibit enlistment in civil wars or in wars involving Commonwealth countries, or indeed in any other conflicts that do not involve a state of war between two

---

[217] As to the workings of this Act, see generally the Diplock Report on the recruitment of British mercenaries in overseas conflicts (Cmnd. 6569 (1976)).

or more *foreign* powers. It thus fails to apply to the principal types of armed conflict in which British citizens are most likely to become involved.[218]

For the purpose of identifying potential offenders, the reference to 'British subjects' in section 4 must now be read in conjunction with section 3(1) of the British Nationality Act 1948 and section 51 of the British Nationality Act 1981. As explained above, this prevents citizens of independent Commonwealth countries from incurring liability in respect of things done or omitted outside the United Kingdom, but has no such application in respect of things done or omitted within the United Kingdom itself. It follows that an Australian mercenary who visits Scotland, and there enlists for service in a foreign war, may by so enlisting commit an offence under English (as well as Scots) law. If, in contrast, he were to enlist somewhere abroad, he would commit no offence under any provision of the Act; but this is all somewhat theoretical, given the inapplicability of the Act to the majority of wars in which any such mercenary or volunteer is likely to enlist.[219]

ENVIRONMENTAL PROTECTION

Protection of Flora and Fauna

Some extraterritorial offences merit only the briefest of mentions. Into this category fall the outdated provisions of the Seal Fisheries (North Pacific) Act 1895 and the Behring Sea Award Act 1894, which give effect to an arbitration between the United Kingdom and the USA and are designed to regulate and in some circumstances prohibit the killing of fur seals in the waters concerned. A flavour of this legislation may be gleaned from the stipulation that 'during the period of time and in the waters in which the fur-seal fishing is allowed, only sailing vessels shall be permitted to carry on or take part in fur-seal fishing operations'.[220] Nevertheless, this legislation remains in force.

---

[218] Notable examples being the Spanish Civil War (volunteers) and more recently the Angolan Civil War (which was the subject of the Diplock Report into the Recruitment of Mercenaries (Cmnd. 6569, 1976). The Diplock Committee observed that 'during the 106 years that it has been upon the statute book there has never been a prosecution, let alone a conviction . . . for an offence in connection with illegal enlistment or recruitment'. That period has since extended for a further 26 years. Other offences under the Act have resulted in prosecutions. See, e.g., *R v. Jameson* [1896] 2 QB 425.

[219] An alternative way of dealing with the embarrassing activities of British mercenaries has been suggested by A.C.E. Lynch, 'British Subjects' Involvement in Foreign Military Clashes' [1978] Criminal Law Review 257. Lynch argues that British citizens, etc., who kill in the course of foreign military enlistment may be guilty of murder by virtue of the Offences Against the Person Act 1861, s. 9. This may be arguable in theory (but see, contra, Brigadier Sir David Hughes-Morgan, [1978] Criminal Law Review 508). In practice it would surely be most unlikely that such a prosecution would ever be launched, or that if launched it could ever succeed before a jury. The position might be different should some kind of war crime or crime against humanity be alleged, but that would be another matter.

[220] Behring Sea Award Act 1894, Sch. 1.

A more modern and relevant provision is section 7 of the Antarctic Act 1994, by which:

(1) No United Kingdom national may in Antarctica—

(a) intentionally kill, injure, capture, handle or molest any native mammal or native bird,

(b) while on foot intentionally disturb a breeding or moulting native bird, or a concentration of native mammals or native birds,

(c) use a vehicle, vessel or aircraft in a manner that disturbs a concentration of native mammals or native birds,

(d) use explosives or firearms in such a manner,

(e) remove or damage such quantities of any native plant that its local distribution or abundance will be significantly affected,

(f) significantly damage a concentration of native plants, or

(g) do anything that is likely to cause significant damage to the habitat of any native mammal, bird, plant or invertebrate,

except in accordance with a permit granted under section 12 or under the written authorisation of another Contracting Party.

The ambit of this provision extends to the whole of Antarctica (in accordance with the 1980 Convention on the Conservation of Antarctic Marine Living Resources) and not merely to the unclaimed sector to which section 21 of the Act applies; and it applies to any United Kingdom national, not merely to scientists and observers to whom sections 23 and 24 apply.

Offences Under the Outer Space Act 1986

Outer space is by no means a lawless frontier. As in Antarctica, activities there are in fact quite closely regulated. In accordance with Article 6 of the 1967 Outer Space Treaty,[221] the Outer Space Act 1986 seeks to ensure that the orderly utilization or exploration of outer space is not prejudiced by the activities of United Kingdom nationals or United Kingdom corporations, anywhere in the world. Such persons must obtain a licence from the Secretary of State before engaging in any activities in outer space, or before launching or operating a 'space object'.[222] This does not apply to persons who act as employees or agents of another. A United Kingdom national requires no licence under the Act if he merely works for NASA.

Offences are governed by section 12 of the Act. These include unlicensed activities and the provision of false information in order to obtain a licence. By section 12(4):

Proceedings for an offence committed outside the United Kingdom may be taken, and the offence may for incidental purposes be treated as having been committed, in any place in the United Kingdom.

---

[221] UKTS 10 (1968); Cmnd. 3519.

[222] By Art. 6 of the Treaty: 'The activities of non-governmental entities in outer space .... shall require authorisation and continued supervision by the appropriate State Party to the Treaty.'

The Act generally has no extraterritorial application to persons other than United Kingdom nationals or corporations, but by section 12(6):

A person other than a person to whom this Act applies is not guilty of an offence under this Act in respect of things done by him outside the United Kingdom, except—
    (a) an offence of aiding, abetting, counselling or procuring, conspiracy or incitement in relation to the commission of an offence under this Act in the United Kingdom; or
    (b) an offence under subsection (3) (liability of directors, officers, &c) in connection with an offence committed by a body corporate which is a person to whom this Act applies.

Unlicensed Deep Sea Mining

In much the same way as the Outer Space Act 1986 prohibits unlicensed activities in space, the Deep Sea Mining (Temporary Provisions) Act 1981 prohibits unlicensed deep sea mining by United Kingdom nationals, United Kingdom corporations, or Scottish firms who are resident in the United Kingdom. By section 1(1) and (2), no such person may explore for or exploit the hard mineral resources of any part of the deep sea bed unless he holds an appropriate licence granted under section 2, or is acting in his capacity as the agent or employee of the holder of such a licence. Breach of the above rules is an offence under section 1(3).

Offences Involving Anti-personnel Mines

By section 2(1) of the Landmines Act 1998, which gives effect to the 1997 Ottawa Convention on Anti-Personnel Mines, it is an offence (subject to certain exceptions) to use, develop, or produce anti-personnel mines, or to possess or participate in the acquisition or transfer of such a mine or of any component thereof. By section 2(2), it is an offence to assist, encourage, or induce any other person to engage in any such conduct. The extraterritorial ambit of these offences is governed by section 3, which provides:

(1) Section 2(1) applies to conduct in the United Kingdom or elsewhere.
(2) Section 2(2) applies to assistance, encouragement and inducements in the United Kingdom or elsewhere, and it so applies irrespective of whether the conduct assisted, encouraged or induced takes place, or (if it takes place) will take place, in the United Kingdom or elsewhere.
(3) Subsections (1) and (2) of s. 2, so far as they apply respectively to—
    (a) conduct outside the United Kingdom, and
    (b) assistance, encouragement and inducements outside the United Kingdom,
impose prohibitions only on United Kingdom nationals, Scottish partnerships and bodies incorporated under the law of a part of the United Kingdom.

Protection of Military Remains

The Protection of Military Remains Act 1986 imposes restrictions on diving or salvage operations and excavations involving aircraft that have crashed, or designated vessels or ships that have been lost, whilst in 'military service',[223] either within United Kingdom or international waters.[224] Aircraft are automatically classified as 'Protected Places', but vessels must be designated. Within a 'Protected Place' any operation involving the unearthing, removal, or salvage, etc., of remains, or entry within a wreck, etc., requires a licence from the Secretary of State. Alternatively, sites may be designated as 'Controlled Sites', within which these actions are also prohibited,[225] as well as any unlicensed diving or salvage operations for the purpose of investigating or recording any remains.[226] To date, only a small number of shipwrecks (not all of them British) have been designated.[227] The Act applies to international waters by virtue of section 3,[228] but if not committed aboard a British-controlled ship (which may be a United Kingdom ship or a vessel exempt from registration under the Merchant Shipping Act 1995) offences are capable of commission only by British (or British overseas, etc.) citizens or by United Kingdom companies.

INCHOATE OFFENCES

The majority of statutes that create extraterritorial offences say nothing about inchoate versions of such offences. Thus, while section 9 of the Offences Against the Person Act 1861 applies to murder or manslaughter committed by British citizens, etc., on land abroad, it makes no express provision as to conspiracy to murder or attempted murder abroad. The obvious implication, one might think, is that the extraterritorial jurisdiction thereby created has no application to inchoate offences. There are a few exceptions. Section 4(1) of the Suppression of Terrorism Act 1978, for example, makes express provision for extraterritorial attempts. Section 4(3), however, makes none; and neither provision refers to cases of

---

[223] As defined in s. 9(2) of the Act.

[224] See Michael Williams, 'War Graves and Salvage: Murky Waters?' (2000) 7(5) *International Maritime Law* 151; and 'Protecting Military Remains: A New Policy for the United Kingdom' (2001) 8(9) *International Maritime Law* 288.

[225] Section 2(1)(a) and (2).   [226] Section 2(3)(a).

[227] See the Protection of Military Remains Act 1986 (Designation of Vessels and Controlled Sites) Order 2002 (SI 2002 No. 1761).

[228] The only wrecks in international waters currently designated are those of *HMS Hood*, sunk in the Denmark Strait in May 1941; *HMS Gloucester*, sunk off Crete in May 1941; *HMS Prince of Wales* and *HMS Repulse*, sunk together off Malaya in December 1941; and *RFA Sir Galahad*, scuttled at sea following damage inflicted during the Falklands War in June 1982. See SI 2002 No. 1761, above.

conspiracy or incitement. Again, the obvious inference is that section 4(1) creates a narrow and limited exception, and that conspiracies are not covered at all.

In the *Pinochet* case,[229] however, the House of Lords appears to have reached a quite different conclusion. It was held that where torture committed abroad was an extraterritorial offence under English law, jurisdiction should equally exist over conspiracy to torture, on the basis of principles established by the Privy Council in *Somchai Liangsiriprasert v. US Government*.[230] Lord Hope said:

> I consider that the common law of England would, applying the rule laid down in *Liangsiriprasert v. US Government*, also regard as justiciable in England a conspiracy to commit an offence anywhere which was triable here as an extra-territorial offence in pursuance of an international Convention, even although no act was done here in furtherance of the conspiracy. I do not think that this would be an unreasonable extension of the rule. It seems to me that on grounds of comity it would make good sense for the rule to be extended in this way in order to promote the aims of the Convention.[231]

If, in other words, a substantive offence has extraterritorial effect by virtue of a provision that is intended to implement a Convention, a conspiracy (or presumably an attempt or incitement) to commit that offence must have a similar extraterritorial effect.

This seems, with respect, to be revolutionary doctrine, and a substantial extension of the much more limited territorial (or cross-frontier) principle laid down in *Liangsiriprasert*. Were it a mere *obiter dictum* or an individual opinion it might have been doubted, but it was clearly more than that, and must accordingly be accepted. Would a similar rule apply to inchoate versions of extraterritorial offences that are not Convention-based? It is difficult to see any good reason why it should not, but Lord Hope appears to have left this issue unresolved.

---

[229] *R. v. Bow Street Metropolitan Stipendiary Magistrate, ex p Pinochet Ugarte (No. 3)* [2000] 1 AC 147. [230] [1991] 1 AC 225.
[231] Ibid., 237–8. A majority of the Appellate Committee agree with Lord Hope's analysis on this issue.

6

Maritime and Aviation Offences

INTRODUCTION

Chapter 3 of this work considered certain issues relating to maritime and aviation offences, namely, the extent to which English criminal law applies in English or Welsh ports and harbours, and within or above the adjacent territorial or internal waters. In contrast, this chapter is concerned with extraterritorial issues. Its primary focus is on things done on or in the sea, or in the air, beyond the territorial limits; but it also addresses offences committed abroad by seamen from United Kingdom ships, together with extraterritorial offences relating to airports and aviation security.

The extent to which English law applies to ships or aircraft beyond the territorial limits varies significantly, even in respect of British ships or aircraft. Distinctions may need to be drawn for jurisdictional purposes between aircraft, ships, and fixed platforms; between British and foreign ships or aircraft; between different categories of ship; between British citizens and others; between a ship's crew and passengers; and between jurisdiction that is statutory and that which is derived from the ancient jurisdiction of the Admiral. Most rules that apply to ships differ from those that apply to aircraft, but a few rules (notably in respect of piracy) apply equally to both.

The rules governing English criminal jurisdiction over ships and aircraft are much more complicated than they need to be. This excessive complexity can in part be attributed to the piecemeal development of the current legislation, much of which appears to have been enacted in the absence of any coherent overall strategy or principle; but further problems may arise as a result of obscure or defective drafting. The Merchant Shipping Act 1995, in particular, contains examples of drafting that seem almost wilfully misleading.

JURISDICTION OVER BRITISH SHIPS

British ships have sometimes been likened to floating British islands,[1] but in *Oteri* v. *The Queen*[2] the Privy Council emphasized that this is at best a

---

[1] As, e.g., in *Forbes* v. *Cochrane* (1824) 2 B & C 448, 464.
[2] [1976] 1 WLR 1272, 1276.

loose metaphor. British ships are not part of the United Kingdom,[3] and one cannot properly describe the jurisdiction exercisable over them when outside British waters as 'territorial'. This is not just a matter of semantics. In 1977, British sailors invited the fugitive train robber, Ronnie Biggs, to visit their frigate, *HMS Danae*, during a goodwill visit to Brazil. On learning of this, senior officers required Biggs to leave. Questions were later asked in Parliament as to why Biggs had not been arrested, but the Government explained that the *Danae* could not be regarded as floating British territory, and that powers of arrest provided under the Criminal Law Act 1967 could not lawfully have been exercised aboard her, given that she was in Brazilian waters at the time.[4] Similarly, provisions dealing with acts committed or events occurring 'within England and Wales' or 'within the United Kingdom' do not automatically apply to acts or events aboard British ships. Specific provision must be made within the relevant legislation (or within legislation dealing with such ships) if such an effect is desired.[5] British ships do, however, sail under the protection of the Crown,[6] and are entitled to fly a British flag.[7] This has important consequences, both under English law and under the rules of public international law.

Jurisdiction of the Flag State under International Law

The right of the 'flag state' to assert and enforce criminal jurisdiction over things done aboard a ship has long been recognized under customary international law, and is now restated in Articles 91 and 92 of the 1982 UNCLOS Convention. Article 91 states that a ship has the nationality of the flag it is entitled to fly. Article 92 provides that 'Ships shall sail under the flag of one state only and, save in exceptional cases expressly provided for in international treaties or in this Convention, shall be subject to its exclusive jurisdiction on the high seas'.

This 'exclusive jurisdiction' involves a package of sovereign powers, including the right to arrest, detain, or requisition the ship, to conduct investigations aboard it, and to prescribe regulations concerning its equipment, manning, and operation. The flag state alone may assert this package of sovereign powers; but Article 92 does not exclude the right of a state to punish one of its own nationals, within its own territory, for a crime previously committed aboard a foreign ship. Most states assert such a right, in some circumstances at least, just as they do in respect of offences committed by their nationals on foreign soil. This is true even of the United Kingdom, as explained below.

---

[3] *R v. Gordon-Finlayson, ex p an Officer* [1941] 1 KB 171, 178.
[4] See *Hansard* (HC), vol. 930, col. 450, 29 April 1977.
[5] As, e.g., in the Suppression of Terrorism Act 1978, s. 4(7).
[6] *Oteri v. The Queen*, fn 2 above.
[7] In some cases, this is a legal requirement.

Article 97 expressly recognizes that the right to punish offences committed at sea is not unique to the flag state. It provides, in respect of collisions or other navigational incidents on the high seas, that penal or disciplinary proceedings against the master or crew of a ship may be instituted 'before the judicial or administrative authorities either of the flag State or of the State of which such person is a national'. The jurisdiction of the alleged offender's state of nationality had previously been recognized by the Permanent Court of International Justice in the *Lotus Case* of 1927,[8] but Article 97 expressly rejects the actual ruling in that case, under which Turkey was held to be entitled to exercise criminal jurisdiction over the navigating officer of a French steamer, which had been in collision with a Turkish vessel on the high seas and caused the deaths of Turkish nationals aboard her. In collision cases, no criminal jurisdiction may now be claimed merely on the basis of the nationality of the victims or by the flag state of the other vessel involved.[9]

Flags of Convenience

As a matter of international law, a state is largely free to determine which ships may claim its nationality, register in its territory, and fly its flag. UNCLOS Article 91 stipulates that there must be a genuine link between the state and the ship, but does not define what form this link should take. In practice, Article 91 does little to prevent merchant ships sailing under flags of convenience, because it is usually possible for ships that are beneficially owned by nationals or corporations of State A to incorporate a company (or subsidiary company) in State B, transfer title in the ship to that company, and then register the ship under State B's flag. One effect of this practice is that a large part of the British merchant fleet has migrated over the years to flags of convenience (such as Liberia, Cyprus, Panama, or The Bahamas) in order to take advantage of the less stringent and costly regulatory regimes operated by those countries, many of which notoriously do little (and could do little if they tried) to enforce their jurisdictional responsibilities under UNCLOS.[10] Ships registered under foreign flags of convenience cannot be regarded as British ships, even if they are indirectly owned by British citizens or companies.[11]

---

[8] *France v. Turkey* (1927) PCIJ Ser. A, No. 10.

[9] See W.E. Beckett, 'Criminal Jurisdiction over Foreigners—the *Franconia* and the *Lotus*' (1927) 8 *British Yearbook of International Law* 108.

[10] As to these duties, see UNCLOS Art. 94. For information as to the problems posed by the misuse of flags of convenience, together with a list of countries that that have been accused by the International Transport Workers' Federation's Fair Practices Committee of providing flags of convenience, see http://www.itf.org.uk/seafarers/foc/foc.htm. See also E. Ellen and D. Campbell, *International Maritime Fraud* (1981), Ch. 6.

[11] Some flags of convenience are those of British overseas territories or possessions, notably Bermuda, Gibraltar, and the Cayman Islands. These are not United Kingdom ships, but they are British ships and fly a modified version of the red ensign.

Admiralty Jurisdiction over British Ships

When considering the ambit of English jurisdiction over crime committed on British ships, most reference works or textbooks concentrate almost exclusively on the jurisdictional provisions contained in the Merchant Shipping Act 1995; but important as these provisions are, they do not apply to all British ships, nor indeed are they wholly confined to British ships. A better starting point is the criminal jurisdiction of the Admiral, which is now exercised by the ordinary criminal courts, and still extends (*inter alia*) over things done aboard any kind of British ship or boat.

Historically, the Admiral's criminal jurisdiction extended both over indictable offences committed on the high seas and (under the statute of 15 Ric 2, c. 3) to offences of murder, manslaughter, or mayhem committed aboard 'great ships' lying within the ports or rivers of the realm.[12] Admiralty jurisdiction is now exercised in England and Wales[13] by the Crown Court,[14] and also by magistrates' courts in cases involving offences triable either way,[15] but for reasons that have previously been explained, purely summary offences have never fallen within this jurisdiction.

The High Seas

Confusingly, the term 'high seas', when used in the context of Admiralty jurisdiction, has a different meaning from that which it bears under international law. To the international lawyer, the high seas used to begin where national territorial limits ended, and for some purposes they are now said to begin only at the outer limits of a state's exclusive economic zone.[16] In the context of Admiralty jurisdiction, however, the high seas have been defined

---

[12] But 'only beneath the bridges of the same rivers nigh to the sea, and in none other places of the same rivers'. The existence of a concurrent Admiralty jurisdiction over offences committed aboard ships lying in rivers, etc, within the realm is no longer a matter of any practical significance, because the courts, offences, and procedure would be no different from those that would apply without it; and the statute was repealed as 'obsolete and unnecessary' by the Criminal Law Act 1967.

[13] Admiralty jurisdiction is not confined to English or even UK courts. See the Admiralty Offences (Colonial) Act 1849, s. 1. In *Oteri v. The Queen* [1976] 1 WLR 1272, Admiralty jurisdiction was exercised by an Australian court over a theft committed aboard the Australian fishing vessel, *Providence*, just outside Australian territorial waters. As the law then stood, the vessel was deemed to be a British ship and the law applied was the English Theft Act 1968. Upholding the conviction, the Privy Council held that 'It has always been the law of England that was applied to persons on British ships within the jurisdiction of the Admiralty'. English and Australian law have each changed in this respect. The *Providence* would no longer be classed as a British ship, and Australian courts would now exercise jurisdiction under Australian legislation, such as the Crimes at Sea Act 1979 (Commonwealth).

[14] Supreme Court Act 1981, s. 46(2).   [15] Magistrates' Courts Act 1980, s. 2(4).

[16] UNCLOS, Art. 86. The UK does not claim an EEZ as such (save in respect of certain overseas territories), but it does claim a 200-mile fishery zone, which is a partial EEZ. This zone would not therefore be categorized as high seas under Art. 86.

as 'all oceans, seas, bays, channels, rivers, creeks and waters . . . where great ships could go, with the exception only of such oceans etc. as are within the body of some county'.[17] In *R* v. *Anderson*,[18] Admiralty jurisdiction was therefore said to prevail over an offence of manslaughter committed by a US citizen aboard a British ship in the Garonne River, some 35 miles from the sea. Bovill CJ said:

Although the prisoner was subject to American jurisprudence as an American citizen, and to the law of France as having committed an offence within the territory of France, yet he must also be considered a subject to the jurisdiction of British law, which extends to the protection of British vessels though in ports belonging to another country.[19]

The court stressed that this Admiralty jurisdiction was independent of any jurisdiction exercisable under the Merchant Shipping Acts, which at that date extended only to offences committed by British subjects, and did not specifically apply to foreign ports or harbours.[20]

One area of uncertainty, as far as Admiralty jurisdiction is concerned, is that of ships lying in navigable rivers above the lowest bridges. The statute of 15 Ric. 2, c. 3 (1391) appeared to exclude any Admiralty claims to jurisdiction in respect of things done above the lowest bridges on such rivers, but this was enacted in order to resolve jurisdictional disputes with the common law courts in respect of things done within the realm of England. What, then, of foreign or Scottish rivers in which the bridges are built high enough for ships to pass beneath them? The issue arose before a Divisional Court in *R* v. *Devon Justices, ex p DPP*,[21] where the offence in question had been committed aboard *HMS Princess Margaret*, at anchor in the Scottish naval base at Rosyth, to landward of the Forth Railway Bridge. It was suggested by counsel that the Act of 1391 could not have envisaged bridges such as this, beneath which the largest ships in the fleet could pass, but the court was reluctant to allow the meaning of a statute to be modified by advances in civil engineering, and carefully avoided deciding the point, relying instead on a separate statutory jurisdiction created by the Naval Discipline Act 1866.[22] The 1391 Act was repealed as 'obsolete or unnecessary' by the Criminal Justice Act 1967, but this does little to resolve the issue, because it is not clear whether the 1391 Act (if applicable at all) had originally extended or restricted the jurisdiction lawfully exercisable by the Admiral prior to its enactment.

---

[17] *The Mecca* [1895] P 95, 107.   [18] (1868) XI Cox CC 198.

[19] Ibid., 204. In *R* v. *Carr and Wilson* (1882) 10 QBD 76, larceny aboard a British ship moored at the quayside in the Dutch port of Rotterdam was held to be an offence within Admiralty jurisdiction.   [20] Merchant Shipping Act 1867 (30 & 31 Vict., c. 124), s. 11.

[21] [1924] 1 KB 503.   [22] See now the Naval Discipline Act 1957, ss. 117–118 (below).

Jurisdiction over 'Her Majesty's Ships and Vessels'

Neither the warships and submarines of the Royal Navy, nor the transport and support vessels of the Royal Fleet Auxiliary Service are 'British ships' within the meaning of the Merchant Shipping Act 1995, section 1, but they are undeniably 'British', and indictable offences committed aboard them must accordingly fall within Admiralty jurisdiction.[23] In practice, jurisdiction over crimes committed aboard 'Her Majesty's ships and vessels'[24] will ordinarily be exercised under the provisions of the Naval Discipline Act 1957, which apply to civil offences as well as to service offences, and to passengers as well as to officers and crew.[25] Admiralty jurisdiction might be invoked, however, should any case arise in which the application of the Naval Discipline Act is in doubt. It is not clear, for example, whether the Act could apply to persons who board (or remain aboard) naval ships or vessels without the appropriate authority.[26] Admiralty jurisdiction must be exercised by the ordinary civilian courts, but is limited in so far as it applies only in respect of indictable offences.

Other British Ships

Naval and fleet auxiliary vessels apart, the concept of a British ship is one that has changed substantially over recent years. The Merchant Shipping Act 1894 originally defined a British ship as a vessel that was owned by British subjects or bodies corporate, and not powered entirely by oars.[27] The term, 'British subjects' included all subjects of the Empire, colonies, and dominions.[28] Registration of such ships was not the key issue as far as jurisdiction was concerned. If a foreign-owned vessel was wrongly registered as British, English criminal law would not ordinarily be applicable to it,[29] but that law *would* apply to any ships that ought to have been so registered, even if they had not been.[30]

---

[23] See *R v. Devon Justices, ex p DPP* [1924] 1 KB 503.

[24] 'Her Majesty's vessels' are defined by s. 132 of the Naval Discipline Act 1957 as ships and vessels, other than Her Majesty's ships, engaged in the naval service of Her Majesty. Apart from Royal Fleet Auxiliaries (which are sometimes armed and sail under the blue ensign) this definition would include merchant or fishing vessels that are 'STUFT' (ships taken up from trade), many examples of which were found in the task force that fought the Falklands War of 1982, including the *SS Canberra* and the ill-fated *MV Atlantic Conveyor*.

[25] Naval Discipline Act 1957, ss. 117–118.　　　[26] See Law Com. No. 91, para. 60.

[27] Rowing boats could not be regarded as 'ships' under the 1894 Act, although Admiralty jurisdiction would arguably have been capable of applying to a British boat, independently of that Act.　　　[28] This explains the ruling in *Oteri v. The Queen* [1976] 1 WLR 1272.

[29] *R v. Bjornsen* (1865) Le & Car 545.

[30] *Oteri v. The Queen*, fn 28 above. See also *R v. Allen* (1866) 10 Cox CC 406.

Section 1(1) of the Merchant Shipping Act 1995 defines British ships rather differently. It does not purport to do so merely for the purposes of the Act itself, but given that it does not include British naval or auxiliary vessels, its application cannot be considered wholly universal. A ship is 'British' under section 1 if:

(a) the ship is registered in the United Kingdom under Part II; or
(b) the ship is, as a Government ship, registered in the United Kingdom in pursuance of an Order in Council under section 308;[31] or
(c) the ship is registered under the law of a relevant British possession;[32] or
(d) the ship is a small ship other than a fishing vessel and—
   (i) is not registered under Part II, but
   (ii) is wholly owned by qualified owners, and
   (iii) is not registered under the law of a country outside the United Kingdom.

By section 1(2), 'qualified owners' are persons qualified to own British ships under regulations made by the Secretary of State;[33] and a 'small ship' means a ship less than 24 metres in length. This excludes small United Kingdom-based craft that are wholly or partially owned by persons who are *not* qualified owners. The term 'ship' now includes every description of vessel used in navigation. A rowing dinghy may thus be a ship in this sense, as may a towed barge or even a floating drilling rig.[34] By section 2 of the 1995 Act, British ships (Government ships excepted) must sail under the red ensign, unless authorized to fly other British national colours, such as the blue ensign.[35]

Admiralty Jurisdiction and Foreign Ships

Crimes of piracy excepted, the Admiral had no inherent jurisdiction over acts committed on foreign ships at sea, although his jurisdiction over acts of murder or mayhem committed aboard ships lying in rivers within the realm extended to foreign ships as well as to English ones. Assuming the majority decision in *R v. Keyn*[36] to have been correct, the Admiral did not

---

[31] Naval vessels do not fall within the definition of 'Government ships' in s. 1(1)(b) and are specifically excluded from the operation of the Act by s. 308(4).

[32] These include British overseas territories, the Channel Islands, and the Isle of Man. Many of these have substantial shipping registers, and some are regarded as flags of convenience.

[33] See the Merchant Shipping (Registration of Ships) Regulations 1993 (SI 1993 No. 3138), reg. 89, as amended. UK nationals, Commonwealth citizens, and EU or European Economic Area nationals exercising freedom of movement or establishment are all qualified owners. By reg. 90, a small ship may be registered if it is owned by one or more persons ordinarily resident in the UK and qualified by virtue of reg. 89.

[34] A rig with legs that can be jacked up when the rig is moved, as opposed to one that is sunk into place on a permanent basis: see *Clark (Inspector of Taxes) v. Perks* [2001] EWCA Civ 1228.

[35] Ships registered in British overseas territories or possessions fly modified version of the red ensign, as do some Manx ships.   [36] (1876) LR 2 Ex D 63.

even possess any general jurisdiction over things done aboard foreign ships within waters adjacent to the shores of England and Wales, although this lacuna was filled by the Territorial Waters Jurisdiction Act 1878, which declared indictable offences committed within British territorial limits to be within Admiralty jurisdiction, even when committed aboard foreign ships. Any criminal jurisdiction exercisable over acts committed aboard foreign ships at sea is therefore statutory, the principal sources being the 1878 Act and the Merchant Shipping Act 1995.

Jurisdiction under the Merchant Shipping Act 1995

The Merchant Shipping Act 1995 contains provisions that create a further basis of jurisdiction over maritime offences and over certain offences committed by seamen ashore. There are four provisions headed 'jurisdiction'. Sections 279 and 280 have been considered elsewhere in this Work.[37] The former appears to be a mere venue provision and deals only with the trial of offences under the Act itself. The latter applies only to ships (and perhaps only to British ships) lying in coastal (that is internal or territorial) waters adjacent to the realm. Sections 281 and 282 are considered below. The Act purports to be a mere consolidation of existing enactments, but in places (notably in section 281) one finds that significant changes have been made to the provisions it purports to consolidate.

United Kingdom Ships and Foreign Ships

Neither section 281 nor section 282 refers to offences committed aboard 'British ships'. They refer, instead, to offences committed aboard 'United Kingdom ships', or in some cases to offences committed by British citizens on 'foreign ships'. The distinction between United Kingdom ships and other British ships first appeared in the Merchant Shipping (Registration etc.) Act 1993, but is now contained in section 1(3) of the 1995 Act, which provides:

A ship is a 'United Kingdom ship' for the purposes of this Act (except sections 85 and 144(3)) if the ship is registered in the United Kingdom under Part II (and in Part V 'United Kingdom fishing vessel' has a corresponding meaning).

This definition excludes not only ships registered in British overseas territories (as clearly it was intended to do) but also Government ships registered under section 308 and many small British vessels (under 24 metres in length) that do not require registration and have not been voluntarily registered

---

[37] See above, pp. 12–14 (s. 279) and 93 (s. 280).

under Part II of the Act. It does, however, include foreign-registered vessels that are 'bareboat chartered-in' by British charterers and temporarily registered under Part II in accordance with section 17 of the Act,[38] and it also includes United Kingdom fishing vessels, which must be registered under Part II, even though for most purposes they are then governed by the regime laid down in Part V.

A 'foreign ship' is defined in section 313 as one that is neither a United Kingdom ship nor a small British ship that has not been registered under the Act. This definition includes ships registered in British possessions, such as Bermuda, Gibraltar, or the Isle of Man. Consequently, a vessel which is a 'British ship' under section 1 of the Act may at the same time be a 'foreign ship' under section 313—a potentially confusing state of affairs. This is not the real problem, however. The real problem is that small, unregistered British ships or boats are neither United Kingdom ships nor foreign ships. This means that such vessels no longer fall within the ambit of the Merchant Shipping Act's principal jurisdictional provisions, which refer in some cases to things done on United Kingdom ships, and in other cases to things done aboard foreign ships, but make no reference at all to things done aboard British ships. This omission cannot have been intended, but it is impossible to construe the Act so as to include them. The implications of this lacuna are not as great as one might at first suppose, because such vessels will still fall within the jurisdiction of the Admiralty, as far as indictable offences are concerned, but summary offences cannot fall within Admiralty jurisdiction. The only jurisdiction provision in the 1995 Act that might apply to such offences when committed aboard unregistered British vessels is section 280 (ships lying off coasts), but there is no reported case in which that provision (or any of its ancestors) has been so applied, and it could not in any case be applicable to vessels lying beyond English territorial waters.

Under section 307, the Secretary of State is empowered to make regulations that would apply designated parts of the Act (or instruments made under it) to designated classes of ships that are not registered in the United Kingdom.[39] The jurisdictional lacuna could thus be filled without the need for new legislation. To date, however, no such regulations have been made that would apply sections 281 or 282 to small, unregistered British vessels or their crews.

---

[38] Bareboat charters involve the hiring of a ship for a stipulated period on terms which give the charterer possession and control of the ship, including the right to appoint the master and crew. During this period, a ship chartered-in and registered under s. 17 will sail under the red ensign, like any other United Kingdom ship.

[39] See, e.g., the Fishing Vessels (Safety of 15–24 Metre Vessels) Regulations 2002 (SI 2002 No. 2201).

Section 281

Section 281 of the 1995 Act, which is derived from section 686 of the Merchant Shipping Act 1894, provides:

Where any person is charged with having committed any offence under this Act then—

(a) if he is a British citizen and is charged with having committed it—
   (i) on board any United Kingdom ship on the high seas,
   (ii) in any foreign port or harbour, or
   (iii) on board any foreign ship to which he does not belong; or
(b) if he is not a British citizen and is charged with having committed it on board any United Kingdom ship on the high seas;

and he is found within the jurisdiction of any court in any part of the United Kingdom which would have had jurisdiction in relation to the offence if it had been committed on board a United Kingdom ship within the limits of its ordinary jurisdiction to try the offence that court shall have jurisdiction to try the offence as if it had been so committed.

Although this section is derived from section 686(1) of the 1894 Act, it differs from the earlier provision in a number of ways. Section 686(1) originally provided:

Where any person, being a British subject, is charged with having committed any offence on board any British ship on the high seas or in any foreign port or harbour or on board any foreign ship to which he does not belong, or, not being a British subject, is charged with having committed any offence on board any British ship on the high seas, and that person is found within the jurisdiction of any court in Her Majesty's dominions, which would have had cognisance of the offence if it had been committed on board a British ship within the limits of its ordinary jurisdiction, that court shall have jurisdiction to try the offence as if it had been so committed.

This did not merely duplicate existing Admiralty jurisdiction, because it was not confined to indictable offences, nor to offences committed on British ships. It enabled a summary offence under English law, committed on a British ship, to be tried by an English magistrates' court, 'as if committed . . . within the limits of its ordinary jurisdiction', and it also enabled jurisdiction to be exercised over offences committed in foreign ports or harbours in cases where Admiralty jurisdiction might otherwise have been in doubt.[40] It even extended to offences committed by British subjects aboard 'foreign ships to which they did not belong'. It applied to the whole of the United Kingdom and to British territories overseas. It thus empowered Scottish courts (for example) to deal with offences against Scots law, should offenders be brought before them.

---

[40] Notably in cases where the ship in question was berthed above the lowest bridging points on a foreign river. See the discussion of *R* v. *Liverpool Justices, ex p Molyneux*, at p. 292 below.

Section 686 originally applied to all kinds of British ship, other than those governed by the Naval Discipline Acts, and references to British subjects originally included the citizens of independent Commonwealth countries,[41] but its ambit was later limited by pre-consolidation amendments contained within Schedule 4 to the Merchant Shipping (Registration etc.) Act 1993. These did not purport to amend the actual wording of section 686(1). Instead, para. 61 of Schedule 4 provided:

Section 686(1) (jurisdiction over offences on board ship) shall—
 (a) so far as it applies to British subjects, apply only to British citizens (within the meaning of the British Nationality Act 1981); and
 (b) so far as it applies to British ships, apply only to United Kingdom ships.

Section 686(1) fell to be construed by the appellate courts on a number of occasions, and much of the case law appertaining to it remains valid in respect of the current provision. In *R* v. *Liverpool Justices, ex p Molyneux,*[42] it was held that the expression 'high seas' must, when used in that section, bear the same wide meaning as it bears in the context of Admiralty jurisdiction. On that basis, the court upheld the conviction of a seaman who had stolen cases of whisky from the British steamer *Kenuta* while she was anchored in the Bahamian port of Nassau. Since Nassau was in a Commonwealth country, it could not be described as a 'foreign port of harbour', but the port was held to form part of the high seas as being a place where great ships could go.

If foreign or Commonwealth ports or harbours were part of the high seas, what was meant by the reference to foreign ports or harbours? It was argued in *Molyneux* that ships lying in a foreign port could not always be regarded as lying on the high seas. Ships berthed in dry docks, or in artificially excavated dock basins, or in areas lying upriver from the lowest bridges could not be said to do so. An alternative explanation, not considered in *Molyneux*, was that the section referred not to British *ships* in foreign ports or harbours, but to British *subjects* in such places. This interpretation was advanced in early editions of *Blackstone's Criminal Practice*,[43] and may perhaps have influenced the draftsman of the 1995 Act, as we shall see, but it was not considered by the Court of Appeal in *R* v. *Cumberworth*,[44] in which it was assumed that section 686(1) was concerned only with offences committed aboard ships.

Cumberworth concerned offences committed by British subjects aboard a foreign ship to which they did not belong. The issue was whether a French ferry in the port of Dieppe fell within the ambit of section 686(1) when its vehicle ramp was lowered onto the quay for loading. The court held that

---

[41] The limitations imposed by the British Nationality Act 1948, s. 3, never applied to jurisdiction under the Merchant Shipping Act 1894.   [42] [1972] 2 QB 384.
[43] See, e.g., the 1st edn (1991), at D1.68.   [44] (1989) 89 Cr App R 187.

the lowering of the ramp made no difference, although dry docking might have done. It was assumed that the offence had to be committed aboard a ship of some kind, and indeed the issue would not have arisen had it been thought that section 686 applied to offences committed by British subjects anywhere within the port of Dieppe.

One further case decided under section 686(1) should be mentioned before we return to the 1995 legislation. This is *R* v. *Kelly*,[45] in which the House of Lords rejected an argument that section 686(1) was nothing more than a venue provision, providing for the trial of acts that were already extraterritorial offences under English law. Their Lordships held that it extended the ambit of ordinary offences (such as criminal damage) that had no extraterritorial ambit of their own. They accordingly upheld the convictions of British subjects who had vandalized fittings on a Danish ferry on the high seas, outside English territorial waters.

Had a similar crime been committed aboard a British ship, there would have been no issue as to jurisdiction. Even if section 686 were construed as a mere venue provision,[46] criminal damage is triable either way, and would therefore fall within Admiralty jurisdiction when committed on any British ship, independently of section 686. The importance of the ruling in *Kelly*, so far as United Kingdom ships are concerned, lies in respect of summary offences. As a result of that ruling, it is no longer possible to dispute the applicability of English law to summary offences committed aboard United Kingdom ships.

Has Section 281 Changed the Law?

A comparison between section 281 of the 1995 Act and the original text of the provision it supplanted reveals a number of apparent differences. Some of these differences result from incorporation of the limitations originally imposed by the Merchant Shipping (Registration etc.) Act 1993 (above), but others require further consideration.

Whereas the old section 686(1) dealt with jurisdiction over offences generally, section 281 of the 1995 Act appears, on its face, to deal only with offences under the Merchant Shipping Act itself. This would totally change the character of the section, and vastly reduce its ambit. The apparent change is, however, an illusion created by perversely obscure drafting. Section 3A of the Magistrates' Courts Act 1980, which was inserted by Schedule 13 to the Merchant Shipping Act 1995, provides that sections 280, 281, and 282 of that Act apply in relation to other offences under the law

---

[45] [1982] AC 665. See Geoffrey Marston, 'Crime by British Passengers on Board Foreign Ships on the High Seas: The Historical Background to Section 686(1)' [1999] *Cambridge Law Journal* 171.

[46] As in *R* v. *Lopez* (1858) Dears & Bell 525. See Glanville Williams, 'Venue and the Ambit of Criminal Law' (1965) 81 *Law Quarterly Review* 276, 395, 410.

of England and Wales as they apply in relation to offences under that Act or instruments under that Act. Similar provision is made, as regards trial on indictment, by section 46A of the Supreme Court Act 1981 (also inserted by Schedule 13 to the 1995 Act).[47]

The editors of *Archbold* have identified another (and this time a material) difference between the old and new provisions:

> Section 686 of the Merchant Shipping Act 1894, as amended, referred to a British citizen being charged with an offence committed 'on board a British ship on the high seas or in any foreign port or harbour' (as to which, see *R v. Cumberworth*). Because of the drafting style adopted in the 1995 Act, there appears to be no requirement that the offence be on a British ship (or any ship) if it is committed in a foreign port or harbour. This was surely unintentional; for otherwise, it would purport to confer jurisdiction on the English courts over any conduct which would be an offence by English law committed within any 'port or harbour' in the world, regardless of whether it was committed on board ship or not, and regardless of the nationality of the ship if it was committed on board ship.[48]

What appears to have happened is that the draftsman sought to improve on the 1894 provision by clarifying the previously ambiguous wording at this point. It is possible that in so doing he correctly divined the intentions of his Victorian predecessor. Contrary to the assumption made in *Archbold*, it is possible that section 686 was indeed intended to apply to cases of misconduct committed by British subjects ashore in foreign ports. Section 687 of the 1894 Act had a comparable effect in relation to offences committed by seamen from British ships, and section 282 of the 1995 Act now replicates this in respect of offences committed by seamen from United Kingdom ships. The problem is that the draftsman evidently overlooked the case law on section 686(1), which had interpreted the section as referring to British ships (and not British subjects) in foreign ports or harbours.[49]

Whether this change was intentional or not, the wording of section 281 is unambiguous, and it is quite impossible to construe it in accordance with the old law. The new and extended meaning is not absurd, nor is it contrary to international law: it is merely different. This does not mean that it is unproblematic. When, for example, is a crime committed in a 'foreign port or harbour'? Many British ports have clearly defined 'port limits', which are marked on Admiralty charts, but the limits of a foreign port may be harder to establish in an English court. It also seems unsatisfactory that ports or harbours in Commonwealth countries should be excluded from the ambit of section 281, save where they form part of the high seas.[50] Although

---

[47] See also the Magistrates' Courts (Northern Ireland) Order 1981 (SI 1981 No. 1675 (NI 26)), s. 17A, and the Judicature (Northern Ireland) Act 1978, s. 46(3A). No such provision is made in respect of Scotland, however.	[48] *Archbold*, § 2–66.

[49] See, e.g., *R v. Cumberworth* (1989) 89 Cr App R 187.

[50] See *R v. Liverpool Justices, ex p Molyneux* [1972] 2 QB 384, p. 292 above.

Commonwealth ships may for jurisdictional purposes be regarded as 'foreign ships', by virtue of section 313 of the Act (even where British-flagged, under section 1), no comparable provision applies to Commonwealth ports or harbours. A British citizen who commits a robbery or rape on dockland within the port of Hamburg commits an offence under English law, by virtue of section 281(a)(ii); but a British citizen who commits a similar robbery ashore within the port of Lagos cannot be indicted under that provision. This, with respect, is absurd and almost certainly unintended. If, however, the robber or rapist is a seaman from a United Kingdom ship, he may instead be indicted under section 282 of the Act, which is examined at pp. 296–8 below.

Application to Foreign Ships: Origins and Rationale

Misconduct committed aboard foreign ships outside English territorial waters would not ordinarily be considered the concern of English law, even when committed by British citizens. It certainly would not fall within Admiralty jurisdiction, unless it amounts to piracy. Why, then, does section 281 contain a special rule in respect of such misconduct; and why does it apply only to those British citizens who 'do not belong' to that ship?

Geoffrey Marston[51] has shown that the explanation for the extension to British subjects (or, now, British citizens) aboard foreign ships, which first appeared in section 11 of the Merchant Shipping Act 1867, can be traced to a series of incidents involving attacks by British sailors on foreign vessels, committed under the pretext of salvage operations, and in particular to an incident involving a French merchant lugger, *La Nymphe*. When the 1867 Bill was before the House of Lords, the Duke of Richmond, President of the Board of Trade, explained the purpose behind the clause that became section 11:

It provided for the punishment of men who committed offences against foreign vessels. On a recent occasion a small French vessel stranded near the English coast was set upon by some men of Harwich, the captain was subjected to violence and the ship was taken possession of; yet the offenders escaped unpunished because their offence was committed on a foreign vessel outside British soil (*sic*). A remedy for this defect in our law was provided in the clause he spoke of, by providing that the offender shall be punished in the same way as if the offence had been committed against an English ship.[52]

---

[51] 'Crime by British Passengers on Board Foreign Ships on the High Seas: The Historical Background to Section 686(1)' [1999] *Cambridge Law Journal* 171.

[52] *Parliamentary Debates* (3rd Series), vol. 188, col. 851. The Duke's account of this incident was not based on any judicial finding, because in unreported civil Admiralty proceedings between the French owners and the Harwich fishermen (who claimed salvage rights) Dr Lushington found it impossible to establish what had happened, and on that basis he dismissed both the salvage claim and a counter claim by the owners. The British Government nevertheless paid compensation to the owners. See Marston, ibid., 177 and 186.

Leaving to one side the question whether such conduct might instead have been dealt with under what is now section 282 of the 1995 Act, or even as piracy,[53] the obvious implication of this tale is that the provision which eventually became section 281(a)(ii) was never intended to apply to British passengers on a foreign ship, but only to British subjects (or now British citizens) who had no business being on that ship at all. Would the House of Lords have upheld the conviction in *R v. Kelly*, had their Lordships been aware of the historical background? Cases in which British citizens board foreign ships without authority, outside British waters, must now be very rare. In contrast, cases such as *Kelly* or *Cumberworth*, in which British passengers misbehave on foreign ships, are not uncommon. The master of a foreign ferry, arriving in England with drunken and violent British passengers aboard, may have no wish to enforce the jurisdiction of the flag state, but may prefer (as in *Kelly*) to hand the offenders over to the English police, with the request that they be dealt with there. In some cases, the offence may come to light, or be reported, only after the voyage has ended. Proceedings under English law may then be considered more convenient than proceedings instigated in the flag state. Had their Lordships ruled that English law did *not* apply to such cases, it is likely that remedial legislation would have been enacted, so as to cure that deficiency.[54]

Section 282

In contrast to section 281, section 282 of the 1995 Act, which supplanted section 687 of the 1894 Act, involved no redrafting of the existing legislation. The original version of section 687 had already been substituted in the pre-consolidation legislation of 1993, and no further modifications were deemed necessary. Section 282, which is headed 'Offences committed by British seamen', provides:

(1) Any act in relation to property or person done in or at any place (ashore or afloat) outside the United Kingdom by any master or seaman who at the time is employed in a United Kingdom ship, which, if done in any part of the United Kingdom, would be an offence under the law of any part of the United Kingdom, shall—

    (a) be an offence under that law, and

    (b) be treated for the purposes of jurisdiction and trial as if it had been done within the jurisdiction of the Admiralty of England.

(2) Subsection (1) above also applies in relation to a person who had been so employed within the period of three months expiring with the time when the act was done.

(3) Subsections (1) and (2) above apply to omissions as they apply to acts.

---

[53] In the *Nymphe* incident, it was observed at the time that a charge of piracy would not be sustainable in court, because the Harwich fishermen had boldly brought their prize into port and claimed salvage rights; and what kind of pirate would dare to do that? The answer, perhaps, is that a very bold pirate might do so—one who was sure that nobody could prove what he had really done.   [54] See Marston, op. cit., fn 51, 195–6.

This differs from the original (pre-1993) text of section 687 in just one substantive respect, namely, in that it applies only to seamen, etc., from United Kingdom ships, rather than to those from British ships; but the drafting has been amended so as to make it clear that it is more than just a venue provision and that it applies to omissions as well as to acts.

Section 687 of the 1894 Act was itself derived without alteration from section 267 of the Merchant Shipping Act 1854, and the law in question has thus been in place for nearly 150 years, but it seems to have been little used, and despite the 1993 redrafting some issues remain unclear. In particular, there appears to be conflict between subsections (1)(a) and (1)(b). The former suggests that a seaman from a United Kingdom ship may be charged with committing abroad *any* offence under United Kingdom law, including (presumably) a purely summary offence, as long as this is an offence 'against property or person'. The latter, however, provides that any such offence must be 'treated for the purposes of jurisdiction and trial as if it had been done within the jurisdiction of the Admiralty of England'. This appears to rule out any trial of a summary offence (such as common assault or battery) because such offences have never fallen within the jurisdiction of the Admiralty, and section 282 does nothing to give any magistrates' courts jurisdiction over a summary offence committed outside its own commission area.[55]

A further area of uncertainty arises in respect of any foreign seaman who may be serving (or who within the last three months has served) aboard a United Kingdom ship. Does section 282 impose liability under English criminal law for an act done by such a person in a foreign port or country, or aboard a foreign ship? There is a strong presumption that Parliament would not seek to apply English criminal law to foreign citizens abroad, and that it would use explicit and unambiguous language if, exceptionally, it wished to do so. On that basis, the better view must be that section 282 does not apply to foreign nationals in respect of things done abroad, unless they are done on a British or United Kingdom ship; but it is regrettable that nothing was done in 1993 or 1995 to clarify the point.[56]

Despite its general obscurity, the rule now contained within section 282 has figured in at least one major case, namely *R* v. *Dudley and Stephens*,[57] in which the defendants, the captain and mate of the British yacht, *Mignonette*, were convicted of murdering the cabin boy, Parker, following the loss of the yacht in a storm. They had survived for many days, adrift in

---

[55] Indictable offences committed within the jurisdiction of the Admiralty are triable in the Crown Court (Supreme Court Act 1981, s. 46) and 'either way' offences are also triable in magistrates' courts, wherever committed (Magistrates' Courts Act 1980, s. 2(3)–(4)).

[56] Especially given that Glanville Williams had identified it as long ago as 1965 (op. cit., fn 46, 413).   [57] (1884) 24 QBD 273, 281.

an open boat, before killing and eating the boy. When counsel argued that 'according to the decision of the majority of the judges in the *Franconia* case there was no jurisdiction in the court at Exeter to try these prisoners', Lord Coleridge CJ (who had dissented in that case) retorted that the minority view had been vindicated, and that the case was in any event distinguishable, involving as it did acts committed by 'English seamen, the crew of an English yacht'. This being the case, his Lordship added, section 267 of the 1854 Act was 'absolutely fatal to this objection'.

If another case were to occur in which one survivor of a British shipwreck were to kill or injure another whilst adrift on the sea (perhaps in a struggle over use or possession of life-saving equipment), could jurisdiction necessarily be asserted under section 282? It is by no means certain that a small, British-owed yacht would be registered in the United Kingdom. As previously explained, registration is mandatory only for vessels that are 24 metres or more in length. Many smaller vessels are registered by choice, but others are not. Even the smallest British-owned craft may be 'British ships', but unless registered they are not United Kingdom ships for the purposes of sections 281 or 282.

All British vessels are subject to the inherent jurisdiction of the Admiralty. Indictable offences committed on such vessels would thus be triable in the ordinary courts. The most serious lacuna in cases of this kind must therefore involve survivors who are in the water, or clinging to wreckage, as where D kills V in the water, in order to steal his lifejacket. This may look like robbery and murder, but D appears to commit no offence unless he belongs to the crew of a United Kingdom ship, or commits the act within British territorial waters.

In contrast, section 282 may apply, in theory, to misconduct committed by a seaman (or even a recently retired seaman) from a United Kingdom ship during a family holiday in Austria. There is no real justification for this, nor indeed is such application intended. It is merely a further by-product of shamefully poor drafting, which manages to makes its ambit both too broad and, in other respects, too narrow.

Ships of 'Convention Countries'

Section 4(7) of the Suppression of Terrorism Act 1978 ensures that, in so far as English criminal jurisdiction extends under section 4(1) to offences committed in Convention countries (or in India), it also extends to offences committed aboard ships, aircraft, or hovercraft registered in such countries, on the same basis (in the case of a crime aboard a ship) as if it were committed 'within the jurisdiction of the Admiralty'. In practice, this jurisdiction would probably be exercised only in cases where extradition proves impossible.

OFFSHORE INSTALLATIONS

The development of the United Kingdom's offshore oil and gas industry during the latter part of the twentieth century[58] necessitated a significant addition to the range of circumstances in which English (or other United Kingdom) law applied to acts committed outside normal territorial limits. Whilst it was understandable that jurisdictional lacunae might be allowed to persist in respect of isolated structures such as the Eddystone lighthouse or Roughs Tower, the importance of the new industry, the hazardous nature of the activities carried out, and the large number of persons working on the new offshore platforms, made it imperative that something was done to bring those platforms within the ambit of the criminal law.

The first provision to apply English or other United Kingdom criminal law to offshore installations lying beyond territorial waters was the Continental Shelf Act 1964, section 3(1), since repealed. The relevant law is now contained within the Criminal Jurisdiction (Offshore Activities) Order 1987.[59] This Order was originally made under the authority of the Oil and Gas (Enterprise) Act 1982, section 22, but that section was repealed and re-enacted in the Petroleum Act 1998, section 10, and the Order now has effect by virtue of the re-enacted provision.[60] The Order applies to the territorial waters of the United Kingdom (no distinction being made, for these purposes, between Scottish, English, or Northern Ireland waters) and also to the waters in any area for the time being designated by Orders made under section 1(7) of the Continental Shelf Act 1964. The Continental Shelf (Designation of Areas) (Consolidation) Order 2000,[61] together with the Continental Shelf (Designation of Areas) Order 2001,[62] designate the areas in question. These are areas of continental shelf adjacent to the United Kingdom, within which the Crown claims rights over the sea bed and subsoil and their natural resources.[63]

By Article 3 of the Criminal Jurisdiction Order:

Any act or omission which—

(a) takes place on, under or above an installation in waters to which this Order applies or any waters within 500 metres of any such installation; and

---

[58] Serious exploration began in 1964, following British ratification of the 1958 Geneva Convention on the Continental Shelf. The first British offshore gas field (West Sole) was discovered in 1965. The first commercial oil production (from the Argyll oil field) began in 1975. See R.B. Clark, *The Waters Around the British Isles* (1987), 38–9.

[59] SI 1987 No. 2198.   [60] Interpretation Act 1978, s. 17(2)(b).

[61] SI 2000 No. 3062.   [62] SI 2001 No. 3670.

[63] By s. 10(8) of the Petroleum Act 1998, an Order may also designate areas in foreign sectors of the continental shelf that comprise any part of a 'cross-boundary field' (as defined in s. 10(9)).

(b) would, if taking place in any part of the United Kingdom, constitute an offence under the law in force in that part,
shall be treated for the purposes of that law as taking place in that part.[64]

The 500-metre zones around such installations, within which United Kingdom criminal law applies, corresponds to the safety zones created by Orders made under section 21 of the Petroleum Act 1987.[65] One feature of such zones is that shipping is excluded from them, and by section 23 an offence is committed by the owner(s) and master of any vessel (British or otherwise) that trespasses within the zone.

A curious feature of the Criminal Jurisdiction Order (and of its parent legislation) is that no distinction is drawn between Scottish adjacent waters and English or other United Kingdom waters. Such a distinction is firmly drawn in most other criminal contexts, as noted in Chapter 3 above, and is particularly conspicuous in the corresponding Civil Jurisdiction (Offshore Activities) Order 1987,[66] where an unusually clear distinction is also drawn between English and Northern Irish waters,[67] but it is absent here. As a result, an unlawful killing on a North Sea oil platform might (in theory) be triable either as manslaughter under English law, or as culpable homicide under Scots law, regardless of whether the platform lies on the English or Scottish side of the border designated in the Civil Jurisdiction Order.

Section 12 of the Petroleum Act 1998 imposes restrictions on the prosecution of some, but not all, types of offence. It provides:

(1) Subject to subsection (2), this subsection applies to—
(a) any offence alleged to have been committed on, under or above an installation in waters to which section 10 applies or any waters within 500 metres of such an installation; and
(b) any offence committed on or as respects an aircraft which is not registered in the United Kingdom which is an offence created by virtue of paragraph 6(5) of Part III of Schedule 13 to the Civil Aviation Act 1982.

(2) Subsection (1) does not apply to any offence to which subsection (5) applies nor to any offence under, or under any provision which has effect under—
(a) the Customs and Excise Acts 1979, or any enactment to be construed as one with those Acts or any of them;
(b) except where it is created by virtue of paragraph 6(5) of Part III of Schedule 13 to the Civil Aviation Act 1982, that Act or any enactment to be construed as one with that Act;

---

[64] 'Installations' include those in transit (e.g., rigs under tow). Police powers are dealt with by Art. 4 of the Order. These may be exercised on, under, or above any installation in waters to which the Order applies, or any waters within 500 metres of such an installation.
[65] See the Offshore Installations (Safety Zones) Order 2002 (SI 2002 No. 1063).
[66] SI 1997 No. 2197.
[67] This defines 'the English area' as such of the offshore area adjacent to England and Wales which lies to the south of the Scottish border and east of the Northern Irish border together with the internal waters of England and Wales in so far as they are tidal or constitute parts of the sea.

(c) the Pilotage Act 1987;

(d) the Value Added Tax Act 1994 or any enactment to be construed as one with that Act;

(e) the Merchant Shipping Act 1995; or

(f) Part III or IV of this Act.

(3) No proceedings for an offence to which subsection (1) applies shall be instituted—

(a) in England and Wales, except by or with the consent of the Director of Public Prosecutions unless prosecution of the offence there requires the consent of the Attorney General;

(b) in Northern Ireland, except by or with the consent of the Director of Public Prosecutions for Northern Ireland unless prosecution of the offence there requires the consent of the Attorney General for Northern Ireland.

(4) Section 3 of the Territorial Waters Jurisdiction Act 1878 (restriction on prosecutions) shall not apply to any proceedings for an offence to which subsection (1) or (5) applies.

(5) This subsection applies to—

(a) any offence under section 23 of the Petroleum Act 1987 (safety zones); and

(b) any offence under any provision made under the Mineral Workings (Offshore Installations) Act 1971 which has effect by virtue of—

(i) paragraph (1) of regulation 6 (savings) of the Offshore Safety (Repeals and Modifications) Regulations 1993; or

(ii) paragraph (1) of regulation 6 (savings) of the Offshore Safety (Repeals and Modifications) Regulations (Northern Ireland) 1993.

The offshore oil and gas industry is a potential target for terrorist attack, and its legal defences have been strengthened accordingly. Offences involving the seizure, destruction, or endangerment of ships or platforms (including foreign ships or platforms in foreign zones) may be punishable under Part II of the Aviation and Maritime Security Act 1990. This legislation is considered elsewhere in this chapter (see pp. 308–9).

PIRACY

Piracy is an ancient crime, which has probably existed for nearly as long as seaborne trade itself. It was the first offence of 'universal jurisdiction', and probably the first extraterritorial offence of any kind, to be recognized under English law, and it later became the first criminal offence to be recognized and defined under international law, but it would be wrong to suppose that the subject is now antiquated or of purely historic interest. According to data compiled by the International Maritime Bureau,[68] there were at least 335 piratical attacks on ships during 2001, 16 of which involved the taking of entire ships or vessels. At least 21 mariners or passengers were murdered in

---

[68] This is the Maritime Bureau of the International Chamber of Commerce (ICC).

the course of such attacks. The previous year was even worse, with 469 attacks and 72 murders.[69] Nevertheless, for reasons that are explained below, only a small number of these attacks would have involved an offence of piracy *jure gentium* (or piracy under international law) which is now the only form of piracy recognized under English criminal law. To put it another way, most cases in which ships are boarded and plundered (or even taken over) by bandits do not amount to piracy under English (or international) criminal law.

Historical Background

Jurisdiction over piracy was originally exercised by the Admiral and his deputies,[70] who asserted the right to try and punish pirates of any nationality, wherever upon the sea and against whatever ships their crimes may have been committed. There were a few cases during the reigns of Edward II and Edward III in which jurisdiction appears to have been exercised over piracy by the Court of King's Bench, but Hale[71] states that this practice 'was interrupted by a special order of the King and his Council in the 35 Edw. 3 and by a *supersedas* issued shortly after'. Since then, maritime piracy has remained an Admiralty offence, albeit that it has long been tried 'according to the course of the common law'[72] and is now triable in the Crown Court, in accordance with the usual rules of evidence and procedure in that court.[73]

As explained in Chapter 3 above, the Admiral's attempts to assert jurisdiction over incidents occurring within creeks, rivers, and harbours lying within the realm of England led to conflicts with the common law courts, and were eventually restrained by the statute of 15 Ric. 2, c. 3, in 1391, under which the Admiral's jurisdiction over such matters was restricted to crimes of murder or mayhem committed aboard great ships lying below the lowest bridges. This does not appear to have prevented the exercise of Admiralty jurisdiction over cases involving piracy committed within the coastal waters of other kingdoms. As late as 1853, the great Admiralty judge, Dr Lushington, could still declare that 'If a robbery be committed in

---

[69] These figures are taken from the IMB Piracy Reporting Centre's annual report for 2001, published in Kuala Lumpur in February 2002. The Centre also publishes daily alerts to vessels in high risk areas, together with a weekly online report, containing reports of recent attacks, missing vessels, and suspicious incidents or warnings (see the ICC's website **www.iccwbo.org** for details).

[70] See Coke, *Institutes*, vol. 4, 143; Stephen, *History of the Criminal Law*, vol. ii, 16.

[71] *Historia Placitorum Coronae*, vol. ii, 12.

[72] Writing in 1805, East (*Pleas of the Crown*, 794) referred to piracy as 'a maritime felony . . . triable under the King's special commission . . . in which . . . two common law judges are constantly included, by whom in effect the prisoners are tried, though the judge of the Admiralty still presides'.   [73] Supreme Court Act 1981, s. 46(2).

creeks, harbours, ports, etc. in foreign countries, the court of Admiralty indisputably has jurisdiction over it, and such offence is consequently piracy'.[74]

The unique breadth of this extraterritorial jurisdiction can in part be explained by the fact that the civil law procedures of the Admiral's court were not constrained by the locally restrictive technicalities of venue. A further consideration was that pirates became regarded by maritime nations as *hostes humani generis*, or enemies of mankind. It was thus accepted that such pirates could be fought, arrested, and punished by the naval forces and courts of any nation that should happen to find them. The seizure and execution of a pirate was considered to be an act that benefited all nations, and it did not matter where or by whom this was done. As the Admiralty judge, Sir Charles Hedge, said in *R* v. *Dawson*[75]:

The King of England hath . . . an undoubted jurisdiction and power in concurrency with other princes and states for the punishment of all piracies and robberies at sea . . . so that if any person whatsoever, native or foreigner . . . shall be robbed or spoiled in . . . any seas, it is piracy within . . . the cognisance of this court.

As a matter of international law, the precise definition of piracy *jure gentium* was by no means clearly or universally understood. Maritime states shared some general understanding of what typical cases of piracy might involve, but there was room for doubt as to whether attacks motivated by considerations other than robbery or depredation could constitute piracy;[76] and there was also room for doubt as to the position in respect of acts done in furtherance of rebellion or insurrection. These doubts were not fully resolved until the concept of piracy was defined by the Geneva Convention on the High Seas in 1958. Under English law, it became possible for piracy to take the form either of piracy *jure gentium*, or of piracy by statute, under which certain acts that did not amount to piracy *jure gentium* were deemed to be piracy under the Piracy Acts of 1698, 1721, or 1744, but this legislation was repealed by the Statute Law (Repeals) Act 1993 and does not warrant further consideration here.

The concept of piracy *jure gentium* has changed significantly over the years.[77] Originally a purely maritime offence, it was extended by the 1958 Geneva Convention on the High Seas so as to include piratical acts committed in respect of aircraft, although in practice this extension was of no great consequence, because acts of airborne piracy are almost unknown.[78]

---

[74] *The Magellan Pirates* (1853) 1 Ecc and Ad 81, 84.   [75] (1696) 13 St Tr 451.

[76] See, e.g., *U S v. Cargo of the Brig Malek Adhel* (1844) 43 US 210.

[77] The changing nature of the offence was noted by the Privy Council in *Re Piracy Jure Gentium* [1934] AC 586, but it has evolved (or mutated) again since that case was decided.

[78] The term, 'air piracy', is popularly used to mean hijacking, but the hijacking of an aircraft (or ship) by its own crew or passengers is a quite different offence from piracy, and is punishable under quite different laws. See below, pp. 316–18.

In a much more important respect, the 1958 Convention adopted a 'narrow' definition of piracy, by excluding depredations committed within the territorial or internal waters of any state, and this narrow definition was incorporated into United Kingdom law by section 4 of the Tokyo Convention Act 1967, which declared that 'for the avoidance of doubt' it should be 'treated as constituting part of the law of nations'. The Geneva definition was restated more or less verbatim in UNCLOS 1982, Articles 101–103; and section 26 of the Merchant Shipping and Maritime Security Act 1997 dutifully substitutes this (again, 'for the avoidance of doubt') as the current definition of piracy under United Kingdom law.

The Modern Definition of Piracy

Even today, the definition of piracy appears to vary according to the context in which it arises. When used in the context of a marine insurance policy, or indeed in common parlance, 'piracy' bears a different (and in may respects wider) meaning from that which it bears under international or criminal law.[79] Most of the attacks recorded in the IMB survey (p. 301 above) would be classed as piracy for the purposes of marine insurance law. Under section 26 of the Merchant Shipping and Maritime Security Act 1997, however, the definition that currently applies for the purposes of the criminal law is that laid down by UNCLOS, Articles 101–103 and reproduced in Schedule 5 to the Act. Article 101 provides that piracy may consist of any of the following acts:

(a) any illegal acts of violence or detention, or any act of depredation,[80] committed for private ends by the crew or the passengers of a private ship or a private aircraft, and directed—

(i) on the high seas, against another ship or aircraft, or against persons or property on board such ship or aircraft;

(ii) against a ship, aircraft, persons or property in a place outside the jurisdiction of any State;

(b) any act of voluntary participation in the operation of a ship or of an aircraft with knowledge of facts making it a pirate ship or aircraft;

(c) any act of inciting or intentionally facilitating an act described in subparagraph (a) or (b).[81]

The term 'high seas', when used in UNCLOS (and thus when used in Schedule 5 to the 1997 Act), has a different meaning from that which it

---

[79] *Athens Maritime Enterprises Corporation v. Hellenic Mutual War Risks Association (Bermuda) Ltd (The Andreas Lemos)* [1983] QB 647 (*per* Staughton J).

[80] In *The Andreas Lemos* (above) Staughton J ruled that non-violent theft (akin to burglary rather than robbery) could not amount to piracy for insurance purposes; but as a matter of criminal law, any private act of depredation launched from another vessel on the high seas should suffice.

[81] Articles 102 and 103 provides ancillary definitions dealing with 'private ships', 'pirate ships', etc.

ordinarily bears under English law. It refers to waters lying beyond the territorial limits of any state, and may even be confined (for most purposes) to waters lying beyond the limits of any exclusive economic zone (or EEZ). UNCLOS, Article 58(2) nevertheless ensures that the rules governing piracy do not cease to apply within the EEZ.[82]

Piracy *jure gentium* is thus defined in terms that exclude any acts done within the territorial jurisdiction of a state—even if that state is the one seeking to exercise jurisdiction. This is an important and very restrictive consideration, because the vast majority of attacks on shipping take place in coastal waters, when the vessels attacked are navigating relatively close to the shore, passing through international straits, riding at anchor offshore, or lying in port. The attackers often board via the anchor chain. In areas that are known to be dangerous, shipping is advised to keep as far to seaward as possible, and to avoid stopping.[83] Attacks committed within the territorial or internal waters of a state may be treated as piracy for insurance purposes, and are certainly so described by the International Maritime Bureau,[84] but do not amount to piracy under international or English criminal law, even if these waters are also major international shipping lanes.[85]

Piracy in English Waters?

In light of the above, it must be considered doubtful whether a charge of piracy could be brought in respect of a vessel that is boarded and plundered by bandits within the territorial waters adjacent to England and Wales itself. Such a crime would be triable as robbery or assault with intent to rob under section 8 of the Theft Act 1968, and this would be the safest option

---

[82] Article 58(2) provides that 'Articles 88–115 and other pertinent rules of international law apply to the exclusive economic zone in so far as they are not incompatible with this Part' (i.e., Pt V).

[83] Ships passing the pirate-infested waters off Somalia are advised to keep at least 50 miles offshore, and on no account to stop or slow down when close inshore. Another heavily infested stretch of water in recent years has been the Malacca Strait, a busy shipping lane which lies between Sumatra and the Malay Peninsula and connects the Andaman and South China Seas.

[84] See also 'Five British Ships in Pirate Attacks' (2002) 151 *Shipping Today and Yesterday* 10. This article notes numerous 'pirate' attacks on British and foreign vessels, but the vast majority appear to be cases of theft or robbery in territorial or internal waters. Some merely involve the furtive theft of ships' stores, which would not appear to be piracy under any accepted definition of the term (see *The Andreas Lemos*, fn 79 above). On the other hand, some cases are reported by the IMB in which ships are fired on, forced to stop, and boarded, even when underway in open water.

[85] In *Archbold*, §25–42, it is argued that 'by the municipal law of England piracy may be committed within the territorial waters of a state, but may only be committed in respect of a ship when it is at sea in the ordinary meaning of that expression or in a geographical position where an attack on her could be described as a maritime offence'. The authorities cited for this proposition are *The Andreas Lemos* (fn 79 above) and *Republic of Bolivia* v. *Indemnity Mutual Marine Assurance Co. Ltd* [1909] 1 KB 785; but these are marine insurance cases, and have little bearing on the definition of piracy under criminal law or international law—as Staughton J expressly acknowledged in *The Andreas Lemos*.

for the prosecution to adopt, but if the bandits were charged with piracy the position would be more complicated. Section 6 of the Territorial Waters Jurisdiction Act 1878, which is still in force, purports to 'preserve' jurisdiction over piracy in United Kingdom territorial waters. It provides:

This Act shall not prejudice or affect the trial in manner heretofore in use of any act of piracy as defined by the law of nations, or affect or prejudice any law relating thereto; and where any act of piracy as defined by the law of nations is also any such offence as is declared by this Act to be within the jurisdiction of the Admiral, such offence may be tried in pursuance of this Act, or in pursuance of any other Act of Parliament, law, or custom relating thereto.

This provision originally ensured that no jurisdiction over acts of piracy committed within British coastal waters was lost as a result of the establishment of the United Kingdom's territorial sea, whilst at the same time it permitted any act of piracy committed within the territorial sea to be prosecuted as robbery, murder, wounding, etc.; but the offence of piracy has been redefined since then, and it is submitted that there is nothing in the 1878 Act that could enable a modern court to overlook this redefinition. The UNCLOS/Maritime Security Act definition does not simply provide that crimes of piracy may not be prosecuted if committed within territorial waters: it defines piracy in such a way that acts of depredation within territorial waters cannot amount to offences of piracy in the first place.

Offences Under Part II of the Aviation and Maritime Security Act 1990

Piracy is no longer the only specific maritime offence to possess a universal or broadly extended ambit under English law. More recently created examples include a series of offences created within Part II of the Aviation and Maritime Security Act 1990, namely: hijacking a ship, contrary to section 9; seizing or exercising control of a fixed platform, contrary to section 10; destroying ships or fixed platforms, or endangering their safety, contrary to section 11(1) or (2); committing acts endangering or likely to endanger safe navigation, contrary to section 12; and threatening to commit a section 11(1) offence, where the making of this threat endangers safety. Under the innocuous marginal heading 'ancillary offences', section 14(1) provides an extended ambit to a wide range of offences of violence, if these are committed (anywhere and by anyone) in connection with offences under sections 9–12 of the Act.

Hijacking of Ships

Section 9 of the 1990 Act, which is closely modelled on the long-established aircraft hijacking offence now contained within section 1 of the Aviation

Security Act 1982, provides:

(1) A person who unlawfully, by the use of force or by threats of any kind, seizes a ship or exercises control of it, commits the offence of hijacking a ship, whatever his nationality and whether the ship is in the United Kingdom or elsewhere, but subject to subsection (2) below.

(2) Subsection (1) above does not apply in relation to a warship or any other ship used as a naval auxiliary or in customs or police service unless—

(a) the person seizing or exercising control of the ship is a United Kingdom national, or

(b) his act is committed in the United Kingdom, or

(c) the ship is used in the naval or customs service of the United Kingdom or in the service of any police force in the United Kingdom.

The hijacking or seizure of a ship by passengers or other persons already aboard it may once have been classed as piracy under English law, but the redefinition of that offence in accordance with the 1958 Geneva Convention (and then with UNCLOS) precluded this. In 1978, the Law Commission first proposed the creation of an offence of maritime hijacking, but the ambit of this offence would have been limited:

(1) to acts committed within United Kingdom territorial waters;

(2) to acts committed in respect of British-controlled vessels; and/or

(3) to acts committed by citizens of the United Kingdom and colonies.[86]

The limitations were perceived to be necessary at that time because no international treaty or rule of customary law permitted states to exercise universal jurisdiction over such offences. There had been few reported instances of maritime hijacking,[87] and the international community does not appear to have addressed the threat of future cases. No mention of hijacking can be found in the 1982 UNCLOS Convention, and the Law Commission's proposal was never implemented.

The seizure of the Italian cruise liner *Achille Lauro* by Palestinian terrorists in 1985, and the subsequent murder of a disabled US citizen by the hijackers, resulted in a major reappraisal of the threat. In November 1985 the problem was considered by the International Maritime Organisation's 14th Assembly, and a proposal by the United States that measures to prevent such unlawful acts should be developed was supported. This led to the adoption of the 1988 Convention on the Suppression of Unlawful Acts

---

[86] Law Com. No. 91, paras 106–113, and cl. 5 of the Draft Criminal Jurisdiction Bill appended to the Report.

[87] A rare example was the 1961 seizure of the Portuguese passenger ship, *Santa Maria*, by hijackers who had boarded her as passengers, and who eventually succeeded in gaining political asylum in Brazil. See Whiteman, *Digest of International Law* (1963), vol. 4, 665.

Against the Safety of Maritime Navigation,[88] which came into force on 1 March 1992. The 1990 Act was passed in order that the United Kingdom might become one of the initial parties to this Convention.

The Convention obliges contracting states either to extradite alleged offenders, or to provide for prosecution in their own courts; and section 9 of the 1990 Act broadly adopts this approach, excluding from its ambit only cases in which foreign warships or naval auxiliary vessels are seized outside British waters by persons who are not United Kingdom nationals. Warships are not protected by the Convention, but acts done in British waters, or by UK nationals, or aboard British ships, are nevertheless within the rightful jurisdiction of the United Kingdom, without it being necessary to rely on the authority of the Convention.

Not all states are parties to the Convention, nor can it be assumed that it represents customary international law. Issues might conceivably arise under international law as to the right of British authorities to prosecute a case involving a ship flying the flag of a state that is not a party to the Convention; but prosecutions for offences under Part II of the 1990 Act require the consent (in England and Wales) of the Attorney-General, who would have to take any such issues into account when deciding whether to give that consent.

Seizing or Exercising Control of a Fixed Platform

The 1988 Convention is supplemented by the Protocol for the Suppression of Unlawful Acts Against the Safety of Fixed Platforms Located on the Continental Shelf, which also came into force on 1 March 1992. In accordance with that Protocol (to which the United Kingdom is a party), section 10 of the 1990 Act provides:

(1) A person who unlawfully, by the use of force or by threats of any kind, seizes a fixed platform or exercises control of it, commits an offence, whatever his nationality and whether the fixed platform is in the United Kingdom or elsewhere.

The offence is punishable, as is hijacking under section 9, by life imprisonment.

The section 10 offence supplements existing offences in so far as it applies to platforms in waters adjacent to England and Wales, but is by no means confined to such platforms. The unlawful seizure an oil or gas platform in (say) Norwegian waters, or on the Norwegian sector of the North Sea continental shelf, now constitutes an offence under English law. No English link need be established, but the Attorney-General's consent would be required (as in prosecutions under section 9), and in practice this consent would

---

[88] (1988) 27 ILM 668. See M. Halberstam, 'Terrorism on the High Seas: the *Achille Lauro*, Piracy and the IMO Convention on Maritime Safety' (1988) 82 *American Journal of International Law* 269.

be granted only if there were some good reason for not extraditing the alleged offenders to Norway.

Destroying Ships or Fixed Platforms or Endangering their Safety

The Convention and Protocol each apply not only to hijacking, etc., but also to a range of other acts, including acts of violence against persons on board ships or platforms; and the placing of devices on board a ship or platform which are likely to destroy or damage it. Such acts are addressed in section 11 of the 1990 Act, which provides:

(1) Subject to subsection (5) below, a person commits an offence if he unlawfully and intentionally—

(a) destroys a ship or a fixed platform,

(b) damages a ship, its cargo or a fixed platform so as to endanger, or to be likely to endanger, the safe navigation of the ship, or as the case may be, the safety of the platform, or

(c) commits on board a ship or on a fixed platform an act of violence which is likely to endanger the safe navigation of the ship, or as the case may be, the safety of the platform.

(2) Subject to subsection (5) below, a person commits an offence if he unlawfully and intentionally places, or causes to be placed, on a ship or fixed platform any device or substance which—

(a) in the case of a ship, is likely to destroy the ship or is likely so to damage it or its cargo as to endanger its safe navigation, or

(b) in the case of a fixed platform, is likely to destroy the fixed platform or so to damage it as to endanger its safety.

As far as foreign warships or naval auxiliaries are concerned, subsection (5) contains restrictions identical to those in section 9(2) (above); but in other respects section 11 applies universally, 'whether any such act . . . is committed in the United Kingdom or elsewhere and whatever the nationality of the person committing the act'.[89]

Other Offences under Part II

The same jurisdictional ambit (that is, universal, save for offences involving foreign naval vessels, etc.) applies to offences under sections 12 and 13 of the 1990 Act, which include various acts endangering or likely to endanger safe navigation at sea (section 12(1)) and threats to commit offences under section 11(1) or 12(1), where these threats are made 'in order to compel any

---

[89] See s. 11(4). By s. 11(7), an 'act of violence' means, in this context, '(a) any act done in the United Kingdom which constitutes the offence of murder, attempted murder, manslaughter, culpable homicide or assault or an offence under section 18, 20, 21, 22, 23, 24, 28 or 29 of the Offences against the Person Act 1861 or under section 2 of the Explosive Substances Act 1883; and (b) any act done outside the United Kingdom which, if done in the United Kingdom, would constitute such an offence . . .'.

other person to do or abstain from doing any act' and are themselves 'likely to endanger the safe navigation of the ship or . . . the safety of the fixed platform'.

Section 14 brings two further types of behaviour within the ambit of English criminal jurisdiction:

(1) Where a person (of whatever nationality) does outside the United Kingdom any act which, if done in the United Kingdom, would constitute an offence falling within subsection (2) below, his act shall constitute that offence if it is done in connection with an offence under section 9, 10, 11 or 12 of this Act committed or attempted by him.

(2) The offences falling within this subsection are murder, attempted murder, manslaughter, culpable homicide[90] and assault[91] and offences under sections 18, 20, 21, 22, 23, 24, 28 or 29 of the Offences against the Person Act 1861 and section 2 of the Explosive Substances Act 1883.

Such offences need not themselves be committed aboard ships or platforms, but must be 'connected' with an actual (or at least an attempted) offence under section 9, etc. An act committed in connection with a contemplated hijacking offence that is never in fact attempted does not appear to be covered by section 14(1); but where section 14(1) does apply, an 'everyday' offence such as assault or malicious wounding becomes an offence of near-universal jurisdiction[92] under English law.[93]

Lastly, section 14(4) makes it an offence for any person in the United Kingdom to induce or assist the commission outside the United Kingdom of any act which would have amounted to an offence under section 9, 11, 12, or 13, but for the fact that it involved a foreign naval vessel, etc. and was therefore excluded under section 9(2), 11(5), 12(6), or 13(4). This recognizes (as indeed do those same provisions) that the limitations of the Convention need not restrict the power of courts in the United Kingdom to deal with terrorist acts committed within the United Kingdom's own territorial limits.

OTHER MARITIME OFFENCES

Drug Trafficking

Sections 18 and 19 of the Criminal Justice (International Cooperation) Act 1990 address the important problem of international drug trafficking.

---

[90] This is an offence under Scots law, and is broadly equivalent to manslaughter under English law.

[91] But not, it seems, assault occasioning actual bodily harm.

[92] It is not quite a universal offence, because the 1861 Act does not extend to Scotland (Offences Against the Person Act 1861, s. 78) and nothing in the 1990 Act gives English courts jurisdiction over acts done in Northern Ireland.

[93] Section 14(1) has effect without prejudice to ss. 281 or 282 of the Merchant Shipping Act 1995 (offences committed on board British ships or by British seamen) or s. 10 of the Petroleum Act 1998 (application of criminal law to offshore installations). See s. 14(3).

By section 18, 'Anything which would constitute a drug trafficking offence if done on land in any part of the United Kingdom shall constitute that offence if done on a British ship'. As far as English law is concerned, that provision appears to do no more than restate what would in any case be the law. Section 19 is a more significant provision, because it extends the ambit of English law to things done aboard certain foreign vessels. It provides:

(1) This section applies to a British ship, a ship registered in a state other than the United Kingdom which is a party to the Vienna Convention (a 'Convention state') and a ship not registered in any country or territory.

(2) A person is guilty of an offence if on a ship to which this section applies, wherever it may be, he—
   (a) has a controlled drug in his possession; or
   (b) is in any way knowingly concerned in the carrying or concealing of a controlled drug on the ship,
knowing or having reasonable grounds to suspect that the drug is intended to be imported or has been exported contrary to section 3(1) of the Misuse of Drugs Act 1971 or the law of any state other than the United Kingdom.

(3) A certificate purporting to be issued by or on behalf of the government of any state to the effect that the importation or export of a controlled drug is prohibited by the law of that state shall be evidence, and in Scotland sufficient evidence, of the matters stated.

Does this apply to things done by foreign citizens aboard foreign ships? Applying general principles of statutory interpretation, the answer might appear to be 'No',[94] but there are other considerations to take into account. Section 19 is one of a series of provisions in the 1990 Act that seek to give effect to the United Kingdom's obligations under the 1988 Vienna Convention Against Illicit Traffic in Narcotic Drugs and Psychotropic Substances.[95] Article 17 of this Convention establishes a scheme under which the authorities of one Convention country may seek and obtain the permission of another Convention country to board and search a vessel flying the flag of that other country and apparently 'exercising freedom of navigation in accordance with international law'. This covers both navigation on the high seas and navigation within the territorial waters of a state. If evidence of involvement in illicit traffic is found, it may then 'take appropriate action with respect to the vessel, persons and cargo on board'. This strongly suggests that it may indeed have been Parliament's intention to assert criminal jurisdiction over such persons, regardless of their nationality; but once again it is to be regretted that the ambit of the legislation was not made more explicit.[96]

Section 19 is supplemented by sections 20 and 21 and by Schedule 3. These deal with enforcement powers and with the need for prosecutions to

---

[94] See above, p. 6.   [95] Cm. 804 (1989).
[96] On the subject of drug trafficking and the Vienna Convention, see further Bantekas, Nash, and Makarel, *International Criminal Law*, 256–61.

be instituted by or with the consent of the Director of Public Prosecutions or Commissioners of Customs and Excise. Schedule 3, paragraph 9, creates a summary offence of obstructing enforcement officers; and this must presumably be capable of commission wherever the officer is lawfully enforcing the Act, including foreign ships that are searched in accordance with section 19 and Schedule 3. Section 21(1) provides a venue in such cases: the offence 'may for all incidental purposes be treated as having been committed in any place in the United Kingdom'. Lastly, by section 21(3):

No proceedings for an offence under section 19 above alleged to have been committed outside the landward limits of the territorial sea of the United Kingdom on a ship registered in a Convention state shall be instituted except in pursuance of the exercise with the authority of the Commissioners of Customs and Excise of the powers conferred by Schedule 3 to this Act and section 3 of the Territorial Waters Jurisdiction Act 1878 (consent of Secretary of State for certain prosecutions) shall not apply to those proceedings.

Marine Pollution by Foreign Ships

United Kingdom ships are subject to English law in respect of oil or other pollution offences whether committed within United Kingdom waters or elsewhere, but as a general rule pollution caused by foreign ships may be so punishable only if committed within United Kingdom territorial or internal waters (excluding Scottish adjacent waters). While this may serve as a starting point, there are several exceptions to the general rule, which are permitted under UNCLOS or other Conventions.[97]

The most important regulations in this context are the Merchant Shipping (Prevention of Oil Pollution) Regulations 1996.[98] These generally apply to foreign ships only if within the United Kingdom's territorial limits, but regulations 12, 13, and 16[99] also prohibit improper discharges of oil or oily mixtures by foreign ships (other than warships) elsewhere, subject to restrictions contained in regulation 38, by which:

(1) No proceedings for an offence of contravening regulation 12, 13 or 16 by a ship which is not a United Kingdom ship, which relates to a discharge in the internal waters, territorial waters or exclusive economic zone of another State shall be instituted unless—

(a) that State, the flag state or a State damaged or threatened by the discharge requests that proceedings be taken; or

(b) the discharge has caused or is likely to cause pollution in the internal waters, territorial sea or controlled waters of the United Kingdom.

---

[97] Notably the 1973 International Convention for the Prevention of Pollution from Ships (the MARPOL Convention).   [98] SI 1996 No. 2154.
[99] Except for reg. 16(6), which is specific to UK ships entering Antarctic waters.

A Greek ship discharging oil into the Black Sea may thus commit an offence under English law, but it is not remotely likely that any prosecution would be instigated under that law.[100]

Regulation 5 of the Merchant Shipping (Dangerous or Noxious Liquid Substances in Bulk) Regulations 1996,[101] which prohibits discharges of noxious liquid substances or pollution hazard substances and improper tank washing, also applies to foreign ships outside United Kingdom waters, but prosecutions in such cases are heavily restricted by regulation 16, particularly in cases where the discharge in question occurred within the internal waters, territorial waters, or exclusive zone of another state, or where the discharge took place outside United Kingdom waters and controlled waters,[102] and the ship was in a port in the United Kingdom at the time of institution of proceedings by reason only of stress of weather or other reason beyond the control of the master or charterer. Broadly similar (but not identical) provisions may be found in the Merchant Shipping (Prevention of Pollution by Garbage) Regulations 1998.[103]

AVIATION SECURITY AND OFFENCES ABOARD AIRCRAFT

Offences committed aboard or against aircraft or air navigation have become a major source of concern over the last few years. Terrorist attacks, involving crimes such as hijacking, bombing, or sabotage, obviously provide the most extreme and dangerous examples, but they are far outnumbered by more mundane offences, many of which are alarming and some of which are potentially very dangerous. Many such offences involve violent and disruptive passengers, who intimidate or physically assault other passengers or cabin staff. Alcohol is often a factor in such incidents, as is the non-smoking rule that applies aboard most airlines serving the United Kingdom. In a typical case, an intoxicated passenger lights up a cigarette, and becomes violent when ordered to extinguish it. The closed environment of an aircraft cabin means that innocent passengers cannot easily get out the way when trouble flares, and such incidents may therefore become extremely distressing for those nearby. Hundreds of such cases are reported each year, although only a minority (notably those in which injuries are inflicted) result in prosecution.[104]

---

[100] By reg. 39, any proceedings for an offence involving a discharge of oil by a foreign ship may be suspended if the flag state then institutes proceedings.

[101] SI 1996 No. 3010.

[102] 'Controlled waters' are waters so designated by the Merchant Shipping (Prevention of Pollution) (Limits) Regulations 1996.   [103] SI 1998 No. 1377.

[104] For a discussion of the issues and statistics as to reported offences, see *Hansard* (HL), 12 January 1999, col. 140.

Other frequently reported incidents involve the misuse of mobile telephones, which may interfere with the aircraft's navigation or radio communications, thus endangering all those aboard. In some cases, passengers refuse to switch off telephones even when reminded of the prohibition against their use.

The Legislation

When considering the ambit of English criminal law in respect of extraterritorial offences committed aboard aircraft,[105] it is necessary to give separate consideration:

(1) to section 92 of the Civil Aviation Act 1982 (as amended), which applies to acts committed aboard a British controlled aircraft in flight or, subject to certain conditions, to acts committed aboard a foreign aircraft that subsequently lands in the United Kingdom; and

(2) to those offences of universal jurisdiction, such as hijacking, which fall within the Aviation Security Act 1982.

Prior to the enactment of the Tokyo Convention Act 1967, serious doubts existed as to whether British civil aircraft fell within the ambit of English criminal law when in flight. The conflict of opinion on that issue between Devlin J in *R v. Martin*[106] and Lord Parker CJ in *R v. Naylor*[107] as to the proper interpretation of the Civil Aviation Act 1949, section 6, is examined in Chapter 1 above. The 1967 Act, which implemented the 1963 Tokyo Convention on Offences aboard Aircraft,[108] resolved any such doubts, except perhaps in respect of aircraft overflying UK territorial waters,[109] and this legislation was later buttressed by the Hijacking Act 1971 and the Protection of Aircraft Act 1973,[110] which addressed the urgent need for universal jurisdiction to be provided in respect of the hijacking and sabotage of civil aircraft.

The legislation that was in place by the end of 1973 was consolidated, with some amendments, in the two Acts of 1982, and later augmented by Part 1 of the Aviation and Maritime Security Act 1990, section 1 of which creates further extraterritorial offences relating to 'endangering safety at aerodromes'.

---

[105] As to the position where offences are committed in the skies above England and Wales, or above territorial waters, see above, pp. 104–6.

[106] [1956] 2 QB 272.   [107] [1962] 2 QB 527.

[108] UKTS 126 (1969); Cmnd. 4230.   [109] See above, p. 105.

[110] These gave effect the 1970 Hague Convention for the Suppression of Unlawful Seizure of Aircraft (UKTS 39 (1972); Cmnd. 4956) and the Montreal Convention for the Suppression of Unlawful Acts against the Safety of Civil Aviation (UKTS 10 (1974); Cmnd. 5524).

Civil Aviation Act 1982, Section 92

By section 92(1)–(1B) of the Civil Aviation Act 1982[111]:

(1) Any act or omission taking place on board a British-controlled aircraft or (subject to subsection (1A) below) a foreign aircraft while in flight elsewhere than in or over the United Kingdom which, if taking place in, or in a part of, the United Kingdom, would constitute an offence under the law in force in, or in that part of, the United Kingdom shall constitute that offence; but this subsection shall not apply to any act or omission which is expressly or impliedly authorised by or under that law when taking place outside the United Kingdom.

(1A) Subsection (1) above shall only apply to an act or omission which takes place on board a foreign aircraft where—
(a) the next landing of the aircraft is in the United Kingdom, and
(b) in the case of an aircraft registered in a country other than the United Kingdom, the act or omission would, if taking place there, also constitute an offence under the law in force in that country.[112]

(1B) Any act or omission punishable under the law in force in any country is an offence under that law for the purposes of subsection (1A) above, however it is described in that law.

As explained in Chapter 3 above, section 92 does not apply to aircraft flying over the United Kingdom itself, because local law (for example, Scots or English law) will then apply.[113] Nor does it apply to military aircraft, or (save where any contrary order is made under section 101 of the Act) to any other aircraft belonging to or exclusively employed in the service of Her Majesty 'in right of the United Kingdom'.[114] It applies to all other British-controlled aircraft, but does not apply to acts aboard a foreign aircraft unless that aircraft then makes the United Kingdom its next landing point. This means that the *actus reus* of the offence depends not just on what the accused does, but on what the aircraft does next. A passenger assaults cabin staff on a US airliner flying over the Atlantic *en route* from London to New York. If the aircraft returns to England (whether because of the incident, or because of an unrelated engine problem) he becomes guilty of an offence under English law; but if it flies on to New York, or diverts to Dublin, he does not.
  A 'British-controlled aircraft' is defined in section 92(5) as an aircraft:

(a) which is for the time being registered in the United Kingdom; or
(b) which is not for the time being registered in any country but in the case of which either the operator of the aircraft or each person entitled as owner to any legal or beneficial interest in it satisfies the following requirements, namely—
    (i) that he is a person qualified to be the owner of a legal or beneficial interest in an aircraft registered in the United Kingdom; and

---

[111] As amended or inserted by the Civil Aviation (Amendment) Act 1996, s. 1.
[112] As to the proof (or presumption) of this, see s. 92(2A)–(2C).
[113] As to the status of aircraft flying over territorial waters, see above, p. 105.
[114] See s. 92(5).

(ii) that he resides or has his principal place of business in the United Kingdom; or

(c) which, being for the time being registered in some other country, is for the time being chartered by demise to a person who, or to persons each of whom, satisfies the requirements aforesaid.

By subsection 92(2)(a), the consent of the Director of Public Prosecutions is required in respect of any prosecutions in England under section 92. Section 92(3) makes provision for venue, which may be important in cases involving summary offences but is unnecessary as far as indictable offences are concerned. A more important question concerns the definition of 'flight'. Section 92(4) provides:

For the purposes of this section the period during which an aircraft is in flight shall be deemed to include any period from the moment when power is applied for the purpose of the aircraft taking off on a flight until the moment when the landing run (if any) at the termination of that flight ends; and any reference in this section to an aircraft in flight shall include a reference to an aircraft during any period when it is on the surface of the sea or land but not within the territorial limits of any country.

This may seem a broad definition, but it is significantly narrower than that which applies for the purpose of offences under the Aviation Security Act 1982 (below).

Offences Under the Aviation Security Act 1982

The principal offences created by the Aviation Security Act 1982 are:

(1) hijacking an aircraft in flight (section 1);
(2) destroying or seriously damaging an aircraft in service (section 2(1)(a));
(3) committing a specified act of violence aboard an aircraft in flight, which is likely to endanger the aircraft (section 2(1)(b));
(4) placing a dangerous or destructive device (such as a bomb) on an aircraft in service (section 2(2));
(5) destroying, or damaging, or interfering with other property (such as radar or air traffic control equipment) where this is likely to endanger the safety of aircraft in flight (section 3(1));
(6) communicating false, misleading, or deceptive information, where this endangers or is likely to endanger the safety of aircraft in flight (section 3(3)); and
(7) possessing prohibited articles (section 4).

These offences all have extraterritorial effect, and for most purposes those in sections 1 and 2 have near-universal application,[115] as do certain ancillary

---

[115] Provisions inserted by the Aviation and Maritime Security Act 1990 create further offences, notably relating to the making of false statements concerning baggage, cargo, or identity documents (ss. 21A and 21B) and unauthorized presence in certain places (ss. 21C and 21D), but none of these provisions appears to have any specific extraterritorial effect.

offences committed aboard an aircraft in connection with a hijacking or attempted hijacking offence under section 1 (section 6(1)).

The Act primarily consolidates the provisions of the Hijacking Act 1971 and the Protection of Aircraft Act 1973. These had been enacted in order that the United Kingdom might ratify the 1970 Hague Convention for Suppression of the Unlawful Seizure of Aircraft[116] and the 1971 Montreal Convention for the Suppression of Unlawful Acts Against the Safety of Civil Aviation.[117] The Conventions may in turn be explained as reactions to a spate of hijackings and acts of sabotage in preceding years, culminating in the notorious 'Dawson's Field' hijackings of September 1970, in which three western airliners, one of them a British VC10, were hijacked by Palestinian terrorists and flown to a remote airstrip in Jordan, where they were destroyed and their passengers and crews held to ransom. The United Nations immediately and unanimously called upon all states 'to take all appropriate measures to deter, prevent or suppress such acts . . . and to provide for the punishment of persons who perpetrate such acts.'[118]

Given the importance that is attached to aviation security and to the fight against terrorism, the extraterritorial jurisdiction provided under the Act is undoubtedly very significant, and its importance cannot be measured merely in terms of prosecutions, of which there are just a handful of reported cases under English law.[119] Even where failures of security allow such offences to occur, it may sometimes be considered more appropriate to extradite alleged offenders to another state that has a greater interest in prosecuting.

Hijacking

Section 1 of the Aviation Security Act 1982 provides:

(1) A person on board an aircraft in flight who unlawfully, by the use of force or by threats of any kind, seizes the aircraft or exercises control of it commits the offence of hijacking, whatever his nationality, whatever the State in which the aircraft is registered and whether the aircraft is in the United Kingdom or elsewhere, but subject to subsection (2) below.

(2) If—

  (a) the aircraft is used in military, customs or police service, or
  (b) both the place of take-off and the place of landing are in the territory of the State in which the aircraft is registered,

---

[116] UKTS 39 (1972); Cmnd. 4956.   [117] UKTS 10 (1974); Cmnd. 5524.

[118] UN General Assembly Resolution No. 2645; (1970) 9 ILM 2288.

[119] See *R v. Moussa Membar and others* [1983] Crim LR 618 (in which it was held that a hijacking offence might still be committed, even if the captain of the aircraft was implicated in it) and *R v. Abdul-Hussain and others* [1999] Crim LR 570 (in which it was held that the defence of duress of circumstances might in some cases be available to persons accused of hijacking). Each of these cases involved the hijacking of foreign aircraft over foreign territory, following which the aircraft in question landed in England. See also *R v. Hindawi* (1988) 10 Cr App R (S) 104, on sentencing in a case involving an attempt to destroy in airliner in flight.

subsection (1) above shall not apply unless—

(i) the person seizing or exercising control of the aircraft is a United Kingdom national; or

(ii) his act is committed in the United Kingdom; or

(iii) the aircraft is registered in the United Kingdom or is used in the military or customs service of the United Kingdom or in the service of any police force in the United Kingdom.

By s. 38(3) of the Act, an aircraft is deemed to be 'in flight' during any period from the moment when all its external doors are closed following embarkation until the moment when any such door is opened for disembarkation. In the event of a forced landing, the flight is deemed to continue until the competent authorities take over responsibility for the aircraft and for persons and property on board.[120]

The limitation imposed under section 1(2)(b) is based squarely on Article 3(3) of the Hague Convention, by which the Convention applies only to cases in which the place of take-off and/or the place of *actual* landing is situated outside the state of registration. Military,[121] police, or customs aircraft are not protected by the Convention, but this does not prevent the United Kingdom from legislating so as to protect its own aircraft in flight; nor does it prevent the extraterritorial application of English (or other United Kingdom) law to United Kingdom nationals who attempt to hijack a foreign military or police aircraft.

Offences Incidental to Hijacking

By section 6(1), various incidental offences committed aboard an aircraft in connection with a hijacking attempt may thereby acquire a universal ambit, similar to that for hijacking itself. Murder is the most significant of these offences, being the only one that is clearly more serious than hijacking itself. Section 6(1) provides:

Without prejudice to section 92 of the Civil Aviation Act 1982 (application of criminal law to aircraft) or to section 2(1)(b) of this Act, where a person (of whatever nationality) does on board any aircraft (wherever registered) and while outside the United Kingdom any act which, if done in the United Kingdom would constitute the offence of murder, attempted murder, manslaughter, culpable homicide or assault or an offence under section 18, 20, 21, 22, 23 28 or 29 of the Offences against the Person Act 1861 or section 2 of the Explosive Substances Act 1883, his act shall constitute that offence if it is done in connection with the offence of hijacking committed or attempted by him on board that aircraft.

---

[120] Contrast the much narrower definition of flight in cases governed by the Civil Aviation Act 1982, s. 92 (p. 316 above).

[121] The term 'military service' includes naval or air force service (s. 38).

Destroying, Damaging, or Endangering the Safety of Aircraft

Section 2 of the 1982 Act provides:

(1) It shall, subject to subsection (4) below, be an offence for any person unlawfully and intentionally—

(a) to destroy an aircraft in service[122] or so to damage such an aircraft as to render it incapable of flight or as to be likely to endanger its safety in flight; or

(b) to commit on board an aircraft in flight any act of violence which is likely to endanger the safety of the aircraft.

(2) It shall also, subject to subsection (4) below, be an offence for any person unlawfully and intentionally to place, or cause to be placed, on an aircraft in service any device or substance which is likely to destroy the aircraft, or is likely so to damage it as to render it incapable of flight or as to be likely to endanger its safety in flight; but nothing in this subsection shall be construed as limiting the circumstances in which the commission of any act—

(a) may constitute an offence under subsection (1) above, or

(b) may constitute attempting or conspiring to commit, or aiding, abetting, counselling or procuring, or being art and part in, the commission of such an offence.

(3) Except as provided by subsection (4) below, subsections (1) and (2) above shall apply whether any such act as is therein mentioned is committed in the United Kingdom or elsewhere, whatever the nationality of the person committing the act and whatever the State in which the aircraft is registered.

(4) Subsections (1) and (2) above shall not apply to any act committed in relation to an aircraft used in military, customs or police service unless—

(a) the act is committed in the United Kingdom, or

(b) where the act is committed outside the United Kingdom, the person committing it is a United Kingdom national.

(5) . . .

(6) In this section 'unlawfully'—

(a) in relation to the commission of an act in the United Kingdom, means so as (apart from this Act) to constitute an offence under the law of the part of the United Kingdom in which the act is committed, and

(b) in relation to the commission of an act outside the United Kingdom, means so that the commission of the act would (apart from this Act) have been an offence under the law of England and Wales if it had been committed in England and Wales or of Scotland if it had been committed in Scotland.

(7) In this section 'act of violence' means—

(a) any act done in the United Kingdom which constitutes the offence of murder, attempted murder, manslaughter, culpable homicide or assault or an offence under section 18, 20, 21, 22, 23, 24, 28 or 29 of the Offences against the Person Act 1861 or under section 2 of the Explosive Substances Act 1883, and

(b) any act done outside the United Kingdom which, if done in the United Kingdom, would constitute such an offence as is mentioned in paragraph (a) above.

---

[122] By s. 38(3)(b), an aircraft shall be taken to be in service both when in flight (see above) and 'during the whole of the period which begins with the pre-flight preparation of the aircraft for a flight and ends 24 hours after the aircraft lands having completed that flight'.

The ambit of the offences created by section 2 differs in two respects from that of hijacking under section 1. The first difference is that acts done against British military aircraft, etc., abroad cannot amount to section 2 offences unless committed by United Kingdom nationals. This is true even of offences committed aboard a British military aircraft in flight. The second difference is that universal jurisdiction may be exercisable under section 2, even in respect of offences committed against foreign aircraft that remain at all material times within their own state of registration. The former distinction is mysterious, but the latter can be explained by reference to Article 4(3) of the Montreal Convention, which expressly permits it. The resulting differences may nevertheless be confusing. If D (who is not a United Kingdom national) attempts to hijack a US airliner shortly after take off from Los Angeles, which then lands in Chicago, he commits no offence of hijacking under English law. He may, however, commit in the process an act of violence that endangers the safety of the flight, so as to make himself guilty of an offence under section 2(1)(b). If, in contrast, D hijacks an RAF military transport over Canada (or over the high seas), he *does* thereby commit an offence of hijacking, but cannot thereby commit any offence under section 2(1)(a), however seriously he endangers the safety of the aircraft.

Lockerbie and the September 11 Hijackings

In recent years, the most notorious crimes against civil aviation have been the destruction of Pan-Am flight 103 over Lockerbie in Scotland in 1988 and, of course, the multiple suicide hijackings of 11 September 2001. Each of these cases involved the murder of persons on the ground as well as of those in the aircraft, and each undoubtedly involved offences that might if required have been triable under English law. There is one surprising difference, however, because the US suicide hijackings involved offences of murder that would be triable (in the case of surviving conspirators or accessories) under English law, whereas the Lockerbie case, much closer to home, did not.

The initial planting of the Lockerbie bomb (by one or more Libyan agents in luggage on a flight from Malta that was then transferred to flight 103 at Frankfurt) was clearly an offence under section 2(2) of the Aviation Security Act 1982, although the defendants were not charged with that offence when indicted before the special Scottish court at Camp Zeist in The Netherlands. The destruction of the aircraft by the explosion of the bomb must equally have involved an offence under section 2(1); but although the defendants were indeed charged with that offence, no verdict on it was returned. The Crown's case was in the end confined to the charge of murder, of which the first defendant was convicted.[123]

---

[123] *HM Advocate v. Abdelbasset Ali Mohamed Al-Megrahi* [1999] Scot HC 248.

While the Aviation Security Act offences involving flight 103 might equally have been triable as offences under English law, none of the 260 murders could have been. As previously explained, murders connected with crimes of hijacking (as, for example, in the September 11 hijackings) are punishable under English law, wherever and by whomsoever committed, by virtue of section 6(1) of the Act, but this provision does not apply to murders, etc. committed in connection with a section 2 offence. The Scottish jurisdiction over the Lockerbie murders was territorial: the victims died either in the skies above Lockerbie, or, in some cases, on the ground at the crash site. That was the sole basis of jurisdiction, to which the 1982 Act was irrelevant. Given that Scots law clearly applied, the non-applicability of English homicide law was irrelevant in that particular case, but it does reveal a surprising state of affairs. It means that if D, a British citizen, plants a bomb on an Israeli airliner at Gatwick or Heathrow, which detonates over the Atlantic Ocean, killing everyone aboard, he is not guilty of murder under English law. He may of course be convicted and imprisoned for an offence under section 2 of the 1982 Act,[124] but a murder conviction might be considered more 'appropriate' on such facts.[125]

Other Acts Endangering or Likely to Endanger the Safety of Aircraft

The 'aviation endangerment' offences created by section 3(1) and (3) of the 1982 Act have a more limited extraterritorial ambit than offences under sections 1 and 2. By section 3(5) and (6).

(5) Subsections (1) and (3) above shall not apply to the commission of any act unless either the act is committed in the United Kingdom, or, where it is committed outside the United Kingdom—

(a) the person committing it is a United Kingdom national; or

(b) the commission of the act endangers or is likely to endanger the safety in flight of a civil aircraft registered in the United Kingdom or chartered by demise to a lessee whose principal place of business, or (if he has no place of business) whose permanent residence, is in the United Kingdom; or

(c) the act is committed on board a civil aircraft which is so registered or so chartered; or

(d) the act is committed on board a civil aircraft which lands in the United Kingdom with the person who committed the act still on board.

---

[124] As in *R v. Hindawi* (1988) 10 Cr App R (S) 104 (sentence of 45 years' imprisonment for an attempt to place a bomb aboard an El-Al airliner at Heathrow; upheld on appeal).

[125] The Offences Against the Person Act 1861, s. 9 (which applies to murders committed by British citizens, etc., on land abroad) would not apply in such a case; nor would s. 4 of the Suppression of Terrorism Act 1978 apply, unless the aircraft in question was registered in a Convention country (or in India): see s. 4(7) (p. 257 above). This explains why no charge of attempted murder was laid in *Hindawi* (above).

(6) Subsection (1) above shall also not apply to any act committed outside the United Kingdom and so committed in relation to property which is situated outside the United Kingdom and is not used for the provision of air navigation facilities in connection with international air navigation, unless the person committing the act is a United Kingdom national.

Offences in Relation to Certain Dangerous Articles

The offence of unlawful possession created by section 4 of the 1982 Act has only a limited and uncertain extraterritorial effect. By section 4(1)(a) it applies 'to aircraft registered in the United Kingdom, whether at a time when the aircraft is in the United Kingdom or not'. Section 4 does not expressly require that the aircraft must be in flight at the time, although such a requirement might perhaps be implied.

Participation in Excluded Offences

Certain acts that are not offences within the normal application of the Aviation Security Act 1982 (because they fall outside the scope of the Conventions) may nevertheless give rise to criminal liability on the part of anyone who induces or assists in their commission from within the United Kingdom. As far as English law is concerned, this means that the assistance, etc., must be provided from within England and Wales. The United Kingdom is of course entitled to apply its territorial law in this way, without reference to the Conventions. Section 6(2) accordingly provides:

It shall be an offence for any person in the United Kingdom to induce or assist the commission outside the United Kingdom of any act which—
(a) would, but for subsection (2) of section 1 of this Act, be an offence under that section; or
(b) would, but for subsection (4) of section 2 of this Act, be an offence under that section; or
(c) would, but for subsection (5) or (6) of section 3 of this Act, be an offence under that section.

Endangering Safety at Aerodromes

Airports are highly vulnerable to terrorist attack, as was demonstrated by incidents at airports in Rome and Vienna during the 1980s, and this led in 1988 to the drafting of a Protocol for the Suppression of Unlawful Acts of Violence at Airports Serving International Civil Aviation.[126] The Protocol supplements the Montreal Convention for the Suppression of Unlawful Acts against the Safety of Civil Aviation, and was implemented

---

[126] Cm. 378 (1988). The Protocol came into force in 1989, but the UK did not become a party until 1990.

into United Kingdom law by Part 1 of the Aviation and Maritime Security Act 1990. For the most part, this legislation merely amends the Aviation Security Act 1982, but section 1(1) and (2) of the 1990 Act create new extraterritorial offences. These provide:

(1) It is an offence for any person by means of any device, substance or weapon intentionally to commit at an aerodrome serving international civil aviation any act of violence[127] which—

(a) causes or is likely to cause death or serious personal injury, and

(b) endangers or is likely to endanger the safe operation of the aerodrome or the safety of persons at the aerodrome.

(2) It is also, subject to subsection (4) below, an offence for any person by means of any device, substance or weapon unlawfully and intentionally—

(a) to destroy or seriously to damage—

(i) property used for the provision of any facilities at an aerodrome serving international civil aviation (including any apparatus or equipment so used), or

(ii) any aircraft which is at such an aerodrome but is not in service, or

(b) to disrupt the services of such an aerodrome,

in such a way as to endanger or be likely to endanger the safe operation of the aerodrome or the safety of persons at the aerodrome.

The extraterritorial ambit of the offences is prescribed by subsections 1(3) and (4), which apply principles previously adopted in the 1982 Act:

(3) Except as provided by subsection (4) below, subsections (1) and (2) above apply whether any such act as is referred to in those subsections is committed in the United Kingdom or elsewhere and whatever the nationality of the person committing the act.

(4) Subsection (2)(a)(ii) above does not apply to any act committed in relation to an aircraft used in military, customs or police service unless—

(a) the act is committed in the United Kingdom, or

(b) where the act is committed outside the United Kingdom, the person committing it is a United Kingdom national.

Consent to Prosecutions

Prosecutions for offences under sections 1–3 or 6 of the Aviation Security Act 1982, or under section 1 of the Aviation and Maritime Security Act 1990, may be instituted only by or with the consent of the Attorney-General.[128]

---

[127] Defined in s. 1(9) as any act which, if committed in the UK, would constitute the offence of murder, attempted murder, manslaughter, culpable homicide or assault; or an offence under ss. 18, 20–24, 28 or 29 of the Offences Against the Person Act 1861 or under s. 2 of the Explosive Substances Act 1883.

[128] Aviation Security Act 1982, s. 8; Aviation and Maritime Security Act 1990, s. 1(7).

7

Rethinking the Ambit of the Criminal Law

INTRODUCTION

The rules which now govern the ambit of English criminal jurisdiction are characterized both by unnecessary complexity and by the lack of any unifying structure or principle. To a large extent, the former is undoubtedly a product of the latter. Much of the complexity arises because there are too many separate and often overlapping rules, which share few common principles and have never been subjected to any thorough consolidation or revision. The relevant law, in other words, is badly in need of clarification, simplification, and reform.

No major obstacles stand in the way of such reform, other than those thrown up by competing demands for Parliamentary time and resources. Many specific reforms or developments have taken place over the last few years, and some of these have been quite substantial. What appears to be lacking, at the moment, is any overall principle or policy, of the kind that might usefully be included in a future Criminal Code.

REFORM AND CODIFICATION

The Law Commission is engaged, once again, on the production of a Draft Criminal Code for England and Wales, beginning as before with general principles of liability. As in the 1989 Draft Code, however, the Commission appears to have no immediate plans to include within it provisions delimiting the territorial and extraterritorial ambit of the criminal law. It is submitted, with respect, that the omission of such provisions would be indefensible. The issues involved are fundamental and should be addressed. One cannot satisfactorily codify the general principles of English criminal law without considering where or to whom that system of law is to apply.

The Draft Criminal Code of 1989

The omission of such issues from the 1989 Draft Code was not the fault of the original Code team. As the Law Commission acknowledged in its introduction to that Code, the team had originally argued that 'The Code must contain general provisions relating to the jurisdiction of the criminal courts, that is to say, the definition of the territory of England and Wales for criminal purposes; and that Part 1 [of the Code] was the appropriate place for them'.[1] Subject to the qualification that it is the ambit of the law itself that is in issue, and not merely the jurisdiction of the courts (or indeed the extent of the realm), it is hard to see how one could seriously challenge that view. In other jurisdictions with established criminal codes, the ambit of the law is almost invariably addressed. The Commission, however, sought the opinions of various Government departments and of the Working Party of the Statute Law Society, and the response from those quarters was by no means favourable.

Some of the Government departments, including the Foreign Office, were unhappy with the team's original proposals in this area, which were derived from the Law Commission's Draft Jurisdiction Bill of 1978.[2] The exact basis of their concerns is not recorded, but the Draft Jurisdiction Bill was undoubtedly flawed in several respects, and would have needed considerable modification and augmentation.[3] Instead of working to improve those original proposals and address any specific concerns, it appears that the Law Commission simply shelved the whole issue, and concluded that there was 'little advantage to be gained by including provisions which would inevitably require reconsideration'.[4]

This was a disappointing and uncharacteristic response. The Codification Project was (and remains) a massive and difficult undertaking. Many of the issues at its heart are more complex and intractable than any concerning the proper ambit of the criminal law. The fact that the Commission gave up so readily on that particular issue may, however, have been linked to the response received from the Statute Law Society's Working Party, who argued that such matters properly belonged within the procedural part of any such Code (that is, within what would have been Part III of the Draft Code, on which little work has ever been done) rather than within Part I, which deals with fundamental principles.

Matters relating to the jurisdiction of the courts should indeed be classed as procedural, but the ambit of the law itself is another matter, as I have attempted to explain in Chapter 1 above. It appears that the Commission was badly advised in this respect, and that it was misled by that advice. Such, however, is the confused thinking that the mislabelling of a concept can induce.[5]

---

[1] See Law Com. No. 177, vol. 1, para. 3.13.   [2] Law Com. No. 91.
[3] See Michael Hirst, 'Territorial Principles and the Law Commission' [1979] *Criminal Law Review* 355 and 781.   [4] Op. cit. fn 1.
[5] Some might argue that codification within the procedural part of the Code would be better than nothing. This is doubtful, however, because it would involve the codification of a fundamental error.

Issues for Future Reform and Codification

If the rules governing the territorial and extraterritorial ambit of the criminal law were ever to be included in a future codification exercise, what form might this codification take? First and foremost, any codification of these rules would need to be preceded by the enactment of substantial reforms. There would be no point in the codification of the current ramshackle rules in all their glory. Indeed, the codification of such an incoherent set of rules would be well-nigh impossible. As the Law Commission explained in 1989, 'the Code cannot reproduce inconsistencies'. The process of reform should therefore be entrusted to a Criminal Jurisdiction Act, the provisions of which could later be incorporated within the main body of the Code. This suggestion may perhaps be dismissed as wishful thinking, because it is unlikely that anything of this sort will be enacted within the foreseeable future; but that does not alter the fact that reform and codification are needed.

It is submitted that the process of reform and codification should address and incorporate the following issues:

The Basic Territorial Ambit of the Law

The delimitation of maritime boundaries lies at the heart of this issue. Boundary issues clearly involve considerations that go well beyond mere matters of criminal law, but everyone concerned must surely have a common interest in establishing clearly defined boundaries for United Kingdom waters. The publication of maritime boundaries and/or bay-closing baselines on Admiralty charts is not merely desirable: it is an international treaty obligation that the United Kingdom has been culpably slow to fulfil.

Much could also be done to simplify or clarify the various jurisdictional regimes that apply within United Kingdom waters. A clear distinction already exists between Scottish adjacent waters and other waters adjacent to the United Kingdom, but no comparable distinction has yet been drawn between waters adjacent to England and Wales and those adjacent to Northern Ireland; nor is it entirely clear whether (or when) English law applies to acts committed in Northern Irish waters. Clarification would be useful here.

Within the waters adjacent to England and Wales, the vast majority of offences under English law should be made capable of commission anywhere within a single, common, and clearly defined territorial area, even if certain offences may in practice be incapable of such wide application.[6] There should be no need to distinguish between different types of offence for that purpose. Summary offences should, in other words, be given the

---

[6] Road traffic offences, for example, must necessarily have a more limited ambit.

same basic territorial ambit as indictable offences, and there should be no separate zones or boundaries within that area, other than those required by international law.[7] Separate concepts or zones of Admiralty and common law jurisdiction, or loosely defined concepts such as that of the *fauces terrae* should therefore be abandoned, and magistrates' courts should acquire the same powers to try summary offences committed in coastal waters as they already possess in respect of offences triable either way.[8] Section 280 of the Merchant Shipping Act 1995 (which deals with ships lying off coasts) may then be repealed as obsolete and unnecessary. Some might argue that it has always been so.

Cross-frontier Crimes

The existing law on cross-frontier offences is unsatisfactory for a number of reasons, but above all it is erratic in its application and seriously in need of rationalization. Buried within the bewildering range of special cases and exceptions discussed in Chapter 4 above, one may find some promising (if still over-complex) examples of a better approach to cross-frontier crime. These are currently of limited application, but might be adapted on a more general basis in order to provide English law with a workable and comprehensive (or 'inclusionary') approach to the assertion of jurisdiction over such crimes. Other countries already have Code provisions that address such issues, and some of these may also merit consideration as possible models for adoption within a future English Code. This is a matter which requires further consideration, and is addressed at greater length later in this chapter (see pp. 340–3).

Ships, Aircraft, and Offshore Installations

Despite the existence of a considerable body of relatively modern legislation dealing with this issue, the maritime ambit of English criminal law still requires clarification and simplification. The provisions of the Merchant Shipping Act 1995 are neither comprehensive nor entirely logical, and do not therefore provide a satisfactory model for future codification. It is absurd, for example, that a summary offence, such as common assault, is incapable of commission aboard a British-owned vessel at sea, unless that vessel has been registered as a United Kingdom ship under Part II of the 1995 Act. Nor, indeed, does a Merchant Shipping Act appear to be the right place to contain rules governing the general maritime ambit of English criminal law. An alternative scheme should therefore be devised, that would

---

[7] International law requires states to distinguish for some purposes between internal and territorial waters, but does not require the adoption of radically different jurisdictional regimes within those zones; nor does it require distinctions to be drawn for that purpose between internal and inland waters.

[8] See the Magistrates' Courts Act 1980, s. 2(3) and (4).

apply equally to all British-owned vessels that are not registered elsewhere in the world. This scheme might, for example, enable acts or omissions that would be offences if committed in any part of the United Kingdom to be punishable in that part of the United Kingdom if committed aboard any such vessel, whether at sea or in a harbour, etc. (not necessarily a 'foreign' harbour) abroad.[9] Offences committed aboard Scottish-based vessels might ordinarily be dealt with under Scots law, but rigid lines of demarcation between English and Scots (or Northern Irish) law might prove troublesome in practice and would be better avoided.

Provisions dealing with aviation are already satisfactory in many respects, but even here clarification is needed on certain issues, notably in respect of aircraft overflying territorial or internal waters. It should be made clear that aircraft overflying English or Welsh waters are subject to the same rules of criminal law as aircraft overflying the territory of England and Wales itself.

Extraterritorial Application

Any reform or codification of this area must at least seek to impose some order or consistency on the disjointed rag-bag of provisions that were considered in Chapter 5 above, but a more radical reform might involve the adoption of a new general principle under which the nationality of the alleged offender would rank alongside territoriality as a general basis for the imposition of criminal liability, at least in respect of offences triable on indictment. Arguments for and against that idea are considered later in this chapter (see pp. 330–40).

Consideration might also be given to adoption of the protective principle jurisdiction, under which acts committed abroad may be regarded as offences under English law, even when committed by foreigners, if those acts threaten legitimate British interests. The counterfeiting of British bank notes abroad provides just one example of conduct that might legitimately be made the subject of such jurisdiction.

Before giving further consideration to these possibilities, however, attention must be given to two related issues. The first concerns acts committed in other parts of the United Kingdom: should English criminal law ever apply to acts committed in Scotland or Northern Ireland? The second concerns issues of nationality and status: to which persons or classes should any nationality-based jurisdiction apply?

Crimes Committed in Other Parts of the United Kingdom

At present, consistency is sadly lacking in this area. Most extraterritorial offences under English law are incapable of commission in Scotland or

---

[9] As to the current distinction between foreign and Commonwealth harbours, see the Merchant Shipping Act 1995, s. 281 and *R v. Liverpool Justices, ex p Molyneux* [1972] 2 QB 384.

Northern Ireland, even if the same conduct constitutes an equivalent offence under Scots or Northern Irish law, and even if it is an offence there by virtue of the very same legislation; but there are some offences, such as bigamy, that appear to defy this rule. As pointed out in Chapter 5 above, it has been held that a British citizen may be convicted in England of an offence of bigamy committed in Scotland, contrary to section 57 of the Offences Against the Person Act 1861, even though that statute is not part of Scots law.[10]

The obvious objection to treating Scotland and Northern Ireland as foreign countries for the purpose of applying extraterritorial provisions of English criminal law is that it would make substantial inroads into the constitutional separation of the relevant legal systems. The more extraterritorial offences that exist under English law, the more extensive these inroads would become. If English law were to adopt a general policy of nationality-based extraterritorial jurisdiction alongside the existing principle of territoriality, that might result in the whole of English criminal law becoming applicable throughout Scotland and Northern Ireland, except in respect of those few persons in Scotland or Northern Ireland who are not United Kingdom nationals. Given that Scots criminal law, in particular, is different from English criminal law in several important respects, it is clear that such a development would cause difficulties, unless some restriction were to be placed on the bringing of prosecutions in England. A possible solution would be for legislation to provide that no prosecution should be brought in England and Wales in respect of acts or omissions in Scotland or Northern Ireland, unless certain conditions are satisfied. These might include:

(1) conditions relating to cross-frontier offences, or to cross-frontier participation in offences committed in England and Wales;[11]
(2) conditions dealing with acts or omissions that are alleged to form part of a series, or of a course of conduct, in which other related acts or omissions are alleged to have taken place in England and Wales; and
(3) conditions dealing with alleged offences (such as 'border' offences) in which there are doubts as to where exactly the offence was committed relative to the border. The rules that currently govern offences committed at unknown localities within the Channel Tunnel System might perhaps be adapted for this purpose.[12]

Nationality and Status

It is submitted that English criminal law should adopt a standard form of British or United Kingdom nationality in the context of extraterritorial

[10] *R v. Topping* (1856) Dears 647 (p. 233 above).
[11] See, e.g., *R v. Robert Millar (Contractors) Ltd* [1970] 2 QB 54.
[12] See above, pp. 101–2.

criminal liability. At present, there are far too many different variants of nationality in use for this purpose, and many offence-creating statutes dating from before 1981 (in particular those dating from before 1948) still refer to obsolete forms of nationality in that context. Nor is that all. Bizarre and almost certainly unintended distinctions must currently be drawn between Commonwealth citizens who commit certain acts (such as murder or bigamy) in foreign or Commonwealth counties and those who commit such acts at sea, or in other parts of the United Kingdom. In the former situation, Commonwealth citizens who are not also British are generally treated as if they were foreigners; but in the latter situation they may sometimes find themselves subject to extraterritorial jurisdiction on the same basis as British citizens. Section 3(1) of the British Nationality Act 1948 clearly needs to be revised in order to avoid such consequences.

It is submitted that any extraterritorial criminal liability that is based on nationality (rather than on universality, or on the protective principle) should ordinarily be limited to United Kingdom nationals or United Kingdom persons (including registered corporations and Scottish partnership firms, where appropriate).[13] Commonwealth citizens who are not United Kingdom nationals should not be subject to any such jurisdiction. Some exceptions to the general rule may need to be preserved, however, notably where the form of nationality or status relied upon is dictated by the terms of an international Convention. The 1977 European Convention on the Suppression of Terrorism, for example, requires the adoption of special rules relating to certain offences committed by the nationals of 'Convention countries' outside the United Kingdom.

ENLARGING THE GENERAL AMBIT OF THE LAW

The potential enlargement or expansion of English criminal jurisdiction has already been discussed at various points in this work, but the principal options for change may usefully be summarized once more. Ignoring the problem of cross-frontier offences for the moment, legislation might be enacted adopting one or more of the following measures:

(1) It might follow the continental practice, and adopt nationality-based jurisdiction on a general or 'wholesale' basis. Assuming that United Kingdom personality would be utilized for that purpose, and that exceptions would be made for acts committed elsewhere within the United Kingdom, this would mean that any act or omission that would amount

---

[13] As to the precise meaning of those terms, see above, pp. 207–8.

to an indictable offence under English law if committed within England and Wales would equally amount to such an offence if committed by a United Kingdom person, anywhere outside the United Kingdom.[14]

(2) In lieu of option (1), reforming legislation might make more extensive and rational use of nationality-based jurisdiction, but without abandoning the general principle of territoriality. Most offences, in other words, would remain narrowly territorial in application,[15] but the exceptions would be more numerous and would share a common framework or format.

(3) In addition to options (1) or (2), legislation might adopt the 'protective principle' of jurisdiction in respect of extraterritorial crimes that threaten important national interests. Whilst English law currently makes no use of that principle, its validity is widely recognized under international law, and adoption should not raise any serious difficulties.

None of these options should be seen as a substitute for extradition in cases where extradition would otherwise be ordered. The United Kingdom has no plans to restrict or prohibit the extradition of its nationals. On the contrary, the Extradition Bill introduced into Parliament in November 2002 is designed to make extradition procedures faster, less complex, and less cumbersome than at present, particularly in respect of 'category 1 territories', such as member states of the European Union. Nevertheless, cases will continue to arise in which extradition is impossible or undesirable, or indeed in which extradition is never sought. As the Government's Interdepartmental Steering Committee explained in its Report[16]:

Although the principle hitherto upheld by the UK that crimes are best prosecuted in the country where they are committed remains important, and equal and parallel principle should be considered: that of ensuring that the criminal is not allowed to escape prosecution. This is a matter which is raised regularly in international fora, particularly within the European Union. . . .

The Case for Wider Nationality-based Jurisdiction

International lawyers who advocate the increased utilization of nationality as a basis for criminal jurisdiction[17] argue that the traditional reliance on

[14] This principle would presumably be restricted to offences triable on indictment, on the basis that most purely summary offences are inherently minor and would not therefore merit the adoption of such extensive (and potentially expensive) extraterritorial jurisdiction.

[15] Special rules must continue to apply to servicemen and Crown servants, etc., when stationed abroad.

[16] *Review of Extraterritorial Jurisdiction* (Home Office, 1996), para. 2.7.

[17] See, e.g., G.R. Watson, 'Offenders Abroad: the Case for Nationality-based Criminal Jurisdiction' (1992) 17 *Yale Journal of International Law* 41; P. Arnell, 'The Case for Nationality-based Jurisdiction' (2001) 50 *International and Comparative Law Quarterly* 955.

territoriality in common law jurisdictions, which once seemed both natural and logical,[18] has increasingly been put under strain by the changing nature of modern society and modern crime. In this context, Arnell[19] cites the 'lessened significance of borders' (especially within the European Union), the greater degree of national awareness and concern over crimes committed in other countries, and the 'internationalisation of criminal law and crime' itself. With respect, while these factors clearly do place a strain on narrowly focused territorial principles, some of them might more logically be used to argue in favour of a more flexible cross-frontier application of territorial principles, or perhaps for some use to be made of the protective principle. When Lord Griffiths declared that 'Crime is now established on an international scale and the common law must face this new reality',[20] he clearly was not calling for greater use of nationality-based jurisdiction, but rather for a broader view to be taken of territorial jurisdiction over international conspiracies. International criminals may not necessarily possess the requisite nationality, but are no less dangerous or troublesome on that account.

Arnell is nevertheless correct in his assertion that the misconduct of United Kingdom nationals abroad has become a matter of national concern. When English football hooligans riot in Belgium, or the activities of English paedophiles in Thailand are exposed by the media, the expectation is that something should be done about it. The same is true of cases in which British companies are shown to have behaved corruptly in seeking contracts abroad. The United Kingdom bears some moral responsibility for the conduct of its nationals abroad, even where it bears no legal responsibility, and this has increasingly been recognized within modern criminal legislation, notably in the Sex Offenders Act 1997 (in respect of sex offences against children) and in the Anti-terrorism, Crime and Security Act 2001 (in respect of overseas corruption). The question is whether this responsibility should be taken further and addressed on a more general basis.

Wholesale Assumption of Jurisdiction, or over Selected Offences Only?

The Government's Interdepartmental Steering Committee concluded in 1996 that whilst existing rules governing extraterritorial criminal jurisdiction were manifestly haphazard and inadequate, the wholesale extension of English criminal law to nationals abroad would be problematic. The Committee therefore recommended that reform should be effected on

---

[18] R.M. Perkins, 'The Territorial Principle in Criminal Law' (1971) 22 *Hastings Law Journal* 1155.   [19] Arnell, op. cit., fn 17, 958–61.
[20] *Somchai Liangsiriprasert v. U S Government* [1991] 1 AC 225.

a selective basis, providing an extraterritorial ambit to individual offences only where some at least of the following tests are satisfied:[21]

(1) The offence is serious;
(2) by virtue of the nature of the offence, witnesses and evidence are likely to be available within the United Kingdom;
(3) there is international consensus as to the reprehensible nature of the crime and the need to take extraterritorial jurisdiction;
(4) the vulnerability of the victim makes it particularly important that offences are prosecuted;
(5) it is in the interests of the standing and reputation of the United Kingdom within the international community; and
(6) there is a danger that such offences would not otherwise be justiciable.

An offence that satisfies one or more of the above tests would not automatically be seen to justify an extraterritorial ambit, 'but it would suggest that action might be justified, particularly if the practical enforcement issues [do] not appear to be insurmountable'.[22]

While not formally implemented, this proposal appears to have been quietly adopted within the law-making process. The first fruits of this adoption were seen the following year in the form of section 7 of the Sex Offenders Act 1997. Indeed, the Committee's Report appears to have been instrumental in persuading the Government to abandon its earlier opposition to the imposition of extraterritorial liability over child-sex offences.[23] With respect, however, such a policy can do little to reduce the complexity and confusion that bedevils this area of law, particularly when no systematic attempt is made to apply it to existing offences.

The Case for Wholesale Assumption

In contrast, much of this complexity and confusion would at once be swept away if all offences triable on indictment (other than those inherently limited to certain localities by virtue of their subject matter) were to be made capable of commission by United Kingdom persons abroad. Such a 'neat' solution has obvious attractions from a codifier's viewpoint; but one must consider whether the practical advantages of such a reform would outweigh the potential disadvantages. The Committee's objections to it must accordingly be examined.

The Committee's first concern was that existing mechanisms for gathering information and evidence from abroad would be overloaded by such a development.[24] This concern appears to have been based on the assumption that it would lead to a large increase in the number of extraterritorial

---

[21] Op. cit., fn 16, para. 2.21.   [22] Ibid., para. 2.22.
[23] See above, pp. 268–9.   [24] Op. cit., fn 16, para. 2.10.

offences investigated and prosecuted, and that this would impose a proportionately large additional strain on the mechanisms in question. A significant increase of this kind might indeed occur—there would be little point in such a radical reform if it did not—but the Continental experience does not suggest that one should expect more than a handful of such prosecutions each year.[25]

In contrast, the mechanisms used for gathering evidence and conducting investigations abroad (which make extensive use of bilateral and multilateral agreements providing for the provision of mutual assistance between contracting states or parties[26]) are already subject to intensive use in connection with the investigation and prosecution of numerous territorial and cross-frontier offences, notably those involving international fraud, smuggling, terrorism, child pornography, and drug trafficking. It is increasingly common for the investigation of such offences to require extraterritorial evidence gathering or international police cooperation,[27] and the strain which this puts on resources may be considerable. The investigation of purely extraterritorial offences is most unlikely to absorb more than a small proportion of the substantial effort currently committed to such matters, even if all indictable offences were to acquire an extraterritorial ambit based on nationality. This is because territorial and cross-frontier offences which threaten interests within the United Kingdom will almost inevitably be of greater and more immediate concern to British investigating authorities, and will be given priority accordingly.

The Committee's second objection was that the wholesale application of English law to offences committed abroad would necessitate major changes to the common law rules of evidence and procedure, because the requirements of a common law system based on oral testimony and cross-examination are 'less well adapted to the requirements of extraterritorial prosecutions than those of a civil law system based on enquiry and

---

[25] This would still be a significant increase, because the current level of extraterritorial prosecutions is very low indeed.

[26] At the time of writing, the law relating to mutual assistance was governed by Pt I of the Criminal Justice (International Cooperation) Act 1990 and by rules made thereunder; but these are likely to be supplanted during 2003 by provisions contained in Pt I of the Crime (International Cooperation) Bill of November 2002. These provisions have been drafted for the purpose of enabling the UK to adopt the mutual legal assistance provisions of the 1990 Schengen Implementing Convention, the 2000 European Convention on Mutual Assistance in Criminal Matters (MLAC) (which in part supplant the Schengen provisions), and certain provisions of the Framework Decision on the execution within the EU of orders freezing property and evidence. It is hoped that the UK will be able to join the Schengen Information System (or SIS), which stores and processes crime-related data from all participating countries. As to mutual legal assistance and international police cooperation generally, see Bantekas, Nash, and Mackarel, *International Criminal Law* (2001), Chapters 8 and 9.

[27] Around half of all cases dealt with by the Serious Fraud Office either involve a cross-frontier element or some need to obtain evidence from abroad, but very few such cases involve 'pure' extraterritorial offences.

investigation'. This objection may be answered, however, in much the same way as the preceding one. If changes are necessary or desirable in order to facilitate the wider use of evidence gathered from abroad then they are already necessary or desirable, because such evidence is already required in respect of numerous prosecutions involving territorial or cross-frontier offences, and these will probably become even more numerous in future years.[28]

The Committee's third objection was that the adoption of such wide jurisdictional powers might encourage other states to decline to prosecute complex offences committed by United Kingdom nationals in their own territories, in the hope that the responsibility and expense of so doing would be taken up by the United Kingdom authorities. This is, with respect, a bizarre argument. Cases do indeed occur in which responsibilities are shirked, or in which it is decided that scarce resources cannot be committed to long, difficult, and expensive investigations. Such cases may occur both at a domestic level and at an international one (particularly where the locus of a transnational crime is difficult to identify); but the Committee offered no evidence to suggest that other countries routinely (if ever) shirk from prosecuting murders or acts of terrorism committed on their territory by British citizens, merely because such acts might instead be dealt with under English law. It is more common to find cases in which various states queue up to assert their respective claims to jurisdiction over the same offences or offenders.[29]

Extraterritorial Application and Cross-frontier Offences

The wholesale adoption of nationality-based jurisdiction might have certain collateral advantages. Many cross-frontier offences, for example, are committed by United Kingdom persons. In such cases, potentially difficult issues concerning the precise *locus* of the crime might simply be avoided if jurisdiction could instead be based on the accused's nationality. The law relating to cross-frontier offences nevertheless requires reform and clarification

---

[28] Measures to liberalize some of the more restrictive English rules of evidence are already in hand, and were put before Parliament in November 2002. Clause 29 of the Crime (International Cooperation) Bill and cl. 98 of the Criminal Justice Bill will, if enacted, do much to facilitate the use of evidence from abroad in criminal trials. The former would enable the Secretary of State to provide for s. 32(1A) of the Criminal Justice Act 1988 (proceedings in which evidence may be given from abroad through a live television link) to apply to a much wider range of criminal proceedings than at present, or even to all criminal proceedings. The latter clause (read in conjunction with cl. 100 of that Bill) would facilitate the wider admission of hearsay evidence, notably where 'the relevant person is outside the United Kingdom and it is not reasonably practicable to secure his attendance'. Each is likely to be enacted during 2003, although they might not then be brought in force for several months.

[29] In contrast, cases have occurred in which English football hooligans were deported from foreign countries without prosecution, even though they could *not* have faced prosecution in England and Wales.

in its own right, and it would be wrong to suppose that a mere extension of nationality-based jurisdiction would provide any real substitute for such important and overdue reforms.

The Case for Adopting the Protective Principle

In comparison with the possible expansion of nationality-based jurisdiction, on the one hand, and the possible expansion of jurisdiction over cross-frontier offences, on the other, the point at issue here is a narrow one. Should English law criminalize acts committed abroad by persons who would not ordinarily fall within the ambit of English criminal jurisdiction, if the acts in question would be criminal if committed in England and Wales and have the potential to damage vital British interests, such as the integrity of its currency?

It is a narrow point, because many acts (such as acts of terrorism) that might otherwise fall naturally within the scope of the 'protective principle' are already covered in other ways. Possible subjects for inclusion within such a principle, were it to be adopted under English law, might include the counterfeiting of British banknotes or coins, the unlawful use or tendering of any such counterfeit currency, and perhaps the forgery, etc., of documents, such as cheques or negotiable instruments, that relate to or directly concern financial interests within the United Kingdom. While many states already criminalize such conduct on a 'protective' basis,[30] without regard to nationality, English law does not. Indeed, English law does not even criminalize acts of counterfeiting committed by United Kingdom nationals abroad. This lacuna could quite easily be filled, although some debate would be needed as to the precise extent of the interests that should be protected in that way.

Inchoate Offences

Whatever approach is adopted in respect of substantive extraterritorial offences, there is a need for clarification as to the status of inchoate versions of any such offences. Where, for example, murder is an extraterritorial offence under English law, is attempted murder, or solicitation to murder, also such an offence? The House of Lords in the *Pinochet* case[31] appear to have assumed that this must be so (at least in respect of jurisdiction exercised in accordance with international conventions) and in policy terms there is

---

[30] See for example Art. 113-10 of the French *Code Penal*, by which French criminal law applies (*inter alia*) to the forgery and counterfeiting of state seals, of coins serving as legal tender, and of banknotes or public papers, when committed by any person outside the territory of the French Republic.

[31] *R v. Bow Street Metropolitan Stipendiary Magistrate, ex p Pinochet Ugarte (No. 3)* [2000] 1 AC 147, 236, *per* Lord Hope.

much to be said in favour of that view; but the question does not seem to have been argued or analysed in any depth or detail, and it would be useful to have it resolved by legislation.

Double Criminality Issues

The principle of double criminality is not generally applied in respect of extraterritorial offences. In respect of several such offences, a defendant may be convicted under English law without any evidence being adduced to show that the conduct in question amounted to an offence under local territorial law. Nor, indeed, would it be a defence in such cases to prove that the conduct in question did *not* amount to an offence under that law.

This seems unfair in principle, although English law is by no means alone in this respect.[32] Where proof of foreign law is required, this may sometimes cause difficulties, as can be seen from extradition cases in which double criminality must routinely be established. Strict evidential requirements as to the content of foreign law might also be seen in some cases as unnecessarily irksome, especially where (as, for example, in simple cases of theft or murder) it might appear safe to assume that local law would proscribe such conduct. A compromise solution might therefore be adopted, under which the courts would presume similarity between the relevant English and local laws, in the absence of evidence to the contrary. Once such evidence is adduced by the defence, it would be for the prosecution to rebut it, as with any other case in which evidential burdens are shouldered by the defence.

Special Cases

It would be necessary to create at least one exception to any such general rule concerning double criminality, namely, in respect of offences against national security. It should be no defence, on a charge brought under the Official Secrets Acts, for the accused to show that the disclosure of British military secrets was lawful in the country where it took place. Special provision may also be needed in respect of conduct committed at a place (say, on the high seas) where no other law applies.

Financial Implications

The costs of implementing any major extraterritorial expansion of English criminal jurisdiction would need to be assessed. Even if the total number of offences actually prosecuted is likely to remain relatively small, the costs involved in investigating a single extraterritorial offence may often be significant, and some of those costs may have to be borne by individual

---

[32] See, e.g., the French *Code Penal*, Art. 113-6, which applies a double-criminality test only to *délits* (misdemeanours) and not to *crimes* (felonies) committed by French citizens abroad.

police forces. In particular, costs may be greatly increased by the need to conduct police enquiries abroad. Where the investigation of an overseas offence is followed by prosecution and trial in England and Wales, further costs will be incurred. The Crown Prosecution Service (or the Serious Fraud Office, Customs and Excise, etc.) would have to cover costs incurred by any foreign-based prosecution witnesses who attend a trial in England, and/or the cost of setting up live television (that is, satellite) links for witnesses who remain abroad. The Lord Chancellor's Department would then have to meet legal aid and court costs, including any additional costs incurred as a result of 'out of hours' sittings that are held to make use of the 'satellite slots' in which evidence is heard from overseas witnesses. It follows that the police and Crown Prosecution Service are likely to approach any complex and potentially lengthy extraterritorial (or cross-frontier) cases very warily. Minor offences that would require extensive foreign investigations are therefore most unlikely to be proceeded with.

On the other hand, the prosecution of major acts of terrorism or fraud may sometimes be thought to justify enormous expenditure, a spectacularly expensive example being the Lockerbie terrorist trial,[33] which was conducted by a Scottish court sitting at Camp Zeist in The Netherlands. A less famous example, which nevertheless illustrates the potentially costly nature of prosecutions for extraterritorial offences, is that of the 'Swindon Strangler', Mohan Singh Kular, whose conviction in England for the murder of his wife during a holiday in the Punjab followed a 16-week investigation in the Punjab by eight officers from the Wiltshire Constabulary, who were escorted everywhere during that investigation by heavily armed Indian police officers. For the trial in the Crown Court at Bristol, 23 Punjabi witnesses were flown to England and fed, clothed, and accommodated at public expense. The four-week trial was then followed by a long series of unreported hearings in the Court of Appeal, at the end of which Kular's conviction was upheld.

The above cases may have been extreme examples, but more routine extraterritorial cases may still involve substantial expenditure. The Interdepartmental Steering Committee used a number of actual and hypothetical examples from English and Scottish cases in order to arrive at an estimate of the additional costs that might typically be incurred through prosecuting such cases. Generalizations are difficult, because some overseas investigations may be much less expensive than others, if only because some foreign countries are more expensive to visit than others. Two overseas murder investigations conducted by British police officers illustrate this very clearly. One involved the despatch of two detectives to The Philippines. This triggered costs of over £6,400 in air flights and subsistence expenses

---

[33] *HM Advocate v. Abdelbaset Ali Mohmed Al Megrahi* [1999] Scot HC 248.

(at 1996 prices), even though the British officers were able to stay in accommodation provided by locally-based Australian officers. In contrast, a Scottish investigation arising from an alleged murder in Benidorm in 1993 proved far less costly, because Benidorm is a cheap tourist destination. Five return flights (for three officers and two pathologists) were procured for just £1,000, giving a total cost of £1,500, including accommodation and subsistence. The case later went to trial, but in stark contrast to Kular's case, all the civil witnesses were from Scotland, and although the accused was eventually acquitted, few extra costs were incurred as a result of the extraterritorial nature of the investigation.

Neither of the above examples includes any allowance for the fact that the officers concerned were unavailable for duties at home. If a 'salary element' is built into the equation this will give a much higher figure that more closely represents the true cost of investigating overseas offences. The Committee used a hypothetical child-sex tourism case as a model. If two British officers (a chief inspector and a sergeant) were flown to Bangkok to conduct a four-day investigation there, the direct costs (at 1996 prices) were estimated at just over £5,600; but the total cost, after incorporating salaries, etc., would have been nearly £10,000 (and would of course be even higher today). Interpreters might also be needed. The Committee concluded that 'Excluding the CPS's administrative costs, this hypothetical case would more than double the cost . . . for an average prosecution. Equivalent costs would be incurred in respect of any defence witnesses and would fall to the legal aid fund'.

The use of live video links, where these are permitted under section 32 of Criminal Justice Act 1988,[34] may reduce trial costs by avoiding the need to bring witnesses to England. In some cases, substantial sums may indeed be saved; but video links require the booking of satellite time, which must be arranged to coincide with the court's schedule and with the witness's availability. In some cases, charges totalling several thousands of pounds may still be incurred.[35] If a pre-booked satellite slot is wasted (say, because the trial is running late) or proves inadequate, a further slot will have to be booked and paid for. This may oblige the court to sit at what would otherwise be considered inconvenient hours, especially where the witness is in a

---

[34] At the time of writing, a witness who is outside the UK may be permitted to give evidence through a live TV link only in cases of murder, manslaughter, or any other unlawful killing, proceedings being conducted by the Serious Fraud Office under s. 1(5) of the Criminal Justice Act 1987, or proceedings for serious and complex fraud in which a notice of transfer to the Crown Court has been issued under s. 4 of that Act; but cl. 29 of the Crime (International Cooperation) Bill, which may become law during the latter part of 2003, will enable the Secretary of State to add to this list of offences, or give s. 32 a more general application.

[35] The Steering Committee provide one example (a serious fraud case involving satellite links to Australia and Canada) in which the cost of the satellite links required was £26,000 (Op. cit., fn 16, para 4.11).

completely different time zone. No provision is currently made or proposed for evidence to be given in English proceedings by means of a simple and inexpensive telephone link, although the Crime (International Cooperation) Bill now before Parliament will make provision for witnesses in the United Kingdom to give evidence by telephone in foreign proceedings, where the relevant foreign law so permits.

While some of these calculations may seem alarming, the history of extra-territorial provisions suggests that the actual utilization of any such general extraterritorial jurisdiction over United Kingdom persons would remain infrequent, and that the overall costs involved would be quite manageable. Even in countries such as The Netherlands, where nationals are never extra-dited and the number of extraterritorial offences prosecuted greatly exceeds that in England, the total number of cases involved remains tiny when viewed as a proportion of all prosecutions. In English law, extraterritorial jurisdiction will doubtless remain a matter of last resort, to be exercised only in serious cases where, for one reason or another, extradition is impos-sible, undesirable, or problematic.

A New Approach to Cross-Frontier Offences

As previously stated, reform of the rules governing cross-frontier offences (including inchoate variants) would in practice be a more important devel-opment than anything concerning 'pure' extraterritorial jurisdiction. In contrast to extraterritorial crime, which rarely even comes to the notice of the authorities in this country, cross-frontier or transnational crime is increasingly common, and is a major source of concern to police forces and other law enforcement agencies throughout England and Wales.[36] While some of the difficulties that arise in such cases (notably those involving overseas investigations and evidence gathering, etc.) are largely unavoid-able, the 'jurisdiction' problems that so often arise in the courts (which are really problems concerning the ambit of the law in question) could largely be eliminated by careful and properly thought-out law reform.

Reform of the Basic Rule

At the heart of any thorough reform in this area, English law should adopt a basic principle of 'inclusionary' jurisdiction over cross-frontier crime. It should accordingly be an offence under English law *either* to initiate, by conduct within England and Wales, the commission of an offence that takes effect abroad, *or* to initiate, by conduct abroad, the commission of an offence that takes effect within England and Wales. It should equally be an

---

[36] This is particularly true of 'frontier' forces and agencies, such as Kent Constabulary, HM Customs and Excise, and the Serious Fraud Office.

offence under English law for 'intermediate' acts or conduct to occur within the jurisdiction, in furtherance of a crime that is both initiated and completed abroad. The 'terminatory' approach which still represents the basic rule today should accordingly be abandoned.

The justification for such a reform is clear. English law has a legitimate concern over any case in which international criminals operating from abroad target victims who are within England and Wales. More specifically, it has a responsibility to protect or secure justice for those victims or potential victims; but it also has both a legitimate concern and a moral responsibility to prohibit and punish conduct within its territory that threatens innocent victims abroad. This responsibility has been recognized for many years, but has only been addressed in a piecemeal fashion. One of the first attempts to address it was in Palmerston's abortive Conspiracy to Murder Bill of 1858, which was a response to the scandal caused by the involvement of Italian emigrés in England in a conspiracy to murder the French emperor, Napoleon III. Since then, there has been much legislation on this subject, but no attempt has ever been made to find a comprehensive solution to the problem.

The New Zealand Crimes Act 1961: a Possible Model?

The drafting of legislation to achieve the requisite reform would require great care. In particular, care must be taken to avoid the complications and lacunae that plague Part I of the Criminal Justice Act 1993. Section 7 of the New Zealand Crimes Act 1961 has often been hailed as a model on which any future English legislation might be based. It provides:

> For the purpose of jurisdiction, where any act or omission forming part of any offence, or any event necessary to the completion of any offence, occurs in New Zealand, the offence shall be deemed to be committed in New Zealand, whether the person charged with the offence was in New Zealand or not at the time of the act, omission, or event.

While this provision has much to commend it in terms of clarity and simplicity, it would be problematic in its application to English law, for much the same reason as Part I of the Criminal Justice Act 1993. The problem, as explained in Chapter 4 above, is that English law does not necessarily define the intended consequences of criminal activity as a constituent or necessary part of the offence in question. In cases involving 'conduct crimes' such as blackmail or theft, for example, the defendant's conduct in posting a letter containing a blackmail demand, or despatching a telex 'appropriating' funds in someone else's bank account, may in itself be sufficient to complete the offence,[37] and while such conduct may well take effect against

---

[37] See *Treacy v. DPP* [1971] AC 537; *R v. Governor of Pentonville Prison, ex p Osman* [1990] 1 WLR 277.

a victim in another jurisdiction, no essential element of the offence would be committed there.[38]

A Canadian Model

This problem was addressed by the Law Reform Commission of Canada in its 1984 Working Paper on *Extraterritorial Jurisdiction*.[39] The Commission drafted the following provision, which has never been implemented but appears, with respect, to resolve the difficulties inherent in the New Zealand approach. It does so by combining the latter with what is essentially a narrowly defined application of the 'effects doctrine'. That doctrine has proved highly controversial when employed by the USA in support of its anti-trust laws, but no real objection could be taken to the way in which it is implemented in the Law Reform Commission's model, which provides:

49 (a) An offence is committed in Canada when it is committed in whole or in part in Canada; and

    (b) it is committed 'in part in Canada' when:

      (i) some of its constituent elements occurred outside Canada and at least one of them occurred in Canada, and a constituent element that occurred in Canada established a real and substantial link between the offence and Canada; or

      (ii) all of its constituent elements occurred outside Canada, but direct substantial harmful effects were intentionally or knowingly caused in Canada

It is submitted that this could easily be adapted as the basis for a workable and 'loophole-free' concept of extended territorial jurisdiction in English law.[40] By requiring any 'effects' relied upon under clause 49 (b)(ii) to be direct, substantial, and intentional, etc., it avoids the potential excesses of the US anti-trust laws. By requiring 'a real and substantial link' between the offence and the territory when relying on the 'constituent element' test, clause 49 (b)(i) also provides some way of controlling the potential excesses of rulings such as *R v. Perrin*.[41]

Inchoate Offences and Participation

The basic rule suggested above would need to be supported by provisions dealing with inchoate offences and secondary or joint participation. As the law now stands, any person who participates abroad in an offence

---

[38] The same objection applies to cl. 112(2) of the unofficial Draft Criminal Law (Scotland) Bill (Christopher Gane *et al.*, 2002), which provides: 'Where an act forming part of an offence, or any event necessary for the completion of an offence, occurs in Scotland, the offence is deemed to be committed in Scotland, whether or not every such act or event occurs in Scotland'.

[39] Working Paper No 37.

[40] Apart from substituting 'England and Wales' for 'Canada', provision should also be made in respect of conduct or results connected with British-controlled ships or aircraft, etc.

[41] [2002] All ER (D) 359 (Mar); [2002] EWCA Crim 747. See above, p. 188.

committed within England and Wales may be prosecuted and convicted under English law.[42] This rule appears broadly satisfactory, and could profitably be retained as part of any future codification, but it should arguably be extended so that it operates in both directions. A person in England who procures the commission of a robbery or murder, for example, should not be immune from punishment under English law merely because the robbery or murder is committed in France or Scotland.

In respect of cross-frontier conspiracies and attempts, extensive 'cross-frontier cover' is already provided by legislation such as section 1A of the Criminal Law Act 1977, and by a line of judicial decisions that follow the precedent set by Lord Griffiths in *Somchai Liangsiriprasert* v. *US Government*;[43] but any future codification should provide the clarity and uniformity that is currently missing, and ensure that all inchoate offences (including common law or statutory offences of incitement or solicitation) possess similarly broad ambits. It should do so, moreover, without resorting to the clumsy and potentially problematic dichotomy adopted in sections 1 and 1A of the 1977 Act, under which prosecutors and courts must draw rigid distinctions between different types of conspiracies, depending on whether the proposed substantive offence would or would not fall within the ambit of English criminal law. What is needed in relation to conspiracy is a single offence that may be committed in any case in which there is a real and substantial link between the conspiracy and the territory of England and Wales.[44]

EUROPEAN UNION FRAUD AND THE *CORPUS JURIS*

When exploring the options for reform of the rules governing the ambit of English criminal law, some consideration must be given to the *Corpus Juris* project, in which a working group of legal scholars, drawn from member states of the European Union and acting at the behest of the European Commission, has produced radical proposals for the investigation and prosecution of fraud against the financial interests of the EU itself.

Historically, the impact of EU law in matters of criminal law has been relatively slight, at least in comparison with the enormous impact it has had in many other areas;[45] but the huge growth of cross-frontier crime within

---

[42] *R* v. *Robert Millar (Contractors) Ltd* [1970] 2 QB 54.
[43] [1991] 1 AC 225.   [44] Or with a British-controlled ship or aircraft, etc.
[45] See Estella Baker, 'Taking European Criminal Law Seriously' [1998] *Criminal Law Review* 361. Some recent UK legislation on issues such as money laundering has nevertheless been influenced by EU considerations or requirements; and parts of European competition law, which prohibit certain restrictive trade practices, arguably create criminal offences in everything but name. Infringements may be investigated and fines imposed by the European Commission, but such procedures are declared to be 'administrative' and thus civil in character. See generally, Hanna Sevenster, 'Criminal Law and EC Law' (1992) 29 *Common Market Law Review* 29; Christopher Harding, 'Exploring the Intersection of European and National Criminal Law' (2000) 25(4) *European Law Review* 374, 378.

Europe poses a significant challenge to the idea that individual criminal jurisdictions can deal adequately with such crime. This is particularly true of crimes committed against, or in connection with, the organs, structures, or agencies of the EU itself. Where such crimes are committed on a transnational basis, as many of them are, it will often be difficult for national prosecutors or police forces to investigate or prosecute them effectively. A case may therefore be made for such crimes to be investigated and prosecuted at a European level, in accordance with a pan-European system of criminal law and procedure, and this indeed is what the *Corpus Juris* scheme proposes.

More specifically, the *Corpus Juris* proposals envisage the creation of a common, unified system of European criminal law and procedure, unfettered by national boundaries within the EU and enforced by a European Public Prosecution Service with jurisdiction to investigate and prosecute offences of fraud, corruption, and price-fixing offences committed against the EU's financial interests in any member states. The original proposals, dating from 1996, were supplemented by a further report in 2000, in which certain difficulties raised by the initial proposal have been reconsidered.[46]

The *Corpus Juris* proposals have yet to be adopted, and may indeed prove very difficult to adopt, if only for political reasons. Because they would deal only with EU fraud, they do not in any event obviate the need for wider reform of the rules governing English criminal jurisdiction, but they might perhaps complement such reforms by providing a more radical solution to one particularly important and troublesome type of problem.

The Problem of EU Fraud

The essence of the problem caused by 'community fraud' has been explained by the European Court of Auditors in these terms:

> Fraud against the Community budget is often transnational. The enforcement agencies, however, operate according to a huge number of different procedures and in dispersed order in a very time-consuming way. In contrast the fraudsters themselves can operate in real time using their international networks of contacts. The procedures in place can simply not cope with new criminal networks.[47]

The scale of the problem is immense, as are the sums involved. The total amount lost through fraud cannot be calculated with any kind of precision, but has officially been estimated at 1.4 per cent of the EU budget, which now runs at over €93 billion per annum. Some estimates put the fraud figure much higher, at nearer 10 per cent of that budget.[48] The complex (and often

---

[46] M. Delmas-Marty, 'Combating Fraud—Necessity, Legitimacy and Feasibility of the *Corpus Juris*' (2000) 37 *Common Market Law Review* 247.

[47] Special Report No. 8/98 [1998] OJ C230/1, para. 7.5.

[48] See the 9th Report of the HL Select Committee on European Communities (8 May 1999).

absurd) systems of regional and agricultural subsidies that form such a large part of EU expenditure tend to encourage fraud, but many of these frauds will never be uncovered, and the estimates given above must therefore involve a substantial element of guesswork.

Measures have already been taken under English law for the purpose of ensuring that English criminal law will apply to transnational EU fraud cases involving a real connection with England and Wales. Section 71 of the Criminal Justice Act 1993 enables participation in foreign EU frauds from within England and Wales to be punished as a substantive offence under English law, while Part I of that Act, which deals more generally with jurisdiction over cross-frontier frauds, ensures that English law can be applied to most EU frauds involving conduct or consequences within England and Wales. Valuable as they are, reforms of this kind nevertheless do little to address the practical problems that may arise when attempts are made to investigate and prosecute cross-frontier fraud. Procedures for securing mutual legal assistance within other EU countries are being improved,[49] but are often over-stretched and may accordingly handicap fraud investigations in cases where time may be of the essence. The advantage of the *Corpus Juris* proposals is that they address problems of legal ambit and problems of investigation and enforcement within a single unified scheme.

The Proposals

The *Corpus Juris* proposals have been analysed in detail elsewhere.[50] Briefly, Part I identifies the specific offences that would acquire a pan-European ambit when committed against EU interests within any member state or states. Such frauds would, however, be tried in national courts and not in a supranational EU tribunal. Some of these offences were not even recognized under English law when the proposals were first drafted, and the proposed European offences still do not wholly correspond with those of English law, partly because the *Corpus Juris* concept of fraud is wider in certain respects. Part II contains proposals for the establishment of the European Public Prosecution Service, which would have jurisdiction to conduct investigations across the EU, acting under judicial control, but in a manner more familiar to continental lawyers than to those accustomed to the English way of things.

Opposition to the *Corpus Juris*

The original *Corpus Juris* proposal was essentially a discussion document, akin to a Green Paper, which its authors recognized would be difficult to

---

[49] See in particular Pt I of the Crime (International Cooperation) Bill of November 2002.

[50] Notably by the House of Lords Select Committee in 1999. See also Evan Bell, 'A European DPP to Prosecute Euro-Fraud?' [2000] *Criminal Law Review* 154.

implement in its existing form. The proposal attracted a great deal of interest and has been subjected to extensive analysis.[51] Within the United Kingdom, much of this analysis has been hostile. Much of the hostility stems from the quite understandable concern that the proposal forms the thin end of a very large wedge, enabling the EU to acquire jurisdiction over an ever-increasing range of criminal investigations and prosecutions within the United Kingdom. Some EU federalists would indeed welcome such a development, but they represent a small minority within the United Kingdom, whereas there are many by whom such a development would be seen as anathema. These essentially political considerations are likely to preclude the voluntary adoption of the proposal within the United Kingdom within the foreseeable future. Nor does it seem likely that anything based on the *Corpus Juris* could be imposed on the United Kingdom without its consent. The House of Lords Select Committee concluded that:

Under Article 280(4) of the amended EC Treaty, the Council [of Ministers] can adopt measures 'in the fields of the prevention of and fight against fraud affecting the financial interest of the Community with a view to affording effective and equivalent protection in the Member States'. But such measures 'shall not concern the application of national criminal law or the national administration of justice'. This proviso . . . precludes the adoption of the *Corpus Juris* in the form of an EC instrument under Article 280(4) and also under Article 308. . . .[52]

On the other hand, the *Corpus Juris* has received a more positive welcome elsewhere within Europe,[53] and it may eventually become difficult for the United Kingdom to resist such proposals, unless more is done to ensure that EU frauds are properly investigated and punished under basic national laws. That would require something more than a mere expansion of the ambit of English or Scots criminal law, but improved measures relating to mutual assistance, extradition, and the sharing of evidence or intelligence have already been proposed, and this may be found to represent a better (or at least a more acceptable) way of dealing with the problem.

CONCLUSION

Some of the issues touched upon in this work could no doubt have been taken further, and other issues have not been touched upon when arguably they should have been. There are issues here that might, for example, be expanded upon or developed by comparative lawyers, legal theorists, or experts in extradition and mutual assistance. My aims and objectives have

---

[51] See op. cit., fn 48, and submissions made to the Select Committee. For an overview of the issues see also Bell, op. cit., fn 50, 163; Harding, op. cit., fn 45, 384.

[52] Op. cit., fn 48, para. 115; but see Bell, op. cit., fn 50, 161.

[53] See Bell, op. cit., fn 50, 167.

been more limited; but I hope that this work at least succeeds in demonstrating the principal rules, faults, and complexities of the current law, both at a general level and in respect of specific persons, places, and offences.

I have also sought to highlight the fundamental importance of ambit in relation to the general part of the criminal law, and in particular to the concept of *actus reus*. Should some at least of the reforms proposed in this work be adopted in future legislation, or better still within a new Criminal Code for England and Wales, that would be a substantial bonus. I trust that the issues will at any rate be addressed within any such Code. A Code that fails to define the ambit of the law it purports to codify must surely be considered incomplete.

Select Bibliography

ARTICLES, NOTES, AND ESSAYS

Akdeniz, Y., 'Section 3 of the Computer Misuse Act 1990: an Antidote for Computer Viruses' [1996] 3 *Web Journal of Current Legal Issues* (online only: see **http://webjcli.ncl.ac.uk/**).

——, 'Governance of Pornography and Child Pornography on the Global Internet: a Multi-layered Approach', in Edwards, L. and Waelde, C. (eds), *Law and the Internet* (Hart, 1997).

Akehurst, M., 'Jurisdiction in International Law' (1972–3) 46 *British Yearbook of International Law* 145.

Alegre, S., 'The Myth and Reality of a Modern European Judicial Space' [2002] *New Law Journal* 986.

Alldridge, P., 'The Sexual Offences (Conspiracy and Incitement) Act 1996' [1997] *Criminal Law Review* 30.

——, 'Sex Offenders Act 1997—Territoriality Provisions' [1997] *Criminal Law Review* 655.

Arnell, P., 'The Case for Nationality-based Jurisdiction' (2001) 50 *International and Comparative Law Quarterly* 955.

Baker, E., 'Taking European Criminal Law Seriously' [1998] *Criminal Law Review* 361.

Beckett, W., 'Criminal Jurisdiction over Foreigners' (1925) 6 *British Yearbook of International Law* 51.

——, 'Criminal Jurisdiction over Foreigners: The *Franconia* and the *Lotus*' (1927) 8 *British Yearbook of International Law* 108.

Bell, E., 'A European DPP to Prosecute Euro-Fraud?' [2000] *Criminal Law Review* 154.

Birnbaum, M., 'Pinochet and Double Criminality' [2000] *Criminal Law Review* 127.

Borrie, G., 'Courts-martial, Civilians and Civil Liberties' (1969) 32 *Modern Law Review* 35.

Brierly, J.L., 'The *Lotus* Case' (1928) 44 *Law Quarterly Review* 154.

Campbell, C., 'Two Steps Backwards: the Criminal Justice (Terrorism and Conspiracy) Act 1998' [1999] *Criminal Law Review* 941.

Cheng, B., 'Crimes Aboard Aircraft' (1959) 12 *Current Legal Problems* 187.

Coleman, J.A. and Hirst, M., 'Indecent Exposure on the Beach' (1983) 147 *Justice of the Peace* 579.

Davis, D., 'Criminal Law and the Internet: The Investigator's Perspective', in Walker, C. (ed.), *Crime, Criminal Justice and the Internet* (*Criminal Law Review* Special Edition, Sweet & Maxwell, 1998) 48.

Delmas-Marty, M., 'Combating Fraud—Necessity, Legitimacy and Feasibility of the *Corpus Juris*' (2000) 37 *Common Market Law Review* 247.

Duffy, H., 'Responding to September 11: the Framework of International Law' (Interights, 2001) (**www.interights.org**).

Edeson, W.R., 'The Prerogative of the Crown to Delimit Britain's Maritime Boundary' (1973) 89 *Law Quarterly Review* 364.

Ellison, L. and Akdeniz, Y., 'Cyberstalking: the Regulation of Harassment on the Internet', in Walker, C. (ed.), *Crime, Criminal Justice and the Internet* (*Criminal Law Review* Special Edition, Sweet & Maxwell, 1998) 29.

Fox, H., 'The Pinochet Case No. 3' (1999) 48 *International and Comparative Law Quarterly* 687.

Gibson, J., 'Territorial Principles and the Law Commission: a Comment' [1979] *Criminal Law Review* 778.

Gilbert, G., 'Crimes Sans Frontiers: Jurisdictional Problems in English Law' (1992) 63 *British Yearbook of International Law* 415.

——, 'Who has Jurisdiction for Cross-frontier Financial Crimes?' [1995] 2 *Web Journal of Current Legal Issues* (online only: see **http://webjcli.ncl.ac.uk**).

Halberstam, M., 'Terrorism on the High Seas: the *Achille Lauro*, Piracy and the IMO Convention on Maritime Safety' (1988) 82 *American Journal of International Law* 269.

Hall, L., 'Territorial Jurisdiction: Criminal Law' [1972] *Criminal Law Review* 276.

Harding, C.S.P., 'Exploring the Intersection of European and National Criminal Law' (2000) 25(4) *European Law Review* 374.

Hirst, M., 'Territorial Principles and the Law Commission' [1979] *Criminal Law Review* 355.

——, 'Territorial Principles and the Law Commission: a Reply' [1979] *Criminal Law Review* 781.

——, 'Jurisdiction over Cross-frontier Offences' (1981) 97 *Law Quarterly Review* 80.

——, 'The Criminal Law Abroad' [1982] *Criminal Law Review* 496.

——, 'Murder in England or Murder in Scotland?' [1995] *Cambridge Law Journal* 488.

——, 'Preventing the Lawful Burial of a Body' [1996] *Criminal Law Review* 96.

——, 'Jurisdiction over Offences of Fraud and Dishonesty' [1999] *Crime Online* Commentary Archive, D1.75. (Online only:see http://grenville.butterworths.co.uk)

——, 'Stolen Goods and Foreign Law' [2000] *Crime Online* Commentary Archive, B4.132.

——, 'Bribery and Corruption in England and Abroad' [2002] *Crime Online* Commentary Archive, B15.1.

——, 'Manslaughter in Spain—Judicial Review of a Decision not to Prosecute' [2002] *Crime Online* Commentary Archive, D1.72.

——, 'Cyberobscenity and the Ambit of English Criminal Law' (2002) 13 *Computers & Law* 25.

Lauterpacht, H., 'Diplomatic Protection and Criminal Jurisdiction over Aliens' (1945–7) 9 *Cambridge Law Journal* 330.

Leigh, L.H., 'Territorial Jurisdiction and Fraud' [1988] *Criminal Law Review* 280.

Leong, G., 'Computer Child Pornography—the Liability of Distributors?', in Walker, C. (ed.), *Crime, Criminal Justice and the Internet* (*Criminal Law Review* Special Edition, Sweet & Maxwell, 1998) 19.

Lew, J., 'The Extraterritorial Criminal Jurisdiction of English Courts' (1978) 27 *International and Comparative Law Quarterly* 168.

Lowe, A.V., 'Blocking Extraterritorial Jurisdiction: the British Protection of Trading Interests Act 1980' (1981) 75 *American Journal of International Law* 257.

——, 'US Extraterritorial Jurisdiction: the Helms-Burton and D'Amato Acts' (1997) 46 *International and Comparative Law Quarterly* 378.

Lynch, A.C.E., 'British Subjects' Involvement in Foreign Military Clashes' [1978] *Criminal Law Review* 257.

McMahon, J., 'Legal Aspects of Outer Space' (1962) 38 *British Yearbook of International Law* 339.

MacNair, M., 'Vicenage and the Antecedents of the Jury' (1999) 17 *Law and History Review* 537.

Marston, G., 'Crimes on Board Foreign Merchant Ships at Sea: Some Aspect of English Practice' (1972) 88 *Law Quarterly Review* 357.

——, 'The Centenary of the *Franconia* Case: The Prosecution of Ferdinand Keyn' (1976) 92 *Law Quarterly Review* 93.

——, 'Crime by British Passengers on Board Foreign Ships on the High Seas: The Historical Background to Section 686(1)' [1999] *Cambridge Law Journal* 171.

——, 'Redrawing the Territorial Sea Baseline in the Firth of Forth' (2002) 51 *International and Comparative Law Quarterly* 279.

Mullan, G., 'The Concept of Double Criminality in the Context of Extraterritorial Crimes' [1997] *Criminal Law Review* 17.

Orchard, G., 'Agreement in Criminal Conspiracy' [1974] *Criminal Law Review* 297.

Penfold, C., 'Nazis, Porn and Politics: Asserting Control over Internet Content' 2001(2) *Journal of Information, Law and Technology* (online only: http://elj.warwick.ac.uk/jilt/).

Perkins, R.M., 'The Territorial Principle in Criminal Law' (1971) 22 *Hastings Law Journal* 1155.

Pritchard, M.J., 'The Army Act and Murder Abroad' (1954) 16 *Cambridge Law Journal* 232.

Seguin, J., 'The Case for Transferring Territorial Jurisdiction in the European Union' (2001) 12 *Criminal Law Forum* 247.

Sevenster, H., 'Criminal Law and EC Law' (1992) 29 *Common Market Law Review* 29.

Shubber, S., 'Is Hijacking of Aircraft Piracy in International Law?' (1968–9) 43 *British Yearbook of International Law* 193.

——, 'Aircraft Hijacking under the Hague Convention 1970—A New Regime?' (1973) 22 *International and Comparative Law Quarterly* 687.

Smith, J.C., 'Theft, Conspiracy and Jurisdiction: Tarling's Case' [1975] *Criminal Law Review* 220.

Sullivan, G.R. and Warbrick, C., 'Territoriality, Theft and *Atakpu*' [1994] *Criminal Law Review* 650.

—— and ——, 'Territorial Jurisdiction: Criminal Justice Act 1993' (1994) 43 *International and Comparative Law Quarterly* 460.

Vince, I., 'Sealand Waives the Rules' (2001) *Code* (issue 1) 40.

Walker, C. and Akdeniz, Y., 'The Governance of the Internet in Europe with Special Reference to Illegal and Harmful Content', in Walker, C. (ed.), *Crime, Criminal Justice and the Internet* (*Criminal Law Review* Special Edition, Sweet & Maxwell, 1998).

Wall, D., 'Policing and the Regulation of the Internet' in Walker, C. (ed.), *Crime, Criminal Justice and the Internet* (*Criminal Law Review* Special Edition, Sweet & Maxwell, 1998) 79.

Warbrick, C., 'International Criminal Law' (1995) 44 *International and Comparative Law Quarterly* 465.

Watson, G.R., 'Offenders Abroad: The Case for Nationality-based Criminal Jurisdiction' (1992) 17 *Yale Journal of International Law* 41.

Wilkinson, G.S., 'The Application of Enactments within English Territorial Waters' (1950) 13 *Modern Law Review* 40.

Williams, D., 'War Graves and Salvage: Murky Waters?' (2000) 7(5) *International Maritime Law* 151.

——, 'Protecting Maritime Military Remains: A New Regime for the United Kingdom' (2001) 8(9) *International Maritime Law* 288.

Williams, G., 'Venue and the Ambit of Criminal Law' (1965) 81 *Law Quarterly Review* 276.

Yang, X., 'Immunity for International Crimes: a Reaffirmation of Traditional Doctrine' [2002] *Cambridge Law Journal* 242.

Books, Reports, and Reference Works

Arlidge, A., *Arlidge & Parry on Fraud* (2nd edn, Sweet & Maxwell, 1996).

Bantekas, I., Nash, S. and Mackarel, M., *International Criminal Law* (Cavendish Publishing, 2001).

Bassiouni, M.C., *Crimes Against Humanity in International Criminal Law* (2nd edn, Martinus Nijhoff, 1999).

Bates, J.H., *United Kingdom Marine Pollution Law* (Lloyd's of London, 1985).

Brierly, J.L., *The Law of Nations: An Introduction to the International Law of Peace* (6th edn, Oxford University Press, 1963).

Brownlie, I., *Principles of Public International Law* (5th edn, Oxford University Press, 1999).

Cameron, I., *The Protective Principle of International Criminal Jurisdiction* (Dartmouth, 1994).

Card, R., *Card, Cross and Jones, Criminal Law* (15th edn, Butterworths, 2001).

Carter, P. and Harrison, R., *Offences of Violence* (2nd edn, Sweet & Maxwell, 1997).

Cassese, A., *International Criminal Law* (Oxford University Press, 2003).

——, Gaeta, P. and Jones, R.W.D., *The Rome Statute of the International Criminal Court—A Commentary* (Oxford University Press, 2002).

Churchill, R. and Lowe, A.V., *The Law of the Sea* (Manchester University Press, 1988).

Clark, R.B., *The Waters Around the British Isles* (Oxford University Press, 1987).

Coke, E., *Institutes of the Laws of England* (vols 3 and 4) (4th edn, 1670).

Criminal Law Revision Committee, 8th Report, *Theft and Related Offences* (Cmnd. 2977, 1966).

——, 14th Report, *Offences Against the Person* (Cmnd. 7844, 1980).

Dinstein, Y. and Tabory, M. (eds), *War Crimes in International Law* (Martinus Nijhoff, 1996).

Dubner, B., *The Law of International Sea Piracy* (Martinus Nijhoff, 1980).

East, E.H., *Treatise of the Pleas of the Crown* (1803) (rep., Professional Books, 1972).

Edwards, L. and Waelde, C. (eds), *Law and the Internet* (Hart, 1997).

Ellen, E. and Campbell, D., *International Maritime Fraud* (Sweet & Maxwell, 1981).

Foster, M., *Crown Law* (Clarendon Press, 1762).

Fulton, T.W., *The Sovereignty of the Sea* (Blackwood, 1911).

Gordon, G., *The Criminal Law of Scotland* (1st edn, W. Green, 1967; also 3rd edn, 2001).

Grabosky, P. and Smith, R., *Crime in the Digital Age* (Federation Press, 1998).

Green, T.A., *Verdict According to Conscience* (University of Chicago Press, 1985).

Griew, E., *The Theft Acts* (7th edn, Sweet & Maxwell, 1995).

Hale, M., *A Treatise de Jure Maris et Brachiorum Ejusdem* (1787) (first published in Moore, S.A., *A History of the Foreshore and the Law Relating Thereto* (Stevens & Haynes, 1888)).

——, *Historia Placitorum Coronae* (first published 1716; edited edn 1736; rep. Professional Books, 1971).

Hall, J.W. (ed.), *The Trial of William Joyce* (Hodge & Co., 1946).

Harris, D.J., *Cases and Materials on International Law* (5th edn, Sweet & Maxwell, 1998).

Harvard Research Group, *Draft Convention on Jurisdiction with Respect to Crime* (reprinted in (1935) 29 *American Journal of International Law* Supp., 480).

Hawkins, W., *Treatise of the Pleas of the Crown* (3rd edn, with additions, B. Nutt, 1739).

Hobday, R. (ed.), *Coulson and Forbes on The Law of Waters and of Land Drainage* (6th edn, Sweet & Maxwell, 1952).

Holdsworth, W., *A History of English Law* (17 vols, Methuen, 1903–1972).

Home Office, *Review of Extraterritorial Jurisdiction: Report of the Interdepartmental Steering Committee* (1996).

Hume, D., *Commentaries on the Law of Scotland Respecting the Description and Punishment of Crimes* (1797).

Jennings, R. and Watts, A. (eds), *Oppenheim's International Law* (9th edn, Longman, 1992).

Kittichaisaree, K., *International Criminal Law* (Oxford University Press, 2001).

Knott, G. (ed.), *The Trial of Roger Casement* (2nd edn, Hodge & Co., 1927).

Lauterpacht, E. (ed.), *British Practice in International Law* (British Institute of International and Comparative Law, 1962–1967).

Lauterpacht, H., *Private Law Sources and Analogies of International Law* (Longmans & Co., 1927).

Law Commission, *The Territorial and Extraterritorial Extent of the Criminal Law* (Law Com. No. 91, 1978).

——, *A Criminal Code for England and Wales* (Law Com. No. 177, 1989).

——, *Jurisdiction over Offences of Fraud and Dishonesty with a Foreign Element* (Law Com. No. 180, 1989).

——, *Legislating the Criminal Code: Corruption* (Law Com. No. 248, 1998).

Law Reform Commission of Canada, *Extraterritorial Jurisdiction* (Working Paper No. 37, 1984).

Lowe, A.V., *Extraterritorial Jurisdiction: An Annotated Collection of Legal Materials* (Grotius, 1983).

McKay, F., *Universal Jurisdiction in Europe* (Redress, 1999).

McWhinney, E., *Aerial Piracy and International Terrorism* (Martinus Nijhoff, 1987).

Marston, G., *The Marginal Seabed* (Oxford University Press, 1981).

Martin, J.M. and Romano, A.T., *Multinational Crime* (Sage, 1992).

Mayson, S., French, D. and Ryan, C., *Company Law* (19th edn, Oxford University Press, 2002).

Meron, T., *War Crimes Law Comes of Age—Essays* (Oxford University Press, 1999).

Milsom, S.F.C., *Historical Foundations of the Common Law* (2nd edn, Butterworths, 1981).

Moore, S.A., *A History of the Foreshore and the Law Relating Thereto* (Stevens & Haynes, 1888).

Murphy, P. (ed.), *Blackstone's Criminal Practice 2003* (Oxford University Press, 2002).

Murray, C. and Harris, L., *Mutual Legal Assistance in Criminal Matters* (Sweet & Maxwell, 2000).

O'Connell, D.P., *The International Law of the Sea* (Oxford University Press, 1984).

Richardson, P.J. (ed.), *Archbold 2003* (Sweet & Maxwell, 2002).

Riesemann, W.M. (ed.), *Jurisdiction in International Law* (Ashgate, 1999).

Robertson, G., *Crimes Against Humanity: The Struggle for Global Justice* (Penguin, 1999).

Rogers, A.P.V., *Law on the Battlefield* (Manchester University Press, 1995).

Schutte, J.J.E., *Extraterritorial Criminal Jurisdiction* (Council of Europe, 1990).

Selden, J., *Mare Clausum Seu de Dominio Maris* (1635).

Shaw, M., *International Law* (4th edn, Cambridge University Press, 1997).

Simester, A.P. and Sullivan, G.R., *Criminal Law, Theory and Doctrine* (Hart Publishing, 2000).

Smith, A.T.H., *Property Offences: The Protection of Property through the Criminal Law* (2nd edn, Sweet & Maxwell, 1994).

Smith, J.C., *The Law of Theft* (8th edn, Butterworths, 1997).

—— and Hogan, B., *Criminal Law* (6th edn, Butterworths, 1988).

——, *Smith & Hogan, Criminal Law* (10th edn, Butterworths, 2002).

Stanbrook, I. and Stanbrook, C., *Extradition Law and Practice* (2nd edn, Oxford University Press, 2000).

Stephen, J.F., *History of the Criminal Law of England* (Macmillan, 1883).

Thayer, L.B., *A Preliminary Treatise on Evidence at the Common Law* (Sweet & Maxwell, 1898).

Various Authors, *Halsbury's Laws of England* (online version, Butterworths, 2002).

Walker, C., *Blackstone's Guide to the Anti-Terrorism Legislation* (Oxford University Press, 2002).

——, (ed.), *Crime, Criminal Justice and the Internet* (*Criminal Law Review* Special Edition, Sweet & Maxwell, 1998).

Wasik, M., *Crime and the Computer* (Oxford University Press, 1991).

Whiteman, M., *Digest of International Law* (US State Dept, 1963).

Williams, G., *Textbook of Criminal Law* (2nd edn, Stevens & Sons, 1983).

Index

Admiralty charts 63, 72–4, 83, 85, 89 *see also* Hydrographic Office
Admiralty jurisdiction 4–5, 33, 66–8
aerodromes, endangering safety at 322–3
air force law *see* military, air force, and naval law
aircraft
  acts endangering 316, 319–22
  British controlled 11–12
  dangerous articles, possession of aboard 322
  foreign controlled 315, 317
  hijacking of 316–18, 320–1
    offences incidental to hijacking 318, 320–1
  Lockerbie and September 11 320–1
  military 320
  piracy involving 303
  sabotage or destruction of 316, 319–22
  UK airspace 104–6
airspace (England and Wales), jurisdiction over 104–6
ambit of criminal law
  ambit and jurisdiction contrasted 1–3, 9–15
  codification, proposed 324–47
  common law offences 2–3
  extraterritorial 201–322
    see also extraterritorial ambit of English law
  international law (or comity), and 9
  reforms, suggested 324–47
  summary offences 14–15, 68–9, 75–6
  territorial principle, reform of 326–7
Antarctica 216–17
anti-personnel mines, offences concerning 279
attempts *see* criminal attempts

bigamy 232–6
border rivers (Esk, Tweed and Sark)
  defined 63–5
  jurisdiction over fishery offences 10, 64–6
  precise location of border within 64
bribery *see* corruption
British nationality *see also* UK nationality
  extraterritorial liability, and 203–8, 225–6, 329–30, 331–6
  forms of 204–5, 329–30
British ships 282–3, 288 *see also* United Kingdom ships

Channel Tunnel 99–102
  frontier control zones within 100
  offences committed within 101–2
commission areas *see* counties and commission areas
common law *see also* venue
  territorial limit of application 2–3
Commonwealth citizens 206–7, 232–3, 277, 292, 330
Commonwealth countries
  distinguished from foreign countries 210, 276, 294–5
computer crime *see* cybercrime and computer misuse
conduct crimes and result crimes 117–29, 135–6, 151, 153, 168
  conduct crimes 119–22, 168
  inchoate offences 135–6, 151, 153
  problems of classification 127–9, 135–6
  result crimes 123–7
conspiracy
  abroad, to commit offence within jurisdiction 136–7, 152–8
  computer misuse 197–8
  conduct crime or result crime 135–6
  defraud, to 138, 175–8
  Group A offences under CJA 1993 175
  within jurisdiction, to commit offence abroad 23, 25, 136–48
Convention countries (Suppression of Terrorism Act 1978) 259
Corpus Juris proposals 343–7
corruption 273–5
counties and commission areas
  foreshore 69–74
  littoral boundaries of 69–76
  Scottish border counties 63
  waters *inter fauces terrae* 74–6
criminal attempts
  computer misuse 197–8
  cross-frontier 134–7, 139, 152–6
  Group A offences under CJA 1993 172–4

cross-frontier offences 7–8, 110–200,
340–3 *see also* conduct crimes and
result crimes
cybercrime and computer misuse 182–98
fraud and dishonesty 158–82
general rule as to 113–29
inchoate 134–58, 342–3
murder and manslaughter 198–200
participation in 129–34, 342–3
perjury 200
proposals for reform of existing rules
327, 340–3
terminatory theory 115–7, 200
Crown Court, jurisdiction of 10–12, 14, 33
Crown servants 209–11
cybercrime and computer misuse 182–98

diplomatic and consular premises
British, abroad 104
foreign, etc., in England and Wales 102–4
diplomatic immunity *see* immunity from
jurisdiction
double criminality 21, 49–50, 337
Draft Criminal Code *see* Law Commission
drug trafficking, international
conspiracies and attempts 154–8
maritime offences 310–12

effects doctrine
jurisdiction under 47–8
England and Wales *see also* border rivers,
territorial waters
airspace above 104–6
Channel Tunnel 99
definition 61–3, 99
distinguished from rest of UK 61
waters adjacent to 76–98
environmental protection 277–80
Esk, river *see* border rivers
European Union, frauds concerning 343–6
extradition 21–2, 49–50 *see also*
double-criminality
extraterritorial ambit of English law 201–322
Admiralty 33
aircraft, offences aboard 313–22
see also aircraft, hijacking, terrorism
Antarctica 216–17
armed forces and accompanying
civilians 211–16
bigamy 232–6
bribery
see corruption
civilian legal systems 33

common law position 5
'Convention countries', offences
committed in 358–60
corruption 273–5
Crown servants 209–11
deep-sea mining, regulation of activities
concerning 279
drug trafficking, maritime 310–12
environmental offences 277–80
extradition, as alternative to 202
see also extradition
financial implications of extending
337–40
foreign enlistment 276–7
genocide and war crimes, etc. 236–45
hostages, taking of 264–6
inchoate offences 280–1
international law, offences under 236–47
internationally protected persons, crimes
against 262–4
maritime 282–313
see also ships, piracy, offshore
installations
military remains, protection of 280
mines, anti-personnel, offences
concerning 279
murder and manslaughter 226–32,
310, 320–1
nationality or status, based on 203–8
Official Secrets Acts, offences
under 221–4
outer space, regulation of activities
concerning 278–9
perjury 272
presumption against, in legislation 6
proposals for extension of 330–46
review of (Home Office, 1996) 144, 164,
201, 268–9, 331
sex offences involving children 268–71
slave trading 246–7
terrorism, legislation concerning 247–68,
see also hijacking
treason and treason felony 218–21
torture 19–20, 38–9, 245–6, 281
venue doctrine, and 28–35, 58–9
wrecks, protected 280

fishery limits
British Fishery Limits 44, 107–9
fishery zones and exclusive economic
zones 106–7
'relevant' British fishery limits 85, 108–9
foreign enlistment 276–7

foreign law
 proof of 24
 recognition of offences under 22–6
foreshore, jurisdiction over 69–74

genocide 236–7, 242–4
 conduct ancillary to 152
Group A offences under CJA 1993 165–78,
  180–1
 excluded offences 179–80
 inchoate offences 172–8
 relevant events 165–72

handling stolen goods
 Group A offence 165, 180–1
 property stolen abroad 24–5, 180–2
hijacking and related offences
 aircraft 317–18, 320–1
 ships etc. 306–8
historical influences on ambit 28–35, 58–9
hostages, taking of 264–6
Hydrographic Office (UK) 72, 86, 93
 see also Admiralty charts

immunity from jurisdiction *see* jurisdictional
  immunities
inchoate offences *see also* conspiracy,
  incitement, attempt
 cross-frontier 134–58, 172–8, 197–8,
  342–3
 extraterritorial 280–1
incitement (solicitation)
 computer misuse 197–8
 Group A offences 174
 murder abroad 148–9
 result crime 135
 sex offences involving children abroad
  139–42
 terrorist offences overseas 149–51
India, application of Suppression of
  Terrorism Act to 259–60, 298
international crime 56–8 *see also*
  cross-frontier offences
International Criminal Court (ICC) 55
international criminal law 54–5
international law, public
 incorporation of within common law
  35–41
 interpretation of statutes, and 34, 39, 41–3
 permissible jurisdiction under 44–55
 territorial limits, and 28, 43–4
 treaties 39–41
international organizations

immunities granted to officers of 18–19
 premises of 104
internationally protected persons, crimes
  against 262–4
internet crime *see* cybercrime and
  computer misuse
islands, British
 Anglesey 61
 Channel Islands (Guernsey, Jersey, etc.)
  61, 206–7
 Isle of Man 61, 83, 107, 288, 290
 Scilly Isles 61
 territorial sea, around 88–9

juries, venue doctrine and 30–3
 see also venue
jurisdiction of courts
 courts-martial 211–15
 Crown Court 10–12, 14, 33
 International Criminal Court (ICC) 55
 jurisdiction distinguished from ambit
  of law 9–12
 magistrates' courts and youth courts 10,
  14–15, 68–9, 75–6, 79
 venue doctrine, and 28–33
jurisdictional immunities 15–21
 consular 18
 diplomatic 16–17
 foreign heads of state and ministers 19–20
 foreign ships 21
 international organization 18–19
 the sovereign (monarch) 16
 visiting forces 21

Law Commission,
 1978 Report (territorial and
  extraterritorial extent) 1, 87, 96–7
 1989 Report (fraud and dishonesty
  offences) 1, 161–3, 165, 167–8,
 Draft Criminal Code 1, 324–6
 Draft Criminal Jurisdiction Bill 325
littoral boundaries 66–93 *see also* territorial
  sea, bays, islands
 counties and commission areas 69
 low-water mark and foreshore 69–72,
  87–8
 waters *inter fauces terrae* 74–6
low-tide elevations
 territorial sea baseline 88–9
low-water mark 69–72, 87–8

media, influence on reform 58
military, air force, and naval law

military, air force, and naval law (*cont.*)
  civil offences under 23, 212–14
  courts-martial 211–15
  standing civilian courts abroad 216
military remains, protection of 280
money laundering offences 26, 180–2
murder and manslaughter *see also* genocide,
      war crimes, etc.
  aircraft, aboard 228, 257, 320–1
  common law 2–3
  conspiracy to murder 23, 142, 148
  cross-frontier killing 117, 198–200
  internationally protected persons, of 262
  offshore installations and structures,
      aboard 96–9, 299–301, 310
  on land outside UK 201, 226–32, 259–60
  Scotland or Northern Ireland 66, 228–30
  ships, aboard 228, 257, 310
  solicitation to murder abroad 148–9
  terrorism legislation, and 248, 256–7,
      259–60
  UN personnel, of 264–5
  uncertain location 66
  unpunishable 23, 148

nationality, British, etc. 203–9
nationality principle of jurisdiction *see also*
      British nationality, UK nationality
  in international law 49–50
  limited use of in English law 3, 7, 49
  wider use of, proposed 330–5
Northern Ireland *see also* United Kingdom,
      offences committed elsewhere within
  airspace above 106, 315
  waters adjacent to 63, 83–5, 108

official secrets offences 221–4
offshore installations and structures 96–9,
      299–301
  seizing or endangering safety of platforms
      308–10
Ordnance Survey mapping
  evidential status of maps 63, 70, 73
  low-water mark on 72–3
  mapping and mereing of boundaries
      63, 70

'passive personality' principle of jurisdiction
  in international law 51–2
  terrorist offences against UK
      nationals 52
perjury and related offences 113, 127,
      200, 272

piracy 53, 301–6 *see also* hijacking
protective principle of jurisdiction
  in international law 48–9
  possible adoption in English law
      331, 336

Scotland
  airspace above 106, 315
  border with England 60–6
    see also border rivers
  offences committed in 5, 61, 126,
      229–30, 233, 259, 275–6, 328–9
  waters adjacent to 83–5
Scots law
  English law, distinguished from 5–6
  fishery offences on border rivers 64–6
sexual offences
  extraterritorial, involving children
      139–42, 268–71
ships *see also* piracy, territorial waters
  Admiralty jurisdiction over 285–9
  British ships 282–3, 288
    see also United Kingdom ships
  fishing boats or vessels 288–90
  flag state, jurisdiction of in international
      law 52–4, 283–4
  flags of convenience 284
  foreign ships
    Admiralty jurisdiction over 288–9
    British citizens aboard 7
    Convention countries, belonging to
        257, 298
    Her Majesty's ships and vessels 283, 287
    naval vessels 53
    pollution offences, committed by
        312–13
    within British waters 21, 37–40, 52
  hijacking of 306–8
  lying off English coast 93–6
  Royal Fleet Auxiliaries 287
  United Kingdom ships 12–14, 68
    foreign ports or harbours, in 291–4
    high seas, on 291–4
    offences committed by seamen from
        296–8
  warships, foreign 53
  wrecks, protected 280
slave trading 246–7
statutory interpretation
  presumption of territoriality 2
summary offences
  jurisdiction over 14–15, 68–9, 75–6, 79
  within territorial waters 62, 68–76, 79

territorial principle of jurisdiction *see also*
  cross-frontier offences
  in international law 45–8
  territorial limits, in English law 60–109
territorial sea or waters (UK) 62, 66–93
  airspace above 105–6
  baselines, from which measured 85–92
  bays of England and Wales 89–93
  breadth of 82
  Franconia case 37–40, 94–5
  history of 77–9
  internal waters, distinguished from 62, 68
  international law and 53, 76–7, 85–6
  islands and low-tide elevations 88–9
  jurisdiction over 76–85
  oil or gas installations 98–9
  police powers within 80
  Roughs Tower ('Sealand') 81, 97–8
  Scottish and Northern Irish waters 83–5
  Secretary of State's certificate as to
    baselines 86–7, 98
  Straits of Dover, seaward limits in 83
  structures in coastal waters 81, 90, 96–8
territoriality, principle of
  defined 3–6
  exceptions to 6–7, 60
  venue doctrine, and 28–33
terrorist offences 247–68
  bombing and explosions 249–50, 258,
    260, 266–7
  fundraising and finance 267–8
  incitement to acts of terrorism overseas
    149–52
  international terrorism, rise of 57–8
  offences involving chemical, biological or
    nuclear devices 250–3
  offences involving misuse of 'peaceful'
    nuclear material 253–4
  offences under the Explosive Substances
    Act 1883 249–50, 260, 262, 265, 267

passive personality jurisdiction over 52
  Suppression of Terrorism Act 1978 254–62
theft
  abroad, proceeds handled, etc., in
    England 24–6, 180–2
  appropriation, locus of 128–9, 171
  conduct crime or result crime 128–9
torture 19–20, 38–9, 245–6, 281
transnational crime *see* cross-frontier
  offences
treason and treason felony 218–21
treaties or conventions *see* international law
Tweed, river *see* border rivers

United Kingdom
  offences committed in Scotland or
    Northern Ireland 126, 229–30, 233,
    259, 275–6, 315, 328–9
United Kingdom nationality 207 *see also*
  nationality
United Nations personnel, offences
  committed against 264–6
universal principle of jurisdiction 54–5,
    202, 236–40, 245–6, 262–8,
    301–5, 316–23 *see also* piracy,
    war crimes, aircraft, hijacking,
    torture

venue doctrine
  influence on territoriality of criminal law
    28–35, 58–9
visiting forces in UK 21

war crimes *see also* genocide
  Geneva Conventions, grave breaches of
    238–40, 243
  International Criminal Court Act 2001
    242–5
  prosecutions and convictions 54–5, 201
  War Crimes Act 1991 201, 240, 242

Lightning Source UK Ltd.
Milton Keynes UK
UKHW02n1441280218
318641UK00003B/190/P